L'EUROPE

■	Le français est la langue officielle
□	Le français est une des langues officielles

NORVÈGE
ESTONIE
GRANDE-BRETAGNE
IRLANDE
Mer du Nord
SUÈDE
DANEMARK
LETTONIE
RUSSIE
LITUANIE
RUSSIE
BIÉLORUSSIE
PAYS-BAS
ALLEMAGNE
POLOGNE
OCÉAN ATLANTIQUE
BELGIQUE
LUXEMBOURG
RÉPUBLIQUE TCHÈQUE
SLOVAQUIE
UKRAINE
FRANCE
SUISSE
AUTRICHE
HONGRIE
MOLDAVIE
SLOVÉNIE
CROATIE
ROUMANIE
ANDORRE
BOSNIE-HERZÉGOVINE
YOUGOSLAVIE
PORTUGAL
ITALIE
Mer Méditerranée
CORSE
BULGARIE
MACÉDOINE
ESPAGNE
ALBANIE
GRÈCE
TURQUIE

0 100 200 milles
0 100 200 kilomètres

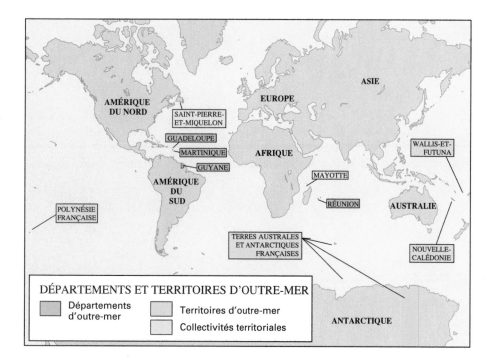

AMÉRIQUE DU NORD
ASIE
EUROPE
SAINT-PIERRE-ET-MIQUELON
WALLIS-ET-FUTUNA
GUADELOUPE
MARTINIQUE
AFRIQUE
GUYANE
MAYOTTE
AMÉRIQUE DU SUD
RÉUNION
AUSTRALIE
POLYNÉSIE FRANÇAISE
NOUVELLE-CALÉDONIE
TERRES AUSTRALES ET ANTARCTIQUES FRANÇAISES
ANTARCTIQUE

DÉPARTEMENTS ET TERRITOIRES D'OUTRE-MER

■	Départements d'outre-mer
■	Territoires d'outre-mer
□	Collectivités territoriales

Entre Amis

Instructor's Annotated Edition

Entre Amis

An Interactive Approach

Fourth Edition

Michael D. Oates
University of Northern Iowa

Larbi Oukada
Indiana University, Indianapolis

Houghton Mifflin Company Boston New York

Components of *Entre amis*, Fourth Edition

- **Student Text with Student Audio CDs/Cassettes**
- **Instructor's Annotated Edition with Student Audio CDs/Cassettes**
- *Cahier d'activités:* **Workbook/Lab Manual/Video Worksheets**
- **Audio Program: CDs or Cassettes**
- **Instructor's Resource Manual (IRM) with Test Bank and Information Gap activities**
- **Instructor's Test Cassette**
- *Pas de problème!* **Video**
- *Entre amis* **Multimedia CD-ROM**
- *Entre amis* **WWW Site with Web-Search Activities, ACE Practice Tests**

Director of World Languages: Beth Kramer
Sponsoring Editor: Randy Welch
Senior Development Editor: Cécile Strugnell
Senior Project Editor: Florence Kilgo
Senior Production/Design Coordinator: Sarah Ambrose
Senior Manufacturing Coordinator: Florence Cadran
Associate Marketing Manager: Claudia Martinez

Credits for text, photos, realia, and illustrations are found following the index at the end of this book.

Printed in the U.S.A.

Library of Congress Catalog Card Number: 2001131538

Student Text ISBN: 0-618-11502-1

Instructor's Annotated Edition ISBN: 0-618-11503-X

1 2 3 4 5 6 7 8 9-DOW-05 04 03 02 01

To the Instructor

Entre amis, Fourth Edition, uses a functional, integrated skills approach to teach French to beginning students. The primary objective of the program is to give students an opportunity to acquire communication skills through interaction with the teacher and with each other in paired activities. Students also develop an awareness of language structure as it relates to French culture. The two are closely integrated throughout each chapter. The use of French gestures to facilitate the presentation and retention of vocabulary is but one illustration of the way that language and culture are interwoven in *Entre amis.* Students compare French grammar and culture to their own and personalize what they practice in their activities.

Main Features

Integration of language and culture. Cultural content is interwoven in language practice throughout the textbook. Culture is an integral part of what students learn, helping to develop their strategic competence and sociolinguistic accuracy.

Functional organization. Each chapter is divided into several *Buts communicatifs,* focusing students on meaningful interaction from the start.

Student-centered approach. The functions and activities of *Entre amis* equip students to exchange information about their own lives. The focus is on the learner's needs: describing personal tastes, activities, possessions, etc.

Interactive activities that work. While personalization is the goal of all of the interactive activities in *Entre amis,* students are never required to use expressions that they have not yet practiced. Grammar and vocabulary are presented in clear contexts before students are required to put them to use.

Manageable grammar and vocabulary. Each chapter introduces structures and expressions related to the targeted functions. The grammar syllabus and vocabulary load are then expanded and reinforced through recycling in subsequent chapters.

Reading as a process. Authentic *lectures* feature pre-reading and post-reading activities. Students are trained to use cognates, context, and their own experience to comprehend material that is above their level of production.

Contextualized writing. The Workbook contains contextualized activities that reinforce what students study in the textbook. Included in each chapter of the Workbook is a *Rédaction,* featuring a process approach to promote the development of the skill of writing.

Francophone culture. Several readings in the chapters of *Entre amis* as well as the five *Escales,* found at the end of every third chapter, familiarize students with the francophone world.

New to the Fourth Edition

- **A New *Entre amis* Multimedia CD-ROM** provides practice for each of the fifteen chapters of the textbook. Each chapter has three sections: 1. video-based skill development, 2. language practice, and 3. multimedia presentation. The CD-ROM also includes a grammar reference, a verb conjugation reference, a glossary of grammatical terms, and bilingual French/English and English/French glossaries.

- **A New *Entre amis* WWW site with two sections:** one for the instructor, the other for the student. The Instructor's Web Site will include Teaching Suggestions, Audio Script, Video Script, and Vignette Script. The Student Web Site includes ACE Practice Tests, Web-Search Activities, lists of Web links to provide additional information about topics presented in the *Escales,* Vocabulary Flash Cards, and other helpful resources.

- **New Video Worksheets,** in the *Cahier d'activités,* reinforce the tie between *Entre amis* and the *Pas de problème!* video, providing lexical and cultural preparation that will increase student comprehension and enjoyment. These Worksheets replace the Video Workbook from earlier editions of ***Entre amis.***

- **New Information Gap activities,** in the Instructor's Resource Manual, provide additional practice of grammar, vocabulary, and communicative strategy. Cued by icons in the Instructor's Edition of the textbook, the Information Gap activities include instructions and worksheets for each chapter.

Revised for the Fourth Edition

- **Three new *Lectures*** have been added to the Student Textbook and several others have been updated.

- **The Student Audio,** packaged with the textbook, offers a choice between CDs and cassettes, and includes all oral presentations and pronunciation sections.

- **An updated *A propos*** includes, in the Instructor's Edition, specific *Comparaison* annotations to invite students to reflect on their own culture in the light of what they are learning.

- **A new first Escale, *La France dans le monde,*** highlights France's role in the European and francophone communities. The other four *Escales* have been updated with new sections.

- **In the Laboratory Manual: New Section C, *Amusons-nous!*** entices students to speak the language through playful, culturally enriching activities. **New speaking activity** in Section B requires students to speak when they answer.

■ **New *Impressions*,** added to the modules of the *Pas de problème!* video. Documentary footage around cultural themes related to ***Entre amis,*** shot partly in France and partly in Guadeloupe. The Guadeloupe sections also include brief interviews with native French speakers.

Chapter Organization

Each of the fifteen chapters of ***Entre amis*** has three main parts: *Coup d'envoi, Buts communicatifs,* and *Intégration.* The following chart illustrates the organization of the chapters and the purpose of each section.

Section	Purpose
Chapter opener	Identification of functions, structures, and cultural content of the chapter Sets the scene
Coup d'envoi	Conceptualized introduction to some of the vocabulary and grammar
*Prise de contact**	Introduction to familiarize students with content
*Conversation**	Model for interaction Role-playing
À propos	Insights into the cultural content of the chapter
À vous!	Initial personalization
Entre amis	Paired activity
*Prononciation**	Explanations and practice to build correct speech
Buts communicatifs	Function-based organizing principle
Introduction*	Familiarization with the function
Grammar	Structures related to the targeted function
Vocabulary	Theme-related vocabulary introduced as needed
Activities	Meaningful practice in communication
Entre amis	Paired activity at the end of the *But Communicatif*
Intégration	Review and development of reading skill
Révision	Additional practice to build control and fluency *Pas de problème!* Video activity
Lecture(s)	Reading(s) with pre- and post-reading activities
Vocabulaire actif	List for review

* Recorded on the student audio packaged with the textbook

Other Program Components

■ **The Instructor's Annotated Edition** contains the student text with marginal annotations providing cultural and phonetic information, suggestions for follow-up activities, and other teaching tips.

■ **The Student Audio** (either CD or cassette) is free with each copy of the student textbook. Cued by an icon in the text, recordings include all oral presentation material (*Prise de contact, Conversations/Lettres,* introductions to the *Buts communicatifs*), pronunciation sections, and poetry readings from the *Intégration* section.

■ **The Cahier d'activités**

■ **Workbook:** The Workbook activities provide students with additional practice of vocabulary and grammar. One or more activities reinforce what has been taught in each section of the chapter. The final activity, *Rédaction*, features pen pals from the francophone countries mentioned in the Escales and provides detailed instructions and suggestions for the writing process and content.

■ **Laboratory Manual and Audio Program:** Activities in the Lab Manual practice listening and speaking, using recordings of the Audio Program available on CDs or cassettes. The script of the Audio program is in the Instructor's Resource Manual and on the new Instructor's Web Site. Section A practices pronunciation, Section B practices listening comprehension and speaking. The new Section C asks students to repeat amusing rhymes, tongue twisters, exchanges, and traditional songs to practice their French.

■ **Vignettes,** recorded in the Audio Program, provide additional listening comprehension practice. They are original mini-dialogues (*vignettes*) that recombine expressions learned in the textbook. Students listen and fill in the blanks to supply the missing words. The script for the vignettes is available in the Instructor's Resource Manual and on the Instructor's Web Site.

■ **Video Worksheets** provide lexical and cultural preparation for the *Pas de problème!* video. Students complete the worksheets, referring as needed to the *Vocabulaire à reconnaître* that lists expressions used in the video and their meaning. Each set of activities ends with a cultural comparison (*Réflexion*). Doing these activities should take no more than fifteen minutes.

The video worksheets in the *Cahier* reinforce the tie between text and video by drawing students' attention to specific cultural components of ***Entre amis.*** Examples include gestures and body language, greetings, communicative strategies, technology, transportation, shopping, and ordering food. The worksheet activities are based on the following correlation chart of text chapters and video modules.

Entre amis	Pas de problème! video	Entre amis	Pas de problème! video
Chapter 1	Introduction to 1:44	Chapter 9	Module 6
Chapter 2	Module 1	Chapter 10	Module 7
Chapter 3	Module 1	Chapter 11	Module 8
Chapter 4	Module 2	Chapter 12	Module 9
Chapter 5	Module 2	Chapter 13	Module 10
Chapter 6	Module 3	Chapter 14	Module 11
Chapter 7	Module 4	Chapter 15	Module 12
Chapter 8	Module 5		

■ **Answer keys,** found in the back of the *Cahier d'activités*, enable students to self-correct when doing the activities of the Workbook, Lab Manual, Vignettes, and Video Worksheets.

- **The Instructor's Resource Manual (IRM) with the Instructor's Test Cassette** contains the Instructor's Guide, Suggestions for teaching with *Entre amis*, and the new Information Gap activities. It includes the Test Bank with explicit suggestions for testing students' speaking ability. **The Instructor's Test Cassette,** packaged with the IRM, facilitates oral testing in a language laboratory and consists of five tests of speaking activities. The Test Bank also includes two written tests for each of the fifteen chapters, three comprehensive tests, and numerous suggestions for quizzes. Also included are the audio script to accompany the Lab Manual, the Vignettes audio scripts, the video transcript, and thirty transparency masters.

- **The Entre amis Multimedia CD-ROM** (see description under "New to the Fourth Edition")

- **The Entre amis WWW site** includes a section for the instructor (see under "New to the Fourth Edition") and one for the student.

The **Student Web Site** includes:

- ACE Practice Tests that check grammar and vocabulary for each of the *Coup d'envoi* and *Buts communicatifs*. Some activities draw examples from the *Pas de problème!* video. Students receive immediate feedback so that they can monitor their own progress. The tests can also be printed or emailed to the instructor upon completion.

- Web-Search Activities, cued in the Student Edition in the *Intégration* section. These require students to search for answers on the Web to questions closely related to the chapter topics. Student answers can also be printed or emailed to the instructor.

- Informative Links to sites that provide additional background to topics addressed in the *Escales* allow students to explore further their interest in France and francophone countries.

Teaching with the *Entre amis* Program

THE INSTRUCTOR AS MODEL, FACILITATOR, AND JUDGE

Comme Maître Jacques dans l'Avare, nous jouons tous plusieurs rôles.

- **Model.** Presenting a clear model for our students is the first of our roles. In addition to introducing the contextualized material that students will practice *(Prise de contact, Conversation,* and *Buts communicatifs)*, we also have many opportunities to "model" attentive listening, patience, enthusiasm, and an ability to laugh at ourselves. Our students will "catch" our attitude toward learning and communicating in French. The Instructor's Resource Manual and the Instructor's part of the web site have suggestions for presenting new material.

- **Facilitator.** With an interactive approach, we spend most of our time involving students in the learning process. In a learner-centered classroom, the accent is on personalization and sharing. The exercises in *Entre amis* were written to facilitate student-to-student interaction. Well-primed, paired activities, followed by a brief closed-book check (follow up), will pay dividends in student progress and enthusiasm. The IRM and the web site have suggestions for planning your class time, warm-up, and follow-up activities.

■ **Judge.** Anticipating possible errors and giving feedback are an integral part of our role as judge. The most appropriate time to invite student questions and to provide correction is immediately following short personalized interaction, e.g., after a communicative activity and before the follow-up. In the IRM there are written tests and quizzes for each chapter in *Entre amis,* as well as detailed suggestions for oral testing.

ENTRE AMIS AND THE NATIONAL STANDARDS[1]

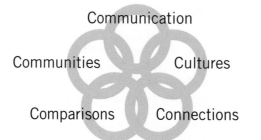

Communication. *This is at the heart of second language study. Students get many opportunities to communicate face-to-face, in writing, and through reading.*

Interpersonal. Contextualized pair practice is an integral part of the *Entre amis* interactive approach. Specific activities include *Prise de contact* (7)[2], *Jouez ces rôles* (8), *À vous* (10), *Entre amis* (10; 48; 102), *Trouvez quelqu'un qui …* (48). Students have many chances to provide and obtain personal information, to express feelings, and to exchange opinions. Activities in this text have truth value, i.e., students are never forced to say "I love spinach" if they really don't.

Interpretive. Students have numerous opportunities to hear and read French. Listening comprehension includes instructor modeling and negotiating of meaning in the *Prise de contact* and initial material in the *Buts communicatifs* as well as on the tapes (lab activities and *vignettes*) and video (*Pas de problème!*). Authentic readings in each chapter feature pre- and post-reading activities that involve students in reading, rereading and interpreting the selections.

Presentational. Students share personal information and ideas in contextualized writing assignments in both the text and the workbook. A process approach to writing is used in the *Rédaction* at the end of each chapter of the workbook and with specific activities in the text, e.g., *Un test de votre personnalité* (97).

---

[1] From the *National Standards in Foreign Language Education,* a collaborative project of ACTFL, AATF, AATG, & AATSP.
[2] Page numbers refer to examples in the text.

Cultures. *Students gain knowledge and understanding of the cultural contexts in which language occurs.*

The *Conversations* and *À propos* sections integrate language and culture. Students are helped to understand the cultural context in which their language practice takes place. Web-search activities, the *Pas de problème!* video, including video worksheets, activities, and **Entre amis** CD-ROM, and the gestures and *Notes culturelles* in the text all reinforce the cultural component of **Entre amis**.

Connections. *Students use their language to access additional knowledge, sometimes unavailable to the monolingual English speaker.*

The fourth edition of **Entre amis** includes a WWW site that expands upon the students' knowledge base. Closely tied to the themes of each chapter, the Web-search activities enable students to access up-to-date information about France and the French-speaking world. These activities require students to use the Internet to examine a variety of sources intended for native speakers and to extract specific information.

Comparisons. *Students compare and contrast the target language and culture with their own.*

Included in the *À propos* section of each chapter in the instructor's edition of **Entre amis** are specific suggestions to involve students in reflecting on their own culture in the light of what they are learning about the target culture. Students are also required to compare and contrast French and English through the grammar sections of the text as well as in numerous student marginal annotations that refer to previously studied material and serve as reminders of grammatical (74; 96; 134) or lexical (70; 101; 118) usage. Similarly, each *Pas de problème!* Video Worksheet includes a *Réflexion* activity.

Communities. *Students have contact with multilingual communities in a variety of contexts and in culturally appropriate ways.*

The *Escale* sections in **Entre amis** are meant to whet students' appetite for a number of areas of the world where French is spoken. WWW activities associated with each chapter as well as informative links with the *Escales* put students in contact with several francophone communities, including the opportunity to interact with other speakers of French beyond their campus.

Suggested Syllabi

The following schedules are meant only as general guidelines. Instructors who wish to make full use of the rich ancillary package that accompanies **Entre amis** are likely to spend more time with each chapter, especially if they wish students to participate more fully in classroom interaction.

Please consult the Instructor's Resource Manual for chapter activities, including detailed lesson plans for the *First Ten Days* and the Test Bank.

Two semesters, meeting 5 days per week

	Semester 1				
Week	Day 1	Day 2	Day 3	Day 4	Day 5
1	1st day	Prelim.	Prelim.	Quiz	Chap. 1
2	But 1	But 2	But 3	But 4	Intég.
3	WWW	Test	Chap. 2	But 1	But 2
4	But 2/3	But 3	But 4	But 4	Intég.
5	WWW	Test	Chap. 3	But 1	But 2
6	But 2	But 3	But 3	Intég.	WWW
7	Oral	Test	Esc. 1	Chap. 4	But 1
8	But 1/2	But 2	But 3	But 4	But 5
9	Intég.	WWW	Test	Chap. 5	But 1
10	But 1/2	But 2	But 3	But 3/4	But 4
11	Intég.	WWW	Test	Chap. 6	But 1
12	But 1	But 2	But 2/3	But 3	But 3
13	Intég.	WWW	Test	Esc. 2	Chap. 7
14	But 1	But 1	But 2	But 2/3	But 3
15	Intég.	WWW	Review	Oral	Test

	Semester 2				
Week	Day 1	Day 2	Day 3	Day 4	Day 5
1	Chap. 8	But 1	But 1	But 2	But 3
2	But 4	Intég.	WWW	Test	Chap. 9
3	But 1	But 1/2	But 2	But 3	But 3
4	Intég.	WWW	Test	Esc. 3	Chap. 10
5	But 1	But 2	But 3	But 3	But 4
6	Intég.	Test	Chap. 11	But 1	But 1/2
7	But 2	But 3	But 3	Intég.	WWW
8	Oral	Test	Chap. 12	But 1	But 1/2
9	But 2	But 3	But 3	Intég.	WWW
10	Test	Esc. 4	Chap. 13	But 1	But 2
11	But 3	But 3/4	But 4	Intég.	WWW
12	Test	Chap. 14	But 1	But 1	But 2
13	But 2/3	But 3	Intég.	WWW	Test
14	Chap. 15	But 1	But 1	But 2	But 2
15	Intég.	WWW	Esc. 5	Oral	Test

Two semesters, meeting 4 days per week

	Semester 1			
Week	Day 1	Day 2	Day 3	Day 4
1	1st day	Prelim.	Prelim.	Quiz
2	Chap. 1	But 1	But 2	But 3
3	But 4	Intég.	Test	Chap. 2
4	But 1	But 2	But 3	But 3/4
5	But 4	Intég.	Test	Chap. 3
6	But 1	But 2	But 2	But 3
7	But 3	Intég.	Test	Chap. 4
8	But 1	But 1/2	But 2	But 3
9	But 4	But 5	Intég.	Test
10	Chap. 5	But 1	But 2	But 3
11	But 3/4	But 4	Intég.	Test
12	Chap. 6	But 1	But 1/2	But 2
13	But 3	But 3	Intég.	Test
14	Chap. 7	But 1	But 1/2	But 2
15	But 3	Intég.	Oral	Test

	Semester 2			
Week	Day 1	Day 2	Day 3	Day 4
1	Chap. 8	But 1	But 1	But 2
2	But 3	But 4	Intég.	Test
3	Chap. 9	But 1	But 1/2	But 2
4	But 3	But 3	Intég.	Test
5	Chap. 10	But 1	But 2	But 3
6	But 3	But 4	Intég.	Test
7	Chap. 11	But 1	But 1/2	But 2
8	But 3	But 3	Intég.	Test
9	Chap. 12	But 1	But 1/2	But 2
10	But 3	But 3	Intég.	Test
11	Chap. 13	But 1	But 2	But 3
12	But 4	Intég.	Test	Chap. 14
13	But 1	But 1	But 2	But 3
14	Intég.	Test	Chap. 15	But 1
15	But 2	Intég.	Oral	Test

Three semesters, meeting 3 days per week*

At some institutions, the introductory-level curriculum covers three semesters. *Entre amis*, with its numerous student-centered interactive activities and process approach to reading and writing, is also ideally suited for use in an extended program. If a student's study of French begins at the college level, we suggest that *Entre amis* be used in conjunction with an intermediate text with a communicative approach, such as *Personnages*, in a four-or-five-semester sequence.

Semester 1			
Week	Day 1	Day 2	Day 3
1	1st day	Prelim.	Prelim.
2	Quiz	Chap. 1	But 1
3	But 2	But 3	But 4
4	Intég.	Test	Chap. 2
5	But 1	But 2	But 3
6	But 3/4	But 4	Intég.
7	Test	Chap. 3	But 1
8	But 2	But 2	But 3
9	But 3	Intég.	Test
10	Esc. 1	Chap. 4	But 1
11	But 1/2	But 2	But 3
12	But 4	But 5	Intég.
13	Test	Chap. 5	But 1
14	But 2	But 3	But 4
15	Intég.	Oral	Test

Semester 2			
Week	Day 1	Day 2	Day 3
1	Chap. 6	But 1	But 1
2	But 2	But 2/3	But 3
3	But 3	Intég.	Test
4	Esc. 2	Chap. 7	But 1
5	But 1	But 2	But 2/3
6	But 3	Intég.	Oral
7	Test	Chap. 8	But 1
8	But 1	But 2	But 3
9	But 4	Intég.	Test
10	Chap. 9	But 1	But 1/2
11	But 2	But 3	But 3
12	Intég.	Test	Esc. 3
13	Chap. 10	But 1	But 2
14	But 3	But 3	But 4
15	Intég.	Oral	Test

Semester 3			
Week	Day 1	Day 2	Day 3
1	Chap. 11	But 1	But 1/2
2	But 2	But 3	But 3
3	Intég.	Test	Chap. 12
4	But 1	But 1/2	But 2
5	But 3	But 3	Intég.
6	Oral	Test	Esc. 4
7	Chap. 13	But 1	But 2
8	But 3	But 3/4	But 4
9	Intég.	Test	Chap. 14
10	But 1	But 1	But 2
11	But 2/3	But 3	Intég.
12	Test	Chap. 15	But 1
13	But 1	But 2	But 2
14	Intég.	Test	Esc. 5
15	Review	Oral	Test

* For a two-semester three-days-per-week syllabus, go to the Instructor's section of the *Entre amis* web site.

Three quarters, meeting 4 days per week

Quarter 1				
Week	**Day 1**	**Day 2**	**Day 3**	**Day 4**
1	1st day	Prelim.	Prelim.	Quiz
2	Chap. 1	But 1	But 2	But 3
3	But 4	Intég.	Test	Chap. 2
4	But 1	But 2	But 2/3	But 3
5	But 4	But 4	Intég.	Test
6	Chap. 3	But 1	But 2	But 2
7	But 3	But 3	Intég.	Test
8	Chap. 4	But 1	But 1	But 2
9	But 2	But 3	But 4	But 5
10	Intég.	Review	Oral	Test

Quarter 2				
Week	**Day 1**	**Day 2**	**Day 3**	**Day 4**
1	Chap. 5	But 1	But 2	But 3
2	But 3/4	But 4	Intég.	Test
3	Chap. 6	But 1	But 2	But 3
4	But 3	Intég.	Test	Chap. 7
5	But 1	But 1/2	But 2	But 3
6	Intég.	Test	Chap. 8	But 1
7	But 1	But 2	But 3	But 4
8	Intég.	Test	Chap. 9	But 1
9	But 1/2	But 2	But 3	But 3
10	Intég.	Review	Oral	Test

Quarter 3				
Week	**Day 1**	**Day 2**	**Day 3**	**Day 4**
1	Chap. 10	But 1	But 2	But 2/3
2	But 3	But 4	Intég.	Test
3	Chap. 11	But 1	But 1/2	But 2
4	But 3	But 3	Intég.	Test
5	Chap. 12	But 1	But 1/2	But 2
6	But 3	But 3	Intég.	Test
7	Chap. 13	But 1	But 2	But 3
8	But 4	Intég.	Test	Chap. 14
9	But 1	But 1	But 2	But 2/3
10	But 3	Intég.	Oral	Test

Three 10-week quarters, meeting 5 days per week

First quarter:	Second quarter:	Third quarter:
1 day for beginning	8 days for chapters 6 to 10	8 days each for chapters 11 to 15
3 days for the Chapitre préliminaire	1 day each for Escales 2 and 3	1 day each for Escales 4 and 5
7–8 days each for chapters 1 to 5	4 days for Web Search/Gap activities	4 days for Web Search/Gap activities
1 day for Escale 1	4 days for testing	4 days for testing
4 days for Web Search/Gap activities		
4 days for testing		

Three 10-week quarters, meeting 3 days per week

First quarter:	Second quarter:	Third quarter:
1 day for beginning	7 days each for chapters 4 to 7	7 days each for chapters 8 to 11
3 days for the Chapitre préliminaire	2 days for testing	2 days for testing
8 days each for chapters 1 to 3		
2 days for testing		

False Beginners

Some students in first-semester French already have had exposure to the French language. They often have a background in grammar but need opportunities to develop their oral skills. Instructors who tailor a course to this type of student are encouraged to use classroom time for personalized interactive practice of French and assign grammar and culture study for out-of-class preparation. Since a copy of the Student Audio is bound with each copy of the text, and grammar and culture are presented in English, **Entre amis** is suited for use with *faux débutants* as well as with true beginners.

Entre Amis

Entre Amis

An Interactive Approach

Fourth Edition

Michael D. Oates
University of Northern Iowa

Larbi Oukada
Indiana University, Indianapolis

Houghton Mifflin Company Boston   New York

Components of *Entre amis*, Fourth Edition

▓ **Student Text with Student Audio**

▓ **Instructor's Annotated Edition with Student Audio**

▓ ***Cahier d'activités:* Workbook/Lab Manual/Video Worksheets**

▓ **Instructor's Resource Manual (IRM) with Test Bank and Information Gap activities**

▓ **Instructor's Test Cassette**

▓ **Audio Program**

▓ ***Pas de problème!* Video**

▓ ***Entre amis* Multimedia CD-ROM**

▓ ***Entre amis* WWW Site with Web-Search Activities and ACE Practice Tests**

Director of World Languages: Beth Kramer
Sponsoring Editor: Randy Welch
Senior Development Editor: Cécile Strugnell
Senior Project Editor: Florence Kilgo
Senior Production/Design Coordinator: Sarah Ambrose
Senior Manufacturing Coordinator: Florence Cadran
Associate Marketing Manager: Claudia Martinez

Credits for text, photos, realia, and illustrations are found following the index at the end of this book.

Printed in the U.S.A.

Library of Congress Catalog Card Number: 2001131538

Student Text ISBN: 0-618-11502-1

Instructor's Annotated Edition ISBN: 0-618-11503-X

1   2   3   4   5   6   7   8   9-DOW-05   04   03   02   01

Contents

To the Student

Entre amis is a first-year college French program centered around the needs of a language learner like you. Among these needs is the ability to communicate in French and to develop insights into French culture and language. You will have many opportunities to hear French spoken and to interact with your instructor and classmates. Your ability to read and write French will improve with practice. The functions and exercises are designed to enable you to share information about your life—your interests, your family, your tastes, your plans.

Helpful Hints

While you will want to experiment with different ways of studying the material you will learn, a few hints, taken from successful language learners, are in order:

En français, s'il vous plaît!   Try to use what you are learning with anyone who is able to converse in French. Greet fellow students in French and see how far you can go in conversing with each other.

Enjoy it.   Be willing to take off the "wise-adult" mask and even to appear silly to keep the communication going. Everybody makes mistakes. Try out new words, use new gestures, and paraphrase, if it helps. Laugh at yourself; it helps.

Bring as many senses into play as possible.   Study out loud, listen to the taped materials, use a pencil and paper to test your recall of the expressions you are studying. Anticipate conversations you will have and prepare a few French sentences in advance. Then try to work them into your conversations.

Nothing ventured, nothing gained.   One must go through lower-level stages before reaching a confident mastery of the language. Study and practice, including attentive listening, combined with meaningful interaction with others will result in an ability to use French to communicate.

Where there's a will, there's a way.   Be resourceful in your attempt to communicate. Seek alternative ways of expressing the same idea. For instance, if you are stuck in trying to say, «Comment vous appelez-vous?» ("What is your name?"), don't give up your attempt and end the conversation. Look for other ways of finding out that person's name. You may want to say, «Je m'appelle John/Jane Doe. Et vous?» or «John/Jane Doe» (pointing to yourself). «Et vous?» (pointing to the other person). There are often numerous possibilities!

Use your imagination.   Some of the exercises will encourage you to play a new role. Add imaginary details to these situations, to your life story, etc., to enliven the activities.

Organization of the Text

The text is divided into fifteen chapters with a brief preliminary chapter plus five *Escales* that provide a glimpse of some of the many places where French is spoken outside of France. Each chapter is organized around a central cultural theme with three major divisions: **Coup d'envoi, Buts communicatifs,** and **Intégration.**

All presentation material, *Prise de contact* and *Conversation* in the *Coup d'envoi,* and the introduction to each *But communicatif* are recorded on the Student Audio shrink-wrapped with your text. Listen to these to prepare for your French class or to review by yourself afterwards.

> **Coup d'envoi** = *Kickoff.*
> **Prise de contact** = *Initial Contact.* See pp. 7, 29, etc.

Coup d'envoi

This section starts the cycle of listening, practicing, and personalizing which will make your learning both rewarding and enjoyable. You will often be asked to reflect and to compare French culture with your own culture.

Prise de contact is a short presentation of key phrases, often illustrated. In this section you are encouraged to participate and respond to simple questions about your family, your life, or your recent activities.

Conversation/Lettre typically shows a language learner in France, adapting to French culture. You will often find this person in situations with which you can identify: introducing himself or asking for directions, for example. Then you will be asked what you would do or say in a similar situation.

The *À propos* section describes particular aspects of French culture closely tied to the *Conversation.* These cultural sections will help you understand why, for example, the French do not usually say "thank you" when responding to a compliment or why meals are structured in France.

The *Il y a un geste* section is a special feature of **Entre amis** and an integral part of every chapter. It consists of photos and descriptions of common French gestures. The primary purpose of the gestures is to reinforce the meaning of the expressions associated with them that you will learn and use throughout the year.

The *Entre amis* activities give you a chance to speak French one-on-one with another student. You are given a role-playing activity that duplicates a real-life situation (ordering a meal in a café, finding out what your partner did yesterday, etc.). These appear several times in each chapter.

The *Prononciation* section helps you to imitate correctly general features of French pronunciation as well as specific sounds. It is important that your speech be readily understandable so that you can communicate more easily with people in French. The Student Audio also practices the pronunciation lesson for each chapter.

Buts communicatifs

> **Buts communicatifs** = *Communicative goals.* See pp. 12, 34, etc.

As was the case in the **Coup d'envoi** section, each of the **Buts communicatifs** sections begins with a presentation, including key phrases that you will use to interact with your instructor and classmates. Material from the **Coup d'envoi** is recycled in the **Buts communicatifs.** The section is divided according to specific tasks, such as asking for directions, describing your weekend activities, and finding out where things are sold. Within this context, there are grammar explanations, exercises, vocabulary, and role-playing activities. The vocabulary is taught in groups of words directly related to each of the functions you are learning. All of these words are then listed at the end of each chapter in the *Vocabulaire actif* section. Each section of the **Buts communicatifs** ends with an *Entre amis* activity that encourages you to put to use what you have just learned.

Intégration

This final section includes one or more reading selections (*Lectures*). These readings are from authentic French materials, such as excerpts from newspapers, magazines, literary texts, or poems. (The poems are recorded on your student audio.) There are activities both before and after each reading to relate the material to your own experience and to help increase your understanding. In addition, there is an activity that corresponds to a specific segment of the *Pas de problème!* video. A list of all the active vocabulary of the chapter is included at the end of this section.

Escales

Escale = *Stop over.*
See pp. 84, 178, etc.

These five magazine-like sections, appearing at intervals between chapters, will give you an appreciation for the widespread use of French throughout the world. You will be introduced to many francophone countries and will enjoy discovering particular aspects of their culture, such as literature, music, art, festivals, sports, food, and traditions.

Appendices

The reference section contains verb conjugations, an appendix of phonetic symbols, a list of professions, a glossary of grammatical terms, French-English and English-French vocabularies, and an index.

Ancillaries

Cahier d'activités

The *Cahier d'activités* combines Workbook, Lab Manual, and Video Worksheets with answer keys for each section so that you can correct yourself as you progress through the chapters.

The Workbook activities will provide you with additional practice for each section of vocabulary and grammar. A final activity, *Rédaction,* will give you writing practice with pen pals from the francophone countries mentioned in the *Escales.* Step-by-step instructions and suggestions will help you through the writing process.

The Laboratory Manual and Audio Program will combine to help you practice your pronunciation and your listening and speaking skills. You will listen to the recordings and instructions of the Audio Program available to you in CDs or cassettes. The Lab Manual will provide you with cues to answer the questions. In the last activity of each chapter, rhymes, tongue twisters, lively exchanges, and traditional songs will motivate you to speak French.

Following the Lab Manual, activities based on *Vignettes,* short skits featuring an exchange between native speakers, provide additional listening practice. The *Vignettes* are also recorded on the Audio Program.

Video worksheets help you to understand the *Pas de problème!* video (see below). A *Vocabulaire à reconnaître* lists new words spoken in the video and their meaning. The worksheets provide simple activities that reinforce the links between the video and what you learned in your textbook.

Pas de problème! Video

The video *Pas de problème!* was filmed in France. Each module introduces young people, French native speakers from different countries, living in France, interacting with each other, and encountering everyday problems that you may experience if you visit France. Between the modules, the video includes *Impressions,* short sections shot in France and in Guadeloupe, that provide insights into the culture and way of life of people in these countries. The themes presented expand on topics addressed in the video or in the textbook. In Guadeloupe, native speakers express their opinion or talk about their own experience as it applies to the chosen themes.

Entre amis Multimedia CD-ROM

This CD-ROM will be a valuable tool for you to practice each of the fifteen chapters of the textbook. Each chapter has three sections: 1. video-based skill development, 2. language practice, and 3. multimedia presentation. The CD-ROM also includes a grammar reference, a verb conjugation reference, a glossary of grammatical terms, and bilingual French/English and English/French glossaries.

Entre amis WWW Site

You may access this site through the Houghton Mifflin WWW site. Icons in the textbook will cue you in to some of the components. At the beginning of the *Intégration* section, an icon indicates web-search activities you can do by accessing the links described. An icon in the *Escales* indicates that the site has links to French WWW sites so that you can look up more information on topics of the *Escale* you are reading. In addition, the WWW site offers interactive ACE Practice Tests that will enable you to check your understanding of the chapter grammar and vocabulary, as well as Vocabulary Flash Cards and other helpful resources.

Acknowledgments

We, the authors, are deeply indebted to the editorial staff of Houghton Mifflin for giving us the opportunity to develop and produce the text. Their encouragement and guidance made **Entre amis,** Fourth Edition possible.

Michael Oates specifically wishes to thank his wife, Maureen O'Leary Oates, for her patience during the development and editing of **Entre amis.** He is grateful for the support of Joye Lore-Lawson, of Indian Hills CC, and Linda Quinn Allen of Iowa State University. Larbi Oukada also wishes to express his gratitude to the following individuals for their contribution to the renovated *Escales*:

Brenda Bertrand, Associate Faculty, IUPUI
Didier Bertrand, Associate Professor, IUPUI
Obioma Nnaemeka, Associate Professor, IUPUI
Page Curry, Associate Faculty, IUPUI DePauw University
Rosalie Vermette, Associate Professor, IUPUI

We would also like to express our sincere appreciation to the following people for their thoughtful reviews of the fourth edition of **Entre amis.**

Martine Howard, Camden County College, New Jersey
Richard Stroik, University of San Diego, CA
Professor Ray Cornelius, Daytona Beach Community College,
   West Campus, FL
Carolyn Jacobs, Houston Community College Central, TX
Rolande Léguillon, University of St. Thomas, Houston, TX
Mike Zoltak, Spokane Community College, WA
Kara Rabbitt, William Patterson University, NJ
Donald Dziekowicz, St. Thomas University, MN

Entre Amis

Au départ

Buts communicatifs

Understanding basic classroom commands

Understanding numbers

Understanding basic expressions of time

Understanding basic weather expressions

Buts communicatifs

Grasping the meaning of spoken French is fundamental to learning to communicate in French. Developing this skill will require patience and perseverance, but your success will be enhanced if you associate a mental image (e.g., of a picture, an object, a gesture, an action, the written word) with the expressions you hear. This preliminary chapter will focus on establishing the association of sound and symbol in a few basic contexts: classroom expressions, numbers, time, and weather.

1 Understanding Basic Classroom Commands

Dans la salle de classe

This icon indicates that this material is recorded on the Student Audio (CD or cassette) provided with each copy of the text.

Point out that accents are part of spelling in French, but that they may be omitted on capital letters.

Listen carefully and watch the physical response of your teacher to each command. Once you have learned to associate the actions with the French sentences, you may be asked to practice them.

Levez-vous!
Allez à la porte!
Ouvrez la porte!
Sortez!
Frappez à la porte!
Entrez!
Fermez la porte!

Allez au tableau!
Prenez la craie!
Écrivez votre nom!
Mettez la craie sur la table!
Donnez la craie à ... !
Donnez-moi la craie!
Asseyez-vous!

This gesture is used in the *Pas de problème* video, *Module 2*.

Il y a un geste

Frapper à la porte.
When knocking on a door (**toc, toc, toc**), the French often use the back of the hand (open or closed).

2 Understanding Numbers

Il y a un geste

Les nombres

0 zéro	10 dix	20 vingt
1 un	11 onze	21 vingt et un
2 deux	12 douze	22 vingt-deux
3 trois	13 treize	23 vingt-trois
4 quatre	14 quatorze	24 vingt-quatre
5 cinq	15 quinze	25 vingt-cinq
6 six	16 seize	26 vingt-six
7 sept	17 dix-sept	27 vingt-sept
8 huit	18 dix-huit	28 vingt-huit
9 neuf	19 dix-neuf	29 vingt-neuf
		30 trente

Teach students to associate the numbers 1–10 with the gestures for counting on the fingers in French.

The gesture on the right is used in the video, *Module 4*.

Compter avec les doigts. When counting, the French normally begin with the thumb, then the index finger, etc. For instance, the thumb, index, and middle fingers are held up to indicate the number three, as a child might indicate when asked his/her age.

3 Understanding Basic Expressions of Time

Quelle heure est-il?

  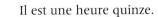 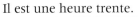

Il est une heure.   Il est une heure dix.   Il est une heure quinze.   Il est une heure trente.

Il est deux heures moins vingt.   Il est deux heures moins dix.   Il est deux heures.   Il est trois heures.

Have students identify the words as masculine (left hand) or feminine (right hand). The same phonetic principle will be used for the adjectives in Chs. 1, 3, & 4.

It is normally easier for students to learn the feminine first and to emphasize the pronunciation of the final consonant. The masculine can often be derived by dropping the final consonant sound.

Practice the French alphabet with the expressions you have learned so far. Read an expression out loud; spell it in French; close your book and try to write it from memory.

Model the alphabet several times for students. Dictate students' names using the French alphabet; ask the class to try to identify the names you spell in French. Follow up by having individuals spell their own names in French.

Masculin ou féminin?

■ You will learn to identify nouns and adjectives in French as masculine or feminine.

Often, the feminine form ends in a consonant sound while the masculine form ends in a vowel sound.

Féminins		*Masculins*	
Françoise	Louise	François	Louis
Jeanne	Martine	Jean	Martin
Laurence	Simone	Laurent	Simon
chaude	froide	chaud	froid
française	intelligente	français	intelligent
anglaise	petite	anglais	petit

L'alphabet français

	prononciation		**prononciation**
A	*ah*	**N**	*enne*
B	*bé*	**O**	*oh*
C	*sé*	**P**	*pé*
D	*dé*	**Q**	*ku*
E	*euh*	**R**	*erre*
F	*effe*	**S**	*esse*
G	*jé*	**T**	*té*
H	*ashe*	**U**	*u*
I	*i*	**V**	*vé*
J	*ji*	**W**	*double vé*
K	*ka*	**X**	*iks*
L	*elle*	**Y**	*i grec*
M	*emme*	**Z**	*zed*

Comment est-ce qu'on écrit **merci?**   *How do you spell "merci"?*
Merci s'écrit M-E-R-C-I.   *"Merci" is spelled M-E-R-C-I.*

4 Understanding Basic Weather Expressions

Quel temps fait-il?

Il fait beau.   Il fait du vent.   Il fait froid.
Il fait du soleil.

Il fait chaud.   Il pleut.   Il neige.

Il y a un geste

Comment? Pardon? An open hand, cupped behind the ear, indicates that the message has not been heard and should be repeated.

Practice the expressions **Comment dit-on ... ?** and **Que veut dire ... ?** to check on the meaning of words already introduced.

VOCABULAIRE

Quelques expressions pour la salle de classe

Pardon? *Pardon?*
Comment? *What (did you say)?*
Répétez, s'il vous plaît. *Please repeat.*
Encore. *Again.*
En français. *In French.*
Ensemble. *Together.*
Tout le monde. *Everybody, everyone.*

Fermez le livre. *Close the book.*
Écoutez. *Listen.*
Répondez. *Answer.*

Comment dit-on «*the teacher*»? *How do you say "the teacher"?*
On dit «le professeur». *You say "le professeur."*

Que veut dire «*le tableau*»? *What does "le tableau" mean?*
Ça veut dire «*the chalkboard*». *It means "the chalkboard."*

Je ne sais pas. *I don't know.*
Je ne comprends pas. *I don't understand.*

Bonjour!

Buts communicatifs
Greeting others
Exchanging personal information
Identifying nationality
Describing physical appearance

Structures utiles
Les pronoms sujets
Le verbe **être**
L'accord des adjectifs
La négation
L'accord des adjectifs (suite)

Culture
Monsieur, Madame et **Mademoiselle**
Le premier contact
La politesse
Le prénom

Prise de contact

Les présentations

See the Instructor's Resource Manual for detailed suggestions on how to teach this lesson.

Mademoiselle Becker

Je m'appelle°
  Lori Becker.
J'habite à° Boston.
Je suis° américaine.
Je suis célibataire°.

Monsieur Davidson

Je m'appelle
  James Davidson.
J'habite à San Francisco.
Je suis américain.
Je suis célibataire.

My name is

I live in
I am
single

Review the Helpful Hints found in the *To the Student* section in the front of your text.

Be sure to learn the vocabulary on the first two pages of each chapter.

Madame Martin

Je m'appelle
  Anne Martin.
J'habite à Angers.
Je suis française.
Je suis mariée°.

Monsieur Martin

Je m'appelle
  Pierre Martin.
J'habite à Angers.
Je suis français.
Je suis marié.

married

Et vous? Qui êtes-vous?°

And you? Who are you?

Conversation

Dans un hôtel à Paris

The *Conversation* is recorded on the Student Audio that accompanies your text.

Listen carefully to your instructor and/or the Student Audio. Will you be able to recall any words immediately after the presentation?

Suggestions for modeling and student practice are found in the Instructor's Resource Manual.

Deux hommes sont au restaurant de l'hôtel Ibis à Paris.

PIERRE MARTIN:	Bonjour°, Monsieur! Excusez-moi de vous déranger.°	*Hello* *Excuse me for bothering you.*
JAMES DAVIDSON:	Bonjour. Pas de problème.°	*No problem.*
PIERRE MARTIN:	Vous permettez?° *(He touches the empty chair.)*	*May I?*
JAMES DAVIDSON:	Certainement. Asseyez-vous là°.	*there; here*
PIERRE MARTIN:	Vous êtes anglais?°	*Are you English?*
JAMES DAVIDSON:	Non, je suis américain. Permettez-moi de me présenter.° Je m'appelle James Davidson. *(They stand up and shake hands.)*	*Let me introduce myself.*
PIERRE MARTIN:	Martin, Pierre Martin. *(A receptionist comes into the room.)*	
LA RÉCEPTIONNISTE:	Le téléphone, Monsieur Davidson. C'est pour vous.° Votre communication de Californie.°	*It's for you.* *Your call from California.*
JAMES DAVIDSON:	Excusez-moi, s'il vous plaît, Monsieur.	
PIERRE MARTIN:	Oui, certainement. Au revoir, Monsieur. *(They shake hands again.)*	
JAMES DAVIDSON:	Bonne journée°, Monsieur.	*Have a good day*
PIERRE MARTIN:	Merci°, vous aussi°.	*Thank you / also; too*

In the **hôtel Ibis** there is a buffet system for meals, with self-seating. The main desk is near the restaurant.

> **Jouez ces rôles.** Role-play the conversation with a partner. Use your own identities.

Why does Pierre Martin say **Bonjour, Monsieur** instead of just **Bonjour**?

a. He likes variety; either expression will do.
b. **Bonjour** alone is a bit less formal than **Bonjour, Monsieur.**
c. He is trying to impress James Davidson.

Only one answer is culturally accurate. Read the information below to find out which one.

Monsieur, Madame et Mademoiselle

A certain amount of formality is in order when initial contact is made with French speakers. It is more polite to add **Monsieur, Madame,** or **Mademoiselle** when addressing someone than simply to say **Bonjour.** James Davidson catches on toward the end of the conversation when he remembers to say **Bonne journée, Monsieur.**

Le premier contact *(Breaking the ice)*

Pierre Martin asks if he can sit at the empty seat. However, the French are usually more reticent than Americans to "break the ice." This may present a challenge to the language learner who wishes to meet others, but as long as you are polite, you should not hesitate to begin a conversation.

La Politesse

See the *Entre amis* web site for additional information.

According to Polly Platt, the five most important words in French are **Excusez-moi de vous déranger.** This is a polite way to interrupt someone in France and a valuable formula for students and tourists who

need to ask for directions or get permission to do something. Remaining polite, even in the face of adversity, is an important survival technique.

Le prénom *(first name)*

It is not unusual to have the French give their last name first, especially in professional situations. Americans are generally much quicker than the French to begin to use another's first name. Rather than instantly condemning the French as "colder" than Americans, the wise strategy would be to refrain from using the first name when you meet someone. It is important to adapt your language usage to fit the culture. "When in Rome, do as the Romans do."

VOCABULAIRE

La politesse

Bonjour, Madame/Monsieur. *Hello, ma'am/sir.*
Excusez-moi. *Excuse me.*
Excusez-moi de vous déranger. *Excuse me for bothering you.*
Je vous demande pardon ... *I beg your pardon ...*
Merci. Vous aussi. *Thanks. You too.*

Pardon. *Pardon me.*
Permettez-moi de me présenter ... *Please allow me to introduce myself ...*
S'il vous plaît. *Please.*
Vous permettez? *May I?*
Bonne journée, Madame/Monsieur. *Have a good day, ma'am/sir.*

Il y a un geste

Le contact physique. James Davidson and Pierre Martin shake hands during their conversation, a normal gesture for both North Americans and the French when meeting someone. However, the French would normally shake hands with friends, colleagues, and their neighbors each time they meet and, if they chat for a while, at the end of their conversation as well. Physical contact plays a very important role in French culture and forgetting to shake hands with a friend would be rude.

These gestures are used in the *Pas de problème* video. For the handshake, see video, *Module 1*. See video, *Modules 8* and *12* for **le téléphone**.

Le téléphone. The French indicate that there is a telephone call by spreading the thumb and little finger of one hand and holding that hand near the ear.

▶ **À vous.** How would you respond to the following?

1. Je m'appelle Alissa. Et vous?
2. Vous êtes français(e)?
3. J'habite à Paris. Et vous?
4. Excusez-moi, s'il vous plaît.
5. Bonne journée.

Model the *Entre amis* activity with a student first. Then have students stand and interact.

Entre amis

Permettez-moi de me présenter

1. Greet your partner.
2. Find out if s/he is French.
3. Give your name and tell where you live.
4. Can you say anything else? (Be sure to shake hands when you say good-bye.)

Point out that in French, **-in**, **-ain**, and **-ent** are nasal *vowel* sounds, even though in writing they end with consonants.

In 1066, the duke of Normandy (William the Conqueror) and his army defeated the English at the Battle of Hastings. A French aristocracy ruled England for the next several centuries.

L'accent et le rythme

■ There is an enormous number of related words in English and French. We inherited most of these after the Norman Conquest, but many are recent borrowings. With respect to pronunciation, these are the words that tend to reveal an English accent the most quickly.

▶ **Compare:**

Anglais	*Français*
CER-tain	cer-TAIN
CER-tain-ly	cer-taine-MENT
MAR-tin	Mar-TIN
a-MER-i-can	a-mé-ri-CAIN

■ Even more important than mastering any particular sound is the development of correct habits in three areas of French intonation.

1. *Rhythm:* French words are spoken in groups, and each syllable but the last is said very evenly.
2. *Accent:* In each group of words, the last syllable is lengthened, thus making it the only accented syllable in the group.
3. *Syllable formation:* Spoken French syllables end in a vowel sound much more often than English ones do.

■ Counting is an excellent way to develop proper French rhythm and accent. Repeat after your instructor:

un DEUX	*un deux TROIS*	*un deux trois QUATRE*
mon-SIEUR	s'il vous PLAÎT	le té-lé-PHONE
mer-CI	cer-taine-MENT	A-sse-yez-VOUS
fran-ÇAIS	té-lé-PHONE	Mon-sieur Mar-TIN

Les consonnes finales

■ A final (written) consonant is normally not pronounced in French.

Françoi~~s~~	permette~~z~~	s'il vou~~s~~ plaî~~t~~
George~~s~~	françai~~s~~	troi~~s~~
Il fai~~t~~ froi~~d~~	américai~~n~~	deu~~x~~

These are the same as the consonants in the English word CaReFuL.

■ There are some words whose final consonant is always pronounced (many words ending in **c, f, l,** or **r,** for instance).

Frédéri**c** neu**f** Miche**l** bonjou**r**

■ When a consonant is followed by **-e** within the same word, the consonant is always pronounced. A single **-s-** followed by **-e** is pronounced as [z]. Two **-ss-** followed by **-e** are pronounced [s].

françai**se** sui**sse** américai**ne** j'habi**te** je m'appe**lle**

The rules governing obligatory **liaison** will be summarized in Ch. 5.

■ When a final silent consonant is followed by a word beginning with a vowel, it is often pronounced with the next word. This is called **liaison.**

vou~~s~~ *(silent)*	vou~~s~~ [z]êtes
deu~~x~~ *(silent)*	deu~~x~~ [z]hommes

Buts communicatifs

1 Greeting Others

> Learn all the words in each *But communicatif.*

le jour° / le matin° / l'après-midi°
    Bonjour, Madame.
    Bonjour, Mademoiselle.

    Bonsoir, Marie.
    Salut°, Marie.

le soir° / la nuit°

    Bonsoir°, Monsieur.
    Bonsoir, Madame.
    Bonsoir, Mademoiselle.

    Bonsoir, Marie.
    Salut, Marie.

day / morning / afternoon

Hi

evening / night

Good evening; Hello

Remarques

1. **Bonjour** and **bonsoir** are used for both formal (**Monsieur, Madame,** etc.) and first-name relationships.
2. The family name (**le nom de famille**) is not used in a greeting. For example, when saying hello to Madame Martin, one says **Bonjour, Madame.**
3. **Salut** is used only in first-name relationships.
4. **M., Mme,** and **Mlle** are the abbreviations for **Monsieur, Madame,** and **Mademoiselle.**

1 **Attention au style.** Greet each of the following people at the indicated time of day. Adapt your choice of words to fit the time and the person being greeted. Be careful not to be overly familiar. If there is more than one response possible, give both.

Modèles: Monsieur Talbot (le matin à 8 heures)
    Bonjour, Monsieur.

    Marie (l'après-midi à 2 heures)
    Bonjour, Marie. ou
    Salut, Marie.

1. Éric (le soir à 7 heures)
2. Mademoiselle Monot (le matin à 9 heures)
3. Monsieur Talbot (l'après-midi à 4 heures)
4. another student (la nuit à l heure)
5. your French teacher (le matin à 11 heures)
6. your best friend (le soir à 10 heures)

2 Exchanging Personal Information

Learn all the words in each *But communicatif.*

Pronounce **appelle** [apεl] and **appelez** [aple].

Remind students to look up the phonetic symbols in Appendix A.

Students will learn in Ch. 5 which prepositions to use with countries.

Comment vous appelez-vous?°
Je m'appelle Nathalie Lachance.

What is your name?

Où habitez-vous?°
J'habite à Laval.
J'habite près de° Montréal.

Where do you live?

near

Êtes-vous célibataire?
Non, je suis mariée.

▶ **Et vous, Monsieur (Madame, Mademoiselle)?**

Remarques

1. **Je m'appelle** and **Comment vous appelez-vous?** should be memorized for now. Note that in **Comment vous appelez-vous?** there is only one **l,** while in **Je m'appelle,** there are two.
2. Use **J'habite à** to identify the *city* in which you live.
3. Use **J'habite près de** to identify the city you live *near.*

2 **Les inscriptions** *(Registration).* You are working at a conference in Geneva. Greet the following people and find out their names and the city where they live.

MODÈLE: Monsieur Robert Perrin (Lyon)

—**Bonjour, Monsieur. Comment vous appelez-vous?**
—**Je m'appelle Perrin, Robert Perrin.**
—**Où habitez-vous?**
—**J'habite à Lyon.**

1. Mademoiselle Chantal Rodrigue (Toulouse)
2. Madame Anne Vermette (Montréal)
3. Monsieur Joseph Guy (Lausanne)
4. Mademoiselle Jeanne Delon (Paris)
5. le professeur de français
6. le président de la République française
7. le président des États-Unis (USA)
8. le premier ministre du Canada

A. Les pronoms sujets

■ The subject pronouns in French are:

singular forms		plural forms	
je (j')	*I*	**nous**	*we*
tu	*you*		
vous	*you*	**vous**	*you*
il	*he; it*	**ils**	*they*
elle	*she; it*	**elles**	*they*
on	*one; someone; people; we*		

Teachers may choose to explain the difference between **h muet** and **h aspiré.** Words beginning with **h aspiré** are noted with an asterisk in the French-English Vocabulary at the end of the book.

See Ch. 3 for a more complete explanation of **tu** and **vous.**

■ Before a vowel sound at the beginning of the next word, **je** becomes **j'**. This happens with words that begin with a vowel, but also with most words that begin with **h-**, which is silent.

J'adore Québec, mais **j'habite** à New York.

■ **Tu** is informal. It is used to address one person with whom you have a close relationship. **Vous** is the singular form used in other cases. To address more than one person, one always uses **vous.**

Tu es à Paris, Michel?
Vous êtes à Lyon, Monsieur?
Marie! Paul! **Vous** êtes à Bordeaux!

Note Whether **vous** is singular or plural, the verb form is always plural.

Gender is explained further with the article **le** in Ch. 2.

■ There are two genders in French: masculine and feminine. All nouns have gender, whether they designate people or things. **Il** stands for a masculine person or thing, **elle** for a feminine person or thing. The plural **ils** stands for a group of masculine persons or things, and **elles** stands for a group of feminine persons or things.

le tableau = **il**   les tables = **elles**
la porte = **elle**   les téléphones = **ils**

■ For a group that includes both masculine and feminine nouns (**Nathalie, Karine, Paul et Marie**), **ils** is used, even if only one of the nouns is masculine.

Karine et Éric? **Ils** sont à Marseille.

■ **On** is a subject pronoun used to express generalities or unknowns, much as do the English forms *one, someone, you, people.* In informal situations, **on** can sometimes be used to mean *we.*

On est à San Francisco.   *We are in San Francisco.*
On est riche en Amérique?   *Are people in America rich?*

B. Le verbe *être*

Il est à Québec.
Je suis à Strasbourg.
Nous sommes à Besançon.

■ The most frequently used verb in French is **être** *(to be)*.

je	**suis**	*I am*	nous	**sommes**	*we are*
tu	**es**	*you are*	vous	**êtes**	*you are*
il	**est**	*he is; it is*	ils	**sont**	*they are (m. or m. + f.)*
elle	**est**	*she is; it is*	elles	**sont**	*they are (f.)*
on	**est**	*one is; people are; we are*			

Review the use of **liaison** on p. 11.

Point out that this is also true of **nous, ils,** and **elles** if they are used before a verb that begins with a vowel sound (see Ch. 2).

■ Before a vowel sound at the beginning of the next word, the silent final consonant of many words (but not all!) is pronounced and is spoken with the next word. This is called **liaison. Liaison** is necessary between a pronoun and a verb.

Vous [z]êtes à Montréal.   On [n]est où?

■ **Liaison** is possible after all forms of **être,** but is common *only* with **est** and **sont.**

Il est [t]à Paris.   Elles sont [t]à Marseille.

3 **Où sont-ils?** *(Where are they?)* Identify the cities where the following people are. Use a subject pronoun in your answer.

MODÈLES: tu (Los Angeles) **Tu es à Los Angeles.**
vous (Québec) **Vous êtes à Québec.**

1. Lori (Boston)
2. Lise et Elsa (Bruxelles)
3. Thierry (Monte Carlo)
4. je (...)
5. Pierre et Anne (Angers)
6. nous (...)
7. Sylvie (Paris)

C. L'accord des adjectifs

Review *Pronunciation,* p. 4.

■ Most adjectives have two pronunciations: one when they refer to a feminine noun and one when they refer to a masculine noun. From an oral point of view, it is usually better to learn the feminine form first. The masculine pronunciation can often be found by dropping the last consonant *sound* of the feminine.

Point out the nasal vowel at the end of **américain.**

Barbara est **américaine.**   Bob est **américain** aussi.
Christine est **française.**   David est **français** aussi.

Choose famous people. Have students make up sentences using **il, elle,** etc.

■ Almost all adjectives change their spelling depending on whether the nouns they refer to are masculine or feminine, singular or plural. These spelling changes may or may not affect pronunciation.

Il est américain.   Elle est américain**e.**
Ils sont américain**s.**   Elles sont américain**es.**

Il est marié.   Elle est mari**ée.**
Ils sont mari**és.**   Elles sont mari**ées.**

■ The feminine adjective almost always ends in a written **-e.** A number of masculine adjectives end in **-e** also. In this case, masculine and feminine forms are identical in pronunciation and spelling.

célibataire   fantastique   optimiste

■ The plural is usually formed by adding a written **-s** to the singular. However, since the final **-s** of the plural is silent, the singular and the plural are pronounced in the same way.

américain américain**s**
américaine américaine**s**

Note If the masculine singular ends in **-s,** the masculine plural is identical.

un homme français deux hommes français

■ Adjectives that describe a group of both masculine and feminine nouns take the masculine plural form.

Bill et Judy sont **mariés.**

VOCABULAIRE

Fiancé(e) is not legally a marital status.

With the exception of **veuve(s)** [vœv] and **veuf(s)** [vœf], the spelling changes in the adjectives listed to the right do not affect pronunciation.

L'état civil *(marital status)*

Femmes	*Hommes*	*Women/men*
célibataire(s)	célibataire(s)	*single*
mariée(s)	marié(s)	*married*
fiancée(s)	fiancé(s)	*engaged*
divorcée(s)	divorcé(s)	*divorced*
veuve(s)	veuf(s)	*widowed*

4 **Quelle coïncidence!** *(What a coincidence!)* State that the marital status of the second person or group is the same as that of the first.

MODÈLES: Isabelle est fiancée. Et Marc? Pierre est marié. Et Chantal et
Il est fiancé aussi. Max?
Ils sont mariés aussi.

1. Anne et Paul sont fiancés. Et Marie?
2. Nous sommes mariés. Et Monique?
3. Nicolas est divorcé. Et Sophie et Thérèse?
4. Je suis célibataire. Et Georges et Sylvie?
5. Madame Beaufort est veuve. Et Monsieur Dupont?

5 **Qui est-ce?** *(Who is it?)* Answer the following questions. Try to identify real people or famous fictional characters. Can you name more than one person? Make sure that the verbs and adjectives agree with the subjects.

Have students ask you the questions first; then (books closed) ask them the questions.

MODÈLE: Qui est fiancé?
Olive Oyl est fiancée. ou **Olive Oyl et Popeye sont
fiancés.**

1. Qui est célibataire? 5. Qui est veuf?
2. Qui est fiancé? 6. Qui est français?
3. Qui est marié? 7. Qui est américain?
4. Qui est divorcé?

6 **Carte de débarquement** *(Arrival form).* When you travel overseas you are usually given an arrival form to fill out. Provide the information requested in the form below.

Carte de débarquement

Nom de famille: _____

Prénom(s): _____

Âge: _____ ans

Nationalité: _____

État civil: _____

Adresse: _____

_____

_____

Code postal: _____

Numéro de téléphone: _____

Motif du voyage: ❑ touristique   ❑ professionnel
                    ❑ transit   ❑ visite privée

Entre amis

Dans un avion *(In an airplane)*

Complete the following interaction with as many members of the class as possible.

1. Greet your neighbor in a culturally appropriate way.
2. Find out if s/he is French.
3. Find out each other's name.
4. Find out the city in which s/he lives.
5. What else can you say?

3 Identifying Nationality

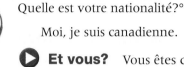

Learn all the words in each *But communicatif.*	

Quelle est votre nationalité?°   *What is your nationality?*

Moi, je suis canadienne.

▶ **Et vous?**   Vous êtes chinois(e)°?   *Chinese*
             Pas du tout!° Je suis ...   *Not at all!*

Remember to pronounce the final consonant in the feminine (see p. 11).

The signs are those used by the **Fédération internationale de l'automobile.**

Senegal and Morocco are two of the French-speaking countries treated in the *Escale* sections of this text.

	Féminin	*Masculin*	
GB	anglaise	anglais	*English*
F	française	français	*French*
J	japonaise	japonais	*Japanese*
SN	sénégalaise	sénégalais	*Senegalese*
USA	américaine	américain	*American*
MA	marocaine	marocain	*Moroccan*
MEX	mexicaine	mexicain	*Mexican*
CDN	canadienne	canadien	*Canadian*
I	italienne	italien	*Italian*
S	suédoise	suédois	*Swedish*
D	allemande	allemand	*German*
E	espagnole	espagnol	*Spanish*
B	belge	belge	*Belgian*
CH	suisse	suisse	*Swiss*
RUS	russe	russe	*Russian*

Remarque   In written French, some feminine adjectives are distinguishable from their masculine form not only by a final **-e,** but also by a doubled final consonant.

un homme canadien   *a Canadian man*
une femme canadie**nne**   *a Canadian woman*

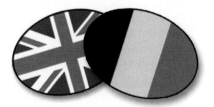

Suggestion for a warm-up: Tell students to pick a nationality. The instructor and/or the class will try to guess it.

7 **Quelle est votre nationalité?** The customs agent needs to know each person's nationality. Your partner will play the role of the customs agent and ask the question. You take the role of each of the following people, and answer.

MODÈLES: Madame Jones et Mademoiselle Jones (GB)
—**Quelle est votre nationalité?**
—**Nous sommes anglaises.**

Maria Gomez (MEX)
—**Quelle est votre nationalité?**
—**Je suis mexicaine.**

1. Jean-François (CDN)
2. Monsieur et Madame Smith (USA)
3. Mademoiselle Nakasone (J)
4. Madame Colon et Mademoiselle Colon (E)
5. Mademoiselle Balke (D)
6. Bruno (SN)
7. Madame Volaro (I)
8. Marie-Christine (F)
9. votre professeur de français
10. vous

Ces trois amis habitent à Paris.

8 **Qui êtes-vous?** *(Who are you?)* Assume the identity of each one of the following people and introduce yourself, indicating your name, your nationality, and the city you are from.

Modèle: Mademoiselle Brigitte Lapointe/Paris (F)
Je m'appelle Brigitte et je suis française. J'habite à Paris.

Extension: Students give their last names first **(Je m'appelle Lapointe, Brigitte Lapointe).**

1. Monsieur Pierre La Vigne/Québec (CDN)
2. Madame Margaret Jones/Manchester (GB)
3. Madame Anne Martin/Angers (F)
4. Monsieur Yasuhiro Saya/Tokyo (J)
5. Madame Mary O'Leary/Boston (USA)
6. Monsieur Ahmed Zoubir/Casablanca (MA)
7. votre professeur de français
8. vous

D. La négation

James Davidson **n'**est **pas** français. Il est américain.
Il **n'**habite **pas** à Paris. Il habite à San Francisco.

■ Two words, **ne** and **pas,** are used to make a sentence negative: **ne** precedes the conjugated verb and **pas** follows it.

Guy et Zoé **ne** sont **pas** mariés.   *Guy and Zoé aren't married.*
Il **ne** fait **pas** très beau.   *It's not very nice out.*

■ Remember that both **ne** and **pas** are necessary in standard French to make a sentence negative.

> **ne** + conjugated verb + **pas**

■ **Ne** becomes **n'** before a vowel sound.

Je **n'**habite **pas** à Paris.   *I don't live in Paris.*
Nathalie **n'**est **pas** française.   *Nathalie is not French.*

Begin exercise 9 as a full-class activity, then put students in groups.

9 **Vous êtes français(e)?** Choose a new nationality and have other students try to guess what it is. If the guess is incorrect, use the negative to respond. If it is correct, say so.

Modèle: —**Vous êtes belge?**
—**Non, je ne suis pas belge.**   ou   **Oui, je suis belge.**

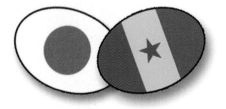

Suggestion: Elicit the questions for 1–8 before pairing students.

10 Ils sont français? Ask your partner whether the following people are French. Choose the correct form of **être** and make sure that the adjective agrees. Your partner will first respond with a negative, and then state the correct information.

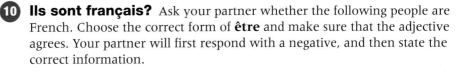

Modèle: —Elles sont françaises?
—Non, elles ne sont pas françaises. Elles sont anglaises.

1.

2.

3.

4.

5.

6.

7.

8.

Entre amis

Une fausse identité: Qui suis-je? *(A false identity: Who am I?)*

1. Pick a new identity (nationality, hometown, marital status) but don't tell your partner what you have chosen.
2. Your partner will guess your new nationality by asking you questions.
3. Your partner will guess your new marital status.
4. Your partner will try to guess which city you live in (one that fits your new nationality).

4 Describing Physical Appearance

Learn all the words in each *But communicatif.*

Try to use **assez** and, in the case of a negative, **pas très** to avoid being overly categorical when describing people.

Voilà° Christine.	Voilà le Père Noël.	*There is; Here is*
Elle est jeune°.	Il est assez° vieux°.	*young / rather / old*
Elle est assez grande°.	Il est assez petit°.	*tall / short; small*
Elle n'est pas grosse°.	Il n'est pas très° mince°.	*fat / very / thin*
Elle est assez jolie°.		*pretty*

▶ **Et vous?** Vous êtes . . .

jeune	*ou*	vieux (vieille)?	
petit(e)	*ou*	grand(e)?	
gros(se)	*ou*	mince?	
beau (belle)	*ou*	laid(e)?°	*attractive or ugly*
Décrivez votre meilleur(e) ami(e).°			*Describe your best friend.*

Il y a un geste

Assez *(sort of, rather; enough).* The gesture for **assez** is an open hand rotated back and forth (palm down).

This gesture is closely related to the gesture for **Ça va (comme ci, comme ça)** taught in Ch. 2.

Adjective placement and the special masculine forms **bel** and **vieil** are taught in Ch. 4. Until Ch. 4, students use adjectives as predicate adjectives only.

Some nouns form the plural in the same way: **le tableau, les tableaux.**

E. L'accord des adjectifs (suite)

■ The masculine forms of some adjectives are not like their feminine forms in either pronunciation or spelling, and so they must be memorized.

belle **beau** vieille **vieux**

■ The masculine plural of some adjectives is formed by adding **-x.** Pronunciation of the plural form remains the same as the singular.

Robert et Paul sont très **beaux.**

■ Masculine singular adjectives that end in **-s** or **-x** keep the same form (and pronunciation) for the masculine plural.

Bill est **gros.** Roseanne et John sont **gros** aussi.
Je suis **vieux.** Georges et Robert sont très **vieux.**

Synthèse: L'accord des adjectifs			
féminin		**masculin**	
singulier	*pluriel*	*singulier*	*pluriel*
petite	petites	petit	petits
grande	grandes	grand	grands
jolie	jolies	joli	jolis
belle	belles	beau	beaux
laide	laides	laid	laids
jeune	jeunes	jeune	jeunes
vieille	vieilles	vieux	vieux
mince	minces	mince	minces
grosse	grosses	gros	gros

11 **Oui, il n'est pas très grand.** The French often tone down what they wish to say by stating the opposite with a negative and the word **très**. Agree with each of the following descriptions by saying the opposite in a negative sentence.

MODÈLE: Michael J. Fox est petit.
        Oui, il n'est pas très grand.

1. Abraham et Sarah sont vieux.
2. Marie-Christine est mince.
3. Goofy est laid.
4. Alissa est petite.
5. Dumbo l'éléphant est gros.
6. L'oncle Sam est vieux.
7. James et Lori sont jeunes.

12 **Décrivez ...** Describe the following people. If you don't know what they look like, guess. Pay close attention to adjective agreement.

MODÈLE: Décrivez James Davidson.   **Il est grand, jeune et assez beau.**

1. Décrivez votre meilleur(e) ami(e).
2. Décrivez votre professeur de français.
3. Décrivez une actrice.
4. Décrivez un acteur.
5. Décrivez Minnie Mouse et Daisy Duck.
6. Décrivez le (la) président(e) de votre université.
7. Décrivez-vous.

Remind students that **assez** is useful when making a judgment. Remind students to use the gesture for **assez.** Also suggest that they can use a negative with **très** if they wish.

Entre amis

Oui ou non?

1. Choose a famous person and describe him/her.
2. If your partner agrees with each description s/he will say so.
3. If your partner disagrees, s/he will correct you.

Intégration

Révision

Suggestion: Encourage students to use the Student Audio and listen once more to the conversation for Ch. 1. This will give them a feeling of confidence and will provide an additional model for timing and fluency.

A Il y a plus d'une façon *(There's more than one way).*

1. Give two ways to say hello in French.
2. Give two ways to break the ice in French.
3. Give two ways to find out someone's name.
4. Give two ways to find out where someone lives.
5. Give two ways to find out someone's nationality.

B L'Inspecteur Clouseau. A bumbling inspector is asking all the wrong questions. Correct him. Invent the correct answer if you wish. Use subject pronouns.

MODÈLES: Vous êtes Mme Perrin?
Non, pas du tout, je ne suis pas Mme Perrin; je suis Mlle Smith.

Madame Perrin est française?
Non, pas du tout, elle n'est pas française; elle est canadienne.

Notice that 1 and 2 are plural. Use **nous** in your answer.

1. Vous êtes Monsieur et Madame Martin?
2. Vous *(pl.)* êtes belges?
3. Madame Martin est veuve?
4. Monsieur et Madame Martin sont divorcés?
5. James et Lori sont mariés?
6. Lori est italienne?
7. James est français?

C Décrivez trois personnes. Choose three people and give as complete a description as you can of each of them. Include at least one famous person.

MODÈLE: **James Davidson est grand, jeune et assez beau. Il est aussi célibataire. Il est américain et il habite à San Francisco.**

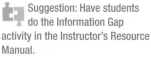 Suggestion: Have students do the Information Gap activity in the Instructor's Resource Manual.

D À vous. How would you respond to the following?

1. Bonjour, Monsieur (Madame, Mademoiselle).
2. Excusez-moi de vous déranger.
3. Vous êtes Monsieur (Madame, Mademoiselle) Dupont?
4. Comment vous appelez-vous?
5. Vous n'êtes pas français(e)?
6. Quelle est votre nationalité?
7. Vous habitez près d'Angers?
8. Où habitez-vous?
9. Vous êtes célibataire?
10. Bonne journée!

Pas de problème!

Preparation for the video: Video worksheet in the *Cahier d'activités*.

Complete the following exercise if you have watched the introduction to the *Pas de problème* video (up to 1:44). Give each person's nationality.

Quelle est la nationalité de Moustafa?
Il est tunisien.

Quelle est la nationalité ...

Answers to video exercise are in the *Cahier d'activités*.

1. de Jean-François?   3. de Bruno?   5. d'Yves?
2. de Marie-Christine?   4. d'Alissa?

Lecture

This first reading is a series of headlines **(manchettes)** taken from the French-language media. It is not vital that you understand every word in order to grasp the general meaning of what you read. The context will often help you guess the meaning.

A **Trouvez les mots apparentés** *(cognates).* In French and English, many words with similar meanings have the same or nearly identical spelling. These words are called cognates. Scan the headlines that follow and find at least fifteen cognates.

B **Sigles** *(Acronyms).* Acronyms are used frequently in French. They are abbreviations made of the first letter of each word in a title and may involve the same letters in their French and English forms. However, the order of the letters is normally different because in French, adjectives usually follow a noun, e.g., **la Croix-Rouge** *(the Red Cross)*. Can you guess the meaning of the following French acronyms?

MODÈLE: ONU (a group of countries)
    UN, the United Nations (Organization)

1. NATO 2. AIDS 3. EU (European Union) 4. Value-added tax 5. DNA 6. In-vitro fertilization 7. International Monetary Fund 8. HIV 9. MRI

1. OTAN (an alliance)
2. SIDA (a disease)
3. UE (a group of European countries)
4. TVA (a special tax)
5. ADN (a way to identify)
6. FIV (a way to conceive)
7. FMI (lends money to poor countries)
8. VIH (a virus)
9. IRM (a body scan to detect illness)

Manchettes

1. Le président américain propose une réduction des armements classiques de l'OTAN

2. Un homme innocenté par des tests d'ADN

3. Des combats violents se déroulent dans le nord de l'Afghanistan

4. Un Allemand pour remplacer le Français à la tête du FMI?

5. L'indifférence de la Banque centrale européenne accentue la baisse de l'euro

6. Mise au point aux États-Unis d'un test prédicatif pour le cancer héréditaire

7. Le jazz fait vibrer La Nouvelle-Orléans d'un air de Mardi Gras

8. Un observatoire national du SIDA va être mis en place

9. Ottawa a entrepris de renforcer son dispositif de défense dans le Grand Nord

10. UN HÉROS INCONNU: Le général canadien qui commanda deux forces de maintien de la paix

Give students 2–3 minutes. Tell them to keep rereading the headlines until you stop them.

C **Les manchettes.** Read the above headlines and decide which ones apply to any of the following categories.

1. Canada
2. the United States
3. politics
4. health and medicine
5. war and peace
6. money

 Dans ces contextes (*In these contexts*). Study the above headlines to help you guess the meaning of the following expressions.

1. armements classiques
2. homme
3. combats violents
4. tête
5. baisse
6. pour
7. nouvelle
8. mis en place
9. renforcer
10. paix

VOCABULAIRE ACTIF

Pour identifier les personnes
Noms

un acteur / une actrice *actor / actress*
une femme *woman*
un homme *man*
un(e) meilleur(e) ami(e) *best friend*
le Père Noël *Santa Claus*
une personne *person (male or female)*
un professeur *teacher (male or female)*
la nationalité *nationality*
un nom *name*
un nom de famille *family name*
un prénom *first name*

Description physique
beau (belle) *handsome (beautiful)*
grand(e) *big; tall*
gros(se) *fat; large*
jeune *young*
joli(e) *pretty*
laid(e) *ugly*
mince *thin*
petit(e) *small; short*
vieux (vieille) *old*

Le jour et la nuit
à ... heure(s) *at ... o'clock*
le jour *day*
le matin *morning*
la nuit *night*
le soir *evening*
l'après-midi *m. afternoon*

D'autres noms
un hôtel *hotel*
une porte *door*
un restaurant *restaurant*
une table *table*
un tableau *chalkboard*
un téléphone *telephone*
l'université *f. university*

Prépositions
à *at; in; to*
de *from, of*
en *in*
près de *near*

Adjectifs de nationalité
allemand(e) *German*
américain(e) *American*
anglais(e) *English*
belge *Belgian*
canadien(ne) *Canadian*
chinois(e) *Chinese*
espagnol(e) *Spanish*
français(e) *French*
italien(ne) *Italian*
japonais(e) *Japanese*
marocain(e) *Moroccan*
mexicain(e) *Mexican*
russe *Russian*
sénégalais(e) *Senegalese*
suédois(e) *Swedish*
suisse *Swiss*

Salutations et adieux
Au revoir. *Good-bye.*
Bonjour. *Hello.*
Bonne journée. *Have a good day.*
Bonsoir. *Good evening.*
Salut! *Hi!*

Pronoms sujets
je *I*
tu *you*
il *he, it*
elle *she, it*
on *one, people, we, they*
nous *we*
vous *you*
ils *they*
elles *they*

État civil
célibataire *single*
divorcé(e) *divorced*
fiancé(e) *engaged*
marié(e) *married*
veuf (veuve) *widowed*

Nombres
un *one*
deux *two*
trois *three*
quatre *four*

À propos de l'identité
Comment vous appelez-vous? *What is your name?*

Je m'appelle ... *My name is ...*
Madame (Mme) *Mrs.*
Mademoiselle (Mlle) *Miss*
Monsieur (M.) *Mr.; sir*
Permettez-moi de me présenter. *Allow me to introduce myself.*
Quelle est votre nationalité? *What is your nationality?*
Vous habitez ... *You live, you reside ...*
Où habitez-vous? *Where do you live?*
J'habite ... *I live, I reside ...*

La politesse
Bonne journée. *Have a good day.*
Excusez-moi. *Excuse me.*
Excusez-moi de vous déranger. *Excuse me for bothering you.*
Je vous demande pardon ... *I beg your pardon ...*
Merci. Vous aussi. *Thanks. You too.*
Pardon. *Pardon me.*
S'il vous plaît. *Please.*
Vous permettez? *May I?*

Verbe
être *to be*

Adverbes
assez *sort of, rather; enough*
aussi *also, too*
certainement *surely, of course*
ne ... pas *not*
là *there; here*
où *where*
très *very*

D'autres expressions utiles
Asseyez-vous. *Sit down.*
C'est ... *It is ...; This is ...*
C'est pour vous. *It's for you.*
entre amis *between friends*
Et moi? *And me?*
Oui ou non? *Yes or no?*
Pas du tout! *Not at all!*
qui *who*
Voilà ... *There is (are) ...; Here is (are) ...*
votre communication de ... *your call from ...*

2 Qu'est-ce que vous aimez?

Coup d'envoi

Prise de contact   ## Quelque chose à boire?

See the suggestions for teaching this lesson in the Instructor's Resource Manual.

Vous voulez ...°

    une tasse° de café?

    un verre° de coca°?

    un verre de vin°?

    une tasse de thé°?

Do you want ...

cup

glass/Coca-Cola

wine

tea

Oui, je veux bien.°

Non, merci.°

Gladly.; Yes, thanks.

No, thanks.

J'aime° le coca.

Je n'aime pas le café.

I like (love)

Est-ce que is often placed at the start of a sentence to make it a question.

Est-ce que vous aimez ...°

    le café? le coca? le vin? le thé?

Do you like ...

Et vous?   Voulez-vous boire quelque chose?°

              Oui, je voudrais ...°

Do you want to drink something?/Yes, I'd like ...

Conversation

Une soirée à Besançon

James Davidson étudie le français à Besançon. Mais il vient de° San Francisco. Au cours d'une soirée°, il aperçoit° Karine Aspel, qui est assistante au laboratoire de langues.

JAMES: Quelle° bonne surprise! Comment allez-vous?°

KARINE: Ça va bien°, merci. Et vous-même°?

JAMES: Très bien ... Votre prénom, c'est Karine, n'est-ce pas?°

KARINE: Oui, je m'appelle Karine Aspel.

JAMES: Et moi, James Davidson.

KARINE: Est-ce que vous êtes américain? Votre français est excellent.

JAMES: Merci beaucoup.

KARINE: Mais c'est vrai!° Vous êtes d'où?°

JAMES: Je viens de° San Francisco. Au fait°, voulez-vous boire quelque chose? Un coca?

KARINE: Merci°, je n'aime pas beaucoup le coca.

JAMES: Alors°, un kir, peut-être°?

KARINE: Je veux bien. Un petit kir, pourquoi pas°?

(James hands a glass of kir to Karine.)

JAMES: À votre santé°, Karine.

KARINE: À la vôtre°. Et merci, James.

he comes from / During a party / notices

What a / How are you?

Fine / yourself

isn't it?

But it's true! / Where are you from?

I come from / By the way

No thanks

Then / perhaps

why not

To your health

To yours

▶ **Jouez ces rôles.** Role-play the above conversation with a partner. Use your own identities. Choose something else to drink.

Il y a un geste

The French often say **Tchin-tchin** as their glasses touch.

À votre santé. The glass is raised when saying *To your health.* Among friends, the glasses are lightly touched as well.

Non, merci. The French often raise the index finger and move it from side to side to indicate *no.* They also may indicate *no* by raising a hand, palm outward, or by shaking their heads as do English speakers. In France, however, the lips are usually well rounded and often are pursed when making these gestures.

> **Why does Karine say Mais c'est vrai! when James says Merci beaucoup?**
>
> a. She misunderstood what he said.
> b. She doesn't mean what she said.
> c. She feels that James doesn't really believe her when she tells him his French is good.

Les compliments

While certainly not averse to being complimented, the French may respond by playing down a compliment, which may be a way of encouraging more of the same. While Americans are taught from an early age to accept and respond *thank you* to compliments, **merci,** when used in response to a compliment, is often perceived by the French as saying "you don't mean it." It is for this reason that Karine Aspel responds **Mais c'est vrai!** insisting that her compliment was true. It is culturally more accurate, therefore, and linguistically enjoyable, to develop a few rejoinders such as **Oh, vraiment?** *(Really?)* or **Vous trouvez?** *(Do you think so?),* which one can employ in similar situations. In this case, a really French response on James's part might be **Mais non! Je ne parle pas vraiment bien. Mon accent n'est pas très bon.** *(But, no! I don't speak really well. My accent's not very good.)*

Merci

The word **merci** is, of course, one of the best ways of conveying politeness, and its use is, by all means, to be encouraged. Its usage, however, differs from that of English in at least one important way: when one is offered something to eat, to drink, etc., the response **merci** is somewhat ambiguous and is often a way of saying *no, thank you.* One would generally say **je veux bien** or **s'il vous plaît** to convey the meaning *yes, thanks.* **Merci** is however the proper polite response once the food, the drink, etc., has actually been served.

Le kir

A popular drink in France, four parts white wine and one part black currant liqueur, **kir** owes its name to **le Chanoine Kir,** a French priest and former mayor of Dijon. It is often served as an **apéritif** *(before dinner drink).*

▶ **À vous.** How would you respond to the following questions?

1. Comment allez-vous?
2. Est-ce que vous êtes français(e)?
3. Votre prénom, c'est ... ?
4. Vous êtes d'où?
5. Voulez-vous boire quelque chose?

Entre amis

À une soirée *(At a party)*

1. Greet another "invited guest."
2. Find out his/her name.
3. Find out his/her nationality.
4. Find out where s/he comes from.
5. What else can you say?

Review the alphabet on p. 4 before doing this activity.

Review what was said about **l'accent et le rythme,** p. 11.

TGV = Train à grande vitesse, a very fast French train; **La SNCF = La Société nationale des chemins de fer français,** the French railroad system.

L'alphabet français (suite)

■ English and French share the same 26-letter Latin alphabet, and although this is useful, it is also potentially troublesome.

■ First, French and English cognates may not be spelled the same. French spellings must, therefore, be memorized.

adresse   personne   appartement

■ Second, because the alphabet is the same, it is tempting to pronounce French words as if they were English. Be very careful, especially when pronouncing cognates, not to transfer English pronunciation to the French words.

téléphone   conversation   professeur

■ Knowing how to say the French alphabet is not only important in spelling out loud. It is also essential when saying the many acronyms used in the French language.

le TGV   les USA   la SNCF

▶ **Quelques sigles.** Read out loud the letters that make up the following acronyms.

1. **SVP**   S'il vous plaît
2. **RSVP**   Répondez, s'il vous plaît
3. **La SNCF**   La Société nationale des chemins de fer français *(French railroad system)*
4. **La RATP**   La Régie autonome des transports parisiens *(Paris subway and bus system)*
5. **Les BD**   Les bandes dessinées *(comic strips)*
6. **Les USA**   Les United States of America *(= Les États-Unis)*
7. **La BNP**   La Banque nationale de Paris
8. **La CGT**   La Confédération générale du travail *(a French labor union)*
9. **BCBG**   Bon chic bon genre *(a French yuppy)*
10. **Le RER**   Le Réseau Express Régional *(a train to the suburbs)*

Accents

Be sure students understand that, unlike in Spanish and some other languages, French accents do *not* mean that a letter or syllable is stressed.

■ French accents are part of spelling and must be learned. They can serve:

1. to indicate how a word is pronounced
   ç → [s]: français
   é → [e]: marié
   è → [ɛ]: très
   ê → [ɛ]: être
   ë → [ɛ]: Noël

2. or to distinguish between meanings
   ou   *or*   la   *the (feminine)*
   où   *where*   là   *there*

French names		**Examples**
´	**accent aigu**	am**é**ricain; t**é**l**é**phone
`	**accent grave**	**à**; tr**è**s; o**ù**
^	**accent circonflexe**	**â**ge; **ê**tes; s'il vous pla**î**t; h**ô**tel; s**û**r
¨	**tréma**	No**ë**l; co**ï**ncidence
¸	**cédille**	fran**ç**ais
-	**trait d'union**	Jean-Luc
'	**apostrophe**	J'aime

Crème s'écrit C–R–E accent grave–M–E.

▶ **Comment est-ce qu'on écrit ... ?**   Your partner will ask you to spell the words below. Give the correct spelling.

MODÈLE: être
         VOTRE PARTENAIRE: **Comment est-ce qu'on écrit «être»?**
                     VOUS: **«Être» s'écrit E accent circonflexe–T–R–E.**

For items 4, 5, 11, & 12, you may wish to teach students to say **deux l, deux s,** and **deux n.**

1. français
2. monsieur
3. belge
4. mademoiselle
5. professeur
6. vieux
7. hôtel
8. très
9. téléphone
10. j'habite
11. canadienne
12. asseyez-vous

Buts communicatifs

1 Asking and Responding to "How are you?"

Questions

more formal	Comment allez-vous?
	Vous allez bien?
first-name basis	Comment ça va?° *How's it going?*
	Ça va?

Réponses

Learn all the words in each *But communicatif.*

Je vais très bien°, merci.	*Very well; I'm fine*
Ça va bien.	
Ça ne va pas mal°.	*Not bad.*
Oh! Comme ci, comme ça.°	*So-so.*
Oh! Pas trop bien.°	*Not too great.*
Je suis assez fatigué(e).°	*I'm rather tired.*
Je suis un peu malade.°	*I'm a little sick.*

Point out that **je vais** is used with adverbs and **je suis** is used with adjectives.

Remarque   It is very important to try to tailor your language to fit the situation. For example, with a friend or another student, you would normally ask **Ça va?** or **Comment ça va?** For someone whom you address as **Monsieur, Madame,** or **Mademoiselle,** you would normally say **Comment allez-vous?**

Il y a un geste

The gesture for **assez** is explained in Ch. 1, p. 22.

This gesture is used in video, *Module 3.*

Ça va.   This gesture implies "so-so" and is very similar to **assez.** Open one or both hands, palms down, and slightly rotate them. This is often accompanied by a slight shrug, and the lips are pursed. One may also say **comme ci, comme ça.**

1 Attention au style.   Greet the following people and find out how they are.

Review activity 1, p. 12.

Have students work with partners and practice responses as well.

MODÈLE: Monsieur Talbot (le matin à 8 h)
   Bonjour, Monsieur. Comment allez-vous?

1. Paul (le soir à 7 h)
2. Mademoiselle Monot (le matin à 9 h 30)
3. Monsieur Talbot (l'après-midi à 4 h)
4. le professeur de français (le matin à 11 h)
5. votre meilleur(e) ami(e) (le soir à 10 h)
6. le (la) président(e) de votre université (l'après-midi à 1 h)

2 **Vous allez bien?** Ask the following people how they are doing. Be careful to choose between the familiar and the formal questions. Your partner will provide the other person's answer.

MODÈLE: Marie (a little sick)
VOUS: **Comment ça va, Marie?**
MARIE: **Oh! je suis un peu malade.**

1. Madame Philippe (tired)
2. Paul (not too great)
3. Monsieur Dupont (sick)
4. Mademoiselle Bernard (very well)
5. Anne (so-so)

6. votre professeur de français (...)
7. votre meilleur(e) ami(e) (...)
8. le (la) président(e) de l'université (...)

Entre amis

Au café

Practice the following situation with as many members of the class as possible. You are in a sidewalk café at one o'clock in the afternoon.

1. Greet your partner in a culturally appropriate manner.
2. Inquire how s/he is doing.
3. Offer him/her something to drink.
4. What else can you say?

2 Giving and Responding to Compliments

Quelques° compliments   *A few*

Vous parlez très bien le français.°   *You speak French very well.*
Vous dansez très bien.
Vous chantez° bien.   *sing*
Vous skiez vraiment° bien.   *really*
Vous nagez comme un poisson.°   *You swim like a fish.*

Quelques réponses

Vous trouvez?°   *Do you think so?*
Pas encore.°   *Not yet.*
Oh! pas vraiment.°   *Not really.*
Oh! je ne sais pas.°   *I don't know.*
C'est gentil mais vous exagérez.°   *That's nice but you're exaggerating.*
Je commence seulement.°   *I'm only beginning.*
Je n'ai pas beaucoup d'expérience.°   *I don't have a lot of experience.*

📼 Examples of the **Vous trouvez?** response are in *Module 4* and *Module 7* of the *Pas de problème* video.

Remarque There are several ways to express an idea. For instance, there are at least three ways to compliment someone's French:

Votre français est excellent.   *Your French is excellent.*
Vous parlez bien le français.   *You speak French well.*
Vous êtes bon (bonne) en français.   *You are good in French.*

3 **Un compliment.** Give a compliment to each of the people pictured below. Another student will take the role of the person in the drawing and will provide a culturally appropriate rejoinder.

MODÈLE: —**Vous parlez bien le français.**
          —**Vous trouvez? Oh! je ne sais pas.**

1.   2.   3.   4.

A. Les verbes en -er

■   All verb infinitives are made up of a **stem** and an **ending.** To use verbs in the present tense, one removes the ending from the infinitive and adds new endings to the resulting stem. Verbs that use the same endings are often classified according to the last two letters of their infinitive. By far the most common class of verbs is the group ending in **-er.**

For a further explanation of any grammatical terms with which you are not familiar, see Appendix *C, Glossary of Grammatical Terms,* at the end of this book.

parler *(to speak)*		
	stem	endings
je	parl	**e**
tu	parl	**es**
il/elle/on	parl	**e**
nous	parl	**ons**
vous	parl	**ez**
ils/elles	parl	**ent**

tomber *(to fall)*		
	stem	endings
je	tomb	**e**
tu	tomb	**es**
il/elle/on	tomb	**e**
nous	tomb	**ons**
vous	tomb	**ez**
ils/elles	tomb	**ent**

■   Whether you are talking to a friend (**tu**), or about yourself (**je**), or about one or more other persons (**il, elle, ils, elles**), the verb is pronounced the same because the endings are silent.

Tu **danses** avec Amy?	*Are you dancing with Amy?*
Je ne **danse** pas du tout.	*I don't dance at all.*
Il **danse** bien, non?	*He dances well, doesn't he?*
Moustafa et Betty **dansent.**	*Moustafa and Betty are dancing.*

■   If you are using the **nous** or **vous** form, the verb is pronounced differently. The **-ez** ending is pronounced [e] and the **-ons** ending is pronounced [ɔ̃].

Vous **dansez** avec Marc?	*Do you dance with Marc?*
Nous ne **dansons** pas très souvent.	*We don't dance very often.*

■ Remember that the present tense has only *one* form in French, while it has several forms in English.

Remember to change **je** to **j'** before a vowel sound. See p. 14.

je **danse**   *I dance, I do dance, I am dancing*
j'**habite**   *I live, I do live, I am living*

■ Before a vowel sound, the final **-n** of **on** and the final **-s** of **nous, vous, ils,** and **elles** are pronounced and linked to the next word.

On [n]écoute la radio?   *Is someone listening to the radio?*
Nous [z]étudions le français.   *We are studying French.*
Vous [z]habitez ici?   *Do you live here?*

VOCABULAIRE

Suggestion: Have students translate a few expressions, e.g., *She dances well, He is watching TV.*

Activités

chanter (une chanson)	*to sing (a song)*
chercher (mes amis)	*to look for (my friends)*
danser (avec mes amis)	*to dance (with my friends)*
écouter (la radio)	*to listen to (the radio)*
enseigner (le français)	*to teach (French)*
étudier (le français)	*to study (French)*
jouer (au tennis)	*to play (tennis)*
manger	*to eat*
nager	*to swim*
parler (français)	*to speak (French)*
patiner	*to skate*
pleurer	*to cry*
regarder (la télé)	*to watch, to look at (TV)*
skier	*to ski*
travailler (beaucoup)	*to work (a lot)*
voyager (souvent)	*to travel (often)*

Note Verbs ending in **-ger** add an **-e-** before the ending in the form used with **nous: nous mangeons, nous nageons, nous voyageons.**

 Comparaisons. Tell what the following people do and then compare yourself to them. Use **Et moi aussi, ...** or **Mais moi, ...** to tell whether or not the statement is also true for you.

MODÈLE: Pierre et Anne/habiter à Angers
     Ils habitent à Angers. Mais moi, je n'habite pas à Angers.

1. vous/nager comme un poisson
2. James/parler bien le français
3. Monsieur et Madame Dupont/danser très bien
4. tu/étudier le français
5. vous/chanter vraiment bien
6. tu/regarder souvent la télévision
7. le professeur/enseigner le français
8. Karine et James/travailler beaucoup
9. Sébastien/patiner/mais/il/tomber souvent

Non, pas du tout. Respond to each question with a negative and follow up with an affirmative answer using the words in parentheses. Supply your own responses for items 5 and 6.

MODÈLE: Je danse *mal,* n'est-ce pas? (bien)
Non, pas du tout. Vous ne dansez pas mal; vous dansez bien.

1. Vous *écoutez* la radio? (regarder la télé)
2. Le professeur *voyage* beaucoup? (travailler)
3. Est-ce que je chante *très mal?* (assez bien)
4. Vous *chantez* avec le professeur? (parler français)
5. Vous habitez *à Paris?* (...)
6. Est-ce que nous étudions *l'espagnol?* (...)

VOCABULAIRE

Des gens que je connais bien
(People that I know well)

mon ami	*my (male) friend*
mon amie	*my (female) friend*
mes amis	*my friends*
ma mère	*my mother*
mon père	*my father*
le professeur	*the (male or female) teacher*
les étudiants	*the students*

Suggestion: Follow up with a stand-up drill; see the Instructor's Resource Manual.

 Mes connaissances. Tell about your family and your acquaintances by choosing an item from each list to create as many factual sentences as you can. You may make any of them negative.

MODÈLE: **Nous ne dansons pas mal.**

	chanter bien
	travailler beaucoup
	écouter souvent la radio
les étudiants	étudier le français
le professeur	skier bien
je	danser mal
nous	patiner beaucoup
ma mère	habiter en France
mon père	parler français
mes amis	nager comme un poisson
	voyager souvent
	pleurer souvent
	regarder souvent la télévision

Explain that, although it is not being practiced here, it is also possible to have a first-name relationship with some people and still use the pronoun **vous**.

This will be explained in Ch. 3, p. 55.

7 **Tu parles bien le français!** Pay compliments to the following friends. Use **tu** for each individual; use **vous** for more than one person.

Modèles: Éric skie bien.
Tu skies bien!

Yann et Sophie dansent bien.
Vous dansez bien!

1. Alissa est très jolie.
2. Christophe parle très bien l'espagnol.
3. David est bon en français.
4. François et Michel parlent bien l'anglais.
5. Ils travaillent beaucoup aussi.
6. Anne et Marie sont vraiment bonnes en maths.
7. Elles chantent bien aussi.
8. Olivier est vraiment très beau.
9. Luc skie comme un champion olympique.

8 **Identification.** Answer the following questions as factually as possible.

Modèle: Qui parle bien le français?
Le professeur parle bien le français.
Mes amis parlent bien le français.

Have students ask you the questions first; then (books closed) ask them the questions.

1. Qui étudie le français?
2. Qui enseigne le français?
3. Qui ne skie pas du tout?
4. Qui chante très bien?
5. Qui joue mal au tennis?
6. Qui regarde souvent la télévision?
7. Qui écoute souvent la radio?

Entre amis

Avec un(e) ami(e)

Practice the following situation with as many members of the class as possible.

1. Pay your partner a compliment.
2. Your partner will give a culturally appropriate response to the compliment and then pay you a compliment in return.
3. Give an appropriate response.

Suggestion: Follow up with a chain drill; see the Instructor's Resource Manual.

3 Offering, Accepting, and Refusing

Point out the pronunciation of eau [o] in the Wisconsin city *Eau Claire*.

NOTE CULTURELLE
Les jeunes Américains aiment beaucoup le lait. Mais, en général, les jeunes Français n'aiment pas le lait.

Pour offrir une boisson°

Voulez-vous boire quelque chose?
Voulez-vous un verre d'orangina°?
Voulez-vous un verre de (d') ... ?
  bière°?
  eau°?
  jus d'orange°?
  lait°?
Voulez-vous une tasse de ... ?
  café?
  chocolat chaud°?
Qu'est-ce que° vous voulez?

To offer a drink

orange soda

beer
water
orange juice
milk

hot chocolate
What

Pour accepter ou refuser quelque chose°

Je veux bien.
Volontiers.°
S'il vous plaît.
Oui, avec plaisir.°
Oui, c'est gentil à vous.°

Merci.
Non, merci.

To accept or refuse something

Gladly.

Yes, with pleasure.
Yes, that's nice of you.

❑ *Boisson à l'orange*
❑ *Jus de pomme*
❑ *1/4 Évian*
❑ *Boisson aux fruits exotiques*

9 **Voulez-vous boire quelque chose?** Use the list of words below to create a dialogue in which one person offers something to drink and the other responds appropriately.

MODÈLES: Coca-Cola
    —Voulez-vous un verre de coca?
    —Volontiers.

    coffee
    —Voulez-vous une tasse de café?
    —Non, merci.

1. water
2. tea
3. orange soda
4. wine
5. milk
6. orange juice
7. hot chocolate
8. beer

Pronounce the menu for students before they begin.

10 **Qu'est-ce que vous voulez?** Examine the drink menu of **La Bague d'or** *(The Golden Ring)* and order something.

Modèles: **Je voudrais une tasse de thé.**
Je voudrais un verre de coca-cola, s'il vous plaît.

La Bague d'or
BRASSERIE ALSACIENNE

Boissons

Vin rouge

Riesling (Vin d'Alsace)

Jus de fruits

Bière (pression)

Café

Thé

Chocolat chaud

Coca-cola

Orangina

Eau minérale (Perrier)

B. L'article défini: *le, la, l'* et *les*

■ You have already learned that all nouns in French have gender — that is, they are classified grammatically as either masculine or feminine. You also know that you need to remember the gender for each noun you learn. One of the functions of French articles is to mark the gender (masculine or feminine) and the number (singular or plural) of a noun.

forms of the definite article	when to use	examples
le (l')	before a masculine singular noun	**le** thé
la (l')	before a feminine singular noun	**la** bière
les	before all plural nouns, masculine or feminine	**les** boissons

■ **Le** and **la** become **l'** when followed by a word that begins with a vowel sound. This includes many words that begin with the letter **h**.

le professeur *but* **l'**étudiant, **l'**ami, **l'**homme
la femme *but* **l'**étudiante, **l'**amie

■ When they are used to refer to specific things or persons, **le, la, l'**, and **les** all correspond to the English definite article *the*.

Le professeur écoute **les** étudiants.   *The teacher listens to the students.*
L'université de Paris est excellente.   *The University of Paris is excellent.*

■ **Le, la, l'**, and **les** are also used before nouns that have a generic meaning, even when in English the word *the* would not be used.

Le lait est bon pour **la** santé.   *Milk is good for your health.*
Elle regarde souvent **la** télé.   *She often watches TV.*
J'étudie **le** chinois.   *I'm studying Chinese.*

Review nationalities, p. 18.   ■ All languages are masculine. Many are derived from the adjective of nationality. All verbs except **parler** require **le** before the name of a language. With **parler, le** is normally kept if there is an adverb directly after the verb, but is normally omitted if there is no adverb directly after the verb.

Ils **étudient le** russe.   *They are studying Russian.*
Ma mère **parle bien le** français.   *My mother speaks French well.*
Mon père **parle** français **aussi.**   *My father speaks French too.*

VOCABULAIRE

Pour répondre à Comment? *(How?)*

très bien	*very well*
(vraiment) bien	*(really) well*
assez bien	*rather well*
un peu	*a bit*
assez mal	*rather poorly*
(vraiment) mal	*(really) poorly*
ne ... pas du tout	*not at all*

11 **Parlez-vous bien le français?** For each language, describe how well you and a friend of yours **(mon ami(e) ____)** speak it.

MODÈLE: l'allemand
Je ne parle pas du tout l'allemand mais mon ami Hans parle très bien l'allemand.

Remind students to use **mais** or **et** when comparing themselves and a friend.

1. le russe   2. l'espagnol   3. l'anglais   4. le français

Remember that **Est-ce que ...?** just signals a question; **Qu'est-ce que ...?** means **What ...?**

12 **Dans la salle de classe.** Practice asking and answering the following questions with your partners.

1. Qu'est-ce que vous étudiez?
2. Étudiez-vous le français le matin, l'après-midi ou le soir?
3. Étudiez-vous aussi l'anglais?
4. Parlez-vous souvent avec le professeur de français?
5. Est-ce que le professeur chante avec la classe?
6. Est-ce que le professeur de français parle anglais?
7. Parlez-vous bien le français?
8. Parlez-vous un peu l'espagnol?

Entre amis

Une réception

You are at a reception at the French consulate.

1. Greet your partner and find out his/her name.
2. Offer him/her something to drink.
3. S/he will accept appropriately.
4. Toast each other.
5. Compliment each other on your ability in French.
6. Respond appropriately to the compliment.

4 Expressing Likes and Dislikes

    Qu'est-ce que tu aimes, Sophie?
        J'aime beaucoup le vin blanc°. J'adore voyager.   *white wine*
        J'aime bien danser.
    Moi aussi°, j'aime voyager et danser. Et qu'est-ce   *Me too*
    que tu n'aimes pas?
        Je n'aime pas le vin rosé. Je déteste le coca. Je
        n'aime pas chanter. Je n'aime pas beaucoup
        travailler.
    Moi non plus°, je n'aime pas travailler.   *Me neither*

▶ **Et vous?**   Qu'est-ce que vous aimez?
              Qu'est-ce que vous n'aimez pas?

Remarques

1. When there are two verbs in succession, the second is not conjugated. It remains in the infinitive form.

    Mon ami **déteste nager** dans l'eau   *My friend hates to swim in cold water.*
      froide.
    Les étudiants **aiment parler** français.   *The students like to speak French.*
    Francis **désire danser.**   *Francis wants to dance.*

2. The use of **le, la, l',** and **les** to express a generality occurs particularly after verbs expressing preferences.

    Marie adore **le** chocolat chaud.   *Marie loves hot chocolate.*
    Elle aime **les** boissons chaudes.   *She likes hot drinks.*
    Mais elle déteste **la** bière.   *But she hates beer.*
    Et elle n'aime pas **l'**eau minérale.   *And she doesn't like mineral water.*

Prime this by having students "predict" your tastes. E.g., **Le professeur adore skier.** Respond **oui** or **non**.

 Qu'est-ce qu'ils aiment? Tell, as truthfully as possible, what the following people like and don't like by combining items from each of the three lists. Guess, if you don't know for certain. How many sentences can you create?

MODÈLES: **Mes amis détestent le lait.**
Je n'aime pas du tout skier.

		skier
mes amis	adorer	travailler
le professeur	aimer beaucoup	la bière
je	ne pas aimer vraiment	le français
nous	ne pas aimer du tout	la télévision
	détester	chanter
		patiner
		danser
		le lait
		l'université
		voyager
		nager
		enseigner

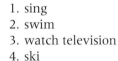 **Vous aimez danser?** Use the words below to interview the person sitting next to you. Find out if s/he likes to dance, to swim, etc. Use **aimer** in every question.

MODÈLE: dance

VOUS: **Vous aimez danser?**
VOTRE PARTENAIRE: **Oui, j'aime (beaucoup) danser.**   ou
Non, je n'aime pas (beaucoup) danser.

Suggestion: Follow up by asking students to share what they learned about their partner, e.g., **Elle aime beaucoup étudier le français.**

1. sing
2. swim
3. watch television
4. ski
5. study
6. study French
7. work
8. travel
9. play tennis
10. speak French

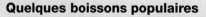

V O C A B U L A I R E

Popular mineral waters are **Vichy, Évian, Vittel, Perrier. Coca** and **orangina** are brand names often used generically.

N O T E   C U L T U R E L L E
La limonade française ressemble beaucoup à la boisson *7-UP.* La boisson américaine *lemonade* est **le citron pressé** en France.
Le café au lait est moitié *(half)* café, moitié lait chaud.

Quelques boissons populaires

le café	*coffee*	le coca	*cola*
le café au lait	*coffee with milk*	la limonade	*lemon-lime soda*
le café crème	*coffee with cream*	l'orangina *m.*	*orangina (an*
le chocolat chaud	*hot chocolate*		*orange soda)*
le citron pressé	*lemonade*		
l'eau minérale *f.*	*mineral water*	la bière	*beer*
le jus d'orange	*orange juice*	le kir	*kir*
le thé	*tea*	le vin	*wine*

 Vous aimez le café? Interview another person to find out which drinks s/he likes or dislikes, then be prepared to report as many answers as you can remember.

16 **En général, les étudiants ...** Decide whether you agree (**C'est vrai**) or disagree (**C'est faux**) with the following statements. If you disagree, correct the statement.

> **MODÈLE:** En général, les étudiants détestent voyager.
> **C'est faux. En général, ils aiment beaucoup voyager.**

1. En général, les étudiants n'aiment pas du tout danser.
2. En général, les étudiants détestent la pizza.
3. En général, les étudiants aiment beaucoup étudier.
4. En général, les étudiants n'aiment pas beaucoup regarder la télévision.
5. En général, les étudiants aiment nager.
6. En général, les étudiants aiment skier.
7. En général, les étudiants aiment beaucoup patiner.
8. En général, les étudiants détestent chanter.
9. En général, les étudiants aiment parler français avec le professeur.
10. En général, les étudiants désirent habiter à New York.

17 **Comment trouvez-vous le café français?** *(What do you think of French coffee?)* Your partner will ask you to give your opinion about something you have tasted. Use **aimer, adorer,** or **détester** in an answer that reflects your own opinion. Or make up an imaginary opinion. You might also say **Je ne sais pas, mais ...** and offer an opinion about something else that is related, instead.

Encourage students to respond **Moi aussi** *or* **Moi non plus** *if they agree with their partner's opinion.*

> **MODÈLE:** les tamalis mexicains
> VOTRE PARTENAIRE: **Comment trouvez-vous les tamalis mexicains?**
> VOUS: **J'aime beaucoup les tamalis mexicains.** ou
> **Je ne sais pas, mais j'adore les enchiladas.**

1. le thé anglais
2. le chocolat suisse
3. la pizza italienne
4. l'eau minérale française
5. le jus d'orange de Floride
6. le café de Colombie
7. la limonade française
8. la bière allemande
9. le vin français

C. Les questions avec réponse *oui* ou *non*

■ In spoken French, by far the most frequently used way of asking a question that can be answered *yes* or *no* is by simply raising the voice at the end of the sentence.

Vous parlez français?	*Do you speak French?*
James habite ici?	*Does James live here?*
Lori est américaine?	*Is Lori American?*
Hélène danse bien?	*Does Hélène dance well?*

■ **Est-ce que** is often placed at the beginning of a sentence to form a question. It becomes **Est-ce qu'** before a vowel sound.

Est-ce que vous parlez français?	*Do you speak French?*
Est-ce que James habite ici?	*Does James live here?*
Est-ce que Lori est américaine?	*Is Lori American?*
Est-ce qu'Hélène danse bien?	*Does Hélène dance well?*

Have students give the probable response to these questions: **Mais oui, je parle français**, etc.

■ The phrase **n'est-ce pas?** (*right?, aren't you?, doesn't he?*, etc.), added at the end of a sentence, expects an affirmative answer.

Tu parles français, **n'est-ce pas?**	*You speak French, don't you?*
James habite ici, **n'est-ce pas?**	*James lives here, doesn't he?*
Lori est américaine, **n'est-ce pas?**	*Lori is American, isn't she?*
Hélène danse bien, **n'est-ce pas?**	*Hélène dances well, doesn't she?*

■ Another question form, which is used more often in written French than in speech and which is characteristic of a more formal speech style, is *inversion* of the verb and its *pronoun* subject. When inversion is used, there is a hyphen between the verb and the pronoun.

Parlez-vous français?	*Do you speak French?*
Aimez-vous chanter?	*Do you like to sing?*
Êtes-vous américain(e)?	*Are you American?*

Note If the third person (**il, elle, on, ils, elles**) is used in inversion, there is always a [t] sound between the verb and the subject pronoun. If the verb ends in a vowel, a written **-t-** is added between the final vowel of the verb and the initial vowel of the pronoun. If the verb ends in **-t,** no extra **-t-** is necessary.

	Enseigne-**t-**il le français?	*Does he teach French?*
	Aime-**t-**elle voyager?	*Does she like to travel?*
But:	Aimen**t-ils** voyager?	*Do they like to travel?*
	Es**t-elle** française?	*Is she French?*
	Son**t-ils** américains?	*Are they American?*

FOR RECOGNITION ONLY:

Some material is taught initially for recognition only. Inversion with a noun is made active in Ch. 5.

• If the subject is a noun, the inversion form can be produced by adding the pronoun of the same number and gender after the verb.

noun + verb + pronoun

Karen est-elle américaine?	*Is Karen American?*
Thierry aime-t-il la bière?	*Does Thierry like beer?*
Nathalie et Stéphane aiment-ils danser?	*Do Nathalie and Stéphane like to dance?*

Comment? *(What did you say?)* We are often obliged to repeat a question when someone doesn't hear or understand us. For each question with inversion, ask a question beginning with **Est-ce que** and a question ending with **n'est-ce pas.**

MODÈLES: James habite-t-il à San Francisco?
> VOTRE PARTENAIRE: **Comment?**
> VOUS: **Est-ce que James habite à San Francisco?**
> VOTRE PARTENAIRE: **Comment?**
> VOUS: **James habite à San Francisco, n'est-ce pas?**

1. James est-il américain?
2. Étudie-t-il le français?
3. Parle-t-il bien le français?
4. Aime-t-il Karine Aspel?
5. Karine est-elle française?
6. Travaille-t-elle beaucoup?

19 Une enquête entre amis *(A survey among friends).* Use the following list to determine the likes and dislikes of two classmates. Be prepared to report back the results of your "survey" to the class. Are there any items on which all the students agree completely?

MODÈLES: skier
> **—Est-ce que tu aimes skier?**
> **—Oui, j'adore skier.**

le jogging
> **—Est-ce que tu aimes le jogging?**
> **—Non, je n'aime pas le jogging.** ou
> **Non, je déteste le jogging. Je n'aime pas les sports.**

1. parler français
2. parler avec le professeur de français
3. voyager
4. regarder la télévision
5. chanter en français
6. la politique
7. l'université
8. étudier le français
9. nager dans l'eau froide
10. travailler beaucoup

20 Les Dupont.* Here are a few facts about the Dupont family. Interview a classmate to find out if this information is also true for him/her.

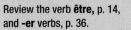
Review the verb **être,** p. 14, and **-er** verbs, p. 36.

MODÈLES: Les Dupont habitent à Marseille.
> VOUS: **Habites-tu à Marseille aussi?**
> VOTRE PARTENAIRE: **Non, je n'habite pas à Marseille.**

Gérard et Martine sont mariés.
> VOUS: **Es-tu marié(e) aussi?**
> VOTRE PARTENAIRE: **Non, je ne suis pas marié(e).** ou
> **Oui, je suis marié(e) aussi.**

1. Martine adore voyager.
2. Gérard Dupont aime la limonade.
3. Les Dupont sont malades.
4. Martine Dupont parle un peu l'espagnol.
5. Monsieur et Madame Dupont aiment beaucoup danser.
6. Les Dupont voyagent beaucoup.

*An **-s** *is not added to family names in French; the article* **les** *indicates the plural.*

Entre amis

À un bal

Practice the following situation with as many members of the class as possible. You are at a dance and are meeting people for the first time. Use **vous.**

1. Say good evening and introduce yourself.
2. Find out if your partner likes to dance.
3. Ask your partner if s/he wants to dance. (S/he does.)
4. Tell your partner that s/he dances well.
5. Offer your partner something to drink.
6. Toast each other.
7. Compliment each other on your ability in French.
8. Respond appropriately to the compliment.

Intégration

Révision

Prime for this activity by eliciting questions. Then have students move about interviewing classmates. Allow 5 minutes, then check to see who has the most answers.

 Suggestion: Have students do the Information Gap activity in the Instructor's Resource Manual.

Remind students of the difference between **Est-ce que** and **Qu'est-ce que,** pp. 40 and 46.

A **Trouvez quelqu'un qui ...** *(Find someone who ...).*
Interview your classmates in French to find someone who ...

MODÈLE: speaks French **Est-ce que tu parles français?**

1. likes coffee
2. swims often
3. doesn't like beer
4. sings poorly
5. studies a lot
6. doesn't ski
7. is tired
8. hates to work
9. likes to travel
10. cries often
11. skates

B **À vous.** How would you respond to the following questions and comments?

1. Parlez-vous français?
2. Comment allez-vous?
3. Où habitez-vous?
4. Voulez-vous boire quelque chose?
5. Si oui, qu'est-ce que vous désirez boire?
6. Vous parlez très bien le français!
7. Vous étudiez l'espagnol, n'est-ce pas?
8. Aimez-vous voyager?
9. Est-ce que vous aimez danser?
10. Qu'est-ce que vous n'aimez pas?

18 **Comment?** *(What did you say?)* We are often obliged to repeat a question when someone doesn't hear or understand us. For each question with inversion, ask a question beginning with **Est-ce que** and a question ending with **n'est-ce pas.**

MODÈLES: James habite-t-il à San Francisco?
VOTRE PARTENAIRE: **Comment?**
VOUS: **Est-ce que James habite à San Francisco?**
VOTRE PARTENAIRE: **Comment?**
VOUS: **James habite à San Francisco, n'est-ce pas?**

1. James est-il américain?
2. Étudie-t-il le français?
3. Parle-t-il bien le français?
4. Aime-t-il Karine Aspel?
5. Karine est-elle française?
6. Travaille-t-elle beaucoup?

19 **Une enquête entre amis** *(A survey among friends).* Use the following list to determine the likes and dislikes of two classmates. Be prepared to report back the results of your "survey" to the class. Are there any items on which all the students agree completely?

MODÈLES: skier   —**Est-ce que tu aimes skier?**
—**Oui, j'adore skier.**

le jogging   —**Est-ce que tu aimes le jogging?**
—**Non, je n'aime pas le jogging.**   ou
Non, je déteste le jogging. Je n'aime pas les sports.

1. parler français
2. parler avec le professeur de français
3. voyager
4. regarder la télévision
5. chanter en français
6. la politique
7. l'université
8. étudier le français
9. nager dans l'eau froide
10. travailler beaucoup

20 **Les Dupont.*** Here are a few facts about the Dupont family. Interview a classmate to find out if this information is also true for him/her.

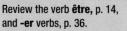
Review the verb **être,** p. 14, and **-er** verbs, p. 36.

MODÈLES: Les Dupont habitent à Marseille.
VOUS: **Habites-tu à Marseille aussi?**
VOTRE PARTENAIRE: **Non, je n'habite pas à Marseille.**

Gérard et Martine sont mariés.
VOUS: **Es-tu marié(e) aussi?**
VOTRE PARTENAIRE: **Non, je ne suis pas marié(e).**   ou
Oui, je suis marié(e) aussi.

1. Martine adore voyager.
2. Gérard Dupont aime la limonade.
3. Les Dupont sont malades.
4. Martine Dupont parle un peu l'espagnol.
5. Monsieur et Madame Dupont aiment beaucoup danser.
6. Les Dupont voyagent beaucoup.

*An **-s** *is not added to family names in French; the article* **les** *indicates the plural.*

Pas de problème!

Complete the following activity if you have watched video *Module 1*. Decide if the following statements are true or false. If a statement is false, correct it.

1. Jean-François et René jouent au tennis.
2. Jean-François joue très bien.
3. Il regarde Nathalie.
4. Marie-Christine est la cousine de Nathalie.
5. Marie-Christine n'aime pas les mélodrames.
6. Les Français détestent les sports.

Lecture

The following reading selection is taken directly from the *Gab*, a weekly newspaper published in Besançon. It is not vital that you understand every word.

A **Étude du vocabulaire.** There are words in French that we refer to as **faux amis** *(false friends, false cognates),* since they mean something different from the English word they seem to resemble. Study the following sentences and match the **faux ami,** in bold print, with the correct meaning in English: *understanding, reading, sensitive.*

> **La lecture** est mon passe-temps préféré.
> Florence est timide et très **sensible.**
> Nous aimons les professeurs **compréhensifs.**

SEUL(E) ET LAS(SE) DE L'ÊTRE*

VOUS ASPIREZ À NOUER UNE RELATION SENTIMENTALE DURABLE
Simplement, facilement, vous pouvez connaître quelqu'un
qui comme vous est motivé par une vie de couple stable.

Depuis 1975
ANDRÉE MOUGENOT CONSEILLÈRE DIPLÔMÉE
10 RUE DE LA RÉPUBLIQUE BESANÇON
fait des heureux

Retournez tout simplement le bon ci-dessous, vous recevrez gratuitement sans aucune marque extérieure un exemple de proposition de mise en relation.

JE SUIS
Nom et prénom..
Adresse

Âge .... Taille ....
Profession ....

JE CHERCHE
Célibataire ☐ Veuf(ve)☐ Divorcé(e) ☐
Âgé de .... ans à........
Études souhaitées ....
Profession souhaitée
....

Autres caractéristiques ....

Célibataire ☐ Veuf(ve) ☐ Divorcé(e) ☐
J'aime recevoir ☐ Sortir ☐ Danser ☐
Le sport ☐ La nature ☐ Bricoler ☐
Jardiner ☐ Voyager ☐ La lecture ☐
La musique ☐

Simple☐ Gai(e)☐ Loyal(e)☐ Calme ☐
Amusant(e)☐ Tendre ☐ Sensible ☐
Compréhensif(ve)☐ Affectueux(se)☐
Sincère ☐ Tolérant(e)☐ Conciliant(e)☐
Passionné(e) ☐Dynamique ☐

*Alone and tired of it.   Le Gab n° 648 (Besançon)

Familles de mots *(Word families).* Can you guess the meanings of the following words? One member of each word family is found in the reading.

1. comprendre, compréhensif, compréhensive, la compréhension
2. recevoir, une réception
3. sortir, une sortie
4. lire, un lecteur, une lectrice, la lecture

C **Autoportrait** *(Self-portrait).* Describe *yourself* using five adjectives from the **Je cherche** section of the reading.

MODÈLE: célibataire, loyal(e), ...

VOCABULAIRE ACTIF

Quelque chose à boire
la bière *beer*
une boisson *drink*
le café *coffee*
le café au lait *coffee with milk*
le café crème *coffee with cream*
le chocolat chaud *hot chocolate*
le citron pressé *lemonade*
le coca *cola*
l'eau *f.* (minérale) *(mineral) water*
le jus d'orange *orange juice*
le kir *kir*
le lait *milk*
la limonade *lemon-lime soda*
l'orangina *m.* *orangina (an orange soda)*
le thé *tea*
le vin (rouge, blanc, rosé) *(red, white, rosé) wine*

Des gens que je connais bien
les étudiants *the students*
ma mère *my mother*
mes amis *my friends*
mon ami(e) *my friend*
mon père *my father*

D'autres noms et pronoms
une chanson *song*
le jogging *jogging*
la pizza *pizza*
un poisson *fish*
la politique *politics*

quelque chose *something*
quelqu'un *someone*
la radio *radio*
une soirée *an evening party*
une tasse *cup*
la télévision (la télé) *television (TV)*
un verre *glass*

Adjectifs
bon (bonne) *good*
chaud(e) *hot*
cher (chère) *dear*
excellent(e) *excellent*
fatigué(e) *tired*
faux (fausse) *false; wrong*
froid(e) *cold*
malade *sick*
vrai(e) *true*

Pour répondre à un compliment
Vous trouvez? *Do you think so?*
Pas encore. *Not yet.*
Oh! Pas vraiment. *Not really.*
Je ne sais pas. *I don't know.*
C'est gentil mais vous exagérez. *That's nice but you're exaggerating.*
Je commence seulement. *I'm only beginning.*
Je n'ai pas beaucoup d'expérience. *I don't have a lot of experience.*

Articles définis
le, la, l', les *the*

D'autres verbes
chanter *to sing*
chercher *to look for*
danser *to dance*
désirer *to want*
écouter *to listen to*
enseigner *to teach*
étudier *to study*
habiter *to live; to reside*
jouer (au tennis) *to play (tennis)*
manger *to eat*
nager *to swim*
parler *to speak*
patiner *to skate*
pleurer *to cry*
regarder *to watch; to look at*
skier *to ski*
tomber *to fall*
travailler *to work*
trouver *to find; to be of the opinion*
voyager *to travel*

Mots invariables
alors *then, therefore, so*
avec *with*
beaucoup *a lot*
bien *well; fine*
comme *like*
en général *in general*
ensemble *together*

ici *here*
mais *but*
mal *poorly; badly*
peut-être *maybe; perhaps*
pour *for; in order to*
pourquoi *why*
seulement *only*
souvent *often*
un peu *a little bit*
vraiment *really*

Pour demander à quelqu'un comment il va

Comment allez-vous? *How are you?*
Vous allez bien? *Are you well?*
(Comment) ça va? *How is it going?*
Je vais très bien. *Very well.*
Ça va bien. *(I'm) fine.*
Comme ci, comme ça. *So-so.*
Assez bien. *Fairly well.*
Je suis fatigué(e). *I am tired.*
Je suis un peu malade. *I am a little sick.*
Pas trop bien. *Not too well.*
Ça ne va pas mal. *I'm not feeling bad.*

Pour offrir, accepter et refuser quelque chose

Voulez-vous boire quelque chose? *Do you want to drink something?*
Je veux bien. *Gladly. Yes, thanks.*
Volontiers. *Gladly.*
S'il vous plaît. *Please.*
Oui, avec plaisir. *Yes, with pleasure.*
Oui, c'est gentil à vous. *Yes, that's nice of you.*
Merci. *No, thank you.*
Non, merci. *No, thank you.*
Je voudrais ... *I would like ...*

Verbes de préférence

adorer *to adore; to love*
aimer *to like; to love*
détester *to hate; to detest*

D'autres expressions utiles

Comment? *What (did you say)?*
est-ce que ... ? *(question marker)*
n'est-ce pas? *right? are you? don't they? etc.*
Comment est-ce qu'on écrit ... ? *How do you spell ... ?*

Comment trouvez-vous ... ? *What do you think of ... ?*
Qu'est-ce que vous aimez? *What do you like?*
Qu'est-ce que vous voulez? *What do you want?*
Vous êtes d'où? *Where are you from?*
Quelle bonne surprise! *What a good surprise!*
À votre santé! *(Here's) to your health!*
À la vôtre! *(Here's) to yours!*
Au fait ... *By the way ...*
Je ne sais pas. *I don't know.*
Je viens de ... *I come from ...*
... s'écrit ... *... is spelled ...*
même(s) *-self (-selves)*
moi aussi *me too*
moi non plus *me neither*

Buts communicatifs
Identifying family and friends
Sharing numerical information
Talking about your home

Structures utiles
L'article indéfini: **un, une** et **des**
Le verbe **avoir**
Les nombres (suite)
Les expressions **il y a** et **voilà**
Les adjectifs possessifs **mon, ton, notre** et **votre**
La négation + **un (une, des)**
La possession avec **de**
Les adjectifs possessifs **son** et **leur**

Culture
La langue et la culture
Les pronoms **tu** et **vous**
Pour gagner du temps

Coup d'envoi

Prise de contact ## Une photo de ma famille

MARIE:	Avez-vous des frères ou des sœurs?°	*Do you have any brothers or sisters? / I have*
CHRISTOPHE:	J'ai° un frère et une sœur.	
MONIQUE:	J'ai une sœur, mais je n'ai pas de° frère.	*I don't have any*
PAUL:	Moi, je n'ai pas de frère ou de sœur.	
MARIE:	Dans° ma famille il y a° cinq personnes.	*In / there are*
	Ma sœur s'appelle° Chantal et mon frère	*My sister's name is*
	s'appelle Robert. Mes parents s'appellent	
	Bernard et Sophie.	

▶ **Et vous?** Avez-vous des frères ou des sœurs?
Avez-vous une photo de votre
   famille?
Qui est sur la photo?°   *Who is in the picture?*

Conversation

L'arrivée à la gare

Lori Becker est une étudiante américaine qui vient en France pour passer un an° dans une famille française. Elle descend du train à la gare° Saint-Laud à Angers. Anne Martin et sa fille, Émilie, attendent° son arrivée.

year
railroad station
are waiting for

Mme Martin:	Mademoiselle Becker?
Lori:	Oui. Bonjour, Madame. Vous êtes bien Madame Martin?°
Mme Martin:	Oui. Bonjour et bienvenue°, Mademoiselle. Vous êtes très fatiguée, sans doute°?
Lori:	Pas trop°. J'ai dormi° un peu dans le train.
Mme Martin:	Mademoiselle Becker, voilà ma fille.
Lori:	Bonjour, tu t'appelles comment?
La petite fille:	Émilie.
Lori:	Et tu as quel âge?°
	The child holds up her thumb and two fingers.
Mme Martin:	Elle a trois ans.
Lori:	Elle est charmante.° Vous avez d'autres enfants°, Madame Martin?
Mme Martin:	Oui, nous avons six enfants.
Lori:	Comment? Combien dites-vous?°
Mme Martin:	Six.
Lori:	Mon Dieu°! Vraiment?
Mme Martin:	Pourquoi? Qu'est-ce qu'il y a?°
Lori:	Euh ... rien°. J'aime beaucoup les enfants.

You're Mme Martin, aren't you?
welcome

probably
too much / I slept

And how old are you?

She's charming.
other children

How many do you say?

God
What's the matter?
nothing

▶ **Jouez ces rôles.** Role-play the conversation exactly as if you were Lori Becker and Mme Martin. Once you have practiced it several times, role-play the conversation using one partner's identity in place of Lori's.

Il y a un geste

Voilà. The open hand is extended, palm up, to emphasize that some fact is evident. **Voilà** is also used to conclude something that has been said or to express that that's how things are.

Why does Lori say "Mon Dieu!"?

a. She is swearing.
b. She is praying.
c. She is expressing surprise.

Why does Lori use tu with Émilie Martin?

a. They have met before and are good friends.
b. She is speaking to a child.
c. Lori considers Émilie an inferior.

La langue et la culture

Each language has its own unique way of expressing reality. The fact that French uses the verb **avoir** *(to have)* when expressing age, whereas English uses the verb *to be,* is only one of many examples that prove that languages are not copies of each other. Similarly, the expression **Mon Dieu!** *(Wow!)* is milder in French than its literal English equivalent *My God!* The French way is not right or wrong, nor is it more or less logical than its English counterpart.

Les pronoms tu et vous

French has two ways of saying *you.* The choice reflects the nature of the relationship, including degree of formality and respect. **Tu** is typically used when speaking to one's family and relatives as well as to close friends, fellow students, children, and animals. **Vous** is normally used when speaking to someone who does not meet the above criteria (e.g., in-laws, employers, teachers, or business acquaintances). It expresses a more formal relationship or a greater social distance than **tu.** In addition, **vous** is always used to refer to more than one person.

Visitors to French-speaking countries would be well advised to use **vous** even if first names are being used, unless they are invited to use the **tu** form. In the *Conversation,* Lori correctly uses **vous** with Madame Martin and **tu** with Émilie.

Pour gagner du temps
(To stall for time)

A helpful strategy for the language learner is to acquire and use certain expressions and gestures that allow him or her to "buy time" to think without destroying the conversational flow or without resorting to English. Like the cup of coffee we sip during a conversation to give us a chance to organize our thoughts, there are a number of useful expressions for "buying time" in French. The number one gap-filler is **euh,** which is the French equivalent of the English *uh* or *umm.*

VOCABULAIRE

Pour gagner du temps
(To stall for time)

alors	*then; therefore, so*	euh	*uh; umm*
ben	*well*	hein?	*huh?*
bon	*good*	mais ...	*but ...*
comment?	*what (did you say)?*	oui ...	*yes ...*
eh bien	*well then*	tiens!	*well, well!*
et ...	*and ...*	voyons	*let's see*

▶ À vous. How would you respond to the following?

1. Comment s'appellent vos parents?
2. Vous avez des frères ou des sœurs?
3. (Si oui) Comment s'appellent-ils (elles)?
4. Où habitent-ils (elles)?

Entre amis

Des frères ou des sœurs?
1. Introduce yourself and tell what you can about yourself.
2. Find out what you can about your partner.
3. Find out if your partner has brothers or sisters.
4. If so, find out their names.

| Prononciation |

L'Accent et le rythme (suite)

■ Remember: When pronouncing French sentences, it is good practice to pay particular attention to the facts that: (1) French rhythm is even (just like counting), (2) syllables normally end in a vowel sound, and (3) the final syllable of a group of words is lengthened.

▶ Count before repeating each of the following expressions.

Review the *Pronunciation* section of Ch. 1.

un, deux, trois, quatre, cinq, SIX

Je suis a-mé-ri-CAIN.
Elle est cé-li-ba-TAIRE.
Vous tra-va-illez beau-COUP?

un, deux, trois, quatre, cinq, six, SEPT

Je m'a-ppelle Ka-rine As-PEL.
Vous ha-bi-tez à Pa-RIS?
Je n'aime pas beau-coup le VIN.

Les sons [e], [ɛ], [ə], [a], [wa]

■ The following words contain some important and very common vowel sounds.

▶ Practice saying these words after your instructor, paying particular attention to the highlighted vowel sound.

[e] • **é**crivez, z**é**ro, r**é**p**é**tez, **é**coutez, nationalit**é**, t**é**l**é**phone, divorc**é**
   • ouvr**ez**, entr**ez**, ferm**ez**, ass**ez**, assey**ez**-vous, excus**ez**-moi
   • présent**er**, habit**er**, écout**er**, arrêt**er**, commenc**er**, continu**er**
   • **et**

Words with [ɛ] in open syllables are omitted, e.g., **est, très, sais.** Instructors can decide whether they wish to stress the [e]/[ɛ] contrast in open syllables.

[ɛ]
- p**e**rsonne, prof**e**sseur, hôt**e**l, univ**e**rsité, **e**spagnol, **e**lle, canadi**e**nne
- cr**è**me, fr**è**re, ch**è**re, discr**è**te
- **ê**tre, **ê**tes
- angl**ai**se, franç**ai**se, célibat**ai**re, l**ai**de, cert**ai**nement

[ə]
- l**e**, l**e**vez-vous, pr**e**nez, r**e**gardez, qu**e**, d**e**, j**e**, n**e**, votr**e** santé, m**e**

Note   encor~~e~~, heur~~e~~, femm~~e~~, homm~~e~~, un~~e~~, ami~~e~~, famill~~e~~, entr~~e~~ amis

[a]
- l**a**, **a**llez, **a**mie, **a**méricain, **a**ssez, m**a**tin, c**a**n**a**dien, qu**a**tre, s**a**lut, d'**a**ccord
- **à**, voil**à**

[wa]
- Franç**oi**s, m**oi**, tr**oi**s, v**oi**là, Madem**oi**selle, au rev**oi**r, bons**oi**r
- v**oy**age

■   Now go back and look at how these sounds are spelled and in what kinds of letter combinations they appear. What patterns do you notice?

■   It is always particularly important to pronounce **la** [la] and **le** [lə] correctly since each marks a different gender, and the meaning of a word may depend on which is used.

la tour = *tower*	**la tour** Eiffel
le tour = *tour, turn*	**le Tour** de France

Buts communicatifs

1 Identifying Family and Friends

—Je vous présente° mon amie, Anne Martin.   *I introduce to you*
  Elle a° une sœur qui habite près d'ici.   *has*
—Votre sœur, comment s'appelle-t-elle?
—Elle s'appelle Catherine.
—Et vous êtes d'où?
—Je suis de Nantes.
—Tiens! J'ai des cousins à Nantes.
—Comment s'appellent-ils?
—Ils s'appellent Dubois.

Point out that the singular **s'appelle-t-il (elle)** and the plural **s'appellent-ils (elles)** are pronounced the same way.

▶ **Et vous?**   Présentez un(e) ami(e).

Remarque   When you use **qui,** the verb that follows agrees with the person(s) to whom **qui** refers.

Elle a des cousins **qui habitent** à Nantes.

Use the drawing to help present the relationships. Then ask students **Comment s'appelle la femme de Pierre Martin?**, etc.

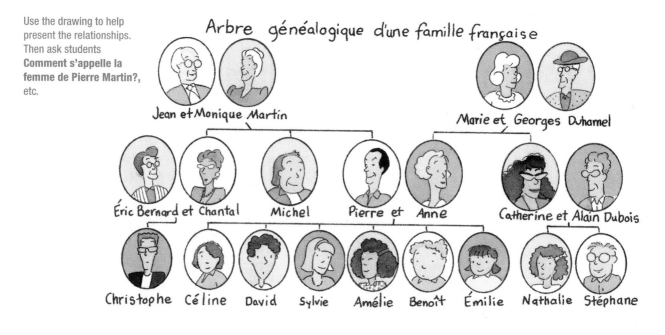

Arbre généalogique d'une famille française

Jean et Monique Martin — Marie et Georges Duhamel

Éric Bernard et Chantal — Michel — Pierre et Anne — Catherine et Alain Dubois

Christophe Céline David Sylvie Amélie Benoît Émilie Nathalie Stéphane

VOCABULAIRE

Une famille française

des parents	*parents; relatives*
un mari et une femme	*a husband and a wife*
un père et une mère	*a father and a mother*
un(e) enfant	*a child (male or female)*
un fils et une fille	*a son and a daughter*
un frère et une sœur	*a brother and a sister*
des grands-parents	*grandparents*
un grand-père	*a grandfather*
une grand-mère	*a grandmother*
des petits-enfants	*grandchildren*
un petit-fils et une petite-fille	*a grandson and a granddaughter*
un oncle et une tante	*an uncle and an aunt*
un neveu et une nièce	*a nephew and a niece*
un(e) cousin(e)	*a cousin (male or female)*
des beaux-parents	*stepparents (or in-laws)*
un beau-père	*a stepfather (or father-in-law)*
une belle-mère	*a stepmother (or mother-in-law)*
un beau-frère	*a brother-in-law*
une belle-sœur	*a sister-in-law*
un demi-frère	*a stepbrother*
une demi-sœur	*a stepsister*

Add **arrière-** before **petit** or **grand** to convey the meaning *great:* **un arrière-petit-fils; une arrière-grand-mère.**

Point out that there is no **-e** on **grand** in the word **grand-mère.**

Notes

1. Most plurals of nouns are formed by adding **-s.** In compound words for family members, an **-s** is added to both parts of the term: **des grands-pères, des belles-mères.**

2. The words **neveu** and **beau** form their plurals with an **-x: des neveux, des beaux-frères.**

3. The word **fils** is invariable in the plural: **des fils, des petits-fils.**

A. L'article indéfini: *un, une* et *des*

■ The French equivalent of the English article *a (an)* is **un** for masculine nouns and **une** for feminine nouns.

un frère	**un** train	**un** orangina
une sœur	**une** table	**une** limonade

By now, students should know the meaning of the word **liaison**; that is, when a silent final consonant is pronounced and linked to a vowel sound that follows it.

The rules governing obligatory **liaison** will be summarized in Ch. 5.

■ The final **-n** of **un** is normally silent. Liaison is required when **un** precedes a vowel sound.

un [n]étudiant

■ The consonant **-n-** is always pronounced in the word **une.** If it precedes a vowel sound, it is linked to that vowel.

une femme   [yn fam]   *But:* une étudiante   [y ne ty djɑ̃t]

■ The plural of **un** and **une** is **des.**

singulier:	un frère	une sœur
pluriel:	**des** frères	**des** sœurs

■ **Des** corresponds to the English *some* or *any.* However, these words are often omitted in English. **Des** is not omitted in French.

J'ai **des** amis à Paris.   *I have (some) friends in Paris.*

■ Liaison is required when an article precedes a vowel sound.

un [n]enfant	un [n]étudiant	un [n]homme
des [z]enfants	des [z]étudiants	des [z]hommes

■ In a series, the article *must* be repeated before each noun.

un homme et **une** femme	*a man and (a) woman*
une mère et **des** enfants	*a mother and (some) children*

1 **Présentations.** How would you introduce the following people?

MODÈLE: Mademoiselle Blondel / F / frère à New York
Je vous présente Mademoiselle Blondel.
Elle est française.
Elle a un frère qui habite à New York.

Review nationalities on p. 18.

1. Madame Brooks / GB / sœur à Toronto
2. Mademoiselle Jones / USA / parents près de Chicago
3. Monsieur Callahan / CDN / frère à Milwaukee
4. Monsieur Lefont / B / fils près d'ici
5. Madame Perez / MEX / petits-enfants près d'El Paso
6. Mademoiselle Keita / SN / cousins à New York
7. un ami
8. une amie
9. votre père ou votre mère

Tout le monde
prend un café.

2 **Quelque chose à boire?** Order the following items.

> **MODÈLE:** citron pressé
> **Je voudrais un citron pressé, s'il vous plaît.**

Review the list of **boissons** on
p. 44

1. thé
2. café
3. bière
4. verre d'eau
5. jus d'orange
6. chocolat
7. coca
8. limonade
9. orangina
10. café crème

B. Le verbe *avoir*

J'ai des cousins à Marseille.	*I have cousins in Marseille.*
Tu as un(e) camarade de chambre?	*Do you have a roommate?*
Nous avons un neveu qui habite près de Chicago.	*We have a nephew who lives near Chicago.*

avoir *(to have)*			
j'	**ai**	nous	**avons**
tu	**as**	vous	**avez**
il/elle/on	**a**	ils/elles	**ont**

Liaison is summarized in the
Pronunciation section of Ch. 5.

■ Liaison is required in **on a, nous avons, vous avez, ils ont,** and **elles ont.**

on [n]a
nous [z]avons

■ Do not confuse **ils ont** and **ils sont.** In liaison, the **-s** in **ils** is pronounced [z] and is linked to the following verb.

Ils [z]ont des enfants.   *They **have** children.*
But: **Il**s **sont** charmants.   *They **are** charming.*

After **pas de,** either the singular or the plural is acceptable. **Je n'ai pas de frère. /Je n'ai pas de frères.**

■ Use **Je n'ai pas de (d') ...** to say *I don't have a ...* or *I don't have any ...*

Je n'ai pas de père.   *I don't have a father.*
Je n'ai pas de frère.   *I don't have any brothers.*
Je n'ai pas d'enfants.   *I don't have any children.*

3 **Un recensement** *(A census).* The following people are being interviewed by the census taker. Follow the model with a partner to complete each interview.

MODÈLE: Mademoiselle Messin / 2 sœurs, 0 frère / Jeanne et Perrine (frères ou sœurs?)
    LE RECENSEUR: **Avez-vous des frères ou des sœurs, Mademoiselle?**
    MLLE MESSIN: **J'ai deux sœurs mais je n'ai pas de frère.**
    LE RECENSEUR: **Comment s'appellent-elles?**
    MLLE MESSIN: **Elles s'appellent Jeanne et Perrine.**

Have students look back at the family tree, p. 58, and tell about Anne Martin's family ties in order to practice additional terms such as **fils, fille,** etc.

1. Monsieur Dubois / 2 frères, 0 sœur / Henri et Luc (frères ou sœurs?)
2. Madame Bernard / 1 enfant: 1 fils, 0 fille / Christophe (enfants?)
3. Monsieur Marot / 2 enfants: 1 fils, 1 fille / Pascal et Hélène (enfants?)
4. vos parents (enfants?)
5. votre meilleur(e) ami(e) (frères ou sœurs?)
6. vos grands-parents (petits-enfants?)
7. vous (?)

Ils ont une petite-fille
qui s'appelle Lara.

④ La famille de David. Use the genealogical chart on page 58 to create sentences describing David's family ties.

MODÈLE: **David a des parents qui s'appellent Pierre et Anne.**

Entre amis

Ta famille

1. Find out if your partner has brothers or sisters.
2. If so, find out their names.
3. Find out where they live.
4. Find out if your partner has children or other family members living with him/her.
5. If so, find out their names.
6. Introduce your partner to another person. Tell as much as you can about your partner and his/her family.

② Sharing Numerical Information

Combien de personnes y a-t-il dans ta famille, Christelle?

Quel âge ont tes parents?

Quel âge a ta sœur?
Quel âge as-tu?
En quelle année es-tu née?

Il y a quatre personnes: mes parents, ma sœur et moi.

Ils ont cinquante ans et quarante-sept ans.

Elle a dix-huit ans.
J'ai vingt ans.
Je suis née°   *I was born*
en mille neuf cent quatre-vingt deux.

▶ Et vous? Combien de personnes y a-t-il dans votre famille? Quel âge ont les membres de votre famille? Quel âge avez-vous?

Remarques

1. The verb **avoir** is used when asking or giving someone's age.

   Quel âge **a** ta camarade de chambre?   *How old is your roommate?*
   Quel âge **a** ton petit ami?   *How old is your boyfriend?*

2. In inversion, remember to insert a **-t-** before the singular forms **il, elle,** and **on.**

        Quel âge ont-elles?   *How old are they?*
   But: Quel âge a**-t-**elle?   *How old is she?*

3. The word **an(s)** must be used when giving someone's age.

   J'ai vingt et un **ans.**   *I am twenty-one.*

VOCABULAIRE À RETENIR

un(e) camarade de chambre *roommate*
un petit ami *boyfriend*
une petite amie *girlfriend*

C. Les nombres (suite)

Review the numbers 0–29 on p. 3

Have students count from 3 to 99 by 3; have them try to guess the age of some famous people.

30 trente	76 soixante-seize
31 trente et un	77 soixante-dix-sept
32 trente-deux	78 soixante-dix-huit
33 trente-trois	79 soixante-dix-neuf
etc.	80 quatre-vingts
40 quarante	81 quatre-vingt-un
41 quarante et un	82 quatre-vingt-deux
42 quarante-deux	83 quatre-vingt-trois
43 quarante-trois	*etc.*
etc.	90 quatre-vingt-dix
50 cinquante	91 quatre-vingt-onze
51 cinquante et un	92 quatre-vingt-douze
52 cinquante-deux	*etc.*
53 cinquante-trois	100 cent
etc.	101 cent un
60 soixante	200 deux cents
61 soixante et un	1.000 mille
62 soixante-deux	1.999 mille neuf cent quatre-vingt-dix-neuf
63 soixante-trois	2.000 deux mille
etc.	2.004 deux mille quatre
70 soixante-dix	100.000 cent mille
71 soixante et onze	100.000.000 un million
72 soixante-douze	1.000.000.000 un milliard
73 soixante-treize	
74 soixante-quatorze	
75 soixante-quinze	

Numbers above 101 repeat the same pattern: **cent vingt *et* un, cent quatre-vingt-un, deux cent vingt *et* un,** etc.

Numbers from 70 to 99 show a different pattern: 70 = 60 + 10; 80 = 4 × 20; 90 = 80 + 10.

■ All numbers are invariable except **un.** Remember to replace the number **un** with **une** before a feminine noun, even in a compound number.

un oncle   trois oncles   vingt et un cousins
une tante   trois tantes   **vingt et une** cousines

You may wish to point out that **quatre** may also be pronounced [kat] before a consonant. Students will hear this in the *Pas de problème* video.

■ When numbers from 1 to 10 stand alone, the final consonants of **un, deux,** and **trois** are silent, but all others are pronounced. The **-x** at the end of **six** and **dix** is pronounced [s].

un   deux   trois
But: quatre   cinq   six   sept   huit   neuf   dix

■ Certain numbers have a different pronunciation when they precede a noun:

- The final consonant of **six, huit,** and **dix** is not pronounced before a consonant.

  six personnes   huit jours   dix verres

- When the following noun begins with a vowel sound, the final consonant is always pronounced and linked to the noun. Note that with **quatre,** both final consonants are linked and the final **-e** is not pronounced.

  un [n]homme   cinq [k]hommes   huit [t]hommes
  deux [z]hommes   six [z]hommes   neuf [f]hommes
  trois [z]hommes   sept [t]hommes   dix [z]hommes
  quatre [tR]hommes   vingt [t]hommes

- The **-f** in **neuf** is pronounced as [v] only before the words **ans** (years) and **heures** (hours).

  neuf [v]ans   neuf [v]heures
  But: neuf [f]enfants   neuf [f]hommes

- The final **-t** in **vingt** is silent when the number stands alone, but is pronounced in the compound numbers built on it.

  vingt   [vɛ̃]
  vingt et un   [vɛ̃ te ɛ̃]
  vingt-deux   [vɛ̃t dø]

■ For numbers ending in 1, from 21 to 71, **et** is used. From 81 to 101 **et** is not used.

  vingt **et** un   But: quatre-vingt-un

You may wish to teach that **quatre-vingts** does not take an -s in the expression **page quatre-vingt.**

■ **Vingt** and **cent** do not add an **-s** if they are *followed* by a number.

  quatre-vingt**s** personnes   But: quatre-vingt-un
  trois cent**s** personnes   But: trois cent cinq

■ **Mille** never adds an **-s.**

  mille personnes   deux **mille** personnes

■ The words **million** and **milliard** are nouns and take an **s** in the plural. If they are followed by another noun, **de** is inserted between the nouns.

  deux millions d'euros

Note   In France, commas and periods used with numbers are the reverse of the system used in North America.

Have students read this sentence out loud. Be sure they correctly identify this as **deux millions.**

  L'état a besoin de **2.000.000,00** d'euros. (deux millions)

■ There are five pairs of numbers in a French telephone number: **02.42.83.21.14.** The first pair indicates the general area of France.

Have students count to 100 by 5's; then have them dictate their phone numbers. When giving American or Canadian phone numbers, give the first three digits together, then the last four in pairs, e.g., 212-3240 **deux cent douze / trente-deux / quarante.**

5 **Les numéros de téléphone.** Pronounce the following phone numbers.

Modèle: 02.81.88.40.01
zéro deux / quatre-vingt-un / quatre-vingt-huit / quarante / zéro un

1. 02.41.93.21.80
2. 04.77.63.06.97
3. 04.42.08.98.89
4. 02.31.86.15.96
5. 04.71.83.61.91
6. 04.67.85.76.90
7. 05.61.10.99.02
8. 02.51.81.95.12
9. 03.88.19.82.43
10. 04.78.87.03.92

6 **Parlez-moi de votre famille** *(Tell me about your family).* Describe the people listed below. Use the model as a guide. If you don't have a brother, etc., say so.

Modèle: un frère
J'ai un frère qui s'appelle Bill.
Il habite à Boston.
Il est grand et assez beau.
Il a vingt-trois ans.

1. une sœur   5. des cousins
2. un frère   6. une cousine
3. un oncle   7. un grand-père ou une grand-mère
4. une tante   8. des parents

NOTE CULTURELLE

En France il y a un **code départemental** pour indiquer où on habite. Le code pour Angers, par exemple, est 49, et pour Besançon le code est 25. Le numéro se trouve sur les plaques d'immatriculation *(license plates)* des voitures et forme aussi les deux premiers chiffres *(numbers)* du **code postal.**

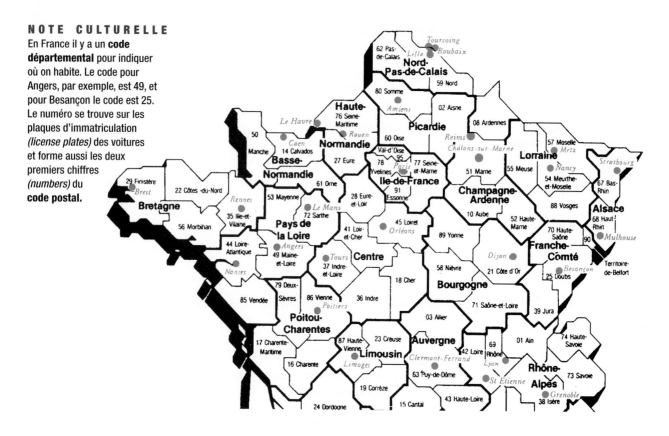

7 **Codes postaux.** The map above shows major cities and the first two numbers of the zip code for several French **départements.** Give the general zip code for the following cities.

Do this in pairs, assigning two or three cities to each team. Use **au nord, au sud, à l'est, à l'ouest de Paris,** to help students locate the cities.

MODÈLE: Nantes

Le code postal pour Nantes est quarante-quatre mille (44000).

1. Dijon
2. Amiens
3. Tours
4. Besançon
5. Angers
6. Le Mans
7. Orléans
8. Nantes
9. Paris
10. Brest
11. Rouen
12. Strasbourg

D. Les expressions *il y a* et *voilà*

Voilà la famille Laplante.
> **Il y a combien de** personnes dans la famille Laplante?
> **Il y a** quatre personnes.
> **Il y a combien de** garçons et **combien de** filles?
> **Il y a** deux filles mais **il n'y a pas de** garçon.

■ **Voilà** can mean either *there is (are)* or *here is (are)*. **Il y a** means *there is (are)*. While **voilà** and **il y a** are both translated *there is* or *there are* in English, they are used quite differently.

■ **Voilà** and **voici** *(here is, here are)* point something out. They bring it to another person's attention. There is usually an accompanying physical movement—a nod of the head, a gesture of the hand toward the person or object, or a pointing of the finger to identify a specific object.

Voici mon fils et ma fille.   *Here are my son and daughter.*
Voilà ma voiture.   *There's my car.*

■ **Il y a** simply states that something exists or tells how many there are.

Il y a un livre sur la table.   *There is a book on the table.*
Il y a quatre filles et deux garçons   *There are four girls and two boys in the*
dans la famille Martin.   *Martin family.*

■ The negative of **il y a un (une, des)** is **il n'y a pas de**.

Il n'y a pas de voiture ici.   *There aren't any cars here.*

Attention   Do not use **de** if **il n'y a pas** is followed by a number.

Il n'y a pas trois voitures dans le   *There aren't three cars in the garage;*
garage; il y a quatre voitures.   *there are four cars.*

■ There are several ways to use **il y a** in a question.

Il y a un livre sur la table?
Est-ce qu'il y a un livre sur la table?   *Is there a book on the table?*
Y a-t-il un livre sur la table?

■ **Il y a** is often used with **combien de**.

Il y a combien de garçons?
Combien de garçons **est-ce qu'il y a?**
Combien de garçons **y a-t-il?**

Lori parle avec Anne Martin. Complete the following sentences using either **il y a** or **voilà.**

MODÈLE: <u>**Voilà**</u> ma fille Émilie.

1. _____deux enfants dans votre famille?
2. Non, Mademoiselle, _____ six enfants.
3. _____ une photo de ma famille.
4. _____ ma mère. Elle est jolie, n'est-ce pas?
5. _____ combien de filles dans votre famille?
6. Où sont-elles? Ah! _____ vos filles!

 À vous. Answer the following questions as factually as possible.

1. Quel âge avez-vous?
2. Combien de personnes y a-t-il dans votre famille?
3. Quel âge ont les membres de votre famille?
4. Combien d'étudiants y a-t-il dans votre classe de français? Combien d'hommes et combien de femmes y a-t-il?
5. Quel âge a votre professeur de français? (Imaginez!)
6. Combien d'oncles et combien de tantes avez-vous? Quel âge ont-ils?

E. Les adjectifs possessifs *mon, ton, notre* et *votre*

—Comment s'appellent **tes** parents?
—**Mes** parents s'appellent Marcel et Jacqueline.
—Combien d'enfants y a-t-il dans **ta** famille?
—Il y a trois enfants dans **ma** famille: deux garçons et une fille.
—Quel âge a **ton** frère? Quel âge a **ta** sœur?
—**Mon** frère a dix-huit ans et **ma** sœur a douze ans.
—Où habitent **vos** grands-parents?
—**Nos** grands-parents habitent à Saumur.

		adjectifs possessifs			
en anglais	*masculin*		*féminin*		*pluriel (m. et f.)*
my	**mon**		**ma**		**mes**
your	**ton**	père	**ta**	mère	**tes**	parents
our	**notre**		**notre**		**nos**
your	**votre**		**votre**		**vos**

■ Possessive adjectives agree in gender and number with the nouns they modify (the "possessions"). **Notre** and **votre** are used for both masculine and feminine singular nouns.

Denise, **ton** père est gentil.	*Denise, your father is nice.*
Alain, **ta** mère est gentille aussi!	*Alain, your mother is nice also!*
Nathalie, **tes** parents sont très gentils.	*Nathalie, your parents are very nice.*

■ In the singular, **ma** and **ta** become **mon** and **ton** when used directly before a feminine word beginning with a vowel sound.

ma meilleure amie   *But:* **mon** amie
ta tante   *But:* **ton** autre tante

■ Liaison occurs if the word following **mon, ton, mes, tes, nos,** or **vos** begins with a vowel sound.

mon petit ami   vos bons amis
But: mon [n]ami   vos [z]amis

■ As with **quatre,** the final **-e** of **notre** and **votre** is not pronounced before a vowel sound, but the final consonants are linked to the next word.

notre [tR]ami

⑩ **Qui?** Try to identify people from among your friends and relatives who "fit" the following questions. Use possessive adjectives in each response. Be sure that verbs agree with subjects, and that adjectives agree with nouns.

Have students ask you the questions first. Then (books closed) ask them the questions.

MODÈLE: Qui chante bien?
       Mes parents chantent bien.   ou   **Notre professeur chante bien.**

1. Qui est grand?
2. Qui parle français?
3. Qui ne skie pas?
4. Qui adore le sport?
5. Qui n'aime pas beaucoup la bière?
6. Qui aime être étudiant(e)?

⑪ **À vous.** Show a real (or imaginary) picture of your family and point out parents, brothers, sisters, cousins, uncles, and aunts. Give each person's age as well.

In place of photos, students could draw stick figure caricatures.

MODÈLE: **Voilà ma sœur, Kristen. Elle a seize ans.**

Entre amis

Dans ta famille

Use possessive adjectives whenever possible.

1. Ask your partner how many people there are in his/her family.
2. Find out the names of his/her brother, sister, etc.
3. Find out how old they are.
4. Find out where they live.
5. Ask if his/her brother, sister, etc. speaks French or studies French.
6. What else can you find out about his/her family members?

Suggest that students consult the list of activities on p. 37 when asking question 6.

3 Talking about Your Home

Habitez-vous dans une maison° ou dans
un appartement°, Lori?   *house*
       apartment
   Nous habitons dans une maison.

Et combien de pièces° y a-t-il dans votre   *rooms*
maison?
   Il y a sept pièces.

Et qu'est-ce qu'il y a chez vous°?   *at your house*
   Chez moi° il y a ...   *at my house*

Bureau can mean either *desk* or *office*. The teacher's office = **le bureau du professeur**. **Chambre** normally implies *bedroom*, not *room* in general.

... dans ma salle de séjour.

... dans ma chambre.

... dans ma cuisine.

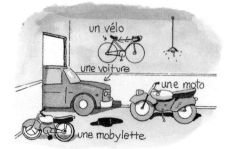

... dans mon garage.

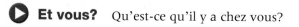

Et vous?   Qu'est-ce qu'il y a chez vous?

12 **Les renseignements** *(Information).* Olivier is giving some information about people in his neighborhood. Help him to complete the sentences. Use the verb **avoir** and a number. Where no number is indicated, use **un, une,** or **des** as appropriate.

> **Modèle:** Les Dufoix / deux enfants / chat
> **Les Dufoix ont deux enfants et un chat.**

1. Charles / radio antique
2. Je / enfants extraordinaires
3. Les Dubois / trois télévisions / stéréo / ordinateur
4. Madame Martin / mari / six enfants
5. Nous / petit appartement / voiture
6. Mes grands-parents / grande maison / quatre chambres
7. Les Martin / chat / chien / deux réfrigérateurs / cuisinière à gaz / lave-vaisselle
8. Madame Davis / voiture japonaise / vélo français

F. La négation + *un (une, des)*

Review the negative of **il y a,** p. 67.

After **pas de,** words may be singular or plural: **pas de frère(s)**

■ After a negation, indefinite articles **(un, une, des)** usually become **de (d').**

Vous avez **un** ordinateur?	Non, je n'ai pas **d'**ordinateur.
Vous avez **une** voiture?	Non, je n'ai pas **de** voiture.
Vous avez **des** frères ou **des** sœurs?	Non, je n'ai pas **de** frère ou **de** sœur.
Y a-t-il **un** lave-vaisselle?	Non, il n'y a pas **de** lave-vaisselle.

Note This rule does not apply after **être.**

Christophe n'est pas **un** enfant.
La voiture n'est pas **une** Ford.
Ce ne sont pas **des** amis.

You may wish to present the **ni ... ni ...** construction for recognition.

■ Also, definite articles **(le, la, l', les)** and possessive adjectives **(mon, ma, mes,** etc.) do not change after a negation.

Je n'aime pas **le** thé.   Mon frère n'aime pas **notre** chien.

■ When contradicting a negative statement or question, use **si** instead of **oui.**

Il n'y a pas de sandwichs ici.	**Si,** il y a des sandwichs.
Vous n'avez pas d'ordinateur?	**Si,** j'ai un ordinateur.
Vous n'aimez pas le café?	**Si,** j'aime le café.

13 **Un riche et un pauvre.** Guy has everything, but Philippe has practically nothing. Explain how they differ.

> **Modèle:** voiture
> **Guy a une voiture, mais Philippe n'a pas de voiture.**

1. appartement
2. machine à laver
3. petite amie
4. ordinateur
5. amis
6. chien

Bavardages *(Gossip).* Someone has made up gossip about you and your neighbors. Correct these falsehoods.

> **MODÈLE:** Monsieur Dupont a des filles.
> **Mais non! Il n'a pas de fille.**

1. Marie a un petit ami.
2. Il y a une moto dans votre garage.
3. Vous détestez le café.
4. Jean-Yves a des enfants.
5. Christophe et Alice ont un chien.
6. Votre voiture est une Renault.

15 As-tu . . . ? Your partner will interview you according to the model. If you really do have the item in question, say so. If not, give a negative answer and then name something that you do have.

> **MODÈLE:** une voiture
> **VOTRE PARTENAIRE: As-tu une voiture?**
> **VOUS: Non, je n'ai pas de voiture mais j'ai une moto.**

1. une maison
2. un chien
3. un cousin à Lyon
4. un ordinateur
5. des amis qui habitent à Paris
6. un frère (une sœur) qui parle français

Follow up by playing the role of a fortune teller. Students have to affirm or deny statements you make, e.g., **Vous avez trois sœurs et deux frères, Vous n'avez pas d'ordinateur.**

16 Une diseuse de bonne aventure. A fortune teller has made the following statements about you. Affirm or deny them. Be careful to use **si** if you wish to contradict a negative statement.

> **MODÈLE:** Vous n'avez pas de frère.
> **Si, j'ai un frère (des frères).** ou
> **Oui, c'est vrai, je n'ai pas de frère.**

1. Vous n'avez pas de sœur.
2. Vous n'habitez pas dans un appartement.
3. Vous n'avez pas de stéréo.
4. Vous n'étudiez pas beaucoup.
5. Le professeur n'est pas gentil.
6. Vous n'aimez pas étudier le français.

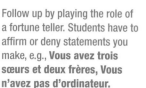 **VOCABULAIRE**

Les pièces d'une maison

You may wish to refer students to p. 154 for the distinction between **salle de bain** and **toilettes**.

un bureau	*office*	les toilettes	*restroom*
une chambre	*bedroom*	un salon	*living room*
une cuisine	*kitchen*	une salle de séjour	*den; living room*
une salle à manger	*dining room*	un sous-sol	*basement*
une salle de bain	*bathroom*	une véranda	*porch*

17 **À vous.** Answer the following questions.

1. Où habitez-vous?
2. Combien de pièces y a-t-il chez vous?
3. Quelles pièces est-ce qu'il y a?
4. Y a-t-il un fauteuil dans votre chambre?
5. Combien de chaises y a-t-il dans votre chambre?
6. Y a-t-il un chien ou un chat dans votre maison?
7. Qu'est-ce qu'il y a dans votre chambre?
8. Qu'est-ce qu'il y a dans le garage du professeur? (Imaginez!)

Entre amis

Une interview

1. Find out where your partner lives.
2. Find out how many rooms s/he has.
3. Ask if s/he has a basement or a porch.
4. Find out if your partner has a refrigerator in his/her room.
5. Find out if s/he has a TV in his/her room.
6. If so, ask if s/he watches television often.
7. Try to find one additional item which your partner has and one item which s/he does not have.
8. Turn to another person and gossip about your partner. Tell what you found out.

G. La possession avec *de*

C'est le mari **de** Mme Martin.	*It's Mme Martin's husband.*
Ce n'est pas la maison **de** René.	*It's not René's house.*
C'est la maison **des** parents **de** René.	*It's René's parents' house.*

Drill **Marie a une sœur** → **Voilà la sœur de Marie.** Other examples: **Alain a une voiture, Monique a un frère, Marc a des amis.**

■ The preposition **de (d')** is used to indicate possession or relationship. French has no possessive *-'s* ending: *Marie's sister* has to be expressed in French as *the sister of Marie.*

la sœur **de** Marie	*Marie's sister*
la voiture **d'**Alain	*Alain's car*

■ If the "owner" is indicated with a proper name, **de (d')** is used without article or possessive adjective. When the word referring to the "owner" is not a proper name, an article or a possessive adjective precedes it: *The grandmother's room* has to be expressed as *the room of the grandmother.*

la chambre de **la** grand-mère	*the grandmother's room*
la moto de **mon** ami	*my friend's motorcycle*

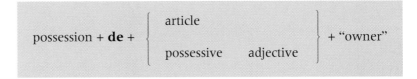

possession + **de** + { article / possessive adjective } + "owner"

■ The preposition **de** contracts with the articles **le** and **les,** but there is no contraction with the articles **la** and **l'**.

Remember that **de l'** could be masculine or feminine.

de + le	→	**du**	du professeur
de + les	→	**des**	des étudiants
de + la	→	**de la**	de la femme
de + l'	→	**de l'**	de l'enfant

Check comprehension by having students translate a few expressions. E.g., *Bill's stereo, the teacher's car.*

C'est une photo **du** professeur.   *It's a picture of the teacher.*
C'est la maison **des** parents d'Éric.   *It's Éric's parents' house.*
C'est le chat **de la** mère de Céline.   *It's Céline's mother's cat.*
C'est la voiture **de l'**oncle de Pascal.   *It's Pascal's uncle's car.*

18 **J'ai trouvé une radio** *(I found a radio).* A number of objects have been found. Ask a question to try to identify the owners. Your partner will answer negatively and will decide who *is* the owner.

MODÈLE: J'ai trouvé une radio. (Jeanne)
  VOUS: **J'ai trouvé une radio. C'est la radio de Jeanne?**
  VOTRE PARTENAIRE: **Non, ce n'est pas la radio de Jeanne. C'est la radio de Kevin.**

Remember to use only **de (d')** with a proper name.

Tell students to use names of students in class for the real owner.

1. J'ai trouvé une voiture. (Madame Dufour)
2. J'ai trouvé une radio. (professeur)
3. J'ai trouvé un chat. (Karine)
4. J'ai trouvé une moto. (l'ami de Michèle)
5. J'ai trouvé un chien. (les parents de Denis)
6. J'ai trouvé une calculatrice. (Frédérique)
7. J'ai trouvé un vélo. (la sœur de Sophie)

19 **Nos possessions.** Complete the following sentences by filling in the blanks.

Ask students to explain the choices they make.

1. Le vélo _____ Laurence est dans le garage.
2. La voiture _____ père _____ Anne est bleue.
3. La photo _____ oncle et _____ tante _____ Guy est sur le bureau _____ grands-parents _____ Guy.
4. Le chat _____ frère _____ Chantal est sur le lit _____ parents _____ Chantal.
5. Où est la calculatrice _____ sœur _____ Sandrine?
6. C'est la stéréo _____ enfants _____ professeur.
7. La moto _____ mon frère est dans notre garage.

Où est-ce? Patrick's family has a number of possessions. Ask where each item is.

MODÈLE: La sœur de Patrick a un vélo. **Où est le vélo de la sœur de Patrick?**

1. Les sœurs de Patrick ont une télévision.
2. Le frère de Patrick a une voiture.
3. L'oncle de Patrick a un chien.
4. Les cousins de Patrick ont une stéréo.
5. Les enfants de Patrick ont un ordinateur.
6. La cousine de Patrick a un appartement.
7. Les parents de Patrick ont une voiture allemande.
8. Le père de Patrick a un bureau.
9. La tante de Patrick a un petit chat.
10. Les parents de Patrick ont une belle maison.

H. Les adjectifs possessifs *son* et *leur*

As-tu une photo de la famille de Léa?	Voilà une photo de **sa** famille.
Où est le père de Léa?	Voilà **son** père.
Où est la mère de Léa?	Voilà **sa** mère.
Où sont les grands-parents de Léa?	Voilà **ses** grands-parents.
Où est la fille de M. et Mme Dupont?	Voilà **leur** fille. C'est Léa!
Où sont les cousins des Dupont?	Voilà **leurs** cousins.

Suggestion for a warm-up: Pair students to show family pictures again: **Voilà ma sœur,** etc. Then have them describe their partner's pictures: **Voilà sa sœur,** etc.

■ **Son, sa,** and **ses** can mean either *his* or *her*. As with **mon, ma,** and **mes,** the choice of form depends on whether the "possession" is masculine or feminine, singular or plural. It makes no difference what the gender of the "owner" is.

son lit	*his bed* or *her bed*
sa chambre	*his room* or *her room*
ses chaises	*his chairs* or *her chairs*

■ **Leur** and **leurs** mean *their* and are used when there is more than one "owner." Both forms are used for either masculine or feminine "possessions."

leur lit   **leur** chambre   **leurs** lits   **leurs** chambres

Note   Be sure not to use **ses** when you mean **leurs.**

ses parents	*his parents* or *her parents*
leurs parents	*their parents*

■ In the singular, **sa** becomes **son** when used directly before a feminine word beginning with a vowel sound.

sa meilleure amie   *But:*   **son** amie

■ Liaison occurs if the word following **son, ses,** or **leurs** begins with a vowel sound.

son petit ami	ses bons amis	leurs parents
But: son [n]ami	ses [z]amis	leurs [z]amis

■ Sometimes the identity of the "owner" would be unclear if a possessive adjective were used. In such cases, it is better to use the possessive construction with **de.**

Robert et Marie habitent avec   *(Robert's mother? Marie's mother?)*
   sa mère.
Robert et Marie habitent avec   *(clearly Marie's mother)*
   la mère **de Marie.**

Synthèse: les adjectifs possessifs				
pronom	masculin	féminin	pluriel (m. et f.)	
je	**mon**	**ma**	**mes**	*my*
tu	**ton**	**ta**	**tes**	*your*
il/elle/on	**son**	**sa**	**ses**	*his/her*
nous	**notre**	**notre**	**nos**	*our*
vous	**votre**	**votre**	**vos**	*your*
ils/elles	**leur**	**leur**	**leurs**	*their*

21 **La chambre de qui?** Clarify the identity of the "owner" in each of the following phrases by completing the following expressions with the appropriate form of de + *article défini.*

Follow-up: (1) Have students translate the possessive adjectives. (2) Close books and reverse the process: **La chambre du frère → sa chambre.**

MODÈLE: sa chambre. La chambre   La chambre **du** frère de
de qui?   Marc.

1. leur photo. La photo de qui?   La photo _____ enfants de ma tante.
2. son nom. Le nom de qui?   Le nom _____ jeune fille.
3. sa moto. La moto de qui?   La moto _____ mari d'Anne.
4. leurs livres. Les livres de qui?   Les livres _____ étudiants.
5. son chien. Le chien de qui?   Le chien _____ oncle d'Isabelle.
6. sa maison. La maison de qui?   La maison _____ ami de Laurent.
7. ses amies. Les amies de qui?   Les amies _____ sœur de Denis.
8. son chat. Le chat de qui?   Le chat _____ petite amie de Jean-Luc.
9. son bureau. Le bureau de qui?   Le bureau _____ professeur.

Comment s'appellent leurs filles?

Be careful to distinguish between **son/sa/ses** and **leur(s)** when asking these questions.

Use p. 58 for review or warm-up:
1. **David (Comment s'appellent ses grands-parents?**, etc.)
2. **Pierre et Anne (... leurs enfants,** etc.)

22 **Comment s'appellent-ils?** Ask the names of the following people, using a possessive adjective in each question. Your partner will supply the answer.

MODÈLES: le cousin de Nathalie? (Stéphane)
> **VOUS: Comment s'appelle son cousin?**
> **VOTRE PARTENAIRE: Il s'appelle Stéphane.**

les cousines de Nathalie? (Christelle et Sandrine)
> **VOUS: Comment s'appellent ses cousines?**
> **VOTRE PARTENAIRE: Elles s'appellent Christelle et Sandrine.**

1. le père de Nathalie? (Michel)
2. la sœur d'Éric? (Isabelle)
3. la mère d'Éric et d'Isabelle? (Monique)
4. les frères de Nathalie? (Christophe et Sébastien)
5. les sœurs de Nathalie? (Sylvie et Céline)
6. le chien de Nathalie? (Fidèle)
7. les grands-parents de Nathalie? (Marie et Pierre Coifard; Louis et Jeanne Dupuis)
8. les parents de votre meilleur(e) ami(e)?
9. les amis de vos parents?

23 **À vous.** Ask and answer the questions using possessive adjectives.

Modèle: Où est la maison de votre ami(e)?
Sa maison est à Denver.

1. Comment s'appelle votre meilleur(e) ami(e)?
2. Quel âge a votre ami(e)?
3. Combien de personnes y a-t-il dans la famille de votre ami(e)?
4. Comment s'appellent les parents de votre ami(e)?
5. Où habitent les parents de votre ami(e)?
6. Qu'est-ce qu'il y a dans la maison des parents de votre ami(e)?

Follow up by having students report on their partner's best friend: **son/sa meilleur(e) ami(e) ...**

Entre amis

Ton (ta) meilleur(e) ami(e)

1. Find out the name of your partner's best friend.
2. Find out where that friend lives.
3. Find out three items of information about that friend's home or possessions.
4. Find out three items of information about that friend's family, e.g., names, ages, activities, etc.

Intégration

Révision

If students write this description, put them in pairs and have each one guess what the other wrote.

Have students interview you to verify their selections, e.g., **Il y a une moto dans votre garage, n'est-ce pas?**

Prime this activity by eliciting the questions first. See p. 48 for suggestions.

A **Ma chambre.** Décrivez votre chambre. Qu'est-ce qu'il y a dans votre chambre?

B **La maison.** Décrivez la maison ou l'appartement de vos parents ou de vos amis. Qu'est-ce qu'il y a dans leur maison?

C **Mon professeur.** Imagine the home, garage, etc. of your French teacher. Make up five different sentences to state what s/he has or does not have.

Modèle: **Il y a une moto dans son garage.**

D **Trouvez quelqu'un qui ...** Interview your classmates in French to find someone who ...

Modèle: speaks French
Est-ce que tu parles français?

1. has a computer
2. has no brothers or sisters
3. has a dog or a cat or a fish
4. likes children a lot
5. is 21 or older
6. has a sister named Nicole
7. has a brother named Christopher
8. lives in an apartment
9. has grandparents who live in another state or province

Suggestion: Have students do the Information Gap activity in the Instructor's Resource Manual.

E **À vous.** Answer the following questions.

1. Combien de personnes y a-t-il dans votre famille?
2. Comment s'appellent deux de vos ami(e)s?
3. Où habitent-ils?
4. Quel âge ont-ils?
5. Sont-ils étudiants? Si oui, ont-ils une chambre à l'université? Étudient-ils le français ou une autre langue?
6. Avez-vous des amis qui ont un appartement? Si oui, qu'est-ce qu'il y a dans leur appartement?
7. Avez-vous un ami qui est marié? Si oui, comment s'appelle sa femme? Quel âge a-t-elle?
8. Avez-vous une amie qui est mariée? Si oui, comment s'appelle son mari? Quel âge a-t-il?
9. Avez-vous des amis qui ont des enfants? Si oui, combien d'enfants ont-ils? Comment s'appellent leurs enfants? Quel âge ont-ils?

Pas de problème!

Preparation for the video:
1. Video worksheet in the *Cahier d'activités*
2. CD-ROM, *Module 1*

Complete the following activity if you have watched video *Module 1*. Answer the following questions.

1. Comment s'appellent les quatre personnes qui jouent au tennis?
2. Comment s'appelle l'amie de Marie-Christine?
3. Qui est la cousine de René?
4. Comment s'appelle le film d'aventures?
5. Comment s'appelle le mélodrame?
6. Quel film est-ce que Marie-Christine préfère?

Lecture I

You may wish to consult the vocabulary on page 72 when labeling the rooms.

A **Ma maison idéale.** Draw a sketch of a home that would be ideal for you. Then label each of the rooms.

B **Étude du vocabulaire.** Study the following sentences and choose the English words that correspond to the French words in bold print: *square meters, fireplace, planted with trees, in new condition, winter, landscaped lot, approximately, stone, in good taste, on one level, roof, country, house, set up/ready-to-use.*

1. Le **pavillon** est situé à la **campagne** à **environ** 30 kilomètres de Paris.
2. Près de la maison il y a un jardin **arboré** et un beau **terrain paysager** de 300 **mètres carrés.**
3. En **hiver,** s'il fait froid, il y a une belle **cheminée** en **pierre** dans la salle de séjour.
4. La cuisine est **aménagée** et équipée **avec goût.**
5. La **toiture** de la maison est **en état neuf.**
6. Les personnes handicapées n'ont pas de problème avec une maison de **plain-pied.**

C **Les pièces.** Read the ads in order to:

1. identify the number of rooms in each home, and
2. make a list of the rooms that are mentioned.

MAISONS À VENDRE

Quelques abréviations: m² (mètres carrés); mn (minutes); s. de b. (salle de bain)

CADRE EXCEPTIONNEL

Belle maison récente, agréable séjour-salon en L 45 m² environ, cuisine aménagée équipée, 3 chambres, belle salle de bain, garage et jardin, mérite votre visite !

ELLE VOUS SÉDUIRA

Aux portes de Cholet, agréable pavillon indépendant sur 500 m² de terrain, cuisine aménagée équipée, beau séjour-salon avec cheminée, 3 chambres, garage 2 voitures et jardin aménagé avec goût.

DE TOUTE BEAUTÉ

Le charme de la campagne à 10 mn de Cholet, belle cuisine aménagée équipée, vaste pièce de réception 90 m² avec superbe cheminée en pierre, salon d'hiver parfaitement exposé, 4 chambres, 2 s. de b., bureau, grand garage, 1 700 m² de terrain paysager, aménagement de goût et de qualité !

EXCEPTIONNELLE

Plain-pied indépendant, séjour-salon, 2 chambres, toiture état neuf, garage et jardin arboré. Affaire à saisir !

D **Inférence.** Reread the ads to try to determine the following information. Be ready to justify your answers by quoting the reading.

1. the newest home
2. the biggest home
3. the largest lot
4. the home that has been remodeled
5. the name of the closest French city
6. the home you would choose and why

E **À discuter.** Aimez-vous ces maisons? Pourquoi ou pourquoi pas?

F **Comparaisons culturelles.** What similarities or differences between French homes and those of your country can you infer from what you have read?

Lecture II

 Étude du vocabulaire. Study the following sentences and choose the English words that correspond to the French words in bold print: *week, live, birth, today, new, is able to, more and more, one out of two.*

1. La **naissance** d'un enfant est une joie pour la famille.
2. Une personne bilingue **peut** parler deux langues.
3. Il y a sept jours dans une **semaine.**
4. **Un** étudiant **sur deux** est un homme.
5. Le **nouveau** professeur est charmant.
6. **Aujourd'hui,** il y a **de plus en plus** d'étudiants qui **vivent** sur le campus.

B **Parcourez la lecture** *(Skim the reading).* Skim the following reading to identify:

1. three types of families
2. the French words for *maternity leave, public day care,* and *nursery school.*

La Famille

À quel âge se marient-ils? L'âge légal du mariage est fixé à dix-huit ans et une jeune fille peut se marier à quinze ans avec l'accord de ses parents. Mais les jeunes se marient de plus en plus tard[1].

	hommes	femmes
en 1968	25 ans	23 ans
aujourd'hui	30 ans	28 ans

(d'après le Quid)

De nouveaux modèles de la famille. Le modèle traditionnel de la famille avec un couple marié et des enfants issus du mariage coexiste de plus en plus avec des modèles nouveaux. Avec le développement de la cohabitation il y a une augmentation du nombre des enfants hors mariage[2]: près de 40% des naissances aujourd'hui. Le nombre des divorces (un divorce sur trois mariages en France et un sur deux à Paris) augmente le nombre des familles monoparentales: 9% des enfants vivent avec un seul[3] de leurs parents. Les remariages multiplient les situations où des enfants vivent avec d'autres enfants issus d'un ou de plusieurs[4] mariages précédents: 11% des enfants vivent dans des familles recomposées. *(d'après Francoscopie)*

Si la mère travaille. Il y a, en France, des conditions qui facilitent la situation de la femme qui continue de travailler après[5] la naissance de son enfant. La femme qui travaille peut avoir un congé de maternité où 84% de son salaire est rémunéré. Elle peut rester[6] à la maison pendant[7] seize semaines: six semaines avant[8] la naissance du bébé et dix semaines après. Pour une femme qui a trois enfants ou plus, la période du congé de maternité est plus longue: huit semaines avant et dix-huit semaines après la naissance. Après son congé de maternité, quand la femme recommence à travailler, elle peut confier son enfant à une crèche collective publique ou choisir[9] une autre solution comme le système des jeunes filles au pair. À deux ans, son enfant peut aller[10] à l'école maternelle où il y a souvent un service de garderie le matin à 7 heures 30 et le soir jusqu'à[11] 19 heures. *(d'après La Civilisation française en évolution II).*

---

1. *late*   2. *out of wedlock*   3. *only one*   4. *several*   5. *after*   6. *remain*   7. *during*   8. *before*
9. *choose*   10. *go*   11. *until*

Questions: Answer the following questions in French.

1. Quel est l'âge légal pour le mariage?
2. Y a-t-il des exceptions?
3. Quel est le pourcentage des divorces à Paris?
4. Est-ce que le nombre de familles avec un parent augmente?
5. Quel pourcentage des enfants n'ont pas de parents mariés?
6. Quelle est la période du congé de maternité pour une femme qui a trois enfants?

 Comparaisons culturelles. What similarities or differences between France and your country can you infer from the reading with respect to:

1. the change in family structure
2. maternity leave and day care
3. the average age for marriage

VOCABULAIRE ACTIF

Possessions

un bureau *desk*
une calculatrice *calculator*
une chaise *chair*
un chat *cat*
un chien *dog*
une cuisinière *stove*
un fauteuil *armchair*
un lave-vaisselle *dishwasher*
un lit *bed*
un livre *book*
une machine à laver *washing machine*
une mobylette *moped, motorized bicycle*
une moto *motorcycle*
un ordinateur *computer*
un réfrigérateur *refrigerator*
un sofa *sofa*
une stéréo *stereo*
un vélo *bicycle*
une voiture *automobile*

La maison ou l'appartement

un appartement *apartment*
un bureau *office*
une chambre *bedroom*
une cuisine *kitchen*
un garage *garage*
une maison *house*
une salle à manger *dining room*

une salle de bain *bathroom*
les toilettes *restroom*
un salon *living room*
une salle de séjour *den; living room*
un sous-sol *basement*
une véranda *porch*

La famille

un beau-père *stepfather (or father-in-law)*
des beaux-parents *(m. pl.) stepparents (or in-laws)*
une belle-mère *stepmother (or mother-in-law)*
une belle-sœur *sister-in-law*
un(e) cousin(e) *cousin*
un(e) enfant *child*
une famille *family*
une femme *wife*
une fille *daughter*
un fils *son*
un frère *brother*
un demi-frère *stepbrother*
une grand-mère *grandmother*
une arrière-grand-mère *great grandmother*
un grand-père *grandfather*
des grands-parents *(m. pl.) grandparents*
un mari *husband*

une mère *mother*
un neveu *nephew*
une nièce *niece*
un oncle *uncle*
des parents *(m. pl.) parents; relatives*
un père *father*
une petite-fille *granddaughter*
un petit-fils *grandson*
des petits-enfants *(m. pl.) grandchildren*
une sœur *sister*
une tante *aunt*

D'autres personnes

un(e) camarade de chambre *roommate*
un(e) étudiant(e) *student*
une fille *girl*
un garçon *boy*
une petite fille *little girl*
un(e) petit(e) ami(e) *boyfriend/girlfriend*

D'autres noms

l'âge *(m.) age*
un an *year*
la gare *(train) station*
un membre *member*
une photo *photograph*
un train *train*

Nombres

trente *thirty*
quarante *forty*
cinquante *fifty*
soixante *sixty*
soixante-dix *seventy*
soixante et onze *seventy-one*
soixante-douze *seventy-two*
quatre-vingts *eighty*
quatre-vingt-un *eighty-one*
quatre-vingt-dix *ninety*
quatre-vingt-onze *ninety-one*
cent *one hundred*
mille *one thousand*
un million *one million*
un milliard *one billion*

Adjectifs possessifs

mon, ma, mes *my*
ton, ta, tes *your*
son, sa, ses *his; her*
notre, nos *our*
votre, vos *your*
leur, leurs *their*

D'autres adjectifs

autre *other*
charmant(e) *charming*
gentil(le) *nice*

Verbes

avoir *to have*
passer (un an) *to spend (a year)*

Prépositions

dans *in*
sur *on*

Conjonction

si *if*

Articles indéfinis

un/une *a, an*
des *some; any*

Adverbes

combien (de) *how many; how much*
comment *how; what*
encore *still; again; more*
trop (de) *too much; too many*

Expressions utiles

Bienvenue! *Welcome!*
chez moi *at my house*
chez vous *at your house*
Comment s'appelle-t-il (elle)? *What's his (her) name?*
Comment s'appellent-ils (elles)? *What are their names?*
Il (elle) s'appelle ... *His (her) name is ...*
Ils (elles) s'appellent ... *Their names are ...*
il y a *there is (are)*
Je suis né(e) *I was born*
Je vous présente ... *Let me introduce you to ...*
Qu'est-ce qu'il y a ... ? *What is there ... ?*
Qu'est-ce qu'il y a? *What's the matter?*
Quel âge avez-vous? (a-t-il?, etc.) *How old are you? (is he?, etc.)*
sans doute *probably*
Si! *Yes!*
sur la photo *in the picture*
voici *here is; here are*
vous dites *you say*

La France et la francophonie

L'importance du français dans le monde

La revue *Language Today* propose un classement des langues les plus importantes. Ce classement est basé sur les critères suivants: le nombre de personnes qui parlent la langue, l'usage de la langue dans les domaines scientifiques et diplomatiques, la puissance économique des nations où on parle la langue, et le prestige social et littéraire de la langue.

LES LANGUES LES PLUS IMPORTANTES

1. l'anglais	6. le chinois
2. le français	7. l'allemand
3. l'espagnol	8. le japonais
4. le russe	9. le portugais
5. l'arabe	10. l'hindi / l'urdu

L'anglicisme: un grand souci. Les Français utilisent un nombre considérable d'expressions d'origine anglo-américaine: **le drugstore, le jogging, le fast food, le footing, le chewing-gum, le jean,** etc. La proportion de ces anglicismes a fait l'objet de mesures législatives en France. En 1993, Jacques Toubon, à l'époque ministre de la Culture de la Francophonie, a proposé un projet de loi sur l'emploi du français car, disait-il, la valeur et le prestige de la langue française, «un élément fondamental de la personnalité et du patrimoine de la France», sont menacés par la domination et la globalisation de l'anglais et par ce que l'écrivain et journaliste René Étiemble a baptisé le «franglais.» Les défenseurs de la loi Toubon (votée le 4 août 1994) pensent qu'il faut défendre le français contre les assauts de l'anglo-américain. Les détracteurs leur opposent que l'anglais ne menace en rien l'intégrité et l'avenir de la langue française, et ils nous rappellent que l'anglais utilise lui-même des mots et des expressions d'origine française comme *à la carte, coup d'état, cul de sac, R.S.V.P., fait accompli, soupe du jour, laissez-faire* et *déjà vu.*

À vous!

1. Pour quelles raisons est-ce que l'anglais est la langue la plus importante?
2. Pourquoi le français est-il numéro deux dans le classement par ordre d'importance?
3. Cherchez d'autres exemples d'expressions françaises utilisées en anglais.

Les origines

Les explorateurs français des XVIe et XVIIe siècles ont étendu l'hégémonie de la France à l'Amérique du Nord (voir Escale 2). Au XIXe siècle, la recherche d'espaces nouveaux, de matière première et de nouveaux marchés commerciaux a incité la France à coloniser plusieurs pays africains et certaines régions de la Caraïbe et de l'Indochine. Après une occupation d'un siècle, la langue française est devenue la langue véhiculaire, voire même la langue officielle, dans la majorité des anciennes colonies.

La francophonie est le terme inventé en 1880 par le géographe Onésime Reclus pour définir l'ensemble des pays où le français est parlé. Parmi les pays francophones il faut citer en Europe la Belgique, le Luxembourg et la Suisse. L'influence et la langue françaises se sont aussi étendues à la Bulgarie, à la Roumanie et, plus loin, à l'Égypte, au Liban et à Madagascar.

La négritude

Quoique l'universalité de la langue française soit perçue comme un avantage par de nombreux Africains des régimes coloniaux, d'autres trouvent que ce «décombre du régime colonial» est source de malaise (*discomfort*). Dans les années 30, de jeunes Antillais et Africains se rencontrent en France où ils font des études et contestent le colonialisme de l'époque. Trois étudiants en particulier, Aimé Césaire de la Martinique, Léon Gontron Damas de Guyane et Léopold Senghor du Sénégal, s'unissent pour publier à Paris en 1932 une petite revue, *Légitime défense*. Ils y lancent un appel à la dignité humaine et invitent leur peuple à être fiers de leurs origines africaines. Le gouvernement français n'a pas été lent à réagir. Les bourses de ces trois étudiants ont été supprimées pendant plusieurs mois, et *Légitime défense* n'a donc eu qu'un seul numéro. Mais la graine était semée, et ces trois mêmes jeunes, à l'esprit indomptable, sont revenus deux ans plus tard et ont fondé avec de nouveaux adeptes le journal *L'Étudiant noir*.

En 1939, Aimé Césaire publie le *Cahier d'un retour au pays natal*. C'est ici que le terme «négritude» apparaît pour la première fois et décrit les objectifs de ce mouvement. Selon Césaire, la négritude est «la simple reconnaissance du fait d'être noir, et l'acceptation de ce fait, de notre destin de noir, de notre histoire et de notre culture». C'est donc ainsi que le mouvement de la négritude est né et que l'âme africaine a commencé à faire entendre sa voix.

Histoire récente

En 1970, l'ensemble des pays francophones, sous l'impulsion des chefs d'État africains Léopold Senghor du Sénégal, Habib Bourguiba de Tunisie et Hanani Diori du Niger, ont souhaité utiliser leur lien linguistique au service de la paix, de la coopération et du développement culturel et économique. Ils ont ainsi créé **l'Agence de la Francophonie**. Cette agence est l'organisation principale des programmes décidés par les pays membres. Elle regroupe 50 États et gouvernements. Elle siège à Lomé (Togo), à Libreville (Gabon) et à Hanoï (Vietnam). Le **Secrétaire général de la Francophonie** et son administration veillent à l'harmonisation des programmes. C'est ainsi que l'Agence de la Francophonie est responsable de la TV5, une chaîne de télévision en langue française, et de l'Université Senghor d'Alexandrie qui a pour vocation d'assurer le perfectionnement des cadres supérieurs des pays francophones de l'Afrique. Parmi ses priorités sont la promotion du français dans le monde, la jeunesse et les technologies nouvelles, et le renforcement de la démocratie et des droits de l'homme.

La France et l'Union européenne

La francophonie n'est pas la seule communauté internationale dont fait partie la France. Depuis 1957, la France forme avec l'Allemagne, l'Italie, la Belgique, les Pays-Bas et le Luxembourg la **Communauté économique européenne.** Dans les années qui suivent, les pouvoirs en commun et les liens économiques et culturels ont augmenté ainsi que le nombre de pays participants. En 1995 l'union inclut quinze pays, et onze d'entre eux ont voté de faire l'unité monétaire en janvier 2002. L'euro est la nouvelle monnaie pour ces pays.

La France et ses partenaires ont lancé une politique ambitieuse pour défendre les intérêts européens, pour renforcer la puissance économique et la croissance de l'emploi et de la formation, pour fortifier les capacités militaires européennes, pour protéger l'environnement, et pour lutter contre le trafic de la drogue. La France a assuré la présidence de l'Union européenne en l'an 2000 et joue un rôle très important dans la promotion d'une Europe forte.

Le bâtiment de l'Union européenne à Strasbourg

L'Hexagone

Benjamin Franklin a écrit: «Tout homme a deux pays: le sien et la France.»

Quelques statistiques

D'après *La Fédération internationale des professeurs de français* (FIPF), cent douze millions de personnes parlent régulièrement le français, une progression de 7,7%. Soixante millions de personnes parlent occasionnellement le français, une progression de 11,8%. Trente-deux millions de personnes apprennent le français dans les pays non-francophones et un million de personnes enseignent le français dans le monde. (*AATF National Bulletin, Vol. 26, No. 4*)

Voir Paris et mourir!

Paris, la «ville lumière», tient son rayonnement universel à ses deux mille ans d'histoire, à sa mode, à son prestige au point de vue art, science et pensée. L'une des plus grandes métropoles mondiales, Paris est devenu, et depuis longtemps, un carrefour et un lieu d'échanges, un grand centre financier, la destination touristique par excellence en France.

La tour Eiffel: emblème de Paris. Par l'audace et l'immensité de sa taille, la tour Eiffel, dès le début de sa construction en 1887, a été l'objet de controverses parmi les Parisiens. De nombreux artistes, hommes de lettres et hommes politiques ont exprimé leur indignation, voire même leur colère. Mais aujourd'hui des millions de personnes visitent cet emblème somptueux de Paris pour admirer la finesse de sa ligne et célébrer le génie de sa construction.

Construite par Gustave Eiffel pour célébrer le centenaire de la Révolution à l'occasion de l'Exposition universelle de 1889

Paris l'ancien et Paris le nouveau. La ville rassemble en contrastes frappants (*striking*) l'architecture ancienne et nouvelle, comme en témoigne le Louvre.

Le Louvre

L'immigration

Il y a toujours eu en France de nombreuses personnes nées à l'étranger qui ont décidé de vivre dans ce pays. Depuis la Seconde Guerre mondiale, la pauvreté des anciennes colonies ainsi que les besoins de main-d'œuvre (*labor*) en France ont causé d'importants flux migratoires. Bientôt le nombre de ces «invités» a fait l'objet de tensions politiques. Aujourd'hui, la question de l'immigration met en conflit la gauche et la droite politiques. Les uns voient dans l'immigration un péril à l'identité nationale. La présence sur le territoire national de communautés étrangères importantes

Le onze tricolore. L'équipe multiethnique de France championne du monde de foot en 1998 est surnommée «Black, Blanc, Beur». Cette équipe, source de fierté nationale, sert aujourd'hui de modèle de la diversité et de l'unité.

risque, selon les slogans du Front national, «de signifier la fin de la France». Les autres pensent que sous ce masque se cachent du racisme, de la xénophobie et de la discrimination. Pour ces derniers l'immigration et la diversité contribuent à la richesse économique et culturelle du pays.

Parmi les immigrés, les nationalités les plus représentées sont les Portugais, les Algériens, les Marocains, les Italiens, les Espagnols, les Turcs et les Tunisiens. Il faut ajouter à cette liste les ressortissants de l'Afrique noire. La présence des Maghrébins et des Africains, qui travaillent pour la plupart comme ouvriers (56%), employés (21%) ou personnel domestique (53% des femmes) et qui occupent souvent des logements défavorisés, suscite beaucoup de polémique.

La France et la technologie

Le train à grande vitesse (TGV), qui circule à 300 km/h (186 *mph*), est un des symboles de la place que la France occupe dans le monde. La technologie du TGV a été exportée aux États-Unis, en Corée du Sud et en Chine. En France, le nouveau TGV Méditerranée a été mis en service en 2001. Marseille et Paris ne sont plus qu'à trois heures de distance.

En aéronautique, malgré (*in spite of*) l'accident tragique qui a eu lieu à Paris en juillet 2000, le Concorde demeure toujours un grand succès de la technologie française. Cet avion supersonique franco-britannique traverse les 5.600 km entre Paris et New York en 3h30. Le nouveau modèle d'Airbus qui sera mis en service en 2005 aura une capacité énorme. Mis à part ces domaines où elle prend la première place en technologie, la France rivalise avec d'autres pays dans d'autres sphères (appareils digitalisés, communications, recherche médicale, par exemple).

Le Tour de France

L'histoire du vélo est très attachée à la France. L'invention de la bicyclette est souvent attribuée à un forgeron (*blacksmith*) écossais, Kirkpatrick Macmillan, mais la popularisation de ce véhicule est due à deux Français, Pierre Michaux et son fils, Ernest. Cette équipe de père et fils construit à Paris en 1861 le premier «vélocipède», un engin avec deux roues (*wheels*) et deux manivelles (*cranks*) attachées à une grande roue. Un an plus tard la famille Michaux fabrique 142 vélos; et, depuis, la production annuelle a considérablement augmenté.

La France est aussi le premier pays à organiser une course cycliste. En 1869, la revue *Vélocipède illustre* sponsorise une course de 80 km entre Rouen et Paris; et en 1903, le Tour de France, ou la Grande Boucle comme on dit aujourd'hui, fait son début. Cette course par étapes est aujourd'hui la plus longue et la plus prestigieuse. Des millions de personnes s'alignent le long des routes pour voir passer les cyclistes pédalant à une vitesse de 40 km à l'heure. Le Tour de France n'est pas seulement une course cycliste mais un symbole de la France et un des plus grands événements sportifs annuels.

L'arrivée du Tour à Paris

Chapitre 4
L'identité

Buts communicatifs
Describing personal attributes
Describing clothing
Describing people and things
Describing what you do at home
Identifying someone's profession

Structures utiles
Quelques groupes d'adjectifs
Ne ... jamais
Les adjectifs de couleur
L'adjectif démonstratif
La place de l'adjectif
Le verbe **faire**
Les mots interrogatifs **qui, que** et **quel**

Culture
Au pair
Le franglais
Les McDo et l'influence américaine
Les cartes postales

Coup d'envoi

Prise de contact

Qu'est-ce que c'est?
(Quel est ce vêtement?°)

What is this article of clothing?

C'est ...

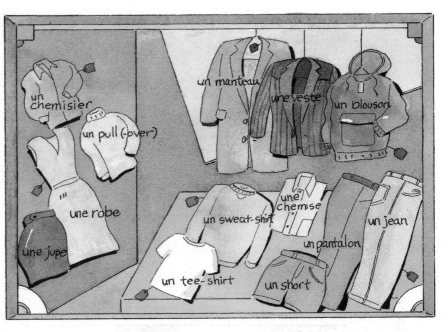

Ce sont°...

These are

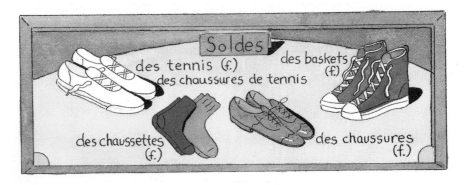

▶ **Et vous?** Qu'est-ce que vous portez aujourd'hui?° *What are you wearing today?*
Moi, je porte ...

Une carte postale au professeur

Lettre

Lori Becker adresse une carte postale à son professeur américain, Madame Walter.

> Chère Madame,   Angers, le 2 octobre
> Me voilà au pair chez¹ les Martin.
> J'aime bien cette² famille! Je
> garde³ deux des enfants et je fais
> quelquefois le ménage.⁴ Ça me donne⁵
> beaucoup de travail mais c'est
> Mme Martin qui fait la cuisine.⁶ Et
> puis les enfants font la vaisselle⁷
> le soir.
>   Quelle belle ville⁹! Et les gens¹⁰ sont
> charmants! Je me sens chez moi¹¹.
> Tout le monde¹² porte un jean et
> un tee-shirt. Et il y a deux McDo à
> Angers! Avec mon meilleur souvenir,
>   Lori

1. *at (the house of)*   2. *this*   3. *look after*   4. *do housework sometimes*   5. *That gives me*
6. *who does the cooking*   7. *then*   8. *do the dishes*   9. *city*   10. *people*   11. *I feel at home*
12. *Everybody*

Compréhension. Taking turns, read the following statements with your partner. Decide whether they are true (**C'est vrai**) or false (**C'est faux**). If a sentence is false, correct it.

1. Lori Becker habite à Angers.
2. Elle habite chez ses parents.
3. Elle travaille pour les Martin.
4. Elle fait la cuisine et la vaisselle.
5. Elle est contente d'être en France.
6. Les vêtements des jeunes Français sont très différents des vêtements des jeunes Américains.

Il y a un geste

This gesture is used in the video, *Module 1*.

Bravo!   The "thumbs up" gesture is used in French to signify approval.

À PROPOS

Pourquoi est-ce que Lori fait le ménage et garde les enfants de Madame Martin?

a. Elle est masochiste.
b. Elle est très gentille et désire aider *(help)* la famille Martin.
c. Il y a souvent des jeunes filles qui habitent avec une famille française et qui travaillent pour payer leur chambre et leurs repas *(meals)*.

Au pair

Many young women from foreign countries work as **jeunes filles au pair** *(nannies)* in France. They are able to spend a year abroad by agreeing to work in a French home. In exchange for room and board, but only a token salary, they do some light housework and help to take care of the children. Lori is **au pair chez les Martin.**

Le franglais

Borrowing inevitably takes place when languages come in contact. The Norman conquest in 1066 introduced thousands of French words into English and many English words have been borrowed by the French. While some of these French cognates are obvious in meaning (**le chewing-gum, un tee-shirt, un sweat-shirt**), others may surprise you: **un smoking,** for instance, means a *tuxedo.* Official measures have been adopted in France to try to stem the flow of English expressions into the French language. Currently, for example, the term **le logiciel** is being encouraged rather than the English cognate **le software.**

Les McDo et l'influence américaine

Lori is, of course, exaggerating when she says **Tout le monde porte un jean.** There has been, however, a change in French cities with respect to clothing style and the use of fast-food restaurants, and many of the French claim this is due to the influence of American culture. Decried by some and praised by others, these changes also reflect the fast-paced life of modern France.

Les cartes postales

When sending postcards, most French people will insert the card in an envelope and put stamp and address on the envelope. This perhaps speeds delivery and ensures privacy.

▶ **À vous.** Describe to your partner what your classmates are wearing.

MODÈLE: **VOTRE PARTENAIRE:** **Qu'est-ce que Sean porte aujourd'hui?**
VOUS: **Il porte ...**

Entre amis

J'aime beaucoup vos chaussures. Elles sont très belles.

1. Compliment your partner on some article of clothing s/he is wearing.
2. S/he should respond in a culturally appropriate manner.
3. Point to two other articles of clothing and ask what they are.
4. If s/he doesn't know, s/he should say **Je ne sais pas.**
5. If s/he *is* able to name the articles, be sure to say that s/he speaks French well.

Prononciation

Les voyelles nasales: [ɛ̃], [ɑ̃] et [ɔ̃]

■ Note the pronunciation of the following words:

[ɛ̃] • **im**possible, **im**probable, **in**telligent, c**in**quante, v**in,** v**in**gt, m**in**ce

• s**ym**pathique, s**ym**phonie, s**yn**thèse

• f**aim,** améric**ain,** maroc**ain,** mexic**ain,** tr**ain**

• h**ein**

• canadi**en,** itali**en,** bi**en,** je vi**en**s, chi**en,** combi**en,** ti**en**s

Some French speakers pronounce the nasal vowel in the words **un** and parf**um** as [ɛ̃]; others pronounce it as [œ̃]. The [œ̃] pronunciation is not being taught at this level.

[ɑ̃] • ch**am**bre, **an,** fr**an**çais, ch**an**ter, m**an**ger, gr**an**d, pend**an**t, étudi**an**te, t**an**te, dem**an**dent

• **en**s**em**ble, m**em**bre, par ex**em**ple, **en, en**core, comm**en**t, souv**en**t

Exception exam**en** [ɛgzamɛ̃]

[ɔ̃] • t**om**ber, c**om**bien, n**om,** prén**om, on, on**t, c**on**versati**on,** n**on, on**cle, **on**ze

■ Now go back and look at how these sounds are spelled and in what kinds of letter combinations they appear. What patterns do you notice?

■ When **-m-** or **-n-** is followed by a consonant or is at the end of a word, it is usually not pronounced. It serves instead to indicate that the preceding vowel is nasal.

c**in**qu**an**te   **en**s**em**ble   c**om**bien   **im**possible

■ When **-m-** or **-n-** is followed by a written vowel (pronounced or not pronounced), the preceding vowel is *not* nasal.

canadien   crème   téléphone
brune   inévitable imaginaire

Note The vowel preceding a written **-mm-** or **-nn-** is also not nasal.

i**nn**ocent   i**mm**obile   co**mm**e   perso**nn**e

Be sure students pronounce nonnasal **i** as [i], not as a short English *i*.

▶ Practice saying the following words after your instructor, paying particular attention to the highlighted vowel sound. In these words, the highlighted vowel sound is *not* nasal.

américain	même	limonade	comme	une
Madame	aime	cousine	comment	lunettes
examen	américaine	inactif	personne	fume

▶ In each of the following pairs of words, one of the words contains a nasal vowel and one does not. Pronounce each word correctly.

1. impossible / immobile
2. minuit / mince
3. faim / aime
4. marocain / marocaine
5. canadienne / canadien
6. une / un

7. ambulance / ami
8. anglaise / année
9. crème / membre
10. dentiste / Denise
11. combien / comment
12. bonne / bon

Buts communicatifs

1 Describing Personal Attributes

Comment est votre meilleur(e) ami(e)? Est-il (elle) ...

calme	ou	nerveux (nerveuse)?	
charmant(e)	ou	désagréable?	
compréhensif (compréhensive)°	ou	intolérant(e)°	*understanding / intolerant*
discret (discrète)	ou	bavard(e)°?	*talkative*
généreux (généreuse)	ou	avare°?	*miserly*
gentil(le)	ou	méchant(e)°?	*mean*
heureux (heureuse)	ou	triste°?	*sad*
intelligent(e)	ou	stupide?	
intéressant(e)	ou	ennuyeux (ennuyeuse)°?	*boring*
optimiste	ou	pessimiste?	
patient(e)	ou	impatient(e)?	
travailleur (travailleuse)°	ou	paresseux (paresseuse)°?	*hard-working / lazy*

▶ **Et vous?** Comment êtes-vous? Comment sont vos professeurs?

Les étudiants sont très bavards et le garçon est un peu impatient.

1 **La famille de Sandrine.** Correct the following false impressions, beginning with **Mais pas du tout!** Make sure each adjective agrees with the noun it modifies.

MODÈLE: Le frère de Sandrine est désagréable.
Mais pas du tout! Il est charmant.

You may also wish to teach the expressions **la barbe** and **Il a un poil dans la main.**

1. Sandrine est paresseuse.
2. Ses parents sont ennuyeux.
3. Leurs enfants sont très stupides.
4. La mère de Sandrine est triste et pessimiste.
5. Ses frères sont désagréables.
6. La sœur de Sandrine est méchante.
7. Son père est impatient.
8. Sa famille est bavarde.

Il y a un geste

Paresseux. The thumb and index finger of one hand "caress" an imaginary hair in the palm of the other hand. This gesture signifies that someone is so lazy that a hair could grow in his/her palm.

Ennuyeux. The gesture for ennuyeux is made by rubbing the knuckles back and forth on the side of the jaw. This rubbing of the "beard" is used to indicate that something is so boring that one could grow a beard while it is happening.

A. Quelques groupes d'adjectifs

Remind students that adjectives ending in **-x** in the masculine singular keep the same form and pronunciation in the masculine plural.

Some feminine adjectives differ from the masculine by a double final consonant as well as by a final **-e.**

Final consonants **c, f, l,** & **r** are usually pronounced: **chic, sportif, intellectuel, travailleur.**

féminin	masculin
discrète(s)	discret(s)
ennuyeuse(s)	ennuyeux
généreuse(s)	généreux
heureuse(s)	heureux
nerveuse(s)	nerveux
paresseuse(s)	paresseux
travailleuse(s)	travailleur(s)
gentille(s)	gentil(s)
intellectuelle(s)	intellectuel(s)
active(s)	actif(s)
compréhensive(s)	compréhensif(s)
sportive(s)	sportif(s)
naïve(s)	naïf(s)
veuve(s)	veuf(s)

■ The **-l** in the masculine form **gentil** is not pronounced. The final consonant sound of the feminine form **gentille** is [j], like the English **y** in *yes*.

gentil   [ʒɑ̃ti]   gentille   [ʒɑ̃tij]

■ In written French, some feminine adjectives (ending in **-e-** + consonant + **-e**) are distinguishable from their masculine forms not only by a final **-e,** but also by a grave accent on the **-e-** before the consonant.

ch**è**re   cher   discr**è**te   discret

■ Some French adjectives are invariable. There is no change to indicate gender or number.

deux femmes **snob**   des chaussures **chic**

2 **Qui est comme ça?** Answer the following questions. Make sure each adjective agrees with the subject.

MODÈLE: Qui est patient dans votre famille?
Ma mère est patiente.
Mes sœurs sont patientes aussi.

If exercise 2 is assigned as written homework, remind students to add an **-s** in the plural, unless the word ends in **-s** or **-x.**

1. Qui est travailleur dans votre famille?
2. Qui est bavard dans votre cours de français?
3. Qui est quelquefois triste?
4. Qui est généreux et optimiste?
5. Qui est sportif?
6. Qui est discret?
7. Qui est snob?
8. Comment sont vos parents?
9. Avez-vous des amis qui sont naïfs?
10. Et-vous? Comment êtes vous?

B. *Ne ... jamais*

Review the formation of the negative in Ch. 1, p. 20.

Mon amie **n'est jamais** méchante.	*My friend is never mean.*
Mon petit ami **ne** porte **jamais** de chaussettes.	*My boyfriend never wears socks.*

■ **Ne ... jamais** *(never)* is placed around the conjugated verb just like **ne ... pas.** It is one of the possible answers to the question **Quand?** *(When?).*

Quand est-ce que tu étudies?
Je **n'**étudie **jamais**!

Note   **Jamais** can be used alone to answer a question.

Quand est-ce que tu pleures?
Jamais!

VOCABULAIRE

Adverbes de fréquence

toujours	*always*	quelquefois	*sometimes*
d'habitude	*usually*	rarement	*rarely*
généralement	*generally*	(ne ...) jamais	*never*
souvent	*often*		

 Comment sont-ils?   Describe the following people with as many true sentences as you can create. Use items from the lists below (or their opposites). Make all necessary changes, paying special attention to the form of the adjectives.

MODÈLE: **Mes parents ne sont jamais impatients.**
Ils sont toujours patients.

Follow up with a stand-up drill. Each student has to give an example: **Mon oncle est généreux; il n'est jamais avare.** See the Instructor's Resource Manual for a description of a stand-up drill.

mes parents		intolérant
je		méchant
mon petit ami	ne ... jamais	triste
ma petite amie	rarement	paresseux
mes amis	quelquefois	bavard
mon professeur	souvent	impatient
nous (les étudiants)	d'habitude	pessimiste
le (la) président(e) de l'université	toujours	ennuyeux
		désagréable
		avare

Un test de votre personnalité. Complete the questionnaire by answering **oui** or **non.** Then read the analysis that follows and write a paragraph to describe yourself.

	oui	*non*
1. Vous parlez beaucoup avec certaines personnes, mais vous refusez de parler avec tout le monde.	_____	_____
2. Vous aimez beaucoup les sports, mais vous détestez étudier et travailler.	_____	_____
3. Vous détestez jouer, danser ou chanter avec les autres, mais vous aimez bien étudier.	_____	_____
4. Vous avez beaucoup d'argent *(money),* mais vous donnez rarement de l'argent à vos amis.	_____	_____
5. Vous n'avez pas d'argent, mais vous n'êtes jamais triste.	_____	_____
6. Votre conversation est toujours agréable et vous parlez avec tout le monde.	_____	_____
7. Vous étudiez beaucoup, vous aimez parler français et vous êtes certain(e) que votre professeur de français est charmant.	_____	_____

Une analyse de vos réponses

1. Si vous répondez **oui** au numéro 1, vous êtes extroverti(e) et bavard(e), mais vous êtes aussi un peu snob.
2. Si vous répondez **oui** au numéro 2, vous êtes sportif (sportive), mais aussi paresseux (paresseuse). Vous n'avez probablement pas de bonnes notes *(good grades).*
3. Un **oui** au numéro 3, et vous êtes introverti(e), mais aussi travailleur (travailleuse). Vous avez probablement des notes excellentes.
4. Un **oui** au numéro 4, et vous êtes avare et pessimiste. Vous n'avez probablement pas beaucoup d'amis.
5. Si vous répondez **oui** au numéro 5, vous êtes d'habitude optimiste et heureux (heureuse), mais peut-être aussi un peu naïf (naïve).
6. Si vous répondez **oui** au numéro 6, vous n'êtes pas du tout ennuyeux (ennuyeuse). Vos amis sont contents d'être avec vous.
7. Enfin *(finally),* si votre réponse est **oui** au numéro 7, vous êtes certainement très intelligent(e), charmant(e) et intéressant(e). Les professeurs de français adorent les étudiant(e)s comme vous.

5 **Cinq personnes que j'aime.** Write a description of five people you like. How much can you tell about each one?

As a warm-up after students have written the assignment, read one or more of the descriptions and see how many details students can remember.

Modèle: Charles Thomas est mon ami.
Charles est petit et un peu gros.
Il est très gentil et intelligent.
Mais il est aussi un peu paresseux.
Voilà pourquoi il n'est pas du tout sportif.

Entre amis

Qui est la personne sur la photo?

1. Show your partner a picture (real or imaginary) of someone.
2. Identify that person (name, age, address).
3. Describe his/her personality.
4. Give a physical description as well.
5. Tell what the person is wearing in the picture.

Suggestion: For #3, have students add *always, seldom,* etc. for each characteristic mentioned.

2 Describing Clothing

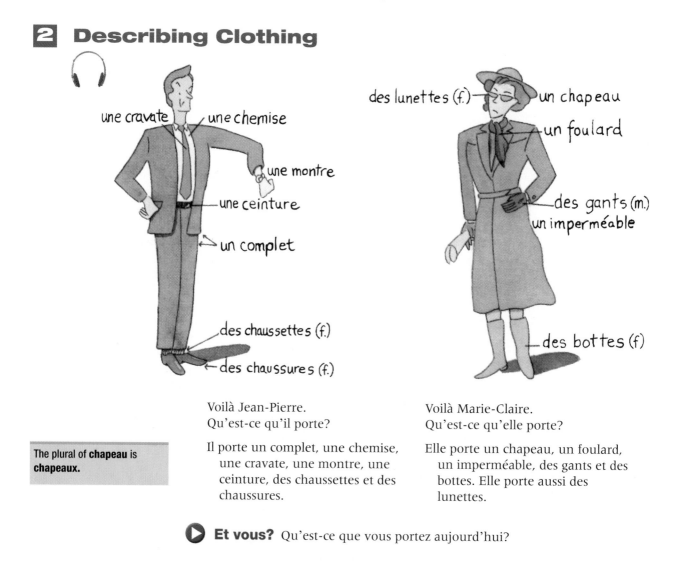

Voilà Jean-Pierre.
Qu'est-ce qu'il porte?

Il porte un complet, une chemise, une cravate, une montre, une ceinture, des chaussettes et des chaussures.

The plural of **chapeau** is **chapeaux.**

Voilà Marie-Claire.
Qu'est-ce qu'elle porte?

Elle porte un chapeau, un foulard, un imperméable, des gants et des bottes. Elle porte aussi des lunettes.

▶ **Et vous?** Qu'est-ce que vous portez aujourd'hui?

6 **Qu'est-ce que c'est?** Identify the following items.

Modèles:

—Qu'est-ce que c'est?
—C'est une ceinture.

—Qu'est-ce que c'est?
—Ce sont des chaussures.

1.

2.

3.

4.

5.

6.

7.

8.

9.

7 **Qu'est-ce qu'ils portent?** Describe the clothing tastes of several people you know. What items of clothing do they wear often, rarely, never?

Modèles: **Mon professeur de français ne porte jamais de jean.**
Je porte souvent un tee-shirt mais je porte rarement un chapeau.

1. mon professeur de français
2. les étudiants de mon cours de français
3. une actrice/un acteur de Hollywood
4. mon/ma meilleur(e) ami(e)
5. les musiciens d'un groupe rock
6. les membres de ma famille
7. moi

C. Les adjectifs de couleur

De quelle couleur est le pantalon de Jean-Pierre?
Il est **gris.** C'est un pantalon **gris.**

De quelle couleur est sa chemise?
Elle est **bleue.** C'est une chemise **bleue.**

De quelle couleur sont ses chaussures?
Elles sont **noires.** Ce sont des chaussures **noires.**

 Et vous? De quelle couleur sont vos vêtements?

VOCABULAIRE

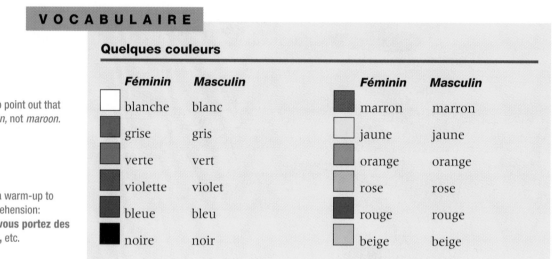

Quelques couleurs

	Féminin	Masculin		Féminin	Masculin
	blanche	blanc		marron	marron
	grise	gris		jaune	jaune
	verte	vert		orange	orange
	violette	violet		rose	rose
	bleue	bleu		rouge	rouge
	noire	noir		beige	beige

Note Plurals of colors are formed by adding **-s.** Exceptions in this list are **gris,** which already ends in **-s, marron,** and **orange,** which are invariable: **des éléphants** *gris,* **des cheveux** *orange,* **des chemises** *marron.*

8 **De quelle couleur sont leurs vêtements?** Ask your partner about the color of the following articles of clothing.

> **MODÈLES:** les chaussures de Jérôme (noir)
> **VOUS:** De quelle couleur sont ses chaussures?
> **VOTRE PARTENAIRE:** Elles sont noires. Ce sont des chaussures noires.
>
> le pull de Martine (bleu)
> **VOUS:** De quelle couleur est son pull?
> **VOTRE PARTENAIRE:** Il est bleu. C'est un pull bleu.

1. la cravate de Denis (jaune et bleu)
2. la robe de Françoise (vert)
3. la veste de Jean (gris)
4. l'imperméable d'Annette (blanc)
5. les chaussettes d'un(e) autre étudiant(e)
6. la chemise d'une autre personne
7. les chaussures de votre partenaire
8. les vêtements du professeur

VOCABULAIRE

Il y a
un
geste

Pour décrire *(to describe)* les vêtements

bon marché	*inexpensive*	ou	cher (chère)	*expensive*
chic	*stylish*	ou	confortable	*comfortable*
élégant(e)	*elegant*	ou	ordinaire	*ordinary, everyday*
propre	*clean*	ou	sale	*dirty*
simple	*simple, plain*	ou	bizarre	*weird, funny-looking*

This gesture is used in video, *Module 7.*

Cher! Similar to its English equivalent, the gesture for **cher!** is made by rubbing the thumb, index, and middle fingers together.

An alternate gesture is to shake the open hand vigorously. See, for example, the gesture **Quelle histoire!**, Ch. 14.

Confortable is not used to describe how a person feels. It is used to describe a thing: **une chemise confortable, une vie confortable.**

Note **Chic** and **bon marché** are invariable. They do not change in the feminine or in the plural: **Ce sont des chaussures *chic,* mais elles sont *bon marché.***

Synthèse: Les adjectifs invariables

bon marché	chic	marron	orange	snob

9 **Au contraire!** Your partner will make a series of statements with which you will disagree. Provide the corrections by following the model.

MODÈLE: la robe de Simone (cher)
VOTRE PARTENAIRE: **La robe de Simone est chère.**
VOUS: **Non, elle n'est pas chère. C'est une robe bon marché.**

1. la veste de Martin (élégant)
2. le sweat-shirt de Monsieur Dupont (propre)
3. la robe de Pascale (chic)
4. les chaussettes du professeur (?)
5. l'imperméable de l'inspecteur Colombo (?)
6. les vêtements de deux autres étudiants (?)

Supply the adjectives for 4–6.

10 **À vous.** Answer the following questions.

Suggestion: Have students describe the clothes of the characters in the video.

1. Qu'est-ce que vous portez aujourd'hui?
2. De quelle couleur sont vos vêtements?
3. Décrivez les vêtements que vous portez.
4. Décrivez les vêtements d'un(e) autre étudiant(e).
5. Qu'est-ce que le professeur porte d'habitude?
6. De quelle couleur sont ses vêtements?
7. Qui ne porte jamais de jean dans votre classe de français?
8. Qui porte rarement des chaussures bon marché?
9. Qu'est-ce qu'on porte pour skier ou pour patiner?

Aimez-vous les défilés de mode *(fashion shows)*? Ce mannequin est chic, n'est-ce pas?

Do this in class as a paired writing exercise. Then read the paragraphs out loud and have the class guess who is being described.

11 **Qui est-ce?** Describe as completely as possible the clothing of a fellow classmate.

MODÈLE: **Cette personne porte un pull jaune et un pantalon vert. Elle porte des chaussures marron. Elle ne porte pas de chaussettes. Ses vêtements ne sont peut-être pas très élégants mais ils sont confortables.**

Entre amis

Au téléphone

You are meeting a friend for dinner in twenty minutes.

1. Call to find out what s/he is wearing.
2. Find out the colors of his/her clothing.
3. Describe what you are wearing as completely as possible.

The French answer the phone by saying **«Allô!»**.

Put students back-to-back when phoning. Have them note each other's description. Follow up with a fashion show: One student reads the description and the other stands and models: **Karen porte ...**

D. L'adjectif démonstratif

Cette femme est très intelligente. *That (this) woman is very intelligent.*
Ce vin est excellent! *This (that) wine is excellent.*
Vous aimez **cet** appartement? *Do you like this (that) apartment?*
Qui sont **ces** deux personnes? *Who are those (these) two people?*

	singulier	pluriel
masculin:	**ce (cet)**	**ces**
féminin:	**cette**	**ces**

■ The demonstrative adjectives are the equivalent of the English adjectives *this (that)* and *these (those).*

ce garçon	*this boy*	or	*that boy*
cet ami	*this (male) friend*	or	*that (male) friend*
cette amie	*this (female) friend*	or	*that (female) friend*
ces amis	*these friends*	or	*those friends*
ces amies	*these (female) friends*	or	*those (female) friends*

■ **Cet** is used before masculine singular words that begin with a vowel sound. It is pronounced exactly like **cette.**

cet homme	*this man*	or	*that man*
cet autre professeur	*this other teacher*	or	*that other teacher*

■ If the context does not distinguish between the meanings *this* and *that* or *these* and *those,* it is possible to make the distinction by adding **-ci** (for *this/these*) or **-là** (for *that/those*) to the noun.

J'aime beaucoup cette chemise-**ci.** *I like this shirt a lot.*
Ces femmes-**là** sont françaises. *Those women are French.*

12 **Au grand magasin** *(At the department store).* While shopping, you overhear a number of comments but are unable to make out all the words. Try to complete the following sentences using one of the demonstrative adjectives **ce, cet, cette,** or **ces,** as appropriate.

1. Vous aimez _____ chaussures? Oui, mais je déteste _____ chemise.
2. _____ pantalon est beau. Mais _____ jupes sont très chères.
3. _____ jean est trop petit pour _____ homme-là.
4. Je ne sais pas comment s'appelle _____ vêtement-là.
5. _____ robes sont jolies, mais _____ sweat-shirt est laid.
6. J'aime beaucoup _____ pull-là, mais je trouve _____ veste trop longue.

Brainstorm with the class for possible reasons for disliking items before putting students in pairs.

13 Non, je n'aime pas ça. Your shopping has made you tired and grouchy. Respond to your friend's questions or comments by saying that you dislike the item(s) in question. Use a demonstrative adjective in each response and invent a reason for your disapproval.

MODÈLE: Voilà une robe rouge.
Je n'aime pas beaucoup cette robe; elle est bizarre.

1. Voilà une belle cravate.
2. Voilà un ordinateur!
3. Oh! la petite calculatrice!
4. C'est un beau chapeau!
5. Tu aimes les chaussures vertes?
6. Voilà des chaussettes blanches intéressantes.
7. J'adore le chemisier bleu.
8. Tu aimes la veste de ce monsieur?

Entre amis

Cette robe est très élégante!

1. Pay your partner at least three compliments on his/her clothing.
2. S/he should respond in a culturally appropriate manner to each compliment.
3. Together, comment on the clothing of one of your neighbors.

3 Describing People and Things

De quelle couleur sont les yeux° et les cheveux° de Michèle?
Elle a les yeux bleus.
Elle a les cheveux blonds.

eyes / hair

De quelle couleur sont les yeux et les cheveux de Thierry?
Il a les yeux verts et les cheveux roux°.

red

De quelle couleur sont les yeux et les cheveux de Monsieur Monot?
Il a les yeux noirs, mais il n'a pas de cheveux.
Il est chauve°.

bald

▶ **Et vous?** De quelle couleur sont vos yeux et vos cheveux?

Remarques

The singular **cheveu** refers to a single strand of hair.

Remember that the masculine plural adjective is used with the words **yeux** and **cheveux**: **les yeux bleus, les cheveux noirs.**

1. Use the definite article **les** with the verb **avoir** to describe the color of a person's hair and eyes.

   Thierry **a les** yeux verts et **les** cheveux roux.

2. The word **cheveu** is almost always used in the plural, which is formed by adding **-x.**

   Michèle a **les cheveux** blonds.

3. Note that the adjective used to describe red hair is **roux** (**rousse**), never **rouge.**

   Il a les cheveux **roux.**   Notre petite-fille est **rousse.**

4. Use the adjective **brun**(**e**) to describe brown hair, never **marron.**

   Alissa a les cheveux **bruns.**   Elle est **brune.**

 Leurs yeux et leurs cheveux. Complete the following sentences with a form of the verb **être** or **avoir,** as appropriate.

1. Mon père _____ les yeux bleus. Il _____ chauve.
2. Brigitte et Virginie _____ les cheveux roux.
3. Vous _____ les yeux noirs.
4. De quelle couleur _____ les yeux de votre mère?
5. Elle _____ les yeux verts.
6. Mes oncles _____ les cheveux blonds, mais ils _____ aussi un peu chauves.

15 **De quelle couleur ... ?** Ask and answer questions with a partner based on the list below. If you don't know the answer, guess.

Follow-up: Have students report as many of their partner's answers as they can.

MODÈLES: vos yeux

> VOUS: **De quelle couleur sont vos yeux?**
> VOTRE PARTENAIRE: **J'ai les yeux verts.**

les cheveux de votre oncle

> VOUS: **De quelle couleur sont les cheveux de votre oncle?**
> VOTRE PARTENAIRE: **Il n'a pas de cheveux. Il est chauve.**

1. vos yeux
2. vos cheveux
3. les yeux de votre meilleur(e) ami(e)
4. les cheveux de votre meilleur(e) ami(e)
5. les yeux et les cheveux d'un(e) autre étudiant(e)
6. les cheveux de vos grands-parents
7. les yeux et les cheveux de vos frères et sœurs (ou de vos amis)

Entre amis

Dans ma famille

1. Find out how many people there are in your partner's family.
2. Find out their names and ages.
3. Find out the color of their hair.
4. Find out their eye color.

Remind students to use the verb **avoir** when talking about age.

E. La place de l'adjectif

un livre **intéressant**	*an interesting book*
une femme **charmante**	*a charming woman*
un **bon** livre	*a good book*
l'**autre** professeur	*the other teacher*

■ Most adjectives (including colors and nationalities) follow the noun they modify.

un homme **charmant**	un garçon **bavard**
une femme **intelligente**	une fille **sportive**
une robe **bleue**	une voiture **française**

■ Certain very common adjectives, however, normally precede the noun.

1. Some that you already know are:

autre	grand	joli
beau	gros	petit
bon	jeune	vieux

2. Two others that usually precede the noun are:

Remember that **nouveau**, like **beau** and **chapeau**, forms the plural by adding **-x.**

masculin singulier	féminin singulier	masculin pluriel	féminin pluriel	équivalent anglais
mauvais	**mauvaise**	**mauvais**	**mauvaises**	*bad*
nouveau	**nouvelle**	**nouveaux**	**nouvelles**	*new*

Point out that students have already learned the special form **cet** to replace **ce** before a noun beginning with a vowel sound.

3. **Beau, vieux,** and **nouveau** each have a special masculine singular form (**bel, vieil, nouvel**) for use when they precede a noun beginning with a vowel sound. These special forms are pronounced exactly like the feminine forms.

un **bel** homme   un **vieil** ami   un **nouvel** appartement

The rules governing **obligatory liaison** will be summarized in Ch. 5.

4. Adjectives ending in a silent consonant are linked by liaison to words beginning with a vowel sound. When linked, a final **-s** or **-x** is pronounced [z] and a final **-d** is pronounced [t].

un mauvais [z]hôtel   deux vieux [z]amis   un grand [t]hôtel

FOR RECOGNITION ONLY:

- In formal spoken and written French, **des** is replaced by **de** if a plural adjective comes *before* the noun.

des professeurs intelligents	**des** voitures françaises
Mais: **de** bons professeurs intelligents	**d'**autres voitures françaises

- A few adjectives can be used either before or after the noun. Their position determines the exact meaning of the adjective.

un **ancien** professeur	*a former teacher*
un château **ancien**	*an ancient castle*
le **pauvre** garçon	*the unfortunate boy*
le garçon **pauvre**	*the boy who has no money*

 16 **C'est vrai.** Restate the following sentence.

Modèles: Les chaussures de Monsieur Masselot sont sales.
 C'est vrai. Il a des chaussures sales.

 L'appartement de Monsieur Masselot est vieux.
 C'est vrai. Il a un vieil appartement.

1. L'appartement de Monsieur Masselot est beau.
2. Les enfants de Monsieur Masselot sont jeunes.
3. La femme de Monsieur Masselot est intelligente.
4. Les parents de Monsieur Masselot sont charmants.
5. Le chat de Monsieur Masselot est gros.
6. Le chien de Monsieur Masselot est méchant.
7. La voiture de Monsieur Masselot est mauvaise.
8. L'ordinateur de Monsieur Masselot est nouveau.
9. L'appartement de Monsieur Masselot est grand.
10. Le réfrigérateur de Monsieur Masselot est petit.
11. La cravate de Monsieur Masselot est bleue.
12. Les chaussettes de Monsieur Masselot sont bizarres.

17 **Quelques compliments.** Select items from each of the lists to pay a few compliments. How many compliments can you create? Make all necessary changes.

Modèles: **C'est une jolie robe.**
 Tu as des chaussures chic.

Remind students of the French reaction to compliments. As an extension, have them respond to their partner's compliments.

You may require students to use **de** instead of **des** before plural adjectives that precede nouns. If you do, remind them that this is a more formal style.

		robe	joli
		maison	élégant
		appartement	bon
		vêtements	magnifique
tu as	un	chemise	intéressant
c'est	une	chemisier	superbe
ce sont	des	chaussettes	beau
		chaussures	chic
		jean	

Review pp. 22, 93, and 104.

18 **Une identité secrète.** Choose the name of someone famous that everyone will recognize. The other students will attempt to guess the identity of this person by asking questions. Answer only **oui** or **non**.

Warm-up: Describe a student (clothing, hair, eyes, etc.) and ask the class to guess his/her identity.

MODÈLE: **C'est une femme?**
Est-ce qu'elle est belle?
A-t-elle les cheveux roux?
Est-ce qu'elle porte souvent des vêtements élégants?
etc.

Suggestion: Model this first by (1) describing your best friend, and (2) role-playing this with one student.

Entre amis

Mon ami(e)

Interview your partner to find out as much as you can about his/her best friend's personality and physical appearance. Inquire also about the clothing that the friend usually wears.

4 Describing What You Do at Home

Que fais°-tu chez toi°, Catherine?   *do / at home*
     Je regarde la télé ou j'écoute la radio.
     J'étudie et je fais mes devoirs°.   *homework*
     Je fais souvent la cuisine°.   *the cooking*
     Je parle avec mes parents.
     Je fais quelquefois la vaisselle°.   *the dishes*
     Je fais rarement le ménage°.   *housework*

▶ **Et vous?** Que faites-vous chez vous?

F. Le verbe *faire*

VOCABULAIRE À RETENIR

courses *shopping*
provisions *grocery shopping*
lessive *wash*

Je déteste **faire** les courses, mais j'aime **faire** la liste.
Ma mère **fait** les provisions.
Mes sœurs **font** la cuisine.
Et c'est moi qui **fais** la vaisselle.
Nous **faisons** tous la lessive.

I hate doing the shopping, but I like making the list.
My mother does the grocery shopping.
My sisters do the cooking.
And I'm the one who does the dishes.
We all do the wash.

faire *(to do; to make)*			
je	**fais**	nous	**faisons**
tu	**fais**	vous	**faites**
il/elle/on	**fait**	ils/elles	**font**

En France, on aime
faire ses provisions
au marché.

■ The **-ai-** in **nous faisons** is pronounced [ə] as in **le, de,** etc.

■ The plural **les devoirs** means *homework*. The singular **la vaisselle** means *the dishes*. The plural **les courses** means *the shopping*.

Je fais **mes devoirs.**	*I do my homework.*
Qui aime faire **la vaisselle?**	*Who likes to do the dishes?*
Nous faisons **nos courses** ensemble.	*We do our shopping together.*

Idiomatic uses of **faire** to describe the weather will be taught in Ch. 7.

■ There are a number of idiomatic uses of the verb **faire.**

Je ne **fais** jamais **la sieste.**	*I never take a nap.*
Veux-tu **faire une promenade?**	*Would you like to take a walk?*
Quel temps fait-il?	*What is the weather like?*
Il fait chaud.	*It's hot out.*
Faites attention!	*Pay attention!* or *Watch out!*

■ A question using **faire** does not necessarily require the verb **faire** in the response.

Que **faites**-vous?
Je *patine,* je *chante,* je *regarde* la télé, j'*écoute* la radio, etc.

19 **Nous faisons beaucoup de choses.** Use the list below to create as many factual sentences as you can.

Modèles: **Mon petit ami ne fait jamais de promenade.**
Ma mère ne fait jamais la sieste.
Nous faisons souvent les courses.

mes amis			la lessive
mon petit ami		toujours	la vaisselle
ma petite amie		d'habitude	la sieste
ma mère	faire	souvent	les courses
mon père		quelquefois	la cuisine
nous (ma famille)		rarement	une promenade
je		ne ... jamais	le ménage
			les provisions
			attention

20 **À vous.** Answer the following questions.

1. Faites-vous toujours vos devoirs pour le cours de français?
2. Quand faites-vous la sieste?
3. Faites-vous une promenade après le dîner?
4. Aux USA, est-ce le mari ou la femme qui fait le ménage d'habitude?
5. Qui aime faire les courses dans votre famille?
6. Aimez-vous faire la cuisine? Si non, qu'est-ce que vous aimez faire?
7. Aimez-vous la cuisine italienne?
8. Qui fait les provisions pour votre famille d'habitude?
9. Qui fait la lessive d'habitude?

Entre amis

Chez toi

1. Find out where your partner lives.
2. Find out who does the grocery shopping and who does the cooking at his/her house.
3. Ask if s/he likes French cooking.
4. Find out what s/he does or doesn't like to do.

5 Identifying Someone's Profession

—Chantal, qu'est-ce que tu veux faire dans la vie?°   *what do you want to do in life?*
—Je voudrais être journaliste. Et toi?
—Je ne sais pas encore.°   *I don't know yet.*

▶ **Et vous?** Qu'est-ce que vous voulez faire dans la vie?

VOCABULAIRE

Quelques professions

architecte	
artiste	
assistant(e) social(e)	*social worker*
athlète	
avocat(e)	*lawyer*
*cadre	*executive*
comptable	*accountant*
cuisinier (cuisinière)	*cook*
*écrivain	*writer*
employé(e)	
fermier (fermière)	*farmer*
fonctionnaire	*civil servant*
homme (femme) d'affaires	*businessman (-woman)*
homme (femme) politique	*politician*

infirmier (infirmière)	*nurse*
*ingénieur	*engineer*
interprète	
journaliste	
*médecin	*doctor*
ouvrier (ouvrière)	*laborer*
patron(ne)	*boss*
pharmacien(ne)	
*professeur	
programmeur (programmeuse)	
secrétaire	
vendeur (vendeuse)	*salesperson*

*Certain professions are used only with masculine articles and adjectives (**un, mon, ce**) for a woman, as well as a man: **Elle est médecin. C'est un médecin.***

A more extensive list of professions can be found in Appendix B at the end of this book.

Nouns of profession, nationality, and religion all act like adjectives when used this way.

Ask students to tell which professions they think are the most interesting: **À mon avis, les professions les plus intéressantes sont ...**

Remarques

1. There are two ways to identify someone's profession:

   • One can use a name or a subject pronoun + **être** + profession, without any article.

Céline **est artiste.**	*Céline is an artist.*
Je **suis pharmacienne.**	*I am a pharmacist.*
Il **est ouvrier.**	*He is a factory worker.*

   • For *he, she,* and *they,* one can also say **c'est** (**ce sont**) + indefinite article + profession.

C'est un professeur.	*He (she) is a teacher.*
Ce n'est pas un employé; c'est le patron.	*He isn't an employee; he's the boss.*
Ce sont des fonctionnaires.	*They are civil servants.*

2. To give more detail, one can use a possessive adjective or an article with an adjective. **C'est** (**ce sont**), not **il/elle est** (**ils/elles sont**), is used.

C'est ton secrétaire?	*Is he your secretary?*
Monique est une athlète **excellente.**	*Monique is an excellent athlete.*
Ce sont des cuisiniers **français.**	*They are French cooks.*

If this is done in pairs, follow up with a stand-up drill. Students have to share something they were told: **Il (elle) voudrait être ... mais il (elle) ne voudrait pas être ...**

21 **Que voulez-vous faire?** Use the list above to select professions that you would like and professions that you would not like.

MODÈLE: **Je voudrais être journaliste mais je ne voudrais pas être écrivain.**

Qu'est-ce qu'il faut faire? *(What do you have to do?)* The
following sentences tell what preparation is needed for different careers.
Complete the sentences with the name of the appropriate career(s).

Modèle: Il faut étudier la biologie pour être **médecin, dentiste** ou
infirmier.

1. Il faut étudier la pédagogie pour être ...
2. Il faut étudier la comptabilité pour être ...
3. Il faut étudier le commerce pour être ...
4. Il faut étudier le journalisme pour être ...
5. Il faut étudier l'agriculture pour être ...
6. Il faut parler deux ou trois langues pour être ...
7. Il faut désirer aider les autres pour être ...
8. Il faut avoir une personnalité agréable pour être ...
9. Il faut faire très bien la cuisine pour être ...

23 **Cinq personnes que je connais** *(Five people I know).* Give a description of five people you know. How much can you tell about each one?
Be sure to include information about what they do and what they want
to do.

Modèle: **Anne Smith est étudiante. C'est une jeune fille travailleuse
et très gentille. Elle a les cheveux roux et les yeux verts.
Elle étudie le français et elle désire être femme d'affaires.
Elle fait bien la cuisine et elle adore la cuisine française.**

G. Les mots interrogatifs *qui, que* et *quel*

Qui fait la cuisine dans votre famille?	*Who does the cooking in your family?*
Que faites-vous après le dîner?	*What do you do after dinner?*
À **quelle** heure dînez-vous?	*At what time do you eat dinner?*

■ **Qui** *(who, whom)* is a pronoun. Use it in questions as the subject of a verb or
as the object of a verb or preposition.

Qui est-ce?	*Who is it?*
Qui regardez-vous?	*At whom are you looking?*
Avec **qui** parlez-vous?	*With whom are you talking?*

■ **Que** *(what)* is also a pronoun. Use it in questions as the object of a verb. It
will be followed either by inversion of the verb and subject or by **est-ce
que.** There are therefore two forms of this question: **Que ... ?** and
Qu'est-ce que ... ?

Que font-ils?	*What do they do?*
Qu'est-ce qu'ils font?	

■ Don't confuse **Est-ce que ... ?** (simple question) and **Qu'est-ce que ... ?**
(What?).

Est-ce que vous voulez danser?	*Do you want to dance?*
Qu'est-ce que vous voulez faire?	*What do you want to do?*
Qu'est-ce qu'il y a?	*What is it? What's the matter?*

■ **Quel** *(which, what)* is an adjective. It is always used with a noun and agrees with the noun.

Quel temps fait-il?   *What is the weather like?*
Quelles actrices aimez-vous?   *Which actresses do you like?*

	singulier	pluriel
masculin	quel	quels
féminin	quelle	quelles

Note   The noun may either follow **quel** or be separated from it by the verb **être.**

Quels vêtements portez-vous?   *Which clothes are you wearing?*
Quelle est votre **adresse?**   *What is your address?*

24 **Quelles questions!** Ask questions using the appropriate form of **quel** with the words provided below.

Modèle: votre profession
            Quelle est votre profession?

1. heure/il est
2. à/heure/vous mangez
3. temps/il fait
4. votre nationalité
5. âge/vous avez
6. vêtements/vous portez/quand il fait chaud
7. votre numéro *(m.)*/de téléphone
8. de/couleur/vos yeux

25 *Qui, que* ou *quel?* Complete the following sentences.

1. _____ fait le ménage chez toi?
2. _____ font tes parents?
3. _____ âge ont tes amis?
4. De _____ couleur sont les cheveux du professeur?
5. Avec _____ parles-tu français?
6. À _____ heure dînes-tu d'habitude?
7. _____ désires-tu faire dans la vie?
8. _____ fais-tu après le dîner?

26 **À vous.** Answer the following questions.

1. Avez-vous des frères ou des sœurs? Si oui, que font-ils à la maison? Qu'est-ce qu'ils désirent faire dans la vie?
2. Que voulez-vous faire dans la vie?
3. Qu'est-ce que vous étudiez ce semestre?
4. Qu'est-ce que votre meilleur(e) ami(e) désire faire dans la vie?
5. Qui fait la cuisine chez vous?
6. À quelle heure faites-vous vos devoirs d'habitude?
7. Que font vos amis après le dîner?
8. Qui ne fait jamais la vaisselle?

27 **Une nouvelle identité.** Give yourself a new identity and give the information requested in the form below as completely as possible.

Consult the list of professions p. 111 and Appendix B when filling this out.

AIR FRANCE
Économique

Pour mieux vous servir, aidez-nous
à vous mieux connaître.

Nom du passager _____

Adresse personnelle _____

_____ Pays _____

Ville _____ N° Tél. _____

Entreprise _____

_____ N° Tél. _____

Adresse professionnelle _____

Pays _____ Ville _____

Profession _____

Vol Air France N° _____ du _____
                                    (jour et mois)

Entre amis

Dans un avion *(In an airplane)*

1. Greet the person sitting next to you on the plane.
2. Find out his/her name and address.
3. Find out what s/he does.
4. What can you find out about his/her family?
5. Find out what the family members do.

Tell students to use the new identity from exercise 27.

Follow up by having students introduce their partners to the class, using their new identities.

Intégration

Révision

A **Portraits personnels.** Provide the information requested below.

1. Décrivez les membres de votre famille.
2. Décrivez votre meilleur(e) ami(e).
3. Décrivez une personne dans la salle de classe. Demandez à votre partenaire de deviner *(guess)* l'identité de cette personne.

B **Trouvez quelqu'un qui ...** Interview your classmates in French to find someone who ...

Prime this activity by eliciting the questions first. See p. 48 for suggestions.

MODÈLE: wants to be a doctor

VOUS: **Est-ce que tu désires être médecin?**
UN(E) AUTRE ÉTUDIANT(E): **Oui, je désire être médecin.** ou
Non, je ne désire pas être médecin.

1. likes to wear jeans and a sweatshirt
2. is wearing white socks
3. never wears a hat
4. has green eyes
5. likes to cook
6. likes French food
7. hates to do housework
8. wants to be a teacher
9. takes a nap in the afternoon

 Suggestion: Have students do the Information Gap activity in the Instructor's Resource Manual.

Item 3: Remind students of the idiomatic use of **faire** in weather expressions: **Il fait chaud.** This will be taught in more detail in Ch. 7.

C **À vous.** Answer the following questions.

1. De quelle couleur sont les vêtements que vous portez aujourd'hui?
2. Qu'est-ce que vos amis portent en classe d'habitude?
3. Quels vêtements aimez-vous porter quand il fait chaud?
4. De quelle couleur sont les yeux et les cheveux de votre meilleur(e) ami(e)?
5. Qui a les yeux bleus et les cheveux bruns?
6. Que faites-vous à la maison?
7. Que font les autres membres de votre famille chez vous?
8. Que voulez-vous faire dans la vie?
9. Qu'est-ce que votre meilleur(e) ami(e) désire faire?

Pas de problème!

Preparation for the video:
1. Video worksheets in the *Cahier d'activités*
2. CD-ROM, *Module 2*

Complete the following exercise if you have watched the video, *Module 2*. Choose the most appropriate answer.

1. Marie-Christine habite dans la rue *(street)* _____. (Bonaparte, Saint-Sulpice, de Tournon)
2. Elle habite _____. (dans une maison, dans un appartement)
3. Il faut _____ pour ouvrir la porte. (la clé, le code, la télécarte)
4. Jean-François est assez _____. (nerveux, calme)
5. _____ est nécessaire pour téléphoner dans une cabine téléphonique. (l'argent, le code, la télécarte)

Lecture I

A **Parcourez les petites annonces.** Glance at the classified ads below to find out what kind of job each one is advertising. Guess which one would pay the most. Which ones require a car? Which ones do not require experience? Which ones are for summer employment only?

Typical salaries in euros per month:
(1) 100 euros
(2) 1000 euros
(3) 1000–1500 euros
(4) 0 euros
(5) 2000–3000 euros
(6) 2000–3000 euros

Offres d'emploi

1 _____
Bébé, un an et demi, cherche fille au pair de nationalité américaine ou canadienne, expérience avec enfants. Appelez Cunin en fin de matinée 02.43.07.47.26.

2 _____
Nous recherchons des secrétaires bilingues. Appelez l'Agence bilingue Paul Grassin au 02.42.76.10.14.

3 _____
Professeurs anglophones pour enseigner l'anglais aux lycéens étrangers en France, école internationale, château. Deux sessions: du 30 juin au 21 juillet; du 25 juillet au 14 août. Tél. 02.41.93.21.62.

4 _____
Famille offre logement et repas en échange de baby-sitting le soir et certains week-ends. Les journées sont libres. Écrivez BP 749, 49000 Angers.

5 _____
Opportunité de carrière. Compagnie internationale, établie depuis 71 ans, est à la recherche de jeunes personnes ambitieuses pour compléter son équipe commerciale. Si vous avez une apparence soignée, si vous êtes positif(ve), si vous possédez une voiture, appelez-nous au 02.41.43.00.22.

6 _____
Vous cherchez un job d'été (juillet et août) bien rémunéré, vous aimez discuter et vous possédez une voiture: venez rejoindre notre équipe de commerciaux. Formation assurée. Débutants acceptés. Tél. 02.41.43.15.80.

B **Cela vous intéresse?** *(Does this interest you?)* Reorder the classified ads above according to how much they appeal to you (which ones you would apply for and in what order). Be prepared to explain your reasons.

You may want students to give their reasons in English to check their comprehension.

C **Votre petite annonce.** Write a classified ad to say you are looking for work in France. Mention your personal description and experience and include the fact that you speak French. Be sure to tell how you can be contacted.

Lecture II

A **Que savez-vous déjà?** Previous knowledge of a topic is a definite asset in understanding a text. Answer the following before reading the poem.

1. Qui est Hamlet et quelle est son expression préférée?
2. Quelle est la nationalité du Hamlet de Shakespeare?
3. Faites une liste de quatre mots qui ont un accent grave.
4. Quelle différence y a-t-il entre **ou** et **où?** Que veulent dire ces deux mots?

B **Étude du vocabulaire.** Study the following sentences and choose the English words that correspond to the French words in bold print: *Do you understand?, so much, pupils, everyone, serious, you can answer, unhappy, What?, day dreaming.*

1. Quand on est étudiant, il y a **tant** de travail à faire!
2. Si vous n'êtes pas absent, **vous pouvez répondre** «présent».
3. Un étudiant qui ne fait pas attention est quelquefois **dans les nuages.**
4. **Hein** ou **quoi** sont souvent des synonymes de «Comment?».
5. À l'université il y a des étudiants; les **élèves** sont généralement à l'école secondaire.
6. Si un professeur désire vérifier si un étudiant ou un élève comprend, il demande: **«Vous y êtes?».**
7. Si un étudiant ne fait pas attention, son professeur risque d'être **mécontent.**
8. La situation est **grave.** Il faut faire très attention.
9. Est-ce que **tout le monde** parle français en France?

L'ACCENT GRAVE

Le professeur

Élève Hamlet!

L'élève Hamlet *(sursautant[1])*

... Hein ... Quoi ... Pardon ... Qu'est-ce qui se passe ... Qu'est-ce qu'il y a ... Qu'est-ce que c'est?

Le professeur *(mécontent)*

Vous ne pouvez pas répondre «présent» comme tout le monde? Pas possible, vous êtes encore dans les nuages.

L'élève Hamlet

Être ou ne pas être dans les nuages!

Le professeur

Suffit. Pas tant de manières. Et conjuguez-moi le verbe être, comme tout le monde, c'est tout ce que je vous demande.

L'élève Hamlet

To be ...

Le professeur

En français, s'il vous plaît, comme tout le monde.

L'élève Hamlet

Bien, monsieur. (Il conjugue:)
Je suis ou je ne suis pas
Tu es ou tu n'es pas
Il est ou il n'est pas
Nous sommes ou nous ne sommes pas ...

Review the meaning of **pauvre** on p. 107.

Le professeur *(excessivement mécontent)*
Mais c'est vous qui n'y êtes pas, mon pauvre ami!

L'élève Hamlet
C'est exact, monsieur le professeur,
Je suis «où» je ne suis pas
Et, dans le fond², hein, à la réflexion,
Être «où» ne pas être
C'est peut-être aussi la question.

Jacques Prévert, Éditions Gallimard

1. *startled* 2. *after all*

 Questions. Répondez.

1. Quelle réponse est-ce qu'on donne d'habitude en classe pour indiquer qu'on n'est pas absent?
2. Dans le poème, est-ce que l'élève Hamlet est en cours de français ou en cours d'anglais? Expliquez votre réponse.
3. Qui est impatient? Justifiez votre réponse.
4. Quel verbe est-ce que Hamlet conjugue?
5. Quelle est l'expression préférée du professeur?
6. Êtes-vous quelquefois comme cet élève Hamlet? Expliquez votre réponse.

D Discussion.

1. Why does Prévert call this poem **l'accent grave?**
2. Describe the personality of each of the characters in this poem.

VOCABULAIRE ACTIF

Quelques professions
un(e) assistant(e) social(e) *social worker*
un(e) avocat(e) *lawyer*
un cadre *executive*
un(e) comptable *accountant*
un cuisinier/une cuisinière *cook*
un écrivain *writer*
un(e) employé(e) *employee*
un fermier/une fermière *farmer*
un(e) fonctionnaire *civil servant*
un homme d'affaires/une femme d'affaires *businessman/business-woman*
un homme politique/une femme politique *politician*
un infirmier/une infirmière *nurse*
un ingénieur *engineer*

un médecin *doctor*
un ouvrier/une ouvrière *laborer*
un(e) patron(ne) *boss*
un vendeur/une vendeuse *salesman/saleswoman*

Description personnelle
avare *miserly*
bavard(e) *talkative*
calme *calm*
chauve *bald*
compréhensif (compréhensive) *understanding*
discret (discrète) *discreet; reserved*
ennuyeux (ennuyeuse) *boring*
extroverti(e) *outgoing*
généreux (généreuse) *generous*
gentil (gentille) *nice*

heureux (heureuse) *happy*
impatient(e) *impatient*
intellectuel (intellectuelle) *intellectual*
intelligent(e) *intelligent*
intéressant(e) *interesting*
intolérant(e) *intolerant*
naïf (naïve) *naive*
sportif (sportive) *athletic*
travailleur (travailleuse) *hard-working*
méchant(e) *nasty; mean*
nerveux (nerveuse) *nervous*
paresseux (paresseuse) *lazy*
patient(e) *patient*
triste *sad*

Activités qu'on fait

les courses *(f. pl.) errands, shopping*
la cuisine *cooking; food*
les devoirs *(m. pl.) homework*
la lessive *wash; laundry*
le ménage *housework*
une promenade *walk; ride*
les provisions *(f. pl.) groceries*
la sieste *nap*
la vaisselle *dishes*

D'autres noms

une adresse *address*
une carte postale *postcard*
les cheveux *(m. pl.) hair*
une chose *thing*
une couleur *color*
le dîner *dinner*
les gens *people*
un magasin *store*
une note *note; grade, mark*
un numéro de téléphone
    telephone number
le temps *weather*
la vie *life*
une ville *city*
les yeux *(m. pl.) eyes*

Adjectifs de couleur

beige *beige*
blanc (blanche) *white*
bleu(e) *blue*
blond(e) *blond*
brun(e) *brown(-haired)*
gris(e) *grey*
jaune *yellow*
marron *brown*
noir(e) *black*
orange *orange*
rose *pink*
rouge *red*
roux (rousse) *red(-haired)*
vert(e) *green*
violet(te) *purple*

Pour décrire les vêtements

bizarre *weird, funny-looking*
bon marché *inexpensive*
cher (chère) *dear; expensive*
chic *chic; stylish*
confortable *comfortable*
élégant(e) *elegant*
ordinaire *ordinary, everyday*
propre *clean*
sale *dirty*
simple *simple, plain*

Vêtements

des baskets *(f.) high-top sneakers*
un blouson *windbreaker, jacket*
des bottes *(f.) boots*
une ceinture *belt*
un chapeau *hat*
des chaussettes *(f.) socks*
des chaussures *(f.) shoes*
une chemise *shirt*
un chemisier *blouse*
un complet *suit*
une cravate *tie*
un foulard *scarf*
des gants *(m.) gloves*
un imperméable *raincoat*
un jean *(pair of) jeans*
une jupe *skirt*
des lunettes *(f. pl.) eyeglasses*
un manteau *coat*
une montre *watch*
un pantalon *(pair of) pants*
un pull-over (un pull) *sweater*
une robe *dress*
un short *(pair of) shorts*
un sweat-shirt *sweatshirt*
un tee-shirt *tee-shirt*
des tennis *(f.) tennis shoes*
une veste *sportcoat*
un vêtement *an article of
    clothing*

D'autres adjectifs

ce/cet (cette) *this; that*
ces *these; those*
mauvais(e) *bad*
nouveau/nouvel (nouvelle) *new*

Pronoms

cela (ça) *that*
toi *you*
tout le monde *everybody*

Verbes

dîner *to eat dinner*
donner *to give*
faire *to do; to make*
garder *to keep; to look after*
porter *to wear; to carry*

Adverbes qui répondent à *Quand?*

aujourd'hui *today*
d'habitude *usually*
généralement *generally*
jamais (ne ... jamais) *never*
quand *when*
quelquefois *sometimes*
rarement *rarely*
toujours *always*

Mots invariables

chez *at the home of*
puis *then; next*

Mots interrogatifs

que ... ? *what ... ?*
qu'est-ce que ... ? *what ... ?*
quel(le) ... ? *which ... ?*

Expressions utiles

Au contraire! *On the contrary!*
avec mon meilleur souvenir *with
    my best regards*
Comment est (sont) ... ? *What is
    (are) ... like?*
De quelle couleur est (sont) ... ?
    What color is (are) ... ?
en classe *in class; to class*
faire attention *to pay attention*
Il fait chaud. *It's hot out.*
Il faut ... *It is necessary ...*
Quel temps fait-il? *What is the
    weather like?*
Qu'est-ce que c'est? *What is this?*

**Buts
communicatifs**
Expressing future time
Telling time
Explaining your
  schedule
Telling where to find
  places

**Structures
utiles**
À + article défini
Le verbe **aller**
L'heure
Les jours de la semaine
Le verbe **devoir**
Quelques prépositions
  de lieu
L'impératif
Les prépositions de lieu
  avec une ville ou un
  pays
Les mots interrogatifs
  où et **quand**

Culture
Quelques malentendus
  culturels
Pour dire *au revoir*

Coup d'envoi

Qu'est-ce que vous allez faire?

Qu'est-ce que tu vas faire° le week-end prochain°, Sylvie?	*What are you going to do / next weekend*
Je vais sortir vendredi° soir.	*I'm going to go out on Friday*
Je vais danser parce que j'adore danser.	
Je vais déjeuner dimanche° avec mes amis.	*I'm going to have lunch on Sunday / I'm going to go to the library.*
Je vais aller à la bibliothèque.°	
Je vais étudier et faire mes devoirs.	
Mais je ne vais pas rester° dans ma chambre tout le week-end°.	*to stay* *the whole weekend*

 Et vous? Qu'est-ce que vous allez faire le week-end prochain? Où allez-vous étudier?

Conversation

Une sortie

C'est vendredi après-midi. Lori rencontre° son amie Denise après° son cours de littérature française.

	meets
	after

LORI: Salut, Denise. Comment vas-tu?

DENISE: Bien, Lori. Quoi de neuf?°   *What's new?*
(*Elles s'embrassent° trois fois°.*)   *kiss / times*

LORI: Pas grand-chose°, mais c'est vendredi et je n'ai *Not much*
pas l'habitude de passer° tout le week-end *I'm not used to spending*
dans ma chambre.
Tu as envie d'aller au cinéma?° *Do you feel like going to the movies?*

DENISE: Quand ça?

LORI: Ce soir ou demain° soir? *tomorrow*

DENISE: Ce soir je ne suis pas libre°. Mais demain *free*
peut-être. Tu vas voir° quel film? *to see*

LORI: Ça m'est égal.° Il y a toujours un bon film au *I don't care.*
cinéma Variétés.

DENISE: D'accord°, très bien. À quelle heure? *Okay*

LORI: Vers 7 heures et demie°. Ça va?° Rendez-vous *Around 7:30 / Okay?*
devant° le cinéma? *in front of*

DENISE: C'est parfait°. *perfect*

LORI: Bonne soirée, Denise, et à demain soir.

▶ **Jouez ces rôles.** Répétez la conversation avec votre partenaire. Utilisez vos noms et le nom d'un cinéma près de chez vous.

Il y a un geste

Au revoir/Salut. When waving good-bye, the open palm, held at about ear level, is normally turned toward the person to whom one is waving. It is often moved toward the other person.

La bise. The French kiss their friends and relatives on both cheeks. This is referred to as **faire la bise.** The number of times that their cheeks touch varies, however, from one region to another: twice in Besançon, three or four times in Angers, and four times in Quimper! In Paris, the number varies from two to four, most likely because people have moved to the capital from different regions.

Pourquoi est-ce que Lori et Denise s'embrassent trois fois?

a. Elles sont superstitieuses.
b. Denise habite à Angers et elle a l'habitude d'embrasser ses amis trois fois.
c. En France on embrasse tout le monde.

Quelques malentendus culturels

A possible misunderstanding may result from the use of expressions that seem to be equivalent in two languages. In the United States, for example, the expression *see you later* is often used as an alternate to *good-bye,* without necessarily implying any real meeting in the near future. This has proven to be frustrating for French visitors, for whom *see you later* is interpreted as meaning *see you soon.* Likewise, any North American who uses the French expression **À tout à l'heure** should realize that this implies that the people in question will be meeting again very soon.

This example is perhaps a useful springboard to understanding one of the basic differences between North Americans and the French: while typically more hesitant to extend an invitation to their home and certainly more reluctant to chat with strangers, once an invitation is extended or a conversation begun, the French take it seriously. North Americans may complain about not being invited to French homes right away, but they themselves have readily and casually extended invitations to "come and see us" and have then been surprised when French acquaintances write to say they are actually coming.

Another source of error for English speakers is the attempt to translate expressions such as *good morning* and *good afternoon* literally when greeting someone. **Bon après-midi** is used only when taking leave of someone. When saying hello, the only common expressions in French are **bonjour, bonsoir,** and **salut.** When saying good-bye, however, the range of possible expressions is much more extensive as can be seen in the list to the right.

Pour dire *au revoir*

à bientôt	*see you soon*
à demain	*see you tomorrow*
à la prochaine	*until next time, be seeing you*
à tout à l'heure	*see you in a little while*
au plaisir (de vous revoir)	*(I hope to) see you again*
au revoir	*good-bye, see you again*
bon après-midi	*have a good afternoon*
bonne journée	*have a good day*
bonne nuit	*pleasant dreams (lit. good night)*
bonne soirée	*have a good evening*
bonsoir	*good evening, good night*
salut	*bye(-bye) (fam.)*
tchao	*bye (fam.)*

À vous. Répondez.

1. Comment allez-vous?
2. Allez-vous rester dans votre chambre ce soir?
3. À quelle heure allez-vous faire vos devoirs?
4. Qu'est-ce que vous allez faire demain soir?
5. Avez-vous envie d'aller au cinéma?

Entre amis

Le week-end prochain

1. Greet your partner.
2. Find out how s/he is doing.
3. Find out what s/he is going to do this weekend.
4. Find out if s/he wants to go to a movie.
5. If so, agree on a time.
6. Be sure to vary the way you say good-bye.

Prononciation

Les syllabes ouvertes

■ There is a strong tendency in French to end spoken syllables with a vowel sound. It is therefore important to learn to link a pronounced consonant to the vowel that follows it.

| il a | [i la] | votre ami | [vɔ tra mi] |
| elle a | [ɛ la] | femme américaine | [fa ma me ʀi kɛn] |

■ The above is also true in the case of liaison. Liaison must occur in the following situations.

Synthèse: Les liaisons obligatoires		
	Alone	**With liaison**
1. when a pronoun is followed by a verb	nous	nous [z]a vons
	vous	vous [z]êtes
2. when a verb and pronoun are inverted	est	est-[t]elle
	ont	ont-[t]ils
	sont	sont-[t]ils
3. when an article or adjective is followed by a noun	un	un [n]homme
	des	des [z]en fants
	deux	deux [z]heures
	trois	trois [z]ans
	mon	mon [n]a mi
	petit	petit [t]a mi
4. after one-syllable adverbs or prepositions	très	très [z]im por tant
	en	en [n]A mé rique
	dans	dans [z]une fa mille

Buts communicatifs

1 Expressing Future Time

Qu'est-ce que tu vas faire samedi° prochain, Julien?	*Saturday*
D'abord° je vais jouer au tennis avec mes amis.	*First (of all)*
Ensuite° nous allons étudier° à la bibliothèque.	*Next / we're going to study*
Je n'aime pas manger seul°, alors après°, nous allons dîner ensemble au restaurant universitaire.	*alone / so after(wards)*
Enfin°, nous allons regarder la télé.	*Finally*

▶ **Et vous?** Qu'est-ce que vous allez faire?

NOTE CULTURELLE
Le restaurant universitaire, qu'on appelle d'habitude **le Resto U,** est très bon marché. C'est parce qu'en France on subventionne *(subsidizes)* en partie les repas *(meals)* des étudiants. Si on a une carte d'étudiant, on bénéficie d'une réduction du prix des repas.

Remember to consult Appendix C, the Glossary of Grammatical Terms, at the end of the book to review any terms with which you are not familiar.

A. À + article défini

Céline ne travaille pas **à la** bibliothèque.	*Céline doesn't work at the library.*
Elle travaille **au** restaurant universitaire.	*She works in the dining hall.*

■ The preposition **à** can mean *to, at,* or *in,* depending on the context. When used with the articles **la** and **l',** it does not change, but when used with the articles **le** and **les,** it is contracted to **au** and **aux.**

à	+	le	**au**	au restaurant
à	+	les	**aux**	aux toilettes
à	+	la	**à la**	à la maison
à	+	l'	**à l'**	à l'hôtel

■ Liaison occurs when **aux** precedes a vowel sound.

aux [z]États-Unis

VOCABULAIRE

Quelques endroits *(A few places)*

A. Sur le campus

un bâtiment	*building*	une librairie	*bookstore*
une bibliothèque	*library*	un parking	*parking lot, garage*
une cafétéria	*cafeteria*	une piscine	*swimming pool*
un campus	*campus*	une résidence	
un couloir	*hall, corridor*	(universitaire)	*dormitory*
un cours	*course, class*	une salle de classe	*classroom*
un gymnase	*gymnasium*	les toilettes *(f. pl.)*	*restroom*

[suite]

V O C A B U L A I R E [suite]

Quelques endroits *(A few places)*

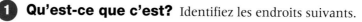

B. En ville

un aéroport	*airport*	une école	*school*
une banque	*bank*	une église	*church*
un bistro	*bar and café*	une épicerie	*grocery store*
une boulangerie	*bakery*	une gare	*railroad station*
un bureau de poste	*post office*	un hôtel	*hotel*
un bureau de tabac	*tobacco shop*	un musée	*museum*
un centre commercial	*shopping center, mall*	une pharmacie	*pharmacy*
un cinéma	*movie theater*	un restaurant	*restaurant*
un château	*chateau, castle*	une ville	*city*

1 **Qu'est-ce que c'est?** Identifiez les endroits suivants.

Modèle: **C'est une église.**

1.

2.

3.

4.

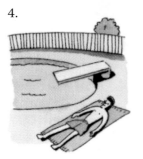

5.

6.

2 **Où vas-tu?** Posez la question. Votre partenaire va répondre d'après le modèle *(according to the model).*

> **MODÈLE:** restaurant (bibliothèque)
> —**Tu vas au restaurant?**
> —**Non, je ne vais pas au restaurant; je vais à la bibliothèque.**

1. bureau de poste (pharmacie)
2. église (centre commercial)
3. restaurant (cinéma)
4. librairie (bibliothèque)
5. hôtel (appartement de ma sœur)
6. gare (aéroport)

3 **Qu'est-ce que vous allez faire?** Indiquez vos projets avec **Je vais à** + article défini et les mots donnés *(given).* Utilisez aussi les mots **d'abord, ensuite** et **après.**

> **MODÈLE:** banque, centre commercial, épicerie
> **D'abord je vais à la banque, ensuite je vais au centre commercial et après je vais à l'épicerie.**

1. école, bibliothèque, librairie
2. banque, restaurant, aéroport
3. bureau de poste, pharmacie, cinéma
4. église, campus, résidence

Entre amis

D'abord, ensuite, après

1. Tell your partner that you are going to go out.
2. S/he will try to guess three places where you are going.
3. S/he will try to guess in what order you are going to the three places.

B. Le verbe *aller*

Je vais en classe à 8 heures.	*I go to class at eight o'clock.*
Allez-vous en ville ce soir?	*Are you going into town this evening?*
Où **allons-nous** dîner?	*Where are we going to eat dinner?*
Les petits Français ne **vont** pas à l'école le mercredi.	*French children don't go to school on Wednesday.*

aller *(to go)*			
je	**vais**	nous	**allons**
tu	**vas**	vous	**allez**
il/elle/on	**va**	ils/elles	**vont**

■ The fundamental meaning of **aller** is *to go.*

> Où **vas-tu?** *Where are you going?*

■ The verb **aller** is also used to discuss health and well-being.

Comment allez-vous?	*How are you?*
Je vais bien, merci.	*I'm fine, thanks.*
Ça va, merci.	*Fine, thanks.*

■ The verb **aller** is also very often used with an infinitive to indicate the future, especially the near future.

Qu'est-ce que **tu vas faire** ce soir?	*What are you going to do this evening?*
Je vais étudier, comme d'habitude.	*I'm going to study, as usual.*
Nous allons passer un test demain.	*We are going to take a test tomorrow.*

Point out the idiomatic expression **passer un test** in the third example.

Note   In the negative of this construction, **ne ... pas** is placed around the verb **aller,** not around the infinitive.

Thierry **ne va pas déjeuner** demain.   *Thierry won't eat lunch tomorrow.*

 Comment vont-ils? Utilisez le verbe **aller** pour poser des questions. Votre partenaire va répondre.

> **Modèle:** ton frère
>
> > **vous: Comment va ton frère?**
> > **votre partenaire: Il va très bien, merci.**   ou
> > **Quel frère? Je n'ai pas de frère.**

Review the possible answers (taught in Ch. 2, p. 35) before doing the exercise.

1. tes amis du cours de français
2. tu
3. ton professeur de français
4. ta sœur
5. ton ami(e) qui s'appelle _____
6. tes grands-parents
7. ta nièce
8. tes neveux

Remind students that if they don't have a niece, etc., they should say so.

VOCABULAIRE

Quelques expressions de temps (futur)

tout à l'heure	*in a little while*
dans une heure	*one hour from now*
ce soir	*tonight*
avant (après) le dîner	*before (after) dinner*
demain (matin, soir)	*tomorrow (morning, evening)*
dans trois jours	*three days from now*
le week-end prochain	*next weekend*
la semaine prochaine	*next week*

Several of these expressions can be preceded by à to mean "See you ..." or "Until ...," e.g., à ce soir, au week-end prochain.

5 **Que vont-ils faire ce soir?** Qu'est-ce qu'ils vont faire et qu'est-ce qu'ils ne vont pas faire? Si vous ne savez pas, devinez *(If you don't know, guess.)*

MODÈLE: mes parents / jouer au tennis ou regarder la télévision
Ce soir, ils vont regarder la télévision; ils ne vont pas jouer au tennis.

1. je / sortir ou rester dans ma chambre
2. le professeur / dîner au restaurant ou dîner à la maison
3. mes amis / étudier à la bibliothèque ou étudier dans leur chambre
4. je / regarder la télévision ou faire mes devoirs
5. mon ami(e) _____ / travailler sur ordinateur ou aller au centre commercial
6. les étudiants / rester sur le campus ou aller au bistro

6 **À vous.** Répondez.

1. Quand allez-vous regarder la télévision?
2. Quand allez-vous sortir avec vos amis?
3. Quand allez-vous passer un test?
4. Quand est-ce que vous allez manger?
5. Où allez-vous déjeuner demain midi?
6. Où et à quelle heure allez-vous dîner demain soir?
7. Allez-vous dîner seul(e) ou avec une autre personne?
8. Quand allez-vous étudier? Avec qui?
9. Qu'est-ce que vous allez faire samedi prochain?
10. Qu'est-ce que vous allez faire dimanche après-midi?

Before putting students in pairs, have them write three things they are going to do this weekend.

Entre amis

Est-ce que tu vas jouer au tennis?

1. Tell your partner that you are not going to stay in your room this weekend.
2. S/he will try to guess three things you are going to do.
3. S/he will try to guess in what order you will do them.

2 Telling Time

Quelle heure est-il maintenant?°

    Il est 10 heures et demie.°

    Je vais au cours de français à 11 heures.

    Je déjeune à midi.°

    Je vais à la bibliothèque à une heure.

    Je vais au gymnase à 4 heures.

    J'étudie de 7 heures à 10 heures du soir.

What time is it now?

It's half past ten.

I eat lunch at noon.

> -- cours de français 11 h
> -- déjeuner 12 h avec Étienne
> -- bibliothèque 13 h
> -- gymnase 16 h

▶ **Et vous?** À quelle heure déjeunez-vous?

           À quelle heure allez-vous à la bibliothèque?

           À quelle heure allez-vous au gymnase?

           À quelle heure allez-vous au cours de français?

           Quelle heure est-il maintenant?

> The distinction between **heure**, **temps**, and **fois** will be explained in Ch. 6.

Remarque   The word **heure** has more than one meaning.

J'étudie trois **heures** par jour.   *I study three hours a day.*

De quelle **heure** à quelle **heure**?   *From what time to what time?*

De 15 **heures** à 18 **heures**.   *From three until six o'clock.*

C. L'heure

■ You have already learned to tell time in a general way. Now that you know how to count to 60, you can be more precise. There are two methods of telling time. The first is an official 24-hour system, which can be thought of as a digital watch on which the hour is always followed by the minutes. The other is an informal 12-hour system that includes the expressions **et quart** *(quarter past, quarter after)*, **et demi(e)** *(half past)*, **moins le quart** *(quarter to, quarter till)*, **midi,** and **minuit** *(midnight)*.

> **VOCABULAIRE À RETENIR**
>
> **quart** *quarter*
> **demi(e)** *half*
> **minuit** *midnight*
> **midi** *noon*

> Review *Understanding Basic Expressions of Time,* p. 3, and numbers, pp. 3, 63.

> The word **heure(s)** is usually represented as **h** (without a period) on schedules, e.g., **5 h 30.**

Système officiel	*Système ordinaire*
neuf heures une	neuf heures une
neuf heures quinze	neuf heures et quart
neuf heures trente	neuf heures et demie
neuf heures quarante-cinq	dix heures moins le quart
douze heures trente	midi et demi
treize heures trente	une heure et demie
dix-huit heures cinquante et une	sept heures moins neuf
vingt-trois heures quarante-cinq	minuit moins le quart

■ In both systems, the feminine number **une** is used to refer to hours and minutes because both **heure** and **minute** are feminine.

1 h 21   **une** heure vingt et **une**

■ In the 12-hour system, **moins** is used to give the time from 1 to 29 minutes *before* the hour. For 15 minutes *before* or *after* the hour, the expressions **moins le quart** and **et quart,** respectively, are used. For 30 minutes past the hour, one says **et demie.**

9 h 40   dix heures **moins** vingt
9 h 45   dix heures **moins le quart**
10 h 15   dix heures **et quart**
10 h 30   dix heures **et demie**

Note   After **midi** and **minuit,** which are both masculine, **et demi** is spelled without a final **-e**: midi **et demi.**

■ The phrases **du matin, de l'après-midi,** and **du soir** are commonly used in the 12-hour system to specify A.M. or P.M. when it is not otherwise clear from the context.

trois heures **du matin** (3 h)   dix heures **du matin** (10 h)
trois heures **de l'après-midi** (15 h)   dix heures **du soir** (22 h)

7 **Quelle heure est-il?** Donnez les heures suivantes. Indiquez l'heure officielle et l'heure ordinaire s'il y a une différence.

Modèle: 13 h 35
              système officiel: **Il est treize heures trente-cinq.**
              système ordinaire: **Il est deux heures moins vingt-cinq de l'après-midi.**

1. 2 h 20   4. 1 h 17   7. 22 h 05   9. 11 h 15
2. 4 h 10   5. 6 h 55   8. 3 h 45   10. 10 h 30
3. 15 h 41   6. 1 h 33

Quelle heure est-il?

If necessary, have students consult the country abbreviations in Ch. 1, p. 18.

Use the maps on the inside covers of this book to locate as many of these places as possible.

 Décalages horaires *(Differences in time).* Vous êtes à Paris et vous voulez téléphoner à des amis. Mais quelle heure est-il chez vos amis? Demandez à votre partenaire.

Décalages horaires
(calculés par rapport à l'heure de Paris)

Anchorage (USA)	− 10		Montréal (CDN)	− 6
Athènes (Grèce)	+ 1		Mexico (MEX)	− 7
Bangkok (Thaïlande)	+ 6		Nouméa	
Casablanca (MA)	− 1		(Nouvelle-Calédonie)	+ 10
Chicago (USA)	− 7		New York (USA)	− 6
Dakar (SN)	− 1		Papeete (Polynésie)	− 11
Denver (USA)	− 8		Saint-Denis (Réunion)	+ 3
Fort-de-France			San Francisco (USA)	− 9
(Martinique)	− 5		Sydney (Australie)	+ 9
Halifax (CDN)	− 5		Tokyo (J)	+ 8
Le Caire (Égypte)	+ 1		Tunis (Tunisie)	0
Londres (GB)	− 1			

Suggestion: Drill the model and do one or two sentences before putting students in pairs.

Follow up (books closed) by redoing several sentences.

MODÈLE: 3 h à Paris/Bangkok?

    VOUS: S'il est trois heures à Paris, quelle heure est-il à Bangkok?

    VOTRE PARTENAIRE: Il est neuf heures à Bangkok.

1. 23 h à Paris/Anchorage?
2. 6 h à Paris/Montréal?
3. 14 h à Paris/Londres?
4. 18 h 30 à Paris/Fort-de-France?

5. 12 h à Paris/Mexico?
6. 3 h 20 à Paris/Chicago?
7. 15 h 45 à Paris/Saint-Denis?
8. 11 h à Paris/Tokyo?

9 **À vous.** Répondez.

1. Quelle heure est-il maintenant?
2. À quelle heure déjeunez-vous d'habitude?
3. Allez-vous faire vos devoirs ce soir? Si oui, de quelle heure à quelle heure?
4. Combien d'heures étudiez-vous par jour?
5. À quelle heure allez-vous dîner ce soir?
6. Allez-vous sortir ce soir? Si oui, à quelle heure? Avec qui?
7. Allez-vous regarder la télévision ce soir? Si oui, de quelle heure à quelle heure? Qu'est-ce que vous allez regarder?

Entre amis

À l'aéroport

1. Ask your partner what time it is.
2. Ask if s/he is going to Paris. (S/he is.)
3. Ask what time it is in Paris now.
4. Ask at what time s/he is going to arrive in Paris.
5. Find out what s/he is going to do in Paris.

3 Explaining Your Schedule

Quel jour est-ce aujourd'hui?
C'est ...

lundi°	*Monday*
mardi°	*Tuesday*
mercredi	
jeudi°	*Thursday*
vendredi	
samedi	
dimanche	

Quel jour est-ce demain?

D. Les jours de la semaine

■ Days of the week are not capitalized in French.

■ The calendar week begins on Monday and ends on Sunday.

❅			janvier			❅
lundi	mardi	mercredi	jeudi	vendredi	samedi	dimanche
		1	2	3	4	5
6	7	8	9	10	11	12
13	14	15	16	17	18	19
20	21	22	23	24	25	26
27	28	29	30	31		

Review the verb **avoir**, p. 60. It is used with **envie, l'intention,** and **l'habitude.** Remember to use **de** + infinitive after these expressions.

■ When referring to a specific day, neither an article nor a preposition is used.

Demain, c'est **vendredi.**	*Tomorrow is Friday.*
C'est **vendredi** demain.	*Tomorrow is Friday.*
J'ai envie de sortir **vendredi** soir.	*I feel like going out Friday evening.*
J'ai l'intention d'étudier **samedi.**	*I plan to study Saturday.*

■ To express the meaning *Saturdays, every Saturday, on Saturdays,* etc., the article **le** is used with the name of the day.

Je n'ai pas de cours **le samedi.**	*I don't have class on Saturdays.*
Le mardi, mon premier cours est à 10 heures.	*On Tuesdays, my first class is at ten o'clock.*
Le vendredi soir, j'ai l'habitude de sortir avec mes amis.	*On Friday nights, I usually go out with my friends.*

■ Similarly, to express the meaning *mornings, every morning, in the morning,* etc., with parts of the day, **le** or **la** is used before the noun.

Le matin, je vais au cours de français.	*Every morning, I go to French class.*
L'après-midi, je vais à la bibliothèque.	*Afternoons, I go to the library.*
Le soir, je fais mes devoirs.	*In the evening, I do my homework.*
La nuit, je suis au lit.	*At night, I'm in bed.*

10 **Le samedi soir.** Utilisez l'expression **avoir envie de** ou **avoir l'habi-tude de,** d'après les modèles.

Follow up by having students give examples describing themselves or their friends.

MODÈLES: les étudiants / envie / sortir ou rester dans leur chambre
Le samedi soir, ils ont envie de sortir; ils n'ont pas envie de rester dans leur chambre.

Ma sœur / l'habitude / aller au cinéma ou faire des devoirs
Le samedi soir, elle a l'habitude d'aller au cinéma; elle n'a pas l'habitude de faire ses devoirs.

1. les étudiants / envie / rester sur le campus ou aller au cinéma
2. je / l'habitude / voir un film ou faire mes devoirs
3. le professeur / l'habitude / préparer ses cours ou regarder la télévision
4. mes amis et moi, nous / envie / dîner entre amis ou dîner seuls
5. mon ami(e) _____ / l'habitude / sortir avec moi ou rester dans sa chambre

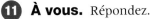

 À vous. Répondez.

Point out that the answers in this activity are of a general nature and will therefore include the article **le** plus the day(s) of the week.

1. Quels sont les jours où vous allez au cours de français?
2. À quelle heure est votre cours?
3. Quels sont les jours où vous n'avez pas de cours?
4. Qu'est-ce que vous avez l'intention de faire le week-end prochain?
5. Avez-vous l'habitude d'aller au gymnase? Si oui, quels jours et à quelle heure?
6. À quelle heure avez-vous votre premier cours le mardi?
7. Quand est-ce que vous allez à la bibliothèque?
8. Quand écoutez-vous la radio?
9. Quand avez-vous envie de regarder la télévision?

VOCABULAIRE

Quelques cours

l'art *(m.)*	*art*	les mathématiques *(f. pl.)*	*math*
la chimie	*chemistry*	la musique	*music*
le commerce	*business*	la pédagogie	*education, teacher*
la comptabilité	*accounting*		*preparation*
la gestion	*management*	la philosophie	*philosophy*
la gymnastique	*gymnastics*	la psychologie	*psychology*
l'histoire *(f.)*	*history*	les sciences *(f. pl.)*	*science*
l'informatique *(f.)*	*computer science*	les sciences économiques *(f. pl.)*	*economics*
la littérature	*literature*	les sciences politiques *(f. pl.)*	*political science*

 Mon emploi du temps *(My schedule).* Indiquez votre emploi du temps pour ce semestre. Indiquez le jour, l'heure et le cours.

MODÈLE: **Le lundi à dix heures, j'ai un cours de français.**
Le lundi à onze heures, j'ai un cours de mathématiques.
Le lundi à une heure, j'ai un cours d'histoire.

13 **As-tu un cours de commerce?** Essayez de deviner *(try to guess)* deux des cours de votre partenaire. Demandez ensuite quels jours et à quelle heure votre partenaire va à ces cours. Votre partenaire va répondre à vos questions.

MODÈLE: **As-tu un cours d'histoire?**
Quels jours vas-tu à ce cours?
À quelle heure vas-tu à ce cours?

E. Le verbe *devoir*

Les étudiants doivent beaucoup travailler.	*Students have to work a lot.*
Vous devez être fatigués.	*You must be tired.*

devoir *(to have to, must; to owe)*			
je	**dois**	nous	**devons**
tu	**dois**	vous	**devez**
il/elle/on	**doit**	ils/elles	**doivent**

■ **Devoir** is often used with the infinitive to express an obligation or a probability.

Vous **devez faire** attention! *(obligation)*	*You must pay attention!*
Lori **doit avoir** vingt ans. *(probability)*	*Lori must be twenty.*

■ **Devoir** plus a noun means *to owe*.

Je dois vingt dollars à mes parents.	*I owe my parents twenty dollars.*

Synthèse: Révision des verbes

	parler	être	avoir	faire	aller	devoir
je	**parle**	**suis**	**ai**	**fais**	**vais**	**dois**
tu	**parles**	**es**	**as**	**fais**	**vas**	**dois**
il/elle/on	**parle**	**est**	**a**	**fait**	**va**	**doit**
nous	**parlons**	**sommes**	**avons**	**faisons**	**allons**	**devons**
vous	**parlez**	**êtes**	**avez**	**faites**	**allez**	**devez**
ils/elles	**parlent**	**sont**	**ont**	**font**	**vont**	**doivent**

GALERIES Lafayette

Envie de communiquer

Envie de regarder

Envie d'écouter

Mais qu'est-ce qu'on doit faire? Utilisez l'expression entre parenthèses pour indiquer ce que chaque personne doit faire.

MODÈLE: Gérard a envie d'aller au cinéma. (étudier)
Gérard a envie d'aller au cinéma mais il doit étudier.

1. Nous avons envie de sortir ce soir. (préparer un examen)
2. Les étudiants ont envie de regarder la télévision. (étudier)
3. Tu as envie de danser ce soir. (faire tes devoirs)
4. J'ai envie de rester au lit. (aller aux cours)
5. Le professeur a envie de faire un voyage. (enseigner)
6. Tes amis ont envie d'aller en ville. (faire la lessive)

 Je dois faire ça cette semaine. Faites une liste de sept choses que
vous devez faire cette semaine (une chose pour chaque jour).

MODÈLE: **Samedi, je dois faire le ménage.**

Follow up by pairing students who will try to guess three items on their partner's list.

16 **Et alors?** Pour chaque phrase, inventez une ou deux conclusions
logiques.

MODÈLE: Lori n'a pas envie de passer le week-end dans sa chambre.
Qu'est-ce qu'elle va faire?
Elle va sortir. ou **Elle a l'intention d'aller au cinéma.**

Follow-up (books closed): Read the questions and brainstorm with students to suggest as many answers as possible.

1. Lori a envie de sortir ce soir. Où va-t-elle? Que fait-elle?
2. Mais son amie Denise n'est pas libre. Qu'est-ce qu'elle doit faire?
3. Lori et Denise font souvent les courses ensemble. Où vont-elles?
4. Aujourd'hui Denise reste dans sa chambre. Pourquoi? Comment va-t-
elle?
5. Lori téléphone à Denise. Pourquoi? De quoi parle-t-elle?

Entre amis

Ton emploi du temps

1. Find out what time it is.
2. Find out what day it is today.
3. Find out what classes your partner has today.
4. Find out when your partner goes to the library.
5. Find out if your partner has to work and, if so, on what days.
6. Find out if your partner feels like going to the movies tonight.

4 Telling Where to Find Places

Où se trouve° la souris?   *is located*

La souris est loin
du fromage.

La souris est près
du fromage.

La souris est devant
le fromage.

La souris est derrière
le fromage.

La souris est sur
le fromage.

La souris est sous
le fromage.

La souris est dans
le fromage.

Où se trouve le
fromage? Le fromage
est dans la souris.

F. Quelques prépositions de lieu

See the video, *Module 4* for examples of people giving directions.

Les toilettes se trouvent **dans** le couloir.	*The restroom is in the hall.*
Les toilettes sont **à côté de** la salle de classe.	*The restroom is next to the classroom.*
Le cinéma se trouve **au** centre commercial.	*The movie theater is at the mall.*
La banque est **à droite** ou **à gauche** du parking?	*Is the bank on the right or on the left of the parking lot?*
Allez **tout droit** et ensuite tournez **à droite.**	*Go straight ahead and then turn to the right.*

à	*at; in; to*		**dans**	*in*
à côté de	*beside*		**entre**	*between; among*
à droite de	*on the right of*	≠	**à gauche de**	*on the left of*
derrière	*behind*	≠	**devant**	*in front of*
loin de	*far from*	≠	**près de**	*near*
sous	*under*	≠	**sur**	*on*

■ **À côté, à droite, à gauche, loin,** and **près** can all drop the **de** and stand alone.

Nous habitons **à côté d'**une église.   *We live next to a church.*
But: **L'église est à côté.**   *The church is next door.*

Note   **À droite** means *to (on) the right,* while **tout droit** means *straight ahead.*

 Où se trouvent ces endroits? Répondez à la question posée par *(asked by)* votre partenaire.

MODÈLE: La bibliothèque (près / bâtiment des sciences)
        VOTRE PARTENAIRE: Où se trouve la bibliothèque?
        VOUS: Elle est près du bâtiment des sciences.

1. le bâtiment administratif (près / bibliothèque)
2. la pharmacie (à côté / église)
3. les résidences universitaires (sur / campus)
4. le restaurant universitaire (dans / résidence)
5. le cinéma (à / centre commercial)
6. le bureau de poste (derrière / pharmacie)
7. le centre commercial (loin / campus)
8. les toilettes (devant / salle de classe)
9. le parking (à gauche / banque)

Review contractions with de, p. 74.

18 **Votre campus.** Faites rapidement le plan *(Draw a map)* de votre campus. Expliquez où se trouvent cinq endroits différents.

MODÈLE: **Voilà la résidence qui s'appelle Brown Hall. Elle est près de la bibliothèque.**

G. L'impératif

Suggestion: Follow up by telling students you are a French-speaking visitor to campus. Have them give directions to specific places.

Regarde!	*Look!*
Regardez!	*Look!*
Regardons!	*Let's look!*
Tourne à gauche!	*Turn to the left!*
Tournez à gauche!	*Turn to the left!*
Tournons à gauche!	*Let's turn to the left!*

You already learned a number of imperatives in the preliminary chapter, p. 2.

■ The imperative is used to give commands and to make suggestions. The forms are usually the same as the present tense for **tu, vous,** and **nous.**

The imperative of **avoir** and **être** will be learned in Ch. 10.

Note   If the infinitive ends in **-er,** the final -s is omitted from the form that corresponds to **tu.**

parler français	tu parle**s** français	*But:* **Parle** français!
aller aux cours	tu va**s** aux cours	*But:* **Va** aux cours!

■ For negative commands, **ne** precedes the verb and **pas** follows it.

Ne regardez **pas** la télévision!
Ne fais **pas** attention à Papa!

19 **En ville.** Regardez le plan (*map*) de la ville. Demandez où se trouvent les endroits suivants. Votre partenaire va expliquer où ils se trouvent.

MODÈLE: cinéma

VOUS: **Où se trouve le cinéma, s'il vous plaît?**
VOTRE PARTENAIRE: **Il est à côté du café. Allez tout droit et tournez à gauche. Il est à droite.**

1. café
2. épicerie
3. église
4. boulangerie
5. bureau de poste

6. bureau de tabac
7. banque
8. cinéma
9. pharmacie
10. hôtel

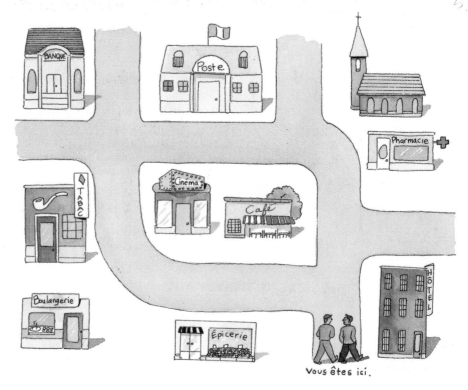

Vous êtes ici.

20 **Qu'est-ce que les bons étudiants doivent faire?** Utilisez l'impératif pour répondre à la question. Décidez ce qu'un bon étudiant doit ou ne doit pas faire.

Suggestion: Have students redo this activity using the **tu** form of the imperative.

MODÈLE: Est-ce que je dois passer tout le week-end dans ma chambre?
Ne passez pas tout le week-end dans votre chambre! ou
Oui, passez tout le week-end dans votre chambre!

1. Est-ce que je dois habiter dans une résidence universitaire?
2. Est-ce que je dois manger à la cafétéria?
3. Est-ce que je dois faire mes devoirs dans ma chambre?
4. Est-ce que je dois étudier à la bibliothèque?
5. Est-ce que je ne dois pas aller au bistro?
6. Est-ce que je ne dois pas parler anglais au cours de français?

Entre amis

Vous êtes un(e) nouvel(le) étudiant(e)

1. Find out where a shopping center is.
2. Find out where the cafeteria is.
3. Find out where the library is.
4. Ask where the restroom is.

Remind students to use one of the polite expressions from p. 9 when stopping someone to ask questions.

H. Les prépositions de lieu avec une ville ou un pays

■ Use **à** to say that you are in a city or are going to a city.

Review the contractions in this chapter on p. 125.

Note In cases where the name of a city contains the definite article **(Le Mans, Le Caire, La Nouvelle-Orléans),** the article is retained and the normal contractions occur where necessary.

> Emmanuelle habite **à La Nouvelle-Orléans.** Nous allons **au Mans.**
> Je suis **à Paris.** Je vais **à New York.**

■ Most countries, states, and provinces ending in **-e** are feminine. An exception is **le Mexique.**

> **la** Belgiqu**e**   **la** Colombi**e** Britannique
> **la** Virgini**e**   **la** Californi**e**
> *But:*   **le Mexique**

■ To say you are in or going to a *country,* the preposition varies. Use **en** before feminine countries or those that begin with a vowel sound. Use **au** before masculine countries which begin with a consonant and use **aux** when the name of the country is plural.

> **en** France   **au** Canada   **aux** États-Unis
> **en** Israël   **au** Mexique   **aux** Pays-Bas

■ To say you are in or going to an American *state* or a Canadian *province,* **en** is normally used before those that are feminine or that begin with a vowel sound. The preposition **au** is often used with masculine provinces that begin with a consonant and with the states of Texas and New Mexico.

> **en** Virginie   **en** Ontario   **au** Manitoba
> **en** Nouvelle-Écosse   **en** Ohio   **au** Nouveau-Mexique

The use of the preposition **de** with countries is introduced in Ch. 7.

Note You may also use **dans l'état de** or **dans la province de.**

> J'habite **dans l'état de** New York.
> Je voyage **dans la province d'**Alberta.

Review the adjectives of nationality in Ch. 1, p. 18.

See how many of the countries listed you can find on the maps on the inside covers of your text.

Quelques langues et quelques pays			
On parle ...	allemand	**en** ...	Allemagne
	anglais		Angleterre
	français et flamand		Belgique
	chinois		Chine
	espagnol		Espagne
	français		France
	anglais et irlandais		Irlande
	italien		Italie
	russe		Russie
	suédois		Suède
	français, allemand et italien		Suisse
On parle ...	français et anglais	**au** ...	Canada
	japonais		Japon
	français et arabe		Maroc
	espagnol		Mexique
	portugais		Portugal
	français et wolof		Sénégal
On parle ...	anglais, espagnol et français	**aux** ...	États-Unis
	hollandais		Pays-Bas

■ When talking about more than one country, use a preposition before each one.

On parle français **en** France, **en** Belgique, **au** Canada, **au** Maroc, **au** Sénégal, etc.

■ When there is no preposition with a country, state, or province, the definite article must be used.

La France est un beau pays.
J'adore **le Canada.**

Note **Israël** is an exception.

Israël est à côté de la Syrie.

21 **Où habitent-ils?** Dans quel pays les personnes suivantes habitent-elles?

Modèle: Vous êtes français.
Vous habitez en France.

1. Lucie est canadienne.
2. Les Dewonck sont belges.
3. Phoebe est anglaise.
4. Pepe et María sont mexicains.
5. Yuko est japonaise.
6. Yolande est sénégalaise.
7. Sean et Deirdre sont irlandais.
8. Caterina est italienne.
9. Hassan est marocain.
10. Nous sommes américains.

Qui sont ces personnes? Où habitent-elles? Vous êtes à l'aéroport d'Orly et vous écoutez des touristes de divers pays. Devinez leur nationalité et où ils vont.

MODÈLE: Il y a deux hommes qui parlent espagnol.
Ils doivent être espagnols ou mexicains.
Ils vont probablement en Espagne ou au Mexique.

1. Il y a un homme et une femme qui parlent français.
2. Il y a deux enfants qui parlent anglais.
3. Il y a une jeune fille qui parle russe.
4. Il y a trois garçons qui parlent arabe.
5. Il y a une personne qui parle suédois.
6. Il y a un homme qui parle allemand.
7. Il y a deux couples qui parlent flamand.
8. Il y a deux jeunes filles qui parlent italien.
9. Il y a un homme et une femme qui parlent japonais.

I. Les mots interrogatifs *où* et *quand*

Remind students that if a third-person verb ends in a vowel, a -**t**- is added between the verb and the pronoun (Ch. 2).

■   A question using **quand** or **où** is formed like any other question, using inversion or **est-ce que**.

Où habitent-ils?   Quand arrive-t-elle?
Où est-ce qu'ils habitent?   Quand est-ce qu'elle arrive?

Review interrogative forms, pp. 45–46.

Note   In **Quand est-ce que,** the -**d** is pronounced [t]. When **quand** is followed by inversion, there is no liaison.

■   With a *noun* subject, the inversion order is *noun + verb + subject pronoun.*

Où **tes parents habitent-ils?**   Quand **ta sœur arrive-t-elle?**

Be sure that students understand that noun inversion is quite limited.

■   In addition, if there is only one verb and no object, the noun subject and the verb may be inverted.

Où **habitent tes parents?**   Quand **arrive ta sœur?**

 Où et quand? Pour chaque phrase, posez une question avec **où.** Votre partenaire va inventer une réponse. Ensuite, posez une question avec **quand.** Votre partenaire va inventer une réponse à cette question aussi.

MODÈLE: Mon frère fait un voyage.
VOUS: **Où est-ce qu'il fait un voyage?**
VOTRE PARTENAIRE: **Il fait un voyage en France.**
VOUS: **Quand est-ce qu'il fait ce voyage?**
VOTRE PARTENAIRE: **Il fait ce voyage la semaine prochaine.**

1. Mon amie a envie de faire des courses.
2. Nous avons l'intention de déjeuner ensemble.
3. Je vais au cinéma.
4. Mon cousin travaille.
5. Mes amis étudient.

24 **À vous.** Répondez.

1. Où les étudiants de votre université habitent-ils?
2. Où se trouve la bibliothèque sur votre campus?
3. Quels bâtiments se trouvent près de la bibliothèque?
4. Où se trouve la salle de classe pour le cours de français?
5. Quand avez-vous votre cours de français?
6. Où les étudiants dînent-ils d'habitude le dimanche soir?
7. Où allez-vous vendredi prochain? Pourquoi?

Entre amis

Un pays où on ne parle pas anglais

1. Tell your partner you are going to a country where English is not spoken.
2. S/he will try to guess where.
3. S/he will try to guess the language(s) spoken there.
4. S/he will ask when you are going to that country.

Intégration

Révision

A **Au revoir.** Quels sont cinq synonymes de l'expression **au revoir?**

B **Les pays.** Répondez.

1. Quels sont cinq pays où on parle français?
2. Nommez deux pays en Europe, deux pays en Asie et deux pays en Afrique.
3. Dans quels pays se trouvent ces villes: Dakar? Genève? Trois-Rivières? Lyon? Montréal? Prairie du Chien? Rabat? Bruxelles? Des Moines? Bâton Rouge?

C **À vous.** Répondez.

1. Qu'est-ce que vous avez envie de faire ce week-end? (trois choses)
2. Qu'est-ce que vous devez faire?
3. Qu'est-ce que vos amis aiment faire le samedi soir?
4. Qu'est-ce que vous faites le lundi? (trois choses)
5. Quels sont les jours où vous allez à votre cours de français?
6. À quelle heure allez-vous à ce cours?
7. Dans quel bâtiment avez-vous ce cours? Où se trouve ce bâtiment?
8. Quel est votre jour préféré? Pourquoi?

Suggestion: Have students do the Information Gap activity in the Instructor's Resource Manual.

D **Trouvez quelqu'un qui ...** Interviewez les autres.

1. Find someone who is studying computer science.
2. Find someone who rarely goes to the library.
3. Find someone who speaks another language.
4. Find someone who plans to go to France or Quebec.
5. Find someone who has to work next weekend.
6. Find someone who is going to go out on Friday evening.
7. Find someone who usually does homework on Friday evening.

Pas de problème!

Preparation for the video:
1. Video worksheet in the *Cahier d'activités*
2. CD-ROM, *Module 2*

Cette activité est basée sur la vidéo *Pas de problème (Module 2)*. Répondez.

1. Qu'est-ce que Jean-François et Marie-Christine vont faire aujourd'hui?
2. Est-ce que Marie-Christine habite Rive *(bank)* gauche ou Rive droite?
3. Quelle est son adresse?
4. Pourquoi est-ce que Jean-François ne téléphone pas tout de suite *(right away)* à Marie-Christine?
5. Où est-ce qu'on va pour trouver des télécartes?
6. Quel est le code pour la porte de chez Marie-Christine?

Lecture I

Before reading, have students locate Anjou, Angers, and the Loire on the map on the inside front cover of the text.

A **Étude du vocabulaire.** Étudiez les phrases suivantes et choisissez *(choose)* les mots anglais qui correspondent aux mots français en caractères gras *(bold print)*: river, friendly, winter, foreign, summer, holiday, king, team, schedule.

1. Le 14 juillet est un **jour férié** parce que c'est la fête nationale française.
2. Il faut consulter l'**horaire** des trains avant d'aller à la gare.
3. La Loire est le **fleuve** le plus long de France.
4. Les Angevins sont très **accueillants.** Ils vous invitent souvent.
5. L'**équipe** canadienne a gagné le match de hockey.
6. Un **roi** est le monarque d'un pays.
7. En **hiver** il fait d'habitude froid et en **été** il fait souvent très chaud.
8. À Paris on rencontre toujours beaucoup d'**étrangers:** des touristes allemands, américains, anglais et des immigrés aussi.

B **Parcourez la publicité.** Lisez rapidement la lecture pour trouver l'adresse et le numéro de téléphone de l'Office de Tourisme.

Vos vacances à Angers

Douces vacances à Angers
Capitale de l'Anjou
Au cœur d'une province accueillante,
Angers vous offre
mille et une promenades.

Angers
Capitale de l'Anjou

Il y a en France, le long d'un fleuve majestueux qu'on appelle la Loire, une vallée célèbre par ses richesses, son climat et sa beauté. C'était dans cette région que les seigneurs, les princes et les rois de France ont fait construire les plus beaux châteaux, les plus belles maisons. C'est dans cette vallée de la Loire que se trouve l'Anjou et la capitale de l'Anjou s'appelle Angers.

VISITES GUIDÉES
Visites panoramiques
Visites à thèmes
Visites «scolaires»

RÉCEPTIF
Forfaits
Séjours à la carte
Événementiel

ACCUEIL
Information
Documentation
Billetterie
Change

ANGERS

TOURISME

Une équipe compétente qui vous simplifie la ville
Place du Président Kennedy - BP 5157 - 49 051 ANGERS Cédex 02
Tél. FRANCE : 02 41 23 51 11 - Fax. FRANCE : 02 41 23 51 10
Tél. FRANCE : 332 41 23 51 11 - Fax. ETRANGER : 332 41 223 51 10
Horaires d'hiver : du lundi au samedi : 9h30 à 18h30 - dimanche : 10h à 13h
Horaires d'été : du lundi au samedi : 9h à 19h - dimanches et jours fériés : 10h à 13h - 14h à 18h

C **Questions.** Relisez toute la lecture et ensuite répondez aux questions suivantes.

1. Où se trouve la ville d'Angers?
2. Qu'est-ce que c'est que la Loire?
3. Pourquoi la vallée de la Loire est-elle célèbre?
4. À quelle heure l'Office de Tourisme ouvre-t-il le dimanche?
5. À quelle heure l'Office de Tourisme ferme-t-il le samedi en été?
6. À quelle heure ferme-t-il le 14 juillet? Pourquoi?

D **Familles de mots.** Essayez de deviner le sens (*try to guess the meaning*) des mots suivants.

Suggestion: Have a team of students write or fax the Office de Tourisme in Angers to request information.

1. accueillir, un accueil, accueillant(e)
2. célébrer, une célébrité, célèbre
3. construire, la construction, constructif, constructive
4. offrir, une offre, offert(e)
5. simplifier, la simplification, simple

Lecture II

A **Trouvez le Cameroun.** Cherchez le Cameroun sur la carte à l'intérieur de la couverture de ce livre. Sur quel continent se trouve ce pays? Quelle est la capitale du Cameroun? Quels sont les pays qui se trouvent près du Cameroun?

B **Étude du vocabulaire.** Étudiez les phrases suivantes et choisissez les mots anglais qui correspondent aux mots français en caractères gras: *birds, against, a cooking utensil, I see, each one, I hear, people, a popular African food, peace, bark, roof.*

1. **J'entends** quelquefois des chiens qui **aboient** quand une voiture passe.
2. Il y a des **oiseaux** sur le **toit** de la maison.
3. **Je vois** des **gens** qui portent des vêtements africains.
4. **Chacun** porte des sandales.
5. Dans leur village on mange du **taro**.
6. On prépare la cuisine avec un **pilon**.
7. Êtes-vous pour ou **contre** la **paix** dans ce pauvre pays?

Village Natal

Ici je suis chez moi,
Je suis vraiment chez moi.
Les hommes que je vois,
Les femmes que je croise[1]
M'appellent leur fils
Et les enfants leur frère.
Le patois qu'on parle est le mien,
Les chants que j'entends expriment[2]
Des joies et des peines qui sont miennes.
L'herbe que je foule reconnaît mes pas[3].
Les chiens n'aboient pas contre moi,
Mais ils remuent la queue[4]
En signe de reconnaissance.
Les oiseaux me saluent au passage
Par des chants affectueux.
Des coups de pilon m'invitent

À me régaler de[5] taro
Si mon ventre est creux[6].
Sous chacun de ces toits qui fument
Lentement dans la paix du soir
On voudra m'accueillir[7].
Bientôt c'est la fête, la fête de chaque soir:
Chants et danses autour du feu[8],
Au rythme du tam-tam, du tambour, du balafon[9].
Nos gens sont pauvres
Mais très simples, très heureux;
Je suis simple comme eux[10]
Content comme eux,
Heureux comme eux.
Ici je suis chez moi,
Je suis vraiment chez moi.

Jean-Louis Dongmo,
Neuf poètes camerounais, Éditions Clé

1. *that I meet*   2. *express*   3. *the grass I walk on recognizes my steps*   4. *wag their tails*   5. *have a delicious meal of*
6. *stomach is empty*   7. *people will welcome me*   8. *around the fire*   9. *musical instruments*   10. *them*

C **Discussion.** Répondez en anglais ou en français.

1. Cherchez les exemples dans le poème qui prouvent que le poète est heureux d'être dans son village.
2. Quelles ressemblances et quelles différences y a-t-il entre le poète et vous?

VOCABULAIRE ACTIF

Adverbes
après *after*
avant *before*
d'abord *at first*
demain *tomorrow*
enfin *finally*
ensuite *next, then*
maintenant *now*

Jours de la semaine
lundi *(m.) Monday*
mardi *(m.) Tuesday*
mercredi *(m.) Wednesday*
jeudi *(m.) Thursday*
vendredi *(m.) Friday*
samedi *(m.) Saturday*
dimanche *(m.) Sunday*

Adjectifs
libre *free*
parfait(e) *perfect*
premier (première) *first*
prochain(e) *next*
seul(e) *alone; only*

Expressions de lieu
à côté *next door; to the side*
à côté de *next to, beside*
derrière *behind*
devant *in front of*
à droite *on (to) the right*
à gauche *on (to) the left*
entre *between, among*
loin *far*
sous *under*
tout droit *straight ahead*

Pays
l'Allemagne *(f.) Germany*
l'Angleterre *(f.) England*
la Belgique *Belgium*
le Canada *Canada*
la Chine *China*
l'Espagne *(f.) Spain*
les États-Unis *(m. pl.) United States*
la France *France*
l'Irlande *(f.) Ireland*
Israël *(m.) Israel*

l'Italie *(f.) Italy*
le Japon *Japan*
le Maroc *Morocco*
le Mexique *Mexico*
les Pays-Bas *(m. pl.) Netherlands*
le Portugal *Portugal*
la Russie *Russia*
le Sénégal *Senegal*
la Suède *Sweden*
la Suisse *Switzerland*

Verbes
aller *to go*
aller en ville *to go into town*
avoir envie de *to want to; to feel like*
avoir l'habitude de *to usually; to be in the habit of*
avoir l'intention de *to plan to*
déjeuner *to have lunch*
devoir *to have to, must; to owe*
faire un voyage *to take a trip*
passer un test *to take a test*
rester *to stay*
tourner *to turn*

Cours
la chimie *chemistry*
le commerce *business*
la comptabilité *accounting*
la gestion *management*
la gymnastique *gymnastics*
l'informatique *(f.) computer science*
la littérature *literature*
la pédagogie *education, teacher preparation*
les sciences *(f.) science*
les sciences économiques *(f.) economics*

Autre préposition
vers (8 heures) *approximately, around (8 o'clock)*

Expressions de temps
Quelle heure est-il? *What time is it?*
Quel jour est-ce? *What day is it?*

Il est ... heure(s). *It is ... o'clock.*
Il est midi (minuit). *It is noon (midnight).*
et demi(e) *half past*
et quart *quarter past, quarter after*
moins le quart *quarter to, quarter till*
ce soir *tonight*
dans une heure (trois jours, etc.) *one hour (three days, etc.) from now*
une minute *minute*
une semaine *week*
tout à l'heure *in a little while*
tout le week-end *all weekend (long)*

D'autres expressions utiles
Cela (ça) m'est égal. *I don't care.*
D'accord. *Okay.*
Je vais sortir. *I'm going to go out.*
Où se trouve (se trouvent) ... ? *Where is (are) ... ?*
pas grand-chose *not much*
Quoi de neuf? *What's new?*
Ça va? *Okay?*
Tu vas voir. *You are going to see.*

D'autres noms
une bise *kiss*
un emploi du temps *schedule*
un film *film, movie*
le fromage *cheese*
un rendez-vous *appointment; date*
une souris *mouse*
un voyage *trip, voyage*
l'arabe *Arabic*
le flamand *Flemish*
le portugais *Portuguese*
le wolof *Wolof*

Endroits
un aéroport *airport*
une banque *bank*
un bâtiment *building*
une bibliothèque *library*
un bistro *bar and café; bistro*
une boulangerie *bakery*

un bureau de poste *post office*
un bureau de tabac *tobacco shop*
une cafétéria *cafeteria*
un campus *campus*
un centre commercial *shopping center, mall*
un château *chateau; castle*
un cinéma *movie theater*
un couloir *hall; corridor*
un cours *course; class*
une école *school*
une église *church*
un endroit *place*
une épicerie *grocery store*
un état *state*

un gymnase *gymnasium*
une librairie *bookstore*
un musée *museum*
un parking *parking lot, garage*
un pays *country*
une pharmacie *pharmacy*
une piscine *swimming pool*
une province *province*
une résidence (universitaire) *dormitory*
un restaurant *restaurant*
une salle de classe *classroom*
les toilettes *(f. pl.) restroom*
une ville *city*

6 Vos activités

Buts communicatifs
Relating past events
Describing your study
  habits
Describing your
  weekend activities

Structures utiles
Le passé composé avec
  avoir
Les verbes **écrire**
  et **lire**
Ne ... rien
Temps, heure et **fois**
Les verbes pronominaux
Jouer de et **jouer à**
Les pronoms accentués
Les verbes **dormir,**
  partir et **sortir**
Les verbes **nettoyer** et
  envoyer

Culture
La maison
Relativité culturelle:
  La maison

Coup d'envoi

Qu'est-ce que tu as fait hier?

Point out the use of **à** before an object with **téléphoner.**

Sébastien, qu'est-ce que tu as fait hier?° *What did you do yesterday?*

> J'ai téléphoné à deux amis.
> J'ai envoyé des messages électroniques°. *sent e-mail*
> J'ai fait mes devoirs.
> J'ai étudié pendant° trois heures. *for*
> J'ai déjeuné à midi et j'ai dîné à 7 heures du soir.
> J'ai regardé un peu la télévision.
> Mais je n'ai pas fait le ménage.
> Et je n'ai pas passé d'examen°. *test*

▶ **Et vous?**   Qu'est-ce que vous avez fait?

Une lettre à des amis

Lori a écrit une lettre à deux de ses camarades du cours de français aux États-Unis.

Angers, le 15 décembre

Chers John et Cathy,

Merci beaucoup de vos lettres. Que le temps passe vite![1] Je suis en France depuis déjà trois mois[2]. Vous avez demandé si j'ai le temps de voyager. Oui, mais je suis très active et très occupée parce qu[3]'il y a toujours tant de[4] choses à faire. C'est la vie, n'est-ce pas?

Dimanche dernier[5], j'ai accompagné ma famille française au Mans chez les parents de Mme Martin. Nous avons passé trois heures à table! Cette semaine, j'ai lu une pièce[6] de Molière pour mon cours de littérature et j'ai écrit une dissertation[7]. J'ai aussi fait le ménage et j'ai gardé[8] les enfants pour Mme Martin. Heureusement, je ne me lève pas tôt[9] le samedi.

Vous avez demandé si j'ai remarqué[10] des différences entre la France et les États-Unis. Eh bien, oui. Chez les Martin, par exemple, les portes à l'intérieur de la maison sont toujours fermées[11], les toilettes ne sont pas dans la salle de bain et les robinets[12] sont marqués «C» et «F». J'ai déjà oublié[13] deux fois[14] que «C» ne veut pas dire «cold». Aïe![15]

Dites bonjour[16] pour moi à Madame Walter, s.v.p. Écrivez-moi à lbecker@wanadoo.fr

Bonnes vacances!

Votre amie «française»,

Lori

---

1. *How time flies!* 2. *I've already been in France for three months* 3. *because* 4. *so many* 5. *last* 6. *I read a play* 7. *I wrote a (term) paper* 8. *watched, looked after* 9. *Fortunately, I don't get up early* 10. *I noticed* 11. *closed* 12. *faucets* 13. *I already forgot* 14. *times* 15. *Ouch!* 16. *Say hello*

 Compréhension. Décidez si les phrases suivantes sont vraies ou fausses. Si une phrase est fausse, corrigez-la.

1. Lori a déjà passé trois mois en France.
2. En France on passe beaucoup de temps à table.
3. Lori a beaucoup de temps libre.
4. On ferme les portes dans une maison française.
5. «C» sur un robinet veut dire «chaud».
6. «F» sur un robinet veut dire «français».

À PROPOS

Comparison: Have students decide if their home corresponds to the description given for North America. Can they mention advantages and disadvantages of each system?

Pourquoi est-ce que les portes sont fermées à l'intérieur d'une maison française?

a. Les Français désirent être différents des autres.

b. Les Français préfèrent l'ordre et l'intimité *(privacy).*

c. Les Français ont peur des voleurs *(are afraid of thieves).*

La maison

Living in France has meant more to Lori than just learning the French language. She has also had the opportunity to become part of a French family and has had to learn to cope with a number of cultural differences. There is no need in French for a separate word to distinguish between *house* and *home.* Both are **la maison,** and **la maison** is seen as a refuge from the storm of the world outside, a place to find comfort and solace and to put order into one's existence. Given the French attitude about **la maison,** it is not surprising to find social and architectural indications of that need for order. There is a set time for meals, and family members are expected to be there. There is an order to a French meal that is quite different from the everything-on-one-plate-at-one-time eating style prevalent in English-speaking North America. The walls around French houses, the shutters on the windows, and the closing of the doors inside the home

are other examples of the French desire for order and clearly established boundaries.

Relativité culturelle: La maison

The home is undoubtedly the scene of the greatest number of cultural contrasts. There are, therefore, some potentially troublesome adjustments.

In France	In North America
Doors are closed, especially the bathroom door, even when no one is in the room.	Doors inside a house are often left open.
Since the toilet is often not in the bathroom, one has to be more specific about whether one is looking for **la salle de bain** or **les toilettes.**	Since the toilet, tub, and shower are all in the bathroom, one person may inconvenience the rest of the family.
Hands can be scalded trying to test "cold" water from a faucet marked "C."	Turning on a faucet marked "C" will not make the water get hot (**chaud**) no matter how long one waits.
There are no screens on windows to keep out insects.	Screens on windows don't allow the wide-open feeling one gets from French windows.
There are almost always walls or a hedge to ensure privacy and clearly mark the limits of one's property.	In many neighborhoods there are no walls to separate houses.
See, for example, p. 80	

Il y a un geste

The **C'est la vie** gesture is used in the video, *Module 11.*

C'est la vie. A gesture often accompanies the expression **C'est la vie:** the shoulders are shrugged, and the head is slightly tilted to one side. Sometimes the lips are pursed as well, and the palms are upturned. The idea is *That's life and I can't do anything about it.*

J'ai oublié! The palm of the hand is raised against the temple. This gesture conveys the meaning that you have forgotten something or have made a mistake.

▶ **À vous.** Donnez une réponse personnelle.

1. Où avez-vous dîné hier soir?
2. Combien de temps avez-vous passé à table?
3. Qu'est-ce que vous avez fait après le dîner?

Entre amis

Hier

1. Ask what your partner did yesterday.
2. S/he will tell you at least two things.
3. Choose one of the things s/he did and find out as much as you can about it (at what time, where, etc.).

Prononciation

Les sons [u] et [y]

■ Because of differences in meaning in words such as **tout** and **tu,** it is very important to distinguish between the vowel sounds [u] and [y]. The following words contain these two important vowel sounds. Practice saying these words after your teacher, paying particular attention to the highlighted vowel sound.

[u] • bonj**ou**r, r**ou**ge, c**ou**rs, éc**ou**ter, j**ou**er, tr**ou**ver, v**ou**lez, je v**ou**drais, t**ou**-j**ou**rs, beauc**ou**p, p**ou**rquoi, s**ou**vent, c**ou**sin, d**ou**te, **ou**vrier, bl**ou**son, c**ou**leur, c**ou**rse, n**ou**veau, auj**ou**rd'hui, c**ou**loir, s**ou**s, t**ou**t, **ou**blié

• **où**

[y] • j**u**s, **u**ne, ét**u**dier, ét**u**diants, t**u,** b**u**reau, calc**u**latrice, voit**u**re, s**u**r, j**u**pe, l**u**nettes, p**u**ll-over, n**u**méro, diffic**u**lté, br**u**ne, st**u**pide, campus, **u**niversi-taire, m**u**sique, R**u**ssie, min**u**te, d**u,** occ**u**pé, j'ai l**u,** littérat**u**re

■ The [u] sound, represented by written **ou** or **où,** is close to the sound in the English word *tooth.*

n**ou**s r**ou**ge **où**

■ The [y] sound is represented by a single written **-u-.** There is, however, no English "equivalent" for this French sound. To produce it, round your lips as if drinking through a straw; then, without moving your lips, pronounce the vowel in the word **ici.**

d**u** **u**ne sal**u**t v**u**e

▶ In each of the following pairs of words, one of the words contains the [u] sound, the other the [y] sound. Pronounce each word correctly.

1. sur / sous
2. jour / jupe
3. vous / vu
4. pure / pour
5. cours / cure
6. russe / rousse
7. roux / rue
8. ou / eu
9. tout / tu

**TOUT MONTRÉAL DANS UNE CARTE.
ET LA CARTE DANS VOTRE POCHE.**

> **Use the Student Audio to help practice pronunciation.**

> Be sure students pronounce [u] and not [ɔ] or [ə] in closed syllables, especially before an **-r.** If necessary, have them pronounce the vowel in open syllables first: **tout, tour; joue, jour; pou, pour.**

Buts
communicatifs

1 Relating Past Events

> Tell students to follow the model when interviewing each other.

Avez-vous déjà[1] nettoyé[2] votre chambre ce semestre?

Oui, j'ai déjà nettoyé ma chambre.
Non, je n'ai pas encore nettoyé ma chambre.

	oui	non
Avez-vous déjà chanté en français?	____	____
Avez-vous déjà dansé la valse?	____	____
Avez-vous déjà mangé des crêpes?	____	____
Avez-vous déjà joué au tennis?	____	____
Avez-vous déjà travaillé dans un restaurant?	____	____
Avez-vous déjà fumé[3] un cigare?	____	____
Avez-vous déjà été absent(e) ce semestre?	____	____
Avez-vous déjà eu un accident?	____	____
Avez-vous déjà fait vos devoirs pour demain?	____	____

1. *already* 2. *cleaned* 3. *smoked*

A. Le passé composé avec *avoir*

Remember to consult Appendix C at the end of the book to review any grammatical terms with which you are not familiar.

Hier soir, **Michel a regardé** la télévision.
Et puis **il a fait** ses devoirs.
Pendant combien de temps **a-t-il étudié?**
Il a étudié pendant deux heures.

Last night, Michel watched television.
And then he did his homework.
How long did he study?

He studied for two hours.

■ The passé composé *(compound past)* is used to tell about or narrate specific events that have already taken place. Depending on the context, its English translation may be any one of several possibilities.

J'ai mangé une pomme.
$\left\{\begin{array}{l}\text{\textit{I ate an apple.}}\\\text{\textit{I did eat an apple.}}\\\text{\textit{I have eaten an apple.}}\end{array}\right.$

Verbs taking the auxiliary **être** will be studied in Ch. 7.

■ The passé composé is formed with the present tense of an auxiliary verb (normally **avoir**) and a past participle.

manger *(au passé composé)*			
j'ai	**mangé**	nous avons	**mangé**
tu as	**mangé**	vous avez	**mangé**
il/elle/on a	**mangé**	ils/elles ont	**mangé**

The conjugation of regular -re and -ir verbs will be taught in Chs. 9 and 12, respectively.

■ The past participles of all **-er** verbs are pronounced the same as the infinitive. They are spelled by replacing the **-er** ending of the infinitive with **-é.**

étudier	+	**-é**	⟶	**étudié**
manger	+	**-é**	⟶	**mangé**
jouer	+	**-é**	⟶	**joué**

In the expression **j'ai eu** *(I had)* the word **eu** is pronounced [y].

■ The past participles of many verbs that *don't* end in **-er** must be memorized.

eu (avoir)	**été** (être)	**fait** (faire)	**dû** (devoir)

J'ai eu la grippe pendant trois jours!
Anne et Guy **ont fait** la cuisine ensemble.
Ils ont **dû** dîner à la maison.

I had the flu for three days!
Anne and Guy did the cooking together.
They must have eaten at home.
They had to eat at home.

Remind students that **devoir** can imply either obligation or probability, p. 136.

■ In the negative, **ne ... pas (ne ... jamais)** is placed around the auxiliary verb.

ne (n') + auxiliary verb + **pas (jamais)** + past participle

Point out that **la plupart de** is usually used with plural nouns and takes a plural verb. The only common exception is **la plupart du temps.**

Il **n'a pas** écouté la radio.
Nous **n'avons pas** fait de promenade.
La plupart des étudiants **n'ont jamais** fumé de cigare.

He didn't listen to the radio.
We didn't take a walk.
Most students have never smoked a cigar.

Review the formation of questions in Ch. 2, pp. 45–46.

■   Questions in the passé composé are formed the way they are in the present tense. Note, however, that in all cases of inversion, only the auxiliary verb and the subject pronoun are involved. The past participle follows the inverted pronoun.

Il a fait ses devoirs?
Est-ce qu'il a fait ses devoirs?
A-t-il fait ses devoirs?
Marc a-t-il fait ses devoirs?

Has he (Marc) done his homework?

1 **Mais il a fait ça hier.** Demandez si David fait les choses suivantes aujourd'hui. Votre partenaire va répondre que David a fait ces choses hier.

MODÈLE: parler à ses parents
VOUS: **Est-ce que David travaille aujourd'hui?**
VOTRE PARTENAIRE: **Non, mais il a travaillé hier.**

1. jouer au tennis
2. être absent
3. avoir une lettre de ses grands-parents
4. dîner avec Véronique
5. manger une pizza
6. faire la vaisselle
7. regarder la télé

2 **Véronique.** Pierre aime Véronique et il vous pose des questions parce qu'elle a dîné avec David hier soir. Répondez à ses questions d'après le modèle.

MODÈLE: Véronique a-t-elle dîné seule? (avec David)
Non, elle n'a pas dîné seule; elle a dîné avec David.

1. Ont-ils dîné au restaurant? (chez David)
2. David a-t-il fait la cuisine? (la vaisselle)
3. Ont-ils mangé un sandwich? (une pizza)
4. Véronique a-t-elle détesté la pizza? (aimé)
5. Ont-ils dansé après le dîner? (regardé la télévision)

3 **La plupart des étudiants.** Qu'est-ce que la plupart des étudiants ont fait hier? Décidez.

Be sure to use plural verb forms with **la plupart des.**

MODÈLE: fumer une cigarette
VOTRE PARTENAIRE: **Est-ce que la plupart des étudiants ont fumé une cigarette hier?**
VOUS: **Non, la plupart des étudiants n'ont pas fumé de cigarette.**

Add the question: **Et vous? Avez-vous fumé une cigarette hier?** Have students answer **Moi aussi** or **Moi non plus** if the answer is the same for them.

1. étudier à la bibliothèque
2. faire leurs devoirs
3. passer un test
4. avoir une bonne note
5. déjeuner avec leurs professeurs
6. travailler après les cours

VOCABULAIRE

Expressions de temps (passé)

Remember that **tout à l'heure** can also refer to the future: *in a little while.* The expression **à tout à l'heure** means *see you soon.*

tout à l'heure	*a little while ago*
ce matin	*this morning*
hier soir	*last night*
hier	*yesterday*
hier matin	*yesterday morning*
lundi dernier	*last Monday*
le week-end dernier	*last weekend*
la semaine dernière	*last week*
le mois dernier	*last month*
l'année dernière	*last year*
il y a deux (trois, etc.) ans	*two (three, etc.) years ago*
il y a longtemps	*a long time ago*
la dernière fois	*the last time*
pendant les vacances	*during vacation*

Notes

1. **Il y a,** used with an expression of time, means *ago*: **il y a deux mois** *(two months ago)*; **il y a trois ans** *(three years ago)*.
2. In general, the word **an** is used when counting the number of years: **un an, deux ans,** etc. The word **année** is normally used when referring to a specific year: **cette année, l'année dernière,** etc. The same distinction is made between **jour** and **journée: Il y a trois jours; une belle journée.**

 Il y a combien de temps? Qu'avons-nous fait? Que n'avons-nous pas fait? Utilisez un élément de chaque colonne pour composer des phrases affirmatives ou négatives.

MODÈLES: **Mes parents ont fait un voyage il y a deux ans.**
Mes parents n'ont jamais parlé français.

	faire un voyage	ne ... jamais
je	avoir des vacances	il y a ...
mes parents	dîner au restaurant	... dernier (dernière)
mon meilleur ami	avoir une lettre	pendant les vacances
ma meilleure amie	être absent(e)(s)	hier (...)
nous	faire la vaisselle	ce matin
	parler français	tout à l'heure
	étudier pendant trois heures	

Do this exercise in pairs. Follow up by having the class interview the instructor.

5 **La dernière fois.** Demandez à votre partenaire quand il (elle) a fait ces choses pour la dernière fois. Il (elle) va répondre.

MODÈLE: être absent(e)

VOUS: **Quelle est la dernière fois que vous avez été absent(e) ce semestre?**

VOTRE PARTENAIRE: **J'ai été absent(e) la semaine dernière.** ou **Je n'ai jamais été absent(e).**

1. étudier seul(e)
2. fumer
3. devoir passer un examen
4. être malade
5. téléphoner à un ami
6. avoir «A» à l'examen
7. passer trois heures à table
8. nager à la piscine
9. manger une pizza

6 **À vous.** Répondez.

1. Pendant combien de temps avez-vous étudié hier soir?
2. Pendant combien de temps avez-vous regardé la télévision?
3. Quelle est la dernière fois que vous avez téléphoné à un(e) ami(e)? Pendant combien de temps avez-vous parlé au téléphone?
4. Quelle est la dernière fois que vous avez eu la grippe? Pendant combien de temps avez-vous été malade?
5. Quelle est la dernière fois que vous avez été absent(e)?
6. Pendant combien de jours avez-vous été absent(e) ce semestre?

Entre amis

Hier soir

1. Find out where your partner ate last night.
2. Find out if s/he watched TV or listened to the radio.
3. If so, find out what s/he watched or listened to.
4. Find out if s/he did his/her homework.
5. If so, find out where.
6. If so, find out how long s/he studied.

Les étudiants font quelquefois leurs devoirs au café.

2 Describing Your Study Habits

	vrai	faux
J'aime étudier seul(e).	____	____
Je fais mes devoirs à la bibliothèque.	____	____
J'écris[1] souvent des dissertations.	____	____
Je ne passe pas beaucoup de temps à faire mes devoirs.	____	____
Je passe au moins[2] trois heures à étudier par jour.	____	____
Je lis[3] au moins un livre par semaine.	____	____
J'écoute la radio pendant que[4] j'étudie.	____	____
Je regarde la télé pendant que j'étudie.	____	____

1. *write* 2. *at least* 3. *read* 4. *while*

Remarque   Use **passer** + unit(s) of time + **à** + infinitive to express how long you spend doing something.

Nous **avons passé deux heures à manger.**	*We spent two hours eating.*
D'habitude, Marc **passe quatre heures à faire** ses devoirs.	*Marc usually spends four hours doing his homework.*

B. Les verbes *écrire* et *lire*

J'aime **lire** des romans policiers.	*I like to read detective stories.*
J'ai passé trois heures à **lire** hier soir.	*I spent three hours reading last night.*
Quelles langues **lisez-vous?**	*What languages do you read?*
Éric lit le journal pendant qu'il mange.	*Éric reads the newspaper while he eats.*
Mes parents n'**écrivent** pas souvent.	*My parents don't write often.*
À qui **écrivez-vous** régulièrement?	*To whom do you write regularly?*
Comment est-ce qu'**on écrit** le mot «lisent»?	*How do you spell the word "lisent"?*

écrire *(to write)*		lire *(to read)*	
j'	**écris**	je	**lis**
tu	**écris**	tu	**lis**
il/elle/on	**écrit**	il/elle/on	**lit**
nous	**écrivons**	nous	**lisons**
vous	**écrivez**	vous	**lisez**
ils/elles	**écrivent**	ils/elles	**lisent**
passé composé: j'**ai écrit**		*passé composé:* j'**ai lu**	

■ Note the pronunciation distinction between the third person singular and plural forms.

il écrit [ekRi]   elle lit [li]
ils [z]écrivent [ekRiv]   elles lisent [liz]

■ The verb **décrire** *(to describe)* is conjugated like **écrire.**

Nous **décrivons** nos familles au professeur.

VOCABULAIRE

Des choses à lire ou à écrire

une bande dessinée	*comic strip*	un magazine	*magazine*
une carte postale	*postcard*	une pièce	*play*
une dissertation	*(term) paper*	un poème	*poem*
un journal	*newspaper*	un roman	*novel*
une lettre	*letter*	un roman policier	*detective story*
un livre	*book*		

See p. 22. The plural of **journal** is **journaux**.

 Qu'est-ce qu'ils lisent? Qu'est-ce qu'ils écrivent? Répondez aux questions. Si vous ne savez pas la réponse, devinez.

1. Combien de livres lisez-vous par semestre?
2. Vos parents écrivent-ils beaucoup de lettres?
3. À qui écrivez-vous des messages électroniques?
4. Qui, dans votre famille, lit des bandes dessinées?
5. Combien de dissertations un étudiant écrit-il par an?
6. Avez-vous déjà écrit une dissertation ce semestre? Si oui, pour quel(s) cours?
7. Avez-vous lu un journal ou un magazine cette semaine? Si non, pourquoi pas?

C. *Ne ... rien*

Suggestion: Play Edith Piaf's recording of **Rien** and show students the words to the song.

■ The opposite of **quelque chose** is **ne ... rien** (*nothing, not anything*).

Mangez-vous **quelque chose?**	*Are you eating something?*
Non, je **ne** mange **rien.**	*No, I am not eating anything.*

■ **Ne ... rien** works like **ne ... pas** and **ne ... jamais;** that is, **ne** and **rien** are placed around the conjugated verb. This means that in the passé composé, **ne** and **rien** surround the auxiliary verb and the past participle follows **rien.**

Je **ne** vais **rien** écrire.	*I'm not going to write anything.*
Je **n'**ai **rien** écrit hier soir.	*I didn't write anything last night.*

■ **Rien** can follow a preposition.

Je **n'**ai pensé **à rien.**	*I didn't think about anything.*
Je **ne** pense **à rien.**	*I'm not thinking about anything.*

Review the use of **ne ... jamais**, p. 96.

■ Unlike English, French allows the use of more than one negative word in a sentence.

Il **ne** fait **jamais rien!**   *He never does anything!*

The use of **rien** as a subject will be studied in Ch. 15.

■ Like **jamais**, **rien** can be used alone to answer a question.

Qu'est-ce que tu as lu? **Rien.**

FOR RECOGNITION ONLY:

- **Quelque chose** and **rien** can be made slightly more specific by the addition of **de** + *masculine adjective* or of **à** + *infinitive*. The two constructions can even be combined.

Jean lit **quelque chose** *d'intéressant.*	Éric **ne** lit **rien** *d'intéressant.*
Il a **quelque chose** *à lire.*	Il **n'**a **rien** *à lire.*
Il a **quelque chose** *d'intéressant à lire.*	Il **n'**a **rien** *d'intéressant à lire.*

 Une personne paresseuse. Éric ne fait rien. Répondez aux questions suivantes avec le mot **rien**.

MODÈLES: Qu'est-ce qu'il fait le vendredi soir?   **Il ne fait rien.**
          Qu'est-ce qu'il a fait vendredi dernier?   **Il n'a rien fait.**
          Qu'est-ce qu'il va faire vendredi prochain?   **Il ne va rien faire.**

1. Qu'est-ce qu'il étudie à la bibliothèque?
2. Qu'est-ce qu'il lit pendant le week-end?
3. Qu'est-ce qu'il va faire cet après-midi?
4. Qu'est-ce qu'il va lire pour ses cours?
5. Qu'est-ce qu'il a écrit pendant les vacances?
6. Qu'est-ce qu'il a lu l'année dernière?

 Ces travailleurs. Sylvie et David sont très travailleurs et la semaine dernière, ils n'ont pas eu le temps de faire des choses amusantes. Posez une question à leur sujet au passé composé. Votre partenaire va utiliser **rien** dans sa réponse.

MODÈLE: regarder quelque chose à la télé
                    VOUS: **Est-ce qu'ils ont regardé quelque chose à la télé?**
         VOTRE PARTENAIRE: **Non, ils n'ont rien regardé.**

Redo Ex. 9 in the near future with **aller: Est-ce qu'ils vont regarder quelque chose? Non, ils ne vont rien regarder.**

1. écouter quelque chose à la radio
2. écrire des poèmes
3. chanter quelque chose ensemble
4. lire un roman policier
5. faire quelque chose en ville

POLICIERS

10 À vous. Répondez.

1. D'habitude qu'est-ce que vous lisez le matin?
2. À qui avez-vous écrit la semaine dernière?
3. Qu'avez-vous lu hier soir?
4. Avez-vous écouté la radio ce matin? Si oui, qu'est-ce que vous avez écouté?
5. Avez-vous des amis qui regardent la télé pendant qu'ils étudient?
6. Qu'est-ce que vous regardez à la télévision pendant que vous étudiez?
7. Combien de temps passez-vous d'habitude à préparer vos cours?
8. Lisez-vous souvent des magazines? Si oui, quels magazines?
9. Combien de dissertations écrivez-vous par semestre?

LIRE GUIDE
WEISBECKER

D. *Temps,* *heure* et *fois*

■ Depending on the context, the French use different words to express what, in English, could always be expressed by the word *time.*

• **L'heure,** as you already know, means *clock time.*

Quelle **heure** est-il? *What time is it?*

Reminder   **Heure** can also mean *hour* or *o'clock.*

J'ai étudié pendant trois **heures.** *I studied for three hours.*
Il est deux **heures.** *It is two o'clock.*

• **La fois** means *time* in a countable or repeated sense.

Combien de **fois** par an? *How many times per year?*
la dernière **fois** *the last time*

• **Le temps** means *time* in a general sense.

Je n'ai pas **le temps** d'étudier. *I don't have time to study.*
Avez-vous **le temps** de voyager? *Do you have time to travel?*
Combien de **temps** avez-vous? *How much time do you have?*

> Remember that **temps** can also mean *weather:* **Quel temps fait-il aujourd'hui?**

 Hier soir. Utilisez **temps, heure** ou **fois** pour compléter ce dialogue.

1. J'ai passé quatre _____ à faire mes devoirs.
2. Avez-vous eu assez de _____ pour regarder la télévision?
3. Non, parce que mes parents ont téléphoné trois _____.
4. À quelle _____ ont-ils téléphoné la première _____?
5. À six _____.
6. Combien de _____ par mois allez-vous chez vos parents?
7. Trois ou quatre _____.
8. Quand avez-vous dîné hier soir? À sept _____.
9. Combien de _____ avez-vous passé à table?
10. Une _____.

12 **À vous.** Répondez.

1. D'habitude combien de temps passez-vous à faire vos devoirs?
2. Pendant combien d'heures avez-vous étudié hier soir? Combien de temps avez-vous passé à faire vos devoirs pour le cours de français?
3. À quelle heure avez-vous dîné? Combien de temps avez-vous passé à table?
4. Combien de temps par semaine passez-vous avec votre meilleur(e) ami(e)?
5. Combien de fois par mois allez-vous au cinéma?
6. Combien de temps avez-vous passé à la bibliothèque la semaine dernière?

Entre amis

Es-tu un(e) bon(ne) étudiant(e)?

1. Find out if your partner spends a lot of time studying.
2. Ask if s/he watches TV while s/he studies.
3. Find out how long s/he studied last night.
4. Ask what s/he read for your French course.
5. Ask your partner how to spell some word in French.
6. Compliment your partner on his/her French.

3 Describing Your Weekend Activities

Qu'est-ce que vous faites pendant le week-end?

	oui	non
Je pars[1] du campus.	——	——
Je sors[2] avec mes amis.	——	——
Je m'amuse[3] bien.	——	——
Je vais au cinéma.	——	——
Je joue du piano.	——	——
Je joue au golf.	——	——
Je fais beaucoup de sport.	——	——
Je dors[4] beaucoup.	——	——
Je me lève tard[5].	——	——
Je ne me couche[6] pas tôt.	——	——
Je nettoie[7] ma chambre.	——	——

1. *leave* 2. *go out* 3. *have fun* 4. *sleep* 5. *late* 6. *go to bed* 7. *clean*

E. Les verbes pronominaux

■ Reflexive verbs **(les verbes pronominaux)** are those whose subject and object are the same. English examples of reflexive verbs are *he cut himself* or *she bought herself a dress.*

■ You have already learned a number of expressions that use reflexive verbs in French.

Comment vous appelez-vous?	*What is your name?*
Je m'appelle ...	*My name is ...*
Comment s'appellent vos amis?	*What are your friends' names?*
Asseyez-vous là!	*Sit there!*

■ Reflexive verbs use an object pronoun **(me, te, se, nous, vous)** in addition to the subject. With the exception of affirmative commands, this pronoun is always placed directly in front of the verb.

s'amuser				se lever			
je	**m'**amuse	nous	**nous** amusons	je	**me** lève	nous	**nous** levons
tu	**t'**amuses	vous	**vous** amusez	tu	**te** lèves	vous	**vous** levez
il/elle/on	**s'**amuse	ils/elles	**s'**amusent	il/elle/on	**se** lève	ils/elles	**se** lèvent

■ Use **est-ce que** or a rising intonation to ask a yes/no question.

Est-ce que tu te lèves tôt le matin? *Do you get up early in the morning?*
Tu t'amuses au cours de français? *Do you have fun in French class?*

■ In the negative, **ne** is placed before the object pronoun and **pas** after the verb.

Je **ne** me lève **pas** tôt. *I don't get up early.*
Mes professeurs **ne** s'amusent **pas.** *My teachers don't have fun.*
Vous **ne** vous couchez **pas** avant *Don't you go to bed before midnight?*
minuit?

■ When the reflexive verb is used in the infinitive form after another verb, the reflexive pronoun agrees with the subject of the sentence.

À quelle heure vas-**tu te** coucher? *At what time are you going to go to bed?*
Je n'aime pas **me** lever tôt. *I don't like to get up early.*
Les étudiants ont l'habitude de *Students are used to having fun on*
s'amuser le samedi soir. *Saturday night.*

 Identifications. Identifiez, si possible, des personnes qui correspondent aux descriptions suivantes.

MODÈLE: une personne qui se lève très tôt le dimanche matin
Mon père se lève très tôt le dimanche matin.

1. une personne qui se couche tôt le dimanche soir
2. une personne qui ne se couche pas s'il y a quelque chose d'intéressant à la télévision
3. deux étudiants qui se couchent tard s'ils ont un examen
4. deux personnes qui s'amusent beaucoup au cours de français
5. deux de vos amis qui ne se lèvent pas tôt le samedi matin
6. une personne qui ne va pas s'amuser pendant les vacances
7. une personne qui se lève quelquefois trop tard pour le cours de français

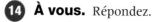 **À vous.** Répondez.

1. Comment vous appelez-vous et comment s'appelle votre meilleur(e) ami(e)?
2. Quel jour est-ce que vous vous couchez tard?
3. Est-ce que vous vous levez tôt ou tard le samedi matin? Expliquez votre réponse.
4. Avez-vous des amis qui ne s'amusent pas beaucoup? Si oui, comment s'appellent-ils?
5. Est-ce que vos professeurs aiment s'amuser en classe?
6. Est-ce que vous vous amusez au cours de français? Pourquoi ou pourquoi pas?
7. À quelle heure est-ce que vous vous levez le lundi matin? Pourquoi?
8. À quelle heure est-ce que vous allez vous coucher ce soir? Expliquez votre réponse.

F. *Jouer de et jouer à*

■ *To play a musical instrument* is expressed by **jouer de** + definite article + musical instrument. The definite article is retained in the negative before the name of the instrument.

Mon frère **joue du** saxophone, mais il ne **joue** pas **de la** guitare.	*My brother plays the saxophone but he doesn't play the guitar.*
De quoi **jouez**-vous?	*What (instrument) do you play?*
Moi, je ne **joue de** rien.	*I don't play any (instrument).*

VOCABULAIRE

Review **de** + article, p. 74, and **à** + article, p. 125.

Quelques instruments de musique

un accordéon	*accordion*	un piano	*piano*
une batterie	*drums*	un saxophone	*saxophone*
une flûte	*flute*	une trompette	*trumpet*
une guitare	*guitar*	un violon	*violin*

Point out that in **le hockey** the article does not change to **l'**. The **h aspiré** is explained in the pronunciation section of Ch. 10.

■ *To play a game* is expressed by **jouer à** + definite article + game.

—Mon amie **joue au** golf le lundi, elle **joue à la** pétanque le mercredi et elle **joue aux** cartes le vendredi soir. Mais elle ne **joue** jamais **aux** échecs.
—**À** quoi **jouez**-vous?
—Moi, je ne **joue à** rien.

VOCABULAIRE

La pétanque may be seen in the video, *Modules 1* & *11*. **La pétanque** is also called **les boules.**

Quelques jeux *(Several games)*

le basket-ball (le basket)	*basketball*
le bridge	*bridge*
les cartes *(f. pl.)*	*cards*
les dames *(f. pl.)*	*checkers*
les échecs *(m. pl.)*	*chess*
le football (le foot)	*soccer*
le football américain	*football*
le golf	*golf*
le hockey	*hockey*
la pétanque	*lawn bowling (bocce)*
le rugby	*rugby*
le tennis	*tennis*

NOTE CULTURELLE
La pétanque est un jeu de boules très populaire en France. On joue à la pétanque à l'extérieur, par exemple près des cafés. Pour marquer des points, il faut placer les boules le plus près possible du cochonnet *(small wooden ball).*

15 **Tout le monde joue.** À quoi jouent-ils? De quoi jouent-ils? Faites des phrases complètes avec les éléments donnés.

Modèles: **Les Canadiens jouent au hockey.**
Ma sœur ne joue pas de l'accordéon.

Follow up by creating "illogical" sentences, e.g., **Tiger Woods joue du violon.** Have students correct them.

les Français			la pétanque
Tiger Woods			l'accordéon
Shaquille O'Neal			le piano
ma sœur			les cartes
mon frère		de	le saxophone
les violonistes	(ne ... pas) jouer	à	le basket-ball
les Américains			la guitare
les Canadiens			les échecs
Martina Hingis			le violon
je			le golf
mon ami(e) ...			le hockey
...			le tennis

16 **À vous.** Répondez.

1. Quel est votre instrument de musique préféré?
2. Quel est votre sport préféré?
3. Jouez-vous d'un instrument de musique? Si oui, de quoi jouez-vous?
4. Êtes-vous sportif (sportive)? Si oui, à quoi jouez-vous?
5. Avez-vous des amis qui jouent aux cartes? Si oui, à quel jeu de cartes jouent-ils?
6. Avez-vous des amis qui jouent d'un instrument de musique? Si oui, de quoi jouent-ils?

G. Les pronoms accentués

Students will learn in Ch. 11 to use stress pronouns in comparisons: **Il est plus grand que** *moi.*

The use of **moi, toi,** etc., after a verb will be presented on pp. 285 and 358.

■ *Stress pronouns* (**les pronoms accentués**) are used in certain circumstances where a subject pronoun cannot be used. Each stress pronoun has a corresponding subject pronoun.

je	→	**moi**	nous	→	**nous**
tu	→	**toi**	vous	→	**vous**
il	→	**lui**	ils	→	**eux**
elle	→	**elle**	elles	→	**elles**

■ Stress pronouns are used in the following circumstances:

• to stress the subject of a sentence

Moi, je n'aime pas le café.   *I don't like coffee.*
Ils aiment le thé, **eux.**   ***They** like tea.*

• in a compound subject

Mes parents et **moi,** nous habitons ici.   *My parents and I live here.*
Monsieur Martin a des enfants?
Oui, sa femme et **lui** ont six enfants.   *Yes, his wife and he have six children.*

• after a preposition

chez **moi**   *at my house*   pour **lui**   *for him*
entre **nous**   *between us*   sans **elles**   *without them*

Note   A stress pronoun after the expression **être à** indicates possession.

Ce livre est **à moi.**   *This book belongs to me.*
Il est **à toi,** ce pull?   *Is this sweater yours?*

• after **c'est** and **ce sont**   Est-ce une photo de Lori?

C'est **moi.**   *It is I (me).*   Ce n'est pas **elle.**   *It is not she (her).*

Note   **C'est** is used with **nous** and **vous. Ce sont** is used only with **eux** and **elles.**

C'est nous.   *It is we (us).*   **Ce sont** eux.   *It is they (them).*

• alone or in phrases without a verb

Lui!   *Him!*
Et **toi?**   *And you?*
Elle aussi.   *So does she. So has she. So is she. She too.*
Moi non plus.   *Me neither. Nor I.*

• with the suffix **-même(s)**

toi-même   *yourself*   **eux**-mêmes   *themselves*

 Eux aussi. La famille de Paul fait exactement ce qu'il fait *(what he does)*. Utilisez un pronom accentué pour répondre à la question. Si la première phrase est affirmative, répondez affirmativement. Si la première phrase est négative, répondez négativement.

MODÈLES: Paul a fait le ménage. Et sa sœur?
Elle aussi.

Paul n'a pas regardé la télévision. Et son frère?
Lui non plus.

1. Paul n'a pas lu le journal ce matin. Et ses sœurs?
2. Paul écrit des lettres. Et ses parents?
3. Paul ne se lève jamais tard. Et sa sœur?
4. Il a déjà mangé. Et son frère?
5. Paul n'aime pas les cigares. Et ses parents?
6. Il va souvent au cinéma le vendredi soir. Et sa sœur?

À vous. Répondez aux questions suivantes. Utilisez un pronom accentué dans chaque réponse.

1. Faites-vous la cuisine vous-même?
2. Déjeunez-vous d'habitude avec votre meilleur(e) ami(e)?
3. Avez-vous dîné chez cet(te) ami(e) hier soir?
4. Avez-vous passé les dernières vacances chez vos parents?
5. Vos amis et vous, allez-vous souvent au cinéma?
6. Faites-vous vos devoirs avec vos amis?

H. Les verbes *dormir, partir* et *sortir*

Je ne **dors** pas bien.	*I don't sleep well.*
Quand **partez-vous** en vacances?	*When are you leaving on vacation?*
Avec qui Annie **sort-elle** vendredi?	*With whom is Annie going out on Friday?*

dormir *(to sleep)*		**partir** *(to leave)*		**sortir** *(to go out)*	
je	**dors**	je	**pars**	je	**sors**
tu	**dors**	tu	**pars**	tu	**sors**
il/elle/on	**dort**	il/elle/on	**part**	il/elle/on	**sort**
nous	**dormons**	nous	**partons**	nous	**sortons**
vous	**dormez**	vous	**partez**	vous	**sortez**
ils/elles	**dorment**	ils/elles	**partent**	ils/elles	**sortent**

■ Note the pronunciation distinction between the third person singular and plural forms.

elle dort [dɔR]	il part [paR]	elle sort [sɔR]
elles dorment [dɔRm]	ils partent [paRt]	elles sortent [sɔRt]

> **Partir** and **sortir** use **être** as the auxiliary in the passé composé and will be studied in the past tense in Ch. 7.

■ The past participle of **dormir** is **dormi**.

J'ai **dormi** pendant huit heures.

 Notre vie à l'université. Utilisez les phrases suivantes pour poser des questions à votre partenaire.

> Remind students to add **vous,** when **toi** is one of the compound subjects.

MODÈLE: tu/sortir souvent

    VOUS: Est-ce que tes amis et toi, vous sortez souvent?

    VOTRE PARTENAIRE: Oui, nous sortons souvent. ou
    Non, nous ne sortons pas souvent.

1. tu / dormir quelquefois pendant les cours
2. tes amis et toi / dormir mal pendant la semaine des examens
3. tu / sortir le vendredi soir avec tes amis
4. tes amis et toi / partir le week-end
5. les étudiants / sortir tous les soirs *(every night)*
6. le professeur de français / partir souvent en vacances

20 **La vie des étudiants.** Répondez aux questions suivantes.

1. Combien d'heures dormez-vous d'habitude par nuit?
2. Pendant combien de temps avez-vous dormi la nuit dernière?
3. Y a-t-il des étudiants qui ne dorment pas le samedi matin? Si oui, pourquoi?
4. Qui dort mal avant un examen important? Pourquoi?
5. Les étudiants sortent-ils quelquefois pendant la semaine? Si oui, où vont-ils? Si non, pourquoi pas?
6. Est-ce que la plupart des étudiants partent le week-end ou est-ce qu'ils restent sur le campus?
7. Quand allez-vous partir en vacances cette année?

I. Les verbes *nettoyer* et *envoyer*

Tu nettoies ta chambre ce matin?	*Are you cleaning your room this morning?*
Oui, mais d'abord **j'envoie** un message électronique.	*Yes, but first I'm sending an e-mail message.*

nettoyer *(to clean)*		**envoyer** *(to send)*	
je	**nettoie**	j'	**envoie**
tu	**nettoies**	tu	**envoies**
il/elle/on	**nettoie**	il/elle/on	**envoie**
nous	**nettoyons**	nous	**envoyons**
vous	**nettoyez**	vous	**envoyez**
ils/elles	**nettoient**	ils/elles	**envoient**
passé composé: j'**ai nettoyé**		j'**ai envoyé**	

■ In the present tense, these verbs are conjugated like **parler,** except that **i** is used in place of **y** in the singular and the third-person plural.

21 **Vrai ou faux?** Faites d'abord des phrases. Ensuite décidez si ces phrases sont vraies ou fausses pour vous. Attention au présent et au passé composé.

MODÈLES: ma sœur / nettoyer ma chambre / le week-end dernier
Elle a nettoyé ma chambre le week-end dernier. (C'est faux!)

ma sœur / nettoyer souvent sa chambre
Elle nettoie souvent sa chambre. (C'est vrai!)

1. les étudiants / nettoyer leur chambre / pendant le week-end
2. je / nettoyer ma chambre / hier
3. nous / envoyer souvent des messages à nos parents
4. nos parents / envoyer des lettres une fois par semaine
5. je / envoyer un message au professeur / il y a trois jours

Entre amis

Le week-end

1. Ask your partner what s/he usually does on weekends.
2. Find out if s/he has fun.
3. Ask if s/he goes out with friends.
4. If so, find out where s/he goes.
5. Find out if s/he gets up early or late on Sunday morning.
6. Find out when s/he cleans her room.
7. What else can you find out?

Intégration www

Révision

Suggestion: Give students time to prepare. Then have individuals give short presentations followed by questions from the class.

A Mon week-end. Que faites-vous d'habitude le week-end? Avez-vous beaucoup de temps libre?

B Notre vie à l'université. Posez des questions. Votre partenaire va répondre. Attention au présent et au passé composé.

MODÈLE: parler français avec tes amis pendant le cours de français
VOUS: **Est-ce que tu parles français avec tes amis pendant le cours de français?**
VOTRE PARTENAIRE: **Oui, je parle français avec eux.** ou
Non, je ne parle pas français avec eux.

1. dormir bien quand il y a un examen
2. aller souvent à la bibliothèque après le dîner
3. écouter la radio quelquefois pendant que tu étudies
4. être absent(e) le mois dernier
5. jouer aux cartes avec tes amis le week-end dernier
6. faire la vaisselle d'habitude après le dîner
7. sortir avec tes amis ce soir

Emmanuel s'amuse bien
au-dessus des Alpes.

Trouvez quelqu'un qui ... Interviewez les autres étudiants pour trouver quelqu'un qui ...

1. écoute la radio pendant qu'il étudie
2. joue de la guitare
3. a eu le temps de lire un livre la semaine dernière
4. a déjà écrit une dissertation ce semestre
5. n'a rien mangé ce matin
6. a eu la grippe l'année dernière
7. a nettoyé sa chambre le week-end dernier
8. ne sort jamais le dimanche soir
9. envoie souvent des messages électroniques à ses professeurs

 À vous. Répondez.

1. Que fait-on pour s'amuser le week-end sur votre campus?
2. Qu'est-ce que la plupart des étudiants font le dimanche soir?
3. Avez-vous regardé la télévision hier soir? Si oui, combien de temps avez-vous passé devant la télévision?
4. Quelle est la dernière fois que vous avez dîné au restaurant? Combien de temps avez-vous passé à table?
5. Combien de fois avez-vous été malade cette année?
6. Jouez-vous d'un instrument de musique? Si oui, de quel instrument jouez-vous?
7. À quoi joue-t-on au Canada et aux États-Unis? Jouez-vous aussi à ce(s) sport(s)?
8. Quelle est la dernière fois que vous avez nettoyé votre chambre?

Suggestion: Have students do the Information Gap activity in the Instructor's Resource Manual.

Pas de problème!

Preparation for the video:
1. Video worksheet in the *Cahier d'activités*
2. CD-ROM, *Module 3*

Cette activité est basée sur la vidéo, *Module 3.* Choisissez la bonne réponse *(Choose the right answer)* pour compléter les phrases suivantes.

1. Marie-Christine admire _____ dans la vitrine *(store window).*
   (un foulard, une carte, un pull)
2. Jean-François et Marie-Christine traversent la ville de Paris pour _____.
   (jouer au tennis, aller au magasin, prendre *(take)* un autobus)
3. Ils ont pris *(took)* _____ ensemble.
   (un autobus, le métro, un taxi)
4. Le métro ferme à _____.
   (minuit, une heure de l'après-midi, une heure du matin)
5. Jean-François a mis *(put)* _____ dans la petite machine.
   (son ticket, sa carte orange)

Lecture I

A **Étude du vocabulaire.** Étudiez les phrases suivantes et choisissez *(choose)* les mots anglais qui correspondent aux mots français en caractères gras *(bold print)*: *saw, to move, the south of France, meals, knife, trees, fingers, all.*

1. Je ne comprends pas **tous** les mots français.
2. Un homme attaque deux jeunes filles au **couteau.**
3. Quand on est paralysé, on n'est pas capable de **bouger.**
4. Les enfants comptent souvent sur les **doigts** pour faire l'addition.
5. Marseille est dans le **Midi** de la France.
6. Nous avons **vu** un film intéressant le week-end dernier.
7. Il y a beaucoup d'**arbres** dans une forêt.
8. Le déjeuner et le dîner sont des **repas.**

B **Parcourez les deux articles.** Skim each of the following selections to find: (1) an example of personal charity and (2) the reward that was given.

UN HOMME COURAGEUX

PARIS: Aziz Soubhane a 17 ans. Il est marocain, mais il habite en France depuis sept ans et fait ses études au Lycée d'enseignement professionnel privé de Notre-Dame, à la Loupe, en Eure-et-Loir.

Aziz a désarmé un homme qui attaquait au couteau deux jeunes filles anglaises dans le métro. Aziz a été le seul à bouger; les autres passagers n'ont pas levé le petit doigt.

Pour son courage, Aziz a reçu le «Prix servir» du Rotary-club de Paris et un chèque de 10.000 francs. C'est l'adjoint au maire de Paris qui a donné le prix à Aziz.

Ce jeune homme est un très bon exemple pour nous.

Les Soldats ont Planté des Arbres

TOULON: L'été dernier, des feux ont détruit une grande partie de la forêt dans le Midi de la France. Le 29 décembre, on a vu des soldats américains aider tous les volontaires de la région à nettoyer la forêt et à replanter des arbres. En une journée, ils ont replanté 5.000 arbres près de la ville d'Hyères, dans la région du Var.

Le 2 janvier, le maire de la ville a donné un grand méchoui à tous les volontaires. Les 165 soldats américains sont en escale à Toulon en ce moment. Ils ont profité de leur temps libre pour aider les Français.

Adjoint au maire = *deputy mayor;* **feux** = *fires;* **méchoui** = *a North African specialty in which a whole lamb is roasted over an open pit of live coals for several hours.*

Point out the locations of Paris and Toulon on the map inside the front cover.

C **Vrai ou faux?** Si une phrase est fausse, corrigez-la.

1. Aziz n'est pas français.
2. Il étudie dans une école publique.
3. Les soldats américains ont aidé les Français.
4. Les soldats ont été obligés d'aider les Français.
5. Les soldats ont travaillé une semaine.

D Questions. Répondez.

1. Qui sont les «bons Samaritains» dans ces deux articles?
2. Qu'est-ce qu'Aziz a fait? Et les soldats américains?
3. Est-ce que les autres personnes dans le métro ont aidé Aziz?
4. Qui a travaillé avec les soldats américains?
5. Qu'est-ce qu'on a donné à Aziz après son acte de courage?
6. Qu'est-ce qu'on a donné aux soldats après leur travail?

E Familles de mots. Essayez de deviner le sens des mots suivants.

1. détruire, la destruction
2. donner, un don, un donneur, une donneuse
3. enseigner, l'enseignement *(m.)*, un enseignant, une enseignante
4. voir, vu, la vue, une vision

F Discussion.

1. Identify three aspects of French culture mentioned in these newspaper articles that are similar to or different from American culture.
2. Are North African people and their cultures viewed favorably or unfavorably in these articles? Explain your answer.

Lecture II

A Étude du vocabulaire. Étudiez les phrases suivantes et choisissez les mots anglais qui correspondent aux mots français en caractères gras: *therefore, head, let go, voice, told.*

1. Le professeur nous a **raconté** une anecdote amusante.
2. Les aviateurs ont **lâché** des bombes sur la ville.
3. Cette chanteuse a une jolie **voix.**
4. As-tu des cachets d'aspirine? J'ai mal à la **tête.**
5. Marc habite à Paris. **Donc** il doit bien parler le français.

Moi

—Comment t'appelles-tu?

Le petit homme lève la tête sans répondre.

Voilà une plaisante question!

—Comment t'appelles-tu?

Il lâche d'une voix triomphante:

—Moi!

—Allons, allons! Tu t'appelles Jean.

—Oui! Jean Moi!

Cette réponse me plaît beaucoup. J'ai formé le projet de la rapporter à un philosophe de mes amis qui étudie ce qu'il appelle «la mentalité des enfants». J'appelle donc mon philosophe au téléphone et je demande: «Qui est à l'appareil[1]?» Une voix grêle et dénaturée[2] me répond: «Moi!» Impossible de raconter mon histoire au philosophe.

Georges Duhamel, *Les Plaisirs et les jeux*

1. *on the phone*   2. *shrill and distorted*

B **Questions.** Choisissez *(Choose)* la meilleure réponse.

1. Le «petit homme» est ...
   a. un garçon   b. un homme qui est petit
2. La question du narrateur est ...
   a. sérieuse   b. juste pour parler avec l'enfant
3. Le narrateur ...
   a. aime la réponse   b. trouve la réponse ridicule
4. Le philosophe trouve la question «Qui est à l'appareil?» ...
   a. sérieuse   b. bizarre

VOCABULAIRE ACTIF

Instruments de musique

un accordéon *accordion*
une batterie *drums*
une flûte *flute*
une guitare *guitar*
un piano *piano*
un saxophone *saxophone*
une trompette *trumpet*
un violon *violin*

D'autres noms

un examen *test, exam*
un exercice *exercise*
un cigare *cigar*
une cigarette *cigarette*
la grippe *flu*
un robinet *faucet*
la valse *waltz*
une crêpe *crepe (pancake)*

Pronoms accentués

moi *I, me*
toi *you*
lui *he, him*
elle *she, her*
nous *we, us*
vous *you*
eux *they, them*
elles *they, them (female)*

Jeux

le basket-ball (le basket) *basketball*
le bridge *bridge*
les cartes *(f. pl.) cards*
les dames *(f. pl.) checkers*
les échecs *(m. pl.) chess*

le football (le foot) *soccer*
le football américain *football*
le golf *golf*
le hockey *hockey*
un jeu *game*
la pétanque *lawn bowling*
le rugby *rugby*
le tennis *tennis*

Choses à lire ou à écrire

une bande dessinée *comic strip*
une carte postale *postcard*
une dissertation *(term) paper*
un journal *newspaper*
une lettre *letter*
un magazine *magazine*
un message électronique *e-mail*
un mot *word*
une pièce *play*
un poème *poem*
un roman *novel*
un roman policier *detective story*

Divisions du temps

une année *year*
une fois *one time*
une journée *day*
un mois *month*
un semestre *semester*
le temps *time; weather*
les vacances *(f. pl.) vacation*

Prépositions

par *per; by; through*
pendant *for; during*
sans *without*

Verbes

accompagner *to accompany*
s'amuser *to have fun*
se coucher *to go to bed*
décrire *to describe*
demander *to ask*
dormir *to sleep*
écrire *to write*
envoyer *to send*
être à *to belong to*
fermer *to close*
fumer *to smoke*
se lever *to get up*
lire *to read*
nettoyer *to clean*
oublier *to forget*
partir *to leave*
préparer (un cours) *to prepare (a lesson)*
remarquer *to notice*
sortir *to go out*
téléphoner (à qqn) *to telephone (someone)*

Expressions de temps

il y a ... ans (mois, etc.) ... *years (months, etc.) ago*
Je suis ici depuis ... mois (heures, etc.). *I've been here for ... months (hours, etc.).*
Pendant combien de temps ... ? *How long ... ?*
tous les soirs *every night*
tout à l'heure *a little while ago; in a little while*

Adverbes de temps

déjà *already*
hier *yesterday*
hier soir *last night*
longtemps *a long time*
récemment *recently*
tard *late*
tôt *early*

D'autres adverbes

au moins *at least*
heureusement *fortunately*
rien (ne ... rien) *nothing, not anything*
tant *so much; so many*

D'autres expressions utiles

À quoi jouez-vous? *What (game, sport) do you play?*
Aïe! *Ouch!*
à l'intérieur de *inside of*
à table *at dinner, at the table*
Bonnes vacances! *Have a good vacation!*
C'est la vie! *That's life!*
De quoi jouez-vous? *What (instrument) do you play?*
Eh bien *Well*
en vacances *on vacation*
faire du sport *to play sports*
la plupart (de) *most (of)*

parce que *because*
par exemple *for example*
Pourquoi pas? *Why not?*
... veut dire ... *... means ...*

escale 2
L'Amérique du Nord

LE FRANÇAIS DANS L'AMÉRIQUE DU NORD: APERÇU HISTORIQUE

1534 Jacques Cartier prend possession de la «Nouvelle-France», territoire des Amérindiens et des Inuits.

1608 Samuel de Champlain fonde la ville de Québec.

1682 Robert Cavelier de La Salle descend le Mississippi. Il nomme le bassin du Mississippi «Louisiane» en l'honneur du roi Louis XIV.

1755 Les Anglais déportent les Acadiens de Nouvelle-Écosse (le «Grand Dérangement»). De nombreux Acadiens s'installent en Louisiane. Le mot «cajun» est une déformation du mot «acadien».

1756–1763 Guerre de Sept Ans: Par le traité de Paris, la France cède (*yields*) son territoire de la Nouvelle-France à la Grande-Bretagne. Création de la province de Québec.

1803 Napoléon vend la Louisiane aux États-Unis pour 15 millions de dollars.

1848 La Grande-Bretagne forme le Canada-Uni. La langue anglaise devient langue officielle.

1921 Suite à la vive réaction des Canadiens français, Londres reconnaît et accepte l'usage de la langue française au Québec.

1966–1970 Développement du mouvement indépendantiste.

1977 La loi 101, la Charte de la langue française, rétablit le français comme seule langue officielle du Québec.

1982 Échec du référendum sur l'indépendance et la souveraineté du Québec désirée par le Parti québécois.

1998 Au référendum sur la souveraineté du Québec, les partisans du maintien de la province dans la confédération canadienne obtiennent une très faible victoire.

Le Québec

Que savez-vous?

Répondez aux questions suivantes. Les réponses se trouvent dans cette escale.

1. Le Québec est-il plus grand que le Texas?
2. Qui a fondé la ville de Québec?
3. Quel pourcentage de la population parle français?
4. Quelle est la plus grande ville du Québec?
5. Quelle est la capitale du Québec?
6. Quelle est la réaction des Québécois face à la suprématie de l'anglais?

REPÈRES: LE QUÉBEC

Population: 6.895.963 habitants; 83% d'origine française, 10% britannique, 7% Inuits ou immigrés francophones

Capitale: Québec

Administration: Province du Canada

Climats: continental, humide et arctique

Religion: 86% de catholiques

Ressources: industrie (forestière, pêcheries, métallurgique, hydroélectrique, minière); agriculture; tourisme

Langue officielle: français; 60% parlent seulement français, 35% parlent français et anglais

Territoire: la plus vaste des dix provinces; aussi grande que l'Alaska

ÉTUDE DU VOCABULAIRE

Quels mots en caractères gras correspondent aux mots suivants: *more, king, century, city, approximately, French-speaking world, most*?

1. La ville de New-York est **plus** grande que Montréal.
2. C'est la **plus** grande ville des États-Unis.
3. La France est une république. Elle n'a pas de **roi**.
4. Il y a **environ** 60 millions de Français en France.
5. Dans les pays de la **francophonie** on parle français.
6. **Un siècle** est une période de 100 ans.

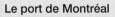

Le port de Montréal

Les Canadiens de Montréal en action

Le vélo est écolo

Le vélo devient un des moyens les plus populaires d'aller à la découverte du Québec! La géographie du Québec présente des reliefs et des paysages qui offrent aux cyclotouristes des promenades très variées et accessibles. La plaine fluviale du Saint-Laurent se prête très bien aux randonnées cyclistes et même les circuits en pays plus montagneux ne découragent pas les amateurs. Le Québec offre un réseau «vert» de plus de 3.000 km d'itinéraires cyclables sillonnant le territoire même dans les régions urbaines. Montréal, avec plus de 300 km de voies cyclables, possède un des réseaux les plus importants en Amérique du Nord. Plusieurs autres villes comme Québec, Laval et Sherbrooke possèdent aussi d'importantes pistes cyclables.

Le hockey: une passion sportive

Le hockey sur glace fait partie de la culture nationale du Canada, où ce sport est immensément populaire. Plus de cinq millions de Canadiens—un sur cinq—ont la passion de ce sport et y participent soit en tant que joueurs professionnels ou amateurs, soit en tant qu'entraîneurs, membres de comités, arbitres ou spectateurs de tous âges. Le Canada a plusieurs *(several)* équipes professionnelles de hockey sur glace. Le hockey sur glace est tellement populaire que la saison de ce sport d'hiver se prolonge jusqu'au mois de juin! L'origine précise du hockey est inconnue. Cependant, c'est à Montréal, la plus grande ville du Québec, que le premier match officiel de hockey a eu lieu au Victoria Rink durant l'hiver de 1875. Aujourd'hui, les habitants de Montréal et du Québec tout entier suivent avec intérêt les matchs de leur équipe favorite, les Canadiens de Montréal. Cette célèbre équipe a gagné la coupe Stanley 24 fois depuis 1916 et a compté plusieurs super-vedettes telles que Maurice «Rocket» Richard, Jean Béliveau et Guy Lafleur.

Et vous?

- **Aimez-vous le hockey sur glace? Jouez-vous à ce sport ou regardez-vous quelquefois des matchs de hockey à la télévision?**
- **Faites-vous du vélo? Si oui, préférez-vous le vélo tout terrain (VTT) ou le vélo de course (*speed bike*)?**
- **Quelles expressions venant de l'anglais sont utilisées en québécois?**

LE FRANÇAIS «QUÉBÉCOIS»

Au Québec, on dit ...	En France, on dit ...
un char	*une voiture*
le gaz	*l'essence*
un chien chaud	*un hot-dog*
jaser	*bavarder*
un melon d'eau	*une pastèque*
les lumières	*les feux (de circulation)*
avoir du fun	*s'amuser*
la poudrerie	*une tempête de neige*
ça mouille	*il pleut*
il fait méchant	*il fait mauvais*
la noirceur	*l'obscurité*
la fin de semaine	*le week-end*
magasiner	*faire des achats*
faire du pouce	*faire de l'autostop*

Le Québec: une province menacée

Au début des années 70, les Canadiens français se considéraient moins comme une minorité de la confédération canadienne, que comme la majorité francophone de la province du Québec. Par leurs efforts, la Charte de la langue française en 1977 a donné au français le statut de seule langue officielle dans la province de Québec, dans le but «d'assurer la qualité et le rayonnement de la langue francaise» dans la civilisation nord-américaine. Malgré la Charte, le Québec est encore menacé par l'invasion anglophone et l'idée d'un Québec indépendant et souverain tente toujours de nombreux citoyens québécois.

La question de séparation fait l'objet d'une guerre continue entre les fédéralistes, représentés par le Parti libéral du Québec (PL), qui veulent rester membres de la Confédération, et les séparatistes ou «souverainistes», représentés par le Parti québécois (PQ), qui veulent préserver leur identité linguistique et culturelle en Amérique du Nord. Lors d'un référendum en 1998, les Québécois s'exprimaient ainsi vis-à-vis de la séparation:

Oui 49.42%   NON 50.58%

Le canadien-français

C'est une langue de France
Aux accents d'Amérique
Elle déjoue[1] le silence
À grands coups de musique
C'est la langue de mon cœur
Et le cœur de ma vie
Que jamais elle ne meure[2]
Que jamais on ne l'oublie

(Michel Rivard, «Le Cœur de ma vie» Les Éditions Sauvages)
1. *thwarts* 2. *May it never die*

Et vous?

Êtes-vous pour ou contre la séparation du Québec du reste du Canada? Expliquez votre réponse.

Dans les villes où ils sont nombreux, les Franco-Américains habitent souvent dans des quartiers séparés, groupés autour d'une église catholique. (Soldier Pond, dans le nord du Maine)

Le Maine

REPÈRES: LE MAINE
Population: 1.253.000 habitants

Population franco-américaine: 348.900 habitants (28% de la population du Maine)

Population qui parle français à la maison: 81.000 (23% de la population franco-américaine)

Villes industrielles «franco-américaines»: Lewiston, Biddeford, Waterville, Augusta

Les Français de la Nouvelle-Angleterre

À partir de 1830 et pendant le siècle suivant, plus d'un million de Canadiens français ont traversé la frontière canado-américaine à la recherche d'une meilleure vie dans les villes industrielles des États-Unis. C'est surtout dans les grandes villes textiles des six états de la Nouvelle-Angleterre que ces immigrés du nord ont transporté leur langue et leur culture. Les francophones de la Nouvelle-Angleterre sont appelés encore aujourd'hui les Franco-Américains.

Le français qu'ils parlent ressemble au français des Québécois. Cette langue française n'est pas un français classique ou littéraire, mais plutôt *(rather)* un français populaire et rural qui a ses origines dans le parler des premiers colons, venus de France au XVIIe siècle. Petit à petit, les Canadiens français ont adapté leur langue aux besoins et aux circonstances de leur situation. Aujourd'hui, le français que parlent les Franco-Américains de la Nouvelle-Angleterre a beaucoup de mots empruntés à l'anglais.

Vrai ou faux?

1. **Les Canadiens français sont venus aux États-Unis pour faire de l'agriculture.**
2. **Le français canadien ressemble au français des anciens colons.**
3. **Dans le Maine, la majorité des familles d'origine canadienne parlent français à la maison.**

La Louisiane

REPÈRES: LA LOUISIANE

Superficie: 125.674 km²

Population: 4.372.035 habitants

Langues: anglais, français, créole

Capitale: Baton Rouge

Ville principale: La Nouvelle-Orléans

Ressources: pétrole, gaz naturel

Population dont la langue au foyer est le français: 572.262 (15% de la population)

Des paroisses «cajun»: Lafayette, Lafourche, Acadia, Vermilion, St. Martin

Que savez-vous?

Répondez aux questions suivantes. Les réponses se trouvent dans cette escale.

1. Qui a découvert la Louisiane?
2. D'où sont les habitants de la Louisiane?
3. Quelle est l'origine du mot cajun?
4. Quelle est la capitale de la Louisiane?
5. Quelles langues parlent-ils?

LE FRANÇAIS «CAJUN»

En Louisiane,

- on prononce le son «h» dans les mots *haut* et *hache*;
- on prononce les consonnes finales et muettes des mots *debout* et *lit*;
- on ne prononce pas le *ne* dans la négation (*e[elle] peut pas aller* pour *elle ne peut pas aller*);
- on crée des combinaisons grammaticales innovatrices (*reparment* pour *réparation* et *jolisit* pour *beauté*);
- on ajoute parfois l'article à la racine du mot (*deleau* pour *de l'eau* et *zoiseau* pour *oiseau*).
- on régularise des conjugaisons (*server* pour *servir*).

En Louisiane, on dit ...	En France, on dit ...
bois	arbre
fréquenter	faire l'amour
dame	femme
naviguer	voyager
un chrétien	une personne
une blonde	une petite amie
chariot	voiture
baler	danser

Laissez les bons temps rouler!

Le Cadien/Cajun*

Dans son poème, *Le Cadien/Cajun*, Christy Dugas Maraist, présidente du Conseil de la Fondation du Monument Acadien, donne plusieurs exemples de différences entre le cadien/cajun et le français standard, comme l'illustre l'extrait suivant:

> ... Écoute, c'est:
> "Attendre," pas "espérer,"
> "Pleurer," pas "brailler,"
> "Penser," pas "jongler."
> Je pense que t'as jamais jonglé de ça.
> Apprends:
> "Lentement," au lieu de
> "doucement,"
> "Gentil," au lieu de "vaillant,"
> "Beaucoup," au lieu de "joliment."
> L'essence ce n'est pas du parfum,
> tu vois.
> Étudie cette liste:
> "Une piastre," c'est "un dollar,"
> C'est une "voiture," pas un "char,"
> Une "fête," c'est un "anniversaire,"
> C'est "pourquoi," pas "quo'faire."
> L'essence va dans ta voiture,
> rappelle-toi!
> Tu me demandes quo'faire
> Tout ça, c'est nécessaire.
> Juste jongle comment vaillant ça
> serait,
> Si tu rencontrais un vrai Français.

Christy Dugas Maraist

* *Cajun* is the english translation of the French *Cadien*.

www

Buts communicatifs
Relating past events (continued)
Describing your background
Stating what you just did

Structures utiles
Le passé composé avec **être**
Le pronom **y**
Le verbe **venir**
Les prépositions de lieu avec une ville ou un pays (suite)
Les mois de l'année, les saisons, le temps
Venir de + infinitif

Culture
L'amabilité
Une technologie de pointe
La télécarte
Le TGV

Coup d'envoi

Prise de contact   **J'ai fait un voyage**

Où es-tu allée l'été° dernier, Stéphanie?   *summer*
    Je suis allée en Europe.

Parle-moi de ce voyage, s'il te plaît.
    Eh bien! Je suis arrivée à Londres le 15
      juin°.   *June*
    J'ai passé quinze jours à voyager en
      Angleterre.
    Puis je suis partie pour Paris le premier
      juillet°.   *July first*
    Je suis restée chez des amis de mes
      parents qui habitent à Paris.
    Je me suis très, très bien amusée.
    Enfin je suis revenue° le 10 août°.   *I came back / August*
    Voilà!

▶ **Et vous?**   Qu'est-ce que vous avez fait pendant les vacances? Êtes-vous
parti(e) en voyage ou êtes-vous resté(e) chez vous?

Conversation

Monsieur et Madame Smith sont arrivés à Angers

Monsieur et Madame Smith, amis de la famille de Lori Becker,
sont partis pour Angers. Là, ils sont descendus du TGV° à la gare got off the high-speed train
Saint-Laud. Monsieur Smith est entré dans une cabine télé-
phonique, a utilisé sa télécarte et a formé le numéro des Martin.

MME MARTIN:	Allô.
M. SMITH:	Madame Martin?
MME MARTIN:	Oui, qui est à l'appareil°?

on the phone

M. SMITH:	Bonjour, Madame. C'est Joseph Smith.
MME MARTIN:	Ah! les amis de Lori. Vous êtes arrivés?
M. SMITH:	Oui, nous sommes un peu en avance°.

early

Nous venons de descendre° du train. we just got off

MME MARTIN:	Mon mari et Lori sont déjà partis vous chercher. Restez là; ils arrivent.
M. SMITH:	D'accord. Merci, Madame. À tout à l'heure.
MME MARTIN:	À tout de suite°, Monsieur. Au revoir.

See you very soon

(Une demi-heure plus tard, chez les Martin)

LORI:	Madame Martin, je vous présente Monsieur et Madame Smith.
MME MARTIN:	Bonjour, Madame. Bonjour, Monsieur. Vous devez être fatigués après votre voyage.
MME SMITH:	Bonjour, Madame. Non, pas trop.
M. MARTIN:	C'est la première fois que vous venez° en France?

come

MME SMITH:	Non, nous sommes déjà venus° il y a deux ans.

came

M. SMITH:	Mais la dernière fois, nous n'avons pas beaucoup voyagé.
MME SMITH:	C'est gentil de vous occuper° de nous.

take care of

Ça ne vous dérange pas trop?

MME MARTIN:	Mais non! Je vous en prie.°

Don't mention it.

The vocabulary in this conversation will reappear in Ex. 3. Be sure students remember it.

▶ **Jouez ces rôles.** Répétez la conversation avec votre partenaire. Une personne joue le rôle des Smith et de Lori et l'autre joue le rôle des Martin. Utilisez vos propres *(own)* noms.

This gesture is used in the video, *Module 2.*

Je vous en prie. With palm open and fingers spread, one hand (or both hands) is held at the waist level and the shoulders are shrugged. The lips are often rounded. This gesture indicates that you are pleased to be of service and that it is not worth mentioning.

Il y a un geste

Pourquoi est-ce que Monsieur Smith utilise une télécarte?

a. Il n'a pas d'argent *(money)* français.
b. Il faut une carte pour utiliser les cabines téléphoniques à la gare Saint-Laud.
c. On peut utiliser des pièces de monnaie ou une carte pour téléphoner dans les cabines téléphoniques.

L'amabilité (Kindness)

The Martins go out of their way to be helpful to Lori's friends. A warm welcome is the norm rather than the exception in Angers. Many *Angevins* serve as host families to foreign students who are enrolled at the *Centre international d'études françaises* or in one of the institutes organized on the campus of the *Université Catholique de l'Ouest.* Others, such as the Martins, employ a **jeune fille au pair** who often becomes a "member" of the family. The tourist who stays only a few days in Paris may not get to appreciate the generosity and the friendliness of the French.

Une technologie de pointe

France is known worldwide for its leadership in art, fashion, perfume, food, and drink. France is also the world's fifth largest economy and fourth largest exporter. It is a leader in transportation (the TGV bullet train), aerospace (Airbus and the Ariane rocket), telecommunications (mobile phones and wireless technology), and civil engineering (the Normandy bridge and the Channel tunnel).

La télécarte

The **télécarte** is an electronic smart card used throughout France for both local and long distance phone calls. It can be purchased in post offices, railroad stations, and tobacco shops in France. Tourists are often caught off guard believing that they will be able to use French coins to make a telephone call. Coin operated phones are becoming increasingly rare in France. In Angers, for example, none of the phone booths at the railroad station accept coins. See video, *Module 2,* where the **télécarte** plays an important role.

Le TGV

France is also a world leader in public transportation *(les transports en commun).* Buses, subways, and trains run well, are on time, and are widely used. Among the latter, the **TGV, Train à Grande Vitesse,** is a spectacular technological achievement and a commercial success! The **TGV Atlantique** is a "bullet train" that serves the western part of France and transports over 40,000 customers per day. With a top speed of over 300 kilometers (200 miles) per hour, it offers exceptional comfort and service. **TGV Atlantique** passengers can even phone to all parts of the world. The **télécarte** is sold in the **TGV** lounge.

Pour utiliser la télécarte:

Décrochez le téléphone.	*Pick up the phone.*
Introduisez votre télécarte.	*Put your telecarte in the slot.*
Composez le numéro.	*Dial the number.*
Attendez que quelqu'un réponde.	*Wait until someone answers.*
Quand vous avez fini, raccrochez le téléphone.	*When you've finished, hang up the phone.*
Reprenez votre télécarte.	*Take your telecarte.*

À vous.   Vous téléphonez à un(e) ami(e). Répondez.

VOTRE AMI(E): Allô.
VOUS: _____

VOTRE AMI(E): Tu es arrivé(e)?
VOUS: _____

VOTRE AMI(E): Où es-tu?
VOUS: _____

VOTRE AMI(E): Reste là. J'arrive.
VOUS: _____

Entre amis

Vous êtes arrivé(e) à la gare

You are a foreign student at a French university and will be staying with a host family.

1. Call your host family and identify yourself.
2. Say that you are at the train station.
3. Reassure them that you are not too tired after your trip.
4. Express your thanks and say "See you very soon."

Prononciation

Les sons [ɔ] et [o]

■ French has an open [ɔ] sound and a closed [o] sound. The following words contain these sounds. Practice saying the words after your instructor, paying particular attention to the highlighted sound.

[ɔ] • **o**range, b**o**nne, c**o**mme, al**o**rs, s**o**mmes, c**o**nnaissez, enc**o**re, p**o**ste, pers**o**nnes, acc**o**rdéon, h**o**ckey, p**o**stale, d**o**rmir, s**o**rtir, n**o**tre, n**o**te, j**o**gging

[o] • radi**o,** pian**o,** m**o**t, v**o**s, gr**o**s

• ch**o**se, quelque ch**o**se, r**o**se

• h**ô**tel, à la v**ô**tre, dr**ô**le

• ch**au**d, f**au**x, **au** fait, d'**au**tres, **au** moins, à g**au**che, il f**au**t, f**au**x, f**au**sse, j**au**ne

• **eau,** b**eau**coup, b**eau,** chap**eau**

▶ Now go back and look at how these sounds are spelled and in what kinds of letter combinations they appear. What patterns do you notice?

■ The sound [ɔ] is always followed by a pronounced consonant.

téléph**o**ne ad**o**re p**o**stale n**o**te d**o**rment m**o**de **o**ctobre

■ The sound [o] is used in several circumstances.

o as the word's final sound	pian**o**, m**o**t
o + [z]	ch**o**se, r**o**se
ô	h**ô**tel, v**ô**tre
au	**au** fait, il f**au**t
eau	l'**eau**, b**eau**coup

■ Say the following pairs of words, making sure to pronounce the [ɔ] and [o] sounds correctly.

1. n**o**s / n**o**tre
2. r**o**binet / r**o**se
3. v**o**tre / v**ô**tre
4. ch**au**d / ch**o**colat
5. b**eau** / b**o**nne

Buts
communicatifs

1 Relating Past Events *(continued)*

Tu es sortie vendredi dernier, Nathalie?
        Oui, je suis sortie.
Où es-tu allée?
        Je suis allée au restaurant et chez des
            amis.
À quelle heure es-tu rentrée° chez toi?   *did you get back*
        Je suis rentrée à minuit.

▶ **Et vous?**   Vous êtes sorti(e) le week-end dernier?
            Si oui, où êtes-vous allé(e)?
            À quelle heure êtes-vous rentré(e)?

A. Le passé composé avec *être*

Review the formation of the **passé composé** with **avoir,** p. 157.

Êtes-vous **arrivée** en train?
Non, je **suis venue** en voiture.

Did you arrive by train?
No, I came by car.

Paul et Karine **sont sortis** hier soir?
Oui, mais ils **sont rentrés** à neuf heures.

Did Paul and Karine go out last night?
Yes, but they came home at nine o'clock.

Remember to consult Appendix C at the end of the book to review any terms with which you are not familiar.

Mon père **est né** à Paris en 1935.
Mais sa famille **est partie** aux États-Unis avant la guerre.
En 1985 il **est tombé** malade.
Il **est mort** en 1986.

My father was born in Paris in 1935.
But his family left for the United States before the war.
He got sick in 1985.
He died in 1986.

■ While most verbs use **avoir** to form the passé composé (see Ch. 6), there are a limited number that use **être.** These verbs are intransitive; that is, they do not take a direct object. The most common are listed on the opposite page.

Ils sont arrivés à la gare.

VOCABULAIRE

You might want to point out that many of these verbs are general terms of movement or change of condition, but that more specific verbs of movement, such as **nager** or **danser**, take **avoir** in the passé composé. For the sake of simplicity, the use of **passer** as an intransitive verb and the use of **monter, descendre, rentrer,** and **sortir** as transitive verbs have been omitted here.

Quelques verbes qui forment le passé composé avec *être*

Infinitif		Participe passé
aller	*to go*	allé
venir	*to come*	venu
devenir	*to become*	devenu
revenir (ici)	*to come back (here)*	revenu
retourner (là)	*to go back; to return (there)*	retourné
rentrer (à la maison)	*to go (come) back; to go (come) home*	rentré
arriver	*to arrive; to happen*	arrivé
rester (à la maison)	*to stay, remain (at home)*	resté
partir	*to leave*	parti
monter (dans une voiture)	*to go up; to get into (a car)*	monté
descendre (d'une voiture)	*to go down; to get out (of a car)*	descendu
tomber	*to fall*	tombé
entrer (dans la classe)	*to enter (the classroom)*	entré
sortir (de la classe)	*to go out (of the classroom)*	sorti
naître	*to be born*	né
mourir	*to die*	mort

Students will not have to use the present tense of **descendre** until Ch. 9, where regular **-re** verbs are introduced. The present tenses of **naître** and **mourir** are not required in this course.

Remember that if a plural subject is of mixed gender, the masculine plural form of the participle will be used.

■ Past participles used with **être** agree in gender and number with the subject, just as if they were adjectives. To show agreement, add **-e** (feminine singular), **-s** (masculine plural), or **-es** (feminine plural).

Masculin	*Féminin*
Je suis **né** à Paris.	Je suis **née** à Paris.
Tu es **né** à New York.	Tu es **née** à New York.
Il est **né** à Montréal.	Elle est **née** à Montréal.
Nous sommes **nés** à Boston.	Nous sommes **nées** à Boston.
Vous êtes **né(s)** à Angers.	Vous êtes **née(s)** à Angers.
Ils sont **nés** à Halifax.	Elles sont **nées** à Halifax.

VOCABULAIRE À RETENIR

à l'heure *on time*
en avance *early*
en retard *late*

■ Most of these verbs are followed by a preposition when they precede the name of a place.

Sandrine est entrée **dans** la salle de classe.

Sandrine went into the classroom.

Moi, je suis arrivé **au** cours de français à l'heure.

I arrived at the French class on time.

Mais Nicolas est retourné **chez** lui pour chercher son livre. Alors, il est arrivé en retard.

But Nicolas went back home for his book. So, he came late.

Review reflexive verbs, p. 165.

■ Reflexive verbs also use **être** to form the passé composé.

Les étudiants **se sont amusés** à la soirée.	*Students had fun at the party.*
Ils ne **se sont** pas **couchés** tôt.	*They did not get to bed early.*
Est-ce que Mélanie **s'est levée** tard le jour suivant?	*Did Mélanie get up late the following day?*
Elle et sa sœur ne **se sont** pas **levées** avant midi.	*She and her sister didn't get up before noon.*

There is no accent on the first **-e-** of the past participle **levé(e)**.

Remember to choose the appropriate object pronoun.

se coucher *(to go to bed)*			
je	**me** suis couché(e)	nous	**nous** sommes couché(e)s
tu	**t'**es couché(e)	vous	**vous** êtes couché(e)(s)
il	**s'**est couché	ils	**se** sont couchés
elle	**s'**est couchée	elles	**se** sont couchées

The rules of past participle agreement with reflexive verbs will be learned in Ch. 13. Until then, only verbs whose reflexive pronoun is a direct object are taught.

1 **Thierry ne fait jamais rien comme les autres.** Expliquez d'après le modèle.

If this exercise is assigned for writing, remind students to make the agreement of the past participle.

> **MODÈLE:** Les autres (partir pour le Canada) / Et Thierry?
> **Les autres sont partis pour le Canada, mais Thierry n'est pas parti pour le Canada.**

1. vous (aller au concert) / Et Thierry?
2. nous (sortir hier soir) / Et Thierry?
3. Marie et Monique (arriver à l'heure) / Et Thierry?
4. ses amis (tomber malades) / Et Thierry?
5. Madame Dubuque (monter dans un taxi) / Et Thierry?
6. les étudiants (rester sur le campus) / Et Thierry?
7. les étudiants (s'amuser) / Et Thierry?

Remember that the past participles of **descendre** and **sortir** are **descendu** and **sorti**.

2 **Le voyage.** Racontez la journée *(Tell about the day)* de Monsieur et Madame Smith. Attention à l'emploi des verbes **avoir** et **être**.

> **MODÈLES:** se lever à 7 heures
> **Ils se sont levés à 7 heures.**
>
> chercher un taxi
> **Ils ont cherché un taxi.**

1. voyager en train
2. arriver à Angers
3. descendre du train à la gare Saint-Laud
4. téléphoner aux Martin
5. monter dans la voiture de Monsieur Martin
6. parler avec Lori Becker
7. aller chez les Martin
8. déjeuner chez les Martin
9. s'amuser

Follow up, books closed, by having students reiterate what the Smiths did.

3 **Qu'est-ce que tu as fait la semaine dernière?** Utilisez **tu** et les expressions suivantes pour interviewer votre partenaire.

> **MODÈLE:** manger une pizza
>
> **VOUS: Est-ce que tu as mangé une pizza la semaine dernière?**
>
> **VOTRE PARTENAIRE: Oui, j'ai mangé une pizza.** ou
> **Non, je n'ai pas mangé de pizza.**

Follow up by asking students to tell two things they learned about their partners.

1. aller au cinéma
2. étudier à la bibliothèque
3. regarder la télévision
4. passer un examen
5. tomber malade
6. entrer dans un bistro
7. descendre en ville
8. lire un journal
9. se lever à 5 heures du matin

4 **La plupart des étudiants.** Qu'est-ce que la plupart des étudiants ont fait la semaine dernière? Utilisez les expressions suivantes pour la question et pour la réponse.

> **MODÈLE:** manger une pizza
>
> —**Est-ce que la plupart des étudiants ont mangé une pizza la semaine dernière?**
> —**Oui, ils ont mangé une pizza.** ou
> **Non, ils n'ont pas mangé de pizza.**

1. aller aux cours
2. faire leurs devoirs
3. nettoyer leur chambre
4. sortir avec leurs amis
5. se coucher tard
6. se lever tôt
7. tomber malades

5 **À vous.** Répondez.

1. Êtes-vous resté(e) sur le campus le week-end dernier?
2. Qu'est-ce que vous avez fait le week-end dernier?
3. Quelle est la dernière fois que vous êtes sorti(e) avec vos amis? Où êtes-vous allés? Qu'est-ce que vous avez fait? À quelle heure êtes-vous rentrés?
4. Vos parents ont-ils déjà visité votre campus? Si oui, quand sont-ils venus?
5. Est-ce que vous arrivez d'habitude à l'heure au cours?
6. Quelle est la dernière fois que vous êtes arrivé(e) en retard au cours?
7. Est-ce que quelqu'un aime arriver en avance au cours de français? Qui est-ce?

6 **Le voyage des Smith.** Racontez l'histoire suivante au passé composé.

Monsieur et Madame Smith passent la nuit à Paris. Ils se lèvent tôt. D'abord ils sortent de leur hôtel. Ensuite ils montent dans un taxi pour aller à la gare Montparnasse. Quand ils arrivent à la gare, ils trouvent leur train et ils cherchent leurs places. Enfin le train part. Ils ne mangent rien pendant le voyage. Après une heure et demie, leur train arrive à la gare Saint-Laud. Monsieur Smith s'occupe de leurs bagages et ils descendent du train.

Entre amis

La dernière fois

1. Find out when the last time was that your partner went out.
2. Ask where s/he went.
3. Find out what s/he did.
4. Find out when s/he got back home.
5. Find out at what time s/he went to bed.

B. Le pronom y

When presenting **y**, give lots of personal examples: **Il y a un cinéma au centre commercial. J'y vais quelquefois. J'y suis allé(e) samedi dernier,** etc.

Ta sœur est **en France?**   Oui, elle **y** est.
Va-t-elle souvent **à Paris?**   Non, elle n'**y** va pas souvent.
Quand pars-tu **en France?**   J'**y** pars dans un mois.

Ton frère est resté **chez lui?**   Non, il n'**y** est pas resté.
Est-il allé **au cinéma?**   Oui, il **y** est allé.

Tu vas rester **dans ta chambre?**   Non, je ne vais pas **y** rester.

This use of **y** is restricted to expressions of place. Point out to students that in these examples **y** answers the question **Où?**

■ **Y** *(There)* is very often used in place of expressions that tell where something is located (**à l'université, dans la voiture,** etc.). The pronoun **y** replaces both the preposition (**à, chez, dans, en, sur,** etc.) and the name of the place.

Nous allons **au cinéma.**   Nous **y** allons.

■ **Y** is placed directly before the conjugated verb. This means that in the passé composé, it goes in front of the auxiliary.

Nous **y** allons la semaine prochaine.   *We are going there next week.*
Nous n'**y** allons pas demain.   *We are not going there tomorrow.*
J'**y** suis allé.   *I went there.*
Ma mère n'**y** est jamais allée.   *My mother has never gone there.*

■ When there is more than one verb, **y** is placed directly in front of the verb to which it is related (usually the infinitive).

Je vais **y** aller.   *I am going to go there.*
Je ne vais pas **y** rester.   *I am not going to stay there.*
J'ai envie d'**y** passer un mois.   *I feel like spending a month there.*
Je n'ai pas l'intention d'**y** habiter.   *I don't plan to live there.*

Drill **j'y vais** and **je n'y vais pas** first. Then do Ex. 7 in groups as a chain exercise.

Review **Quelques endroits,** pp. 125–126.

7 **Non, je n'y vais pas.** Un(e) étudiant(e) demande **Vas-tu à la pharmacie?** Un(e) autre répond **Non, je n'y vais pas; je vais ... (au centre commercial, à l'église,** etc.). Inventez au moins 10 questions.

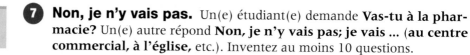

8 **Tu y vas souvent?** Demandez si votre partenaire fait souvent les choses suivantes. Votre partenaire va utiliser **y** dans chaque *(each)* réponse.

MODÈLE: aller au cinéma
VOUS: **Tu vas souvent au cinéma?**
VOTRE PARTENAIRE: **Oui, j'y vais souvent.**   ou
Non, je n'y vais pas souvent.

1. aller chez le médecin
2. étudier à la bibliothèque
3. dîner au restaurant
4. arriver au cours en retard

5. monter dans ta voiture
6. retourner chez tes parents
7. aller à la poste

9 **Tu y es allé(e) hier?** Refaites l'exercice 8, mais posez les questions au passé composé. Votre partenaire va utiliser **y** dans chaque réponse.

MODÈLE: aller au cinéma
VOUS: **Es-tu allé(e) au cinéma hier?**
VOTRE PARTENAIRE: **Oui, j'y suis allé(e).**   ou
Non, je n'y suis pas allé(e).

Suggestion: This activity could be done in the future: **Vas-tu aller au cinéma demain?**

COMMENT S'Y PERDRE, COMMENT S'Y RETROUVER

10 **À vous.** Répondez. Utilisez **y** dans chaque réponse.

1. Êtes-vous sur le campus maintenant?
2. Êtes-vous allé(e) à la bibliothèque hier soir? Si oui, à quelle heure y êtes-vous entré(e)? Combien de temps y êtes-vous resté(e)?
3. Combien de fois par semaine allez-vous au cours de français? Y allez-vous demain?
4. Êtes-vous resté(e) chez vous pendant les dernières vacances?
5. La plupart des étudiants ont-ils dîné au restaurant hier soir?
6. Avez-vous envie d'aller un jour en France? Y êtes-vous déjà allé(e)? Si oui, combien de temps y avez-vous passé?
7. Allez-vous au cinéma ce soir? Si oui, avec qui y allez-vous?

Entre amis

Au campus et à la maison

Use **y,** if possible, in your answers.

1. Ask if your partner went to the library last night.
2. Find out if s/he is going there this evening.
3. Find out the same information with respect to the gymnasium, the post office, and the grocery store.
4. Find out if your partner is going home next weekend.
5. Find out when s/he went home last.
6. Find out what s/he did when s/he went home.

Review the vocabulary on pp. 125–126.

2 Describing Your Background

D'où viennent ces personnes?

Alain et Sylvie viennent de Nantes.
Tom vient d'Angleterre. Il vient de Londres.
Mike vient des États-Unis et Rose vient du Canada.
Il vient de l'état d'Iowa et elle vient de la province d'Ontario.

Et vous? D'où venez-vous?

C. Le verbe *venir*

Est-ce que **Monique vient** de France?	*Does Monique come from France?*
Non, **elle vient** du Canada.	*No, she comes from Canada.*
Elle est devenue médecin.	*She became a doctor.*
Elle n'est pas ici mais **elle revient** à 6 heures.	*She isn't here but she's coming back at six o'clock.*

venir *(to come)*			
je	**viens**	nous	**venons**
tu	**viens**	vous	**venez**
il/elle/on	**vient**	ils/elles	**viennent**

passé composé: je **suis venu(e)**

This is similar to the distinction between **américain** and **américaine**, pp. 92–93.

■ Note the pronunciation distinction between the third person singular and plural forms.

vient [vjɛ̃] viennent [vjɛn]

■ The verbs **revenir** *(to come back)* and **devenir** *(to become)* are conjugated like **venir**.

11 **Les gens partent.** Demandez quand ils reviennent. Votre partenaire va répondre.

MODÈLE: Marie-Dominique (à 15 h 30)
VOUS: **Quand est-ce qu'elle revient?**
VOTRE PARTENAIRE: **Elle revient à quinze heures trente.**

1. Stéphanie (à 12 h 45)
2. Colette et Karine (à midi)
3. nous (la semaine prochaine)
4. tu (ce soir)
5. le patron (demain matin)
6. vos amis (mercredi)
7. vous (dans une heure)
8. ta sœur et toi (tout de suite)

D. Les prépositions de lieu avec une ville ou un pays (suite)

You have already learned to use prepositions to express *to* or *at* with a city, state, province, or country (see Ch. 5).

D'où viennent vos parents?
Mon père est originaire **du** Canada.
Ma mère vient **des** États-Unis.
Je viens **de** Bruxelles.
Monsieur et Madame Luc viennent **de** France.

Where do your parents come from?
My father is a native of Canada.
My mother comes from the United States.
I come from Brussels.
Monsieur and Madame Luc come from France.

■ To tell where a person is *from,* some form of **de** is used.

• **de** with cities:
  de Paris, **d'**Angers

• **de** with feminine countries or countries that begin with a vowel sound:
  de France, **d'**Iran

• **du** with masculine countries:
  du Mexique, **du** Canada

• **des** with plural countries:
  des États-Unis

■ To say that someone is from a U.S. state or Canadian province, **de** is normally used before those that are feminine or that begin with a vowel sound. The preposition **du** is often used with masculine states and provinces that begin with a consonant.

de Géorgie   **d'**Iowa   **du** Kansas
de Terre-Neuve   **d'**Alberta   **du** Québec

Note You may also use **de l'état de** or **de la province de** to say which U.S. state or Canadian province someone is from.

Mon meilleur ami vient **de l'état d'**Arizona.
Je viens **de la province d'**Ontario.

See Ch. 5 for a list of countries already studied, p. 142.

■ Use the expression **d'où** with **venir** to inquire where someone comes from.

D'où vient Guy—du Canada ou de France?

Review prepositions of place, p. 138.

Synthèse: Les prépositions de lieu		
	Je viens ...	J'habite ... / Je vais ...
ville	**de**	**à**
pays féminin ou pays qui commence par une voyelle	**de**	**en**
pays masculin	**du**	**au**
pays pluriel	**des**	**aux**

One can also say **la Hollande** for **les Pays-Bas.**

Je viens **d'**Atlanta. Je vais **à** New York.
María vient **d'**Espagne. Elle habite **en** France.
Emilio téléphone **du** Mexique **au** Canada.
Nous venons **des** États-Unis. Nous allons **aux** Pays-Bas en vacances.
John vient **de l'état de** Nebraska mais il habite **dans l'état d'**Arizona.
Denise vient **de la province d'**Ontario, mais elle habite **dans la province de** Québec.

Have students explain the choice of each preposition in these examples.

12 **André va voyager.** Il a l'intention de donner de ses nouvelles *(keep in touch)* à ses parents et à ses amis. Qu'est-ce qu'il va faire?

> **MODÈLE:** écrire / Italie
> **Il va écrire d'Italie.**

1. téléphoner / Allemagne
2. poster une lettre / Moscou
3. écrire une carte postale / Japon
4. téléphoner / Mexique
5. écrire / état de New York
6. écrire un message / province d'Ontario
7. poster une cassette / Liverpool

13 **André est retourné chez lui.** Il a contacté ses parents et ses amis pendant son voyage. Qu'est-ce qu'il a fait?

> **MODÈLE:** écrire / Rome
> **Il a écrit de Rome.**

1. téléphoner / Berlin
2. poster une lettre / Russie
3. écrire une carte postale / Tokyo
4. téléphoner / Mexico
5. écrire / États-Unis
6. écrire un message / Canada
7. poster une cassette / Angleterre

Remind students that **le Mexique** is the country. **Mexico** is used only for *Mexico City.*

D'où viennent-ils? La liste des passagers du vol *(flight)* Air France n° 0748 inclut des personnes de différents pays. Expliquez d'où viennent ces personnes et où elles habitent maintenant.

MODÈLE: Sandrine (Paris / New York)
Sandrine vient de Paris, mais elle habite à New York maintenant.

Habiter may be used with a direct object. In this text it is taught with a preposition.

1. Ralph (Canada / États-Unis)
2. Alice (Belgique / France)
3. Helmut et Ingrid (Allemagne / Italie)
4. William (Angleterre / Irlande)
5. José et María (Mexique / États-Unis)
6. Gertrude (Ontario / Manitoba)
7. Judy et Bill (Michigan / Allemagne)

 À vous. Répondez.

1. De quelle ville venez-vous?
2. De quelle(s) ville(s) viennent vos parents?
3. D'où vient votre meilleur(e) ami(e)?
4. D'où viennent vos grands-parents?
5. D'où vient votre professeur de français? (Devinez.)
6. D'où viennent deux autres étudiants du cours de français?

VOCABULAIRE

Les mois de l'année, les saisons, le temps

Les mois de l'année	Les saisons	Le temps
janvier	l'hiver	Il fait froid.
février		Il neige.
mars		Il fait du vent.
avril	le printemps	Il pleut.
mai		Il fait frais.
juin		
juillet	l'été	Il fait beau.
août		Il fait du soleil.
septembre		Il fait chaud.
octobre	l'automne	Il fait encore beau.
novembre		Il commence à faire froid.
décembre		Il fait mauvais.

The opposite of **Il fait beau** is **Il fait mauvais.**

Note The negation of **il fait du vent** is **il ne fait pas** *de* **vent.**

E. Les mois de l'année, les saisons, le temps

■ Names of months begin with lowercase letters in French. Use the preposition **en** before the months to mean *in*.

en février   **en** août   **en** septembre

■ Use **en** also with all seasons except **le printemps.**

en été   **en** automne   **en** hiver
But: **au** printemps

Point out that there are two ways of expressing dates in English *(May third, the third of May)* while there is only one way in French.

■ The French represent the date by giving the day first, then the month.

Amy est née **le premier mai.**	*Amy was born on the first of May.*
Mon anniversaire est **le dix février.**	*My birthday is the tenth of February.*
Le bébé est né **le vingt-cinq avril.**	*The baby was born on April twenty-fifth.*

Note   Use **le premier** (*... first, the first of ...)*, but then **le deux, le trois,** etc.

La fête nationale suisse est **le premier** août.

VOCABULAIRE

Quelques dates

le premier janvier	le Jour de l'An
le premier juillet	la fête nationale canadienne
le quatre juillet	la fête nationale américaine
le quatorze juillet	la fête nationale française
le premier novembre	la Toussaint
le vingt-cinq décembre	Noël

 En quelle saison sont-ils nés? Expliquez quand et en quelle saison les personnes suivantes sont nées.

Follow-up: Have students tell their birthdays.

MODÈLE: Monique (15/4)
           Elle est née le quinze avril. Elle est née au printemps.

1. Martin Luther King, fils (15/1)
2. Maureen (10/2) et Michel (23/9)
3. Anne (25/8) et Stéphanie (13/7)
4. George Washington (22/2)
5. vous

Quelle est la date? Votre partenaire va poser une question. Donnez la réponse.

> **MODÈLE:** Noël
> **VOTRE PARTENAIRE: Quelle est la date du jour de Noël?**
> **VOUS: C'est le vingt-cinq décembre.**

1. ton anniversaire
2. l'anniversaire de ton (ta) meilleur(e) ami(e)
3. le Jour de l'An
4. le commencement du printemps
5. le commencement de l'été
6. le commencement de l'automne
7. le commencement de l'hiver
8. le commencement des vacances d'été à ton université
9. la fête nationale américaine
10. la fête nationale canadienne
11. la fête nationale française

 Quel temps fait-il? Posez des questions. Si votre partenaire ne sait pas la réponse, il (elle) va deviner.

> **MODÈLE:** février / chez toi
> **VOUS: Quel temps fait-il en février chez toi?**
> **VOTRE PARTENAIRE: Il fait froid et il neige.**

1. été / chez toi
2. hiver / Montréal
3. automne / Chicago
4. printemps / Washington, D.C.
5. août / Maroc
6. avril / Paris
7. décembre / Acapulco

 À vous. Répondez.

1. En quelle saison êtes-vous né(e)?
2. En quel mois êtes-vous né(e)?
3. En quel(s) mois les membres de votre famille sont-ils nés?
4. En quelle saison est-ce qu'il pleut chez vous?
5. En quelle saison est-ce qu'il commence à faire froid chez vous?
6. Quelle est votre saison préférée? Pourquoi?
7. Qu'est-ce que vous avez fait l'été dernier?

Entre amis

D'où viennent-ils?

1. Find out where your partner comes from.
2. Find out if that is where s/he was born.
3. Find out where your partner lives now.
4. Find out his/her birthdate.
5. Find out if your partner has ever gone to France, Canada, or some other French-speaking country.

3 Stating What You Just Did

Tu as déjà mangé, Thierry?

    Oui, il y a une demi-heure. Je viens de manger.°   *I just ate.*

Tes amis ont téléphoné?

    Oui, il y a dix minutes. Ils viennent de téléphoner.°   *They just called.*

▶ **Et vous?** Qu'est-ce que vous venez de faire?

    Est-ce que vous venez de parler français?

F. *Venir de* + infinitif

■ **Venir de** followed by an infinitive means *to have just*.

Je **viens d'arriver.**	*I have just arrived.*
Ils **viennent de manger.**	*They just ate.*
Mon frère **vient de se coucher.**	*My brother just went to bed.*
Qu'est-ce que tu **viens de faire?**	*What did you just do?*

 20 Qu'est-ce qu'ils ont fait? Chaque phrase est assez vague. Posez une question qui commence par **Qu'est-ce que** pour demander une précision. Ensuite votre partenaire va suggérer *(suggest)* une réponse à la question.

Point out that the question is in the **passé composé**.

MODÈLE: Mes amis viennent de manger quelque chose.

        VOUS: Qu'est-ce qu'ils ont mangé?

    VOTRE PARTENAIRE: Ils ont mangé une pizza.

1. Pierre vient de lire quelque chose.
2. Nous venons de regarder quelque chose.
3. Je viens d'étudier quelque chose.
4. Mon frère et ma sœur viennent de trouver quelque chose.
5. Je viens d'écrire quelque chose.
6. Nous venons de faire quelque chose.

21 **Elle vient de téléphoner.** Votre camarade de chambre vient de rentrer chez vous. Répondez **oui** à ses questions et utilisez **venir de** dans chaque réponse.

MODÈLE: Martine a téléphoné?
Oui, elle vient de téléphoner.

1. Est-elle rentrée chez elle?
2. Est-ce qu'elle a déjà dîné?
3. Vous avez parlé de moi?
4. A-t-elle trouvé ma lettre?
5. Est-ce qu'elle a lu ma lettre?
6. Tu as expliqué pourquoi je n'ai pas téléphoné?

22 **La naissance** *(birth)* **de Vianney.** Vous êtes le frère de Brigitte et vos parents vous téléphonent de la maternité *(maternity hospital).* Vous posez des questions au passé composé. Votre partenaire joue le rôle des parents et utilise **venir de** pour répondre.

MODÈLE: Vous / monter à la salle d'attente *(waiting room)*
LE FRÈRE: Est-ce que vous êtes montés à la salle d'attente?
LES PARENTS: Oui, nous venons de monter à la salle d'attente.

1. Brigitte / avoir son bébé
2. Vianney / naître
3. le médecin / partir
4. vous / entrer dans la chambre de Brigitte
5. Matthieu, Antoine et Julien / parler avec leurs parents
6. Chantal / téléphoner

Matthieu Monnier est né le 17 mai 1989. Ses frères s'appellent Antoine, Julien et Vianney. Antoine est né le 4 avril 1991, Julien le 29 mars 1993 et Vianney le 18 mai 1997. Ils habitent à Angers avec leurs parents, Brigitte et Jean-Philippe.

Using this model, have students compose their own birth announcement.

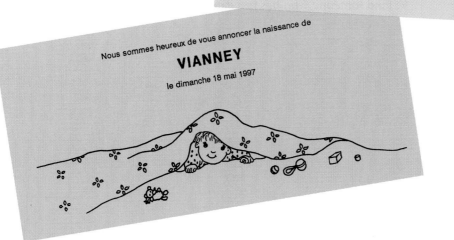

Intégration www

Révision

A **Les mois et les saisons**

1. Nommez les mois de l'année.
2. Nommez les saisons de l'année.
3. Parlez du temps qu'il fait pendant chaque *(each)* saison.
4. Pour chaque saison, mentionnez une activité qu'on fait.

Partners should answer only **oui** or **non** to questions asked.

B **Le week-end dernier.** Faites une liste de vos activités du week-end dernier. Essayez ensuite de deviner ce que votre partenaire a écrit.

C **À vous.** Répondez.

1. Quelle est la date de votre anniversaire?
2. De quel pays venez-vous?
3. Dans quelle ville êtes-vous né(e)?
4. D'où viennent vos parents?
5. Quand les membres de votre famille sont-ils nés?
6. À quelle heure êtes-vous arrivé(e) au cours de français la dernière fois? Y êtes-vous arrivé(e) en retard, à l'heure ou en avance?
7. Êtes-vous déjà allé(e) dans un pays où on parle français? Si oui, où, et avec qui?
8. Qu'est-ce que vous venez d'étudier au cours de français?
9. Avez-vous déjà voyagé en train ou en avion? Où êtes-vous allé(e)?

Suggestion: Have students do the Information Gap activity in the Instructor's Resource Manual.

D **Trouvez quelqu'un qui ...** Interviewez les autres étudiants.

1. Find someone who was born in another state or province.
2. Find someone who comes from a large city.
3. Find someone who has been to a French-speaking country.
4. Find someone who spent last summer on campus.
5. Find someone who did not go out last Friday evening.
6. Find someone who stayed in his/her room last night.
7. Find someone who went to the library last night.
8. Find someone who did not watch television last night.
9. Find someone who has just eaten.

Pas de problème!

Cette activité est basée sur la vidéo, *Module 4.* Choisissez la bonne réponse pour compléter les phrases suivantes.

1. Jean-François a l'intention d'acheter *(buy)* _____.
   (du pain, des croissants, des pâtisseries)
2. Il est _____ quand Jean-François parle avec l'artiste pour la première fois.
   (9 h 15, 9 h 45, 8 h 45)
3. L'artiste se trouve _____.
   (à Montparnasse, au Quartier Latin, à Montmartre)
4. L'artiste dessine *(is drawing)* _____.
   (Notre-Dame, le Sacré-Cœur, la Sainte-Chapelle)
5. Jean-François parle _____ fois avec lui.
   (deux, trois, quatre)
6. C'est _____.
   (mercredi, vendredi, dimanche)
7. L'homme qui entre dans la boulangerie avant Jean-François veut _____ croissants.
   (deux, trois, quatre)

Lecture I

A **Étude du vocabulaire.** Étudiez les phrases suivantes et choisissez les mots anglais qui correspondent aux mots français en caractères gras: *second, according to, in fact, only, understand, such as, remember, following.*

1. D'abord, nous faisons cet exercice. Ensuite nous allons faire l'exercice **suivant.**
2. Il est important de **se rappeler** que cinq et demi s'écrit 5,5 en France mais 5.5 aux États-Unis.
3. Il est souvent difficile de **comprendre** ces différences culturelles.
4. **D'après** les experts, il fait plus chaud au mois d'août qu'au mois de juillet.
5. Y a-t-il **seulement** vingt-huit jours au mois de février?
6. **En effet** il y a d'habitude 28 jours dans le **deuxième** mois de l'année.
7. Dans certaines villes, **telles que** Paris, Lyon et Montréal, il y a un métro.

B **Identifiez les pays.** Combien de pays y a-t-il dans l'Union européenne? Combien de ces pays se trouvent sur la carte au début du livre?

Les femmes parlementaires européennes

Les femmes représentent cinquante-deux pour cent de la population française mais, d'après des statistiques récemment publiées dans le magazine *L'Express,* les femmes françaises constituent seulement 5,5 pour cent des parlementaires en France. C'est en effet le plus petit pourcentage de femmes parlementaires des quinze pays de l'Union européenne.

Tableau I.	À l'Assemblée nationale		
	pays	*femmes députés*	*pourcentage de l'Assemblée*
1	la Suède	151	43
2	le Danemark	59	34
3	la Finlande	67	33,5
4	les Pays-Bas	43	28,5
5	l'Allemagne	176	26,5
6	l'Autriche	47	25,7
7	l'Espagne	76	22
8	le Luxembourg	11	18
9	le Portugal	31	13,5
10	la Belgique	18	12
11	l'Irlande	20	12
12	la Grande-Bretagne	63	10
13	l'Italie	60	9,5
14	la Grèce	17	5,6
15	la France	32	5,5

NOTE CULTURELLE
En France, en octobre 2000, le pourcentage de femmes parlementaires avait un peu changé. Il y avait (*there were*) cinquante-sept femmes députées à l'Assemblée nationale et vingt femmes au Sénat. Consultez les activités WWW pour le Chapitre 7 pour trouver combien il y a de femmes parlementaires aujourd'hui en France.

Tableau II.	Au Sénat ou dans les Chambres hautes		
	pays	*femmes sénateurs*	*pourcentage du Sénat*
1	les Pays-Bas	43	22,5
2	l'Autriche	13	20,3
3	la Belgique	13	18,3
4	l'Allemagne	12	17,4
5	l'Espagne	31	15
6	l'Irlande	8	13
7	l'Italie	26	8
8	la Grande-Bretagne	82	6
9	la France	18	5,6

Née au Sénégal de père militaire avant l'indépendance, Ségolène Royal fait ses études en France en sciences politiques, économiques et administratives. Elle est députée socialiste depuis 1988.

Pour bien comprendre ces statistiques, il faut d'abord se rappeler que, dans certains pays y compris la France, il y a deux chambres parlementaires; dans d'autres, telles que la Suède et le Danemark, il y en a seulement une. Donc il y a quinze pays qui ont représentation à l'Assemblée nationale (tableau I), mais seulement neuf qui ont un Sénat (tableau II). En France, il y a 577 députés à l'Assemblée nationale et 303 sénateurs.

L'Express, juin 1996

 Vrai ou faux? Décidez si les phrases suivantes sont vraies ou fausses. Si une phrase est fausse, corrigez-la.

1. Il y a plus de cinquante pour cent de femmes dans la population française.
2. Il y a neuf pays qui n'ont pas de chambre correspondant à l'Assemblée nationale.
3. Il y a 545 députés hommes en France.
4. Les Suédois ont le plus grand pourcentage de sénateurs féminins.
5. La Hollande est un des pays de l'Union européenne.
6. L'Irlande a le plus petit nombre de femmes sénateurs.
7. La France a le plus petit nombre de députées.

D Discussion.

1. Y a-t-il beaucoup, assez ou trop peu de femmes parlementaires dans votre pays? Expliquez votre réponse.
2. Comparez votre pays aux différents pays de l'Union européenne.

Lecture II

A **Parlons du genre** *(gender).* Identifiez les mots suivants qui sont masculins, féminins ou peuvent *(can)* être les deux.

	M	F	M/F
1. personne	———	———	———
2. enfant	———	———	———
3. professeur	———	———	———
4. artiste	———	———	———
5. victime	———	———	———
6. médecin	———	———	———
7. ingénieur	———	———	———

B **Faites une liste.** Faites une liste de toutes les expressions que vous connaissez *(that you know)* qui commencent par «Il».

Suggestion: Use the poem for a
Concours de prononciation
(see the Instructor's Resource
Manual).

IL

Il pleut Il pleut
Il fait beau
Il fait du soleil
Il est tôt
Il se fait[1] tard
Il
Il
Il
toujours Il
Toujours Il qui pleut et qui neige
Toujours Il qui fait du soleil
Toujours Il
Pourquoi pas Elle
Jamais Elle
Pourtant[2] Elle aussi
Souvent se fait[3] belle!

Jacques Prévert, Éditions Gallimard

1. *is getting*   2. *However*   3. *makes herself*

C **Discussion.** Quel est le point de vue du poète? Êtes-vous d'accord avec lui? Pourquoi ou pourquoi pas?

VOCABULAIRE ACTIF

Les mois de l'année
janvier *(m.) January*
février *(m.) February*
mars *(m.) March*
avril *(m.) April*
mai *(m.) May*
juin *(m.) June*
juillet *(m.) July*
août *(m.) August*
septembre *(m.) September*
octobre *(m.) October*
novembre *(m.) November*
décembre *(m.) December*

Les saisons de l'année
le printemps *spring*
l'été *(m.) summer*
l'automne *(m.) fall*
l'hiver *(m.) winter*
une saison *season*

Expressions météorologiques
Il fait froid. *It's cold.*
Il fait chaud. *It's hot (warm).*
Il fait frais. *It's cool.*
It fait beau. *It's nice out.*
Il fait mauvais. *The weather is bad.*
Il fait du soleil. *It's sunny out.*
Il fait du vent. *It's windy.*
Il pleut. *It's raining.*
Il neige. *It's snowing.*

Il commence à faire froid. *It's starting to get cold.*

Expressions de temps
à l'heure *on time*
en avance *early*
en retard *late*
une demi-heure *half an hour*
puis *then; next*
tout de suite *immediately; right away*
À tout de suite. *See you very soon.*

D'autres noms
un anniversaire *birthday*
un avion *airplane*
un bébé *baby*
la fête nationale *national holiday*
une guerre *war*
le monde *world*
une place *seat*
un problème *problem*
une victime *victim (male or female)*

Expressions utiles
Ça ne vous dérange pas? *That doesn't bother you?*
D'où venez-vous? *Where do you come from?*
en voiture *by car*
être originaire de *to be a native of*

Je vous en prie. *Don't mention it; You're welcome; Please do.*
Parlez-moi de ce voyage. *Tell me about this trip.*
Qui est à l'appareil? *Who is speaking (on the phone)?*
suivant(e) *following; next*
y *there*

Verbes
arriver *to arrive; to happen*
commencer *to begin*
descendre *to go down; to get out of*
devenir *to become*
entrer *to enter*
monter *to go up; to get into*
mourir *to die*
naître *to be born*
poster *to mail*
rentrer *to go (come) back; to go (come) home*
retourner *to go back; to return*
revenir *to come back*
tourner *to turn*
venir *to come*
venir de ... *to have just ...*

Quelques fêtes
la Toussaint *All Saints Day*
le Jour de l'An *New Year's Day*
Noël *Christmas*

8 On mange bien en France

Coup d'envoi

　## Quelque chose à manger?

 Use the video, *Modules 4,* **La boulangerie,** & *10,* **Le marché,** to help set the scene for this chapter.

Tu as faim°, Bruno?   *You are hungry*
  Qu'est-ce qu'il y a?
Il y a ...
  du pain° .   *bread*
  des hors-d'œuvre°.   *appetizers*
  de la soupe.
  du poisson.
  de la viande°.   *meat*
  des légumes°.   *vegetables*
  de la salade.
  du fromage.
Qu'est-ce que tu vas prendre?°   *What are you going to have?*

▶ **Et vous?**   Qu'est-ce que vous allez prendre?
     Je voudrais ...
     Merci, je n'ai pas faim.
     Je regrette° mais j'ai déjà mangé.   *I'm sorry*

Conversation

L'apéritif chez les Aspel

James Davidson est invité à prendre l'apéritif° chez Monsieur et Madame Aspel, les parents de Karine. Monsieur Aspel lui offre quelque chose à boire.

have a before-dinner drink

M. ASPEL: Que voulez-vous boire, James? J'ai du vin, de la limonade, du jus de pomme°, de la bière ...

apple

JAMES: Quel choix!° Comment s'appelle ce vin?

What a choice!

M. ASPEL: C'est du beaujolais. Et voilà une bouteille° de bordeaux.

bottle

JAMES: Alors, un peu de beaujolais, s'il vous plaît.

M. ASPEL: Bien sûr°, voilà.

Of course

(James lève° son verre et Monsieur Aspel verse° du vin.)

lifts/pours

JAMES: Merci beaucoup.

M. ASPEL: Je vous en prie.

(Un peu plus tard)

M. ASPEL: Alors, que pensez-vous° de ce petit vin?

what do you think

JAMES: Il est délicieux.

M. ASPEL: Encore à boire?°

More to drink?

JAMES: Non, merci.

M. ASPEL: C'est vrai?

Remind students of the gesture for **Non, merci,** taught in Ch. 2.

JAMES: Oui, vraiment. Sans façon.°

Honestly.

M. ASPEL: Alors, je n'insiste pas.°

I won't insist.

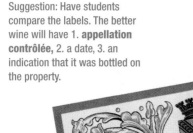 **Jouez ces rôles.** Répétez la conversation avec votre partenaire. Utilisez vos noms.

Suggestion: Have students compare the labels. The better wine will have 1. **appellation contrôlée,** 2. a date, 3. an indication that it was bottled on the property.

Pourquoi est-ce que James lève son verre quand Monsieur Aspel va verser du vin?

a. James est très poli. Cela fait partie *(is part of)* du savoir-vivre *(code of good manners)*.

b. C'est plus facile *(easier)* pour Monsieur Aspel.

c. James ne veut pas renverser *(knock over)* son verre.

L'apéritif

A before-dinner drink is often offered. This might be **un kir, un porto** *(port wine),* **un jus de pomme,** etc.

L'art d'apprécier le vin

Wine is an integral part of French social life and there are a number of polite gestures, such as lifting one's glass when wine is to be poured, that are associated with wine appreciation.

Tout se fait autour d'une table (Everything takes place around a table)

It does not take long in France to realize how much time is spent sitting around a table. Not only is a table the place to enjoy a meal or share a drink, it is also a primary spot for business deals, serious discussion, pleasant companionship, courtship, and child rearing! It is not surprising, therefore, to find that the table has a place of honor in France, whether it is in **la cuisine, la salle à manger, le restaurant, le café, le bistro,** or **la cafétéria.**

Un repas français (A French meal)

A good example of the presence of structure in French lives is the order of a French meal. There

are as many as five separate courses at both lunch and dinner, although these are not necessarily heavy meals. After the **hors-d'œuvre,** the **plat principal** is served. There may be more than one **plat principal** (e.g., fish *and* meat). **La salade** normally comes next, followed by **le fromage** and **le dessert.** In a light meal, either the cheese or the dessert may be omitted.

Any variation in the order of the French meal is almost always minor. In some regions, such as **Angers,** the salad is often eaten with the main course. The number of courses in a French meal reflects not only the French feeling for structure, but also the French appreciation of savoring each taste individually.

Sans façon

Refusing additional servings is often quite difficult in France. The French are gracious hosts and are anxious that their guests have enough to eat and drink. There is therefore a need to find ways to convey politely that you are full. Do not, incidentally, say **Je suis plein(e)** (literally, *I am full*), since this would convey that you were either drunk or pregnant. When all else fails (e.g., **Merci; Non, merci; Vraiment; Je n'ai plus faim/soif; J'ai très bien mangé/bu,** etc.), the expression **Sans façon** *(Honestly; No kidding)* will usually work. Of course, if you feel like having a second serving, you may say **Volontiers!** or **Je veux bien.**

In France	In North America
Eating several courses, even light ones, means that you have to stop after each course and wait for the next. Much more time is spent at the table.	Everything may be served at once and, therefore, much less time is spent at the table.
A green salad is served *after* (occasionally with) the **plat principal.** It is not eaten as a first course.	If there is a salad, it is eaten at the start of the meal.
There is only one type of dressing (oil and vinegar) served with a salad.	There is a variety of salad dressings available. What is referred to as *French dressing* is nothing like what is served with a salad in France.
Bread is always served with the meal, usually without butter, and is bought fresh every day.	Bread is not always served with the meal.
Coffee is not served during lunch or dinner. It is served, without cream, at the end of these meals.	Coffee is occasionally served right away at the start of the meal.
Café au lait is served only at breakfast. This mixture of 1/2 coffee and 1/2 warm milk is often served in a bowl.	Many people put milk in their coffee at every meal.

Additional information, including information on table manners, will be found in Ch. 13.

En France, on boit beaucoup d'eau minérale.

Il y a un geste

Encore à boire?   A fist is made with the thumb extended to somewhat resemble a bottle. Then the thumb is pointed toward a glass as an invitation or a request to have more to drink.

À vous.   Répondez.

1. Que voulez-vous? J'ai de la limonade, du jus de pomme, ...
2. Bien sûr, voilà.
3. Aimez-vous la limonade, le jus de pomme, ... ?
4. Encore à boire?

Entre amis

Tu as faim?

1. Find out if your partner is hungry. (S/he is.)
2. Ask if s/he wants something to eat.
3. S/he will ask what there is.
4. Tell what there is.
5. Find out what s/he is going to have.

Prononciation

Les sons [k], [s], [z], [ʃ], [ʒ] et [ɲ]

■ The following words contain some related French consonant sounds. Practice saying the words after your instructor, paying particular attention to the highlighted sound. As you pronounce the words for one sound, look at how that sound is spelled and in what kinds of letter combinations it appears. What patterns do you notice?

[k]
- **c**afé, en**c**ore, bi**c**yclette, chi**c**
- cin**q**, **qu**el**qu**efois
- **k**ir, vod**k**a

[s]
- **s**a, **s**ur, di**s**cret, **s**kier, conver**s**ation, val**s**e, fil**s**, mar**s**
- pre**ss**é, poi**ss**on
- **c**itron, exer**c**ice, bi**c**yclette
- **ç**a, fran**ç**ais, gar**ç**on
- si**x**, di**x**, soi**x**ante

[z]
- mai**s**on, va**s**e, poi**s**on, maga**s**in
- **z**éro, sei**z**e, maga**z**ine

[ʃ]
- **ch**aud, blan**ch**e, mé**ch**ant
- **sh**ort, sweat-**sh**irt

[ʒ]
- **j**ouer, tou**j**ours, dé**j**euner, dé**j**à
- oran**g**e, **g**énéral, gara**g**e, refri**g**érateur

[ɲ]
- espa**gn**ol, Allema**gn**e, rensei**gn**ement

■ In most situations, **-s-** is pronounced [s]. But when it appears between two vowels, it is pronounced as [z].

soir	**s**alade	**s**eul	cla**ss**e	con**s**idération

But: va**s**e   pré**s**ente   rai**s**on   cho**s**e   mu**s**ée

■ As in English, **-c-** is usually pronounced [k], but becomes [s] when it precedes the letters **-e, -i,** or **-y.** To create the [s] sound of **-c-** in some words where it is not followed by **e, i,** or **y,** it is written as **ç.**

en**c**ore	**c**assis	**c**omment	Maro**c**	**c**rème

But: Fran**c**e   voi**c**i   bi**c**yclette   fran**ç**ais   Fran**ç**ois

■ Finally, as in English, the letter **-g-** is usually pronounced [g], but becomes [ʒ] when it precedes the letters **-e, -i,** or **-y.** To create the [ʒ] sound of **-g-** in some words where it is not followed by **e, i,** or **y,** an **-e** is added after it.

re**g**arder	**g**olf	**g**uitare	**g**rippe	é**g**lise

But: **g**entil   oran**g**ina   **g**ymnase   man**g**eons   voya**g**eons

▶ Pronounce the following words correctly.

1. chocolat, commerce, chaussures, citron, bicyclette, ça, garçon, chercher, chance, avec
2. cinq, cinquante, quelques, pourquoi, Belgique, quart, chaque, question, banque
3. kir, vodka, skier, baskets, hockey
4. excellent, saxophone, examen, exercice, six, dix, soixante
5. Sénégal, orange, mangeons, voyageur, garage, gauche, âge, ménage, agent, gymnastique
6. surprise, Suisse, sous, semestre, saison, sieste, poisson, plaisir, ensuite
7. conversation, télévision, fonctionnaire, attention, provisions, dissertation
8. zéro, onze, magazine, douze
9. jupe, jeune, je, janvier, aujourd'hui, déjeuner, déjà
10. espagnol, Allemagne, accompagner, renseignement

En été, on commence souvent le repas par un demi-melon bien froid. C'est délicieux.

1 Ordering a French Meal

Client(e)	Serveur/Serveuse°	waiter / waitress
Qu'est-ce que vous avez comme ...	Il y a ...	
hors-d'œuvre?	des crudités°.	raw vegetables
	du pâté°.	pâté (meat spread)
	de la salade de tomates.	
soupes?	de la soupe aux légumes.	
	de la soupe à l'oignon°.	onion
plats principaux?	de la truite°.	trout
	du saumon°.	salmon
	du bœuf°.	beef
	du porc.	
	du poulet°.	chicken
légumes?	des haricots verts°.	green beans
	des petits pois°.	peas
	des épinards°.	spinach
	des frites°.	French fries
	du riz°.	rice
fromages?	de l'emmental°.	Swiss cheese
	du camembert.	
	du chèvre°.	goat cheese
	du brie.	
desserts?	des fruits.	
	de la glace°.	ice cream
	des pâtisseries°.	pastries
	de la tarte°.	pie
	du gâteau°.	cake

Garçon is the traditional way of referring to a waiter; however, the word **serveur** is increasingly used.

Point out the pronunciation of **oignon** [ɔɲɔ̃].

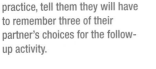

Before pairing students for practice, tell them they will have to remember three of their partner's choices for the follow-up activity.

▶ **Et vous?** Avez-vous décidé? Qu'est-ce que vous allez commander? Je vais prendre ...

Remarques

1. The words **hors-d'œuvre** and **haricot** begin with the letter **h-** but are treated as if they began with a pronounced consonant. Liaison does not take place after words like **les** and **des,** nor is the letter **-e** dropped in words like **le** and **de.**

   Nous aimons **les/hors-d'œuvre.**   Il n'y a pas **de haricots.**

2. **Hors-d'œuvre** is invariable in the plural.

   un **hors-d'œuvre**   des **hors-d'œuvre**

A. L'article partitif

Apportez-moi **du** pain, s'il vous plaît.	*Bring me some bread, please.*
Vous voulez **de la** glace?	*Do you want (some) ice cream?*
Vous avez **de l'**eau minérale?	*Do you have (any) mineral water?*
Je vais manger **des** frites.	*I'm going to eat (some) French fries.*

■ You have already learned about definite articles and indefinite articles in French. There is a third type of article in French called **l'article partitif** *(the partitive article)* that is used when a noun represents a certain quantity, or a part, of a larger whole. In English, we sometimes use the words *some* or *any* to represent this idea, but sometimes we use no article at all.

Je voudrais **du** gâteau.	*I would like cake (but just some of it).*
Le professeur a **de la** patience.	*The professor has patience (not all the patience in the world, just a portion of it).*
Jean a **des** livres.	*Jean has books (but not all the books in the whole world).*

partitive article	when to use	examples
du	before a masculine singular noun	**du** pain
de la	before a feminine singular noun	**de la** salade
de l'	before a masculine or feminine singular noun that begins with a vowel sound	**de l'**eau
des	before all plural nouns, masculine or feminine	**des** frites

Write these sentences on the board, then drill: 1. **Est-ce qu'il y a du café?** (glace/légumes/eau/fromage/etc.) 2. **Il n'y a pas de café.** (glace/légumes/etc.)

■ Like the indefinite article, the partitive article usually becomes **de** after a negation.

Est-ce qu'il y a **de l'**eau minérale?	*Is there any mineral water?*
Non, il n'y a **pas d'**eau minérale.	*No, there isn't any mineral water.*
Il y a **des** légumes?	*Are there any vegetables?*
Non, il n'y a **pas de** légumes.	*No, there aren't any vegetables.*

Note This rule does not apply after **être**.

Ce n'est pas **du** vin, ce n'est pas **de la** limonade, ce n'est pas **de l'**eau. C'est **du** lait.

■ In a series, the article must be repeated before each noun.

Vous voulez **de la** glace, **de la** tarte ou **du** gâteau?

Be sure to use the contractions **l'**, **de l'**, and **d'** before a vowel.

Synthèse: Les articles

	définis	indéfinis	partitifs
masculin singulier	le	un	du
féminin singulier	la	une	de la
pluriel	les	des	des
dans une phrase négative	le/la/les	de	de

Review the definite article, p. 41, and the indefinite article, p. 59.

Voici un des desserts préférés des Français. Ces gâteaux font venir l'eau à la bouche, n'est-ce pas?

Follow-up: Use the items in the pictures to drill and contrast:
1. *J'aime **le** pain.*, etc., and
2. *Je **voudrais** du pain.*, etc.

1 **Qu'est-ce que c'est?** Identifiez les choses suivantes.

MODÈLES:

C'est du pain.   **Ce sont des petits pois.**

Before pairing students for practice, tell them they will have to remember their partner's choices for the follow-up: **Qu'est-ce que votre partenaire va prendre?**

Remind students that the definite article is used to express a preference and that it does not change after a negation (see Ch. 2).

 Qu'est-ce que vous commandez? Dites au garçon ou à la serveuse que vous aimez la catégorie indiquée. Ensuite demandez quels sont les choix. Il (elle) va mentionner deux choix. Décidez.

MODÈLE: vegetables

> VOUS: **J'aime beaucoup les légumes. Qu'est-ce que vous avez comme légumes?**
> SERVEUR/SERVEUSE: **Nous avons des petits pois et des épinards.**
> VOUS: **Je voudrais des petits pois, s'il vous plaît.**

1. appetizers   3. fish   5. wine
2. meat   4. vegetables 6. cheese
                                    7. desserts

 Ils viennent de pique-niquer. Qu'est-ce qu'ils ont apporté *(brought)*? Qu'est-ce qu'ils n'ont pas apporté?

MODÈLE: Les Delille (pain, salade)
> **Les Delille ont apporté du pain, mais ils n'ont pas apporté de salade.**

1. Séverine (salade, fromage)
2. Roland (haricots verts, petits pois)
3. Serge et Christelle (fromage, vin rouge)
4. Patricia (poisson, viande)
5. Vous (... , ...)

4 Un(e) touriste va au restaurant. Jouez la scène suivante avec votre partenaire en complétant les phrases avec **du, de la, de l', des, de** ou **d'.**

—Vous avez décidé?
—Oui, je voudrais _____ pâté _____ truite, _____ frites et _____ épinards.
—Et comme boisson?
—Apportez-moi _____ café, s'il vous plaît.
—Mais c'est impossible! Il n'y a jamais _____ café avec le plat principal.
—Qu'est-ce qu'il y a?
—Nous avons _____ vin ou _____ eau minérale.
—Vous n'avez pas _____ orangina?
—Si, si vous insistez. Et comme dessert?
—Je crois que je voudrais _____ gâteau.
—Nous n'avons pas _____ gâteau. Il y a _____ glace et _____ fruits.
—Merci, je ne vais pas prendre _____ dessert.

B. *Ne ... plus*

■ The opposite of **encore** is **ne ... plus** *(no more, not any more, no longer).*

Avez-vous **encore** soif?   *Are you still thirsty?*
Non, je **n'**ai **plus** soif et je **n'**ai   *No, I'm not thirsty any more and I'm no*
plus faim.   *longer hungry.*

■ **Ne … plus** works like the other negations you have learned; that is, **ne** and **plus** are placed around the conjugated verb. This means that in the passé composé, **ne** and **plus** surround the auxiliary verb and the past participle follows **plus**.

Remember that the partitive article becomes **de** after a negation: **plus** *de* **glace, plus** *de* **dessert.**

Je regrette; nous **n'**avons **plus** de glace.	*I'm sorry; we have no more ice cream.*
Je **ne** vais **plus** manger de dessert.	*I am not going to eat any more dessert.*
Delphine **n'**a **plus** dîné dans ce restaurant-là.	*Delphine did not eat in that restaurant again.*

5 **Encore à manger ou à boire?** Offrez encore à manger ou à boire. Votre partenaire va refuser poliment.

MODÈLES: bière
    —**Encore de la bière?**
    —**Sans façon, je n'ai plus soif.**

glace
    —**Encore de la glace?**
    —**Merci, je n'ai plus faim.**

1. café
2. eau
3. limonade
4. pâté

5. viande
6. frites
7. tarte
8. poisson

9. légumes
10. beaujolais
11. salade
12. fromage

6 **Le restaurant impossible.** Il n'y a plus beaucoup à manger ou à boire. Le serveur (la serveuse) répond toujours **Je regrette** et suggère autre chose. Insistez! Expliquez que vous n'aimez pas ce qu'il (elle) propose.

MODÈLE: poisson (viande)
    VOUS: **Avez-vous du poisson?**
    SERVEUR/SERVEUSE: **Je regrette, nous n'avons plus de poisson; mais nous avons de la viande.**
    VOUS: **Mais je voudrais du poisson! Je n'aime pas la viande.**

1. coca (vin)
2. soupe (hors-d'œuvre)
3. épinards (frites)
4. truite (saumon)
5. pâté (crudités)

6. pâtisseries (glace)
7. chocolat chaud (café)
8. haricots verts (petits pois)
9. orangina (limonade)

Il y a un geste

L'addition, s'il vous plaît *(Check, please).*
When the French want to signal to a waiter or waitress that they want the check, they pretend to be writing on the open palm of one hand. This is discreetly held up for the waiter to see.

Entre amis

L'addition, s'il vous plaît

You have just finished your meal in a French restaurant. You signal the waiter/waitress.

1. Ask the waiter/waitress for your bill.
2. S/he will verify the items you ordered.
3. Confirm or correct what s/he says.

Suggestion: Give partners time to invent **"une addition."** The one who "verifies" should pretend to read the items on the bill.

C. Le verbe *prendre*

Nous prenons souvent un repas ensemble.	*We often have a meal together.*
Je prends un café.	*I'm having a cup of coffee.*
Mes amis ne **prennent** pas le petit déjeuner.	*My friends don't eat breakfast.*
Qui a pris mon dessert?	*Who took my dessert?*

prendre *(to take; to eat, drink)*			
je	**prends**	nous	**prenons**
tu	**prends**	vous	**prenez**
il/elle/on	**prend**	ils/elles	**prennent**

passé composé: j'**ai pris**

Drill: **Je ne prends pas le petit déjeuner. (Vous/Nous/Mes parents/etc.)**

■ Note the pronunciation distinction between the third person singular and plural forms.

il prend   [prã]   ils prennent   [prɛn]

■ The verbs **apprendre** *(to learn)* and **comprendre** *(to understand; to include)* are conjugated like **prendre.**

Quelle langue **apprenez-vous?**	*What language are you learning?*
J'apprends le français.	*I'm learning French.*
Peggy comprend bien le français.	*Peggy understands French well.*
Comprennent-ils toujours le professeur?	*Do they always understand the teacher?*
Pardon, **je** n'**ai** pas **compris.**	*Excuse me, I didn't understand.*
Le service est **compris.**	*The service (tip) is included.*

VOCABULAIRE À RETENIR

apprendre *to learn*
comprendre *to understand; to include*

Note   *To learn to do something* is **apprendre à** + infinitive.

Nous **apprenons à parler** français.   *We are learning to speak French.*

7 **Les voyageurs.** Les personnes suivantes vont voyager. Expliquez quelle langue elles apprennent.

Review **langues et pays,** in Ch. 5.

MODÈLE: Je vais en France.
    Alors j'apprends à parler français.

1. Mes parents vont en Italie.
2. Mon cousin va en Allemagne.
3. Ma sœur va au Mexique.
4. Mon oncle et ma tante vont en Russie.

5. Mes amis et moi allons en Belgique.
6. Vous allez en Chine.
7. Je vais au Maroc.

8 **La plupart des étudiants.** Interviewez votre partenaire à propos des étudiants de votre cours de français. Attention au présent et au passé composé.

MODÈLES: apprendre le français
    —Est-ce que la plupart des étudiants apprennent le français?
    —Bien sûr, ils apprennent le français.

apprendre le français à l'âge de quinze ans
    —Est-ce que la plupart des étudiants ont appris le français à l'âge de quinze ans?
    —Non, ils n'ont pas appris le français à l'âge de quinze ans.

1. prendre quelquefois un verre de vin au petit déjeuner
2. prendre le petit déjeuner ce matin
3. comprendre toujours le professeur de français
4. apprendre l'espagnol à l'âge de cinq ans
5. prendre souvent un taxi
6. prendre un taxi hier
7. comprendre cet exercice

9 **À vous.** Répondez.

1. Vos amis prennent-ils le petit déjeuner d'habitude? Si oui, qu'est-ce qu'ils prennent comme boisson?
2. D'habitude, qu'est-ce que vous prenez comme boisson au petit déjeuner? au déjeuner? au dîner?
3. Qu'est-ce que vous avez pris comme boisson ce matin?
4. Qu'est-ce que la plupart des Français prennent comme boisson au dîner?
5. Qu'est-ce que vous allez prendre si vous dînez dans un restaurant français?
6. Si vous commandez un dessert, que prenez-vous d'habitude?
7. Comprenez-vous toujours les menus qui sont en français?
8. Avez-vous appris à faire la cuisine?

Entre amis

Tu comprends les serveurs de restaurant?

1. Ask if your partner is learning French.
2. Find out if s/he understands French waiters.
3. Ask if s/he is hungry. (S/he is.)
4. Invite your partner to go to a French restaurant.
5. Discuss what you are going to have.

2 Discussing Quantities

Qu'est-ce que tu manges, Solange?
Je mange …
    beaucoup de frites.
    un peu de gâteau.
    peu d'épinards.
    très peu de moutarde°.   *mustard*
Je mange …
    un morceau° de pizza.   *piece*
    une tranche de jambon°.   *slice of ham*
    une assiette° de crudités.   *plate*
    une boîte de bonbons°.   *box of candy*

Et vous? Qu'est-ce que vous mangez?
Je mange …
Qu'est-ce que vous buvez°?   *you drink*
Je bois° …   *I drink*

Remarque The plural of **un morceau** is **des morceaux.**

Thomas a mangé cinq **morceaux** de pizza.

D. Les expressions de quantité

Point out that the plural **œufs** is pronounced [ø]. The final **-fs** is silent.

■ You have already been using expressions of quantity throughout this course. There are two kinds of expressions of quantity: specific measures (**une tasse, un verre,** etc.) and indefinite expressions of quantity (**assez, beaucoup,** etc.).

■ To use these expressions of quantity with nouns, insert **de** (but no article) before the noun.

Une bouteille de vin, s'il vous plaît.   *A bottle of wine, please.*
Une douzaine d'œufs, s'il vous plaît.   *A dozen eggs, please.*
Il faut **un kilo de porc.**   *We need a kilo of pork.*
Trois kilos de pommes de terre aussi.   *Three kilos of potatoes also.*
Je voudrais **un morceau de pain.**   *I'd like a piece of bread.*
Ils n'ont pas **beaucoup d'amis.**   *They don't have a lot of friends.*
Combien de frères ou **de sœurs**   *How many brothers or sisters do*
  avez-vous?   *you have?*

■ **Trop, beaucoup, assez,** and **peu** can be used with either singular or plural nouns. *Un* **peu** can only be used with singular nouns, those that cannot be counted. To express the idea of a small amount with a plural noun (which *can* be counted), use **quelques** *(a few, some)* without **de.**

Voulez-vous **un peu de** fromage?   *Would you like a little cheese?*
But: Voulez-vous **quelques** frites?   *Would you like a few French fries?*

■ The indefinite expressions of quantity can also be used with verbs, without the addition of **de.**

Je chante **beaucoup.**   *I sing a lot.*
Rip van Winkle a **trop** dormi.   *Rip van Winkle slept too much.*
Nous avons **assez** travaillé!   *We have worked enough!*

■ To express how much you like or dislike a thing, the definite article (not **de**) is used before the noun.

Je n'aime pas **beaucoup le** lait.   *I don't much like milk.*
Mon frère aime **trop la** glace.   *My brother likes ice cream too much.*

The expression of quantity, in such cases, is really modifying the verb.

■ **Peu de** can be introduced by the word **très** to make it more emphatic. **Très** cannot be used with the other expressions of quantity.

L'ex-président mange **très peu de** brocoli.

E. Le verbe *boire*

Quel vin **boit-on** avec du poisson?
Nous buvons un peu de thé.
Nos amis mangent de la salade et **ils boivent** de l'eau.
Hélène a trop **bu!**

boire *(to drink)*			
je	**bois**	nous	**buvons**
tu	**bois**	vous	**buvez**
il/elle/on	**boit**		
ils/elles	**boivent**		
passé composé: j'**ai bu**			

■ Note the pronunciation distinction between the third person singular and plural forms.

elle boi~~t~~   [bwa]   elles boi**v**e~~nt~~   [bwav]

You may wish to point out that the expression «**Les goûts et les couleurs**» is a French idiomatic expression: "People have different tastes."

❿ Les goûts et les couleurs *(Tastes and colors).* Donnez des précisions en utilisant *(by using)* les expressions de quantité entre parenthèses.

> **Modèles:** Nous buvons du vin. (peu) Nous aimons les fruits. (beaucoup)
> **Nous buvons peu de vin.** **Nous aimons beaucoup les fruits.**

1. Ma sœur boit de l'orangina. (trop)
2. Elle aime l'orangina. (beaucoup)
3. Nos parents prennent du café. (un peu)
4. Vous avez de la salade? (assez)
5. Jean n'aime pas le vin. (beaucoup)
6. Il boit de l'eau. (peu)
7. J'aime le poisson. (assez bien)
8. Du vin blanc, s'il vous plaît. (un verre)
9. Marie désire des hors-d'œuvre. (quelques)
10. Je voudrais de la viande et du vin. (quatre tranches / une bouteille)

⓫ Dans ma famille. Décrivez les habitudes de votre famille.

> **Modèles:** **Nous mangeons beaucoup de glace.**
> **Ma sœur boit très peu de lait.**

Do in pairs. Follow with a stand-up drill in which each student gives one true example.

mes parents		trop	épinards
ma sœur		beaucoup	fruits
mon frère	manger	assez	limonade
je	boire	peu	lait
nous		très peu	glace
		jamais	salade
			poisson
			eau
			chocolat chaud
			pommes de terre

⓬ Sur le campus. Utilisez une expression de quantité pour répondre à chaque question.

> **Modèle:** Les étudiants ont-ils du temps libre?
> **Ils ont très peu de temps libre.**

Poll students after doing Ex. 12: **Combien ont des amis qui boivent du thé?**, etc.

1. Avez-vous des amis à l'université?
2. Est-ce que les étudiants de votre université boivent de la bière?
3. Aiment-ils le coca light?
4. Est-ce que vos amis boivent du thé?
5. Vos amis mangent-ils du fromage?
6. Les étudiants mangent de la pizza, n'est-ce pas?
7. Les étudiants ont-ils des devoirs?

13 **L'appétit vient en mangeant** *(Eating whets the appetite).* Complétez les paragraphes avec **le, la, l', les, du, de la, de l', des, de** et **d'**.

1. Françoise est au restaurant. Elle va manger _____ hors-d'œuvre, _____ poisson, _____ viande, _____ salade, un peu _____ fromage et beaucoup _____ glace. Elle va boire _____ vin blanc avec _____ poisson et _____ vin rouge avec _____ viande et _____ fromage. Mais elle ne va pas manger _____ soupe parce qu'elle n'aime pas _____ soupe.

2. Monsieur et Madame Blanc ne boivent jamais _____ café. Ils détestent _____ café mais ils aiment beaucoup _____ thé. Quelquefois ils boivent _____ vin, mais jamais beaucoup. Leurs enfants adorent _____ orangina et _____ coca-cola classique. Mais il n'y a jamais _____ orangina ou _____ coca chez eux. Les parents pensent que _____ coca et _____ orangina ne sont pas bons pour les jeunes enfants. Alors leurs enfants boivent _____ lait ou _____ eau.

NOTE CULTURELLE
Les Québécois disent «déjeuner» pour **petit déjeuner,** «dîner» pour **déjeuner** et «souper» pour **dîner.**

Read these menus to your students and have them guess the meanings of the unfamiliar words: for instance, **canneberge** *(cranberry),* **sirop d'érable** *(maple syrup).*

Le petit déjeuner à Paris

du pain
un croissant
du beurre
de la confiture
du café au lait
du thé
du chocolat chaud

Le petit déjeuner à Québec

du jus de fruits (orange, pomme, canneberge)
des céréales (froides ou chaudes)
un œuf
du jambon ou du bacon
du pain grillé
des crêpes
du beurre
de la confiture
du sirop d'érable
du café
du thé
du lait
du chocolat chaud

Entre amis

Tu prends le petit déjeuner d'habitude?

Use the breakfast menu on the previous page, if possible.

1. Find out if your partner usually has breakfast.
2. Find out if s/he had breakfast this morning.
3. If so, find out what s/he ate.
4. Ask what s/he drank.

3 Expressing an Opinion

NOTE CULTURELLE
Le croque-monsieur *(open-faced toasted ham and cheese sandwich):* Un des choix les plus populaires dans les cafés et les bistros de France. C'est une tranche de pain au jambon et au fromage qu'on fait griller.

Miam°, je trouve ce croque-monsieur délicieux!   *Yum*
Qu'en penses-tu°, René?   *What's your opinion?*
    Je suis d'accord avec toi. Je le trouve très bon.°   *I think it's very good.*

Comment trouves-tu ces épinards?
    Ils sont bons. Je les aime bien.

Que penses-tu de la pizza aux anchois°?   *anchovies*
    Berk°, je la trouve affreuse°.   *Yuck / awful*

▶ **Et vous?**   Que pensez-vous du thé au citron? Est-il ... délicieux? bon? affreux?
Que pensez-vous des croissants français? Sont-ils ... délicieux? bons? affreux?
Que pensez-vous de la glace au chocolat? Est-elle ... délicieuse? bonne? affreuse?
Que pensez-vous des soupes froides? Sont-elles ... délicieuses? bonnes? affreuses?

F. Les pronoms objets directs *le, la, les*

J'aime beaucoup mes amis.   *I like my friends a lot.*
Je **les** aime beaucoup.   *I like them a lot.*

Mes amis étudient le français.   *My friends study French.*
Ils **l'**étudient.   *They study it.*

Ils ne regardent pas souvent la télé.   *They don't watch TV often.*
Ils ne **la** regardent pas souvent.   *They don't watch it often.*

■ A direct object pronoun replaces a noun that is the direct object of a verb (where no preposition precedes the noun). Object pronouns are placed directly in front of the verb.

Direct object pronouns	examples of nouns	examples of pronouns
le	Je déteste **le fromage.**	Je **le** déteste.
la	Je trouve **cette pâtisserie** affreuse.	Je **la** trouve affreuse.
l'	Je n'aime pas **la bière.**	Je ne **l'**aime pas.
les	J'adore **les croque-monsieur.**	Je **les** adore.

NB: Use **l'** in place of **le** or **la** if the following word begins with a vowel sound.

Other direct object pronouns will be studied in Chapter 10.

14 **Qu'en penses-tu?** *(What do you think of it/of them?)* Vous êtes à une soirée avec un(e) ami(e). Donnez votre opinion des choix indiqués et demandez l'opinion de votre ami(e). Suivez les modèles.

> **MODÈLES:** hors-d'œuvre
>> **VOUS:** Que penses-tu de ces hors-d'œuvre?
>> **VOTRE AMI(E):** Je les trouve très bons. Qu'en penses-tu?
>> **VOUS:** Je suis d'accord. Ils sont délicieux.
>
>> pâtisserie
>> **VOUS:** Que penses-tu de cette pâtisserie?
>> **VOTRE AMI(E):** Je la trouve affreuse. Qu'en penses-tu?
>> **VOUS:** Je ne suis pas d'accord. Elle est excellente.

Tell students to pretend that they are official food tasters.

1. fromage	3. café	5. fruits *(m.)*	7. légumes *(m.)*	9. viande
2. bière	4. glace	6. poisson	8. croque-monsieur	10. salade

Entre amis

Que penses-tu de ... ?

1. Give your partner something to eat and drink.
2. Toast your partner.
3. Ask what s/he thinks of the food you offered.
4. Find out what s/he thinks of the drink.
5. Offer some more.

Suggestion: Remind students to use expressions such as **Je l'aime, Je le trouve ...** , etc.

Review the verb **avoir**, p. 60.

G. Quelques expressions avec *avoir*

■ A number of idiomatic expressions in French use **avoir** with a noun where English would use *to be* with an adjective.

Use **très** with **faim, soif,** etc. to express the meaning *very.*

Feelings		*Opinions/Judgments*	
j'ai faim	*I am hungry*	j'ai raison	*I am right*
j'ai soif	*I am thirsty*		*I am wise*
j'ai froid	*I am cold*	j'ai tort	*I am wrong*
j'ai chaud	*I am hot*		*I am unwise*
j'ai sommeil	*I am sleepy*		
j'ai peur	*I am afraid*		

■ **Peur, raison,** and **tort** can be used alone, but are often followed by **de** and an infinitive. **Peur** can also be followed by **de** and a noun.

Paul **a tort de** fumer.	*Paul is wrong to smoke.*
Tu **as raison d'**étudier souvent.	*You are wise to study often.*
Nous **avons peur d'**avoir une mauvaise note.	*We are afraid of getting a bad grade.*
Je **n'ai pas peur des** examens.	*I am not afraid of tests.*

■ When an infinitive is negative, both **ne** and **pas** precede it.

Il a eu tort de **ne pas étudier.** *He was wrong not to study.*

15 **Explications.** Donnez une explication ou exprimez votre opinion. Complétez les phrases suivantes avec une des expressions idiomatiques qui emploient le verbe **avoir.**

MODÈLE: Olivier ne porte pas de manteau en novembre. Il ...
Il a froid. ou **Il a tort.**

1. Je suis fatigué. J' ...
2. Ah! Quand nous pensons à une bonne pizza au fromage, nous ...
3. Christelle pense qu'on parle espagnol au Portugal. Elle ...
4. Mon frère ... des gros chiens.
5. Vous pensez que notre professeur est charmant? Ah! Vous ...
6. Nous allons boire quelque chose parce que nous ...
7. Cet après-midi je voudrais aller à la piscine. J' ...
8. C'est le mois de décembre et nous ...

16 **Si c'est comme ça** *(If that's the way it is).* Utilisez une ou deux expressions avec **avoir** pour compléter les phrases suivantes.

MODÈLE: Si on travaille beaucoup, on ...
Si on travaille beaucoup, on a faim et soif.

1. On a envie de manger quelque chose si on ...
2. Si on ne va pas aux cours, on ...
3. Si on ne porte pas de manteau en décembre, on ...
4. Si on pense que deux fois quatre font quarante-quatre, on ...
5. S'ils font leurs devoirs, les étudiants ...
6. Si on porte beaucoup de vêtements en été ...
7. Si on ne boit pas d'eau, on ...
8. Si on pense que les professeurs sont méchants, on ...

17 **À vous.** Répondez.

1. À quel(s) moment(s) de la journée avez-vous faim? Que faites-vous quand vous avez faim?
2. À quel(s) moment(s) de la journée avez-vous soif? Que faites-vous?
3. Où vont les étudiants de votre université quand ils ont soif?
4. À quel(s) moment(s) de la journée avez-vous sommeil? Que faites-vous?
5. Pendant quels cours avez-vous envie de dormir?
6. Quels vêtements portez-vous si vous avez froid?
7. Que faites-vous si vous avez chaud?
8. Avez-vous peur d'avoir une mauvaise note?
9. Avez-vous peur avant un examen? Si oui, de quels examens avez-vous peur?
10. Vos professeurs ont-ils toujours raison?

Entre amis

Un examen

1. Tell your partner that there is a test next week.
2. Find out if s/he is afraid.
3. Find out if s/he is going to study this weekend.
4. Depending on the answer, say whether you think s/he is wise or unwise.

4 Expressing a Preference

Quelle sorte° de sandwichs préfères-tu, Valérie?   *type*
  Je préfère les sandwichs au fromage.

Quelle sorte de pizzas préfères-tu?
  Je préfère les pizzas aux champignons°.   *mushrooms*

Quelle sorte de glace préfères-tu?
  Je préfère la glace à la fraise°.   *strawberry*

▶ **Et vous?**   Que préférez-vous?
          Moi, je préfère les sandwichs ...

au beurre°	*with butter*
au beurre d'arachide°	*with peanut butter*
à la confiture°	*with jam*
au fromage	
au jambon	
à la mayonnaise	
à la moutarde	
au pâté	

Point out the French
pronunciation of **pizza** [pidza].

Et je préfère les pizzas ...

au fromage
aux champignons
aux oignons
aux anchois
à l'ail°   *with garlic*

Point out that **ail** is pronounced
the same as **Aïe!** [aj].

Et je préfère la glace ...

au chocolat
à la vanille
à la fraise
au café

Review the use of **à** with the
definite article, p. 125.

Remarque   Use **à** and the definite article to specify ingredients.

une omelette **au fromage**	*a cheese omelet*
une crêpe **à la confiture**	*a crepe with jam*
une pizza **aux champignons**	*a mushroom pizza*
un croissant **au beurre**	*a croissant made with butter*

Quel choix! Vous êtes dans une pizzeria à Paris. Demandez à la serveuse ou au serveur le choix qu'elle (il) offre. Elle (il) va répondre. Ensuite commandez quelque chose.

> **MODÈLE:** pizzas
>
> **VOUS:** Quelles sortes de pizzas avez-vous?
> **SERVEUSE/SERVEUR:** Nous avons des pizzas au jambon, aux champignons et au fromage.
> **VOUS:** Je voudrais une pizza au fromage et au jambon, s'il vous plaît.

1. sandwichs 3. pizzas 5. crêpes
2. omelettes 4. glaces 6. croissants

19 **Mes préférences.** Écrivez trois petits paragraphes pour décrire ...

1. les choses que vous aimez beaucoup.
2. les choses que vous mangez si vous avez très faim.
3. les choses que vous ne mangez jamais.

Have students guess each other's choices.

H. Les verbes comme *préférer*

Vous préférez la glace ou la pâtisserie?	*Do you prefer ice cream or pastry?*
Je préfère la glace.	*I prefer ice cream.*
Espérez-vous aller en France un jour?	*Do you hope to go to France sometime?*
Oui, et **j'espère** aller au Canada aussi.	*Yes, and I hope to go to Canada also.*
Répétez, s'il vous plaît.	*Repeat, please.*
Les étudiants **répètent** après leur professeur.	*The students repeat after their teacher.*

> **VOCABULAIRE À RETENIR**
>
> **préférer** *to prefer*
> **espérer** *to hope*
> **répéter** *to repeat*
> **exagérer** *to exaggerate*

■ The verbs **préférer** *(to prefer)*, **espérer** *(to hope)*, **répéter** *(to repeat; to practice)*, and **exagérer** *(to exaggerate)* are all conjugated as regular **-er** verbs except that before a silent ending (as in the present tense of the **je, tu, il/elle/on,** and **ils/elles** forms), the **-é-** before the ending becomes **-è-.**

> **Préférer** usually is followed by **le, la, les,** when used with a noun.

préférer *(to prefer)*			
silent endings		pronounced endings	
je	**préfère**	nous	**préférons**
tu	**préfères**	vous	**préférez**
il/elle/on	**préfère**		
ils/elles	**préfèrent**		
passé composé: j'**ai préféré**			

20 **Vos amis et vous.** Interviewez une autre personne d'après le modèle.

MODÈLE: la truite ou les anchois

> **VOUS:** **Est-ce que vos amis préfèrent la truite ou les anchois?**
> **VOTRE PARTENAIRE:** **Ils préfèrent la truite.**
> **VOUS:** **Et vous, qu'est-ce que vous préférez?**
> **VOTRE PARTENAIRE:** **Moi, je préfère les anchois.**
> **VOUS:** **Berk!**

Have students report back to their partners as many of their partners' answers as they can remember. Then have them prepare a list of the items they agree on: **Nous préférons ...**

1. le samedi soir ou le lundi matin
2. faire la vaisselle ou faire la cuisine
3. New York ou Los Angeles
4. la politique ou les mathématiques
5. partir en vacances ou travailler
6. étudier ou jouer au tennis
7. le cinéma ou le théâtre
8. le petit déjeuner ou le dîner
9. voyager ou rester à la maison
10. les sandwichs ou les omelettes
11. le coca ou le coca light
12. apprendre les mathématiques ou apprendre le français
13. regarder la télévision ou écouter la radio

21 **Microconversation: Vous déjeunez au restaurant.** Qu'est-ce qu'il y a à à manger et à boire? Il y a toujours un choix. Vous préférez autre chose, mais il faut choisir *(you have to choose)*. Suivez *(follow)* le modèle.

Review the choices on p. 215.

MODÈLE: le fromage

> **VOUS:** **Qu'est-ce que vous avez comme fromage?**
> **SERVEUR:** **Nous avons du brie et du camembert.**
> **VOUS:** **Je préfère le chèvre. Vous n'avez pas de chèvre?**
> **SERVEUR:** **Je regrette, mais le brie et le camembert sont très bons.**
> **VOUS:** **Très bien, je vais prendre du brie, s'il vous plaît.**
>
> *(Un peu plus tard)*
>
> **SERVEUR:** **Comment trouvez-vous le brie?**
> **VOUS:** **Je pense qu'il est excellent!**

1. les hors-d'œuvre   2. la viande   3. les légumes
4. le fromage   5. les desserts

Entre amis

Au snack-bar

1. Find out if your partner is hungry. (S/he is.)
2. Find out if s/he likes sandwiches, pizza, ice cream, etc.
3. Find out what kind of sandwich, etc., s/he prefers.
4. Tell your partner what you are going to order.

Intégration  www

Révision

If students do this in writing,
they can then try to guess the
items on their partner's list.

A À la carte

1. Nommez trois sortes de pizzas.
2. Nommez trois sortes de sandwichs.
3. Nommez trois sortes de légumes.
4. Nommez trois sortes de plats principaux.

B À vous. Répondez.

1. Où allez-vous si vous avez faim ou soif?
2. Aimez-vous les sandwichs? Si oui, quelle sorte de sandwich préférez-vous?
3. Qu'est-ce que vous préférez comme pizza? Qu'est-ce que vos amis préfèrent?
4. Si vous allez au restaurant, qu'est-ce que vous commandez d'habitude? Qu'est-ce que vous refusez de manger?
5. Avez-vous pris le petit déjeuner ce matin? Si oui, qu'est-ce que vous avez mangé? Qu'est-ce que vous avez bu?
6. Qu'est-ce que vous buvez le soir d'habitude? Qu'est-ce que vos amis boivent?
7. Qu'est-ce que vous pensez du vin de Californie? du vin de New York? du vin français?
8. Qu'est-ce que vous pensez du fromage américain? du fromage français?
9. Que pensez-vous des repas au restaurant universitaire?
10. À quel moment avez-vous sommeil? Pourquoi?
11. Qu'est-ce que vous espérez faire dans la vie?

Suggestion: Have students
do the Information Gap
activity in the Instructor's
Resource Manual.

On trouve en France beaucoup de restaurants vietnamiens ou marocains. Les propriétaires sont généralement immigrés de ces pays francophones.

Canard à l'orange = *duck in orange sauce;*
omelette norvégienne = *baked Alaska*

The difference between un menu and une carte is explained in Ch. 13.

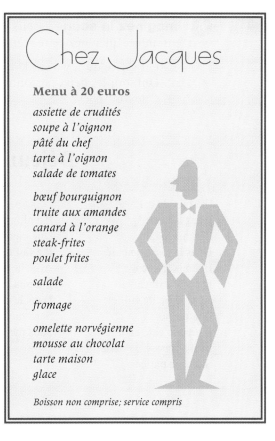

Chez Jacques

Menu à 20 euros

assiette de crudités
soupe à l'oignon
pâté du chef
tarte à l'oignon
salade de tomates

bœuf bourguignon
truite aux amandes
canard à l'orange
steak-frites
poulet frites

salade

fromage

omelette norvégienne
mousse au chocolat
tarte maison
glace

Boisson non comprise; service compris

Suggestion: Select an item that has "run out," e.g., **la truite.** When the waiter/waitress tells you (as chef) that someone has selected this item, tell him/her **il n'y a plus de ...** The waiter/waitress then has to inform the "customer."

Entre amis

Le menu, s'il vous plaît

You are a waiter (waitress). Use the menu provided and wait on two customers. When you have finished taking their order, tell the chef (the teacher) what they are having.

Pas de problème!

Preparation for the video:
1. Video worksheet in the *Cahier d'activités*
2. CD-ROM, *Module 5*

NOTE CULTURELLE
«Faire le pont» *(bridge):* Si, par exemple, on a un jour de congé *(holiday)* le mardi, on ne travaille pas le lundi. Comme cela, on a quatre jours de suite *(in a row)* sans travail: le week-end plus lundi et mardi.

Cette activité est basée sur la vidéo, *Module 5*. Répondez.

1. Quelle est la nationalité de Bruno?
2. Qu'est-ce que les quatre jeunes personnes commandent au café?
3. Quel temps fait-il?
4. Quels sont les quatre jours mentionnés par Marie-Christine pour expliquer le mot «pont»?
5. Qui a un ami qui s'appelle Noël?
6. Pourquoi est-ce qu'ils ne partent pas en voiture?
7. Comment vont-ils voyager?
8. Qui ne va pas voyager? Pourquoi pas?

A **Imaginez la scène.** Deux personnes prennent le petit déjeuner ensemble. Imaginez cette scène. Répondez aux questions suivantes.

1. Qu'est-ce qu'il y a sur la table?
2. Qui sont les deux personnes?
3. Que font-elles?
4. Que boivent-elles?
5. De quoi est-ce qu'elles parlent?
6. Quel temps fait-il?

Déjeuner du Matin

Il a mis[1] le café
Dans la tasse
Il a mis le lait
Dans la tasse de café
Il a mis le sucre
Dans le café au lait
Avec la petite cuiller[2]
Il a tourné
Il a bu le café au lait
Et il a reposé[3] la tasse
Sans me parler

Il a allumé[4]
Une cigarette
Il a fait des ronds[5]
Avec la fumée
Il a mis les cendres[6]
Dans le cendrier[7]
Sans me parler
Sans me regarder

Il s'est levé
Il a mis
Son chapeau sur sa tête[8]
Il a mis
Son manteau de pluie[9]
Parce qu'il pleuvait[10]
Et il est parti
Sous la pluie
Sans une parole[11]
Sans me regarder
Et moi j'ai pris
Ma tête dans ma main[12]
Et j'ai pleuré.

Jacques Prévert

---

1. *He put* 2. *spoon* 3. *he set down* 4. *He lit* 5. *rings* 6. *ashes* 7. *ashtray* 8. *head*
9. *rain* 10. *it was raining* 11. *a word* 12. *hand*

B **Questions.** Répondez.

1. Où sont ces personnes?
2. Qui sont les deux personnes? (Imaginez)
3. Quels problèmes y a-t-il? (Imaginez)
4. Est-ce que ce poème est triste? Expliquez votre réponse.

Be prepared with props: a cup, a spoon, a cigarette and ashtray, etc.

C **Jouez cette scène.** Faites tous les gestes nécessaires et présentez le poème *Déjeuner du Matin* sans parler.

A **Étude du vocabulaire.** Étudiez les phrases suivantes et choisissez les mots anglais qui correspondent aux mots français en caractères gras: *not including, in force, until, way, leisure activities, valid.*

1. Cette carte visa est **valable?** Oui, **jusqu'au** mois de juillet.
2. Les **loisirs** comprennent les promenades, les jeux de cartes, etc.
3. Jean-François joue au tennis d'une **façon** bizarre.
4. C'est le prix **hors**-taxe ou est-ce que les taxes sont comprises?
5. La nouvelle loi entre **en vigueur** le premier janvier.

B **Un coup d'œil sur la lecture.** Lisez rapidement la publicité et faites une liste des avantages du Week-end Privilège.

The *Entre amis* web site contains a link to the Hôtel Royal, including up-to-date information concerning special offers.

C **Vrai ou faux?** Décidez si les phrases suivantes sont vraies ou fausses d'après la lecture. Si une phrase est fausse, corrigez-la.

1. Cette offre comprend une nuit à l'hôtel et deux repas.
2. Il faut payer le double si deux personnes restent dans une chambre.
3. L'hôtel Royal est un hôtel de luxe.
4. Si on est seul, cette offre n'est pas valable.
5. Le Week-end Privilège comprend deux nuits à l'hôtel.
6. En novembre le prix change.
7. Au dîner, le vin est compris dans le repas.

Week-End Privilège à Deauville

La meilleure façon de savourer un Week-End, c'est de commencer par se faire inviter à dîner.

Pour 160 €, votre **Week-End Privilège** comprend : Une nuit en chambre tradition, les petits déjeuners continentaux, la revue-spectacle «Hello Deauville» du Casino de Deauville, l'accès à tout un ensemble d'activités sportives et de loisirs et **un dîner**** **pour 2 personnes offert au restaurant "Côté Royal".**

LUCIEN BARRIÈRE

Hôtel Royal ★★★★

Réservations au 02 31 98 66 93

*Prix par personne en chambre double.
Offre exceptionnelle valable jusqu'au 31 octobre, non cumulable avec d'autres offres en vigueur.
** Dîner offert sur la base du menu "Côté Royal" hors boissons.

You may wish to point out the **petit déjeuner à Paris,** p. 225.

D **Discussion.** Répondez.

1. En quoi consiste un petit déjeuner continental? Faites une liste.
2. Cherchez Deauville dans une encyclopédie. Expliquez son intérêt touristique.
3. Est-ce que cette offre est vraiment exceptionnelle? Expliquez votre réponse.

VOCABULAIRE ACTIF

Boissons
un apéritif *before-dinner drink*
du beaujolais *Beaujolais*
du bordeaux *Bordeaux*

Hors-d'œuvre ou soupe
des crudités *(f. pl.) raw vegetables*
un hors-d'œuvre *appetizer*
du pâté *pâté (meat spread)*

de la salade de tomates *tomato salad*
de la soupe *soup*
de la soupe aux légumes *vegetable soup*

Viandes
du bœuf *beef*
du jambon *ham*

du poulet *chicken*
du porc *pork*
de la viande *meat*

Poissons
des anchois *(m. pl.) anchovies*
du saumon *salmon*
de la truite *trout*

Légumes

de l'ail *(m.) garlic*
du brocoli *broccoli*
des épinards *(m. pl.) spinach*
des frites *(f. pl.) French fries*
des haricots verts *(m. pl.) green beans*
un légume *vegetable*
un oignon *onion*
des petits pois *(m. pl.) peas*
une pomme de terre *potato*
du riz *rice*

Fromages

du brie *Brie*
du camembert *Camembert*
du chèvre *goat cheese*
de l'emmental *(m.) Swiss cheese*

D'autres choses à manger

du beurre *butter*
du beurre d'arachide *peanut butter*
des céréales *(f. pl.) cereal*
des champignons *(m.) mushrooms*
de la confiture *jam*
un croissant *croissant*
un croque-monsieur *open-faced toasted ham and cheese sandwich*
de la mayonnaise *mayonnaise*
de la moutarde *mustard*
un œuf *egg*
une omelette *omelet*
du pain *bread*
du pain grillé *toast*
de la salade *salad*
un sandwich *sandwich*
une tomate *tomato*

Desserts

un bonbon *candy*
une crêpe *crepe, French pancake*
un dessert *dessert*
des fraises *(f.) strawberries*

un fruit *fruit*
du gâteau *cake*
de la glace (à la vanille) *(vanilla) ice cream*
des pâtisseries *(f.) pastries*
une pomme *apple*
de la tarte *pie*

Quantités et mesures

une assiette *plate*
une boîte *box; can*
une bouteille *bottle*
une douzaine *dozen*
un kilo *kilogram*
un morceau *piece*
une tranche *slice*

D'autres noms

l'addition *(f.) (restaurant) bill, check*
un choix *choice*
le déjeuner *lunch*
un garçon *waiter; boy*
le petit déjeuner *breakfast*
le plat principal *main course, main dish*
un repas *meal*
un serveur *waiter*
une serveuse *waitress*
le théâtre *theater*

Adjectifs

affreux (affreuse) *horrible*
délicieux (délicieuse) *delicious*
quelques *a few; some*

Verbes

apporter *to bring*
apprendre *to learn; to teach*
avoir chaud *to be hot*
avoir faim *to be hungry*
avoir froid *to be cold*
avoir peur *to be afraid*

avoir raison *to be right; to be wise*
avoir soif *to be thirsty*
avoir sommeil *to be sleepy*
avoir tort *to be wrong; to be unwise*
boire *to drink*
commander *to order*
comprendre *to understand*
espérer *to hope*
penser *to think*
préférer *to prefer*
prendre *to take; to eat, to drink*
répéter *to repeat; to practice*

Adverbes

naturellement *naturally*
peu (de) *little; few*
plus (ne ... plus) *no more; no longer*

Expressions utiles

à propos de *regarding, on the subject of*
au contraire *on the contrary*
Berk! *Yuck! Awful!*
bien sûr *of course*
Encore à boire (manger)? *More to drink (eat)?*
Encore de ... ? *More ... ?*
Je n'insiste pas. *I won't insist.*
je regrette *I'm sorry*
Le service est compris. *The tip is included.*
Miam! *Yum!*
Quelle(s) sorte(s) de ... ? *What kind(s) of ... ?*
Qu'en penses-tu? *What do you think of it (of them)?*
Qu'est-ce que vous avez comme ... ? *What do you have for (in the way of) ... ?*
sans façon *honestly; no kidding*
si vous insistez *if you insist*

9 Où est-ce qu'on l'achète?

Buts communicatifs
Finding out where things are sold
Describing an illness or injury
Making a purchase

Structures utiles
Les verbes en **-re**
Depuis
Le verbe **acheter**
Le pronom relatif

Culture
La pharmacie
Le tabac
Les petits magasins
On achète des fleurs.

Coup d'envoi

Prise de contact   Les achats

Où est-ce qu'on achète° des journaux?   *buy*
    On peut° aller ...   *you can*
        au bureau de tabac.
        à la gare.
        au kiosque°.   *newsstand*
Où est-ce qu'on achète des cadeaux°?   *gifts*
    On peut aller ...
        chez un fleuriste°.   *florist's shop*
        dans une boutique.
        dans un grand magasin°.   *department store*
        au marché aux puces°.   *flea market*
Où est-ce qu'on achète quelque chose à manger?
    On peut aller ...
        au marché°.   *(open-air) market*
        au supermarché.
        à l'épicerie.

▶ **Et vous?**   Qu'est-ce que vous voulez acheter?
             Où allez-vous faire cet achat°?   *purchase*

GALERIES Lafayette

DEPUIS 1893
LES BOUTIQUES DU CHÂTEAU

THE DEPARTMENT STORE CAPITAL OF FASHION.
LE GRAND MAGASIN CAPITALE DE LA MODE

À la pharmacie

Joseph Smith est un touriste. Il désire acheter un journal américain et il pense qu'on achète les journaux à la pharmacie. Mais en France on n'y vend pas de journaux.

JOSEPH SMITH:	Bonjour, Monsieur. Vous avez le *Herald Tribune?*
PHARMACIEN:	Comment? Qu'est-ce que vous dites?° — *What are you saying?*
JOSEPH SMITH:	Je voudrais acheter le *Herald Tribune.*
PHARMACIEN:	Qu'est-ce que c'est?
JOSEPH SMITH:	C'est un journal.
PHARMACIEN:	Mais on ne vend° pas de journaux ici, Monsieur. — *sell*
JOSEPH SMITH:	Vous n'en° avez pas? — *any*
PHARMACIEN:	Non, Monsieur. C'est une pharmacie. Nous vendons seulement des médicaments°. — *medicine*
JOSEPH SMITH:	Mais aux États-Unis on achète des journaux à la pharmacie.
PHARMACIEN:	Désolé°, Monsieur, mais nous sommes en France. — *Sorry*
JOSEPH SMITH:	Pouvez-vous me dire° où on peut trouver des journaux, s'il vous plaît? — *Can you tell me*
PHARMACIEN:	Ça dépend°. Si vous cherchez un journal d'un autre pays, il faut aller au bureau de tabac qui est dans la rue° de la Gare. — *depends* / *street*
JOSEPH SMITH:	Merci, Monsieur. Vous êtes très aimable°. — *kind*

▶ **Jouez ces rôles.**   Répétez la conversation avec votre partenaire. Utilisez le nom de votre journal préféré.

📼 This gesture is used in the video, *Modules 1 & 4.*

Il y a un geste

Désolé(e).   When saying **désolé(e)**, the shoulders are hunched and the upturned palms are often raised. Sarcasm is added to the gesture by also pursing one's lips and raising one's eyebrows.

Pourquoi le pharmacien ne vend-il pas de journal à Monsieur Smith?

a. Parce que Monsieur Smith est américain.
b. Parce que le pharmacien ne comprend pas Monsieur Smith quand il parle français.
c. Parce qu'on vend les journaux dans un magasin différent.

Quel est le meilleur cadeau si on est invité à dîner dans une famille française?

a. une boîte de bonbons
b. une bouteille de vin
c. un bouquet de fleurs

La pharmacie

Pharmacists in France don't sell magazines, newspapers, candy, drinks, or greeting cards. They will fill a prescription and are much less reticent than North American pharmacists to suggest treatments for nonserious illnesses, including a cold, a sore throat, and a headache. In this respect French pharmacies are a convenient and helpful solution for travelers who become ill.

Le tabac

One can buy magazines, newspapers, and postcards at the tobacco shop. Among the most popular English language publications available in France are the *International Herald Tribune* and the international edition of *Time* magazine. Since **le bureau de tabac** is under state license, one can also purchase stamps and cigarettes. Smoking is more widespread in France than in North America. While there have been some efforts to suggest that smoking is bad for your health, the state monopoly on the sale of tobacco has meant that, until recently, little was done to restrict the purchase or the use of cigarettes. However, for several years smoking has been confined to specific areas in public places. Fines can be levied on those who refuse to obey.

Use the video, *Modules 7,* **Les boutiques et les petits magasins,** and *11,* **Le tabac,** to help set the scene.

Les petits magasins

Although supermarkets (**supermarchés**) and even larger, all-in-one **hypermarchés** are found in every French city, the tourist in France will readily discover a variety of shops that specialize in one type of food. **La boulangerie** *(bakery),* **la pâtisserie** *(pastry shop),* **la boucherie** *(butcher),* **la charcuterie** *(pork butcher, delicatessen),* and **l'épicerie** *(grocery store)* are found in most neighborhoods. Not only, for example, do the French buy fresh bread daily, they will also go out of their way and pay a bit more, if necessary, to get bread that they consider more tasty. The French often use the possessive adjective to refer to **mon boulanger** *(my baker),* a phenomenon that is very rare or nonexistent in North America.

On achète des fleurs

Flower shops play an important role in French culture. More than any other gift, flowers are the number one choice when one is invited to dinner. Unless you plan on giving a dozen, choose an uneven **(impair)** number of flowers. Various reasons are given for the custom of offering three, five, or seven flowers rather than an even number. These include the implication that the donor has carefully selected them or that they may be more attractively arranged.

Une réponse homéopathique
...à la décalcification.

Ceci est un médicament. LHF: 4 rue Rabelais - 92600 Asnières

Laboratoires Homéopathiques de France

▶ **À vous.** Entrez dans une pharmacie et essayez d'acheter *(try to buy)* un magazine—*Time, Paris Match, Elle,* etc. Répondez au pharmacien.

PHARMACIEN:	Bonjour, Monsieur (Madame/Mademoiselle).
VOUS:	_____
PHARMACIEN:	Comment? Qu'est-ce que vous dites?
VOUS:	_____
PHARMACIEN:	Mais on ne vend pas de magazines ici.
VOUS:	_____

Entre amis

Au tabac

Your partner will take the role of the proprietor of a tobacco shop.

1. Ask if s/he has a certain newspaper or magazine.
2. S/he will say s/he doesn't.
3. Ask if s/he has bread, milk, wine, etc.
4. S/he will say s/he is sorry, but s/he doesn't.
5. Find out where you can find the things you are looking for.
6. Get directions.

Prononciation

Use the Student Audio to help practice pronunciation.

Le son [R]

■ The most common consonant sound in French is [R]. While there are acceptable variations of this sound, [R] is normally a friction-like sound made in roughly the same area of the mouth as [g] and [k]. Keeping the tongue tip behind the lower teeth, the friction sound is made when the back of the tongue comes close to the back part of the mouth (pharynx). Use the word **berk!** to practice several times. It might also be helpful to use the following process: (1) say "ahhh ... ," (2) change "ahhh ... " to "ahrrr ... " by beginning to gargle as you say "ahhh ... ," (3) add [g] at the beginning and say **gare** several times, (4) say **garçon.** Then practice the following words.

- pou**r**, su**r**, bonjou**r**, bonsoi**r**
- ga**r**çon, me**r**ci, pa**r**lez
- **r**usse, **r**ien, **R**obert, **r**ouge
- t**r**ès, t**r**ois, c**r**ois, d**r**oit, f**r**ère, éc**r**ire
- vot**r**e, quat**r**e, not**r**e, prop**r**e, septemb**r**e

The poem **Il pleure dans mon cœur** at the end of this chapter will provide further practice for the [R].

Buts
communicatifs

1 Finding Out Where Things Are Sold

Qu'est-ce qu'on vend à la pharmacie?
On y vend ...
des médicaments.
des cachets d'aspirine°.   *aspirin tablets*
des pastilles°.   *lozenges*
du dentifrice°   *toothpaste*
des pilules°.   *pills*
du savon°.   *soap*
Qu'est-ce qu'on vend au bureau de tabac?
On y vend ...
du tabac°.   *tobacco*
un paquet° de cigarettes.   *pack*
des timbres°.   *stamps*
des télécartes.
des journaux.
des magazines.
des cartes postales.

Contrary to the general rule requiring a pronounced final **-c** (**avec, chic, Luc, Marc,** etc.), **tabac** has a silent final **-c.**

Point out that this is true for **blanc** & **franc** as well.

A. Les verbes en -*re*

J'**attends** mon amie avec impatience.	*I'm anxiously waiting for my friend.*
Entendez-vous son train?	*Do you hear her train?*
Elle **a répondu** «oui» à mon invitation.	*She responded "yes" to my invitation.*
Elle aime **rendre visite** à ses amis.	*She likes to visit her friends.*
La voilà. Elle **descend** du train.	*There she is. She's getting off the train.*
J'espère qu'elle n'**a** pas **perdu** sa valise.	*I hope she hasn't lost her suitcase.*

<table>
<tr><th colspan="6" style="text-align:center">vendre (to sell)</th></tr>
<tr><td>je</td><td>vend</td><td>s</td><td>nous</td><td>vend</td><td>ons</td></tr>
<tr><td>tu</td><td>vend</td><td>s</td><td>vous</td><td>vend</td><td>ez</td></tr>
<tr><td>il/elle/on</td><td>vend</td><td></td><td>ils/elles</td><td>vend</td><td>ent</td></tr>
<tr><td colspan="6" style="text-align:center">passé composé: j'ai vendu</td></tr>
</table>

> Be careful to distinguish between the endings for **-re** verbs and those of **-er** verbs, p. 36.

■ A number of frequently used verbs are conjugated like **vendre**.

VOCABULAIRE

> Be careful to avoid confusing **attendre** and **entendre**. Review the nasal vowels on p. 92. **Entendre** begins with a nasal vowel.

Quelques verbes réguliers en -*re*

attendre (un ami)	*to wait (for a friend)*
descendre	*to go down; to get out of*
entendre (un bruit)	*to hear (a noise)*
perdre (une valise)	*to lose (a suitcase)*
rendre (les devoirs)	*to give back (homework)*
rendre visite à quelqu'un	*to visit someone*
répondre (à une question)	*to answer (a question)*

> The verb **visiter** is normally reserved for use with *places*. **Rendre visite à** is used with *persons*.

■ The singular (**je, tu, il/elle/on**) forms of each of these verbs are pronounced alike.

je perds	tu perds	il perd	[pɛR]
je rends	tu rends	elle rend	[Rɑ̃]

■ There is no ending added to the stem in the **il/elle/on** forms of regular **-re** verbs. In inversion of the **il/elle/on** form, the **-d** is pronounced [t].

	vend**ons** [vɑ̃dɔ̃]	vend**ent** [vɑ̃d]	
But:	vend-on [vɑ̃tɔ̃]	vend-elle [vɑ̃tɛl]	

■ Past participles of regular **-re** verbs are formed by adding **-u** to the present tense verb stem.

vend**u**   perd**u**   répond**u**

■ **Rendre visite** and **répondre** are used with the preposition **à** before an object.

J'**ai rendu visite à** mon frère.   *I visited my brother.*
Anne **répond** toujours **aux**   *Anne always answers the teacher's*
questions du professeur.   *questions.*

■ **Attendre** does not use a preposition before an object.

J'**attends** mes amis.   *I am waiting for my friends.*

■ In the expressions **perdre patience** and **perdre courage** the article or possessive adjective is omitted.

    Le professeur a **perdu patience** avec moi.
But: J'ai **perdu** *mes* devoirs.

1 **Mes professeurs et moi.** Indiquez si *oui* ou *non* vos professeurs font les choses suivantes. Et vous, est-ce que vous les faites?

Modèle: perdre des livres
    Mes professeurs ne perdent jamais de livres, mais moi, je perds quelquefois des livres.

1. perdre patience
2. attendre les vacances avec impatience
3. répondre à beaucoup de questions
4. rendre visite à des amis
5. vendre des livres

2 **Un petit sketch: Au bureau de tabac.** Lisez ou jouez le sketch suivant et répondez ensuite aux questions.

M. SMITH:	Madame, est-ce que vous avez le *Herald Tribune?*
LA MARCHANDE:	Non, Monsieur. Je n'ai plus de journaux américains.
M. SMITH:	Où est-ce que je peux acheter un journal américain, s'il vous plaît?
LA MARCHANDE:	Il faut aller à la gare.
M. SMITH:	Pourquoi à la gare?
LA MARCHANDE:	Parce qu'on vend des journaux d'autres pays à la gare.
M. SMITH:	Merci, Madame.
LA MARCHANDE:	Je vous en prie, Monsieur.

Questions

1. Quelle sorte de journal Joseph cherche-t-il?
2. La marchande vend-elle des journaux?
3. A-t-elle le *Herald Tribune?* Expliquez.
4. Où Joseph va-t-il aller? Pourquoi?
5. Où vend-on des journaux dans votre ville?
6. Quel journal préférez-vous?

3 **À vous.** Répondez.

1. Où vend-on des cigarettes dans votre pays?
2. Qu'est-ce que les pharmaciens vendent dans votre pays?
3. À qui rendez-vous visite pendant les vacances?
4. Attendez-vous les vacances avec impatience? Pourquoi (pas)?
5. Dans quelles circonstances perdez-vous patience?
6. Est-ce que vous répondez rapidement aux lettres de vos amis?
7. À qui avez-vous répondu récemment?

Entre amis

Des achats

Your partner will take the role of a pharmacist.

1. Find out if s/he has postcards, stamps, cigarettes, bread, meats, gifts, etc. (S/he doesn't.)
2. Find out where these items are sold.
3. Ask directions to one of the stores.

2 Describing an Illness or Injury

le dos

les cheveux *(m.pl.)*

un œil (les yeux)

une oreille

la tête

le nez

les dents *(f.pl.)*

une épaule

un bras

l'estomac *(m.)*

un genou

une jambe

la bouche

la gorge

une main

un pied

Jacques, qu'est-ce que tu as?° Tu as l'air° malade.
    J'ai mal au dos° depuis° hier. J'ai trop fait de gymnastique.
Oh là là! Moi aussi, mais j'ai mal aux jambes, moi!

what's the matter with you? / You look / My back hurts / since

▶ **Et vous?** Avez-vous eu la grippe cette année? Avez-vous souvent mal à la tête?
    Et les étudiants? S'ils étudient trop, ont-ils mal aux yeux?

Remarques

1. Like the word **tabac, estomac** has a silent final **-c.**
2. **Si** *(if)* becomes **s'** only before the words **il** and **ils.** Before other words beginning with vowels, it does not elide.

> **Si on** a mal à la tête, on prend des cachets d'aspirine.
> **Si elle** est malade, elle doit rester au lit.

But: **S'il** est malade, il doit rester au lit.

Review the contractions on p. 125.

3. **Avoir mal à** is used with the definite article and a part of the body to express that one has a sore hand, arm, etc.

Mon fils **a mal au bras.**	*My son's arm hurts.*
J'**ai mal à la gorge.**	*I have a sore throat.*
Avez-vous **mal aux dents?**	*Do you have a toothache?*

The masculine form of the adjective can also be used after **avoir l'air** to make agreement with the word **air.**

4. **Avoir l'air** *(to seem, appear, look)* is often followed by an adjective.

Hélène **a l'air sportive.**   Jean-Yves **a l'air fatigué.**

VOCABULAIRE

Qu'est-ce que vous avez?

Je suis malade.	*I'm sick.*
J'ai de la fièvre.	*I have a fever.*
J'ai un rhume.	*I have a cold.*
J'ai la grippe.	*I have the flu.*
J'ai le nez qui coule.	*I have a runny nose.*
Je tousse.	*I am coughing.*
J'ai mal ...	
à l'estomac.	*I have a stomachache. My stomach hurts.*
aux oreilles.	*My ears hurt.*
au pied.	*I have a sore foot. My foot hurts.*
Je suis ...	
déçu(e).	*I'm disappointed.*
déprimé(e).	*I'm depressed.*
triste.	*I'm sad.*

4 **Ça ne va pas.** Complétez les phrases suivantes.

> **MODÈLE:** Si on a de la fièvre, ...
>
> **Si on a de la fièvre, on est malade.** ou
> **Si on a de la fièvre, on a peut-être la grippe.**

To review the parts of the body, play «**Jacques a dit**» *(Simon says)*, using **Touchez ...** Alternate: Play a game of charades in which students act out particular illnesses. The rest of the class has to guess what's wrong.

1. Si on regarde trop la télévision, ...
2. Si on danse trop souvent, ...
3. Si on boit trop, ...
4. Si on a le nez qui coule, ...
5. Si on tousse beaucoup, ...
6. Si on mange trop, ...
7. Si on fume trop, ...
8. Si on écrit trop, ...
9. Si on étudie trop, ...
10. Si on fait une trop longue promenade, ...
11. Si on entend trop de bruit, ...
12. Si on mange trop de bonbons, ...
13. Si on skie mal, ...
14. Si on passe trop d'examens, ...

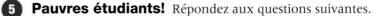

5 **Pauvres étudiants!** Répondez aux questions suivantes.

1. Que prenez-vous si vous avez la grippe?
2. Est-ce que vous restez au lit si vous êtes malade?
3. Qu'est-ce que vous faites si vous avez un rhume?
4. Quand les étudiants ont-ils mal à la tête?
5. Quand les étudiants ont-ils mal aux pieds?
6. Quand les étudiants ont-ils mal à l'estomac?
7. Fumez-vous des cigarettes? Pourquoi ou pourquoi pas?

Encourage students to use **ça dépend** to show that some of their answers may not be clear-cut.

6 **Aïe!** Utilisez les expressions suivantes pour faire des phrases, mais ajoutez une explication *(add an explanation)* avec **si** ou **parce que.**

Modèles: **Les étudiants ont mal aux yeux s'ils étudient trop.**
J'ai mal à la tête parce que je passe trop d'examens.

les étudiants je un(e) de mes ami(e)s	avoir mal	la tête le dos les bras les yeux la main les jambes les pieds les dents la gorge l'estomac le nez l'épaule le genou	si ... parce que ...

B. *Depuis*

Depuis combien de temps habites-tu ici?	*How long (for how much time) have you been living here?*
J'habite ici **depuis un an.**	*I've been living here for a year.*
Depuis quand étudies-tu le français?	*How long (since when) have you been studying French?*
J'étudie le français **depuis septembre.**	*I've been studying French since September.*

■ Use **depuis combien de temps** or **depuis quand** with the present tense to ask about something that has already begun but is *still continuing.* **Depuis combien de temps** asks for the length of time so far and **depuis quand** asks for the starting date.

> verb (present tense) + **depuis** + { length of time
starting date

Depuis combien de temps ... ?	*For how much time ... ?*
Depuis quand ... ?	*Since when ... ?*

Review expressions of time in Ch. 6, p. 159.

■ In the affirmative, the English translation of the present tense verb and **depuis** is usually *has (have) been ... ing for* a certain length of time or *since* a certain date.

Chantal **habite** à Chicago **depuis un an.**	*Chantal has been living in Chicago for a year.*
Chantal **habite** à Chicago **depuis février dernier.**	*Chantal has been living in Chicago since last February.*

■ To state that something has *not* happened for a period of time, however, the negative of the passé composé is used with **depuis.**

Je **n'ai pas été** malade **depuis** six mois.	*I haven't been sick for six months.*
Mes parents **n'ont pas écrit depuis** deux semaines.	*My parents haven't written for two weeks.*

Attention   **Depuis** is used to talk about situations that are still going on. To ask or state how much time was spent doing something that has already been *completed*, use **pendant** with the passé composé.

J'étudie depuis deux heures.	*I've been studying for two hours (and I haven't finished yet).*
But: **J'ai étudié pendant** deux heures.	*I studied for two hours (and now I'm finished).*

7 **Ils sont tous malades. Qu'est-ce qu'ils doivent faire?** D'abord utilisez les expressions entre parenthèses pour indiquer depuis combien de temps chaque personne est malade. Ensuite répondez aux questions qui suivent.

Modèle: Virginie (pieds / deux jours)
Virginie a mal aux pieds depuis deux jours.
Qui doit changer de chaussures?
Virginie doit changer de chaussures.

1. Michel (gorge / deux heures).
2. Madame Matté (dents / une semaine).
3. Anne (yeux / un mois).
4. Monsieur Monneau (fièvre / ce matin).
5. Guy (genou / trois mois).

Questions

1. Qui doit changer de lunettes?
2. Qui doit se coucher et doit rester au lit?
3. Qui ne doit plus jouer au tennis?
4. Qui ne doit plus fumer et doit prendre des pastilles?
5. Qui doit aller chez le dentiste?

8 **Comment allez-vous?** Utilisez les expressions suivantes pour faire des phrases.

> MODÈLES: **Mon frère est malade depuis trois mois.**
> **Je n'ai pas été malade depuis cinq ans.**
> **Je n'ai pas eu mal à la tête depuis cinq ans.**

		malade
je		rhume
ma sœur	(ne ... pas) avoir	fièvre depuis ...
mon frère	(ne ... pas) être	déprimé(e)
un(e) des mes ami(e)s		mal ...
		fatigué(e)

9 **Une interview.** Posez des questions logiques avec **depuis** ou **pendant**. Votre partenaire va répondre.

> MODÈLES: parler français
>> VOUS: **Depuis combien de temps parles-tu français?**
>> VOTRE PARTENAIRE: **Je parle français depuis six mois.**
>
> regarder la télé hier soir
>> VOUS: **Pendant combien de temps as-tu regardé la télé hier soir?**
>> VOTRE PARTENAIRE: **J'ai regardé la télé pendant une heure.**

1. étudier le français
2. étudier hier soir
3. habiter à l'adresse que tu as maintenant
4. écouter la radio ce matin
5. être étudiant(e) à cette université
6. faire cet exercice

Entre amis

Tu es malade depuis longtemps?

1. Greet your partner and inquire about his/her health. (S/he is sick.)
2. Find out what the matter is.
3. Find out how long s/he has been sick.
4. Suggest a remedy.

3 Making a Purchase

Où vas-tu Alain?
> Je vais faire des achats.

De quoi as-tu besoin?°   *What do you need?*
> J'ai besoin de toutes sortes de choses.°   *I need all kinds of things.*
> J'ai besoin de pain, de bœuf, de saucisses°,   *sausages*
>   de légumes et de fruits.
> J'ai besoin d'un livre et de fleurs° aussi.   *flowers*
> Je vais acheter° ...   *to buy*
>> du pain à la boulangerie,
>> du bœuf à la boucherie,
>> des saucisses à la charcuterie°,   *delicatessen*
>> des légumes et des fruits à l'épicerie,
>> des fleurs chez un fleuriste
>> et un livre à la librairie.
> Alors, j'ai besoin d'argent° pour payer   *money*
>   tout cela.

▶ Et vous? De quoi avez-vous besoin?

NOTE CULTURELLE
À la boucherie, on vend de la viande de bœuf et on vend aussi du mouton. On y trouve des steaks, des rôtis *(roasts)*, etc. À la charcuterie, on vend de la viande de porc et on vend aussi du poulet et du lapin *(rabbit)*. On y trouve du jambon, des pâtés variés, du bacon, des saucisses, du saucisson *(salami)*, etc.

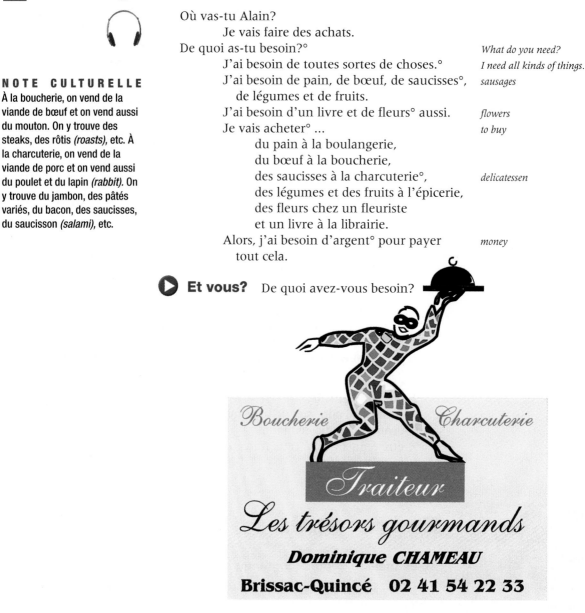

Boucherie   Charcuterie

Traiteur

Les trésors gourmands

Dominique CHAMEAU

Brissac-Quincé   02 41 54 22 33

Remarques

1. **Avoir besoin** *(to need)* works much like **avoir envie.** It is used with **de** and an infinitive or a noun. If **avoir besoin** is used with a noun, the definite article is usually omitted.

   J'**ai besoin d'**étudier.   *I need to study.*
   Nous **avons besoin de** légumes et   *We need vegetables and mineral*
   d'eau minérale.   *water.*

2. Use **un (une)** with **avoir besoin d'** to say that *one* item is needed.

   Vous **avez besoin d'une** feuille   *You need a sheet of paper.*
   de papier.

Tu as besoin
d'autre chose?

10 **Où faut-il aller?** Où est-ce qu'on trouve les produits suivants? Suivez *(follow)* le modèle.

MODÈLE: pâté   **Si on a besoin de pâté, il faut aller à la charcuterie.**

1. épinards
2. médicaments
3. un kilo d'oranges

4. un rôti de bœuf
5. croissants
6. fleurs

7. jambon
8. un livre
9. cigarettes

After students have worked in pairs, have a stand-up drill. Each student has to say a sentence starting with **Si ...**

Entre amis

Je viens d'arriver

You are new in town and need some information. Your partner will play the role of a neighbor.

1. Tell your neighbor that you are going shopping.
2. Tell him/her what you need.
3. Ask where to buy it.
4. Be sure to express your gratitude for your neighbor's help.

C. Le verbe *acheter*

Mon père va **acheter** une autre voiture.
Nous **achetons** nos livres à la librairie.
On **achète** un journal au bureau de tabac.
J'**ai acheté** cinq kilos de pommes de terre.

Review the formation of **préférer**, p. 230.

■ As you have already learned with **préférer,** certain verbs change their spelling of the verb stem of the present tense depending on whether or not the ending is pronounced.

Vous préf**é**rez le blanc ou le rouge?   Je préf**è**re le rouge.

Rules governing mute [ə] will be presented in Ch. 15.

■ The verb **acheter** also contains a spelling change in the verb stem of the present tense. When the ending is not pronounced, the **-e-** before the **-t-** becomes **-è.**

	acheter *(to buy)*		
silent endings		pronounced endings	
j'	achète	nous	achetons
tu	achètes	vous	achetez
il/elle/on	achète		
ils/elles	achètent		

passé composé: j'**ai acheté**

11 **Nous achetons tout ça.** On fait des achats. Utilisez les expressions suivantes pour faire des phrases. Utilisez la forme négative, si vous voulez.

MODÈLES: **J'achète de la glace pour mes amis.**
Nous n'achetons jamais de cigarettes pour nos amis.

Review the possessive adjectives on p. 76.

je		glace		
nous		cigarettes		amis
le professeur		cachets d'aspirine		classe *(f.)*
mes amis	acheter	magazines		parents
ma mère		pommes	pour	professeur
mon père		timbres		famille
les étudiants		pain		moi
		bonbons		nous
		médicaments		
		fleurs		

Have students redo this exercise in the **passé composé**.

 Pourquoi y vont-ils? Demandez ce que ces personnes achètent. Votre partenaire va répondre.

MODÈLE: Je vais au bureau de tabac.

> VOUS: **Qu'est-ce que tu achètes au bureau de tabac?**
>
> VOTRE PARTENAIRE: **J'achète des timbres.**

Both **un** and **une** may be used with fleuriste.

1. Je vais à la boucherie.
2. Nous allons à la pharmacie.
3. Mon père va au supermarché.
4. Nous allons dans un grand magasin.
5. Les étudiants vont à la boulangerie.
6. Paul va à l'épicerie.
7. Ces deux femmes vont au bureau de tabac.
8. Marie va à la librairie près de l'université.
9. Je vais chez un fleuriste.

VOCABULAIRE

NOTE CULTURELLE
Depuis 2002, **l'euro** est la seule monnaie officielle de la France et de la plupart des pays de l'Union européenne. Il existe huit pièces de monnaie et sept billets, d'une pièce de 1 cent jusqu'à un billet de 500 euros.

See the *Entre amis* web site for Web search activities with links to up-to-date information concerning the euro and the European Union.

Pour payer les achats

de l'argent *(m.)*	*money*
un billet	*bill (paper money)*
la monnaie	*change; currency*
une pièce (de monnaie)	*coin*
un euro	*euro*
un dollar	*dollar*
une carte de crédit	*credit card*
un chèque	*check*
un chèque de voyage	*traveler's check*
coûter	*to cost*
payer	*to pay*

You might wish to point out that **payer** takes a direct object, even when the object is a purchase: **Nous payons nos achats** = *We pay **for** our purchases.*

Note **Payer** is often found with a spelling change. Before silent endings, the **-y-** becomes **-i-: je paie, tu paies,** etc. *But:* **nous payons, vous payez.**

13 **Un petit sketch: Au bureau de tabac de la gare.** Lisez ou jouez le sketch. Ensuite répondez aux questions.

Joseph Smith parle avec un marchand de journaux au bureau de tabac de la gare.

M. SMITH:	Vous vendez des journaux américains?
LE MARCHAND:	Ça dépend du journal.
M. SMITH:	Avez-vous le *Herald Tribune?*
LE MARCHAND:	Oui, nous l'avons.
M. SMITH:	Bien. Je vous dois combien?
LE MARCHAND:	Un euro dix.
M. SMITH:	Voilà, Monsieur.
LE MARCHAND:	C'est parfait, Monsieur. Merci.
M. SMITH:	Au revoir, Monsieur. Bonne journée.
LE MARCHAND:	Merci. Vous aussi, Monsieur.

Questions

1. Où Joseph achète-t-il son journal?
2. Quel journal demande-t-il?
3. Est-ce que le marchand a ce journal?
4. Combien coûte le journal?
5. Est-ce que Joseph l'achète?

VOCABULAIRE

Mots utiles pour faire des achats

une barquette	*small box; mini crate*
une boîte	*box; can*
un bouquet	*bouquet*
une bouteille	*bottle*
un kilo	*kilogram (2.2 pounds)*
un litre	*liter*
une livre	*pound*
un paquet	*package*

14 **Ça coûte combien?** Demandez combien coûte l'objet. Votre partenaire va donner la réponse en euros.

MODÈLE: bonbons (3€ le paquet)
VOUS: **Combien coûte un paquet de bonbons?**
VOTRE PARTENAIRE: **Les bonbons coûtent trois euros le paquet.**

> Notice the use of the *indefinite* article in the question and the *definite* article in the answer.

1. bordeaux (7€ le litre)
2. fromage Pont l'Évêque (3€ la livre)
3. fraises d'Espagne (1€ la barquette)
4. orangina (2€ la bouteille)
5. jambon de Bayonne (10€ le kilo)
6. cigarettes (3€ le paquet)
7. œufs (2€ la douzaine)
8. fleurs (8€ le bouquet)

15 **En ville.** Vous avez besoin de plusieurs *(several)* choses. Utilisez les deux listes suivantes pour trouver l'adresse et le numéro de téléphone des magasins nécessaires.

Go over this listing with students before attempting the activity.

MODÈLE: pour acheter des médicaments

Pour acheter des médicaments, l'adresse est un, place de la Laiterie. Téléphonez au zéro deux/quarante et un/quatre-vingt-sept/cinquante-huit/trente-neuf.

Review numbers on pp. 3 and 63.

Place de la Laiterie		Rue de la Gare	
1 PHARMACIE GODARD	02.41.87.58.39	1 PHOTO PLUS	02.41.87.67.31
4 CHEVALIER, Yves		2 MOD COIFFURE	02.41.88.00.03
bureau de tabac	02.41.87.48.37	3 CRÉDIT AGRICOLE	02.41.88.12.56
5 BANQUE NATIONALE DE PARIS	02.41.88.00.23	4 CATFISH	
7 ARMORIC POISSONNERIE	02.41.88.39.84	restaurant grill	02.41.87.14.87
9 BOUCHERIE DU RONCERAY	02.41.87.57.28	5 PHARMACIE DE LA GARE	02.41.87.66.67
11 FAÏENCERIE DU RONCERAY	02.41.87.40.29	6 LE FLORENTIN	
15 SALOUD, Gérard		fleuriste	02.41.87.41.72
assurances	02.41.87.50.27	7 LE RELAIS	
18 COLIN, Jean		hôtel	02.41.88.42.51
boulangerie-pâtisserie	02.41.88.01.62	8 CINÉMA LE FRANÇAIS	02.41.87.66.66
19 VERNAUDON, Michel		9 LE PEN DUICK	
vêtements	02.41.87.01.96	restaurant	02.41.87.46.59
21 DACTYL BURO ANJOU		10 BAR BRASSERIE LE SIGNAL	02.41.87.49.41
machines bureaux	02.41.88.59.52		

1. pour acheter un kilo de bœuf
2. pour acheter un paquet de cigarettes
3. pour acheter du pain
4. pour demander à quelle heure le film va commencer
5. pour acheter un bouquet de fleurs
6. pour réserver une table pour dîner
7. pour acheter un pull ou un pantalon
8. pour acheter du saumon
9. pour acheter des euros si on a des dollars

Le restaurant Catfish se trouve dans la rue de la Gare.

16 **Une révision des nombres.** Répondez.

1. Quelle est votre adresse?
2. Quel est votre code postal?
3. Quel est votre numéro de téléphone?
4. Quel est le numéro de téléphone de votre meilleur(e) ami(e)?
5. En quelle année êtes-vous né(e)?
6. Combien de jours y a-t-il dans une année?
7. Combien de pages y a-t-il dans ce livre de français?
8. Combien de minutes y a-t-il dans une journée?
9. En quelle année Christophe Colomb est-il arrivé au Nouveau Monde?
10. Combien d'étudiants y a-t-il sur ce campus?

D. Le pronom relatif

Point out that students have already been using relative pronouns. See, for example, pp. 57 and 230. Relative pronouns will also be studied in Ch. 14.

■ Relative pronouns like *who, whom, which,* and *that* relate or tie two clauses together. They refer to a word in the first clause.

Le cadeau est sur la table. Il est pour ma sœur.	
La cadeau **qui** est sur la table est pour ma sœur	*The gift (that is) on the table is for my sister.*
Le cadeau est pour ma sœur. Je l'ai acheté ce matin.	
Le cadeau **que** j'ai acheté ce matin est pour ma sœur.	*The gift (that) I bought this morning is for my sister.*

■ The choice of the relative pronoun **qui** or **que** depends on its function as subject or object.

■ **Qui** *(who, that, which)* replaces a person or a thing that is the *subject* of a relative clause.

Une boulangerie est un magasin **qui** vend du pain.

■ **Que/qu'** *(whom, that, which)* replaces a person or a thing that is the *object* of a relative clause.

Le Monde est un journal **que** je lis avec intérêt.
Le Monde est un journal **qu'**on achète souvent.
Voilà un professeur **que** les étudiants aiment beaucoup.

■ Although the relative pronoun may be omitted in English, it is never omitted in French.

C'est le magasin **que** je préfère.   *It's the store (that) I prefer.*

FOR RECOGNITION ONLY:

The relative pronoun **dont** *(whose, of which, about which)* is normally used when the French expression would require the preposition **de.** In the following example, one needs to remember that **besoin** is used with **de.**

C'est le livre **dont** j'ai besoin.   *It's the book (that) I need.*

Identifications. Identifiez la personne ou la chose qui correspond à la description.

> **MODÈLE:** quelqu'un qui parle français depuis longtemps
> **Le professeur de français est quelqu'un qui parle français depuis longtemps.**

1. un magasin qui vend des médicaments
2. quelque chose qu'on vend à l'épicerie
3. un restaurant que vous recommandez pour sa cuisine italienne
4. un livre que vous avez déjà lu et que vous recommandez
5. quelque chose que vous mangez souvent
6. quelque chose dont on a besoin pour payer ses achats au centre commercial
7. quelqu'un qui parle français avec vous
8. une personne qui vend des fleurs
9. quelque chose qu'on achète à la librairie
10. quelque chose dont les étudiants ont besoin pour être heureux

18 **Définitions.** Décrivez les personnes ou les choses suivantes.

> **MODÈLES:** un McDo   **C'est un restaurant qui vend des Big Macs.**
> un professeur **C'est une personne qui enseigne.**
> ma mère   **C'est une personne que j'aime.**

Suggestion: Have students work in pairs to create these definitions. Then brainstorm with the class to elicit as many definitions as possible for each item.

1. un bureau de tabac
2. une pizza aux anchois
3. une pharmacienne
4. la France
5. mon professeur de français
6. un francophone
7. un supermarché

Entre amis

Vous entrez dans un bureau de tabac

Your partner takes the role of a merchant.

1. Ask if s/he has a specific English-language magazine (name it).
2. Your partner will inquire what it is.
3. Identify it. How much can you say?
4. Your partner will say s/he is sorry but that s/he doesn't have it.
5. Find out the name of the French magazines s/he has.
6. Select one and find out how much it costs.
7. Pay for it.

Intégration

Révision

If students do this in writing, they can then try to guess the items on their partner's list.

A **Des renseignements.** Préparez une liste de cinq renseignements pour des touristes qui vont en France.

MODÈLE: **Si on a besoin de pain, on peut aller à la boulangerie.**

B **À vous.** Répondez.

1. Êtes-vous souvent malade?
2. Que prenez-vous si vous avez la grippe?
3. Que faites-vous quand vous avez mal à la tête?
4. Aimez-vous les cigarettes? Fumez-vous? Si oui, depuis combien de temps? Si non, avez-vous déjà fumé? Pendant combien de temps?
5. Où faites-vous vos provisions? Qu'est-ce que vous y achetez?
6. Quelle est votre adresse? Depuis quand y habitez-vous?
7. Comment s'appelle le magasin qui vend du pain?
8. Qu'est-ce que c'est qu'une épicerie?

 Suggestion: Have students do the Information Gap activity in the Instructor's Resource Manual.

C **Je fais des achats.** En groupes de deux ou trois. Un membre du groupe fait une liste de cinq endroits différents où il va faire des achats et, pour chaque endroit, la chose qu'il va acheter. Les autres membres du groupe vont deviner *(guess)* 1. où il va faire ses achats, et 2. ce qu'il achète. Il répond seulement par oui ou par non.

MODÈLE: **Est-ce que tu achètes quelque chose à la librairie?**
Est-ce que tu achètes un livre?

Pas de problème!

Preparation for the video:
1. Video worksheet in the *Cahier d'activités*
2. CD-ROM, *Module 6*

Cette activité est basée sur la vidéo, *Module 6*. Choisissez la bonne réponse pour compléter les phrases suivantes.

1. Bruno rend visite à _____.
   (Alissa, Nogent, Noël)
2. Avec ses amis, il visite le château _____.
   (Sainte-Jeanne, Saint-Jean, Nogent)
3. Le château se trouve en _____.
   (Normandie, Picardie, Alsace)
4. Dans la salle des gardes, ils admirent _____.
   (la fenêtre, la forêt, la cheminée)
5. La maison de Noël se trouve _____ derrière la forêt.
   (à droite, à gauche, tout droit)

Lecture I

A **Étude du vocabulaire.** Étudiez les phrases suivantes et choisissez les mots anglais qui correspondent aux mots français en caractères gras: *grief, love, hate, rain, roofs, gentle, ground, heart.*

1. J'aime le son de la **pluie** qui tombe sur les **toits** des maisons.
2. L'**amour** et la **haine** sont deux émotions opposées. Quand on aime, c'est l'**amour** et quand on déteste, c'est la **haine.**
3. Le **cœur** fait circuler le sang dans les veines et les artères.
4. La **terre** noire de l'Iowa est très fertile.
5. La mort du président nous a plongés dans le **deuil.**
6. Une voix **douce** est agréable à entendre.

B **Anticipez le contenu.** Avant de lire le poème, répondez aux questions suivantes.

1. Aimez-vous la pluie?
2. Pleut-il souvent là où vous habitez?
3. Quand il pleut, êtes-vous content(e), triste ou indifférent(e)? Expliquez.

Suggestions: Have students make a list of the words that rhyme. Have them make lists of words containing the sounds [R] or [l]. Give a prize to the first student who can recite the poem from memory. Have a **Concours de prononciation** (see the Instructor's Resource Manual).

Il pleure dans mon cœur

Il pleure dans mon cœur
Comme il pleut sur la ville,
Quelle est cette langueur
Qui pénètre mon cœur?

Ô bruit doux de la pluie
Par terre et sur les toits!
Pour un cœur qui s'ennuie[1]
Ô le chant de la pluie!

Il pleure sans raison
Dans ce cœur qui s'écœure[2].
Quoi! nulle trahison[3]?
Ce deuil est sans raison.

C'est bien la pire peine[4]
De ne savoir[5] pourquoi,
Sans amour et sans haine,
Mon cœur a tant de peine.

Paul Verlaine

---

1. *is saddened*   2. *is depressed*   3. *no treason*   4. *the worst suffering*   5. *not to know*

C **Discussion.** Répondez.

1. Quelle est la réaction du poète à la pluie? Quelles expressions utilise-t-il pour exprimer cette émotion?
2. Est-ce que le poète sait pourquoi il a cette réaction à la pluie? Expliquez.

D **Familles de mots.** Essayez de deviner le sens des mots suivants.

1. pleuvoir, la pluie, pluvieux (pluvieuse)
2. aimer, l'amour, aimable, amoureux (amoureuse)
3. s'ennuyer, l'ennui, ennuyeux (ennuyeuse)
4. peiner, la peine, pénible

Lecture II

A **Étude du vocabulaire.** Étudiez les phrases suivantes et choisissez les mots anglais qui correspondent aux mots français en caractères gras: *flight, sponsoring, places, beat, billboard, sidewalks, samples, building.*

1. Nos joueurs de basket-ball espèrent **battre** leurs adversaires.
2. Un **vol** est un voyage en avion.
3. Un **immeuble** est un grand bâtiment où les gens travaillent ou habitent.
4. Les gens restent sur les **trottoirs** parce que les rues sont dangereuses.
5. Le mot **lieux** est souvent un synonyme pour le mot *endroits.*
6. Les représentants commerciaux donnent des **échantillons** pour encourager les gens à acheter leurs produits.
7. Sur le **panneau d'affichage** de la bande dessinée, on peut lire: «Le tabac tue».
8. Le **parrainage** d'une équipe de football coûte quelquefois très cher à une entreprise.

Devinez de quoi il s'agit. Lisez rapidement le titre et la première phrase de chaque article pour identifier le sujet des articles et les deux pays qu'il concerne.

Hystérie Anti-Tabac

Le Canada est en train de battre les États-Unis en matière d'hystérie anti-tabac. Le conseil municipal de Toronto—la capitale économique et financière du pays—a adopté un règlement draconien contre les fumeurs: depuis le 1er janvier 1997, le Torontois a seulement sa maison, sa voiture ou la rue pour prendre sa bouffée[1] de nicotine. La croisade contre[2] la cigarette ne date pas d'hier. La compagnie aérienne nationale Air Canada a été la première à l'interdire[3] sur les vols transatlantiques. Dans les hôtels, le principe des chambres fumeurs et non fumeurs est en vigueur. Les immeubles du gouvernement fédéral sont des zones strictement non-fumeurs. On voit, sur les trottoirs des grandes villes, les fumeurs irréductibles faire la pause cigarette avant de regagner leur bureau[4].

Les mesures du président

Principales mesures annoncées par la Maison-Blanche, pour limiter l'accès des adolescents au tabac:

- les distributeurs automatiques sont interdits dans certains lieux fréquentés par les jeunes;
- les échantillons et paquets de moins de 20 cigarettes sont interdits;
- les publicités pour le tabac sont interdites dans un rayon[5] de 500 mètres autour des établissements scolaires et des terrains de jeux;
- sauf[6] dans les lieux interdits aux moins de 18 ans, et à condition qu'elles ne soient[7] pas visibles de l'extérieur, les publicités sur les panneaux d'affichage et les lieux de vente doivent se limiter à des textes en noir et blanc;
- la publicité dans les publications dont les lecteurs sont constitués en grande partie d'adolescents (plus de 15%) doit se limiter à des textes en noir et blanc;
- le parrainage d'événements sportifs est interdit.

d'après *Le Point*

---

1. *puff*   2. *crusade against*   3. *to forbid it*   4. *go back to their office*   5. *in a radius*   6. *except*
7. *provided that they are*

Dans quel article?   Relisez les deux articles et décidez si les idées suivantes se trouvent dans l'article sur le Canada ou dans l'article sur les États-Unis.

1. On n'accepte pas d'annonces publicitaires pour les cigarettes près des écoles.
2. Certains fumeurs continuent à fumer avant d'entrer dans le bâtiment où ils travaillent.
3. Il n'y a plus de publicité en couleur pour les cigarettes dans les magazines lus par les jeunes.
4. Cette mesure stricte a été appliquée juste après Noël.
5. On ne permet plus que les entreprises qui vendent du tabac sponsorisent les matchs de tennis, de base-ball, etc.
6. Dans les endroits où vont les jeunes, on ne vend plus de cigarettes dans des machines.
7. On n'accepte plus depuis longtemps que les gens fument dans les avions s'ils font un voyage dans un autre pays.
8. Il n'est plus permis de donner des cigarettes gratuites pour encourager les individus à fumer.

D Familles de mots.   Essayez de deviner le sens des mots suivants.

1. interdire, interdit(e), une interdiction
2. vendre, la vente, un vendeur, une vendeuse
3. fumer, un fumeur, une fumeuse, la fumée
4. conseiller, le conseil, un conseiller, une conseillère
5. distribuer, un distributeur, la distribution

VOCABULAIRE ACTIF

Argent
l'argent *(m.) money*
un billet *bill (paper money)*
une carte de crédit *credit card*
un chèque *check*
un chèque de voyage *traveler's check*
un centime *centime*
un dollar *dollar*
un euro *euro*
la monnaie *change*
une pièce (de monnaie) *coin*

Adjectifs
aimable *kind; nice*
déçu(e) *disappointed*
déprimé(e) *depressed*
désolé(e) *sorry*
long (longue) *long*

Magasins
une boucherie *butcher shop*
une boutique *(gift, clothing, etc.) shop*
une charcuterie *pork butcher's; delicatessen*
un grand magasin *department store*
un kiosque *newsstand*
un marché *(open-air) market*
un marché aux puces *flea market*
une pâtisserie *pastry shop; pastry*
un supermarché *supermarket*

À la pharmacie
un cachet d'aspirine *aspirin tablet*
un dentifrice *toothpaste*
un médicament *medicine*
une pastille *lozenge*
une pilule *pill*
un savon *bar of soap*

Parties du corps
la bouche *mouth*
un bras *arm*
une dent *tooth*
le dos *back*
une épaule *shoulder*
l'estomac *(m.) stomach*
un genou *knee*
la gorge *throat*
une jambe *leg*
une main *hand*
le nez *nose*
un œil *eye*
une oreille *ear*
un pied *foot*
la tête *head*

D'autres noms

un achat *purchase*
une barquette *small box*
un billet *ticket*
un bouquet *bouquet*
un bruit *noise*
un cadeau *gift*
un code postal *zip code*
un coin *corner*
une feuille *leaf; sheet (of paper)*
une fièvre *fever*
une fleur *flower*
un(e) fleuriste *florist*
l'impatience (f.) *impatience*
un litre *liter*
une livre *pound*
un(e) marchand(e) *merchant*
le papier *paper*
un paquet *package; pack*
un rhume *a cold*
une rue *street*
une sardine *sardine*
une saucisse *sausage*
le tabac *tobacco; tobacconist's shop*
un timbre *stamp*
une valise *suitcase*

Verbes

acheter *to buy*
attendre *to wait (for)*
avoir besoin de *to need*
avoir l'air *to seem, appear, look*
avoir mal (à) *to be sore, to have a pain (in)*
coûter *to cost*
dépendre *to depend*
entendre *to hear*
payer *to pay (for)*
perdre *to lose*
perdre patience *to lose (one's) patience*
rendre *to give back*
rendre visite à quelqu'un *to visit someone*
répondre (à) *to answer*
réserver *to reserve*
tousser *to cough*
vendre *to sell*

Préposition

depuis *for; since*

Expressions utiles

avec intérêt *with interest*
Ça dépend. *That depends.*
C'est bien simple. *It's quite simple.*
De quoi avez-vous besoin? *What do you need?*
Depuis combien de temps? *For how much time?*
Depuis quand? *Since when?*
je peux *I can*
le nez qui coule *runny nose*
Oh là là! *Oh dear!*
on peut *one can*
Pouvez-vous me dire ... ? *Can you tell me ... ?*
Qu'est-ce que tu as? *What's the matter (with you)?*
Qu'est-ce que vous dites? *What are you saying?*
Vous n'en avez pas? *Don't you have any?*

escale 3
L'Afrique noire francophone

LE SAVEZ-VOUS?
Dans quels pays de l'Afrique noire parle-t-on français? Pourquoi?

Formée en majeure partie d'anciennes *(former)* colonies françaises, l'Afrique noire francophone consiste en deux grandes régions: l'Afrique occidentale, qui va de la Mauritanie au golfe de Guinée, et l'Afrique équatoriale, qui regroupe les pays du Tchad au Congo et l'ancien Congo belge (voir la carte de l'Afrique à la fin du livre). Le climat est tropical dans le nord de cette vaste région, désertique dans le centre, plus humide près de l'océan. Vers le sud, le désert fait place à la savane, puis à la forêt équatoriale.

CHRONOLOGIE

Préhistoire L'Afrique, berceau *(cradle)* de l'humanité, riche en souvenirs préhistoriques.

Ier–Xe siècles Civilisations Nok au Nigéria, Ifé au Bénin.

XIe–XIVe siècles Dans la région des fleuves Sénégal et Niger, s'établissent les empires du Ghana, du Mali, du Songhaï. L'Islam, introduit par des caravanes arabes, devient la religion dominante.

XIVe–XVe siècles Civilisations yoruba au Bénin et bantoue au royaume du Kongo.

XVe–XVIIIe siècles Explorateurs et marchands d'Europe établissent des centres de commerce le long des côtes africaines. La traite des esclaves se développe.

1659 La France fonde la ville de Saint-Louis au nord de Dakar.

1858–1958 La France s'établit en Afrique occidentale et équatoriale.

1908 La Belgique acquiert le Congo belge.

1960 Indépendance de la plupart des colonies africaines.

Sanctuaire Yoruba

Léopold Sédar Senghor

La négritude dans l'Afrique indépendante

Vers 1960, au lendemain de l'indépendance, le mouvement de la négritude prend un caractère nouveau. Ce n'est plus une protestation contre le racisme, mais la défense des anciennes traditions dans un monde qui non seulement se modernise à une vitesse vertigineuse, mais qui devient aussi de plus en plus uniforme. Le but du mouvement devient d'intégrer l'Afrique dans le monde moderne avec son commerce et son industrie sans perdre les légendes, les valeurs, la perspective unique de l'univers de l'Afrique ancienne.

Les problèmes et les contradictions engendrés par le régime colonial et l'influence européenne font place aujourd'hui en Afrique à de nouveaux défis. Comment rester africain tout en adoptant un style de vie urbain et moderne? Les femmes, silencieuses par le passé, prennent la plume et revendiquent leurs droits. Parmi celles-ci, Mariama Bâ adresse le problème que pose le concubinage pour la femme moderne; Calixthe Beyala (Grand Prix du Roman de l'Académie française en 1996 pour son roman *Les honneurs perdus*) décrit le monde cruel et insensé des bidonvilles (*shantytowns*) des grandes agglomérations africaines et l'exploitation entre Africains où la femme est plus que jamais victime de l'homme. Dans cette littérature nouvelle, un thème constant se retrouve: celui d'une lutte pour une identité qui ne se soumet à aucun pouvoir opprimant.

Poème de la négritude

Le mouvement de la négritude inspire beaucoup d'auteurs noirs. Ici Bernard Dadié, de la Côte d'Ivoire, exprime sa fierté (*pride*) d'être noir.

> *Je vous remercie mon Dieu de m'avoir créé noir,*
> *D'avoir fait de moi*
> *la somme de toutes les douleurs,*
> *mis sur ma tête,*
> *Le Monde.*
> *J'ai la livrée du Centaure*
> *Et je porte le Monde depuis le premier matin.*
>
> *Le blanc est une couleur de circonstance*
> *Le Noir, la couleur de tous les jours*
> *Et je porte le Monde depuis le premier soir.*
>
> *Je suis content*
> *de la forme de ma tête*
> *faite pour porter le Monde,*
> *satisfait de la forme de mon nez*
> *Qui doit humer tout le vent du Monde,*
> *heureux*
> *de la forme de mes jambes*
> *prêtes à courir toutes les étapes du Monde.*

Calixthe Beyala

Le français en Afrique

La colonisation a formé des liens contradictoires entre la France et l'Afrique. Dans la majorité des anciennes colonies d'Afrique, le français est la langue officielle ou la langue véhiculaire. Pour plusieurs intellectuels et hommes politiques africains, ce «décombre du régime colonial» est une source de malaise. Il faudrait, pensent-ils, s'exprimer dans la langue maternelle. Pour d'autres, comme le président du Sénégal, Abdoulaye Wade, la présence et l'universalité de la langue française, perpétuée et célébrée par l'institution de la francophonie, est un avantage commercial et politique. Le français représente un outil de modernité et une solution pratique à la communication dans les pays plurilingues de l'Afrique noire. «Je suis», écrivait Abdoulaye Wade dans *L'Express* du 13 juillet 2000, «de la génération des Africains qui ont appris l'histoire de France dans des manuels qui com-

mençaient par le fameux 'Nos ancêtres, les Gaulois'. Toutefois, la signification qui en a été donnée a été biaisée par la doctrine anticolonialiste. En effet, aucun d'entre nous, élèves, n'a un seul moment pensé qu'il descendait des Gaulois. Nous savions parfaitement que l'on nous prêtait ou donnait des manuels écrits pour les petits Français. Nous trouvions ces Gaulois, avec leurs longues barbes, laids et probablement très sales. Nos professeurs, français ou sénégalais, le savaient tout aussi bien. Ce que nous avons malgré tout apprécié, dans ces manuels contestés, c'était que la France ne faisait pas de discrimination dans la qualité de l'enseignement qu'elle nous dispensait. »

À vous!

À votre avis, la langue française représente-t-elle un avantage ou un inconvénient pour les pays de l'Afrique noire francophone?

Quelques Pays où le français est la langue officielle

REPÈRES:	LE BÉNIN	LE BURKINA	LE CONGO-BRAZZAVILLE
Nom officiel:	République du Bénin	Burkina Faso	République du Congo
Capitale:	Porto-Novo	Ouagadougou	Brazzaville
Superficie:	112.622 km²	274.200 km²	341.821 km²
Population:	4,5 millions	10,1 millions	2,8 millions

	LE CONGO-KINSHASA	LA CÔTE D'IVOIRE	LE MALI
Nom officiel:	République démocratique du Congo	République de Côte d'Ivoire	République du Mali
Capitale:	Kinshasa	Yamoussoukro	Bamako
Superficie:	2.344.885 km²	322.462 km²	1.241.231 km²
Population:	51,9 millions	20 millions	8,8 millions

La femme africaine, mythe ou réalité?

L'Afrique, continent de contrastes frappants et de diversités bouleversantes, regroupe des pays où l'on parle des milliers de langues indigènes et où on adopte des langues européennes comme langues officielles, le résultat de plusieurs années de colonisation. Étant donné la diversité qui marque ce continent, peut-on parler à juste titre de *la* femme africaine? Allons en Afrique *la* chercher.

Notre avion vient d'atterrir à l'aéroport de Dakar. Après avoir passé par la douane, je retrouve mon amie sénégalaise, Aminata. Nous étions copines de chambre quand j'étais étudiante à Paris. Aminata avait souvent le mal du pays; sa famille lui manquait beaucoup. Le soir, elle me parlait de sa famille; une grande famille qui se composait non seulement de la mère, du père, des frères et des sœurs mais aussi des grands-parents, tantes, oncles, nièces, neveux, cousins et cousines. Sa famille avait une grande importance dans sa vie, j'en étais persuadée.

Deux semaines après avoir reçu son diplôme, Aminata a regagné le Sénégal et s'est vite mariée avec son petit ami, Samba. En trois ans elle a eu deux garçons. Je n'étais pas surprise parce que je savais qu'Aminata était obsédée par une seule idée, devenir maman. Mais Aminata est aussi devenue directrice d'une banque. Et son mari, Samba, est professeur de chimie à l'Université Cheikh Anta Diop. Ils ont acheté une grande maison près de la plage où ils mènent une vie tranquille avec leurs enfants et la mère d'Aminata, qui a soixante-douze ans. Samba et Aminata ne veulent plus d'enfants; leurs deux fils, Michel et Antoine, leur suffisent. Samba et Aminata s'entendent bien; ils font le ménage ensemble. Samba adore faire la cuisine et j'ai pris du poids à cause de ses plats appétissants. La mère d'Aminata est veuve. Elle habite chez sa fille depuis six ans et y restera pour le reste de sa vie.

Trois jours après mon arrivée à Dakar, Aminata et moi allons rendre visite à son oncle qui habite dans un village à soixante-dix kilomètres de Dakar. Au grand

portail de la concession, Aïssatou nous accueille chaleureusement. Aminata me la présente comme la première femme de son oncle. «Première femme? Ton oncle est-il divorcé?» lui dis-je. «Non, il ne l'est pas. Tu sais, plus de 80 pour cent des Sénégalais sont musulmans et pas mal parmi eux sont polygames», dit-elle. Me voyant étonnée, elle me dit: «Oui, mon oncle, Modou, est polygame; il a quatre femmes—Aïssatou, Ndèye, Fatou and Nabou.»

Modou et ses deux frères, Ousseynou et Mawdo, vivent ensemble avec leurs familles dans une concession d'une dizaine de maisons qui entourent une grande cour. Au milieu se trouve un grand arbre à l'ombre duquel des femmes font la lessive en bavardant et des enfants écoutent attentivement des contes. Dans la concession, il n'y a que les femmes et les filles qui font le ménage. Mais toutes les femmes de Modou travaillent pour s'assurer l'indépendance financière. Ndèye est fermière, et le jour où nous visitons leur petit village, elle travaille dans sa ferme à cinq kilomètres du village. Fatou est commerçante et va souvent au marché vendre du poisson. Pendant qu'elles travaillent, Ndèye et Fatou ne s'inquiètent pas de leurs enfants (il y en a treize) parce que leurs coépouses, Aïssatou et Nabou, s'occupent d'eux. «Eh bien, ma poulette, tu vois que la polygamie a ses avantages», me dit Aminata d'un ton moqueur.

Au bout de deux semaines de séjour au Sénégal, je fais connaissance de plusieurs femmes africaines dans des situations différentes—il y en a qui ont des coépouses mais Aminata a un mariage monogame; il y en a qui habitent dans les grandes villes mais d'autres vivent dans des petits villages qui facilitent la coexistence de la tradition et la modernité. Malgré toutes ces différences, il y a des ressemblances—les femmes travaillent et, par conséquent, ont une indépendance économique appréciable; elles ont un grand respect pour la maternité et les personnes âgées. Finalement, la question se pose: Avons-nous découvert *la* femme africaine? À vous la parole!

Obioma Nnaemeka

www

10 Dans la rue et sur la route

Buts communicatifs
Giving reasons; making excuses
Expressing familiarity and judgment
Giving orders and advice
Describing ways of doing things

Structures utiles
Les verbes **vouloir** et **pouvoir**
Le verbe **connaître**
Les pronoms objets directs (suite)
L'impératif (suite)
Le subjonctif (*an overview*)
Les pronoms à l'impératif
Les nombres ordinaux
Le verbe **conduire**
Les adverbes

Culture
Conduire en France
Les expressions de tendresse

Coup d'envoi

Prise de contact

Les indications

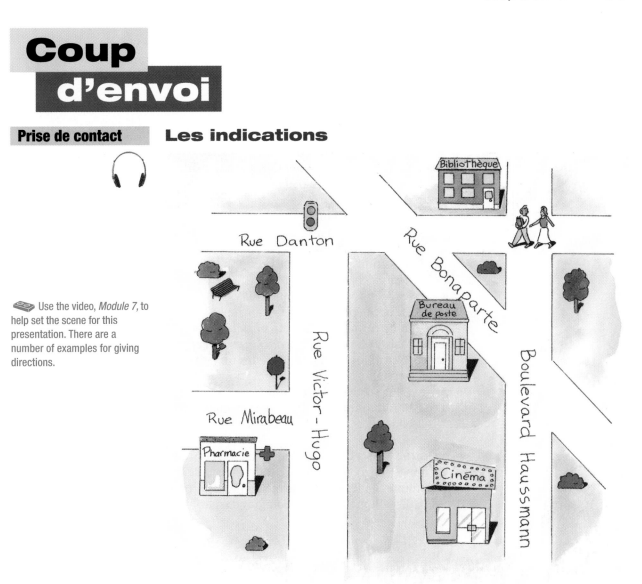

Use the video, *Module 7*, to help set the scene for this presentation. There are a number of examples for giving directions.

Remind students how to interrupt someone politely, p. 9.

Review the directions in Ch. 5, p. 138.

VOCABULAIRE À RETENIR

dans la rue *on the street*
sur l'avenue *on the avenue*
sur le boulevard *on the boulevard*
sur la route *on the highway*

Pardon, pouvez-vous me dire où se trouve la pharmacie?

Oui, c'est dans la rue Mirabeau.
Prenez la rue Danton.
Continuez jusqu'au feu°.   *until the traffic light*
Puis, tournez à gauche. C'est la rue Victor-Hugo.
Ensuite, la rue Mirabeau est la première rue à
   droite après le stop°.   *stop sign*

▶ **Et vous?**   Pouvez-vous me dire où se trouve la poste?
                Où se trouve le cinéma, s'il vous plaît?
                Pour la bibliothèque, s'il vous plaît?

Do this using local landmarks, streets, etc.

Conversation

Un père très nerveux

Michel Avoine est très nerveux parce que sa fille apprend à conduire°.   *to drive*

CATHERINE: Papa, est-ce que je peux conduire?

MICHEL: Tu veux° conduire, ma chérie°?   *You want/honey*
Eh bien, attache ta ceinture de sécurité° et   *seat belt*
prends le volant°. Mais fais attention!   *steering wheel*

CATHERINE: Chut!° Pas de commentaires, s'il te plaît.   *Shh!*
Laisse-moi tranquille.°   *Leave me alone.*

MICHEL: D'accord, démarre°. Regarde à gauche, à   *start*
droite et dans ton rétroviseur°.   *rearview mirror*
Avance lentement°, ma fille.   *slowly*
Change de vitesse.° Continue tout droit.   *Shift; change speed.*
Ne conduis pas si vite°.   *so fast*
(un peu plus tard)
Ne prends pas le sens interdit°.   *one-way street*
Prends la première rue à gauche.
Et ne regarde pas les garçons qui passent.

CATHERINE: Mais, tais-toi!° Tu n'arrêtes° pas de parler!   *keep quiet!/stop*

MICHEL: Excuse-moi, ma puce°. Je suis un peu   *(lit.) flea*
nerveux.
C'est promis, plus un mot°.   *not one more word*

CATHERINE: Plus un mot, mon œil!° Je te connais° trop   *my eye!/I know you*
bien.

▶ **Jouez ces rôles.**   Répétez la conversation avec votre partenaire.
Changez ensuite de rôle: c'est un fils qui demande à sa maman s'il peut
conduire. Faites les changements nécessaires: par exemple, la mère appelle
son fils «mon chéri» et «mon grand».

Il y a un geste

Chut!   The index finger is raised to the lips to indicate that silence is in order.

Tais-toi!   The thumb and fingers are alternately opened and closed to tell someone to "shut up."

Mon œil!   There is a gesture meaning that one does not believe what was said. The index finger is placed under an eyelid and pulls down slightly on the skin.

Pourquoi est-ce que Michel est nerveux?

a. Sa fille conduit très mal.
b. Tous les pères sont nerveux.
c. On conduit vite en France et il est important d'être prudent.

Michel appelle sa fille «ma puce». Pourquoi?

a. C'est une expression de tendresse (*term of endearment*).
b. Il est sexiste. Les puces sont petites et il pense que sa fille est inférieure.
c. Les Français aiment beaucoup les insectes.

Conduire en France

One of the most unsettling discoveries one makes on a trip to France is the speed at which most people drive. Much has already been written about the French **appétit de la vitesse.** For example, Daninos's Major Thompson (see the **Lecture,** page 292) complains about the "peaceful citizen" who "can change in front of your eyes into a demonic pilot." That this can be the case, in spite of a very demanding driver's license test, a very elaborate and expensive training period in **l'auto-école,** the fact that one must be eighteen to get a license, and the fact that one must be at least sixteen years old to have a learner's permit and be accompanied by someone who is at least twenty-eight years old while learning to drive, may justify Major Thompson's comment that **Les Français conduisent plutôt bien, mais follement** (*The French drive rather well, but wildly*).

Les expressions de tendresse

Ma chérie, ma puce, mon chéri, and **mon grand** are common terms of endearment, but there are many others. Among couples, **mon chou** (*honey*, literally *my cabbage*) is very frequent. It is most likely a shortened form of **chou à la crème** (*cream puff*). In French families such expressions seem to be more frequently used than is the case among members of North American families. Terms of endearment are perhaps the verbal equivalent of the greater amount of physical contact found in France.

Quelques expressions de tendresse		
femme	*homme*	*femme ou homme*
ma chérie	mon chéri	mon chou
ma puce (*flea*)	mon grand	mon cœur (*heart*)
ma biche (*deer*)	mon lapin (*rabbit*)	mon ange (*angel*)
		mon bijou (*jewel*)

VATEL AUTO-ECOLE

PRÈS DE LA FACULTÉ DES LETTRES

5, RUE CONSTANTINE - TOURS

COURS DE CODE PAR AUDIOSCOPE

**FORMATION TRADITIONNELLE
OU ACCÉLÉRÉE SUR DEMANDE
FORFAIT SUR 2 SEMAINES**

SUR FORD FIESTA

▶ **À vous.**   Votre ami(e) apprend à conduire. Répondez à ses questions.

1. Est-ce que je peux conduire?
2. Tu vas attacher ta ceinture de sécurité?
3. Où allons-nous?
4. Où se trouve cet endroit?

Entre amis

Votre partenaire conduit

1. Ask if your partner wants to drive. (S/he does)
2. Tell your partner to take the wheel.
3. Tell him/her to start the car.
4. Tell him/her to look left and right.
5. Tell him/her to move ahead slowly.
6. Tell him/her to take the first street on the right.
7. Ask if s/he is nervous.

Instruct the student who is "driving" to respond each time with a gesture: Pretend to take the wheel, turn an imaginary key, etc.

Prononciation

La lettre *h*

■ The letter **h** is never pronounced in French. There are, however, two categories of **h-** words:

1. Some **h-** words act *as if they began with a vowel:* These words are said to begin with **h muet** *(mute h)*. Elision (dropping a final vowel and replacing it with an apostrophe) and liaison (pronouncing a normally silent final consonant and linking it to the next word) both occur before **h muet,** just as they would with a word beginning with a vowel.

d'habitude	**l'**heure	**j'**habite
un [n]homme	elle est [t]heureuse	deux [z]heures

2. Some **h-** words act *as if they began with a consonant:* These words are said to begin with **h aspiré** *(aspirate h)*. Elision and liaison do not occur before **h aspiré.**

pas **de** haricots	**le** huit décembre	**le** hockey
un/hamburger	les/haricots	des/hors-d'œuvre

■ In addition, note that the combination **-th-** is pronounced [t].

   thé   **Th**omas   a**th**lète   biblio**th**èque   ma**th**s

Buts
communicatifs

1 Giving Reasons; Making Excuses

Tu vas à la boum°, Brigitte?   *to the party*
Oui, j'ai envie de danser.
Oui, je veux m'amuser.
Oui, je veux être avec mes amis.
Je regrette. Je ne peux pas° sortir ce soir.   *I am unable to, I can't*

▶ **Et vous?** Voulez-vous aller danser?
Je veux bien! J'adore danser.
Je regrette. Je ne sais pas danser.
Non, je suis trop fatigué(e).
Je voudrais bien, mais j'ai besoin d'étudier.
Voulez-vous sortir ce soir? Pourquoi ou pourquoi pas?

Il y a un geste

Invitation à danser. When inviting someone to dance, the index finger is pointed toward the floor and makes a small circular motion.

The imperfect of **vouloir** and **pouvoir** will be taught in Ch. 11.

Suggestion: Contrast the sound [ø] in the singular with the [œ] sound in the 3rd person plural. This contrast will be the focus of the pronunciation section in Ch. 13.

A. Les verbes *vouloir* et *pouvoir*

Mes amis veulent sortir tous les soirs.	*My friends want to go out every night.*
Mais **ils ne peuvent pas.**	*But they can't.*
As-tu pu parler avec Paul?	*Were you able to talk to Paul?*
J'ai voulu mais **je n'ai pas pu.**	*I wanted to (I tried to) but I wasn't able to.*

Veux and **peux** are pronounced like **deux.**

vouloir *(to want; to wish)*		pouvoir *(to be able; to be allowed)*	
je	**veux**	je	**peux**
tu	**veux**	tu	**peux**
il/elle/on	**veut**	il/elle/on	**peut**
nous	**voulons**	nous	**pouvons**
vous	**voulez**	vous	**pouvez**
ils/elles	**veulent**	ils/elles	**peuvent**
passé composé: j'**ai voulu**		*passé composé:* j'**ai pu**	

**VOCABULAIRE
À RETENIR**

J'ai voulu *I tried*
J'ai pu *I succeeded*
Je n'ai pas pu *I failed*

■ **Vouloir** and **pouvoir** are frequently followed by an infinitive.

Qui **veut sortir** ce soir?	*Who wants to go out tonight?*
Je **ne peux pas sortir** ce soir.	*I can't go out tonight.*

■ The passé composé of **vouloir, j'ai voulu,** means *I tried.* The passé composé of **pouvoir, j'ai pu,** means *I succeeded,* and the negative **je n'ai pas pu** means *I failed.*

■ **Vouloir** can also be used with a noun or pronoun, often to offer something or to make a request.

Voulez-vous **quelque chose** à boire?   *Do you want something to drink?*

Remind students that the phrase **je veux bien** is often used when accepting an offer, p. 29.

Note   When making requests, it is more polite to use **je voudrais** instead of **je veux.**

Je voudrais un verre d'eau.   *I'd like a glass of water.*

 Pourquoi y vont-ils? Expliquez où vont les personnes suivantes et pourquoi. Utilisez le verbe **aller** et le verbe **vouloir** dans chaque phrase.

Follow-up: Make up illogical sentences that students must correct, e.g., **On va au cinéma parce qu'on veut danser.**

Modèle: **Les étudiants vont à la boum parce qu'ils veulent danser.**

		à la résidence		étudier
		à la bibliothèque		acheter quelque chose
		à la boum		danser
		au restaurant		écouter un sermon
on		aux cours		dormir
je		à l'église		parler avec des amis
nous	aller	au bistro	vouloir	manger
tu		à la piscine		boire
vous		à la patinoire		prendre un avion
les étudiants		au cinéma		patiner
		au centre com-mercial		nager
				voir un film
		en France		visiter des monuments
		à l'aéroport		apprendre quelque chose

 Un petit sketch. Lisez ou jouez le sketch suivant. Répondez ensuite aux questions.

Deux étudiants parlent de leurs activités.

JACQUES: Je peux porter ta veste grise?
CHRISTOPHE: Oui, si tu veux. Pourquoi?
JACQUES: Ce soir je sors.
CHRISTOPHE: Je vais être indiscret. Et tu vas où?
JACQUES: Les étudiants organisent une boum.
CHRISTOPHE: Tu y vas avec qui?
JACQUES: J'y vais seul, mais je crois que Sandrine a l'intention d'y aller aussi.
CHRISTOPHE: Et tu vas pouvoir l'inviter à danser, bien sûr?
JACQUES: Je voudrais bien danser avec elle. Mais elle a beaucoup d'admirateurs.
CHRISTOPHE: Tu as pu danser avec elle la dernière fois?
JACQUES: Non, elle n'a pas voulu. Mais cette fois, ça va être différent.

Questions

1. Qui va à la boum?
2. Avec qui y va-t-il?
3. Quels vêtements veut-il porter?
4. Avec qui Jacques veut-il danser?
5. Pourquoi est-ce qu'il n'a pas pu danser avec Sandrine la dernière fois?

3 **Pourquoi pas?** Utilisez le verbe **pouvoir** à la forme négative et l'expression **parce que** pour expliquer pourquoi quelque chose n'est pas possible.

MODÈLE: **Tu ne peux pas sortir parce que tu es trop fatigué(e).**

If you do this in pairs, follow with a stand-up drill. Students must give an example before sitting down.

| tu
vous
mes amis
mon ami(e)
je
nous
les étudiants | ne pas
pouvoir | aller à un
  concert
sortir
dîner
voyager
jouer aux cartes
étudier
venir au cours
danser
regarder la
  télévision
skier | avoir la grippe
avoir un rhume
être malade(s)
être trop fatigué(e)(s)
ne pas avoir d'argent
avoir sommeil
avoir besoin d'étudier
être occupé(e)(s)
ne pas avoir le temps
avoir mal aux yeux
avoir mal aux pieds
ne pas être libre(s) |

4 **Qu'est-ce qu'il a?** Raymond répond toujours «non». Utilisez les expressions suivantes avec **vouloir** ou **pouvoir** pour expliquer quelle excuse il peut avoir.

Drill the model sentence before doing the activity.

MODÈLE: Si nous l'invitons à manger quelque chose, ...
Si nous l'invitons à manger quelque chose, Raymond va répondre qu'il ne veut pas manger parce qu'il n'a pas faim.

1. Si nous l'invitons à boire quelque chose, ...
2. Si nous l'invitons à chanter une chanson, ...
3. Si nous l'invitons à danser la valse, ...
4. Si nous l'invitons à nager à la piscine, ...
5. Si nous l'invitons à aller à un match de football, ...
6. Si nous l'invitons à faire du ski, ...
7. Si nous l'invitons à dîner chez nous, ...
8. Si nous l'invitons à étudier avec nous, ...

Entre amis

Pourquoi pas?

1. Ask if your partner can go to a movie with you. (S/he can't.)
2. Find out why not.
3. Suggest other activities. How many excuses can s/he find?

2 Expressing Familiarity and Judgment

Tu connais Éric, Céline?
> Oui, je le connais.

Tu connais ses parents?
> Je les connais mais pas très bien.

Tu connais la ville de Boston?
> Non, je ne la connais pas.

Et vous? Vous connaissez la ville de Paris?
Vous connaissez le Québec?

> *Le* **Québec** refers to the province of Quebec. *Quebec City* is referred to simply as **Québec.**

B. Le verbe *connaître*

Est-ce que **vous connaissez** Paris?	*Do you know Paris?*
Anne ne **connaît** pas cette ville.	*Anne doesn't know that city.*
Je connais cet homme.	*I know that man.*
J'ai connu cet homme à Paris.	*I met that man in Paris.*

connaître			
(to know, be acquainted with, be familiar with)			
je	**connais**	nous	**connaissons**
tu	**connais**	vous	**connaissez**
il/elle/on	**connaît**	ils/elles	**connaissent**
passé composé: j'**ai connu**			

Students already know the phrase **Je ne sais pas.** A clear distinction will be made between **je sais** and **je connais** in Ch. 12.

■ There is a circumflex accent on the **-i-** only in the verb stem of the **il/elle/on** form and in the infinitive.

> Je **connais** bien la mentalité américaine.
> *But:* Il ne **connaît** pas l'histoire de France.

■ **Connaître** denotes familiarity and means *to know, be acquainted with (a person, a place, a concept, a thing).* It is always accompanied by a direct object and cannot stand alone.

The special meanings of **pouvoir** and **vouloir** in the passé composé were taught on p. 274.

Connaissez-vous **les parents de Thomas?**	*Do you know Thomas's parents?*
Non, mais je connais **leur maison.**	*No, but I'm familiar with their house.*

The use of **savoir** in the passé composé will be taught in Ch. 12.

Note In the passé composé, **connaître** denotes a first meeting.

J'**ai connu** Robert en janvier.   *I met Robert in January.*

Review the direct object pronouns on p. 226.

C. Les pronoms objets directs (suite)

Connais-tu Christelle?	*Do you know Christelle?*
Non, je ne **la** connais pas personnellement.	*No, I don't know her personally.*
Est-ce qu'elle **te** connaît?	*Does she know you?*
Non, elle ne **me** connaît pas.	*No, she doesn't know me.*
Tu **nous** invites chez toi?	*Are you inviting us to your house?*
Non, ce soir je ne peux pas **vous** inviter.	*No, tonight I can't invite you.*
As-tu acheté ton livre?	*Did you buy your book?*
Je **l'**ai acheté mais je ne **l'**ai pas encore lu.	*I bought it but I haven't read it yet.*

See Appendix C for grammatical terms.

Pronoms objets directs

singulier		pluriel	
me (**m'**)	*me*	**nous**	*us*
te (**t'**)	*you*	**vous**	*you*
le (**l'**)	*him; it*	**les**	*them*
la (**l'**)	*her; it*		

■ Remember that object pronouns are placed directly in front of the verb.

Aimes-tu *les sandwichs?*	Oui, je **les** aime.
Connais-tu *ma mère?*	Non, je ne **la** connais pas.

■ When used with a verb followed by an infinitive, direct object pronouns are put directly in front of the verb to which they are related (usually the infinitive).

Pascale veut **me** connaître?	Oui, elle veut **vous** connaître.
Je vais demander *l'addition.*	Je vais **la** demander.
Nous ne pouvons pas regarder *la télévision.*	Nous ne pouvons pas **la** regarder.
J'ai envie d'écouter *la radio.*	J'ai envie de **l'**écouter.

■ Direct object pronouns can be used with **voici** and **voilà**.

Où est Robert? **Le** voilà!	*Where is Robert? There he is!*
Vous venez? **Nous** voilà!	*Are you coming? Here we are.*

■ In the passé composé, object pronouns are placed directly in front of the auxiliary verb.

Marc a acheté *son livre?*	Oui, il **l'**a acheté.
As-tu aimé *le film?*	Non, je ne **l'**ai pas aimé.

FOR RECOGNITION ONLY:

The past participle agrees in gender and number with a *preceding* direct object.

Tu n'as pas **écouté** *la radio*.   *But:* Tu ne *l'*as pas écouté**e**.

Nous avons **attendu** *nos amis*.   *But:* Nous *les* avons attendu**s**.

5 **C'est vrai?** D'abord utilisez le verbe **connaître** pour faire des phrases à la forme affirmative. Ensuite utilisez un pronom objet dans une deuxième phrase pour dire si c'est vrai ou faux.

MODÈLE: je / la Côte-d'Ivoire
       Je connais la Côte-d'Ivoire.
       C'est faux. Je ne la connais pas.   ou
       C'est vrai. Je la connais.

1. nos parents / notre professeur de français
2. notre professeur de français / nos parents
3. nous / l'avenue des Champs-Élysées
4. je / les amis de mes parents
5. mon ami(e) ... / le musée du Louvre
6. les étudiants / le (la) président(e) de l'université

6 **Qui les connaît?** Interviewez un(e) partenaire. Utilisez le verbe **connaître**. Employez un pronom objet dans votre réponse.

MODÈLES: tu / mes amis
       VOUS: **Est-ce que tu connais mes amis?**
       VOTRE PARTENAIRE: **Oui, je les connais.**   ou
       Non, je ne les connais pas.

       tes amis / me
       VOUS: **Est-ce que tes amis me connaissent?**
       VOTRE PARTENAIRE: **Oui, ils te connaissent.**   ou
       Non, ils ne te connaissent pas.

1. tu / mes parents
2. tes parents / me
3. tes amis / le professeur de français
4. le professeur de français / tes amis
5. tu / les autres étudiants de notre cours de français
6. les autres étudiants de notre cours de français / te
7. le (la) président(e) de notre université / nous
8. nous / le (la) président(e) de notre université

7 **Pourquoi ou pourquoi pas?** Répondez en utilisant un pronom objet direct. Ensuite expliquez votre réponse.

MODÈLES: Aimez-vous étudier le français?
Oui, j'aime l'étudier parce que j'ai envie de le parler.

Voulez-vous faire la vaisselle?
Non, je ne veux pas la faire parce que c'est ennuyeux.

1. Aimez-vous faire les courses?
2. Allez-vous regarder la télévision ce soir?
3. Voulez-vous connaître la ville de Paris?
4. Pouvez-vous chanter *la Marseillaise*?
5. Préférez-vous faire vos devoirs à la bibliothèque?
6. Comprenez-vous l'espagnol?
7. Me comprenez-vous?

8 **Une devinette** *(A riddle).* À quoi correspond le pronom? Devinez!

MODÈLE: On le trouve dans la classe de français.
On trouve le livre de français dans la classe de français. ou
On trouve Mike dans la classe de français.

Do this first in pairs; then redo as a teacher-led activity to elicit as many answers as possible.

1. On le prend le matin.
2. On la regarde quelquefois.
3. On l'écoute souvent.
4. On peut les faire à la bibliothèque.
5. On le lit pour préparer ce cours.
6. On aime le parler avec le professeur.
7. Les étudiants l'adorent.
8. On la fait après le dîner.
9. On les achète à la librairie.

Entre amis

Une enquête: vous êtes journaliste

Find out the following information. Your partner should use an object pronoun whenever possible.

1. Find out if your partner knows a specific radio program (choose one).
2. If so, find out if s/he listens to it often.
3. Find out if your partner knows a TV program (choose one from tonight's schedule.)
4. Ask if s/he is going to watch it this evening.
5. Find out why or why not.
6. Find out if s/he listens to the radio while s/he studies.
7. Find out if s/he watches TV while s/he studies. If not, inquire why not.

3 Giving Orders and Advice

Remind students of the gesture
for **tais-toi (taisez-vous),** p. 270.

Quelqu'un parle au chauffeur°:
    Démarrez!
    Changez de vitesse!
    Continuez tout droit!
    Prenez à droite!
    Arrêtez au stop!
    Reculez!°
    Faites attention aux voitures!

driver

Back up!

Le chauffeur répond
    Taisez-vous!°

Keep quiet!

Taisez-vous is the **vous** form
of the imperative **tais-toi,**
used on p. 270.

▶ **Et vous?** Parlez au chauffeur!

D. L'impératif (suite)

Fais attention!	*Pay attention!*
Faites attention!	*Pay attention!*
Faisons attention!	*Let's pay attention!*

Ne sors pas!	*Don't go out!*
Ne sortez pas!	*Don't go out!*
Ne sortons pas!	*Let's not go out!*

Review the imperative on
p. 139.

■ The imperative is used to give commands and to make suggestions. The forms are usually the same as the present tense for **tu, vous,** and **nous.**

The use of pronouns with the
imperative will be taught on
p. 285.

■ **Être** and **avoir** have irregular imperatives:

être	avoir
sois	aie
soyez	ayez
soyons	ayons

Sois gentil!	*Be nice!*
Soyons sérieux!	*Let's be serious!*
Ayez pitié de nous!	*Have pity on us!*
N'**aie** pas peur!	*Don't be afraid!*

Follow with two chain drills:
A. One student gives an order to
the next, who responds **Mais je
ne veux pas ...** Tell students to
try to avoid orders that have
already been given.
B. Reverse the process: the first
student says **Je ne veux pas ...**
and the next gives the order to
do so.

9 **Le pauvre professeur.** Les étudiants refusent de faire ce qu'il veut. Utilisez **Mais je ne veux pas ...** et répondez.

Modèle: Écoutez!
    Mais je ne veux pas écouter.

1. Allez en classe!
2. Prenez ce livre!
3. Écrivez votre dissertation!
4. Lisez ce roman!
5. Parlez à votre professeur!

6. Soyez raisonnable!
7. Arrêtez de parler!
8. Ayez pitié de vos professeurs!
9. Faites attention!
10. Sortez de cette classe!

Remember that the final **-s** is omitted from the **tu** form of the imperative if the infinitive ends in **-er**.

10 **Un père exaspéré.** Michel trouve que sa fille n'est pas raisonnable. Il décide que sa fille peut faire ce qu'elle veut.

MODÈLE: Je veux aller au cinéma.
Alors, va au cinéma!

1. Je ne peux rien manger.
2. Je ne veux pas faire la vaisselle.
3. Je veux regarder la télévision.
4. Je ne veux pas étudier.
5. Je ne peux pas écrire de rédaction.
6. Je ne veux pas avoir de bonnes notes en français.
7. Je ne veux pas être raisonnable.

11 **Des touristes.** Vous aidez des touristes francophones près de votre campus. Répondez et expliquez aux touristes où il faut aller.

MODÈLE: Où est le centre commercial, s'il vous plaît?
Prenez la rue Main. Ensuite tournez à gauche dans la rue Madison.

1. Pouvez-vous me dire où je peux trouver un supermarché?
2. Je voudrais trouver une pharmacie, s'il vous plaît.
3. Y a-t-il un bureau de poste dans cette ville?
4. Y a-t-il un arrêt d'autobus près d'ici?
5. Où sont les toilettes, s'il vous plaît?
6. Connaissez-vous un restaurant près d'ici?

E. Le subjonctif: un bref aperçu *(an overview)*

■ You have learned to use the infinitive after a number of verbal expressions. This happens when both verbs have the same subject or when the first verb is an impersonal expression with no specific subject.

Je veux parler français.　　*I want to speak French.*
Il faut étudier.　　*One (You, We, etc.) must study.*

It is not vital that students be able to use the subjunctive at this point. They must, however, be able to recognize it and, in the case of expressions that "give advice," they must be able to replace it with an imperative. Active formation of the subjunctive will be required when it is reintroduced in Ch. 13.

■ Expressions that are used to give advice to someone, however, are frequently followed by **que** plus the subject and its verb in a form called the subjunctive.

Je veux **que vous parliez** français.　　*I want you to speak French.*
Il faut **qu'on étudie.**　　*One (You, We, etc.) must study.*

■ The stem of the subjunctive is usually the same as the stem of the **ils/elles** form of the present tense. Except for **avoir** and **être,** the endings of the subjunctive are the same for all verbs.

-e	-ions
-es	-iez
-e	-ent

The subjunctive of **-ir** verbs will be introduced in Ch. 14.

■ Here are the subjunctive forms of regular **-er** and **-re** verbs.

-er verbs (parlent)		
que je	parl	**e**
que tu	parl	**es**
qu'il/elle/on	parl	**e**
que nous	parl	**ions**
que vous	parl	**iez**
qu'ils/elles	parl	**ent**

-re verbs (vendent)		
que je	vend	**e**
que tu	vend	**es**
qu'il/elle/on	vend	**e**
que nous	vend	**ions**
que vous	vend	**iez**
qu'ils/elles	vend	**ent**

■ Note that the subjunctive forms for **je, tu, il/elle/on,** and **ils/elles** of regular **-er** verbs look and sound the same as the present tense.

Il faut que tu **changes** de vitesse.　　*You must change gears.*
Je veux qu'elle **invite** sa cousine.　　*I want her to invite her cousin.*

■ The **nous** and **vous** forms of the subjunctive look and sound different from the present tense because of the **-i-** in their endings.

Le prof veut **que nous parlions** français.　　*The teacher wants us to speak French.*
Il faut **que vous étudiiez**.　　*It is necessary that you study. (You have to study.)*

Note the double **-i-** in the **nous** and **vous** forms of **étudier**.

The entire subjunctive conjugation of **avoir** and **être** will be given in Ch. 13.

■ The subjunctive forms of **avoir** and **être** are very similar to their imperative forms.

Il ne faut pas que vous **ayez** peur.　　*You must not be afraid.*
Il est important qu'ils ne **soient** pas en retard.　　*It is important that they not be late.*
Il vaut mieux que vous **soyez** à l'heure.　　*It's better that you be on time.*

VOCABULAIRE

Ordres et Conseils

il est essentiel que	*it is essential that*
il est important que	*it is important that*
il est indispensable que	*it is essential that*
il est nécessaire que	*it is necessary that*
il faut que	*it is necessary that; (someone) must*
il ne faut pas que	*(someone) must not*
il vaut mieux que	*it is preferable that; it is better that*
je préfère que	*I prefer that*
je veux que	*I want*
je voudrais que	*I would like*

■ With the above expressions, it is important to remember that, if there is no change of subjects, the infinitive is used. The preposition **de** is, however, required after **il est nécessaire/important/essentiel/ indispensable.**

Je ne veux pas **perdre** mon temps.	*I don't want to waste my time.*
Il est important d'**étudier** beaucoup.	*It's important to study a lot.*

■ When the above expressions are followed by **que** and a change of subjects, the subjunctive must be used.

Ma mère ne veut pas **que je perde** mon temps.	*My mother doesn't want me to waste my time.*
Il est important **que j'étudie** beaucoup.	*It's important that I study a lot.*

 Ils veulent que je fasse tout ça? Tout le monde vous demande de faire quelque chose. Décidez si vous êtes d'accord.

> **MODÈLE:** Votre père veut que vous étudiiez beaucoup.
> **Très bien, je vais étudier beaucoup.** ou
> **Mais je ne veux pas étudier beaucoup.**

1. Vos parents veulent que vous restiez à la maison.
2. Votre mère veut que vous rendiez visite à vos grands-parents.
3. Vos parents ne veulent pas que vous vendiez vos livres.
4. Vos parents ne veulent pas que vous sortiez tous les soirs.
5. Votre professeur veut que vous ayez «A» à votre examen de français.
6. Vos parents ne veulent pas que vous fumiez.
7. Vos professeurs ne veulent pas que vous perdiez vos devoirs.
8. Vos parents veulent que vous attachiez votre ceinture de sécurité.

13 Conseils aux étudiants de première année. Ces recommandations de l'administration et des professeurs sont-elles pertinentes? Quelle est votre opinion? Utilisez l'impératif dans chaque réponse et faites tous les changements nécessaires.

> **MODÈLE:** Il ne faut pas que les étudiants sortent souvent.
> **C'est un bon conseil. Ne sortez pas souvent!** ou
> **C'est un mauvais conseil. Sortez souvent, si vous voulez.**

1. Il est important que les étudiants étudient le français.
2. Il ne faut pas qu'ils soient absents.
3. Il est essentiel qu'ils dorment huit heures par jour.
4. Il faut qu'ils mangent au restaurant universitaire.
5. L'administration veut que les étudiants habitent dans une résidence universitaire.
6. Il vaut mieux qu'ils prennent le petit déjeuner.
7. Il est important qu'ils aient de bonnes notes.
8. Il est absolument indispensable qu'ils écoutent leurs professeurs.

F. Les pronoms à l'impératif

Allez-y and **Vas-y** are often used to mean *Go ahead*.

The imperative forms of reflexive verbs will be taught again in Ch. 13.

■ In an affirmative sentence, an object pronoun follows the imperative.

Je peux prendre la voiture?	**Prends-la!**	**Prenez-la!**
Je veux acheter ce livre.	**Achète-le!**	**Achetez-le!**
Je vais porter ces chaussures.	**Porte-les!**	**Portez-les!**
Je vais au cinéma.	**Vas-y!***	**Allez-y!**
Je m'amuse bien.	**Amuse-toi!**	**Amusez-vous!**
Je me lève.	**Lève-toi!**	**Levez-vous!**

Note   Used after a verb, **me** and **te** become **moi** and **toi**.

Regardez-**moi!**   *Look at me!*   Écoute-**moi!**   *Listen to me!*

*While the final **-s** of the **tu** form of verbs that end in **-er** is dropped in the imperative (see p. 139), it is retained when it is followed by a pronoun beginning with a vowel.

Point out that this is the same as the general rule for other forms of the verb.

■ If the sentence is negative, the object pronoun precedes the verb.

Je ne veux pas acheter ce livre.	**Ne l'achète pas!**	**Ne l'achetez pas!**
Je ne veux pas porter ces chaussures.	**Ne les porte pas!**	**Ne les portez pas!**
Vous me regardez tout le temps.	**Ne me regarde pas!**	**Ne me regardez pas!**
Je ne veux pas aller au cinéma.	**N'y va pas!**	**N'y allez pas!**
Je ne me lève pas.	**Ne te lève pas!**	**Ne vous levez pas!**

14 **La voix de ma conscience** *(The voice of my conscience).* Qu'est-ce que votre conscience vous dit de faire ou de ne pas faire? Utilisez un pronom objet avec l'impératif.

Votre conscience est une bonne amie. Alors, quand elle vous parle, elle utilise **tu**.

MODÈLE: Je vais manger ces bonbons.   **Mange-les!** ou
Ne les mange pas!

1. Je ne vais pas faire mes devoirs.
2. Je veux prendre la voiture de mon ami(e).
3. Je ne veux pas attacher ma ceinture de sécurité.
4. Je vais boire cette bouteille de vin.
5. Je veux acheter ces vêtements.
6. Je veux faire la sieste.
7. Je ne veux pas me lever pour aller au cours.
8. Je vais regarder la télévision.
9. Je peux aller au cinéma?
10. Je vais m'amuser ce soir.

G. Les nombres ordinaux

Prends la **première** rue à gauche.
C'est la **deuxième** fois que je viens en France.
Elle habite dans la **quatrième** maison.
Victor Hugo est né au **dix-neuvième** siècle *(century).*

■ To form most ordinal numbers, one simply adds **-ième** to the cardinal number. The abbreviated form is a numeral followed by a raised **e.**

deux	⟶	**deuxième**	2^e
trois	⟶	**troisième**	3^e

For cardinal numbers such as **vingt et un,** the ordinal number is formed according to the normal rule: **vingt et un** → **vingt et unième (21ᵉ).**

■ There are a few exceptions.

1. The ordinal number for **un (une)** is **premier (première).** It is the only ordinal number whose ending is altered to show gender agreement with the noun it modifies.

    un (une) ⟶ **premier (première)** 1ᵉʳ (1ʳᵉ)

2. **Cinq** and numbers built on **cinq** add a **-u-** before the ending.

    cinq ⟶ **cinq*u*ième** 5ᵉ

3. **Neuf** and numbers built on **neuf** change the **-f-** to **-v-** before the ending.

    neuf ⟶ **neu*v*ième** 9ᵉ

4. Cardinal numbers ending in **-e** drop the **-e** before the ending.

    quatre ⟶ **quatrième** 4ᵉ
    onze ⟶ **onzième** 11ᵉ
    douze ⟶ **douzième** 12ᵉ

■ In dates, **le premier** is used, as in English, to express the meaning *the first,* but the cardinal numbers are used for the rest of the days in the month.

    le **premier** mai   *But:* le **deux** mai, le **trois** mai

Remember that **Premier** agrees in the feminine: Elizabeth **Première.**

■ This is also true when talking about monarchs. **Premier (Première)** is used for *the First,* but the cardinal numbers are used thereafter. Note that the definite article is not used in French.

    François **Premier**   *But:* Henri **Quatre**

⓯ Prononcez et écrivez. Lisez ces expressions et écrivez en toutes lettres.

MODÈLE: le 21ᵉ siècle
le vingt et unième siècle

1. Henri Iᵉʳ
2. la 2ᵉ année consécutive
3. la 3ᵉ fois
4. le 1ᵉʳ mois de l'année
5. Louis XV
6. la 6ᵉ fois
7. le 20ᵉ siècle
8. la 1ʳᵉ rue à droite
9. le 25 décembre

⓰ Le calendrier. Répondez.

MODÈLE: Quelle est la date de Noël?
C'est le vingt-cinq décembre.

Review days, p. 133, and months, p. 197.

1. Quelle est la date d'aujourd'hui?
2. Quelle est la date du Jour de l'An?
3. Quelles sont les dates de votre fête nationale et de la fête nationale française?
4. Quelle est la date de votre anniversaire?
5. Quelle est la date de l'anniversaire de mariage de vos parents?
6. Quel est le troisième mois de l'année?
7. Quel est le dernier jour de l'année?
8. Quel est le cinquième jour de la semaine en France?
9. Quel est le cinquième jour de la semaine pour vous?

Entre amis

Excusez-moi de vous déranger

You are visiting a French-speaking city.

1. Stop a native and explain that you don't know the city.
2. Ask for directions to a good restaurant, a good hotel, and a post office.
3. Be sure to thank the native properly.

4 Describing Ways of Doing Things

À quelle vitesse conduisez-vous?
  Moi, je conduis ...
    comme un escargot°.   *like a snail*
    lentement.
    tranquillement°.   *calmly*
    prudemment°.   *prudently*
    vite.
    à toute vitesse°.   *at top speed*
    comme un fou (une folle)°.   *like a crazy person*

Comment vos amis conduisent-ils?

Il y a un geste

À toute vitesse. A closed fist is held at chest level and moved horizontally away from the body and back in a few rapid motions. This suggests a rapid speed. It may also be used to describe someone who has a "hard-driving" personality.

H. Le verbe *conduire*

Est-ce que tu as peur de **conduire**?
Je conduis très souvent.
Hier, **nous avons conduit** une voiture de sport.

conduire *(to drive)*			
je	**conduis**	nous	**conduisons**
tu	**conduis**	vous	**conduisez**
il/elle/on	**conduit**	ils/elles	**conduisent**
passé composé: j'**ai conduit**			

■ The verb **conduire** is not used to tell that you drive to a destination. It is used alone or with adverbs or direct objects. To tell *where* you are driving, use **aller en voiture.**

　　　Il **conduit** une Renault.　　　*He drives a Renault.*
But:　Il **va** à Monte-Carlo **en voiture.**　　*He is driving to Monte Carlo.*

17 **Comment ces gens conduisent-ils?** Votre partenaire va vous poser des questions. Répondez. Si vous ne savez pas, inventez une réponse.

MODÈLE:　votre tante
　　　　　VOTRE PARTENAIRE: **Comment votre tante conduit-elle?**
　　　　　　　　　　　VOUS: **Ma tante conduit à toute vitesse.**

1. les étudiants de cette université
2. le professeur de français
3. les professeurs (en général)
4. les femmes
5. les hommes

6. les Français
7. les Américains
8. votre meilleur(e) ami(e)
9. vous

Entre amis

Vous donnez des conseils au chauffeur

1. Be a back-seat driver. Tell your partner that s/he is driving too fast.
2. Tell him/her to go slowly.
3. Tell him/her to pay attention.
4. Tell him/her to shift.
5. Tell him/her where to go and how to drive.

I. Les adverbes

■ While there are exceptions, most French adverbs end in **-ment.**

Avance **lentement!**　　Tu vas trop **rapidement.**

■ If the masculine singular form of the adjective ends in a consonant, **-ment** is added to the feminine form.

premier (première)	⟶	**premièrement**	*first*
sérieux (sérieuse)	⟶	**sérieusement**	*seriously*
attentif (attentive)	⟶	**attentivement**	*attentively*
personnel (personnelle)	⟶	**personnellement**	*personally*

■ The suffix **-ment** is added to the masculine singular form of an adjective if it ends in a vowel.

vrai	⟶	**vraiment**	*truly*
facile	⟶	**facilement**	*easily*
absolu	⟶	**absolument**	*absolutely*

Exception　fou (folle) ⟶ **follement**　　*crazily*

If necessary, consult Appendix C at the end of the book to review the distinction between an adjective and an adverb.

Point out that this [a] is also found in the word **femme**.

■ For masculine adjectives ending in **-ant** or **-ent**, the adverbs will end in **-amment** or **-emment** respectively. The first vowel in both spellings is pronounced [a].

constant $\longrightarrow$ **constamment** *constantly*
patient $\longrightarrow$ **patiemment** *patiently*
prudent $\longrightarrow$ **prudemment** *prudently*

The comparative forms **meilleur(e)** and **mieux** will be taught in Ch. 11.

■ Several of the most common adverbs are completely different from their corresponding adjectives.

bon $\longrightarrow$ **bien** *well* Loïc danse **bien**.
mauvais $\longrightarrow$ **mal** *poorly* Il chante **mal**.
petit $\longrightarrow$ **peu** *little* Et il mange très **peu**.

Note **Rapide** has two corresponding adverbs: **rapidement** and **vite**.

18 **Tout le monde est chauffeur.** Décrivez les chauffeurs suivants. Pour chaque adjectif, faites une phrase avec le verbe **être** et un adjectif, et puis une autre phrase, avec le verbe **conduire** et un adverbe.

Modèle: ma tante/lent **Ma tante est lente. Elle conduit lentement.**

nous (les étudiants)	rapide
mon oncle	sérieux
ma tante	bon
mon père	prudent
ma mère	patient
je	nerveux
le professeur	admirable
les hommes	raisonnable
les femmes	parfait
	tranquille
	attentif
	fou

19 **Identification.** Identifiez des personnes qui correspondent aux questions suivantes.

Have students ask you the questions first. Then follow up, books closed, by asking them the questions.

Modèle: Qui conduit lentement?
Mes parents conduisent lentement. ou
Mon oncle conduit lentement.

1. Qui conduit nerveusement?
2. Qui parle rapidement le français?
3. Qui fait bien la cuisine?
4. Qui parle constamment?
5. Qui apprend facilement les maths?
6. Qui travaille sérieusement?
7. Qui écoute patiemment?
8. Qui étudie attentivement?
9. Qui chante mal?
10. Qui écrit peu?

Entre amis

Vous êtes journaliste

1. Find out if your partner speaks French.
2. Explain that you are a reporter for a newspaper called *L'Équipe (The Team)*.
3. Get permission to ask a few questions.
4. Find out if s/he plays tennis, swims, skates, or skis.
5. If so, find out how well and how often.
6. Double-check the answers by reporting back what your partner has told you.

Intégration www

Révision

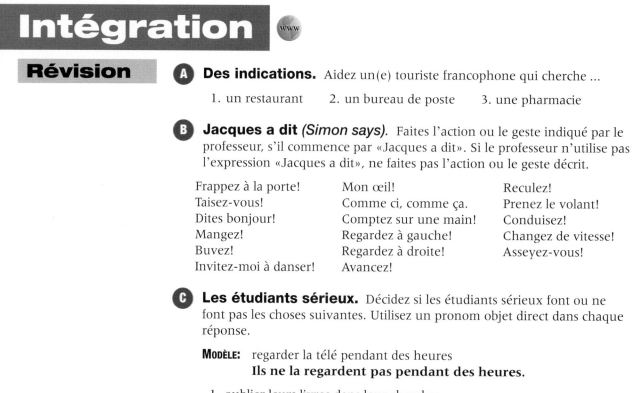

A **Des indications.** Aidez un(e) touriste francophone qui cherche ...

  1. un restaurant   2. un bureau de poste   3. une pharmacie

B **Jacques a dit** *(Simon says).* Faites l'action ou le geste indiqué par le professeur, s'il commence par «Jacques a dit». Si le professeur n'utilise pas l'expression «Jacques a dit», ne faites pas l'action ou le geste décrit.

Frappez à la porte!	Mon œil!	Reculez!
Taisez-vous!	Comme ci, comme ça.	Prenez le volant!
Dites bonjour!	Comptez sur une main!	Conduisez!
Mangez!	Regardez à gauche!	Changez de vitesse!
Buvez!	Regardez à droite!	Asseyez-vous!
Invitez-moi à danser!	Avancez!	

C **Les étudiants sérieux.** Décidez si les étudiants sérieux font ou ne font pas les choses suivantes. Utilisez un pronom objet direct dans chaque réponse.

MODÈLE: regarder la télé pendant des heures
Ils ne la regardent pas pendant des heures.

  1. oublier leurs livres dans leur chambre
  2. conduire follement la voiture de leurs parents
  3. pouvoir facilement apprendre le subjonctif
  4. vouloir étudier le français
  5. faire toujours leurs devoirs
  6. passer la nuit à regarder la télévision

D **La voiture de votre professeur de français.** Répondez.

Suggestion: Have students do the Information Gap activity in the Instructor's Resource Manual.

1. Comment? Vous voulez conduire ma voiture?
2. Avez-vous votre permis de conduire?
3. Depuis combien de temps l'avez-vous?
4. Conduisez-vous souvent les voitures des autres?
5. Vous allez attacher votre ceinture de sécurité?
6. Prenez le volant.
7. Faites bien attention aux autres voitures, n'est-ce pas?
8. Soyez prudent(e), s'il vous plaît.

Pas de problème!

Preparation for the video:
1. Video worksheet in the *Cahier d'activités*
2. CD-ROM, *Module 7*

Cette activité est basée sur la vidéo, *Module 7*. Choisissez la bonne réponse pour compléter les phrases suivantes.

1. Quand Alicia dit que les cartes sont jolies, Bruno répond _____.
   (Merci, Tu trouves?, Tu as raison)
2. Bruno veut envoyer _____ à sa mère.
   (un cadeau, une carte postale, une lettre)
3. Une femme explique à Bruno que la poste se trouve à _____ mètres.
   (100, 500, 50)
4. On vend de la porcelaine _____.
   (dans les boutiques, dans les petits magasins, à la pharmacie)
5. Bruno a acheté _____ carte(s) postale(s).
   (une, deux, douze)
6. Pour poster ses cartes postales et son colis, Bruno doit payer _____ francs.
   (59, 69, 79)

Lecture I

A **Étude du vocabulaire.** Étudiez les phrases suivantes et choisissez les mots anglais qui correspondent aux mots français en caractères gras: *more, convinced, rather, hates, approximately, those, latecomer, less, thus, bother.*

1. Un avion est **plus** rapide qu'un train.
2. L'état de Rhode Island est **moins** grand que le Texas.
3. Notre professeur **exècre** le tabac. Les cigarettes le rendent malade.
4. Pourquoi est-ce que vous me parlez **ainsi**? Qu'est-ce que je vous ai fait?
5. Mon frère est toujours **retardataire.** Il n'arrive jamais à l'heure.
6. Est-ce que cela vous **dérange** si je fume?
7. **Ceux** qui étudient sont **ceux** qui ont les meilleures notes.
8. Christian chante **plutôt** mal, mais il aime chanter quand même.
9. Il y a **à peu près** trente personnes au restaurant.
10. Je suis **convaincu** que le professeur veut que j'étudie beaucoup.

B **Qu'en pensez-vous?** Quelle est la réputation des Français au volant? Quelle est la réputation des chauffeurs californiens? des chauffeurs new-yorkais? Et vous, comment conduisez-vous?

Vous voulez prendre le volant?

La France au volant

Il faut se méfier des[1] Français en général, mais sur la route en particulier. Pour un Anglais qui arrive en France, il est indispensable de savoir d'abord qu'il existe deux sortes de Français: les à-pied et les en-voiture. Les à-pied exècrent les en-voiture, et les en-voiture terrorisent les à-pied, les premiers passant instantanément dans le camp des seconds si on leur met un volant entre les mains. (Il en est ainsi au théâtre avec les retardataires qui, après avoir dérangé douze personnes pour s'asseoir, sont les premiers à protester contre ceux qui ont le toupet[2] d'arriver plus tard.)

Les Anglais conduisent plutôt mal, mais prudemment. Les Français conduisent plutôt bien, mais follement. La proportion des accidents est à peu près la même dans les deux pays. Mais je me sens[3] plus tranquille avec des gens qui font mal des choses bien[4] qu'avec ceux qui font bien de mauvaises choses.

Les Anglais (et les Américains) sont depuis longtemps convaincus que la voiture va moins vite que l'avion. Les Français (et la plupart des Latins) semblent encore vouloir prouver le contraire.

Pierre Daninos, *Les Carnets du Major Thompson*

---

1. *watch out for*   2. *nerve*   3. *feel*   4. *do good things poorly*

C **Vrai ou faux?** Décidez si les phrases suivantes sont vraies ou fausses d'après la lecture. Si une phrase est fausse, corrigez-la.

1. Les Français sont dangereux quand ils conduisent.
2. Les Anglais sont de bons conducteurs *(drivers)* mais ils conduisent plutôt vite.
3. En France, ceux qui marchent n'apprécient pas beaucoup ceux qui sont au volant.
4. Ceux qui conduisent adorent les à-pied.
5. Les Anglais ont moins d'accidents que les Français.
6. L'avion va plus vite que la voiture mais les Américains ne le comprennent pas encore.

Questions. Répondez.

1. Pourquoi dit-on qu'il y a deux sortes de Français?
2. Quelle transformation y a-t-il quand un Français prend le volant?
3. Les retardataires sont-ils hypocrites? Expliquez votre réponse.
4. Quelles différences y a-t-il entre les Anglais et les Français?
5. Qui sont les Latins?
6. Qui sont ceux qui font mal des choses qui sont bonnes?

 Familles de mots. Essayez de deviner le sens des mots suivants.

1. conduire, un conducteur, une conductrice, la conduite
2. exister, l'existence, l'existentialisme
3. retarder, un(e) retardataire, un retard
4. terroriser, un(e) terroriste, le terrorisme, la terreur

Lecture II

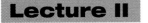 **Les voitures françaises.** Lisez la lecture suivante et identifiez deux marques *(makes)* de voitures françaises.

R (Renault).

AUTOMOBILES	
Vends Renault Espace RN 21 Turbo D, mod 96, 8.000 kms, bleue, climatisée, airbag, radio. Tél. 02.43.81.75.79 ap. 18h.	Vends Laguna ii TD 2.2 RXE 7 cv, janvier 1999, 25.000 km, ABS, climatisation automatique, airbags, direction assistée, vitres électriques avant. Pare-brise athermique. Radio commande au volant. Etat neuf. 20.000€. Tél. 02.41.58.87.18 le soir.
Vends Renault 9 GTL, 68.000 kms, 5 vitesses, vitres teintées électriques, gris métallique, direction assistée, toit ouvrant. Tél. 02.41.34.63.23 après 20h.	
Vds Mercedes C 250 D Élégance 95, 1ᵉ main, 44.000 kms, état neuf, clim, radio (Sony), alarme, radiocommandée, vert métal. Tél. 02.41.64.35.70.	Xantia turbo D VSX Export, année modèle 1996, gris Quartz, 97.500 km, suspension hydractive, direction assistée, climatisation régulée, radio commande volant, 4 vitres électriques, ABS, pastille verte, verrouillage et anti-démarrage par plip HF. Non fumeur. Parfait état, entretien Citroën, contrôle technique ok. Disponible 15 avril. Tél. 02.41.62.53.58.
VDS R5 pour pièces détachées, roulante mais accidentée, petit prix. Tél. 02.41.32.51.61.	
Vds Renault Twingo, 6 mois, noire, toit ouvrant, bag, 3.200 kms, 10.000€. Tél. 02.43.75.64.98.	

 Pouvez-vous décider?

1. Quelle est probablement la plus vieille voiture?
2. Quelle voiture est probablement la plus chère?
3. Quelle voiture est probablement la moins chère?
4. Quelle voiture n'est pas française?
5. Quelles voitures ne sont certainement pas rouges?
6. Quelles voitures sont confortables quand il fait chaud?
7. Quels propriétaires ne sont pas chez eux pendant la journée?

Follow-up: Read a student's ad out loud. Others will try to guess who wrote it or will summarize it.

Une voiture à vendre. Écrivez une petite annonce pour une voiture que vous voulez vendre.

VOCABULAIRE ACTIF

Sur la route

un arrêt (d'autobus) *(bus) stop*
arrêter *to stop*
à toute vitesse *at top speed*
attacher *to attach; to put on*
avancer *to advance*
une ceinture de sécurité *safety belt, seat belt*
changer (de) *to change*
un chauffeur *driver*
comme un fou *like a crazy person*
conduire *to drive*
démarrer *to start a car*
un feu *traffic light*
jusqu'au feu *until the traffic light*
un permis de conduire *driver's license*
reculer *to back up*
une route *highway*
un rétroviseur *rearview mirror*
le sens interdit *one-way street*
un stop *stop sign*
la vitesse *speed*
un volant *steering wheel*

D'autres noms

l'année scolaire (f.) *school year*
un anniversaire de mariage *wedding anniversary*
une boum *party*
un commentaire *commentary*
un conseil *(piece of) advice*
un escargot *snail*
un fou (une folle) *fool; crazy person*
un match *game*
une patinoire *skating rink*
un(e) propriétaire *owner*
un siècle *century*

Adjectifs

attentif (attentive) *attentive*
constant(e) *constant*
fou (folle) *crazy; mad*
lent(e) *slow*
neuf (neuve) *brand-new*
prudent(e) *cautious*
raisonnable *reasonable*
rapide *rapid; fast*
sérieux (sérieuse) *serious*
tranquille *calm*

Verbes

avoir pitié (de qqn.) *to have pity (on s.o.); to feel sorry (for s.o.)*
connaître *to know; be acquainted with; be familiar with*
inviter *to invite*
laisser *to leave; to let*
pouvoir *to be able; to be allowed*
vouloir *to want; to wish*

Adverbes

absolument *absolutely*
constamment *constantly*
follement *in a crazy manner*
lentement *slowly*
patiemment *patiently*
personnellement *personally*
prudemment *prudently*
rapidement *rapidly*
sérieusement *seriously*
si *so*
vite *quickly; fast*

Pronoms objets directs

me *me*
te *you*
le *him; it*
la *her; it*
nous *us*
vous *you*
les *them*

Des ordres et des conseils

il est essentiel que *it is essential that*
il est important que *it is important that*
il est indispensable que *it is essential that*
il est nécessaire que *it is necessary that*
il faut que *it is necessary that; (someone) must*
il ne faut pas que *(someone) must not*
il vaut mieux que *it is preferable that; it is better that*
je préfère que *I prefer that*
je veux que *I want*
je voudrais que *I would like*

Expressions utiles

C'est promis. *It's a promise.*
Chut! *Shh!*
je veux m'amuser *I want to have fun*
Laisse-moi (Laissez-moi) tranquille! *Leave me alone!*
(mon/ma) chéri(e) *(my) dear, honey*
Mon œil! *My eye!*
ma puce *honey (lit. my flea)*
Plus un mot. *Not one more word.*
Tais-toi! (Taisez-vous!) *Keep quiet!*

Comme si c'était hier

Coup d'envoi

Prise de contact   ## Quand vous étiez jeune

Qu'est-ce que tu faisais° quand tu avais seize ans°,   *used to do / were sixteen*
   Caroline?
         J'allais au lycée°.   *high school*
         J'étudiais l'anglais et les mathématiques.
         J'habitais une petite maison.
         Je sortais quelquefois avec mes amis.
         Nous allions au cinéma ensemble.
         Mais je n'avais pas encore mon permis de
            conduire.

 Et vous?   Qu'est-ce que vous faisiez quand vous aviez seize ans?

Conversation	**L'album de photos**	

Lori et son amie Denise sont en train de° regarder un album de photos.   *in the process of*

LORI: C'est une photo de toi?

DENISE: Oui, c'était° au mariage de ma sœur.   *it was*

LORI: Elle est plus âgée que° toi?   *older than*

DENISE: Oui, de deux ans.

LORI: Ah! La voilà en robe de mariée°, n'est-ce pas?   *wedding dress*
Comme elle était belle!°   *How beautiful she was!*

DENISE: Tu vois° la photo de ce jeune homme en   *You see*
smoking°? C'est mon beau-frère.   *in a tuxedo*

LORI: Il avait l'air jeune.

DENISE: Il n'avait que vingt ans.°   *He was only twenty.*
À mon avis°, il en avait assez de° porter son   *In my opinion / he was fed up*
smoking.   *with*

LORI: Il faisait chaud?

DENISE: Très! Et il avait déjà porté° son smoking pour le   *had already worn*
mariage à la mairie°.   *town hall*

LORI: Quand est-ce que ce mariage a eu lieu°?   *took place*

DENISE: Il y a deux ans.

LORI: Alors, c'est ton tour°. Quand est-ce que tu vas   *turn*
épouser° ton petit ami?   *marry*
(Elles rient.°)   *They laugh.*

DENISE: Lori, occupe-toi de tes oignons!°   *mind your own business!*

▶ **Jouez ces rôles.**   Répétez la conversation avec votre partenaire. Remplacez «mariage de ma sœur» par «mariage de mon frère». Faites tous les changements nécessaires.

Il y a un geste

J'en ai assez.   The right hand is raised near the left temple. The hand is open but bent at a right angle to the wrist. The gesture is made by twisting the wrist so that the hand passes over your forehead, implying that you are "fed up to here."

À PROPOS

Comparison: Have students describe family gatherings in their country: Who attends? On what occasions? Ask students to comment on the following issues with respect to their country: marriage (where and at what age?); the availability of day care; unemployment.

Pourquoi le beau-frère avait-il déjà porté son smoking à la mairie?

a. Il aimait beaucoup porter un smoking.
b. C'est normal. On porte toujours des vêtements élégants à la mairie.
c. Il y a eu deux cérémonies de mariage: à la mairie et à l'église.

La famille

Quite attached to home, family, and friends, the French are usually very fond of weddings, family reunions, picnics, social gatherings, etc., which provide an opportunity to nurture the close relationships found within the circle of their social and emotional ties. In general, these family and friendship bonds seem stronger and longer-lasting than those typically found in English-speaking North America. The French are often equally attached to the region in which they live. It is therefore rather common, for example, to find homes that have been lived in by successive generations of the same family.

Les jeunes

High unemployment (over 12% in 1997) and the increasing length of their studies have meant that few young adults are able to become financially independent of their families. At age twenty-two, 60% of the men and 45% of the women are still living with their parents. Very few students, for example, are able to have a part-time job or purchase a car. Fortunately public transportation is widely available and universities are inexpensive.

Le mariage en France

In order to be legally married in France, all couples are wed in a civil ceremony at the town hall. The mayor (**le maire**), or the mayor's representative, performs the ceremony and the couples express their consent by saying **oui.** Many couples choose to have a religious ceremony as well. This takes place at the church, temple, or mosque, after the civil ceremony.

Currently the average age for marriage is approximately 30 (men) and 28 (women). (See **Lecture II, "La famille",** p. 81.) Since after marriage two women out of three continue to work and the birth rate has fallen to 1.8 children per family, attempts have been made by the government to help couples who have children. There are paid maternity (or paternity) leaves, public day care centers, and subsidies to families with more than two children. Nursery schools accept children as young as two years of age and, if parents wish, will supervise the children, at school, from 7:30 AM until 7 PM.

▶ **À vous.** Répondez.

Have students repeat the questions after you before doing this exercise.

1. Où habitiez-vous quand vous aviez seize ans?
2. Comment s'appelaient vos amis?
3. À quelle école alliez-vous?
4. Qu'est-ce que vous étudiiez?

Entre amis

Une vieille photo

1. Show your partner an old photo of a group of people.
2. Tell who the people are.
3. Tell how old each one was in the photo.
4. Describe what they were wearing.
5. Tell where they lived.

If they do not have a photo, give students a few seconds to draw stick figures of a group of people.

Prononciation

🎧 Use the Student Audio to help practice pronunciation.

Help students avoid pronouncing a short, English *i* in place of the French [i] in words such as **aspirine** and **visiter.**

Les sons [i] et [j]

■ Two related sounds in French are the pure vowel sound [i] (as in the English word *teeth*), and the semi-consonant/semi-vowel [j] (as in the English word *yes*). Practice saying the following words after your instructor, paying particular attention to the highlighted sound. As you pronounce the words for one sound, look at how that sound is spelled and in what kinds of letter combinations it appears. What patterns do you notice?

[i]
- **i**l, **i**c**i,** r**i**z, p**i**zza, pol**i**tique, asp**i**r**i**ne
- su**i**s, fru**i**t, depu**i**s, tru**i**te, condu**i**re, ju**i**llet
- br**i**e, am**i**e, Soph**i**e
- S**y**lvie, bic**y**clette, **y**

[j]
- mar**i**é, jan**vi**er, **hi**er, **mi**am, **ki**osque, nat**i**onal, mons**i**eur, b**i**en
- déta**il,** somme**il,** **œil,** trava**ill**e, Marse**ill**e, feu**ill**e
- gent**ill**e, f**ill**e, past**ill**e, van**ill**e, ju**ill**et
- **y**eux, essa**y**er, pa**y**er

The uses of [l] and [j] are further covered in Ch. 12.

■ The [i] sound is represented by written -i- or -y- in the following situations:

1. **i** not in combination with another vowel: mer**ci,** av**ri**l, f**i**lle
2. **i** following a **u**: p**ui**s, br**ui**t, tr**ui**te
3. final **-ie**: br**ie,** étud**ie**
4. **-y-** between two consonants: il **y** va, S**y**lvie

■ The [j] sound is required in the following circumstances:

1. **i-** before a pronounced vowel in the same syllable: p**i**ed, v**i**ande, mar**i**age
2. **-il, -ill** after a pronounced vowel in the same syllable: trava**il,** conse**ill**er, œ**il**
3. **-ll** after [i]: fi**ll**e, jui**ll**et

Exceptions   mi**ll**ion, mi**ll**iard, mi**ll**e, vi**ll**e, vi**ll**age, tranqui**ll**e

4. initial **y-** before a vowel, **-y-** between two vowels: **y**eux, essa**y**er.

Note   Between the sound [i] at the end of one syllable and another vowel at the beginning of the next syllable, [j] is pronounced even though there is no letter representing the sound.

quatrième [ka tRi jɛm]

Point out that linking takes place before **yeux: les yeux.**

▶ **Practice the following words.**

1. Sylvie, yeux, bicyclette, y, payer
2. télévision, brioche, nuit, addition, cuisine, principal, délicieux, insister, feuille
3. pitié, amie, papier, pièce, prier, pâtisserie, client, habitiez, impatient, oublier
4. milliard, juillet, ville, fille, bouteille, travail, travaille, conseil, allions, vanille, mille, œil, oreille, tranquille, gentil, gentille, million

Buts
communicatifs

1 Describing Conditions and Feelings in the Past

🎧 Quand vous étiez jeune, ...

	oui	non
aviez-vous un chien ou un chat?	____	____
étiez-vous souvent malade?	____	____
habitiez-vous une grande ville?	____	____
aviez-vous beaucoup d'amis?	____	____
regardiez-vous beaucoup la télé?	____	____

Faisiez is pronounced [fəzje]; see also p. 109.

Que faisiez-vous après l'école?
Comment s'appelaient vos voisins°?   *neighbors*
À votre avis, quelle était la meilleure émission°   *best program*
   de télé?

A. L'imparfait

■ You have already been using one past tense, the passé composé, to relate what happened in the past. The imperfect (**l'imparfait**) is a past tense used to describe conditions and feelings and to express habitual actions.

1. Describing conditions

Ma sœur **était** belle.	*My sister was beautiful.*
Mon beau-frère **avait** l'air jeune.	*My brother-in-law seemed young.*
Léa **portait** une jolie robe.	*Léa was wearing a pretty dress.*
Anne **était** malade.	*Anne was sick.*
Il **pleuvait.**	*It was raining.*
Il y **avait** trois chambres dans notre maison.	*There were three bedrooms in our house.*

2. Describing feelings

Ma sœur **était** nerveuse.	*My sister was nervous.*
Mon beau-frère en **avait** assez.	*My brother-in-law was fed up.*
Je **détestais** les épinards.	*I used to hate spinach.*
Tout le monde **était** heureux.	*Everybody was happy.*

3. Expressing habitual past actions

Nous **regardions** des dessins animés le samedi.	*We used to watch cartoons on Saturday.*
À cette époque, Marie **sortait** avec Paul.	*Back then, Marie used to go out with Paul.*

But:	Nous **avons regardé** des dessins animés samedi.	*We watched cartoons (last) Saturday. (once, not a repeated event)*
	Marie **est sortie** avec Paul vendredi dernier.	*Marie went out with Paul last Friday. (one day, not habitually)*

Review uses of the passé composé, pp. 157–158.

■ To form the imperfect tense, take the **nous** form of the present tense, drop the **-ons** ending, and add the endings **-ais, -ais, -ait, -ions, -iez, -aient.**

jouer (jou~~ons~~)		
je	**jou**	**ais**
tu	**jou**	**ais**
il/elle/on	**jou**	**ait**
nous	**jou**	**ions**
vous	**jou**	**iez**
ils/elles	**jou**	**aient**

avoir (av~~ons~~)		
j'	**av**	**ais**
tu	**av**	**ais**
il/elle/on	**av**	**ait**
nous	**av**	**ions**
vous	**av**	**iez**
ils/elles	**av**	**aient**

aller (all~~ons~~)		
j'	**all**	**ais**
tu	**all**	**ais**
il/elle/on	**all**	**ait**
nous	**all**	**ions**
vous	**all**	**iez**
ils/elles	**all**	**aient**

■ Impersonal expressions also have imperfect tense forms.

infinitive	present	imperfect	
neiger	il neige	**il neigeait**	*it was snowing*
pleuvoir	il pleut	**il pleuvait**	*it was raining*
falloir	il faut	**il fallait**	*it was necessary*
valoir mieux	il vaut mieux	**il valait mieux**	*it was better*

■ **Être** is the only verb that has an irregular stem: **ét-.** The endings are regular.

J'**étais** malade.
Nous **étions** désolés.

■ The **je, tu, il/elle/on,** and **ils/elles** forms of the imperfect all sound alike because the endings are all pronounced the same.

je **jouais**   tu **jouais**   il **jouait**   elles **jouaient**

Note that the **nous** and **vous** forms of the imperfect of most verbs are identical to the subjunctive forms. See Ch. 10, p. 283.

■ The **-ions** and **-iez** endings are pronounced as one syllable, with the letter **-i-** pronounced [j].

vous habit**iez**   [a bi tje]
nous all**ions**   [a ljɔ̃]

■ You have already learned that if the present tense stem of a verb ends in **-g,** an **-e-** is added before endings beginning with **-o-.** This is also true in other tenses before endings beginning with **-a-** or **-u-.**

present: nous mang**e**ons
imperfect: je mang**e**ais   tu mang**e**ais   il mang**e**ait   ils mang**e**aient
(*But:* nous mangions, vous mangiez)

■ Similarly, if the stem of a verb ends in **-c,** a **-ç-** is used instead before endings beginning with **-a-, -o-,** or **-u-.**

present: nous commen**ç**ons
imperfect: je commen**ç**ais   tu commen**ç**ais   il commen**ç**ait
(*But:* nous commencions, vous commenciez)

Les petits Français commencent l'école plus tôt que les petits Américains. Ils peuvent entrer à l'école maternelle à l'âge de deux ans.

Do this activity in pairs. Follow with a stand-up drill.

1 **Quand ils étaient jeunes.** Qu'est-ce que ces personnes faisaient ou ne faisaient pas quand elles étaient jeunes? Si vous ne savez pas, devinez. Utilisez **et** ou **mais** et la forme négative pour les décrire.

MODÈLE: mes amis / aller à l'école / conduire
Quand mes amis étaient jeunes, ils allaient à l'école mais ils ne conduisaient pas.

1. mes amis / regarder souvent des dessins animés / lire beaucoup
2. nous / aller à l'école / faire toujours nos devoirs
3. je / manger beaucoup de bonbons / avoir souvent mal aux dents
4. je / me coucher tôt / être toujours raisonnable
5. mes parents / se connaître depuis longtemps / sortir ensemble
6. le professeur de français / avoir de bonnes notes / aller souvent à la bibliothèque

2 **Ma grand-mère.** Transformez le paragraphe suivant à l'imparfait.

Ma grand-mère habite dans une petite maison qui est très jolie et qui a deux chambres. Dans cette région, il pleut souvent et en hiver, quand il neige, on reste à la maison. Ma grand-mère est fragile et elle travaille très peu. Elle est petite et assez vieille. Elle a soixante-quinze ans et elle est seule à la maison depuis la mort de mon grand-père. Mais quand je vais chez elle, nous parlons de beaucoup de choses et quelquefois nous chantons. Elle veut toujours nous préparer quelque chose à manger, mais je fais la cuisine moi-même. Ensuite nous mangeons ensemble. Je l'aime beaucoup et elle m'aime beaucoup aussi.

3 **Quand vous aviez quatorze ans.** Répondez.

Follow up by having the class interview first the teacher (with books open) and then another student (with books closed).

1. Qui était président des États-Unis quand vous aviez quatorze ans?
2. Quelles émissions regardiez-vous à la télé?
3. Quels acteurs et quelles actrices étaient populaires?
4. Quel âge avaient les autres membres de votre famille quand vous aviez quatorze ans?
5. Qu'est-ce que vous faisiez le vendredi soir?
6. Qu'est-ce que vous aimiez manger? Qu'est-ce que vous détestiez?
7. Qui faisait la cuisine pour vous?
8. À quelle école alliez-vous?
9. Comment s'appelaient vos voisins?

B. *Ne ... que*

Sylvie **n'**a **que** dix-huit ans.	*Sylvie is only eighteen.*
Ses parents **n'**ont **qu'**une fille.	*Her parents have only one daughter.*
Il **n'**y a **que** trois personnes dans la famille.	*There are only three people in the family.*

■ **Ne ... que,** a synonym of **seulement,** is used to express a limitation. **Ne** comes before the verb and **que** is placed directly before the expression that it limits.

Il **ne** sort **qu'**avec Renée.	*He goes out only with Renée.*
Il **ne** sort avec Renée **que** le vendredi soir.	*He goes out with Renée on Friday nights only.*

Review **il y a** + expressions of time, p. 159.

Suggestion: Follow up (books closed) by asking how old the people were *ten* years ago. Require **ne ... que** in each answer.

④ Quel âge avaient-ils il y a cinq ans? Décidez quel âge tout le monde avait il y a cinq ans. Si vous ne savez pas *(If you don't know),* devinez. Utilisez **ne ... que.**

Modèle: votre frère   **Il y a cinq ans, mon frère n'avait que seize ans.**

1. vous
2. votre meilleur(e) ami(e)
3. votre mère ou votre père
4. les étudiants de cette classe

5. votre acteur préféré
6. votre actrice préférée
7. le professeur de français (Imaginez.)

Entre amis

Quand tu étais enfant

1. Find out where your partner lived ten years ago.
2. Ask how old s/he was.
3. Ask what s/he did on Saturdays.
4. Find out what her/his school's name was.
5. Ask if s/he had a dog or a cat. If so, find out its name.
6. Find out who his/her neighbors were.

② Setting the Scene in the Past

Quand vous êtes arrivé(e) sur ce campus pour la première fois ...

c'était en quelle saison?
c'était en quel mois?
quel âge aviez-vous?
étiez-vous seul(e) ou avec des amis?
quel temps faisait-il?
quels vêtements portiez-vous?

C. L'imparfait et le passé composé

Review the passé composé, pp. 157 and 188–189.

■ The **imparfait** is often used to give background information that "sets the scene" for some other verb in the past. This scene-setting information describes what was going on. It describes the conditions surrounding some other action. If the other verb specifies what *happened*, it is in the **passé composé.**

J'étais en train de faire mes devoirs quand **Alain a téléphoné.**

Il était huit heures quand **Renée est arrivée.**

Jeanne avait quinze ans quand **elle a commencé** à fréquenter les garçons.

I was (busy) doing my homework when Alain telephoned.

It was eight o'clock when Renée arrived.

Jeanne was fifteen when she started dating boys.

■ For weather expressions:

- Use the **imperfect** when the weather sets the scene for another past action.

Il faisait beau quand **nous sommes sortis.**   *It was nice outside when we went out.*

Il pleuvait quand **nous sommes rentrés.**   *It was raining when we got home.*

Il neigeait. Alors **Karine a décidé** de porter ses bottes.   *It was snowing. So Karine decided to wear her boots.*

- Use the **passé composé** when you simply state what the weather was like at a specific time.

Hier, **il a plu** à Paris, mais **il a neigé** dans les montagnes. **Il a fait beau** à Nice.

5 **Qu'est-ce qu'elle faisait?** Utilisez les expressions suivantes pour créer des phrases logiques.

MODÈLE: **Léa faisait du ski quand elle est tombée.**

| Léa | être en train d'étudier
regarder la télévision
être en train de lire
conduire
manger
boire
faire la sieste
écrire une lettre
prendre le petit déjeuner
descendre d'une voiture | quand | son fiancé
ses parents
je
elle
nous
ses amis | entrer
partir
arriver
tomber
avoir un accident
perdre patience
téléphoner |

6 **Les Lauprête ont fait un voyage.** Quel temps faisait-il? Complétez les phrases suivantes.

MODÈLE: faire du vent / sortir de chez eux
Il faisait du vent quand les Lauprête sont sortis de chez eux.

1. pleuvoir / prendre le taxi
2. faire beau / arriver à l'aéroport
3. faire chaud / monter dans l'avion
4. faire froid / descendre de l'avion
5. neiger / commencer à faire du ski

Point out that a weather report would normally use the passé composé.

Follow up (with books closed) by asking students to try to recall some of the sentences other students created.

Do this activity in pairs. Then follow up (with books closed) by redoing the exercise as a teacher-led activity. Ask periodically **Comment est-ce qu'on écrit** *pleuvait?* (*pris, faisait,* etc.).

7 **Dernière sortie au restaurant.** Décrivez la dernière fois que vous êtes allé(e) au restaurant.

1. Quel jour est-ce que c'était?
2. Quel temps faisait-il?
3. Quels vêtements portiez-vous?
4. Quelle heure était-il quand vous êtes arrivé(e)?
5. Étiez-vous seul(e)? Si non, qui était avec vous?
6. Environ combien de personnes y avait-il au restaurant?
7. Quelle était la spécialité du restaurant?
8. Comment était le serveur (la serveuse)?
9. Aviez-vous très faim?
10. Qu'est-ce que vous avez commandé?
11. Comment était le repas?

UN SIECLE DE MOULES ET DE FRITES, ÇA SE FÊTE !

Léon de Bruxelles a 100 ans ! En famille ou entre amis, profitez de ce centenaire pour découvrir nos savoureuses spécialités de moules, nos plats gourmands typiquement belges ... sans oublier nos inimitables frites ! Chez Léon de Bruxelles, on fait la fête tous les jours !

Léon de Bruxelles 1893

La Brasserie Belge

8 **Renseignements.** Écrivez un petit paragraphe pour chaque numéro. Expliquez les conditions et ce qui est arrivé.

MODÈLE: Quand je suis tombé(e), ...
> (Qu'est-ce que vous faisiez? Avec qui étiez-vous? Qu'est-ce que vous avez dit?)
> **Quand je suis tombé(e), je faisais du ski. J'étais seul(e) et j'ai dit «Aïe!».**

1. Quand j'ai trouvé mon ami, ...
   (Qu'est-ce qu'il portait? Où allait-il? Avec qui était-il? Qu'est-ce que vous avez fait?)
2. Quand ma mère a téléphoné, ...
   (Quelle heure était-il? Que faisiez-vous? Qu'est-ce qu'elle voulait? Qu'est-ce que vous avez répondu?)
3. Quand mon cousin (mon ami(e), mon frère, etc.) a eu son accident, ...
   (Où était-il? Qu'est-ce qu'il faisait? Quel âge avait-il? Quel temps faisait-il? Qu'est-ce qu'il a fait après?)
4. Quand je suis entré(e) dans la classe, ...
   (Quelles personnes étaient là? Qu'est-ce qu'elles portaient? Quelle heure était-il? Avec qui avez-vous parlé?)

Entre amis

Tu t'es bien amusé(e)?

1. Find out when the last time was that your partner went out.
2. Ask where s/he went and what s/he did.
3. Find out what s/he was wearing.
4. Find out what the weather was like.
5. Ask if s/he had fun.
6. Ask at what time s/he got home.
7. Find out if s/he was tired when s/he got home.

Before pairing students, have them identify the verb tense for each sentence.

Que faisiez-vous
à cet âge-là?

3 Making Comparisons

Est-ce que ta vie était différente quand tu avais
seize ans, Christine?

> Pas vraiment. À cette époque°, je   *Back then*
>> travaillais autant° que maintenant.   *as much*
> Et j'étudiais aussi° souvent que   *as*
>> maintenant.
> Mais j'étais moins° active.   *less*
> Et j'avais plus° de soucis°.   *more / worries*

▶ **Et vous?**

Quand vous n'aviez que seize ans, ...
est-ce que vous étudiiez moins que maintenant?
faisiez-vous autant de sport?
aviez-vous plus de temps libre que maintenant?
est-ce que vous aviez moins de soucis?
étiez-vous plus heureux (heureuse) que maintenant?
étiez-vous aussi grand(e)?
sortiez-vous plus souvent que maintenant?
est-ce que vous parliez aussi couramment° le   *fluently*
   français?

D. Le comparatif

■ To make comparisons, the French use the words **plus** *(more)* and **moins**
(fewer; less). They also use **autant** *(as much; as many)* for comparing verbs and
nouns and **aussi** *(as)* for comparing adjectives and adverbs. All comparatives
may be followed by **que** *(than, as)* and a second term of comparison.

Donald a plus d'argent (**que** d'amis).	*Donald has more money (than friends).*
Je travaille autant (**que** lui).	*I work as much (as he).*
Guy parle moins souvent avec moi (**qu'**avec Anne).	*Guy talks less often with me (than with Anne).*
Éric est aussi pauvre (**qu'**avant).	*Éric is as poor (as before).*

Review the forms of stressed pronouns, Ch. 6, p.168.

Note   When a personal pronoun is required after **que,** a stress pronoun
is used.

Tu bois plus de café **que moi.**	*You drink more coffee than I.*
Nous avons moins d'enfants **qu'eux.**	*We have fewer children than they.*

■ To compare how much of a particular action people do, the words **plus,**
moins, and **autant** are used *after a verb.*

René **parle plus** que son père.	*René talks more than his father.*
Il **parle moins** que sa mère.	*He talks less than his mother.*
Il **parle autant** que moi.	*He talks as much as I.*

Review the use of expressions of quantity, Ch. 8, p. 222.

■ To compare how much of something one has, eats, drinks, etc., the expressions of quantity **plus de, moins de,** and **autant de** are used *before a noun.*

Je mangeais **plus de pommes** que d'oranges.	*I used to eat more apples than oranges.*
André a **moins de soucis** qu'il y a trois ans.	*André has fewer worries than three years ago.*
J'ai **autant de responsabilités** que vous.	*I have as many responsibilities as you.*

■ To compare descriptions of people, things, or actions, the words **plus,**
moins, and **aussi** are used *before an adjective or an adverb.*

Je suis **plus âgé** que mon frère.	*I am older than my brother.*
Ma mère est **moins grande** que mon père.	*My mother is not as tall as my father.*
Lisa parle **aussi couramment** que Pierre.	*Lisa speaks as fluently as Pierre.*

Monique a quinze jours de vacances. Décidez si Monique a plus, moins ou autant de vacances que les autres.

> **MODÈLE:** Ses parents ont un mois de vacances.
> **Monique a moins de vacances qu'eux.**

NOTE CULTURELLE
Les Français utilisent souvent l'expression **huit jours** comme synonyme d'**une semaine.** De la même manière, on utilise l'expression **quinze jours** à la place de **deux semaines.**

1. Alice a huit jours de vacances.
2. Nous avons deux mois de vacances.
3. Tu as un jour de vacances.
4. Son frère a deux semaines de vacances.
5. Vous avez trente jours de vacances.
6. Je n'ai pas de vacances.
7. Michel et Jean ont trois mois de vacances.
8. Philippe a une semaine de vacances.
9. Ses amies ont quinze jours de vacances.

 À mon avis. Utilisez un élément de chaque colonne pour faire des phrases logiques.

> **MODÈLES:** **À mon avis, les étudiants ont autant de soucis que les professeurs.**
> **À mon avis, ma mère conduit aussi rapidement que mon père.**

les étudiants / les professeurs			responsabilités
ma mère / mon père		plus (de)	soucis
le président des États-Unis / moi	avoir	moins (de)	argent
mes amis / moi		autant (de)	travail
les femmes / les hommes			temps libre
un patron / un employé			
un pilote / une hôtesse de l'air	conduire	plus	rapidement
les parents / les enfants		moins	prudemment
nous / notre professeur		aussi	attentivement
			nerveusement
			follement

 À mon avis et de l'avis du professeur. Donnez votre opinion et devinez l'opinion du professeur. Attention aux adjectifs!

> **MODÈLE:** la musique classique / la musique pop / beau
> **À mon avis, la musique pop est aussi belle que la musique classique.**
> **De l'avis du professeur, la musique classique est plus belle que la musique pop.**

1. la statue de la Liberté / la tour Eiffel / beau
2. les jeunes filles / les garçons / travailleur
3. cette université / l'université de Paris / important
4. une moto / un vélo / dangereux
5. un chien / un chat / intelligent
6. un examen / un médicament / affreux
7. un restaurant français / un restaurant mexicain / chic
8. la télévision / un livre / ennuyeux

Entre amis

Il y a dix ans

1. Find out where your partner lived ten years ago.
2. Find out if s/he had more free time than now.
3. Find out if s/he had fewer worries.
4. Find out if s/he had more friends.
5. Find out if s/he had as much homework.
6. Find out if s/he spoke French as fluently.

E. Le comparatif de *bon* et de *bien*

Danielle est une **meilleure** étudiante que sa sœur.	*Danielle is a better student than her sister.*
Elle conduit **mieux** que sa sœur.	*She drives better than her sister.*

■ The comparative forms of the *adjective* **bon(ne)** are **moins bon(ne), aussi bon(ne),** and **meilleur(e).** Like all adjectives, these agree with the noun they modify.

Est-ce que sa sœur est **aussi bonne** que Danièle?	*Is her sister as good as Danièle?*
Non, comme étudiante, elle est **moins bonne.**	*No, as a student, she's worse.*
Danièle est **meilleure.**	*Danièle is better.*

Review the distinction between adjectives and adverbs in Appendix C at the end of the book.

■ The comparative forms of the adverb **bien** are **moins bien, aussi bien,** and **mieux.** Like all adverbs, these are invariable.

Marc travaille **moins bien** que Paul.	*Marc doesn't work as well as Paul.*
Monique travaille **aussi bien** que Paul.	*Monique works as well as Paul.*
Marc travaille bien. Paul travaille **mieux.**	*Marc works well. Paul works better.*
Chantal chante **mieux** que son frère.	*Chantal sings better than her brother.*

Attention

1. Both French and English have two separate words to distinguish between an adjective and an adverb when indicating quality.

Pascal est un **bon** étudiant.	Pascal parle **bien** le français.
*Pascal is a **good** student.*	*Pascal speaks French **well**.*

2. In English, however, the comparative form of both *good* and *well* is the same word: *better.* In French, there is still a separate word for each.

Tom est un **meilleur** étudiant.	Tom parle **mieux** le français.
*Tom is a **better** student.*	*Tom speaks French **better**.*

Follow-up: Have students compare themselves to a sibling. Alternate: Redo the exercise. Change **son frère David** to **sa sœur Stéphanie** and inform students that she is on a par with her brother (use **aussi bonne,** etc.).

12 **Deux frères.** Pauvre François! Son frère David fait toujours mieux que lui. Comparez-les.

MODÈLE: François est bon en anglais.
Oui, mais son frère David est meilleur en anglais que lui.

1. François parle bien l'anglais.
2. François a une bonne voiture.
3. François a une bonne note en anglais.
4. François joue bien au tennis.
5. François conduit attentivement.
6. François est un bon étudiant.
7. François chante bien.
8. François est intelligent.

13 **Nos meilleurs amis et nous.** D'abord faites une comparaison entre vous et votre meilleur(e) ami(e). Ensuite encouragez votre partenaire à faire la même chose.

MODÈLE: chanter bien

VOUS: Moi, je chante mieux que mon meilleur ami (ma meilleure amie). Et toi?

VOTRE PARTENAIRE: Moi, je chante moins bien que lui (qu'elle).

1. être bon(ne) en maths
2. parler bien le français
3. être patient(e)
4. conduire bien
5. être un(e) bon(ne) étudiant(e)
6. être grand(e)
7. danser bien
8. être bavard(e)

Follow up by having students share two things they learned about their partner.

F. Le superlatif

Mathusalem est **la personne la plus âgée** de la Bible.
Job est **la personne la moins impatiente** de la Bible.
Le Rhode Island est **le plus petit état** des États-Unis.
Les Canadiens sont **les meilleurs joueurs** de hockey du monde.

■ Superlatives are preceded by a definite article and may be used with an expression including **de** *(in, of)* plus a noun to make the extent of the superlative clear.

C'est **la meilleure** chanson (**de** l'année).	*It's the best song (of the year).*
De tous les étudiants, c'est lui qui étudie **le plus attentivement.**	*Of all the students, he's the one who studies the most attentively.*
Elle voyage **le moins** (**de** sa famille).	*She travels the least (in her family).*
De tous les enfants, c'est Joël qui a demandé **le plus** de cadeaux.	*Of all the children, it's Joel who asked for the most gifts.*

■ With the superlative of an adverb, a verb, or an expression of quantity, **le** is always used.

De tous les membres de ma famille, c'est mon frère qui fait *le* **plus de voyages.**	*Of all my family members, it's my brother who takes the most trips.*
Ma sœur voyage *le* **moins.**	*My sister travels the least.*
Elle voyage *le* **moins fréquemment.**	*She travels the least frequently.*

Point out that the possessive adjective can be used in place of the definite article. Students have already been using the superlative in the expression **votre meilleur(e) ami(e).**

Review the adjectives that normally precede a noun, Ch. 4, pp. 106–107.

■ With a superlative *adjective*, the definite article agrees with the adjective.

le plus petit   la plus petite
le moins grand   la moins grande

les plus petits   les plus petites
les moins grands   les moins grandes

Note   Superlative adjectives are placed either before or after the noun according to where they would be placed normally.

1. If the adjective follows the noun, the definite article must be repeated.

   La Tour d'Argent est *le restaurant le plus chic* de Paris.
   Les romans policiers sont *les romans les plus intéressants.*
   Sandrine est *l'étudiante la moins paresseuse.*

2. If the adjective precedes the noun, only one definite article is used.

   Paris et Lyon sont *les plus grandes villes* de France.
   Le français est *la plus belle langue* du monde.
   C'est *le moins bon restaurant* de la ville.

14 **Quelle exagération!** Aimez-vous votre cours de français? Exagérez un peu. Utilisez le superlatif dans les phrases suivantes.

MODÈLE: C'est un cours important.
   C'est le cours le plus important du monde!

Try to use other endings besides **du monde.** For instance, **de l'université, des États-Unis,** etc.

1. C'est un cours intéressant.
2. C'est un bon cours.
3. C'est un professeur intelligent.
4. Ce sont des étudiants travailleurs.
5. Ce sont de bons étudiants.
6. Ce sont de belles étudiantes.
7. Ce sont de beaux étudiants.
8. C'est un livre bizarre.

15 **Quel est le plus ... ?** Répondez à ces questions. Si vous ne savez pas, devinez.

MODÈLE: Quel est le plus grand état des États-Unis?
   L'Alaska est le plus grand état des États-Unis.

Answers: (1) New York, Toronto; (2) Montréal

1. Quelle est la plus grande ville des États-Unis? du Canada?
2. Quelle est la plus grande ville francophone du monde après Paris?
3. Qui est la meilleure actrice de votre pays?
4. Quel est le film le plus ennuyeux de cette année?
5. Qui est la femme politique la plus célèbre du monde?
6. Qui est la personne la moins âgée de cette classe?
7. Quelle est l'émission de télévision la plus intéressante le jeudi soir?

Rien que des superlatifs! Donnez votre opinion personnelle. Faites des phrases au superlatif.

Modèles: un bon restaurant (de la ville)
  Joe's Diner est le meilleur restaurant de la ville.

  un sport intéressant (du monde)
  Le golf est le sport le plus intéressant du monde.

1. une bonne actrice (de mon pays)
2. un professeur charmant (de cette université)
3. un film ennuyeux (de cette année)
4. un bel acteur (de mon pays)
5. une mauvaise chanson (de cette année)
6. une personne amusante (de ma famille)

 Microconversation: Tu n'es jamais d'accord (in agreement) **avec moi.** Utilisez les expressions suivantes pour compléter la conversation.

Review the gesture for **non**, Ch. 2, p. 30.

Modèle: le meilleur restaurant
  VOTRE PARTENAIRE: Quel est le meilleur restaurant de la ville?
  VOUS: C'est le restaurant qui s'appelle *Chez Tony.*
  VOTRE PARTENAIRE: Mais non! C'est le plus mauvais restaurant.
  VOUS: Tu n'es jamais d'accord avec moi!

1. le meilleur bistro de la ville
2. le cours le plus intéressant de cette université
3. le bâtiment le plus laid de cette université
4. la plus belle ville du pays
5. le meilleur supermarché de la ville
6. le professeur le plus charmant de cette université

18 **À vous.** Répondez.

1. Quel est le mois que vous aimez le mieux? Pourquoi?
2. Quel est le mois que vous aimez le moins? Pourquoi?
3. Quelle est l'émission de radio que vous écoutez le plus? Pourquoi l'écoutez-vous?
4. Quelle est l'émission de télévision que vous regardez le plus?
5. Quelle est la meilleure équipe de football de votre pays?
6. Qui fait le mieux la cuisine de votre famille?
7. Qui est la personne la plus gentille de votre famille?
8. Quelle personne conduit le plus rapidement de votre famille?

A useful structure is ... **que j'aime le mieux (le plus, le moins).**
Le printemps est la saison **que j'aime le mieux.**
L'hiver est la saison **que j'aime le moins.**

Entre amis

Description d'une famille

1. Find out how many people there are in your partner's family.
2. Find out who is the oldest, tallest, shortest, youngest.
3. Find out who sings the best, who dances the best.
4. Find out who is the most generous and who is the most stingy.
5. Find out who gives the most presents and who gives the least.

Intégration

Révision

A Quelles différences!

1. Nommez trois choses que vous faisiez quand vous étiez à l'école secondaire et que vous ne faites plus maintenant.
2. Nommez trois différences entre vous et un autre membre de votre famille.
3. Quelles différences y a-t-il entre un chien et un chat?
4. Quelles différences y a-t-il entre un avion et un train?

B Un sondage. Complétez le formulaire suivant.

1. Le plus bel homme du monde: _____
2. La plus belle femme du monde: _____
3. Le meilleur groupe rock: _____
4. Le meilleur chanteur: _____
5. La meilleure chanteuse: _____
6. La meilleure émission de télévision: _____
7. L'émission la moins intéressante: _____
8. Le meilleur film: _____
9. Le livre le plus intéressant: _____
10. Le sport que vous aimez le mieux: _____
11. La personne que vous admirez le plus: _____
12. Le moment le plus ennuyeux de votre journée: _____

Follow-up: Put students in pairs and have them try to guess each other's answers.

C À vous. Répondez.

1. Quel âge aviez-vous quand vous avez commencé vos études au lycée?
2. Où habitiez-vous à cette époque?
3. Avez-vous changé d'adresse depuis?
4. Combien de personnes y avait-il dans votre famille?
5. Quelle était votre émission de télévision préférée?
6. Comment s'appelait votre meilleur(e) ami(e)?
7. Quelle était la chanson la plus populaire quand vous étiez au lycée?
8. Quels cours aimiez-vous le mieux quand vous étiez au lycée? Pourquoi?
9. Écoutiez-vous la radio aussi souvent que maintenant?

Suggestion: Have students do the Information Gap activity in the Instructor's Resource Manual.

Pas de problème!

Preparation for the video:
1. Video worksheet in the
Cahier d'activités
2. CD-ROM, *Module 8*

Cette activité est basée sur la vidéo, *Module 8*. Choisissez la bonne réponse pour compléter les phrases suivantes.

1. Noël doit payer _____ francs pour faire le plein d'essence *(gas)*.
   (105, 115, 150)
2. Noël vient d'acheter _____.
   (une nouvelle voiture, une nouvelle batterie, un nouveau système électrique)
3. Émile va regarder. Il faut qu'il ouvre _____.
   (le capot *(hood)*, le système électrique, la batterie)
4. La voiture ne démarre pas parce que _____ ne marche *(work)* pas.
   (le capot, le système électrique, la batterie)
5. Émile peut la réparer _____.
   (tout de suite, ce soir, demain)
6. Sur l'autoroute, la vitesse est limitée à _____ kilomètres à l'heure.
   (300, 130, 103)
7. Sur les routes nationales, la vitesse est limitée à _____ kilomètres à l'heure.
   (70, 80, 90)

Lecture I

 Étude du vocabulaire. Étudiez les phrases suivantes et choisissez les mots anglais qui correspondent aux mots français en caractères gras: *especially, earth, to send, when, rather, beyond, around, full, happiness.*

1. Quel **bonheur lorsque** les étudiants sont en vacances!
2. Elle était fatiguée **au-delà** des limites de ses forces.
3. Les tasses étaient **remplies** de café.
4. Il faisait froid? Non, il faisait **plutôt** chaud.
5. La **terre** de l'Iowa est fertile, **surtout** quand elle est noire.
6. Marie va **envoyer** une lettre à sa mère.
7. Marc a regardé **autour** de lui pour voir s'il connaissait des gens.

B **Parcourez cette sélection.** Lisez rapidement la lecture suivante pour trouver un ou deux exemples de l'amour et du courage d'Aïda.

La Grand-mère Aïda

*Marie-Célie Agnant est née à Port-au-Prince, en Haïti, mais habite actuellement à Montréal. Dans **La Dot de Sara** (Sara's Dowry) elle raconte l'histoire de quatre générations de femmes haïtiennes.*

Grand-mère Aïda c'était comme la bonne terre. Amoureuse de la vie, généreuse et intelligente. Elle donnait, donnait, la femme Aïda, pour le plaisir de donner, pour l'amour de l'amour, l'amour de la tendresse, pour l'amour sans raison d'aimer, au-delà de la raison et de l'amour, cet amour de la vie pour ce qu'elle est véritablement: trésor, mystère, beauté, bonheur simple dans le tourbillon[1] de l'existence, au milieu des siens[2]: enfants, petits-enfants, nièces et neveux. Aïda, les jupes toujours remplies d'enfants. Et lorsque j'y pense, au fait, qu'avait-elle d'autre, qu'avions-nous d'autre? ...

Grand-mère Aïda m'avait élevée au doigt et à la baguette[3], comme cela se faisait dans ce temps-là. Ma mère à moi, Man Clarisse, n'avait pas survécu à ma naissance[4]. Elle avait été emportée par une septicémie[5], dit-on, quelque temps après que je sois née et n'avait jamais voulu révéler le nom de celui qui l'avait mise en mal d'enfant[6]. Elle avait alors vingt ans. Comme tant d'autres, elle avait dû se dire que les enfants, c'est plutôt l'affaire des femmes. Il y avait autour de nous et avec nous cette communauté de commères, matantes et marraines[7], qui étaient pour moi comme autant de mamans. Elle avait tenu[8], grand-mère, à m'envoyer à l'école. À l'époque, c'était un grand pas[9], comme on dit, car les petites filles—et croyez-moi, cela n'a pas beaucoup changé—on les gardait surtout pour aider à la maison, ou à faire marcher le commerce. L'école, lorsqu'on le pouvait, on y envoyait plutôt les futurs messieurs. S'il y avait quelque argent à investir, mieux valait l'employer à garnir la caboche[10] des petits hommes, ceux qui, pensait-on, devaient par la suite sauver la famille de la faim en devenant agronomes[11], avocats, ingénieurs, et peut-être même médecins.

Envoyer les enfants à l'école, c'était, disait-on, comme mettre de l'argent en banque. J'y suis allée, moi, jusqu'à la deuxième année du secondaire, puis à l'école d'économie domestique du bourg, chez madame Souffrant. C'était énorme.

Marie-Célie Agnant, *La Dot de Sara*

---

1. *whirlwind*   2. *surrounded by her family*   3. *had raised me strictly*   4. *hadn't survived my birth*
5. *blood poisoning*   6. *the one who had made her pregnant*   7. *neighbors, aunts and godmothers*
8. *had insisted on*   9. *step*   10. *head*   11. *by becoming agricultural specialists*

 Vrai ou faux? Décidez si les phrases suivantes sont vraies ou fausses. Si une phrase est fausse, corrigez-la.

1. La narratrice est la fille d'Aïda.
2. On sait le nom du père de la narratrice.
3. Elle a sans doute appris à faire la cuisine dans une école spécialisée.
4. Sa mère était assez âgée quand elle est morte.
5. Les garçons devaient, plus tard, gagner de l'argent pour la famille.
6. Il était normal que les filles fassent des études.
7. Aïda s'occupait de beaucoup d'enfants.

Discussions. Relisez la lecture et cherchez des exemples ...

1. pour comparer Aïda et les grands-mères que vous avez connues.
2. de généralisations/stéréotypes en ce qui concerne les hommes et les femmes.
3. de ressemblances ou de différences entre la culture haïtienne et la culture de votre pays.

E **Familles de mots.** Essayez de deviner le sens des mots suivants.

1. aimer, l'amour, aimable, amoureux (amoureuse)
2. naître, la naissance, né(e)
3. raisonner, la raison, raisonnable
4. la vérité, véritable, véritablement, vrai(e)

Lecture II

A **Parcourez les annonces personnelles.** Lisez rapidement la lecture pour identifier 1. la personne la plus âgée et 2. la personne la plus égoïste.

ANNONCES PERSONNELLES	
Jeune homme, 20 ans, bien physiquement et moralement, bonne situation[1], cherche en vue mariage jeune fille 18–22 ans, réponse assurée, joindre photo qui sera retournée. Ecr. Réf. 5093	Jeune fille, 27 ans, désire rencontrer jeune homme, âge en rapport[2], joindre photo si possible. Ecr. Réf. 5095
Dame agréable, élégante, sans enfants, jeune de cœur[3], désire rencontrer, pour sorties amicales, Monsieur, cinquante–soixante ans, bien[4] sous tous rapports[5], libre, optimiste, aimant[6] la nature, joindre photo qui sera retournée, discrétion absolue, mariage exclu. Ecr. Réf. 5094	Homme, 37 ans, propriétaire appartement, voiture, passé irréprochable, intelligent, éducation, très gentil cœur, très sympathique[7], se marierait[8] av. J.F., même[9] secrétaire, ouvrière, mais affectueuse, douce[10], très sincère, réponse assurée dans l'immédiat, discrétion. Ecr. Réf. 5096

1. *job*   2. *similar*   3. *heart*   4. *nice*   5. *in every respect*   6. *who likes*   7. *likeable*   8. *would marry*   9. *even*   10. *sweet*

B **Vrai ou faux?** Relisez les annonces personnelles et ensuite décidez si les phrases suivantes sont vraies ou fausses. Si une phrase est fausse, corrigez-la.

1. Tous les auteurs des annonces parlent de mariage.
2. Ils demandent tous qu'une photo accompagne la réponse.
3. La plus jeune personne travaille.
4. Les deux femmes sont moins discrètes que les deux hommes.
5. La personne la plus riche est une femme.
6. La personne la plus matérialiste est un homme.

 Inventez une annonce personnelle. Inventez une annonce pour vous ou pour un(e) ami(e). Utilisez la lecture comme modèle.

VOCABULAIRE ACTIF

Noms

un chanteur/une chanteuse
  singer
un dessin animé *cartoon*
une émission *(de télé) (TV)*
  program
une équipe *team*
une hôtesse de l'air *(female) flight*
  attendant
un lycée *senior high school*
le maire *mayor*
la mairie *town hall*
le mariage *marriage; wedding*
un pilote *pilot*
une responsabilité *responsibility*
une robe de mariée *wedding dress*
un smoking *tuxedo*
un souci *worry; care*
une statue *statue*
un tour *turn, tour*
une tour *tower*
un voisin/une voisine *neighbor*

Pour faire une comparaison

aussi ... *as ...*
autant *as much*
mieux *better*
moins *less*
plus *more*

Adjectifs

âgé(e) *old*
amusant(e) *amusing, funny; fun*
dangereux (dangereuse)
  dangerous
meilleur(e) *better*
pauvre *poor*
populaire *popular*
préféré(e) *favorite*
sincère *sincere*

Verbes

avoir lieu *to take place*
en avoir assez *to be fed up*
épouser (quelqu'un) *to marry*
  (someone)
être en train de *to be in the*
  process of
fréquenter (quelqu'un) *to date*
  (someone)
neiger *to snow*
pleuvoir *to rain*

Expressions utiles

à cette époque *at that time;*
  back then
à mon (ton, etc.) avis *in my (your,*
  etc.) opinion
Comme il (elle) était ... !
  How ... he (she) was!
huit jours *one week*
il neigeait *it was snowing*
il pleuvait *it was raining*
j'aime le mieux (le plus)
  I like best
j'aime le moins *I like least*
ne ... que *only*
Occupe-toi de tes oignons! *Mind*
  your own business!
parler couramment *to speak*
  fluently
quinze jours *two weeks*
toute la famille *the whole family*
tu vois *you see*

Buts communicatifs
Making a request
Making a restaurant or hotel reservation
Making a transportation reservation

Structures utiles
Le verbe **savoir**
Les verbes réguliers en **-ir (-iss-)**
L'adjectif **tout**
Le futur
Le futur avec **si** et **quand**

Culture
Pour répondre au téléphone
La politesse (rappel)
À l'hôtel
Mince!

Coup d'envoi

Prise de contact ## Au restaurant ou à l'hôtel

Puis-je° réserver une table?   *May I*
       Pour combien de personnes?
       Pour quel jour?
       Et pour quelle heure?
       À quel nom°, s'il vous plaît?   *In what name*
Puis-je réserver une chambre?
       Pour combien de personnes?
       Pour quelle(s) nuit(s)?
       À quel nom, s'il vous plaît?

| **Conversation** | # Une réservation par téléphone |

Joseph Smith téléphone pour réserver une table pour demain soir dans un restaurant à Angers. Mais le restaurant sera° fermé demain.

°will be

MME DUPONT: Allô! Ici le restaurant La Pyramide. J'écoute.

JOSEPH SMITH: Bonjour, Madame. Je voudrais réserver une table pour demain soir.

MME DUPONT: Je regrette, Monsieur. Nous serons fermés demain.

JOSEPH SMITH: Mince!° Je ne savais pas° que vous fermiez le mardi. Qu'est-ce que je vais faire? Vous serez ouvert après-demain?°

°Darn it! / I didn't know

°You will be open the day after tomorrow?

MME DUPONT: Mais oui, Monsieur.

JOSEPH SMITH: Bien, alors puis-je réserver une table pour après-demain?

MME DUPONT: Oui, c'est pour combien de personnes?

JOSEPH SMITH: Cinq. Une table pour cinq personnes.

MME DUPONT: À quel nom, s'il vous plaît?

JOSEPH SMITH: Au nom de Smith.

MME DUPONT: Pouvez-vous épeler° le nom, s'il vous plaît?

°spell

JOSEPH SMITH: S-M-I-T-H.

MME DUPONT: Et pour quelle heure?

JOSEPH SMITH: Pour huit heures, si possible.

MME DUPONT: Très bien, Monsieur. C'est entendu°. Une table pour cinq pour vingt heures.

°agreed

JOSEPH SMITH: Je vous remercie° beaucoup. Au revoir, Madame.

°thank

MME DUPONT: Au revoir, Monsieur. À mercredi soir.

Review the French alphabet on p. 4.

▶ **Jouez ces rôles.** Répétez la conversation avec votre partenaire. Utilisez vos propres *(own)* noms et demandez une réservation pour neuf heures. Faites tous les changements nécessaires.

Il y a un geste

This gesture is used in each video module. See especially *Modules 2 & 3.*

Qu'est-ce que je vais faire? The mouth is open, with a look of exasperation. An alternate gesture is to expel air through slightly pursed lips.

À PROPOS

Comment dit-on «second floor» en français?

a. le premier étage
b. le deuxième étage
c. le troisième étage

Pourquoi est-ce que Joseph dit «Mince!»?

a. Il n'est pas gros.
b. Il mange trop et doit maigrir *(lose weight)*.
c. Il regrette que le restaurant ferme le mardi.

Pour répondre au téléphone

Allô is only used, in French, when responding to the phone. Likewise, **J'écoute** *(lit. I'm listening)* and **Qui est à l'appareil?** *(Who is on the phone?)* are appropriate in this context. See p. 175 for an example of the latter.

La politesse (rappel)

Remember to use **je voudrais,** and not **je veux,** when making a polite request. Respect and politeness will not fail to make a good impression in France. Conversely, impatience and lack of courtesy will be met with similar treatment. Review the polite expressions on p. 9.

À l'hôtel

Most French hotels have private bathrooms, but there are exceptions. It is still possible to find hotels in which the toilet and the showers are located down the hall from the room. However, every room will have a sink of its own.

The first floor of any French building is called **le rez-de-chaussée** and the second floor is **le premier étage.** If your room is **au deuxième étage,** you will need to climb two flights of stairs, not one. In an elevator, you must remember to press **RC** and not **1** if you wish to get to the ground floor.

In order to conserve electricity, many French hotels have installed **minuteries.** These are hall lights that stay lit for only one minute. Unsuspecting tourists are occasionally surprised to have the hall light go off before they can get their door key in the lock.

Mince!

This is one of a number of euphemisms used to avoid another "five-letter word." Other inoffensive expressions used to express disappointment are **zut!** and **flûte!** *(darn, shucks).*

À vous. Vous avez téléphoné à l'hôtel de Champagne pour réserver une chambre. Parlez avec la réceptionniste.

RÉCEPTIONNISTE: Allô! Ici l'hôtel de Champagne.
VOUS: _____

RÉCEPTIONNISTE: Ce soir?
VOUS: _____

RÉCEPTIONNISTE: Pour combien de personnes?
VOUS: _____

RÉCEPTIONNISTE: Et à quel nom?
VOUS: _____

RÉCEPTIONNISTE: Épelez le nom, s'il vous plaît.
VOUS: _____

RÉCEPTIONNISTE: Très bien. C'est entendu.
VOUS: _____

Entre amis

Vous êtes hôte/hôtesse au restaurant

You are speaking on the telephone to a customer. Your partner will take the role of the customer.

1. Ask if s/he wants to reserve a table.
2. Find out how many there are in the party.
3. Find out at what time s/he wishes to dine.
4. Find out his/her name.
5. Find out how to spell the name.
6. Repeat back the information you received.

Prononciation

Use the Student Audio to help practice pronunciation.

Les sons [l] et [j]

■ You learned in Chapter 11 that the letter **l** in certain situations is pronounced [j], as in the English word *yes*. However, in many cases it is pronounced [l], as in the French word **la**.

■ While the [l] sound is somewhat close to the sound of **l** in the English word *like*, it is far from that in the English word *bull*. Special attention is therefore necessary when pronouncing [l], especially at the end of a word. To produce the [l] sound, the tongue must be in a curved, convex position. Practice saying the following words:

la   pi**l**ote   b**l**eu   que**l**   e**ll**e

■ Now practice saying the following words after your instructor, paying particular attention to the highlighted sound. As you pronounce the words for one sound, look at how that sound is spelled and in what kinds of letter combinations it appears. What patterns do you notice?

[j]
- déta**il**, somme**il**, œ**il**, sole**il**, trava**ill**e, ore**ill**e, feu**ill**e, me**ill**eur
- genti**ll**e, fi**ll**e, pasti**ll**e, vani**ll**e, cédi**ll**e, ju**ill**et, bi**ll**et

[l]
- **l**e, **l**a, **l**es, **l**'air, **l**à, **l**ycée, **l**aisser, **l**ent, **l**entement, **l**ongue
- pi**l**ote, déso**l**é, faci**l**e, popu**l**aire, fidè**l**e, fo**l**ie, vo**l**ant, épau**l**e, pi**l**u**l**e
- i**l**, ba**l**, posta**l**, que**l**
- p**l**eut, p**l**us, b**l**eu, c**l**ient
- do**ll**ar, inte**ll**igent, a**ll**emand, appe**ll**e, e**ll**e, fo**ll**e, mademoise**ll**e

■ Remember that the [j] sound is required for the letter **l** in the following circumstances:

1. **-il** or **-ill** after a pronounced vowel in the same syllable: trav**ail,** conse**ill**er
2. **-ll** after [i]: f**ill**e, ju**ill**et

> Be sure to distinguish between **gentil** [ʒɑ̃ti] and **gentille** [ʒɑ̃tij].

Exceptions   mi**ll**ion, mi**ll**iard, mi**ll**e, vi**ll**e, tranqui**ll**e, vi**ll**age

■ In a few words, the letter **l** is silent: genti**l,** fi**l**s

■ In all other cases, the letter **l** or the combination **ll** is pronounced as [l]—that is, at the beginning or end of a word, between two vowels, or following a consonant.

le   il   pilule   inutile   pleut   dollar

■ Pronounce the following sentences correctly.

1. Les lilas sont merveilleux.
2. Il habite dans un village près de Marseille.
3. Le soleil m'a fait mal aux yeux.
4. Aïe! J'ai mal à l'oreille!
5. Ma fille Hélène travaille au lycée.

Buts
communicatifs

1 Making a Request

—C'est ici le bureau des renseignements°?　　　　　　*information*
—Oui.
—Puis-je vous demander quelques renseignements?
—Mais certainement. Allez-y.
—Pourriez-vous me dire° où sont les toilettes?　　　　*Could you tell me*
—Elles sont dans le couloir.
—Pouvez-vous m'indiquer où se trouve la gare?
—Oui, elle est tout près°. Quand vous sortirez,　　　　*very near*
　tournez à gauche dans la rue.
—Savez-vous° si le bureau de poste est ouvert toute　　*Do you know*
　la journée°?　　　　　　　　　　　　　　　　　　*all day long*
—Oui, il reste ouvert. Il ne ferme pas à midi.
—Je voudrais savoir à quelle heure les banques
　ferment.
—Elles ferment à 17 heures.
—La pharmacie est ouverte jusqu'à quelle heure?
—Jusqu'à 19 heures.
—Merci, vous êtes très aimable.
—De rien.° Je suis là pour ça.　　　　　　　　　　*You're welcome.*

The final **-e** in **Puis-je ...** is silent: [pɥiʒ]. When inverted, **je** does not change before a vowel.

Remarque   When asking permission to do something, you may use **Est-ce que je peux ... ?** or **Puis-je ... ?**

Est-ce que je peux conduire?   *May I drive?*
Puis-je avoir un verre d'eau?   *May I have a glass of water?*

VOCABULAIRE

Pour demander un service

faire une demande	*to make a request*
poser une question	*to ask a question*
demander un renseignement	*to ask for information*
réserver une place	*to reserve a seat*
louer une voiture	*to rent a car*
recommander un bon restaurant	*to recommend a good restaurant*
commander un repas	*to order a meal*
confirmer un départ	*to confirm a departure*

Review possible answers before doing the exercise: **Oui, allez-y!**; **Si vous voulez**; etc.

Do the exercise in pairs. Follow up with a role-play: The teacher plays an English-speaking tourist and selects a student as "interpreter" to translate his/her questions and the "native's" responses.

1 **Allez-y!** Utilisez la liste suivante pour faire une demande. Votre partenaire va vous donner la permission.

MODÈLE: ask you for information
> **VOUS:** Est-ce que je peux vous demander un renseignement, s'il vous plaît?
> **VOTRE PARTENAIRE:** Mais certainement.   ou   Allez-y!

1. speak with you
2. ask a question
3. ask something
4. read your newspaper
5. have a glass of water
6. order something
7. watch television

Follow-up: A student answers one question and then addresses the next question to someone else.

2 **Il n'y en a plus** *(There are no more).* Utilisez les listes suivantes pour faire des demandes. Ensuite votre partenaire va expliquer qu'il n'y en a plus.

MODÈLE: **VOUS:** Puis-je réserver une table?
VOTRE PARTENAIRE: Je regrette. Il n'y a plus de tables.

	réserver	un journal
	louer	un verre d'eau
	commander	une chambre
puis-je	avoir	un vélo
	acheter	une tasse de café
	demander	une voiture
	boire	une place

> The word **carte** has various meanings depending on the context: **carte postale** *(postcard)*, **jouer aux cartes** *(cards)*, **carte** *(map)* **de France**. In Ch. 13, it will be used in a restaurant setting: **à la carte**.

3 **Microconversation: Pour aller au château de Rigny.** Utilisez la carte *(map)* suivante pour expliquer quelles routes il faut prendre pour aller des villes indiquées au château de Rigny.

MODÈLE: la route de Paris au château de Rigny

> **TOURISTE:** **Puis-je vous demander un renseignement?**
> **GUIDE:** **Certainement. Allez-y.**
> **TOURISTE:** **Pouvez-vous m'indiquer la route de Paris au château de Rigny?**
> **GUIDE:** **Oui, regardez la carte. Prenez l'autoroute 6 et l'autoroute 38 jusqu'à Dijon et ensuite prenez la départementale 70 jusqu'au château de Rigny.**
> **TOURISTE:** **Je vous remercie. Vous êtes bien aimable.**

NOTE CULTURELLE

Les routes de France sont marquées **A** pour autoroute, **N** pour route nationale et **D** pour route départementale. On dit, par exemple, **l'autoroute A six, la nationale cinquante-sept** ou **la départementale quatre cent soixante-quinze**. Il faut payer pour utiliser l'autoroute.

1. la route de Besançon au château de Rigny
2. la route de Langres au château de Rigny
3. la route de Vesoul au château de Rigny
4. la route de Troyes au château de Rigny
5. la route de Belfort au château de Rigny
6. la route de Nancy au château de Rigny

Entre amis

Quelques renseignements

You are a French-speaking tourist in your partner's hometown.

1. Find out if s/he speaks French.
2. Get permission to ask a question.
3. Find out if there is a hotel nearby.
4. Get directions to the hotel.
5. Ask if s/he can recommend a good restaurant.
6. Ask directions on how to get there.
7. Express your gratitude for her/his help.

A. Le verbe *savoir*

Cette femme **sait** bien **danser**.	*That woman really knows how to dance.*
Savez-vous **comment** elle s'appelle?	*Do you know her name?*
Je **sais que** son prénom est Sophie.	*I know her first name is Sophie.*
Je ne **sais** pas **si** elle est célibataire.	*I don't know if she is single.*

savoir *(to know)*			
je	**sais**	nous	**savons**
tu	**sais**	vous	**savez**
il/elle/on	**sait**	ils/elles	**savent**

passé composé: j'**ai su** *(I found out, I learned)*

■ The verb **savoir** *(to know)* is used to express a skill or knowledge of a fact. It is used alone (**Je sais / Je ne sais pas**), or is followed by an infinitive, by the words **que** *(that)* or **si** *(if, whether),* or by question words such as **où, comment, combien, pourquoi, quand, quel.**

Je ne **savais** pas **que** tu venais.	*I didn't know that you were coming.*
Je ne **savais** pas **si** tu venais.	*I didn't know whether you were coming.*
Je ne **savais** pas **quand** tu venais.	*I didn't know when you were coming.*

Note   Followed by an infinitive, **savoir** means *to know how (to do something).*

Savez-vous parler espagnol?	*Do you know how to speak Spanish?*

Review the use of **connaître**, Ch. 10, p. 277.

■ The verbs **connaître** and **savoir** are used in different circumstances. Both are used with direct objects, but **connaître** (which means *to know* in the sense of *to be acquainted with, to be familiar with*) is used in general with people and places, while **savoir** is used with facts.

Vous **connaissez** ma sœur?	*Do you know my sister?*
Je ne **sais** pas son nom.	*I don't know her name.*

The special meanings of **vouloir** and **pouvoir** in the passé composé were learned in Ch. 10, p. 274.

■ The passé composé of **savoir** means *found out, learned.*

Je l'**ai su** hier.	*I found it out yesterday.*

4 **C'est inutile** *(It's useless).* On suggère que vous demandiez quelques renseignements. Répondez que c'est inutile. Ensuite utilisez le verbe **savoir** pour expliquer pourquoi c'est inutile.

Remind students of the pronunciation of **inutile**, [in], not [ɛ̃], where **in-** precedes a vowel. This was practiced on p. 92.

Modèle: Demandons à Jacques comment s'appelle cette jeune fille.
     C'est inutile! Jacques ne sait pas comment elle s'appelle.

1. Demandons à Jacques si Jeanne va à la boum.
2. Demandons à nos amis où habite le professeur.
3. Demandons au professeur le nom de cette voiture.
4. Demandons à ces personnes quand le film va commencer.
5. Demandons à Jean-Michel où sont les toilettes.
6. Demandons à Françoise la date du concert.
7. Demandons à nos amis pourquoi ils sont déprimés.

Une interview. Interviewez votre partenaire. Attention aux verbes **savoir** et **connaître**.

MODÈLES: où j'habite

> **VOUS:** **Sais-tu où j'habite?**
> **VOTRE PARTENAIRE:** **Non, je ne sais pas où tu habites.** ou
> **Oui, je sais où tu habites.**

mes parents

> **VOUS:** **Connais-tu mes parents?**
> **VOTRE PARTENAIRE:** **Non, je ne les connais pas.** ou
> **Oui, je les connais.**

1. danser le tango
2. quelle heure il est
3. la famille du professeur
4. parler espagnol
5. la ville de Québec
6. mon adresse
7. pourquoi tu étudies le français
8. la différence entre **savoir** et **connaître**

 Un petit sketch: À la boum. Lisez ou jouez le sketch suivant et ensuite répondez aux questions.

Georges parle avec son ami Thomas à la boum. Ils regardent une jeune fille.

GEORGES: Est-ce que tu connais cette jeune fille?

THOMAS: Oui, je la connais, mais je ne sais pas comment elle s'appelle.

GEORGES: Elle est jolie, n'est-ce pas?

THOMAS: Oui. Sais-tu si elle danse bien?

GEORGES: Je ne sais pas mais je vais l'inviter.

THOMAS: Bonne chance!

Questions (Répondez à l'imparfait):

1. Qui connaissait la jeune fille?
2. Savait-il comment elle s'appelait?
3. Qu'est-ce que Thomas voulait savoir?
4. Qu'est-ce que Georges allait faire?

VOCABULAIRE À RETENIR
Bonne chance *Good luck*

MOI, JE SAIS OÙ JE VAIS.

ÉCOLE SUPÉRIEURE D'INFORMATIQUE DE COMMERCE ET DE GESTION

ESIG

7 **Vous connaissez ce restaurant?** Complétez les phrases suivantes avec la forme convenable de **savoir** ou de **connaître**.

1. _____-vous s'il y a un bon restaurant près d'ici?
2. Oui, je _____ un restaurant qui est excellent, mais je ne _____ pas s'il est ouvert le mardi.
3. Je vais téléphoner à mon frère. Il _____ bien la ville et il va certainement _____ quel jour le restaurant est fermé. Est-ce que vous _____ mon frère?
4. Je le _____ un peu, mais je ne _____ pas comment il s'appelle.
5. Il s'appelle Paul. Vous _____ où nous habitons, n'est-ce pas?
6. Non, mais je _____ que ce n'est pas loin d'ici.

8 **À vous.** Répondez.

1. Connaissez-vous le président (la présidente) de votre université?
2. Savez-vous comment il (elle) s'appelle?
3. Vos parents savent-ils que vous étudiez le français?
4. Savent-ils à quelle heure vous allez au cours de français?
5. Connaissent-ils vos amis?
6. Vos amis savent-ils faire du ski?
7. Savez-vous s'ils étudient le français?
8. Connaissiez-vous ces amis quand vous étiez au lycée?
9. Est-ce qu'ils savent la date de votre anniversaire?
10. Saviez-vous parler français quand vous étiez au lycée?

Entre amis

Connais-tu X? Sais-tu si ... ?

1. Find out if your partner knows some person (name someone). Keep asking until you find someone s/he knows.
2. Ask if your partner knows if that person speaks French.
3. Ask if your partner knows that person's family.
4. Find out if your partner knows the person's age, address, whether s/he likes pizza, etc.

2 Making a Restaurant or Hotel Reservation

Il vous reste° des chambres, s'il vous plaît?	*Do you still have*
Oui, pour combien de personnes?	
Non, je regrette. Nous sommes complets°.	*full*
Quel est le prix° d'une chambre avec salle de bain?	*price*
... euros par nuit.	
Est-ce que le petit déjeuner est compris dans le prix de la chambre?	
Oui, tout est compris.	
Non, il y a un supplément° de 3 euros.	*extra charge*
Puis-je demander d'autres serviettes°?	*towels*
Mais certainement.	
Je regrette. Il n'y en a plus.°	*There are no more.*

VOCABULAIRE

Review the distinction between **les toilettes** and **la salle de bain**, p. 154.

À l'hôtel

une clé	*key*	une serviette	*towel*
un couloir	*hallway*	un supplément	*extra charge*
une douche	*shower*	les toilettes	*restroom, toilet*
le premier étage	*second floor*	complet (complète)	*full*
le rez-de-chaussée	*first floor*	compris(e)	*included*
une salle de bain	*bathroom*		

 Microconversation: Il vous reste des chambres? Complétez la conversation avec les détails suivants. Décidez ensuite combien de chambres il vous faut.

Demonstrate the model with a student. Then have two students perform No. 1 for the class, before putting students in pairs. Follow-up (books closed): Have pairs of students ad-lib, choosing their own answers.

MODÈLE: trois personnes / une nuit / 50€ (60€) / p.déj. (4€)

TOURISTE: **Il vous reste des chambres?**
HÔTELIER: **Oui, pour combien de personnes?**
TOURISTE: **Pour trois personnes.**
HÔTELIER: **Très bien. Pour combien de nuits?**
TOURISTE: **Pour une seule nuit. Quel est le prix des chambres, s'il vous plaît?**
HÔTELIER: **Cinquante euros pour une chambre pour une personne ou soixante euros pour une chambre pour deux personnes.**
TOURISTE: **Est-ce que le petit déjeuner est compris?**
HÔTELIER: **Non, il y a un supplément de quatre euros.**
TOURISTE: **Très bien. Je vais prendre une chambre pour une personne et une chambre pour deux personnes.**

1. une personne / deux nuits / 40€ / p.déj. 5€
2. quatre personnes / une semaine / 45€ (60€) / tout compris
3. deux personnes / une nuit / 40€ (50€) / p.déj. 4€
4. vingt-cinq étudiants / un mois / 25€ (30€) / tout compris

 Si vous alliez à l'hôtel. Posez des questions. Votre partenaire va donner une réponse appropriée.

MODÈLE: You want to know if there are any rooms left.
VOUS: **Est-ce qu'il vous reste des chambres?** ou
Avez-vous encore des chambres?
VOTRE PARTENAIRE: **Oui, certainement.**

Do this exercise in pairs. Follow up with the teacher again playing an English-speaking tourist and selecting an "interpreter" from among the students.

You want to know ...

1. where the toilet is.
2. if there is a bathroom in the room.
3. if there is a shower in the bathroom.
4. if you can have extra towels.
5. how much the room costs.
6. if breakfast is included in the price.
7. at what time you can have breakfast.
8. if there is a television set in the room.

Entre amis

À l'hôtel Ibis

Your partner will take the role of a hotel clerk.

1. Find out if there are still rooms available.
2. Find out the price.
3. Find out if breakfast is included.
4. Ask if the toilet and shower are in the room.
5. Ask if you can have extra towels.

B. Les verbes réguliers en *-ir (-iss-)*

Qu'est-ce que vous **choisissez?**	*What do you choose?*
J'**ai** déjà **choisi** une pâtisserie.	*I have already chosen a pastry.*
Nous **finissons** à cinq heures.	*We finish at five o'clock.*
Obéis à ta mère!	*Obey your mother!*
Ralentissez, s'il vous plaît.	*Please slow down.*
Avez-vous **réussi** à votre examen?	*Did you pass your test?*

■ You have already learned several French verbs whose infinitives end in **-ir.**

sortir	je sors	nous sortons	ils sortent
partir	je pars	nous partons	ils partent
dormir	je dors	nous dormons	ils dorment

■ There is a larger group of French verbs that also have infinitives ending in **-ir** but that are conjugated differently.

choisir *(to choose)*					
je	**chois**	**is**	nous	**chois**	**issons**
tu	**chois**	**is**	vous	**chois**	**issez**
il/elle/on	**chois**	**it**	ils/elles	**chois**	**issent**

passé composé: j'**ai choisi**

■ Because there are a number of verbs formed in this way, these **-ir** verbs are said to be *regular*. The following verbs are conjugated like **choisir.**

VOCABULAIRE

Quelques verbes réguliers en *-ir (-iss-)*

finir	*to finish*
grossir	*to put on weight*
maigrir	*to take off weight*
obéir (à quelqu'un)	*to obey (someone)*
ralentir	*to slow down*
réussir (à un examen)	*to succeed; to pass (an exam)*

Drill **J'obéis toujours au professeur** with other subjects.

■ When used with an infinitive, **finir** and **choisir** are followed by **de,** and **réussir** is followed by **à.**

Nous **avons fini de** manger.	*We finished eating.*
Karine **a choisi d'**aller au centre commercial.	*Karine decided to go to the mall.*
Elle **a réussi à** trouver des desserts délicieux.	*She succeeded in finding delicious desserts.*

■ The past participle of regular **-ir (-iss-)** verbs is formed by adding **-i** to the present tense verb stem.

choisi   fini   obéi

> *Choisissez une orientation pour votre épargne. Nos spécialistes feront le reste.*
>
>

Review the partitive article, p. 216.

11 **Qu'est-ce qu'ils choisissent d'habitude?** Posez la question et votre partenaire va répondre.

MODÈLE: tu / pâté ou soupe à l'oignon?
> **VOUS:**   **Est-ce que d'habitude tu choisis du pâté ou de la soupe à l'oignon?**
> **VOTRE PARTENAIRE:**   **D'habitude je choisis du pâté.**

1. tu / crudités, soupe ou pâté?
2. les végétariens / viande ou poisson?
3. les enfants / épinards ou frites?
4. le professeur de français / camembert ou fromage américain?
5. tes amis / glace, fruits, tarte ou gâteau?
6. tu / café ou thé?

12 **À vous.** Répondez.

1. Est-ce que vous choisissez un dessert d'habitude?
2. Qu'est-ce que vous avez choisi comme dessert la dernière fois que vous avez dîné au restaurant?
3. Qu'est-ce que vos amis choisissent comme dessert?
4. Est-ce que vous avez tendance à grossir?
5. Réussissez-vous à maigrir quand vous voulez?
6. Que peut-on choisir au restaurant si on veut grossir?
7. Que peut-on choisir au restaurant si on veut maigrir?
8. Finissez-vous toujours votre repas?
9. Finissiez-vous toujours votre repas quand vous étiez jeune?

Entre amis

À la fin du repas

1. Tell your partner s/he has lost weight.
2. Find out whether s/he is going to finish his/her cheese.
3. Encourage him/her to choose a dessert.
4. Say that s/he is not going to get fat.

C. L'adjectif *tout*

Il y a des toilettes dans **toutes** les chambres.	*There are toilets in all the rooms.*
Je parle avec mes amis **tous** les jours.	*I speak with my friends every day.*
Nous regardons la télévision **tous** les soirs.	*We watch television every evening.*
J'ai passé **toute** la journée à la bibliothèque.	*I spent the whole day at the library.*
Tout le monde aime dîner au restaurant.	*Everybody likes to dine out.*

■ **Tout** *(all, every, each, the whole)* is often used as an adjective. In those cases it is usually followed by one of the determiners: **le, un, ce,** or **mon, ton, son, notre, votre, leur.** Both **tout** and the determiner agree with the noun they modify.

	masculin	féminin
singulier	**tout**	**toute**
pluriel	**tous**	**toutes**

■ In the singular, the meaning of **tout** is usually *the whole* or *all ... (long).*

toute la journée	*all day (long)*
toute l'année	*all year*
toute la classe	*the whole class*
tout le temps	*all the time*
tout le monde	*everybody* (literally, *the whole world*)

■ In the plural, the meaning of **tout** is usually *all* or *every.*

tous mes amis	*all my friends*
tous les hommes et **toutes** les femmes	*all (the) men and all (the) women*
tous les deux	*both (masc.)*
toutes les deux	*both (fem.)*
toutes ces personnes	*all these people*
toutes sortes de choses	*all sorts of things*
tous les jours	*every day*
toutes les semaines	*every week*
tous les ans	*every year*

■ Only when **tous** is used as a pronoun is the final **-s** pronounced.

Mes amis sont **tous** ici.   [tus]   *My friends are all here.*

 Toute la famille Jeantet. Complétez les phrases avec la forme convenable de l'adjectif **tout.**

1. Monsieur et Madame Jeantet parlent anglais, _____ les deux.
2. _____ le monde dit qu'ils sont très gentils.
3. _____ leurs filles ont les yeux bleus.
4. Elles passent _____ leur temps à regarder la télévision.
5. _____ la famille va en Angleterre _____ les ans.
6. Ils achètent _____ sortes de choses.
7. Les filles Jeantet écrivent une carte postale à _____ leurs amis.
8. Elles sont contentes de voyager, _____ les trois.

 À votre avis. Ajoutez **tout** et posez une question. Votre partenaire va décider ensuite si la généralisation est vraie ou fausse.

MODÈLE: Les hommes sont beaux.
VOUS: **Est-ce que tous les hommes sont beaux?**
VOTRE PARTENAIRE: **Oui, à mon avis tous les hommes sont beaux.**   ou
    Non, à mon avis tous les hommes ne sont pas beaux.

1. Les femmes sont belles.
2. Les repas au restaurant universitaire sont délicieux.
3. Les professeurs sont gentils.
4. Le campus est très beau.
5. Tes amis adorent parler français.
6. Ta famille chante bien.
7. Tes cours sont intéressants.

Entre amis

La Pyramide

Call the restaurant La Pyramide and ask if the restaurant is open every day. Then make a reservation.

Put students' chairs back-to-back when they are "telephoning."

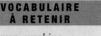

VOCABULAIRE À RETENIR

fumeur *smoking*
non fumeur *non-smoking*

Restaurant LA PYRAMIDE

Cuisine française traditionnelle
Recommandé par les meilleurs guides

Réservation: 02-41-83-15-15

Restaurant non fumeur
Ouvert tous les jours

3 Making a Transportation Reservation

Bonjour, Madame.
    Bonjour, Monsieur. Puis-je avoir un billet° *ticket*
      pour Strasbourg, s'il vous plaît?
Un aller simple°? *one way*
    Oui, un aller simple.
    Non, un aller-retour°. *round trip*
En quelle classe?
    En première.
    En seconde.
Quand partirez-vous?° *When will you leave?*
    Tout de suite.° *Right away.*
    Bientôt.
    Dans quelques jours.
Très bien. N'oubliez pas de composter° votre billet. *punch, stamp*

Margin notes (left column):

Point out that **aller simple** is two separate words, while **aller-retour** is one word containing a hyphen.

seconde: [səgɔ̃d]

You might wish to explain that tickets are stamped or punched by inserting them into a machine in the railroad station.

Use video, *Module 5*, to help set the scene. Alissa and Bruno are going to purchase train tickets.

NOTE CULTURELLE
Les billets de train peuvent être utilisés pendant quelques mois. Il est donc nécessaire de composter le billet le jour où on prend le train. Si on oublie de le composter, on peut être obligé de payer une amende *(fine)*.

Remarque   **Second(e)** is normally used in place of **deuxième** when there are only two in a series. Note that the **c** is pronounced [g].

Un billet en **seconde** classe, s'il vous plaît.

Bonjour, Madame. Puis-je avoir un billet?

15 **Microconversation: Nous prenons le train.** Réservez des places dans le train. Complétez la conversation avec les catégories suivantes.

Margin note (left column):

Do the exercise in pairs. Follow up with the teacher playing the **guichetier** (**guichetière**) and having students line up at the "ticket window."

MODÈLE: 1 / Paris 17 h / ven. / 1ʳᵉ / vous ne fumez pas
      VOUS: Puis-je réserver une place?
    EMPLOYÉ(E): Dans quel train, s'il vous plaît?
      VOUS: Le train pour Paris qui part à 17 heures.
    EMPLOYÉ(E): Quel jour, s'il vous plaît?
      VOUS: Vendredi.
    EMPLOYÉ(E): Et en quelle classe?
      VOUS: En première.
    EMPLOYÉ(E): Fumeur ou non fumeur?
      VOUS: Non fumeur.
    EMPLOYÉ(E): Très bien, une place en première classe non fumeur dans le train pour Paris qui part à 17 heures vendredi.

1. 1 / Marseille 11 h / lun. / 2ᵉ / vous ne fumez pas
2. 4 / Dijon 18 h / dim. / 2ᵉ / vous fumez
3. 15 / Biarritz 8 h / sam. / 2ᵉ / vous ne fumez pas
4. 2 / Madrid 23 h / merc. / 1ʳᵉ / vous ne fumez pas

16 **Un petit sketch: On confirme un départ.** Lisez ou jouez le sketch et ensuite répondez aux questions.

Un touriste téléphone à la compagnie Air France.

VOCABULAIRE
À RETENIR

un vol *flight*

L'EMPLOYÉ: Allô, Air France. J'écoute.
LE TOURISTE: Bonjour, Monsieur. Je voudrais confirmer un départ, s'il vous plaît.
L'EMPLOYÉ: Très bien, Monsieur. Votre nom, s'il vous plaît?
LE TOURISTE: Paul Schmitdz.
L'EMPLOYÉ: Comment? Pouvez-vous épeler votre nom, s'il vous plaît?
LE TOURISTE: S-C-H-M-I-T-D-Z.
L'EMPLOYÉ: Très bien. Votre jour de départ et le numéro de votre vol?
LE TOURISTE: Mardi prochain, et c'est le vol 307.
L'EMPLOYÉ: Très bien, Monsieur Schmitdz. Votre départ est confirmé.
LE TOURISTE: Merci beaucoup.
L'EMPLOYÉ: À votre service, Monsieur.

Questions (Répondez au passé)

1. Pour quelle compagnie l'employé travaillait-il?
2. Quelle était la première question de l'employé?
3. Quand le vol partait-il?
4. Quel était le numéro du vol?

Entre amis

Confirmez votre départ

1. Call Air Canada.
2. State that you wish to confirm your departure.
3. Identify yourself and your flight number.
4. Verify the time of departure.
5. Find out at what time you need to arrive at the airport.
6. End the conversation appropriately.

D. Le futur

Nous **aurons** notre diplôme en juin.	*We will get our diplomas in June.*
Nous **irons** en France l'été prochain.	*We will go to France next summer.*
Nous **prendrons** l'avion pour Paris.	*We will take the plane to Paris.*
J'espère qu'il ne **pleuvra** pas.	*I hope it won't rain.*
Nous **passerons** une nuit à l'hôtel Ibis.	*We will spend a night at the Ibis Hotel.*

Review the formation of the near future, Ch. 5, p. 128.

■ You have already learned to express future time by using **aller** plus an infinitive.

Ils **vont sortir** ensemble. *They are going to go out together.*

■ Another way to express what will take place is by using the future tense.

Ils **sortiront** ensemble. *They will go out together.*

> The future has only three different pronounced endings: [e] **-ai, -ez;** [a] **-as, -a;** and [ɔ̃] **-ons, -ont.**

■ To form the future tense for most verbs, take the infinitive and add the endings **-ai, -as, -a, -ons, -ez, -ont.** For infinitives ending in **-e**, drop the **-e** before adding the endings. Note that the future endings are similar to the present tense of the verb **avoir.**

finir					
je	**finir ai**	nous	**finir ons**		
tu	**finir as**	vous	**finir ez**		
il/elle/on	**finir a**	ils/elles	**finir ont**		

vendre					
je	**vendr ai**	nous	**vendr ons**		
tu	**vendr as**	vous	**vendr ez**		
il/elle/on	**vendr a**	ils/elles	**vendr ont**		

> Review the formation of **acheter,** Ch. 9, p. 252.

■ Verbs like **acheter** keep their spelling change in the future, even for the **nous** and **vous** forms.

J'achèterai une voiture l'année prochaine.
Nous achèterons une Renault.
Les étudiants **se lèveront** tard pendant les vacances.

> You may wish to point out that verbs like **préférer** do *not* have a spelling change in the future.

■ All future stems end in **-r** and the future endings are always the same. There are, however, a number of verbs with irregular stems.

infinitive	stem	future
être	**ser-**	je **serai**
avoir	**aur-**	j'**aurai**
faire	**fer-**	je **ferai**
aller	**ir-**	j'**irai**
venir (devenir)	**viendr- (deviendr-)**	je **viendrai** (je **deviendrai**)
pouvoir	**pourr-**	je **pourrai**
savoir	**saur-**	je **saurai**
vouloir	**voudr-**	je **voudrai**

■ Here are the future forms of two impersonal expressions.

> For the future of verbs not mentioned here, tell students to see the Appendix. This includes **mourir** and **payer**, as well as many regular verbs students have learned actively.

infinitive	present	future
pleuvoir	il pleut	**il pleuvra**
falloir	il faut	**il faudra**

 Pendant les vacances. Qu'est-ce que tout le monde fera? Utilisez le futur au lieu *(in place)* du verbe **aller** plus l'infinitif.

MODÈLE: Nous n'allons pas étudier. **Nous n'étudierons pas.**

1. Joe va voyager avec ses parents.
2. Ils vont faire un voyage en France.
3. Ils vont visiter Paris.
4. Je vais les accompagner.
5. Nous allons prendre un avion.
6. Nous allons partir bientôt.
7. Une semaine à l'hôtel à Paris va coûter cher.
8. Je vais acheter des souvenirs.
9. Il va falloir que j'achète une autre valise.
10. Il ne va pas pleuvoir.

Follow-up: Students use the questions to interview first the instructor (with books open) and then another student (with books closed).

18 **À vous.** Répondez.

1. Est-ce que vous resterez sur le campus l'été prochain?
2. Est-ce que vous travaillerez? Si oui, où? Si non, pourquoi pas?
3. Est-ce que vous ferez un voyage? Si oui, où?
4. Qu'est-ce que vous lirez?
5. Qu'est-ce que vous regarderez à la télévision?
6. À qui rendrez-vous visite?
7. Sortirez-vous avec des amis? Si oui, où irez-vous probablement?
8. Serez-vous fatigué(e) à la fin des vacances?
9. J'espère qu'il fera beau pendant les vacances.

E. Le futur avec *si* et *quand*

The **si**-clause may either precede or follow the main clause.

■ When a main clause containing a *future* tense verb is combined with a clause introduced by **si** *(if),* the verb in the **si**-clause is in the *present* tense. English works the same way.

Si-clauses with the imperfect will be taught in Ch. 15. You might also want to point out that **si** + present tense can also be used with an imperative (**Si tu ne veux pas le savoir, ne m'écoute pas**).

Nous ferons un pique-nique demain **s'il fait beau.**	*We will have a picnic tomorrow if it is nice out.*
Si tu veux, nous sortirons vendredi soir.	*If you want, we will go out on Friday night.*
Si tu travailles cet été, est-ce que tu gagneras beaucoup d'argent?	*If you work this summer, will you earn a lot of money?*

■ However, when a main clause with a future tense verb is combined with a clause introduced by **quand,** the verb in the **quand** clause is in the *future.* Be careful not to allow English to influence your choice of verb tense. English uses the present in this case.

VOCABULAIRE À RETENIR

gagner de l'argent
to earn money
gagner à la loterie
to win the lottery

Quand il fera beau, nous ferons un pique-nique.	*When it is nice out, we will have a picnic.*
Aurez-vous beaucoup d'enfants **quand vous serez marié(e)?**	*Will you have a lot of children when you are married?*
Quand j'aurai le temps, j'écrirai.	*When I have time, I will write.*
Quand je gagnerai à la loterie, je ferai un long voyage.	*When I win the lottery, I will take a long trip.*

Beaucoup d'étudiants feront les vendanges *(grape harvest)* en automne. Ils veulent gagner de l'argent.

19 **Si nous gagnons beaucoup d'argent.** Utilisez **si** avec l'expression **gagner beaucoup d'argent** et complétez les phrases suivantes.

> **MODÈLE:** moi / acheter des vêtements
> **Si je gagne beaucoup d'argent, j'achèterai des vêtements.**

1. mes amis / être très contents
2. le professeur de français / habiter dans un château
3. les étudiants du cours de français / aller en France
4. nous / dîner dans les meilleurs restaurants
5. moi / arrêter de travailler
6. ma meilleure amie / faire un long voyage

Follow up with a contest: Who can create the most sentences that begin with **Si je gagne beaucoup d'argent ...**?

20 **Quand ferons-nous tout cela?** Combien de phrases logiques pouvez-vous faire? Chaque phrase commence par **quand**.

> **MODÈLE:** **Quand j'aurai faim, j'irai au restaurant.**

Follow work in pairs with a stand-up drill. Each student must give one sentence before sitting down.

quand	mes amis	réussir aux examens	avoir ... ans
	je	avoir faim	boire ...
	mon ami(e)	avoir un diplôme	acheter ...
	nous	être riche(s)	(ne ... pas) travailler
	les étudiants	parler bien le français	aller ...
		avoir soif	chanter
		finir d'étudier	être fatigué(e)(s)
		gagner de l'argent	manger ...
			faire un voyage ...

21 **Qu'est-ce que tu feras?** Utilisez les expressions suivantes pour interviewer votre partenaire.

> **MODÈLE:** quand / avoir le temps / écrire à tes parents
> **VOUS:** **Quand tu auras le temps, écriras-tu à tes parents?**
> **VOTRE PARTENAIRE:** **Oui, quand j'aurai le temps, j'écrirai à mes parents.**

Suggestion: Brainstorm with students to elicit all the questions before pairing students.

1. si / être libre / écrire à tes parents
2. quand / finir tes études / avoir quel âge
3. quand / travailler / gagner beaucoup d'argent
4. si / être marié(e) / faire la cuisine
5. quand / faire la cuisine / préparer des spécialités françaises
6. si / avoir des enfants / être très content(e)
7. quand / parler français / penser à cette classe

Entre amis

Quand auras-tu ton diplôme?

1. Find out when your partner will graduate.
2. Find out what s/he will do afterwards.
3. Ask if s/he will travel. If so, ask where s/he will go.
4. Ask what s/he will buy, if s/he has enough money.

Intégration

Révision

A **Au téléphone.** «Téléphonez» à votre partenaire et jouez les rôles suivants.

1. Réservez une table au restaurant.
2. Réservez une place dans un train.
3. Confirmez un départ en avion.
4. Réservez une chambre d'hôtel.

B **Diseur (diseuse) de bonne aventure** *(fortuneteller).* Écrivez cinq phrases pour prédire l'avenir *(predict the future)* d'un(e) de vos camarades de classe.

MODÈLE: **Tu parleras français comme un Français.**

C **À vous.** Répondez.

1. En quelle année avez-vous fini vos études au lycée?
2. Saviez-vous déjà parler français?
3. Est-ce que vous réussissiez toujours à vos examens quand vous étiez au lycée?
4. Quand finirez-vous vos études universitaires?
5. Qu'est-ce que vous ferez quand vous aurez votre diplôme?
6. Où irez-vous si vous faites un voyage?
7. Quelles villes visiterez-vous si vous avez le temps?
8. Qui fera le ménage quand vous serez marié(e)?

Pas de problème!

Cette activité est basée sur la vidéo, *Module 9*. Choisissez la bonne réponse pour compléter les phrases suivantes.

1. D'abord, Yves et Moustafa faisaient des recherches _____.
   (au musée, à la librairie, à la bibliothèque)
2. Moustafa faisait une étude sur _____.
   (la lecture, l'agriculture, l'architecture)
3. Le Louvre est aujourd'hui _____.
   (un musée, un château, une pyramide)
4. La Pyramide du Louvre est fermée _____.
   (le lundi, le mardi, le mercredi)
5. Moustafa a décidé de faire une description de _____ de la Pyramide.
   (l'intérieur, l'extérieur)
6. Le passant a expliqué à Yves et à Moustafa que l'entrée du musée était _____.
   (à côté d'eux, devant eux, derrière eux)

Lecture I

A **Étude du vocabulaire.** Étudiez les phrases suivantes et choisissez les mots anglais qui correspondent aux mots français en caractères gras:
holiday, until, schedule, except, beginning on, run.

1. J'ai téléphoné à l'aéroport pour savoir **l'horaire** des vols.
2. Nous serons en France **à partir du** 10 juin.
3. Certains trains ne **circulent** pas le week-end.
4. Tout le monde est venu **sauf** Christian. Pourquoi est-ce qu'il n'est pas venu?
5. Le magasin est ouvert **jusqu'à** dix-huit heures.
6. Le quatorze juillet est la **fête** nationale en France.

In activity B: 1. St-Laud, 2. quatre.

B **Parcourez l'horaire.** Lisez rapidement pour trouver le nom de la gare d'Angers et le nombre de trains qui vont de Montparnasse à Angers.

L'horaire des trains (Paris-Nantes)

Numéro de train		3741	3741	8849	8955	8957	13557	86743	6816/7	8859	86745	86745	86745	3789	8863	8967	8869	8975	8679	566/7
Notes à consulter		1	2	3	4	5	6	7	8	9	10	11	12	13	14	9	15	16	9
				TGV	TGV	TGV			TGV						TGV	TGV	TGV	TGV	TGV	TGV
Paris-Montparnasse 1-2	D	16.43	16.43	16.50	17.25	17.30			17.50			18.10	18.25	18.40	18.45	19.25	19.50			
Massy	D																			21.02
Versailles-Chantiers	D																			
Chartres	D	17.30	17.30																	
Le Mans	A	18.27	18.27	17.44					18.44				19.55		19.39					
Le Mans	D		17.46			17.53	18.27		18.46	18.54	18.54	19.21	19.57		19.41					
Sablé	A					18.16	19.00			19.29	19.29	19.56	20.21		20.00					
Angers-St-Laud	A		18.24						19.02	19.23		20.02	20.46		20.21					22.28
Ancenis	A												21.20		20.45					
Nantes	A			19.01	19.27	19.29			19.43	20.01			21.39	20.27	20.39	21.03	21.27	21.49			23.04

Notes :

1. Circule : jusqu'au 3 juil   : les ven;les 4, 11, 18 et 25 sept - Départ de Paris Montp 3 Vaug.- ☎ ♿assuré certains jours.
2. Circule : du 10 juil au 28 août   : les ven- ☎.
3. Circule : tous les jours sauf les sam, dim et fêtes et sauf le 13 juil   - ☎- ♿.
4. Circule : les ven- ☎- ♿.
5. Circulation périodique- ☎- ♿.
6. Circule : les lun, mar, mer, jeu sauf les 8 juin, 13 et 14 juil   - 🚲.
7. Circule : tous les jours sauf les sam, dim et fêtes- 🚲.
8. Circule : jusqu'au 3 juil   : les ven, dim et fêtes sauf le 7 juin ;Circule du 4 juil au 6 sept : tous les jours;à partir du 11 sept   : les ven et dim- ☎- ♿.
9. ☎- ♿.
10. Circule : tous les jours sauf les ven, dim et fêtes- 🚲.
11. Circule : les dim et fêtes- 🚲.
12. Circule : les ven- 🚲.
13. Circule : les ven- ☎.
14. Circule : tous les jours sauf les ven, dim et fêtes;Circule les 7 juin, 12 juil et 15 août   - ☐1reCL assuré certains jours-☎- ♿.
15. Circule : les ven- ☐1reCL-☎- ♿.
16. Circulation périodique- ☐1reCL assuré certains jours-☎- ♿.

C **Questions.** Répondez.

1. Quel est le train le plus rapide entre Paris-Montparnasse et Angers?
2. Quel est le train le moins rapide entre Paris-Montparnasse et Angers? Pourquoi?
3. Combien d'arrêts y a-t-il pour ce train?
4. Combien de temps le TGV prend-il entre Massy et Angers?
5. Quels sont les trains qui offrent des facilités aux handicapés?
6. Quels trains ne circulent pas le samedi?
7. Si on est au Mans, quels trains peut-on prendre pour Angers?
8. Si on part de Paris-Montparnasse, quels trains peut-on prendre si on veut arriver pour dîner à Angers à vingt heures?

Lecture II

Suggestion: Have students review Escale 3: L'Afrique noire francophone.

A **Étude du vocabulaire.** Étudiez les phrases suivantes et choisissez les mots anglais qui correspondent aux mots français en caractères gras: *full board, huts, dugout canoe, housing, mattress, bush country, river, water skiing, wind surfing, beach.*

1. Les Sénégalais circulent beaucoup en **pirogue** le long de leurs rivières.
2. Un **fleuve** est une grande rivière qui rejoint la mer.
3. La **brousse** est une région qui se trouve loin des villes.
4. Les habitants des villages africains vivent dans des **cases.**
5. Sur le lac, les plus sportifs peuvent faire du **ski nautique** ou, quand il y a du vent, de la **planche à voile.**
6. L'**hébergement** pendant le séjour peut se faire dans un hôtel ou dans des bungalows près de l'hôtel.
7. À l'hôtel, on peut choisir la **pension complète** ou prendre ses repas dans les restaurants de la ville.
8. En vacances, de nombreux touristes aiment passer leur temps au bord de la mer à la **plage.**
9. Si on ne veut pas avoir mal au dos, il vaut mieux avoir un **matelas** sur son lit.

B **Parcourez la lecture.** Lisez rapidement la lecture pour trouver ...

1. quatre types de transport.
2. cinq endroits à visiter qui se trouvent sur la carte.

Séjours organisés au Sénégal

Brousse et plage

Une semaine: 3 nuits en brousse en pension complète à l'hôtel Le Pélican/4 nuits à l'hôtel Village Club Les Filaos.

L'hôtel Le Pélican à 2 h 30 de Dakar au bord du fleuve Saloum joint le confort aux charmes de la vie africaine. Un site géographique exceptionnel, la province du Siné Saloum est réputée pour la richesse de sa faune et de sa flore.

L'hôtel Village Club Les Filaos se trouve à 73 kilomètres au sud de Dakar, en bordure de plage. Ses bungalows sont entièrement équipés, notamment avec salle de bain et toilettes privées. Restaurants, piscines. Sports et loisirs gratuits: tennis, planches à voile, volley-ball, pétanque. Sports et loisirs payants: ski nautique, excursions.

Le Circuit Cap Vert

Deux semaines. Ce circuit traverse une très belle région du Sénégal, sauvage et peu fréquentée par les touristes: le pays Bassari. Le déplacement se fait en minibus. Ce type de voyage vous fera côtoyer en permanence les habitants du pays et favorisera les contacts avec une population toujours accueillante. Il procure un confort limité. Les voyageurs sont hébergés dans des cases, des écoles ou en bivouac. Un sac de couchage et un petit matelas de mousse sont indispensables. Une réunion de préparation avec votre accompagnateur aura lieu deux à trois semaines avant le départ.

Itinéraire type: Visite de Dakar et de l'île de Gorée, descente en taxi-brousse sur Thiès (visite du marché), Saint-Louis (marché), Mlomp (cases à étages), Elinkine (promenade en pirogue), île de Karabane (baignade), parc de Basse Casamance, Gambie, région du Siné Saloum (promenade en pirogue), Toubakouta, Koalack, M'Bour-Dakar.

Le prix comprend:

- l'assistance à l'aéroport
- les transports au Sénégal, la nourriture et l'hébergement (petits hôtels, chez l'habitant)
- un accompagnateur
- l'assurance

Le prix ne comprend pas:

- le transport aérien
- les boissons

C **Vrai ou faux?** Décidez si les phrases suivantes sont vraies ou fausses. Si une phrase n'est pas vraie, corrigez-la.

1. L'hôtel Le Pélican se trouve à Dakar.
2. Il y a beaucoup d'animaux et de plantes dans la région de Siné Saloum.
3. Il ne sera pas nécessaire de payer pour faire usage de la planche à voile.
4. Les participants seront hébergés dans des hôtels de luxe pour toute la durée du circuit Cap Vert.
5. Beaucoup de touristes ont déjà fait ce voyage et connaissent le pays Bassari.
6. Il est peu probable qu'on doive passer la nuit dans des cases pendant le circuit.
7. Le voyage en avion est compris dans le prix du circuit.
8. Les repas sont compris dans le prix du circuit, mais pour les boissons il faudra payer un supplément.

D **Discussion.** Lequel des deux séjours préférez-vous? Expliquez votre réponse.

VOCABULAIRE ACTIF

Les voyages
un aller-retour *round-trip ticket*
un aller simple *one-way ticket*
l'autoroute (f.) *turnpike, through-way, highway*
un billet *ticket*
une carte *map*
composter (un billet) *to punch (a ticket)*
confirmer (un départ) *to confirm (a departure)*
le départ *departure*
en première *in first class*
en seconde *in second class*
fumeur *smoking (car)*
non fumeur *non-smoking (car)*
ralentir *to slow down*
un renseignement *item of information*
la route *route, way, road*
le vol *flight*

Adjectifs
complet (complète) *full; complete*
inutile *useless*
ouvert(e) *open*
riche *rich*
tout (toute/tous/toutes) *all; every; the whole*

D'autres noms
une demande *request*
un diplôme *diploma*
un pique-nique *picnic*

Expressions utiles
Allez-y. *Go ahead.*
Allô! *Hello! (on the phone)*
après-demain *day after tomorrow*
À quel nom … ? *In whose name … ?*
avoir tendance à *to tend to*
Bonne chance! *Good luck!*
Comment je vais faire? *What am I going to do?*
De rien *You're welcome*
entendu *agreed; understood; O.K.*
Il n'y en a plus. *There is (are) no more.*
Il vous reste … ? *Do you still have … ?*
Mince! *Darn it!*
Pourriez-vous me dire … ? *Could you tell me … ?*
Puis-je … ? *May I … ?*
tous (toutes) les deux *both*
tout de suite *right away*
tout près *very near*

À l'hôtel
une clé *key*
une douche *shower*
un étage *floor*
le prix *price*
le rez-de-chaussée *ground floor*
une serviette *towel*
un supplément *extra charge; supplement*

Verbes
choisir *to choose*
épeler *to spell*
faire une demande *to make a request*
finir *to finish*
gagner (à la loterie) *to win (the lottery)*
gagner (de l'argent) *to earn (money)*
grossir *to put on weight*
indiquer *to tell; to indicate; to point out*
louer *to rent*
maigrir *to lose weight*
obéir *to obey*
poser une question *to ask a question*
recommander *to recommend*
remercier *to thank*
réussir *to succeed; to pass*
savoir *to know*

escale 4
Le Maghreb

Que savez-vous?

Répondez aux questions suivantes. Les réponses se trouvent dans cette escale.

1. Quels sont les trois pays du Maghreb?
2. Quelles civilisations se sont établies au Maghreb dans l'antiquité?
3. Quels événements historiques ont le plus marqué les pays du Maghreb?

Avenue Bourguiba à Tunis

CHRONOLOGIE

- Premiers habitants de la région: les Berbères
- 814 avant J.-C. Empire carthaginois; site ancien de Carthage près de Tunis.
- 264–146 avant J.-C. Guerres puniques entre Carthage et Rome; destruction de Carthage.
- Colonie romaine jusqu'à l'invasion des Vandales en 439.
- Conquête arabe à la fin du VIIᵉ siècle; islamisation.
- Formation d'empires berbères s'étendant à l'Andalousie (Espagne).
- Au XVIᵉ siècle, domination turque. Le Maghreb fait partie de l'Empire ottoman.
- Retour au nomadisme. Rivalités des pays européens pour contrôler la région.
- Période coloniale: En 1830, l'Algérie est, en fait, un département français.
- Protectorat français en Tunisie en 1881 et au Maroc en 1912.
- 1954–1962: Guerre d'indépendance en Algérie.
- 1956: Indépendance de la Tunisie et du Maroc.

Vrai ou faux?

1. Le Maroc est le plus grand pays du Maghreb.
2. Le Maroc est très proche de l'Espagne.
3. Il y a de nombreux Berbères en Tunisie.
4. L'Algérie et le Maroc ont approximativement la même population.

REPÈRES:	LE MAROC	L'ALGÉRIE	LA TUNISIE
Superficie:	710.850 km², comparable à celle du Texas	environ 2.381.740 km², plus de trois fois le Texas	163.610 km²; un peu plus grand que la Géorgie
Population:	environ 30 millions	environ 29 millions	près de 9 millions
Ethnicité:	99% Arabes et Berbères; quelques Harratins (noirs) dans le sud	83% Arabes, 16% Berbères surtout dans les montagnes de l'Atlas, 1% Européens	98% Arabes, 2% Européens
Capitale:	Rabat	Alger	Tunis
Langues:	arabe, français, berbère, un peu d'espagnol	arabe, français, berbère	arabe, français

On mange le couscous assis par terre autour du grand plat et on se sert avec la main droite seulement.

ÉTUDE DU VOCABULAIRE

Identifiez dans les phrases suivantes les mots en caractères gras qui correspondent aux mots suivants: *mix, baste, hollow, cooked, wash, layer, spicy, dough.*

1. Pour éviter les microbes, on recommande de manger la viande bien **cuite**.
2. Quand un plat a beaucoup de sauce liquide, on le sert dans un plat **creux**.
3. En Inde on aime la cuisine **épicée**.
4. Il faut **laver** les légumes avant de les préparer.
5. Pour faire un gâteau, on **mélange** la farine, le beurre, le lait avec les œufs pour faire une **pâte**.
6. Un gâteau d'anniversaire a souvent une **couche** de sucre glacé et des décorations.
7. Quand la viande est rôtie au feu ouvert, il faut bien **l'arroser** pour qu'elle ne sèche pas.

La cuisine maghrébine
«Bismillah!»[1]

Voici la description de quelques plats traditionnels de la cuisine maghrébine.

- **Le couscous:** Semoule cuite à la vapeur et servie dans un grand plat creux avec carottes, navets (*turnips*), aubergines (*eggplants*), courgettes (*zucchinis*) et une viande bien cuite, généralement du mouton ou du bœuf; le tout arrosé d'un bouillon épicé pour donner un plat exotique. Après le couscous, on sert un thé à la menthe (*mint*) bien chaud et très sucré. On mange ce plat le vendredi midi (jour de la grande prière de la semaine) ainsi que les jours de fête.
- **Le tagine:** plat savoureux fait avec du foie de veau (*calf's liver*) avec petits pois et raisins secs ou du foie de poulet aux amandes et aux prunes (*plums*). Son goût sucré en fait un plat délicieux.
- **La harira:** soupe, probablement d'origine berbère, qui est le repas favori des musulmans durant le mois du Ramadan[2].

- **Le méchoui[3]:** mouton couvert d'un mélange de paprika, cumin, beurre et sel et rôti tout entier à feu vif pendant deux heures pour obtenir une viande tendre. On le sert aux fêtes religieuses et aux grandes occasions.
- **La bastela:** Entre de fines couches d'une pâte presque transparente appelée «warka», on place des amandes et du poulet ou parfois du pigeon. On le sert aussi aux réunions importantes dans une large assiette avec une couche de sucre glacé et de la cannelle (*cinnamon*) en poudre.
- **Desserts:** Pâtisseries au miel (*honey*), noix (*nuts*) et amandes, qui se servent avec du thé à la menthe.

---

1. Bismillah! *Praise be to God!* 2. Ramadan: Holy month during which Muslims do not eat or drink from sunrise to sunset. 3. Méchoui: Review the reading in Ch. 6, p. 174.

La littérature maghrébine d'expression française

Que savez-vous?

1. **Pourquoi les auteurs maghrébins publient-ils leurs œuvres en français?**
2. **Parmi les écrivains suivants, lesquels sont du Maghreb? Ousmane Sembène, Tahar Ben Jelloun, Pham duy Khiêm, Assia Djebar, Aimé Césaire?**
3. **Que signifie «littérature maghrébine»?**

Tahar Ben Jelloun

La littérature francophone des Maghrébins s'est développée après la Seconde Guerre mondiale[1]. Elle attire[2] l'attention sur la misère et les désillusions de l'après-guerre, l'espoir et l'identité nationale des pays récemment émancipés, le conflit entre les valeurs et le style de vie occidentaux et la culture et les traditions orientales. Depuis l'indépendance de l'Algérie, de la Tunisie et du Maroc, les écrivains et les intellectuels de ces pays ont animé à travers leurs écrits des discussions passionnantes sur l'effet du colonialisme, la coexistence du moderne et du traditionnel, et la situation souvent marginalisée de la femme. Cette littérature s'est rarement contentée d'être un témoignage[3] sociologique; elle a souvent été une revendication personnelle à caractère autobiographique, en même temps qu'une critique sociale audacieuse.

Ces auteurs publient leurs œuvres en arabe et en français et s'adressent ainsi au monde occidental aussi bien qu'à leurs compatriotes. Il faut se rappeler que la majorité d'entre eux ont reçu leur formation dans des écoles françaises. Élèves doués[4], ils ont souvent bénéficié de bourses[5] pour faire leurs études universitaires en France. Plusieurs des écrivains maghrébins d'expression française témoignent de la présence en France d'une immigration nombreuse d'origine maghrébine; cette littérature «beure»[6] révèle l'identité incertaine des jeunes gens, enfants de deux cultures, souvent exilés dans des HLM[7] de banlieue.

---

1. *world*   2. *attracts*   3. *testimony*   4. *talented*   5. *scholarships*
6. Beur: *first generation born of North African immigrants*
7. HLM (habitation à loyer modéré): *inexpensive housing*

À vous!

1. Selon l'article, quels sont les trois thèmes principaux trouvés dans la littérature maghrébine?
2. Pourquoi le thème de «l'identité» est-il important?
3. Expliquez comment les écrits sociologiques dans la littérature maghrébine ont souvent un caractère autobiographique et de critique sociale.

Tahar Ben Jelloun et la migration linguistique

Né à Fès en 1944, Tahar Ben Jelloun a fait des études de philosophie et de psychiatrie sociale, d'abord à Rabat au Maroc et ensuite à Paris, où il vit actuellement. Mais la littérature est sa vocation principale. Il a publié plusieurs romans et recueils de poésie et d'essais. En 1987, il a reçu le prix Goncourt, le plus prestigieux prix littéraire français, pour son roman *La Nuit sacrée*.

Ben Jelloun essaye de rattacher sa culture d'origine et son expression en langue française. Ainsi, il a libéré ses écrits de contraintes politiques. Ben Jelloun refuse d'être catégorisé comme écrivain marocain, francophone ou français. Cette question n'a pas de sens, explique-t-il. «Les intellectuels n'étant pas des douaniers, ils n'ont pas à nous demander sans arrêt d'exhiber un passeport.»

Ses romans traitent en effet de thèmes interlinguistiques et interculturels: l'homme dépaysé, l'homme dépossédé de ses racines et de son identité, les difficultés de la vie d'émigré et les problèmes de ceux qui vivent en dehors de leur culture maternelle. C'est ainsi que Ben Jelloun explique la schizophrénie culturelle de l'émigré: «Ne me dites pas pourquoi j'écris en français, mais comment j'habite cette langue. Certes, c'est encore une histoire d'amour, une histoire où les conflits sont violents et fréquents. Rien n'est acquis. La séduction est un travail quotidien, une exigence plus qu'une esthétique.»

À vous!

1. Quelle est la source d'inspiration créatrice de Tahar Ben Jelloun?
2. Où habite-t-il actuellement?
3. Pourquoi les émigrés se sentent-ils parfois schizophrènes?
4. Pourquoi est-ce que des intellectuels comme Ben Jelloun n'ont pas besoin de s'attacher à une nationalité particulière?

Assia Djebar: romancière et cinéaste algérienne

Née en 1936 et éduquée en Algérie, d'abord à l'école coranique puis au lycée français, Assia obtient une bourse d'étude et part en France à 19 ans. Elle interrompt ses études pour participer à la grève (*strike*) des étudiants en Algérie en 1956. En 1958, elle fait des études supérieures d'histoire en Tunisie et poursuit des enquêtes (*surveys*) dans les camps de réfugiés à la frontière algéro-tunisienne pendant la guerre d'indépendance. L'expérience des réfugiés se retrouve dans plusieurs de ses romans.

Dans *Femmes d'Alger dans leur appartement,* Assia Djebar rassemble plusieurs nouvelles, où elle se met «à l'écoute» de ses sœurs algériennes, femmes de tout âge, de toutes conditions, «dont les corps sont prisonniers, mais les âmes (*souls*) plus que jamais mouvantes.» Ces femmes sont cloîtrées dans le silence. Pour sortir des siècles d'ombre (*shadows*), il faut:

> Parler, parler sans cesse d'hier et d'aujourd'hui,
> parler entre nous [...] et regarder [...] hors des murs
> et des prisons.

Ces récits de femmes, elle les traduit d'un «arabe féminin» autant dire d'un «arabe souterrain».

Comme pour beaucoup d'autres auteurs maghrébins, écrire en français, la langue des colonisateurs, a pour Assia une signification très particulière. Au début de son roman, *L'Amour, la fantasia* (1985), elle décrit «la fillette arabe allant pour la première fois à l'école [française], mais dans la main du père.» C'est donc le père qui l'a introduite à cette langue et à cette culture[1]. Elle explique qu'en étudiant le français, «son corps s'occidentalisait à sa manière». Pour elle, s'exprimer en français, langue de l'ancien conquérant, représente un dévoilement, une mise à nu, mais aussi un exil de l'enfance. Ce n'est pas du nom de son père qu'elle signe ses œuvres mais d'un pseudonyme. Parler d'elle-même, hors de la tradition, n'est possible qu'en français, cette langue qui est pour elle à la fois libération et dissimulation.

1. Jean Déjeux, *La littérature féminine de langue française au Maghreb*, p. 199.

À vous!

1. **Dans quels pays est-ce qu'Assia Djebar a fait ses études?**
2. **Qui sont les personnages principaux dans les œuvres d'Assia Djebar?**
3. **Pourquoi est-ce qu'Assia Djebar fait référence à la langue arabe comme «arabe souterrain»?**

Fatima Bellahcène

Cette libération du silence est évoquée dans le poème d'une autre jeune Algérienne, qui se voit traitée en étrangère par sa famille parce qu'elle est écrivain.

L'Étrangère

Vous dites j'ai changé
Comme tous les autres
Je me suis trahie[1].
Non, je n'ai pas changé
J'ai seulement appris à parler.
Vous avez cru que j'étais un livre ouvert,
Un livre aux feuilles blanches[2],
Parce que je me taisais,
Parce que derrière mon silence, je me terrais[3].
[...]

Actualités de l'émigration, no. 80

1. *betrayed*   2. *blank pages*   3. *I kept hidden*

À vous!

1. **Expliquez la métaphore d'un «livre aux feuilles blanches».**
2. **Avez-vous remarqué des ressemblances entre les œuvres de Djebar et de Bellahcène?**
3. **Pouvez-vous expliquer comment la culture traditionnelle du Maghreb a contribué au silence des femmes?**
4. **À votre avis, est-ce que la situation des femmes maghrébines ressemble à celle des femmes de votre pays?**

13 Ma journée

Buts communicatifs
Describing a table setting
Describing one's day
Describing past activities
Expressing one's will

Structures utiles
Le verbe **mettre**
Les verbes pronominaux (suite)
Les verbes **se promener, s'inquiéter, s'appeler** et **s'asseoir**
Le passé des verbes pronominaux
Le subjonctif (suite)

Culture
L'étiquette à table
Au menu ou à la carte?

Coup d'envoi

Prise de contact

Bon appétit!

You may wish to tell students that French monograms are placed *on the back* of spoons and forks, proof that they traditionally face down when set on a table.

You learned in Ch. 9 that **genou** means *knee.* In the plural, it can refer to either *lap* or *knees.*

Avant de manger

Mettez° une nappe° sur la table.	*Put / tablecloth*
Mettez des assiettes sur la nappe.	
Mettez un verre et une cuiller° devant chaque assiette.	*spoon*
Mettez une fourchette° à gauche de l'assiette.	*fork*
Mettez un couteau° à droite de l'assiette.	*knife*

À table

Asseyez-vous.	
Mettez une serviette° sur vos genoux°.	*napkin / lap*
Coupez° le pain.	*Cut*
Mettez un morceau de pain sur la nappe à côté de l'assiette.	
Versez° du vin dans le verre.	*Pour*
Levez° votre verre et admirez la couleur du vin.	*Lift*
Humez° le vin.	*Smell*
Goûtez-le.°	*Taste it.*
Bon appétit!	

Nous nous mettons à table

Monsieur et Madame Smith et Monsieur et Madame Martin sont arrivés au restaurant, mais Lori n'est pas encore là.

MAÎTRE D'HÔTEL:	Bonsoir, Messieurs, Bonsoir, Mesdames. Vous avez réservé?
M. SMITH:	Oui, Monsieur, au nom de Smith.
MAÎTRE D'HÔTEL:	Très bien, un instant, s'il vous plaît. *(Il vérifie sa liste.)* C'est pour cinq personnes, n'est-ce pas?
MME SMITH:	C'est exact.°
MAÎTRE D'HÔTEL:	Vous voulez vous asseoir°?
M. SMITH:	Volontiers, notre amie ne va pas tarder°.
MAÎTRE D'HÔTEL:	Par ici°, s'il vous plaît. *(ensuite)* Voici votre table. *(Ils s'asseyent.°)*
M. SMITH:	Merci beaucoup, Monsieur. *(Le maître d'hôtel sourit° mais ne répond pas. Il s'en va°.)*
MME MARTIN:	C'est très gentil à vous de nous inviter.
MME SMITH:	Mais c'est un plaisir pour nous.
M. MARTIN:	Voilà Lori qui arrive. Bonsoir, Lori. *(Lori serre la main à Monsieur et Madame Martin et fait la bise à Monsieur et Madame Smith.)*
LORI BECKER:	Excusez-moi d'être en retard.
MME MARTIN:	Ne vous inquiétez pas°, Lori. Nous venons d'arriver.

That's right.

to sit down

won't be long

This way

They sit down.

smiles
leaves

Don't worry

▶ **Jouez ces rôles.** Répétez la conversation avec vos partenaires. Ensuite imaginez une excuse pour Lori. Pourquoi est-elle arrivée en retard?

This gesture is used in video, *Modules 2, 6, & 7.*

While perhaps not an obvious gesture, this is culturally pertinent to our students, who may expect a verbal response every time they say **merci.**

Il y a un geste

Il n'y a pas de quoi. Although the French have numerous spoken formulae that convey the idea of *You're welcome* (**Il n'y a pas de quoi, De rien, Je vous en prie,** etc.), they frequently respond with only a discreet smile. This smile is often unnoticed by North Americans, who may interpret the lack of a verbal response to their "thank you" as less than polite.

Pourquoi Monsieur Smith n'avance-t-il pas la chaise de sa femme quand elle va s'asseoir?

a. Ce n'est pas l'habitude en France.
b. Il a oublié de le faire.
c. Il est marié depuis longtemps.

Quelle est la différence entre un menu et une carte dans un restaurant?

a. C'est la même chose, mais un menu est plus élégant qu'une carte.
b. C'est la même chose, mais une carte est plus élégante qu'un menu.
c. Un menu propose deux ou trois repas à prix fixe. Une carte donne la liste de tous les plats.

Pourquoi le maître d'hôtel ne répond-il pas quand Monsieur Smith dit merci?

a. Il est impoli.
b. Il ne dit rien mais il répond par un sourire (smile).
c. Parce que Monsieur Smith n'est pas français.

L'étiquette à table

When Mrs. Smith is about to be seated, it is very likely that the gentlemen will not pull out her chair as a courtesy as might be the case in a North American setting. This is simply not done in France.

While the table is set, as in North America, with the forks to the left and the knives to the right, there are differences: forks are often turned tines down; glasses are above the plate rather than to one side; teaspoons are placed between the glass and the plate. If soup is served, the soup spoon is not held sideways but rather placed, tip first, in the mouth.

The French do not pick up a slice of bread and bite off a piece. Rather, they break off a small bite-sized piece and may even use this as a utensil to guide food onto the fork. From time to time, this piece is eaten and another piece broken off. Review page 211 for additional information.

Au menu ou à la carte?

La carte lists all of the dishes that the restaurant prepares. Customers can choose any combination of items they wish (**à la carte**). **Le menu** has one or more set (complete) lunches or dinners at a set price. There might, for example, be **le menu à 15€** and **le menu à 20€.** Each **menu** will include three or more courses, with or without beverage. Menus are usually by far the less expensive way to order food in France.

In France	In North America
Ice cubes are not readily available at restaurants.	Ice water is often served automatically with meals. Cold drinks are very common.
Dinner is often at 8:00 P.M. or later.	Dinner is often at 6:00 P.M. or earlier.
Meals may last two hours or more.	Meals may last only 20 or 25 minutes.
Bread is placed on the tablecloth instead of on a plate.	Bread is not always served with a meal. When it is served, it is always kept on the plate.
People keep both hands above the table while eating.	People put one hand in their lap while eating.
The service charge, or tip, is already included in the bill (**le service est compris**).	The tip is often not included in the bill.

351

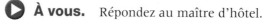 **À vous.** Répondez au maître d'hôtel.

1. Bonsoir, Monsieur (Madame / Mademoiselle). Vous avez réservé?
2. Pour deux personnes?
3. Vous voulez vous asseoir?
4. Par ici, s'il vous plaît. Voici votre table.

Entre amis

Au restaurant

You are the maître d'hôtel at a restaurant. Your partner is a customer.

1. Ask if s/he has made a reservation. (S/he has.)
2. Find out for how many people.
3. Ask if the others have already arrived.
4. Ask him/her if s/he wants to sit down.
5. Tell him/her "This way, please."

Prononciation

Les voyelles arrondies [ø] et [œ]

- Lip rounding plays a much greater role in the accurate pronunciation of French than it does in English. French has rounded vowels that are produced in the front part of the mouth, a combination that does not exist in English. Use the word **euh** to practice. This word is prevalent and is very characteristic of the normal position for French pronunciation: the lips are rounded and the tongue is behind the lower teeth.

- For the [ø] sound in **euh,** round your lips and then try to say **et.** For the [œ] sound in **neuf,** the lips are more open than for **euh.** There is, moreover, always a pronounced consonant after the vowel sound in words like **neuf, sœur,** etc.

[ø]   • **eu**h, d**eu**x, v**eu**t, p**eu**t, bl**eu,** ennuy**eu**x, pl**eu**t

[œ]   • n**eu**f, s**œu**r, b**eu**rre, profess**eu**r, h**eu**re, v**eu**lent, p**eu**vent, pl**eu**re

▶ **Listen and repeat.**

1. Est-ce que je peux vous aider?
2. La sœur du professeur arrive à neuf heures.
3. Ils veulent du beurre sur leur pain.
4. Les deux portent un pull bleu.
5. «Il pleure dans mon cœur comme il pleut sur la ville.» *(Verlaine)*

Remind students that this poem is in Ch. 9.

Buts communicatifs

1 Describing a Table Setting

Où est-ce qu'on met la nappe? On la met sur la table.
Où est-ce qu'on met l'assiette? On la met sur la nappe.
Où est-ce qu'on met le couteau? On le met à droite de l'assiette.
Où est-ce qu'on met la cuiller? On la met entre l'assiette et le verre.
Où est-ce qu'on met la serviette? On la met sur ses genoux.
Où est-ce qu'on met les mains? On les met sur la table.
Où est-ce qu'on met le pain? On le met sur la nappe, à côté de l'assiette.

Use video, *Module 10* to help introduce the table setting.

▶ **Et vous?** Qu'est-ce qu'on met à gauche de l'assiette?
Où est-ce qu'on met les verres?

A. Le verbe *mettre*

Je vais **mettre** mon pyjama. *I'm going to put on my pajamas.*
Nous **mettons** un maillot de *We put on a bathing suit to go to the pool.*
bain pour aller à la piscine.
J'**ai mis** le sel, le poivre et le *I put the salt, pepper, and sugar on*
sucre sur la table. *the table.*

Notice that, like the **-re** verbs, p. 243, the endings for **mettre** are **-s, -s, –, -ons, -ez, -ent.** The plural stem, however, has **-tt-**.

mettre *(to put, place, lay; to put on)*			
je	**mets**	nous	**mettons**
tu	**mets**	vous	**mettez**
il/elle/on	**met**	ils/elles	**mettent**
passé composé: j'**ai mis**			

VOCABULAIRE À RETENIR

le chauffage *heat*
la climatisation *air conditioning*

■ **Mettre** can also mean *to turn on* (*the radio, the heat,* etc.) and is used in the expression **mettre la table** to mean *to set the table.*

Qui **a mis** la table ce soir? *Who set the table this evening?*
Mets le chauffage; j'ai froid. *Turn on the heat; I'm cold.*
Mais je viens de **mettre** la *But I just turned on the air*
climatisation. *conditioning.*

1 **Qu'est-ce qu'ils mettent?** Indiquez les vêtements que mettent les personnes suivantes.

> **Modèles:** Qu'est-ce que vos amis mettent pour nager?
> **Ils mettent un maillot de bain.**

Review articles of clothing on pp. 89 and 98.

1. Qu'est-ce que les étudiants mettent pour aller à leurs cours?
2. Qu'est-ce que le professeur de français met pour aller au cours de français?
3. Qu'est-ce que vous mettez s'il neige?
4. Qu'est-ce que vous mettez s'il fait chaud?
5. Qu'est-ce qu'on met pour faire du jogging?
6. Qu'est-ce que vos amis mettent s'ils vont à une boum?
7. Que mettez-vous si vous allez dîner dans un restaurant très chic?

2 **Un petit test de votre savoir-vivre.** Choisissez une réponse pour chaque question et ensuite lisez l'analyse de vos réponses.

Do this first with books closed. The teacher reads the question and students suggest answers before they see the answers in the book.

1. Que mettez-vous quand vous allez dîner au restaurant?
   a. des vêtements chic
   b. un jean et des baskets
   c. un bikini
   d. rien

2. Que buvez-vous pendant le repas?
   a. du vin ou de l'eau
   b. du lait ou du café
   c. du whisky
   d. de l'eau dans un bol

3. Où mettez-vous le pain pendant le repas?
   a. sur la nappe à côté de l'assiette
   b. dans mon assiette
   c. dans l'assiette de mon (ma) voisin(e)
   d. sous la table

4. Où est votre main gauche pendant que vous mangez?
   a. sur la table
   b. sur mes genoux
   c. sur le genou de mon (ma) voisin(e)
   d. sous la table

5. Combien de temps passez-vous à table?
   a. entre une et deux heures
   b. entre 25 et 45 minutes
   c. Ça dépend du charme de mon (ma) voisin(e).
   d. cinq minutes

Remember that you learned in Ch. 8 *not* to say **Je suis plein(e),** literally *I am full,* because in French it can mean either *I am drunk* or *I am pregnant.*

6. Que dites-vous à la fin du repas?
   a. C'était très bon.
   b. Je suis plein(e).
   c. Veux-tu faire une promenade, chéri(e)?
   d. Oua! oua! *(bow-wow!)*

Résultats

a. Si vous avez répondu **a** à toutes les questions, vous êtes peut-être français(e) ou vous méritez de l'être.
b. Si vous avez répondu **b,** vous êtes probablement américain(e), comme la personne qui a écrit ce questionnaire.
c. Si votre réponse est **c,** vous êtes trop entreprenant(e) *(forward, bold)* et vous dérangez beaucoup votre voisin(e).
d. Si votre réponse est **d,** vous vous identifiez beaucoup aux chiens.

Follow-up: With books open, the class interviews the teacher, then (books closed) they interview another student.

3 **À vous.** Répondez.

1. Mettez-vous du sucre ou de la crème dans votre café?
2. Que mettez-vous dans une tasse de thé?
3. Où met-on le pain quand on mange à la française?
4. Que faut-il faire pour mettre la table?
5. À quel moment de l'année met-on le chauffage dans la région où vous habitez? À quel moment de l'année met-on la climatisation?
6. En quelle saison met-on un gros manteau?
7. Quels vêtements les étudiants mettent-ils d'habitude sur votre campus?
8. Quels vêtements avez-vous mis hier? Pourquoi avez-vous décidé de porter ces vêtements-là?

Entre amis

L'éducation d'un(e) enfant

You are a French parent instructing your child (your partner) on table manners. Remember to use **tu**.

1. Tell your child to put the napkin on his/her lap.
2. Tell him/her to put a piece of bread on the table.
3. Tell him/her not to play with the bread.
4. Tell him/her to put water in his/her glass.
5. Find out what s/he did at school today.

2 Describing One's Day

You may wish to teach **se doucher** as well. It seems to be used less frequently than **prendre une douche.**

Le matin

7 h	Je me réveille tôt et je me lève.
7 h 10	Je me lave ou je prends une douche.
7 h 25	Je m'habille.
7 h 35	Je me brosse les cheveux.
7 h 50	Après avoir mangé°, je me brosse les dents.

After eating

L'après-midi

3 h	Je me repose.
5 h	Je m'amuse avec mon chien.

Le soir

11 h	Je me couche assez tard et je m'endors.

Et vous? À quelle heure vous réveillez-vous?
Que faites-vous le matin? l'après-midi? le soir?

Review pp. 165 and 189.

Remarque **Tôt** and **tard** mean *early* and *late* in the day. They should not be confused with **en avance** and **en retard,** which mean *early* and *late* for a specific meeting, class, etc.

Il se lève **tard!** (à midi)
Il est **en retard.** (pour son cours de français)

The conjugations of **se promener, s'inquiéter,** and **s'appeler,** which have spelling changes in their stems, and the conjugation of **s'asseoir,** are given on p. 360.

V O C A B U L A I R E

Quelques verbes pronominaux

se réveiller	*to wake up*
se laver	*to get washed*
se brosser (les dents, les cheveux)	*to brush (one's teeth, one's hair)*
s'habiller	*to get dressed*
s'amuser	*to have fun*
se souvenir (de)	*to remember*
s'inquiéter	*to worry*
s'asseoir	*to sit down*
se promener	*to take a walk, ride*
se dépêcher	*to hurry*
s'appeler	*to be named*
s'endormir	*to fall asleep*
se reposer	*to rest*

Review **Les verbes pronominaux,** Ch. 6, p. 165.

B. Les verbes pronominaux (suite)

■ Remember that the reflexive pronouns are **me, te, se, nous, vous,** and **se.**

se laver *(to get washed, to wash oneself)*			
je	**me** lave	nous	**nous** lavons
tu	**te** laves	vous	**vous** lavez
il/elle/on	**se** lave	ils/elles	**se** lavent

s'endormir *(to fall asleep)*			
je	**m'**endors	nous	**nous** endormons
tu	**t'**endors	vous	**vous** endormez
il/elle/on	**s'**endort	ils/elles	**s'**endorment

Note The reflexive pronoun always changes form as necessary to agree with the subject of the verb, even when it is part of an infinitive construction.

Je vais **m'**amuser.   **Tu** vas **t'**amuser aussi.   **Nous** allons **nous** amuser!

■ Many verbs can be used reflexively or nonreflexively, depending on whether the object of the verb is the same as the subject or not.

Jean **se lave** avant de manger. (*Jean* is the subject *and* the object.)
Mais: Jean **lave sa voiture.** (*Jean* is the subject but *sa voiture* is the object.)

Noëlle adore **se promener.** (*Noëlle* is the subject *and* the object.)
Mais: Noëlle refuse de **promener le chien.** (*Noëlle* is the subject but *le chien* is the object.)

Past tenses of reflexive verbs are covered on pp. 190 and 362.

■ Like all other object pronouns, the reflexive pronoun is always placed immediately before the verb (except in an affirmative command). This rule is true, no matter whether the verb is in an affirmative, interrogative, negative, or infinitive form.

Comment **vous** appelez-vous?	*What is your name?*
Tu veux **t'**asseoir?	*Do you want to sit down?*
Ne **s'**amusent-ils pas en classe?	*Don't they have fun in class?*
Je ne **m'**appelle pas Aude.	*My name is not Aude.*
Roman ne **se** réveille jamais très tôt.	*Roman never wakes up very early.*
Nous allons **nous** promener.	*We are going to take a walk.*
J'ai décidé de ne pas **me** lever.	*I decided not to get up.*

Review the imperative with pronouns, Ch. 10, p. 285. Remember that when **me** and **te** follow the verb they become **moi** and **toi**.

■ As you have already seen (see Ch. 10), when the imperative is affirmative, the object pronoun is placed after the verb. This is true even when the object pronoun is a reflexive pronoun.

Dépêche-**toi**!	*Hurry (up)!*
Dépêchez-**vous**!	*Hurry (up)!*
Dépêchons-**nous**!	*Let's hurry!*

Remind students not to use the imperative of reflexive verbs when they mean to use an interrogative: **Lavez-vous!** vs. **Vous lavez-vous?**

■ You also know that if the imperative is negative, normal word order is followed and the object pronoun precedes the verb.

Ne **te** dépêche pas.	*Don't hurry.*
Ne **vous** dépêchez pas.	*Don't hurry.*
Ne **nous** dépêchons pas.	*Let's not hurry.*

4 **Vrai ou faux?** Décidez si les phrases suivantes sont vraies. Si elles ne sont pas vraies, corrigez-les.

> **MODÈLE:**   Vous vous réveillez toujours tôt le matin.
> **C'est faux. Je ne me réveille pas toujours tôt le matin.**

1. Vous vous brossez les dents avant le petit déjeuner.
2. On se lave normalement avec de l'eau froide.
3. Les étudiants de votre université se douchent une fois par semaine.
4. Ils s'habillent avant la douche.
5. Vous vous endormez quelquefois en classe.
6. Vous vous reposez toujours après les repas.
7. D'habitude, on se brosse les cheveux avec une brosse à dents.
8. Les professeurs se souviennent toujours des noms de leurs étudiants.

5 **Nos activités de chaque jour.** Faites des phrases logiques. Vous pouvez utiliser la forme négative.

> MODÈLE: **Ma sœur se brosse les cheveux trois fois par jour.**

	se laver	tôt
	s'amuser	tard
	se dépêcher	le matin
nous	se coucher	le soir
les étudiants	prendre une douche	dans un fauteuil
mon père	s'habiller	dans la salle de bain
ma mère	s'endormir	avec de l'eau chaude
je	se réveiller	avec de l'eau froide
ma sœur	se brosser les cheveux	une (deux, etc.) fois par jour
mon frère	se brosser les dents	avec une brosse à cheveux
	se mettre à table	avec une brosse à dents
	se reposer	

6 **Fais ce que tu veux.** Utilisez l'impératif et l'expression **Eh bien, ...** pour encourager les autres à faire ce qu'ils veulent.

> MODÈLES: Je voudrais m'asseoir.   Je ne voudrais pas me lever.
>   **Eh bien, assieds-toi.**   **Eh bien, ne te lève pas.**

1. Je voudrais me coucher.
2. Je ne voudrais pas me dépêcher.
3. Je ne voudrais pas me brosser les dents.
4. Je voudrais m'amuser.
5. Je ne voudrais pas me lever à 7 heures.
6. Je ne voudrais pas étudier.
7. Je voudrais sortir avec mes amis.
8. Je voudrais m'endormir en classe.

C. Les verbes *se promener, s'inquiéter, s'appeler* et *s'asseoir*

■ Some reflexive verbs contain spelling changes in the verb stem of the present tense.

Review **se lever,** p. 165, **préférer,** p. 230, and **acheter,** p. 252.

■ Like **se lever** and **acheter, se promener** changes **-e-** to **-è-** before silent endings.

	se promener *(to take a walk, ride)*		
je	me prom**è**ne	nous	nous promenons
tu	te prom**è**nes	vous	vous promenez
il/elle/on	se prom**è**ne		
ils/elles	se prom**è**nent		

■ Like **préférer, s'inquiéter** changes **-é-** to **-è-** before silent endings.

	s'inquiéter *(to worry)*		
je	m'inqui**è**te	nous	nous inquiétons
tu	t'inqui**è**tes	vous	vous inquiétez
il/elle/on	s'inqui**è**te		
ils/elles	s'inqui**è**tent		

You may wish to point out that, like **acheter,** the spelling change occurs in the future for **se lever, se promener,** and **s'appeler: Je me lèverai tôt.; Elle s'appellera Dubois.** However, like **préférer,** there is no change in the future for **s'inquiéter: Je ne m'inquiéterai plus.**

■ **S'appeler** changes **-l-** to **-ll-** before silent endings.

	s'appeler *(to be named)*		
je	m'appelle	nous	nous appelons
tu	t'appelles	vous	vous appelez
il/elle/on	s'appelle		
ils/elles	s'appellent		

Note **S'asseoir** is irregular and is conjugated as follows:

	s'asseoir *(to sit down)*		
je	m'**assieds**	nous	nous **asseyons**
tu	t'**assieds**	vous	vous **asseyez**
il/elle/on	s'**assied**	ils/elles	s'**asseyent**

La journée des étudiants. Utilisez des verbes pronominaux pour compléter les phrases suivantes.

MODÈLE: Nous _____ à nos places.
Nous nous asseyons à nos places.

1. Le soir, les étudiants ne _____ pas avant minuit parce qu'ils ont beaucoup de travail.
2. S'ils sont en retard pour un cours, ils _____.
3. Ils _____ s'il y a un examen.
4. Le week-end, les étudiants _____.
5. Le samedi matin, ils font la grasse matinée; ils ne _____ pas avant 10 heures.
6. Ils _____ très tard et ils _____ tout de suite.
7. Ils _____ en jean normalement parce que les jeans sont confortables.

 Pour avoir du succès à l'université. Vous êtes très docile et vous répondez systématiquement que vous êtes d'accord. Utilisez le futur.

MODÈLE: Ne vous couchez pas trop tard.
D'accord, je ne me coucherai pas trop tard.

Review the future on p. 336.

1. Ne vous endormez pas pendant le cours de français.
2. Ne vous lavez pas avec de l'eau froide.
3. Amusez-vous bien pendant le week-end.
4. Dépêchez-vous pour ne pas être en retard.
5. Levez-vous avant 8 heures.
6. Ne vous inquiétez pas quand vous avez un examen.
7. Ne vous promenez pas après 22 heures.

9 **Un petit sondage** *(A small poll).* Vous êtes journaliste. Interviewez une autre personne (votre partenaire). Demandez ...

MODÈLE: s'il (si elle) se lève tôt
VOUS: **Est-ce que vous vous levez tôt le samedi matin?**
VOTRE PARTENAIRE: **Non, je me lève assez tard.**

Follow up by having the class interview the teacher (with books open) and then another student (with books closed).

1. s'il (si elle) parle français
2. comment il (elle) s'appelle
3. comment il (elle) va
4. s'il (si elle) est fatigué(e)
5. à quelle heure il (elle) se lève en semaine
6. à quelle heure il (elle) se couche
7. s'il (si elle) se lève tôt ou tard le samedi matin
8. s'il (si elle) s'endort à la bibliothèque
9. avec quel dentifrice il (elle) se brosse les dents
10. s'il (si elle) s'inquiète quand il y a un examen
11. depuis quand il (elle) étudie le français

Entre amis

Et ta journée?

Interview your partner about his/her typical day.

1. Find out at what time your partner wakes up.
2. Find out what s/he does during the day.
3. Find out at what time your partner goes to bed.

3 Describing Past Activities

La dernière fois que j'ai dîné au restaurant avec des amis ...

	oui	non
ils y sont arrivés avant moi.	____	____
je me suis dépêché(e) pour arriver à l'heure.	____	____
mes amis s'inquiétaient parce que j'étais en retard.	____	____
nous nous sommes mis à table à huit heures.	____	____
je me suis bien amusé(e).	____	____
nous nous sommes promenés après le repas.	____	____
je me suis couché(e) assez tôt.	____	____

D. Le passé des verbes pronominaux

■ The imperfect tense of reflexive verbs is formed in the same way as that of simple verbs. The reflexive pronoun precedes the verb.

> There are no spelling changes in the imperfect for stem changing verbs; **s'appeler: Il s'appelait Pierre; se lever: Je me levais tôt.**

s'inquiéter *(inquiétons)*			
je	**m'inquiétais**	nous	**nous inquiétions**
tu	**t'inquiétais**	vous	**vous inquiétiez**
il/elle/on	**s'inquiétait**	ils/elles	**s'inquiétaient**

> Review the passé composé of **se coucher** in Ch. 7, p. 190.

■ All reflexive verbs use the auxiliary **être** to form the passé composé. The past participle agrees in gender and number with the preceding direct object (usually the reflexive pronoun).

se reposer			
je	**me**	**suis**	**reposé(e)**
tu	**t'**	**es**	**reposé(e)**
il/on	**s'**	**est**	**reposé**
elle	**s'**	**est**	**reposée**
nous	**nous**	**sommes**	**reposé(e)s**
vous	**vous**	**êtes**	**reposé(e)(s)**
ils	**se**	**sont**	**reposés**
elles	**se**	**sont**	**reposées**

> The past participle of stem changing verbs is not affected by spelling changes; it is based on the infinitive: **promené, inquiété, appelé.**

Delphine **s'est couchée** tôt parce qu'elle était fatiguée.

Nous **nous sommes** bien **amusé(e)s** le week-end dernier.

> **Note**   Except for **s'asseoir,** the past participles of reflexive verbs are formed by the normal rules. The past participle of **s'asseoir** is **assis.**

Les deux femmes se sont **assises** à côté de moi.

■ In the negative, **ne ... pas** (**jamais,** etc.) are placed around the reflexive pronoun and the auxiliary verb.

Les enfants **ne** se sont **pas** couchés.
Je **ne** me suis **jamais** endormi(e) en classe.

■ In questions with inversion, as in all cases of inversion, the *subject* pronoun is placed after the auxiliary verb. The *reflexive* pronoun always directly precedes the auxiliary verb.

À quelle heure **t'es-tu** couchée, Christelle?
Vos amies **se** sont-**elles** reposées?

> Reflexive pronouns are object pronouns, just like **le, la, les.** They follow the same general placement rules. See Ch. 10, p. 278.

> Indirect object pronouns will be presented in Ch. 14.

FOR RECOGNITION ONLY:

• The past participle of a reflexive verb agrees with a preceding direct object. In most cases, the direct object is the reflexive pronoun, which precedes the past participle.

Claire **s'**est lavée.	*Claire washed **herself.***
Nous **nous** sommes amusés.	*We had a good time. (We amused **ourselves.**)*

• However, with some reflexive verbs (such as **se laver** and **se brosser**), the direct object often follows the verb and the reflexive pronoun is not the direct object. The past participle *does not agree* with a reflexive pronoun that is not a direct object.

> Ask students: *What did Claire wash? (her hair); What did she brush? (her teeth).*

Claire s'est lavé **les cheveux.**	*Claire washed **her hair.***
Elle s'est brossé **les dents.**	*She brushed **her teeth.***

 Mais oui, Maman.   Madame Cousineau pose beaucoup de questions à sa fille. Utilisez l'expression entre parenthèses pour répondre à ces questions.

> **Modèle:**   Tu t'es réveillée à 7 heures? (mais oui)
> **Mais oui, je me suis réveillée à 7 heures.**

1. Est-ce que tu t'es lavée ce matin? (mais oui)
2. Tu ne t'es pas dépêchée? (mais si!)
3. As-tu pris le petit déjeuner? (mais oui)
4. À quelle heure es-tu partie pour l'école? (à 7 heures 45)
5. Est-ce que tu t'es amusée à l'école? (non)
6. Tu ne t'es pas endormie en classe? (mais non)
7. À quelle heure es-tu rentrée de l'école? (à 5 heures)
8. Est-ce que tu as fait tes devoirs? (euh ... non)

Le professeur et ses
étudiants s'amusent
après le cours.

 Vous aussi? Décidez si les phrases suivantes sont vraies pour vous. Utilisez **Moi aussi, Moi non plus** ou **Pas moi** pour répondre. Si vous choisissez **Pas moi,** ajoutez une explication.

MODÈLE: Les professeurs se sont bien amusés le week-end dernier.
**Pas moi, je ne me suis pas amusé(e). J'ai étudié pendant
tout le week-end.**

1. Les professeurs se sont couchés avant minuit hier.
2. Ils se sont réveillés à 8 heures ce matin.
3. Ils ont pris le petit déjeuner.
4. Ils ont pris une douche ensuite.
5. Ils sont allés à leur premier cours à 9 heures.
6. Ils ne se sont pas assis pendant leurs cours.
7. Ils se sont bien amusés en classe.
8. Ils ont bu du café après le cours.

12 Votre vie sur le campus. Vous êtes journaliste. Interviewez un(e) étudiant(e). Demandez ...

MODÈLES: s'il (si elle) s'est levé(e) tôt ce matin.
Vous êtes-vous levé(e) tôt ce matin?

ce qu'il (elle) a mangé.
Qu'est-ce que vous avez mangé?

1. s'il (si elle) arrive quelque-fois en retard en classe.
2. s'il (si elle) s'est dépêché(e) ce matin.
3. où il (elle) va pour s'amuser.
4. ce qu'il (elle) a fait hier soir.
5. s'il (si elle) s'est amusé(e) hier soir.
6. à quelle heure il (elle) s'est couché(e).
7. s'il (si elle) s'est endormi(e) tout de suite.
8. combien d'heures il (elle) a dormi.
9. s'il (si elle) se repose d'habitude l'après-midi.
10. s'il (si elle) s'inquiète avant un examen.

Entre amis

Hier

1. Find out at what time your partner got up yesterday.
2. Find out what clothing s/he put on.
3. Ask if s/he took a walk.
4. Find out what else s/he did.
5. Ask if s/he had fun.
6. Find out at what time s/he went to bed.

4 Expressing One's Will

Que veux-tu que je fasse°, Emmanuelle?   *What do you want me to do*

Je voudrais ...
    que tu ailles° au marché.   *go*
    que tu achètes des fruits et des légumes.
    que tu fasses la cuisine.
    que tu mettes la table.

▶ **Et vous?**   Que voulez-vous que vos amis fassent?

E. Le subjonctif (suite)

Review Ch. 10, pp. 282–284.

Je voudrais **que mes amis fassent** la cuisine pour moi.
Je voudrais **que mon ami** me **téléphone.**
Je voudrais **que vous veniez** au centre commercial avec moi.

■ You have already learned that the subjunctive is used after the word **que** in the second clause of a sentence in situations in which you are advising others. It is also used in other situations, such as when you are telling others what you want them to do.

VOCABULAIRE

La volonté *(will)*

exiger que	*to demand that*	souhaiter que	*to wish, hope that*
vouloir que	*to want*	préférer que	*to prefer that*
désirer que	*to want*		

Review With the exception of **être** and **avoir,** the subjunctive endings are always **-e, -es, -e, -ions, -iez, -ent.** The stem is usually formed by taking the present tense **ils/elles** form and dropping the **-ent** ending.

chanter (ils chantent)			vendre (ils vendent)			choisir (ils choisissent)		
que je	chant	**e**	que je	vend	**e**	que je	choisiss	**e**
que tu	chant	**es**	que tu	vend	**es**	que tu	choisiss	**es**
qu'il/elle/on	chant	**e**	qu'il/elle/on	vend	**e**	qu'il/elle/on	choisiss	**e**
que nous	chant	**ions**	que nous	vend	**ions**	que nous	choisiss	**ions**
que vous	chant	**iez**	que vous	vend	**iez**	que vous	choisiss	**iez**
qu'ils/elles	chant	**ent**	qu'ils/elles	vend	**ent**	qu'ils/elles	choisiss	**ent**

Point out the resemblance between the present indicative of the **-er** verbs, p. 36, and the subjunctive.

Note Even many irregular verbs follow this basic rule.

écrire	(ils écrivent)	que j'**écrive,** que nous **écrivions**
lire	(ils lisent)	que je **lise,** que nous **lisions**
partir	(ils partent)	que je **parte,** que nous **partions**
connaître	(ils connaissent)	que je **connaisse,** que nous **connaissions**
conduire	(ils conduisent)	que je **conduise,** que nous **conduisions**
mettre	(ils mettent)	que je **mette,** que nous **mettions**

Suggestion: Have students supply the **je** and **nous** forms for the verbs named here.

■ Some verbs have one stem for **je, tu, il/elle/on,** and **ils/elles** forms and another stem for **nous** and **vous.** Many of these are the same verbs that have two stems in the present tense. Some verbs of this type that you have already learned are **venir, prendre, boire, préférer, acheter,** and **se lever.**

venir					
(ils	viennent)		(nous	venons)	
que je	**vienn**	**e**	que nous	**ven**	**ions**
que tu	**vienn**	**es**	que vous	**ven**	**iez**
qu'il/elle/on	**vienn**	**e**			
qu'ils/elles	**vienn**	**ent**			

Aille, ailles, aille, and **aillent** are pronounced like **aïe!** (ouch!) and **ail** (garlic): [aj].

Note **Aller** also has two stems (**aill-,** which is irregular, and **all-**).

You might also want to mention that **vouloir** is also of this type, having **veuill-** and **voul-** as its two stems.

aller					
(aill-)			(nous	allons)	
que j'	**aill**	**e**	que nous	**all**	**ions**
que tu	**aill**	**es**	que vous	**all**	**iez**
qu'il/elle/on	**aill**	**e**			
qu'ils/elles	**aill**	**ent**			

You might also want to mention that **pouvoir** is also of this type, having **puiss-** as its stem.

■ Some verbs have totally irregular stems. Their endings, however, are regular.

faire *(fass-)*		
que je	**fass**	e
que tu	**fass**	es
qu'il/elle/on	**fass**	e
que nous	**fass**	ions
que vous	**fass**	iez
qu'ils/elles	**fass**	ent

savoir *(sach-)*		
que je	**sach**	e
que tu	**sach**	es
qu'il/elle/on	**sach**	e
que nous	**sach**	ions
que vous	**sach**	iez
qu'ils/elles	**sach**	ent

Aie, aies, ait, and **aient** are pronounced like **est** *(is).*

■ Only **être** and **avoir** have irregular stems *and* endings.

être	
que je	**sois**
que tu	**sois**
qu'il/elle/on	**soit**
que nous	**soyons**
que vous	**soyez**
qu'ils/elles	**soient**

avoir	
que j'	**aie**
que tu	**aies**
qu'il/elle/on	**ait**
que nous	**ayons**
que vous	**ayez**
qu'ils/elles	**aient**

Review the use of the infinitive and the use of the subjunctive on p. 284.

Attention If there is not a change of subjects, the infinitive must be used.

Je voudrais **téléphoner** à mon ami.	*I would like to call my friend.*
Je voudrais **parler** avec lui.	*I would like to speak with him.*
Mais: Je voudrais que mon ami fasse la cuisine.	*I would like my friend to cook.*

13 **Nos professeurs sont si exigeants!** *(Our teachers are so demanding!)* Utilisez les expressions suivantes pour faire des phrases.

MODÈLE: les professeurs / vouloir / les étudiants / venir aux cours
Les professeurs veulent que les étudiants viennent aux cours.

1. les professeurs / désirer / les étudiants / faire leurs devoirs
2. les professeurs / vouloir / les étudiants / avoir de bonnes notes
3. les professeurs / exiger / les étudiants / être à l'heure
4. notre professeur / vouloir absolument / nous / parler français en classe
5. notre professeur / désirer / nous / réussir
6. notre professeur / souhaiter / nous / aller en France
7. notre professeur / préférer / nous / habiter chez une famille française
8. notre professeur / souhaiter / nous / savoir parler comme les Français

14 **Que veulent-ils que je fasse?** Tout le monde veut que vous fassiez quelque chose. Faites des phrases pour expliquer ce qu'ils veulent. Vous pouvez utiliser la forme négative si vous voulez.

MODÈLES: **Mes amis désirent que je sorte tous les soirs.**
Ma mère ne veut pas que je conduise vite.
Mon père préfère que je n'aie pas de voiture.

mes amis	exiger		étudier beaucoup
	vouloir		sortir tous les soirs
mon père	désirer	que je	aller au bistro
ma mère	souhaiter		tomber malade
	préférer		être heureux/heureuse
			avoir une voiture
			conduire vite
			faire la cuisine
			partir en vacances
			m'amuser beaucoup
			m'inquiéter quand il y a un examen
			acheter moins de vêtements

Il faut qu'elles se dépêchent parce qu'elles vont bientôt se mettre à table.

Un petit sketch: Une fille au pair. Lisez ou jouez le sketch suivant et répondez ensuite aux questions.

MME MARTIN:	Je serai absente toute la journée.
LORI:	Très bien, Madame. Que voulez-vous que je fasse aujourd'hui?
MME MARTIN:	Je préparerai le dîner, mais je voudrais que vous alliez au marché.
LORI:	D'accord.
MME MARTIN:	Vous pouvez aussi y envoyer les enfants. J'ai laissé ma liste sur la table de la cuisine.
	(Elle regarde sa montre.)
	Aïe! Il faut que je parte. Au revoir, Lori. Au revoir, les enfants.
	(après le départ de Mme Martin)
LORI:	David! Sylvie! Dépêchez-vous! Votre mère veut que vous achetiez six tomates et un kilo de pommes de terre. Et n'oubliez pas de dire «s'il vous plaît» et «merci» à la dame au marché.
DAVID ET SYLVIE:	Mais Lori!
LORI:	Dépêchez-vous! Et mettez vos manteaux! Il pleut.
DAVID ET SYLVIE:	Où est l'argent?
LORI:	Attendez, le voilà. *(Elle donne l'argent aux enfants.)* Allez-y! Il ne faut pas que vous oubliiez la monnaie.

(margin note:) Point out **-ii-** in the subjunctive of **oublier.** Can students recall another verb in **-ier** (e.g., **étudier**)?

Questions

1. Que faut-il que Lori fasse?
2. Est-il nécessaire qu'elle aille au marché elle-même?
3. Pourquoi veut-elle que les enfants mettent leurs manteaux?
4. Pourquoi les enfants ne partent-ils pas tout de suite?

🔟 **Fais comme il faut.** Votre mère vous donne des conseils. Utilisez un verbe de volonté avec **que** et le subjonctif. Qu'est-ce qu'elle dit?

MODÈLES: ne pas t'endormir en classe
Je souhaite que tu ne t'endormes pas en classe.

conduire lentement
J'exige que tu conduises lentement.

1. prendre le petit déjeuner
2. ne pas boire de bière
3. mettre un chapeau s'il fait froid
4. aller aux cours tous les jours
5. savoir l'importance d'une bonne éducation
6. ne sortir avec tes ami(e)s que le week-end
7. être prudent(e)
8. rentrer tôt
9. ne pas te lever tard

17 **À vous.** Répondez.

1. Que voulez-vous que vos parents fassent pour vous?
2. Qu'est-ce qu'ils veulent que vous fassiez pour eux?
3. Où voulez-vous que vos amis aillent avec vous?
4. Que voulez-vous que vos amis vous donnent pour votre anniversaire?
5. Quels vêtements préférez-vous mettre pour aller à vos cours?
6. Quels vêtements préférez-vous que le professeur mette?
7. Qu'est-ce que le professeur veut que vous fassiez?

Entre amis

Des projets pour visiter la ville de Québec

1. Tell your partner that your teacher wants you to go to Québec.
2. Tell your partner that you want him/her to come with you.
3. Explain that you have to speak French there.
4. Tell your partner that your teacher wants you to leave next week.

Intégration

Révision

A **Pour mettre la table.** Que faut-il qu'on fasse pour mettre la table à la française? Donnez une description complète.

MODÈLE: **Il faut qu'on mette une nappe sur la table.**

B **Ma journée.** D'abord décrivez votre journée habituelle. Ensuite décrivez votre journée d'hier.

C **Catégories.** Interviewez les étudiants de votre cours de français. Pouvez-vous trouver une personne pour chaque catégorie? *Attention:* Certains verbes ne sont pas des verbes pronominaux.

Have students stand and move about when interviewing the others. Give a prize to those who find a person for all the categories.

MODÈLE: quelqu'un qui se lève avant 7 heures du matin
VOUS: **Te lèves-tu avant 7 heures du matin?**
UN(E) AUTRE ÉTUDIANT(E): **Oui, je me lève avant 7 heures du matin.**
ou
Non, je ne me lève pas avant 7 heures du matin.

1. quelqu'un qui se lève avant 7 heures du matin
2. quelqu'un qui se couche après minuit
3. quelqu'un qui s'endort quelquefois en classe
4. quelqu'un qui lave sa voiture une fois par mois
5. quelqu'un qui se brosse les dents avant le petit déjeuner
6. quelqu'un qui se réveille quelquefois pendant la nuit

7. quelqu'un qui se promène après le dîner
8. quelqu'un qui promène souvent son chien
9. quelqu'un qui s'amuse au cours de français
10. quelqu'un qui s'inquiète s'il (si elle) est en retard
11. quelqu'un qui s'assied toujours à la même place au cours de français

 Suggestion: Have students do the Information Gap activity in the Instructor's Resource Manual.

D **À vous.** Répondez.

1. Que font les étudiants de votre université pour s'amuser?
2. Qu'est-ce que les professeurs veulent que leurs étudiants fassent?
3. Qu'est-ce que vos parents ne veulent pas que vous fassiez?
4. Dans quelles circonstances vous dépêchez-vous?
5. À quel(s) moment(s) de la journée vous brossez-vous les dents?
6. Avez-vous quelquefois envie de vous endormir en classe? Pourquoi ou pourquoi pas?

Pas de problème!

Preparation for the video:
1. Video worksheet in the *Cahier d'activités*
2. CD-ROM, *Module 10*

Cette activité est basée sur la vidéo, *Module 10*. Écoutez attentivement pour savoir si les choses suivantes sont mentionnées. Cochez *(check)* les expressions que vous entendez.

__ les anchois
__ les champignons
__ les desserts
__ le fromage
__ les légumes
__ le pâté
__ les pommes de terre
__ la salade
__ les croissants
__ les concombres
__ le fromage de brebis

__ les artichauts
__ la charcuterie
__ les épinards
__ les fruits
__ les melons
__ la pâtisserie
__ le porc
__ les sardines
__ le thon
__ les tomates
__ les saucisses

__ les bananes
__ les cornichons
__ les fraises
__ le gâteau
__ les œufs
__ les petits pois
__ le poulet
__ le saumon
__ la truite
__ les framboises
__ le fromage de chèvre

__ le bifteck
__ la tarte
__ les frites
__ la glace
__ le pain
__ le poisson
__ le riz
__ la soupe
__ la viande
__ les radis
__ le fromage de vache

Lecture I

A **Étude du vocabulaire.** Étudiez les phrases suivantes et choisissez les mots qui correspondent aux mots français en caractères gras: *sand, those, burning, gently, shovel, lived, erased, pick up, sea.*

1. Le professeur a écrit une phrase au tableau et ensuite il a **effacé** la phrase.
2. Marie, regarde ta chambre! Tu as laissé tes vêtements sur ton lit. **Ramasse**-les tout de suite!
3. **Ceux** qui habitent près de la **mer** peuvent souvent s'amuser dans l'eau.
4. Quand nous étions jeunes, nous **vivions** heureux avec notre famille.
5. En été, les enfants aimaient bien nager dans la **mer** ou jouer avec une **pelle** dans le **sable.**
6. Quand il faisait très chaud, le **sable** était **brûlant.** On ne pouvait pas marcher sans chaussures.
7. Parlez **doucement!** Les enfants dorment.

B **Pensez à la saison.** À quelle saison pensez-vous quand vous entendez les expressions suivantes?

1. la mer et le sable
2. le soleil brûlant
3. les feuilles mortes
4. le vent du nord
5. la belle vie
6. la nuit froide
7. les jours heureux

Les Feuilles mortes

Oh! Je voudrais tant que tu te souviennes
Des jours heureux où nous étions amis.
En ce temps-là la vie était plus belle
Et le soleil plus brûlant qu'aujourd'hui.
Les feuilles mortes se ramassent à la pelle,
Tu vois, je n'ai pas oublié.
Les feuilles mortes se ramassent à la pelle,
Les souvenirs et les regrets aussi
Et le vent du nord les emporte[1]
Dans la nuit froide de l'oubli.
Tu vois, je n'ai pas oublié
La chanson que tu me chantais.

C'est une chanson qui nous ressemble,
Toi, tu m'aimais, et je t'aimais.
Nous vivions tous les deux ensemble,
Toi, qui m'aimais; moi, qui t'aimais.
Mais la vie sépare ceux qui s'aiment
Tout doucement, sans faire de bruit
Et la mer efface sur le sable
Les pas des amants désunis.[2]

Jacques Prévert

*If you have a recording of **Les Feuilles mortes** (there are several available), play it for your students.*

If students do not recognize "Autumn Leaves," ask them to give the poem an English title. Have students brainstorm to suggest songs they know that have a similar theme.

*Use the poem for a **Concours de prononciation** (see the Instructor's Resource Manual).*

---

1. *carries away*   2. *the footprints of separated lovers*

C **À votre avis.** Relisez le poème et faites deux listes: (1) des expressions qui vous semblent tristes ou nostalgiques et (2) des expressions qui vous semblent plus heureuses.

Lecture II

A **Étude du vocabulaire.** Étudiez les phrases suivantes et choisissez les mots qui correspondent aux mots français en caractères gras: *corn, dry, dust, maid, rooms, harvest.*

1. C'était une maison avec quatre **pièces:** deux chambres, une cuisine et une salle de séjour.
2. Il y a longtemps que j'ai nettoyé cette chambre. Les meubles sont couverts de **poussière.**
3. Sans pluie, toute la région était **sèche.**
4. L'automne est la saison de la **récolte** du **maïs** dans l'Iowa.
5. Quelquefois les familles ont une **bonne** pour les aider au ménage.

B **Situez ces expressions.** Étudiez les expressions suivantes qui sont utilisées dans la lettre que Madame Nabi a envoyée du Burkina Faso. Ensuite cherchez-les dans sa lettre.

barrage *dam*, bouillie de mil *millet porridge*, dolo *a type of punch*, ignames *yams*, marmite *large pot*, occasions de rencontre *chances to meet others*, oseille *sorrel*, pagne *(grass) skirt*, Pâques *Easter*, prière *prayer*, tamarin *tamarind fruit*, tarissent *dry up*, tuteurs, *legal guardians*, volaille *poultry*

Une lettre du Burkina Faso

Madame Nabi adresse une lettre à son amie américaine où elle lui parle de sa vie au Burkina Faso. Madame Nabi et son mari s'occupent d'un CSPS, Centre de santé et promotion sociale, pour procurer à leurs compatriotes aide et conseils au point de vue santé.

Zitenga, le 3 avril 1997

À Madame Baer

Je suis ravie de vous écrire cette lettre. Vous avez le bonjour de mon mari, M. Nabi, et de mon bébé, Wen Danga Benaja (puissance de Dieu, en mooré), qui a quatre mois. Mon bonjour également à toute votre famille et à tous ceux et celles qui vous sont chers. Nous vous ferons découvrir le Burkina par notre correspondance.

Nous habitons à Zitenga, qui est à 53 km au nord de la ville d'Ouagadougou, capitale du Burkina Faso. Ce village se trouve dans la province d'Oubritenga, une des 45

Les notables du village habillés pour la fête

provinces du pays. Nous avons un climat sahélien[1]: il pleut de juin à octobre, il fait froid de novembre à janvier et chaud de février à mai. Pendant la saison froide, le vent, qu'on appelle le Harmattan et qui vient du désert, couvre tout de poussière. Les villageois sont des cultivateurs, surtout de mil, d'arachides et de riz, et des éleveurs de moutons, de bœufs et de volailles. En saison sèche, on fait du jardinage et du commerce.

Le village respecte la hiérarchie traditionnelle. Le chef est généralement le plus vieux de la tribu et c'est lui qui est gardien de la tradition. Parmi les principales religions, l'animisme, la plus ancienne, est en voie de disparaître. Les gens qui la pratiquent adorent des idoles et placent leur confiance dans les ancêtres. Il y a aussi des catholiques, des protestants et des musulmans; ces derniers sont les plus nombreux. Les ethnies existantes sont les Mossis, qui sont en majorité, et les Peuhls qui sont nomades. On parle le mooré, le foulfouldé (peuhl) et le français.

Les occasions de rencontre sont surtout les fêtes traditionnelles mossis, dont le Basga, fête des récoltes où les vieux animistes préparent des boissons comme le dolo fait à base de sorgho rouge. Il y a aussi la fête musulmane du Ramadan et la Tabaski, fête des moutons. Les Chrétiens fêtent Noël et Pâques. Après un décès dans le village, on se réunit pour fêter le mort et demander à Dieu de l'accepter dans sa maison. On prépare un repas avec poulet et mouton, on boit le dolo, et on assiste à la danse des masques, exécutée au rythme des tams-tams. Ces masques sont des objets sacrés qui ne sortent que pour les funérailles et certaines fêtes mossis. Les jours de grands marchés, tous les 21 jours, le vendredi, les jeunes organisent des fêtes, les Damandassés, qui sont l'occasion pour eux de montrer leurs beaux habits, leurs belles robes et pagnes. C'est l'occasion aussi pour garçons et filles de se lier d'une amitié qui peut souvent aller jusqu'au mariage. Les Damandassés commencent après les récoltes à quatre heures de l'après-midi et durent jusqu'au petit matin.

Les maisons sont construites en "banco" ou terre séchée au soleil. Notre maison a deux pièces et un salon. J'y habite avec mon mari, mon bébé, ainsi que la femme d'un grand frère de mon mari, trois élèves (ma petite sœur qui fait la sixième, et une fille et un garçon qui font la cinquième, dont nous sommes les tuteurs), deux garçons qui nous aident pour les travaux domestiques et la construction, une bonne et un homme de 45 ans qui est chez nous depuis trois mois. En tout nous sommes onze dans la famille.

Mme Nabi et sa petite sœur dans les champs

Nous commençons chaque journée par une prière protestante de 6h à 6h30. Puis, mon mari et moi, nous allons au Centre de santé et de promotion sociale[2], où nous sommes agents de santé. À 12h30 c'est le déjeuner, et de 15h à 17h nous repartons au CSPS. Vers 19h c'est le dîner. Nous nous couchons chaque soir vers 22h, si nous n'avons pas de malade à surveiller au dispensaire. Quand on a un peu de temps, on lit un bon roman.

Le repas du matin, c'est la bouillie de mil préparée avec le jus de tamarin, cuite avec du sucre. Très rarement, on prend du café, du lait ou du pain. À midi, on prépare du riz avec sauce ou haricots; ou bien des ignames avec sauce tomate ou simplement salées, avec de l'huile d'arachide. Le soir, on mange du tô. Le tô est fait avec de la farine de maïs ou de mil, de l'eau et du jus de tamarin. On y ajoute une sauce faite avec des légumes tels que de l'oseille, des oignons, des tomates, ou de la viande ou du poisson fumé. On utilise aussi l'huile ou la pâte d'arachide. On mange assis par terre autour de la marmite et on prend la nourriture avec la main droite. Les femmes et les hommes mangent séparément.

Nous cherchons l'eau de boisson à un forage (une pompe) assez loin de chez nous, parce que le forage du dispensaire est en panne et nous n'avons pas les moyens suffisants pour le réparer. En plus des forages, les habitants puisent l'eau des puits, des mares ou des marigots[3]. Malheureusement ces sources d'eau tarissent très vite. Les femmes portent l'eau sur leur tête. Ceux qui ont les moyens vont à *l'eau avec des charrettes. Les légumes frais, qu'on achète au marché, viennent des villages environnants où il y a des barrages et donc des terres irriguées. Le problème de l'eau est crucial à Zitenga.*

Je remercie Madame Baer des cadeaux qu'elle a offerts à mon bébé. Si vous voulez d'autres détails, vous pouvez nous écrire. Nous vous souhaitons courage dans votre travail et surtout bonne réception de cette lettre.

Madame Nabi, née Ouedraogo Abzèta, Zitenga

---

1. *climate of transition between the desert and damper regions*   2. *M. Nabi is head of the Center, but not a doctor. His wife has nursing skills. Two midwives do pre-natal and post-natal counseling, including family planning. A second man does vaccination tours, and a third is a fix-it person and also gives shots and does circumcisions.*   3. *dead branch of a river bed*

 Vrai ou faux? Décidez si les phrases suivantes sont vraies ou fausses d'après la lecture. Si une phrase est fausse, corrigez-la.

1. Madame Nabi habite une grande maison.
2. Il y a plus de protestants que de membres d'autres religions.
3. On ne parle que le français au Burkina Faso.
4. La famille se met à table pour manger.
5. On utilise une fourchette, un couteau et une cuiller et on mange «à la française».
6. Les légumes frais viennent du jardin des Nabi.
7. Madame Nabi et son mari travaillent dans une sorte de clinique.
8. Ils se lèvent avant six heures du matin.
9. Pour avoir de l'eau, on doit simplement ouvrir le robinet dans la cuisine.

 Questions. Répondez.

1. Combien d'hommes et combien de femmes habitent la maison de Madame Nabi?
2. D'après cette lettre, combien de langues est-ce qu'on parle au Burkina Faso?
3. Quelles sont les quatre religions dont parle Madame Nabi?
4. Quelles sont les différentes sortes de viande mentionnées dans cette lettre?
5. Quels sont les besoins essentiels pour les gens du village?

E **Cherchez des exemples.** Relisez la lettre et cherchez des exemples ...

1. qui indiquent que le Burkina Faso se trouve en Afrique.
2. qui prouvent que le Burkina Faso est un pays pauvre.
3. qui montrent l'influence de l'Islam au Burkina Faso.
4. qui révèlent la foi *(faith)* et la charité des Nabi.

VOCABULAIRE ACTIF

À table
un bol *bowl*
un couteau *knife*
une cuiller *spoon*
une fourchette *fork*
une nappe *tablecloth*
le poivre *pepper*
le sel *salt*
une serviette *napkin*
le sucre *sugar*

Au restaurant
une carte *(à la carte) menu*
un menu *(fixed price) menu*

D'autres noms
une brosse à cheveux (à dents)
   hairbrush (toothbrush)
le chauffage *heat*
la climatisation *air conditioning*
une dame *lady*
les genoux *(m. pl.) lap; knees*
un maillot de bain *bathing suit*
un pyjama *(pair of) pajamas*
des skis *(m.) skis*
une soirée *evening party*
un sourire *smile*

La routine quotidienne
se brosser (les dents) *to brush*
   (one's teeth)
se coucher *to go to bed*
s'endormir *to fall asleep*
s'habiller *to get dressed*
se laver *to get washed; to wash up*
se lever *to get up; to stand up*
se mettre à table *to sit down to eat*
se promener *to take a walk, ride*
se reposer *to rest*
se réveiller *to wake up*

Expressions utiles
à la française *in the French style*
Bon appétit! *Have a good meal.*
C'est exact. *That's right.*
de rien *you're welcome; don't men-*
   tion it; not at all
Excusez-moi (nous, etc.) d'être
   en retard. *Excuse me (us, etc.) for*
   being late.
Il n'y a pas de quoi. *Don't mention*
   it.; Not at all.
il sourit *he smiles*
Par ici. *(Come) this way.; Follow me.*

Verbes
s'appeler *to be named; to be called*
s'asseoir *to sit down*
couper *to cut*
se dépêcher *to hurry*
exiger (que) *to demand (that)*
goûter *to taste*
s'inquiéter *to worry*
laver *to wash*
lever *to lift; to raise*
mettre *to put; to place; to lay*
mettre la table *to set the table*
mettre le chauffage *to turn on the*
   heat
souhaiter (que) *to wish; to hope*
   (that)
se souvenir (de) *to remember*
tarder *to be a long time coming*
verser *to pour*

Buts communicatifs
Describing interpersonal relationships
Describing television programs
Expressing emotion

Structures utiles
Le verbe **dire**
Les pronoms objets indirects
Les verbes **voir** et **croire**
Les interrogatifs **quel** et **lequel**
Le pronom relatif (suite)
Le subjonctif (suite)
Le pronom **en**

Culture
La télévision française
Qu'est-ce que les Français regardent à la télé?
Les faux amis

Une histoire d'amour

David et Marie sortent ensemble.

Ils s'entendent° très bien.	*get along*
Ils s'embrassent°.	*kiss*
Ils s'aiment.	
Il lui° a demandé si elle voulait l'épouser.	*her*
Elle lui° a répondu que oui.	*him*
Il lui a acheté une très belle bague de fiançailles°.	*engagement ring*
Ils vont se marier.	

▶ Et vous? Connaissez-vous des couples célèbres° qui sont fiancés? *famous*
Connaissez-vous des couples célèbres qui sont mariés?
Connaissez-vous des couples célèbres qui sont divorcés?

M. et Mme Jean-Pierre Delataille   *M. et Mme Émile Baron*

ont l'honneur de vous annoncer le mariage de leurs enfants

Marie et David

et vous prient d'assister ou de vous unir d'intention à la Messe de Mariage

qui sera célébrée le samedi 13 juillet 2002 à 17 heures, en l'Église St-Gervais.

27, rue Mahler—75004 Paris   *27, rue des Tournelles—75004 Paris*

Conversation

Quelle histoire!

Lori et son amie Denise sont assises à la terrasse d'un café. Denise lui demande si elle a regardé le feuilleton° d'hier soir. — soap opera, series

DENISE: Encore à boire, Lori?

LORI: Non, vraiment, sans façon.

DENISE: Au fait, tu as regardé le feuilleton hier à la télé?

LORI: Lequel?° — *Which one?*

DENISE: *Nos chers enfants.*

LORI: Non. Qu'est-ce qui est arrivé?° — *What happened?*

DENISE: David et Marie ne s'aiment plus. Marie a un petit ami maintenant.

LORI: Eh! ça devient sérieux.

DENISE: Tu ne sais pas tout. Ils vont divorcer. David lui a dit qu'il allait partir.

LORI: Il est sans doute très malheureux°, n'est-ce pas? — *unhappy*

DENISE: Bien sûr. Il dit que le mariage est une loterie. Pour se consoler le plus vite possible, il a mis une annonce° dans le journal local. — *advertisement*

LORI: Ça, c'est original°. Et il y a des candidates? — *a novel idea*

DENISE: Oui, trois femmes lui ont répondu et veulent le rencontrer°. — *meet*

LORI: Sans blague?° — *No kidding?*

DENISE: Je te le jure.° C'est passionnant! — *I swear.*

LORI: Quelle histoire!

▶ **Jouez ces rôles.** Répétez la conversation avec votre partenaire. Remplacez ensuite *David* par *Marie* et *Marie* par *David*, par exemple: **Elle lui a dit qu'elle allait partir.** Faites tous les changements nécessaires.

The **Quelle histoire!** gesture is used in the video, *Modules 1 & 6.*

Point out the relationship between **jurer** and the English word *jury.*

Il y a un geste

Je te le jure. An outstretched hand, palm down, means *I swear,* perhaps originally meaning "I would put my hand in the fire (if it were not true)."

Quelle histoire! To indicate that something is amazing, exaggerated, or far-fetched, the French hold the hand open with fingers pointing down and shake the wrist several times. Other expressions used with this gesture are **Oh là là!** *(Wow!, Oh dear!)* and **Mon Dieu!** *(My goodness!).*

À PROPOS

Comparison: Have students describe their TV viewing. What do they watch and how much time do they spend watching TV? How do their viewing habits compare with those of the French?

Comment dit-on «passionnant» en anglais?

a. passionate   b. amazing   c. exciting

Que veut dire «sans doute»?

a. certainement b. probablement c. peut-être

En France il y a cinq chaînes (channels) de télévision nationales. Sur ces cinq, _____ sont des chaînes publiques.

a. Deux   b. Trois   c. Quatre

La télévision française

Until recently, commercials **(la publicité),** if allowed at all, were grouped into relatively lengthy segments and shown between programs. Today, however, commercials often interrupt programs, especially on the private channels. As in North America, many viewers cope by channel "surfing" **(zapper).**

Of the five major channels available to all, only two **(TF1** and **M6)** are private. The others **(France 2, France 3,** and **Arte/La 5)** are public. In addition to commercials and government subsidies, public television is financed in France (and in most European countries) by a user tax. Everyone who has a color TV set, currently 96% of French households, must pay 700 francs per year.

France 2 programming, especially the evening news **(le Journal de vingt heures),** is made available throughout the francophone world and in most other countries. It may be found on the French-language channels in Canada and on SCOLA and the International channel in the United States.

Recently cable TV watching and Internet use have increased considerably in France. French has become, after English, the second language of the World Wide Web.

Les faux amis (False cognates)

It is estimated that as much as 50% of our English-language vocabulary comes from French. Most of these words are true cognates and facilitate comprehension. There are, however, a number of false cognates whose meaning *in a given context* is quite different from what we might expect. Some examples are given on page 381.

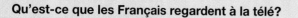

Qu'est-ce que les Français regardent à la télé?

Si on ne considère que les chaînes nationales TF1, France 2, France 3, Arte/La Cinquième et M6, les Français regardent, en moyenne *(on the average),* 1.051 heures de programmes par an, dont 272 h. de fiction (feuilletons, etc.); 152 h. de magazines, de documentaires et de débats; 151 h. de journaux télévisés (informations); 99 h. de publicité; 88 h. de films; 86 h. de jeux; 71 h. de sport; 54 h. de variétés; 31 h. d'émissions pour enfants; 2 h. de théâtre et de musique classique; 45 h. d'autres programmes. *(d'après le Quid)*

VOCABULAIRE

Quelques faux amis

actuellement	*now*
une annonce	*advertisement*
arriver	*to happen*
assister (à)	*to attend*
attendre	*to wait for*
un avertissement	*warning*
compréhensif (-ve)	*understanding*
confus(e)	*ashamed, embarrassed*
demander	*to ask*
une émission	*program*
formidable	*wonderful*
une histoire	*story*
un journal	*newspaper*
original(e)	*novel, odd; different*
passionnant(e)	*exciting, fascinating*
passer un examen	*to take a test*
rester	*to stay*
sans doute	*probably*

Review *cognate*, p. 25 and *false cognate*, p. 49.

 À vous. Répondez.

1. Avez-vous un feuilleton préféré? Si oui, lequel?
2. Que pensez-vous des feuilletons en général?
3. Quel feuilleton aimez-vous le moins?

Entre amis

Mon émission préférée

1. Ask your partner what his/her favorite TV show is.
2. Find out why s/he likes it.
3. Find out if s/he watched it this week.
4. If so, find out what happened. If not, ask what happened the last time s/he watched it.

Prononciation

La tension

■ There is much more tension in the facial muscles when speaking French than when speaking English. Two important phenomena result from this greater tension.

1. *There are no diphthongs (glides from one vowel sound to another) in French.* French vowels are said to be "pure." The positions of mouth and tongue remain stable during the pronunciation of a vowel, and therefore one vowel sound does not "glide" into another as often happens in English.

▶ **Contrast:**

English	French
day	des
aut**o**	aut**o**

■ Notice that in the English word *day,* the **a** glides into an **ee** sound at the end, and that in the English word *auto,* the **o** glides to **oo.**

▶ Now practice "holding steady" the sound of each of the vowels in the following French words.

étudiant, am**é**ricain, sant**é**, soir**ée**, dans**er**, parl**ez**, l**es**, j'**ai**
ch**o**se, styl**o**, tr**o**p, zér**o**, **au**ssi, ch**au**d, b**eau**, mant**eau**

2. *Final consonants are completely released.* The pronunciation of final French consonants is much more "complete" than is the case for those of American English.

■ Note that in American English, the final consonants are often neither dropped nor firmly enunciated. In similar French words, the final consonants are all clearly pronounced.

▶ **Contrast:**

English	French	English	French
ro**b**	ro**be**	home	ho**mme**
gran**d**	gran**de**	American	américai**ne**
ba**g**	ba**gue**	gri**p**	gri**ppe**
be**ll**	be**lle**	intelligen**t**	intelligen**te**

Now practice "releasing" the highlighted final consonant sounds below so that you can hear them clearly.

Item 5: Be sure there is liaison after **un** but not after **et.**

1. u**n**e gran**d**e fille
2. Elle s'appelle Michè**l**e.
3. un pi**qu**e-ni**qu**e
4. une ba**gu**e de fiançailles
5. un ho**mm**e et une fe**mm**e
6. sa ju**p**e verte

1 Describing Interpersonal Relationships

L'histoire d'un divorce

David et Marie ne s'entendent plus très bien.
Ils se fâchent°.   *get angry*
Ils se disputent°.   *argue; fight*
Il ne lui envoie plus de fleurs.
Elle ne lui parle plus.
Il lui a dit° qu'il ne l'aime plus.   *He told her*
Ils vont se séparer.
Ils ont même° l'intention de divorcer.   *even*

Review also p. 378

 Et vous? Choisissez un couple (de Hollywood, de Washington, de vos amis, etc.) que vous connaissez. Comment s'appellent-ils? Est-ce qu'ils s'entendent bien? Est-ce qu'ils se disputent quelquefois? Décrivez ce couple.

A. Le verbe *dire*

David **dit** qu'il va partir.   *David says (that) he's going to leave.*
Dites à Marie de faire attention. *Tell Marie to watch out.*

dire *(to say; to tell)*			
je	**dis**	nous	**disons**
tu	**dis**	vous	**dites**
il/elle/on	**dit**	ils/elles	**disent**
passé composé: j'**ai dit**			

■ The verb **dire** should not be confused with the verb **parler.** Both can mean *to tell,* but they are used differently.

• **Dire** can be followed by a quote or by an item of information (sometimes contained in another clause introduced by **que**).

Bruno **dit bonjour** à Alissa.	*Bruno **says hello** to Alissa.*
Il **lui dit un secret.**	*He **tells her a secret.***
Il **dit qu'il l'aime.**	*He **says that he loves her.***
Il **dit** toujours **la vérité.**	*He always **tells the truth.***

• **Parler** can stand alone or can be followed by an adverb, by **à** (or **avec**) and the person spoken to, or by **de** and the topic of conversation.

Bruno **parle** (lentement).	*Bruno **is speaking** (slowly).*
Il **parle à** Alissa.	*He **is talking to** Alissa.*
Il **parle de** lui-même.	*He **is telling about** himself.*

Note When the meaning is *to tell (a story),* the verb **raconter** is used.

Raconte-nous une histoire.   *Tell us a story.*

1 **Qu'est-ce qu'ils disent?** Quelles sont les opinions de chaque personne? Utilisez le verbe **dire** et le verbe **être** dans chaque phrase.

MODÈLE: Ma grand-mère / le rap / facile ou difficile à comprendre
Ma grand-mère dit que le rap est difficile à comprendre.

1. je / la publicité à la télé / très bonne ou très mauvaise
2. nos grands-parents / nous / charmants ou désagréables
3. nous / le cours de français / formidable ou ennuyeux
4. le professeur de français / nous / travailleurs ou paresseux
5. mes professeurs / je / intelligent(e) ou stupide
6. mes amis / le football à la télé / passionnant ou affreux

2 **À vous.** Répondez.

1. Que dites-vous quand vous avez une bonne note à un examen?
2. Que dit votre professeur de français quand vous entrez en classe?
3. Que dites-vous quand vous êtes en retard à un cours?
4. Que dites-vous à un(e) ami(e) qui vous téléphone à 6 heures du matin?
5. De quoi parlez-vous avec vos amis?
6. Vos professeurs racontent-ils quelquefois des histoires en classe? Si oui, quelle sorte d'histoires?
7. Comment dit-on «Oh dear!» en français?
8. Dites-vous toujours la vérité?

Follow up, books closed, by asking students to recall these examples or to make up others.

3 **Le perroquet et la fourmi** *(the parrot and the ant).* **Quelle histoire!** Utilisez les verbes **dire, parler** et **raconter** pour compléter le paragraphe suivant.

Mon frère _____ qu'il adore les histoires drôles. Hier soir, par exemple, il m'a _____ l'histoire d'une femme anglaise qui achète un perroquet qui ne _____ que le français. Mais la pauvre dame ne peut rien _____ en français et ne peut pas _____ avec lui. Un jour, la dame va boire un verre de lait mais dans le verre il y a une fourmi. Le perroquet veut _____ à la dame de ne pas boire le lait; il _____ FOURMI!! parce qu'il ne _____ pas anglais. La dame pense que le perroquet a _____ «For me!» et elle part chercher un verre de lait pour son perroquet. J'ai _____ à mon frère que je n'apprécie pas beaucoup les histoires qu'il _____.

B. Les pronoms objets indirects

David parle *à Marie.* — *David is speaking to Marie.*
Il **lui** dit qu'il l'aime. — *He tells **her** that he loves her.*
Il **lui** demande l'épouser. — *He asks **her** to marry him.*
Il **lui** achète une bague de fiançailles. — *He buys **her** an engagement ring.*
Ils écrivent *à leurs parents.* — *They write to their parents.*
Ils **leur** disent qu'ils vont se marier. — *They tell **them** that they are going to get married.*

Il lui a demandé si elle voulait se promener.

■ Indirect object nouns in French are preceded by the preposition **à.** Many verbs take indirect objects, either in addition to a direct object or with no direct object.

VOCABULAIRE

Quelques verbes qui prennent un objet indirect

acheter		*to buy*
demander		*to ask*
dire		*to say; to tell*
donner		*to give*
écrire		*to write*
emprunter	quelque chose **à quelqu'un**	*to borrow*
envoyer		*to send*
montrer		*to show*
prêter		*to lend*
raconter		*to tell*
rendre		*to give back*
vendre		*to sell*
obéir		*to obey*
parler	**à quelqu'un**	*to speak, talk*
répondre		*to respond, answer*
téléphoner		*to telephone*

> Two additional expressions that you have already learned take a specific direct object plus an indirect object: **poser une question à quelqu'un; rendre visite à quelqu'un.** J'ai posé une question **au professeur.** *(I asked the teacher a question.)* Vas-tu rendre visite **à tes parents?** *(Are you going to visit your parents?)*

Note Do not be confused by verbs that take an indirect object in French but a direct object in English.

Paul obéit **à ses parents.**	*Paul obeys his parents.*
Je téléphone **à Brigitte.**	*I call Brigitte.*
Marc rend visite **à ses amis.**	*Marc visits his friends.*

■ Indirect object nouns can be replaced in sentences by indirect object pronouns.

> Review the direct object pronouns on pp. 226 and 278.

me (m')	*(to) me*	**nous**	*(to) us*
te (t')	*(to) you*	**vous**	*(to) you*
lui	*(to) him; (to) her*	**leur**	*(to) them*

> Point out that the indirect object pronouns are *personal* pronouns. Remind students that they have already learned (Ch. 7) to substitute the pronoun **y** for **à** + an object, place, etc.

Note The indirect object pronouns **me, te, nous,** and **vous** are identical to the direct object pronouns. But unlike direct objects, **lui** is used for both *(to) him* and *(to) her*, and **leur** is used for *(to) them.*

Alain a-t-il téléphoné **à Pierre?**	Oui, il **lui** a téléphoné.
A-t-il téléphoné aussi **à Anne?**	Oui, il **lui** a téléphoné aussi.
A-t-il téléphoné **à Guy et à Ariel?**	Oui, il **leur** a téléphoné après.
Vous a-t-il parlé de tout ça?	Non, il ne **m'**a pas parlé de ça.
	Ariel **m'**a dit ça.

Note Often in English, the preposition *to* is omitted. Also, in some contexts indirect object pronouns may mean *for someone*, *from someone*, etc.

Est-ce que je **t'**ai donné de l'argent?	*Did I give you some money? (= to you)*
Mais non, tu **m'**as emprunté 5 dollars!	*No, you borrowed 5 dollars from me!*
Alors, je **t'**achèterai quelque chose.	*Then I'll buy you something. (= for you)*

■ Like a direct object pronoun, an indirect object pronoun is almost always placed directly *before* the verb.

Nous **lui** répondons tout de suite.	*We answer him (her) right away.*
Ils ne **nous** ont pas téléphoné.	*They didn't telephone us.*
Vous dit-elle la vérité?	*Is she telling you the truth?*
Elle va **leur** rendre visite.	*She is going to visit them.*
Ne **m'**écris pas.	*Don't write to me.*

Note Also like direct object pronouns, indirect object pronouns follow the verb *only* in affirmative commands, and in that case **me** and **te** become **moi** and **toi**.

Écris-**lui** immédiatement!	*Write to him immediately!*
Donne-**moi** de l'eau, s'il te plaît.	*Give me some water, please.*

Synthèse: Object pronouns

direct:	**me**	**te**	**le/la**	**nous**	**vous**	**les**
indirect:	**me**	**te**	**lui**	**nous**	**vous**	**leur**
reflexive:	**me**	**te**	**se**	**nous**	**vous**	**se**

Carrefour vous simplifie la vie!
Tout en faisant vos courses, vous pouvez aussi...

4 **Le professeur et les étudiants.** Utilisez les expressions suivantes pour faire des phrases. Utilisez un pronom objet indirect dans chaque phrase et utilisez la forme négative si vous voulez.

MODÈLES: **Le professeur leur parle toujours en français.**
Les étudiants ne lui rendent jamais visite.

		dire bonjour	
		parler en français	
		écrire des lettres	toujours
		téléphoner	d'habitude
le professeur	leur	rendre visite	souvent
les étudiants	lui	poser des questions	quelquefois
		demander un conseil	rarement
		raconter des histoires	jamais
		obéir	
		donner des tests faciles	

Vrai ou faux? Décidez si les phrases suivantes sont vraies ou fausses. Ensuite répondez chaque fois avec un pronom objet indirect. Si une phrase est fausse, corrigez-la.

MODÈLES: Le professeur dit toujours bonjour aux étudiants.
C'est vrai. Il leur dit toujours bonjour.

Le président vous a téléphoné.
C'est faux. Il ne m'a pas téléphoné.

1. Le professeur de français ne donne pas beaucoup de devoirs aux étudiants.
2. Le professeur vous pose beaucoup de questions.
3. Les étudiants répondent toujours correctement au professeur.
4. Vous écrivez quelquefois des lettres à vos amis.
5. Vos amis vous répondent chaque fois.
6. Vous téléphonez souvent à votre meilleur(e) ami(e).
7. Vous ne rendez jamais visite à vos cousins.
8. Vous montrez toujours vos notes à vos parents.
9. Vos parents vous prêtent souvent leur voiture.

 Faites-le donc! *(Then do it!)* Encouragez la personne d'après les modèles. Utilisez des pronoms objets indirects.

MODÈLES: Je vais rendre visite à Jean.
Eh bien, rendez-lui donc visite!

Je voudrais poser une question au professeur.
Eh bien, posez-lui donc une question!

1. Je vais parler à Claire.
2. Je voudrais répondre au professeur.
3. Je vais rendre visite à mes grands-parents.
4. Je vais prêter ma voiture à mon amie.
5. J'ai envie de vous poser une question.
6. Je voudrais dire bonjour à Thierry.
7. J'ai envie de téléphoner à mes parents.

7 **Non, ne le faites pas!** Employez encore les phrases de l'activité 6 pour dire à la personne de *ne pas* faire ce qu'elle veut faire. Utilisez des pronoms objets indirects.

MODÈLES: Je vais rendre visite à Jean.
Mais non, ne lui rendez pas visite!

Je voudrais poser une question au professeur.
Mais non, ne lui posez pas de question!

La voiture de Paul. Remplacez chaque expression en italique par un des pronoms suivants: **le, la, les, lui** ou **leur**.

MODÈLES: Les parents de Paul ont acheté une voiture *à leur fils*.
Les parents de Paul lui ont acheté une voiture.

Ils aiment beaucoup *leur fils*.
Ils l'aiment beaucoup.

1. Il a dit merci *à ses parents*.
2. Georges a demandé *à Paul* s'il pouvait conduire *la voiture*.
3. Paul a prêté sa voiture *à Georges*.
4. Georges rend visite *à sa petite amie*.
5. Elle aime beaucoup *la voiture*.
6. Elle demande *à Georges* si elle peut conduire *la voiture*.
7. Il prête la voiture *à sa petite amie*. Elle dit merci *à Georges*.
8. Il dit *à son amie* de prendre *le volant*.
9. Elle va rendre la voiture *à Georges* la semaine prochaine.

 Je vais le faire. Répondez affirmativement à chaque ordre par l'expression **Je vais** + un infinitif. Remplacez les expressions en italique par un pronom objet direct ou indirect.

MODÈLES: Il faut que vous téléphoniez *à Léa!*   Il faut que vous écriviez
D'accord, je vais lui téléphoner.   *votre nom.*
D'accord, je vais l'écrire.

1. Il faut que vous obéissiez *à vos parents!*
2. Il faut que vous prêtiez votre livre *à votre voisine!*
3. Il faut que vous regardiez *cette émission!*
4. Il faut que vous écriviez une lettre *à vos grands-parents!*
5. Il faut que vous disiez *la vérité!*
6. Il ne faut pas que vous demandiez *à Agnès* quel âge elle a!
7. Il ne faut pas que vous buviez *ce verre de vin!*
8. Il faut que vous posiez une question *au professeur!*
9. Il faut que vous *me* répondiez!

⑩ À vous. Répondez.

Remind students of the expression **Occupez-vous de vos oignons!** and allow them to use this answer if the questions are too personal.

1. Téléphonez-vous souvent à vos amis?
2. À qui avez-vous parlé récemment?
3. Qu'est-ce que vous lui avez dit?
4. Qu'est-ce que vous lui avez demandé?
5. Qu'est-ce qu'il vous a répondu?
6. Allez-vous rendre visite à des amis bientôt?
7. Si oui, quand est-ce que vous leur rendrez visite? Si non, comment les contacterez-vous?
8. Que prêtez-vous à vos amis?
9. Qu'est-ce que vous empruntez à vos parents?

Entre amis

Votre meilleur(e) ami(e)

Talk to your partner about his/her best friend. Use indirect object pronouns where appropriate.

1. Find out the name of your partner's best friend.
2. Ask if your partner wrote to him/her this week.
3. Ask if your partner visited him/her this week.
4. Ask if your partner called him/her this week.
5. If so, try to find out what your partner said to his/her friend.

2 Describing Television Programs

Quelles émissions y a-t-il à la télévision?
> Il y a ...
>> les informations, par exemple, *le Journal du soir*.
>> la météorologie, par exemple, *le Bulletin météo*.
>> les sports, par exemple, *le Tour de France*.
>> les films, par exemple, *Tous les matins du monde*.
>> les pièces, par exemple, *L'Avare* de Molière.
>> les feuilletons, par exemple, *Le Fond du problème*.
>> les dessins animés, par exemple, *Popeye*.
>> les jeux, par exemple, *la Roue de la fortune*.
>> la publicité, par exemple, les spots publicitaires pour Perrier, Coca-Cola.

Et vous? Qu'est-ce que vous regardez à la télévision?

11 À vous. Répondez.

1. Combien de temps par jour passez-vous à regarder la télévision?
2. Que regardez-vous à la télévision?
3. Quelles sont les émissions que vous ne regardez presque *(almost)* jamais?
4. Quelle émission trouvez-vous la plus drôle?
5. Quelle émission trouvez-vous la plus ennuyeuse?
6. Regardez-vous quelquefois des feuilletons? Si oui, quel feuilleton préférez-vous?
7. Que pensez-vous de la publicité à la télévision?
8. Voudriez-vous qu'il y ait plus, autant ou moins de sports à la télévision? Pourquoi?

Students have already learned:
je voudrais.

C. Les verbes *voir* et *croire*

Je **crois** qu'il va neiger. Qu'en pensez-vous?	*I think it's going to snow. What do you think?*
On **verra.**	*We'll see.*
Je **crois** que je **vois** nos amis.	*I think (that) I see our friends.*
Avez-vous déjà **vu** ce film?	*Did you already see this film?*
Je **crois** que oui.	*I believe so.*
Non, je ne **crois** pas.	*No, I don't believe so.*

Note the use of **que** in the expression **Je crois que oui.**

Point out that **voir** means *to see* and **regarder** means *to look at.* You may also wish to point out that **croire** and **penser** often have the same meaning, but that there are differences, e.g., **je le crois** *(I believe him),* **je pense à lui** *(I think about him).*

■ The verbs **voir** and **croire** have similar present tense conjugations.

voir *(to see)*		croire *(to believe, think)*	
je	**vois**	je	**crois**
tu	**vois**	tu	**crois**
il/elle/on	**voit**	il/elle/on	**croit**
nous	**voyons**	nous	**croyons**
vous	**voyez**	vous	**croyez**
ils/elles	**voient**	ils/elles	**croient**
passé composé: j'**ai vu**		*passé composé:* j'**ai cru**	

■ The future tense verb stem for **voir** is irregular: **verr-.** The future of **croire** is regular.

Je vous **verrai** demain.	*I will see you tomorrow.*
Mes amis ne me **croiront** pas.	*My friends won't believe me.*

■ The subjunctive forms of **voir** and **croire** have two stems just like other verbs that have two present tense stems.

Il faut que je le **voie.**	Il faut que vous le **voyiez** aussi.
Je veux qu'il me **croie.**	Je veux que vous me **croyiez.**

12 **Que croient-ils?** Tout le monde a son opinion. Utilisez le verbe **croire** et identifiez ce qui, à votre avis, correspond à la description donnée.

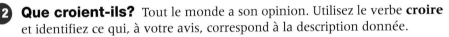

Follow up by having students tell you where they agreed or disagreed with their partner.

Modèle: mon père / la meilleure équipe de football
Mon père croit que les New York Giants sont la meilleure équipe de football.

1. je / l'émission la plus intéressante le jeudi soir
2. nous / le cours le plus ennuyeux
3. le professeur de français / les étudiants les plus travailleurs
4. mes parents / la chose la plus importante de ma vie
5. mes amis / le feuilleton le plus passionnant
6. je / le plus mauvais film de cette année

13 **Que croyez-vous?** Est-ce que la phrase est vraie pour la plupart des étudiants de votre cours de français? Si oui, répondez **Je crois que oui.** Si non, répondez **Je ne crois pas** et corrigez la phrase.

MODÈLE: La plupart des étudiants croient que le professeur de français est méchant.
> **Je ne crois pas. Ils croient que le professeur est très gentil.**

1. La plupart des étudiants voient leurs parents tous les jours.
2. La plupart des étudiants verront un film le week-end prochain.
3. La plupart des étudiants ont déjà vu un film français.
4. La plupart des étudiants veulent voir un pays où on parle français.
5. La plupart des étudiants verront la tour Eiffel un jour.
6. La plupart des étudiants croient que les femmes conduisent mieux que les hommes.
7. La plupart des étudiants croyaient au Père Noël quand ils étaient petits.
8. La plupart des étudiants croient actuellement au Père Noël.

14 **À vous.** Répondez.

1. Quel film avez-vous vu la dernière fois que vous êtes allé(e) au cinéma?
2. Qui voyez-vous tous les jours?
3. Qui avez-vous vu hier?
4. Quelle note croyez-vous que vous aurez en français?
5. Quand croyez-vous que vous irez en Europe?
6. Qu'est-ce que vous verrez si vous y allez?
7. Qui croit au Père Noël?

D. Les interrogatifs *quel* et *lequel*

Review **quel**, p. 113.

■ You have already learned to use the adjective **quel** *(which? what?).* **Quel** always occurs with a noun and agrees with that noun.

Quel feuilleton avez-vous vu?
De **quelle** actrice parlez-vous?
Quels acteurs préférez-vous?
Quelles sont vos émissions préférées?

■ **Lequel** *(which one)* replaces **quel** and the noun it modifies. Both parts of **lequel** show agreement.

Vous avez vu le feuilleton?	**Lequel?** (Quel feuilleton?)
Que pensez-vous de cette actrice?	**Laquelle?** (Quelle actrice?)
Ces acteurs sont formidables.	**Lesquels?** (Quels acteurs?)
Ce sont vos émissions préférées?	**Lesquelles?** (Quelles émissions?)

	singulier	pluriel
masculin	**lequel**	**lesquels**
féminin	**laquelle**	**lesquelles**

■ Do not use the indefinite article (**un, une, des**) when **quel** is used in an exclamation.

Quelle histoire!   *What a story!*
Quel cours!   *What a course!*
Quels étudiants!   *What students!*

■ **Lequel** is often followed by the preposition **de** to name the group from which the choice is to be made.

Laquelle *de vos amies* s'appelle Mimi?   *Which of your friends is named Mimi?*

Lesquels *de vos professeurs* parlent français?   *Which of your teachers speak French?*

FOR RECOGNITION ONLY:

• When **lequel, lesquels,** and **lesquelles** are preceded by the prepositions **à** or **de,** the normal contractions are made. No contraction is made with **laquelle.**

à + lequel	→	**auquel**	de + lequel	→	**duquel**
à + lesquels	→	**auxquels**	de + lesquels	→	**desquels**
à + lesquelles	→	**auxquelles**	de + lesquelles	→	**desquelles**

Alexis parle d'un film, mais **duquel** parle-t-il?
Il parle aussi des émissions de télé, mais **desquelles?**
Auxquelles de ces émissions vous intéressez-vous?

 Dans une salle bruyante *(In a noisy room).* On fait du bruit et vous n'entendez pas bien les réponses de votre partenaire. Demandez-lui de répéter. Utilisez une forme de **quel** dans la première question et une forme de **lequel** dans la deuxième.

Modèle: ville

           VOUS: **Quelle ville préfères-tu?**
    VOTRE PARTENAIRE: **Je préfère Québec.**
           VOUS: **Laquelle?**
    VOTRE PARTENAIRE: **Québec.**

1. émission	5. voiture	9. feuilleton
2. ville	6. acteurs	10. cours
3. dessin animé	7. actrices	11. dessert
4. film	8. chanson	12. sports

Microconversation: Non, je n'ai pas pu. Interviewez votre parte-naire d'après le modèle. Faites tous les changements nécessaires.

> **MODÈLE:** regarder le feuilleton
>> **VOUS:** **As-tu regardé le feuilleton hier?**
>> **VOTRE PARTENAIRE:** **Lequel?**
>> **VOUS:** **«Mes chers enfants».**
>> **VOTRE PARTENAIRE:** **Non, je n'ai pas pu le regarder.**

1. voir le match (de basket-ball, de base-ball, etc.)
2. regarder les informations
3. voir la pièce
4. regarder l'émission
5. regarder les dessins animés
6. voir le film

17 **À vous.** Répondez.

1. Y a-t-il des mois de l'année plus agréables que les autres? Lesquels?
2. Quel est le mois le moins agréable, à votre avis?
3. Lequel des membres de votre famille est le plus jeune?
4. Laquelle des actrices célèbres trouvez-vous la plus belle?
5. Lequel des acteurs célèbres trouvez-vous le plus beau?
6. Lesquels de vos amis voyez-vous tous les jours?
7. Auxquels envoyez-vous des messages électroniques?

E. Le pronom relatif (suite)

■ Relative pronouns like *who, whom,* and *which* relate or tie two clauses to-gether. They refer to a word in the first clause.

Review relative pronouns on p. 256.

(J'ai des amis. Ils habitent en France.)
J'ai des amis **qui** habitent en France.   *I have friends who live in France.*
(J'ai des amis. Vous les connaissez bien.)
J'ai des amis **que** vous connaissez bien.   *I have friends whom you know well.*

■ The choice of the relative pronoun **qui** or **que** depends on its function as subject or object.

- **Qui** *(who, that, which)* replaces a person or a thing that is the *subject* of a relative clause.

«La Roue de la fortune» est une émission **qui** est très populaire.

- **Que** *(whom, that, which)* replaces a person or a thing that is the *object* of a relative clause.

Le film **que** j'ai vu était très intéressant.

■ Past participles conjugated with **avoir** agree with a preceding direct object. Therefore, a past participle will agree with **que** in a relative clause.

Review agreement on p. 279.

la pièce que j'ai vu**e**   *the play I saw*
la robe qu'elle a mis**e**   *the dress she put on*
les fleurs que tu as achet**ées**   *the flowers you bought*

■ Although the relative pronoun may be omitted in English, it is never omitted in French.

C'est l'émission **que** je préfère.   *It's the program (that) I prefer.*

■ Preceded by a preposition, **qui** is normally used with persons and **lequel, laquelle,** etc., is used with things.

la personne **avec qui** j'ai dansé   *the person with whom I danced*
la question **à laquelle** j'ai déjà répondu   *the question I already answered*

■ **Dont** *(whose, of which, about which)* is normally used to replace a relative pronoun and the preposition **de** that precedes it.

(l'émission de laquelle nous avons parlé)
l'émission **dont** nous avons parlé   *the program we spoke about*
(l'annonceur de qui je me souviens bien)
l'annonceur **dont** je me souviens bien   *the announcer I remember well*

N O S   P A R T E N A I R E S

buzz™   AEROPORT DE BORDEAUX
Chambre de Commerce et d'Industrie de Bordeaux

La compagnie qui, sur Bordeaux-Londres, vous offre l'essentiel

18 **Identifiez-les.** Quelles sont les personnes ou les choses suivantes?

Modèle: une personne que vous avez vue à la télé
          Jay Leno est une personne que j'ai vue à la télé.

1. une émission qui est très populaire à la télé
2. une émission que vous refusez de regarder à la télé
3. le dernier film que vous avez vu
4. une personne que vous connaissez qui n'aime pas regarder la télé
5. la publicité qui est la plus ennuyeuse de la télé
6. le dessin animé que vous croyez le plus drôle
7. l'actrice ou l'acteur que vous préférez
8. une émission de télévision dont vous avez parlé avec vos amis
9. une personne avec qui vous êtes allé(e) au cinéma

Entre amis

Un film que j'ai vu

1. Find out the name of the last film that your partner saw.
2. Ask if s/he saw it on TV or at the movies.
3. Ask if s/he liked the film.
4. Find out the names of the actors who were in the film.
5. Find out all you can about this film.

3 Expressing Emotion

Êtes-vous d'accord avec les sentiments exprimés dans les phrases suivantes?
Qu'en pensez-vous?[1]

	oui	non
Je suis fâché(e) que les professeurs donnent tant de devoirs!	——	——
Je regrette que mes notes ne soient pas meilleures.	——	——
C'est dommage qu'il y ait tant d'émissions sportives à la télévision.	——	——
C'est ridicule qu'il y ait tant de publicité à la télévision.	——	——
Je suis désolé(e) que tant de gens n'aient pas assez à manger.	——	——
Le professeur est ravi que je fasse des progrès.	——	——

1. *What's your opinion (about them)?*

Review the forms and uses of the subjunctive in Chs. 10 & 13.

F. Le subjonctif (suite)

■ The subjunctive forms for **vouloir** and **pouvoir** are as follows:

vouloir				
	(veuill-)		(nous	voulons)
que je	**veuill**	**e**	que nous	**voul** **ions**
que tu	**veuill**	**es**	que vous	**voul** **iez**
qu'il/elle/on	**veuill**	**e**		
qu'ils/elles	**veuill**	**ent**		

pouvoir *(puiss-)*				
que je	**puiss** **e**	que nous	**puiss** **ions**
que tu	**puiss** **es**	que vous	**puiss** **iez**
qu'il/elle/on	**puiss** **e**	qu'ils/elles	**puiss** **ent**

■ In addition to expressing necessity and will, the subjunctive is also used to express emotion.

Je suis content(e) que vous **soyez** ici. *I am happy (that) you are here.*
Je regrette que Luc ne **puisse** pas venir. *I am sorry Luc can't come.*

■ If there is no change of subjects, the preposition **de** plus the infinitive is used instead of the subjunctive.

Je suis content(e) **d'être** ici. *I am happy to be here.*
Luc regrette **de ne pas pouvoir** venir. *Luc is sorry he can't come.*

VOCABULAIRE

Pour exprimer un sentiment

Je suis ravi(e) que	*I am delighted that*
C'est formidable que	*It's great that*
C'est chouette que	*It's great that*
Je suis content(e) que	*I am happy that*
Ce n'est pas possible que	*It's not possible that*
C'est incroyable que	*It's unbelievable that*
C'est dommage que	*It's too bad that*
C'est ridicule que	*It's ridiculous that*
Je suis triste que	*I am sad that*
Je regrette que	*I am sorry that*
Je suis désolé(e) que	*I am very sorry that*
Je suis fâché(e) que	*I am angry that*

 Des réactions différentes. Décidez si votre professeur est content et si vous êtes content(e) aussi.

> **MODÈLE:** J'ai beaucoup de devoirs.
> **Mon professeur est content que j'aie beaucoup de devoirs. Mais moi, je ne suis pas content(e) d'avoir beaucoup de devoirs.**

1. Je vais souvent à la bibliothèque.
2. Je sais parler français.
3. Je lis *Entre amis* tous les soirs.
4. Je suis un(e) bon(ne) étudiant(e).
5. J'ai «A» à mon examen.
6. Je sors tous les soirs.
7. Je fais régulièrement des rédactions.
8. Je peux aller en France cet été.
9. Je veux étudier le français en France.

20 Votre réaction, s'il vous plaît. Choisissez une expression pour réagir *(react)* aux phrases suivantes.

> **MODÈLE:** Véronique va en Floride. Mais il pleut.
> **C'est formidable qu'elle aille en Floride. Mais c'est dommage qu'il pleuve.**

1. Les vacances commencent bientôt. Mais les examens vont avoir lieu avant les vacances.
2. Tous les professeurs sont généreux et charmants. Mais ils donnent beaucoup de devoirs.
3. Les étudiants de cette classe font toujours leurs devoirs. Mais il sont fatigués.

㉑ Test psychologique. Expliquez les causes de vos réactions. Faites deux ou trois phrases chaque fois.

Modèle: Je suis triste …

Je suis triste que mon petit ami (ma petite amie) ne m'aime plus.
Je suis triste que tout le monde me déteste.
Je suis triste de ne pas avoir de bons amis.

1. C'est ridicule …   3. Je suis ravi(e) …   5. C'est chouette …
2. Nous regrettons …   4. C'est dommage …

㉒ En groupes *(3 ou 4 étudiants).* Une personne dira une phrase au présent ou au futur (par exemple: **J'ai chaud** ou **Je sortirai ce soir**). Une autre personne réagira (par exemple: **C'est dommage que tu aies chaud** ou **Je suis content(e) que tu sortes ce soir**). Combien de phrases pouvez-vous former?

G. Le pronom *en*

On vend des journaux ici?	*Do you sell newspapers here?*
Non, on n'**en** vend pas. Vous **en** trouverez à la gare.	*No, we don't sell any. You will find some at the station.*
Vous avez du brocoli?	*Do you have any broccoli?*
Oui, j'**en** ai.	*Yes, I have some.*
Il y a beaucoup de fruits cette année?	*Is there a lot of fruit this year?*
Oui, il y **en** a beaucoup.	*Yes, there is a lot (of it).*
Vous avez des oranges?	*Do you have any oranges?*
Oui. Combien **en** voulez-vous?	*Yes. How many (of them) do you want?*
J'**en** voudrais six.	*I would like six (of them).*

■ The pronoun **en** takes the place of a noun that is preceded by some form of **de** (e.g., **de, du, de la, de l', des**) or by a number (e.g., **un, une, deux, trois**), or by an expression of quantity (e.g., **beaucoup de, trop de**).

Vous avez **du** camembert?	Oui, j'**en** ai.
Noël a **une** voiture?	Oui, il **en** a une.
Nous avons **assez de** livres?	Oui, nous **en** avons assez.

■ When a noun is preceded by a number or a quantity word, the number or quantity word must be included in a sentence with **en**.

Vous avez **une** maison?	*Do you have a house?*
Oui, j'**en** ai **une**.	*Yes, I have one.*

Vous avez **deux** valises?	*Do you have two suitcases?*
Non, je n'**en** ai pas **deux**.	*No, I don't have two (of them).*
Je n'**en** ai qu'**une**.	*I have only one.*
Mon père **en** a **beaucoup**.	*My father has a lot (of them).*

Note To say *I don't have any*, use **Je n'en ai pas.**

■ **En** is also used to replace **de** plus an infinitive or **de** plus a noun with expressions of emotion.

Hervé est triste **de partir**?	Oui, il **en** est triste.
Es-tu contente **de tes notes**?	Oui, j'**en** suis ravie.

23 **Sondage** *(Poll).* Utilisez les expressions suivantes pour interviewer votre partenaire. Il (elle) va utiliser **en** dans chaque réponse.

> **MODÈLE:** voitures
>
> VOUS: **Combien de voitures as-tu?**
> VOTRE PARTENAIRE: **J'en ai une.** ou **Je n'en ai pas.**

1. frères	5. professeurs
2. sœurs	6. voitures
3. enfants	7. cours
4. camarades de chambre	8. cartes de crédit

24 **Quelles réactions!** Composez deux phrases affirmatives ou négatives. La première peut être au présent, à l'imparfait ou au passé composé. Utilisez **en** dans la deuxième.

> **MODÈLE:** **Mes amis n'ont pas gagné à la loterie.**
> **Ils en sont désolés.**

Remember that **confus** is a false cognate, p. 381.

	être fiancé(e)(s)	
	se marier	ravi
	attendre un bébé	content
je	réussir à un examen	triste
mes amis	avoir une mauvaise note	désolé
un(e) de mes ami(e)s	divorcer	fâché
	gagner à la loterie	confus
	arriver en retard	

25 **À vous.** Répondez. Utilisez **en** dans chaque réponse.

1. Combien de tasses de café buvez-vous par jour?
2. Buvez-vous du thé?
3. Voulez-vous du chewing-gum?
4. Êtes-vous content(e) de vos notes?
5. Combien de personnes y a-t-il dans votre famille?
6. Combien de maillots de bain avez-vous?
7. Quelle est votre réaction quand vous avez «A» à l'examen?

Entre amis

Les examens finals

Use **en** whenever possible.

1. Find out how many courses your partner has this semester.
2. Ask if s/he is pleased (happy) with his/her courses.
3. Ask if s/he is pleased (happy) with his/her grades.
4. Find out how many final exams s/he will have.
5. Ask if s/he is afraid of them.

Intégration www

Révision

A **Décrivez-les.** Inventez une description pour les couples suivants.

1. un couple qui va se marier.
2. un couple qui divorce.
3. un couple qui habite chez les parents du mari.

B **Un feuilleton.** Choisissez un feuilleton que vous connaissez. Décrivez-le à votre partenaire.

C **Mes réactions.** Quelles sont vos réactions aux circonstances suivantes?

MODÈLE: Le professeur vous annonce qu'il n'y aura pas de cours demain.
J'en suis ravi(e)! Je lui dis «Merci beaucoup!». C'est chouette qu'il n'y ait pas de cours.

1. Le professeur vous dit qu'il y aura un examen demain.
2. On vous téléphone pour vous annoncer que vous venez de gagner à la loterie.
3. Vous vous êtes disputé(e) avec votre ami(e) et il (elle) vous envoie un message électronique pour vous demander pardon.
4. Vos parents veulent vous parler de vos études et de ce que vous allez faire dans la vie.
5. Une amie vous annonce que son petit ami ne veut plus la voir.
6. Vous dormez et le téléphone sonne à trois heures du matin. Vous y répondez et une personne que vous ne connaissez pas vous demande si vous voulez acheter une encyclopédie.

Pas de problème!

Cette activité est basée sur la vidéo, *Module 11*. Choisissez la bonne réponse pour compléter les phrases suivantes.

1. Dans ce contexte, le mot «papillon» veut dire _____.
   (une cravate, un insecte, une contravention)
2. Le conducteur doit _____ francs.
   (450, 65, 75)
3. Il dit qu'on lui a donné un papillon pour _____ minutes de stationnement.
   (5, 10, 15)
4. L'homme qui a eu la contravention est de nationalité _____.
   (française, suisse, belge)
5. D'après cette vidéo, il faut que cet homme aille _____ pour acheter un timbre fiscal.
   (à la poste, au tabac, à la gare)

Lecture I

A **Que regardez-vous?** Faites une liste des cinq émissions de télé de votre pays qui sont, à votre avis, les plus intéressantes.

B **Parcourez les listes d'émissions.** Lisez rapidement les listes d'émissions pour identifier (1) le jour de la semaine et (2) les différents sports qui sont mentionnés.

La télévision

Les deux colonnes suivantes sont tirées du site web de Yahoo! France.

TF1		**France 2**	
08h10	Disney! (dessin animé)	08h30	Les voix bouddhistes
09h57	Météo	08h45	Connaître l'Islam
10h00	Motocross: Championnat du Monde 250cc	09h15	À bible ouverte
11h00	Téléfoot: Championnat de France	09h30	Orthodoxie
12h15	Le juste prix (jeu)	10h00	Présence protestante
12h50	À vrai dire: Aménager la cuisine	10h30	La Présence du Seigneur
12h55	Météo	11h00	Messe célébrée en la cathédrale St.-Michel
13h00	Le journal	12h00	Cérémonie du Souvenir
13h15	Au nom du sport	13h00	Le journal de treize heures
13h55	Formule 1: Grand Prix d'Italie	13h25	Météo 2
15h40	Dingue de toi (série, comédie)	13h30	Rapport du Loto
17h00	Dawson: La nouvelle Ève (série, comédie)	13h35	Vivement dimanche
17h55	Trente millions d'amis (magazine, animalier)	15h35	Le singe araignée d'Amazonie
18h55	L'euro en poche (magazine, économique)	16h35	Snoops
19h55	Être heureux comme (magazine, culturel)	17h20	Nash Bridges
20h00	Le journal	18h15	Stade 2
20h35	Au nom du sport (magazine, sportif)	19h25	Vivement dimanche prochain
20h40	Le résultat des courses (magazine, sportif)	20h00	Le journal de vingt heures
20h45	Le temps d'un tournage (magazine, cinéma)	20h45	Météo 2
20h50	Météo	20h55	Urgences
20h55	Boomerang (film, comédie)	21h45	Urgences
23h00	Les films dans les salles (magazine, cinéma)	22h35	Urgences
23h05	Le messager de la mort (film, policier)	23h20	Les documents du dimanche

C **À vous de juger.** Lesquelles des émissions intéresseront probablement une personne qui ...

Point out that three episodes of **Urgences** *(ER)* are shown back-to-back, which is typical in France.

1. pratique sa religion?
2. aime les sports?
3. aime l'émission américaine *ER*?
4. veut gagner de l'argent?
5. veut savoir le temps qu'il fera demain?
6. veut savoir ce qui se passe dans le monde?
7. aime les animaux?
8. est un enfant?

Inférence. Relisez la lecture et cherchez des exemples qui aident à identifier une des chaînes comme privée et l'autre comme publique.

 Écrivez un téléguide. Indiquez le(s) jour(s) et l'heure, le nom et une description pour les cinq émissions de télévision que vous avez choisies dans l'activité A.

 Étude du vocabulaire. Étudiez les phrases suivantes et choisissez les mots qui correspondent aux mots français en caractères gras: *native, earn, be bored, although, run over, masterpiece.*

1. On **s'ennuie** si on travaille tout le temps sans jamais prendre de vacances.
2. «Hamlet» est un **chef d'œuvre** de Shakespeare.
3. Attention quand vous traversez la rue. Une voiture peut vous **écraser.**
4. J'ai quitté ma ville **natale** il y a quinze ans.
5. Marc veut **gagner** assez d'argent pour pouvoir acheter une voiture.
6. Cet homme est gentil **quoiqu'**un peu bizarre.

 Avant de lire. Réfléchissez aux films que vous avez vus.

1. À votre avis, quel est le meilleur film de cette année?
2. Quel film trouvez-vous le plus bizarre?
3. Quel film trouvez-vous le plus comique?
4. Quel est le film le plus violent?
5. Combien de fois êtes-vous allé(e) au cinéma le mois dernier?
6. Quel est le dernier film que vous avez vu?

 Parcourez la liste des films. Lisez rapidement pour identifier les films et les acteurs que vous connaissez.

AU CINÉMA

«LE HUITIÈME JOUR»: Harry est un cadre stressé. Sa vie de routine est troublée par un accident: il écrase un chien et rencontre Georges, un mongolien qui lui redonne goût à la vie. Un regard tendre et plein de fantaisie sur la rencontre de deux univers. Avec Daniel Auteuil, Pascal Duquenne. Gaumont à 12h30, 18h, 21h.

«JANE EYRE»: L'héroïne du chef-d'œuvre de Charlotte Brontë prend les traits de Charlotte Gainsbourg dans ce film néo-romantique où une jeune fille sortie d'un triste orphelinat trouve un emploi de préceptrice chez un homme étrange. De Franco Zeffirelli avec Charlotte Gainsbourg, William Hurt. Montparnasse à 18h30, 21h.

«PRINCESSES»: Apparemment, elles n'avaient rien en commun si ce n'est la jeunesse et la beauté. L'une sage, l'autre rebelle, deux jeunes femmes apprennent qu'elles sont demi-sœurs et que leur père est recherché pour meurtre. Dans l'urgence et la peur d'une issue fatale, elles partent à sa recherche, sur les traces d'un passé encore douloureux. Avec ce film, Sylvie Verheyde joue sur le registre du film noir en imposant le chaos comme moteur de l'action. Avec Emma de Caunes, Jean-Hugues Anglade et Karole Rocher. Cyrano à 14h, 16h, 18h, 20h, 22h.

«LA COUPE D'OR»: L'intrigue: au début du vingtième siècle, un beau prince italien follement amoureux d'une séduisante Américaine se voit dans l'obligation d'épouser la fille d'un richissime collectionneur new-yorkais. Mais la maîtresse, pugnace, parvient, pour ne pas s'éloigner de son amant, à se faire épouser du père de la mariée, compatriote fortuné et ... veuf bien conservé! Le jeu est dangereux et les quatre protagonistes ont beaucoup à perdre. Un drame britannique de James Ivory avec Kate Beckinsale, James Fox, Anjelica Huston et Nick Nolte. Danton à 11h45, 14h15, 16h50, 19h25, 22h.

«APPARENCES»: C'est une belle maison, près d'un lac du Vermont, quoiqu'un peu isolée. C'est un beau couple: lui, brillant et séduisant, mais un peu obsédé par le travail; elle, une belle femme qui-a-tout-pour-être-heureuse. Une porte qui s'ouvre seule, un visage apparu dans l'eau du bain et quelques murmures dans une pièce doivent-ils suffire à vous faire croire que votre nouvelle voisine est morte assassinée? Oui, dans ce film à suspense où le spectateur nage en plein mystère et en fausses déductions ... Un film de Robert Zemeckis avec Harrison Ford, Michelle Pfeiffer, Miranda Otto et James Remar. UGC Maillot à 10h55, 13h30, 16h10, 18h50, 21h25.

«ENDURANCE»: C'est l'histoire incroyable mais authentique d'Haile Gebreselassie, ce jeune Éthiopien, pratiquement inconnu du grand public jusqu'aux Jeux Olympiques d'Atlanta, où il a remporté la course du 10.000 mètres, pulvérisant le précédent record. Derrière cet hommage au champion, interprété par lui-même, il y a un portrait de la vie en Afrique de l'Est. Une comédie dramatique de Leslie Woodhead avec Yonas Zergaw, Shawanness Gebreselassie et Tedesse Haile. L'Arlequin à 18h10 (début 10mn après), 20h10 (début 10mn après), 22h10 (début 10mn après).

«MAUVAISE FILLE»: Film de Régis Franc avec Daniel Gélin et Florence Pernel. Rose, dix-huit ans, s'ennuie dans sa Camargue natale entre un père dépressif, un frère macho et un amoureux ennuyeux. Variétés à 20h15.

«CHIEN ET CHAT»: Film de Philippe Galland. Avec Roland Giraud et André Dussolier. Un officier de la gendarmerie et un commissaire de police unissent leurs forces pour sauver leurs deux enfants compromis dans un trafic de drogue. Les Halles à 19h45, 22h.

«LE BRASIER»: Comme beaucoup de Polonais, Pavlak est venu en France avec son fils Viktor pour travailler à la mine. Pour gagner un peu plus d'argent, il participe à des combats de boxe. Un film d'Éric Barbier avec Jean-Marc Barr, Marushka Detmers et Thierry Fortineau. Vox à 14h30, 21h30.

Whenever possible, have students give reasons to justify their answers.

 Questions. Choisissez parmi *(among)* les films mentionnés dans la lecture.

1. Dans quel film est-ce que le personnage principal est un champion sportif?
2. Dans quel film est-ce que le personnage principal est un handicapé mental?
3. Dans quel film est-ce que le personnage principal est un immigré?
4. Quel films peuvent vous faire peur? Justifiez votre réponse.
5. Quel film a l'air le plus intéressant?
6. Quel film a l'air le plus violent?
7. Quels films est-ce qu'on ne peut voir que le soir?

E **Familles de mots.** Essayez de deviner le sens des mots suivants.

1. débuter, un débutant, une débutante, le début
2. droguer, un drogué, une droguée, la drogue
3. s'ennuyer, ennuyé(e), ennuyeux, ennuyeuse, l'ennui
4. employer, un employé, une employée, un emploi
5. épouser, un époux, une épouse
6. séduire, séduisant(e), un séducteur, une séductrice, la séduction

VOCABULAIRE ACTIF

À propos de la télévision
une annonce *advertisement*
une chaîne (de télé) *(TV) channel*
un feuilleton *soap opera; series*
les informations (f. pl.) *news*
la météo(rologie) *weather forecast*
la publicité *publicity; commercial*

D'autres noms
un avertissement *warning*
un revenant *ghost*
la vérité *truth*

Adjectifs
célèbre *famous*
chouette *great (fam.)*
confus(e) *ashamed; embarrassed*
drôle *funny*
fâché(e) *angry*
formidable *terrific*
incroyable *unbelievable, incredible*
malheureux (malheureuse) *unhappy*
original(e) *different, novel; original*
passionnant(e) *exciting*
ravi(e) *delighted*
ridicule *ridiculous*

Relations personnelles
s'aimer *to love each other*
une bague (de fiançailles) *(engagement) ring*

se disputer *to argue*
un divorce *divorce*
divorcer *to get a divorce*
s'embrasser *to kiss*
s'entendre (avec) *to get along (with)*
se fâcher *to get angry*
se faire des amis *to make friends*
se marier (avec) *to marry*
rencontrer *to meet*
se séparer *to separate (from each other)*

D'autres verbes
assister (à) *to attend*
se consoler *to console oneself*
croire *to believe, think*
dire *to say; to tell*
emprunter *to borrow*
s'intéresser à *to be interested in*
montrer *to show*
prêter *to lend*
raconter (une histoire) *to tell (a story)*
regretter *to be sorry*
voir *to see*

Adverbes
actuellement *now*
même *even*
presque *almost*

Pronoms objets indirects
me *(to) me*
te *(to) you*
lui *(to) him; (to) her*
nous *(to) us*
vous *(to) you*
leur *(to) them*

D'autres pronoms
en *some; of it (them); about it (them)*
dont *whose, of which*
lequel/laquelle/lesquels/lesquelles *which*

Expressions utiles
C'est dommage. *That's (It's) too bad.*
Je crois que oui. *I think so.*
Je ne crois pas. *I don't think so.*
Je te le jure. *I swear (to you).*
Quelle histoire! *What a story!*
Qu'est-ce qui est arrivé? *What happened?*
Sans blague! *No kidding!*

Qu'est-ce que je devrais faire?

Buts communicatifs
Seeking and providing information
Making basic hypotheses

Structures utiles
L'imparfait, le passé composé (suite) et le plus-que-parfait
Le verbe **devoir** (suite)
Les pronoms interrogatifs
Ne ... personne et **ne ... rien**
Le conditionnel
Si hypothétique

Culture
Les accidents de la route
Les agents et les gendarmes
Les contraventions

Coup d'envoi

Prise de contact

Use the video, *Module 8,* **La voiture,** to help set the scene.

Qu'est-ce qui est arrivé?

Qu'est-ce qui est arrivé, Emmanuelle?

    J'ai eu un accident.

    L'autre conducteur (conductrice)° n'a pas   *driver*
        vu ma voiture.

    Il (elle) a freiné° trop tard.   *braked*

    Sa voiture a dérapé°.   *skidded*

    Il (elle) a heurté° ma voiture.   *struck; hit*

Pourquoi l'accident a-t-il eu lieu?

    Le conducteur (la conductrice) ne faisait pas
        attention.

    Il (elle) croyait que personne° ne venait.   *nobody*

    Il (elle) ne regardait pas à droite.

    Il (elle) roulait° trop vite.   *was going*

    Il (elle) avait trop bu°.   *had had too much to drink*

    Il (elle) était ivre°.   *drunk*

Et vous.   Avez-vous déjà eu un accident?

               Avez-vous déjà vu un accident?

               Si oui, qu'est-ce qui est arrivé?

VOTRE SÉCURITÉ

Sur route, sur mer, en montagne, la majorité des accidents sont dûs à des imprudences caractérisées.

Alors soyez attentifs aux conseils que vous rappelleront la Sécurité Routière et la Gendarmerie Nationale.

Sur route

Méfiez-vous de la conduite en plein soleil après un repas, des routes de nuit après une journée d'activité. Bouclez votre ceinture, respectez les limitations de vitesse :
– pas plus de 60 km/h en agglomération,
– pas plus de 90 km/h sur route,
– pas plus de 130 km/h sur autoroute.
Minitel : 36 15 ROUTE.

Conversation

Un accident a eu lieu

James Davidson vient d'avoir un accident de voiture. Il en parle avec son voisin Maurice.

MAURICE: Mais qu'est-ce que tu as? Tu es tout pâle!

JAMES: C'est que j'ai eu très peur ce matin.

MAURICE: Qu'est-ce qui est arrivé?

JAMES: J'ai eu un accident de voiture.

MAURICE: Mon Dieu!

JAMES: J'allais au travail quand l'accident a eu lieu. L'autre ne faisait pas attention. Ce chauffard° avait brûlé un stop° parce qu'il allait trop vite. *bad driver / had run through a stop sign*

MAURICE: Quel imbécile!

JAMES: Oui, et nous sommes entrés en collision.

MAURICE: Quel idiot! Et personne n'a vu l'accident?

JAMES: Si! Heureusement il y avait deux témoins° et puis un gendarme qui était juste derrière moi. *witnesses*

MAURICE: Quelle chance! Qu'est-ce que le gendarme a fait?

JAMES: Il m'a assuré° qu'il avait tout vu° et que c'était la faute° de l'autre. *assured / had seen everything / fault*

MAURICE: J'espère que le gendarme lui a donné une bonne contravention°! *ticket*

Use the video, *Module 11*, to show an example of someone who has received a **contravention.**

▶ **Jouez ces rôles.** Répétez la conversation avec votre partenaire. Ensuite Maurice parle avec deux personnes (James et Karine étaient dans la voiture). Faites tous les changements nécessaires, par exemple **nous** à la place de **je.**

À PROPOS

Comparison: Have students describe their own driving habits or those of their friends with respect to speeding, wearing a seat belt, stopping at a stop sign, etc. Have them describe current speed limits in town and on highways in their country.

Essayez de classifier les infractions *(violations)* **suivantes d'après leur fréquence.**

a. ne pas s'arrêter à un feu rouge ou à un stop

b. dépasser le degré légal d'alcool dans le sang *(blood)*

c. dépasser la limite de vitesse

d. ne pas porter de ceinture de sécurité

Les agents et les gendarmes

The **agent de police** is often found directing traffic at major intersections in French cities. Since the **agents** are normally on foot, they are often stopped by tourists in need of information. The **gendarme,** often found in the countryside and in small towns, is actually part of the French military and is stationed in separate quarters in the **gendarmerie. Gendarmes** are similar to state police in that they are usually on motorcycles or in patrol cars. They would therefore normally be the ones to investigate an accident.

Les accidents de la route

Environ huit mille personnes sont tuées tous les ans dans des accidents de la circulation *(traffic)* en France. Entre 1987 et 1997, ces accidents ont fait plus de 222.000 morts et 5.383.000 blessés, ce qui est très grave. Avec près de 150 décès par million d'habitants, la France a la quatrième place des quinze pays de l'Union européenne, après le Portugal, la Grèce et le Luxembourg. *(d'après Francoscopie)*

Reread **Votre Sécurité** on p. 406 to determine the speed limits in France.

Les contraventions

There are approximately 15 million traffic tickets given in France per year. Of these, 9 million are for illegal parking and 1 million for exceeding the speed limit. The record for a speeding ticket is 243 KPH (over 150 MPH) for which the speeder received a year in prison and a 100.000 franc fine. In addition, approximately 660.000 tickets for not wearing a seat belt and 100.000 for drunken driving are given in an average year. Besides the parking tickets, the following were the most frequent traffic violations in France in a recent year: (1) speeding (43%); (2) not wearing a seat belt while riding in a car, or a helmet when on a motorcycle (24%); (3) failure to give right of way or to stop at a light or a stop sign (13%); (4) failure to pass the alcohol test (7%). Eighty-one percent of those committing a traffic violation were men.

408

J'ai eu très peur. To indicate fear, the open hand is held fingers facing up; the hand is lowered with the fingers "trembling."

Quel imbécile! To indicate that someone has done something stupid, touch your index finger to your temple. The finger is either tapped on the temple or twisted back and forth.

Ivre. To indicate that someone has had too much to drink, one hand is cupped in a fist, and placed loosely on the nose and rotated.

Il y a un geste

 À vous. Répondez.

1. Quand avez-vous eu peur?
2. Pour quelle raison avez-vous eu peur?
3. Qu'est-ce que vous avez fait?

Entre amis

C'était la faute du professeur

1. Tell your partner that you had an accident.
2. Explain that you hit the teacher's car.
3. Say that it was the teacher's fault.
4. Explain that s/he was going too slowly.

Prononciation

La voyelle [ə]

■ As you have already learned, the letter **-e-** can stand for any one of the sounds [e], [ɛ], [ɑ̃], and [ɛ̃], depending on the spelling combinations of which it is a part. You have also seen, however, that the letter **-e-** sometimes represents the sound [ə]. The symbol [ə] stands for a vowel called "unstable **e**" or "mute **e.**" It is called unstable because it is sometimes pronounced and sometimes not.

▶ Look at the following pairs of examples and then read them aloud. A highlighted **-e-** represents a pronounced [ə]. An **-e-** with a slash through it represents a silent [ə]. Compare especially changes you find in the same word from one sentence of the pair to the other.

L**e** voilà!	Mais l̸e voilà!
C**e** film est très bon.	Moi, j̸e n'aim̸e pas c̸e film.
D**e**main, vous l̸e trouv̸erez.	Vous l̸e trouv̸erez d̸emain.
D**e**nis̸e est américain̸e?	Ell̸e est française.
R**e**gardez cett̸e femm̸e.	Vous r̸egardez cett̸e femm̸e?
Nous pr**e**nons l̸e train vendr̸edi.	Nous arriv̸erons sam̸edi.
Votr**e** pèr̸e est charmant.	Votr̸e ami̸e est charmant̸e.
Voilà un̸e tass̸e d**e** café.	Nous n̸e voulons pas d̸e café.
C'est un̸e bagu̸e d**e** fiançaill̸es.	Mais il n'y aura pas d̸e mariag̸e.
Qu'est-c̸e qu**e** tu veux?	Elle a dit qu̸e tu voulais m̸e voir.
d**e** rien	Il finit d̸e rir̸e.
vous s**e**riez	vous s̸erez

*You may wish to explain the change from **votre** to **vot'** before a consonant in familiar French.*

■ In general, [ə] is *silent* in the following circumstances.

Have students identify examples of each circumstance in the sentences above.

1. at the end of a sentence
2. before or after a pronounced vowel
3. when it is preceded by only one pronounced consonant sound

■ In general, [ə] is *pronounced* in the following circumstances.

1. when it is in the first syllable of a sentence
2. when it is preceded by two pronounced consonant sounds (even if there is an intervening silent [ə]) and followed by at least one pronounced consonant
3. when it precedes the combination [Rj]

You may wish to point out that **ex-** + *vowel* = [ɛgz-] *and* **ex-** + *consonant* = [ɛks-].

Note When the letter **-e-** is followed *in the same word* by two consonants or by **-x,** it is normally pronounced [ɛ].

elle	av**e**rtissement	c**e**tte	pr**e**nnent	v**e**rser	m**e**rci
exiger	**e**xcusez-moi	**e**xact	**e**xamen		

▶ **Écoutez et puis répétez.**

*Remind students that **faisait** has a "mute e". See p. 300.*

1. L'autre conducteur ne faisait pas attention.
2. Qu'est-ce que votre frère a fait?
3. Est-ce que tu regardes des feuilletons le vendredi ou le samedi?
4. De quelle ville venez-vous?
5. Vous venez de Paris, n'est-ce pas?

Buts communicatifs

1 Seeking and Providing Information

Avez-vous entendu parler d'un accident?
Avez-vous vu un accident?

Est-ce que quelqu'un a été blessé°?	*wounded*
Est-ce que quelqu'un a été tué°?	*killed*
Est-ce qu'il y a eu beaucoup de morts°?	*deaths*
Où est-ce que l'accident a eu lieu?	
Quelle heure était-il?	
De quelle couleur étaient les voitures?	
De quelle marque° étaient les voitures?	*make; brand*
De quelle année étaient les voitures?	
Est-ce qu'il avait plu?°	*Had it rained?*
La chaussée° devait être glissante°, n'est-ce pas?	*pavement / slippery*
Y avait-il d'autres témoins?	

A. L'imparfait, le passé composé (suite) et le plus-que-parfait

Review the comparison of the passé composé and imperfect, Ch. 11, p. 304.

■ It is perhaps helpful, when trying to remember whether to use the imperfect or the passé composé, to think of the analogy with a stage play.

• In a play, there is often scenery (trees, birds singing, the sun shining, etc.) and background action (minor characters strolling by, people playing, working, etc.). This scenery and background action are represented by the imperfect.

Il **était** tôt.	*It was early.*
Il **faisait** froid.	*It was cold out.*
James **allait** au travail.	*James was going to work.*
Un autre conducteur ne **faisait** pas attention.	*Another driver wasn't paying attention.*

Que faisaient les acteurs dans la pièce *(play)*?

• Likewise, in a play, there are main actors upon whom the audience focuses, if even for a moment. They speak, move, become aware, act, and react. The narration of these past events requires the passé composé.

Qu'est-ce qui lui **est arrivé?**	*What happened to him?*
Il **a eu** un accident.	*He had an accident.*
Ils **sont entrés** en collision.	*They collided.*
Un gendarme lui **a donné** une contravention.	*A policeman gave him a ticket.*

■ The pluperfect **(le plus-que-parfait)** is used to describe a past event that took place prior to some other past event. This tense normally corresponds to the English *had* plus a past participle.

Il **avait plu** (avant l'accident).	*It had rained (before the accident).*
La dame **était arrivée** (avant moi).	*The lady had arrived (before me).*

■ To form the **plus-que-parfait,** use the **imparfait** of **avoir** or **être** and the past participle.

étudier	arriver	se lever
j'avais étudié	j'étais arrivé(e)	je m'étais levé(e)
tu avais étudié	tu étais arrivé(e)	tu t'étais levé(e)
il/on avait étudié	il/on était arrivé	il/on s'était levé
elle avait étudié	elle était arrivée	elle s'était levée
nous avions étudié	nous étions arrivé(e)s	nous nous étions levé(e)s
vous aviez étudié	vous étiez arrivé(e)(s)	vous vous étiez levé(e)(s)
ils avaient étudié	ils étaient arrivés	ils s'étaient levés
elles avaient étudié	elles étaient arrivées	elles s'étaient levées

 Voilà pourquoi. Répondez aux questions suivantes. Essayez de trouver des raisons logiques.

MODÈLE: Pourquoi Laurent a-t-il téléphoné à Mireille?
Il lui a téléphoné parce qu'il voulait sortir avec elle.   ou
Il lui a téléphoné parce qu'il la trouvait gentille.

1. Pourquoi Laurent et Mireille sont-ils sortis samedi soir?
2. Pourquoi ont-ils mis leur manteau?
3. Pourquoi sont-ils allés au restaurant?
4. Pourquoi n'ont-ils pas pris de dessert?
5. Pourquoi ont-ils fait une promenade après?

2 **Pourquoi pas, Amélie?** Utilisez la forme négative. Expliquez pourquoi Amélie n'a pas fait les choses suivantes.

> **MODÈLE:** prendre le petit déjeuner
> **Amélie n'a pas pris le petit déjeuner parce qu'elle n'avait pas faim.** ou
> **Amélie n'a pas pris le petit déjeuner parce qu'elle a oublié.**

Brainstorm with the class to find as many reasons as possible for each thing Amélie did not do.

1. aller au cinéma
2. étudier dans sa chambre
3. regarder son émission préférée
4. danser avec Gérard
5. nager
6. avoir un accident
7. boire du vin

3 **Quel chauffard!** Utilisez le plus-que-parfait pour indiquer ce que le mauvais chauffeur avait fait avant l'accident.

> **MODÈLE:** ne pas être prudent
> **Il n'avait pas été prudent.**

1. aller au bistro
2. boire de la bière
3. ne pas attacher sa ceinture
4. oublier de faire attention
5. brûler un stop
6. se regarder dans le rétroviseur

B. Le verbe *devoir* (suite)

Review **devoir**, Ch. 5, p. 136.

Où est Céline?	*Where is Céline?*
Je ne sais pas. Elle **doit** être malade.	*I don't know. She **must** be sick.*
Mais elle **devait** apporter des fleurs pour le prof!	*But she **was supposed to** bring flowers for the teacher!*
Oui, je sais. Puisqu'elle n'est pas venue, j'**ai dû** aller les acheter.	*Yes, I know. Since she didn't come, I **had to** go buy them.*
Maintenant tout le monde me **doit** 5 francs pour le bouquet.	*Now everybody **owes** me 5 francs for the bouquet.*

■ The past participle of **devoir** is **dû.** When it has a feminine agreement, however, it loses the circumflex: **due.** This often occurs when the past participle is used as an adjective.

l'argent **dû** à mon frère   la pollution **due** à l'industrie

■ The future tense verb stem for **devoir** is irregular: **devr-.**

Elle **devra** travailler dur.   *She'll have to work hard.*

■ Like other verbs with two stems in the present tense, **devoir** has two stems in the subjunctive.

que je **doive**   que nous **devions**

■ The passé composé and the imperfect can both mean *had to* or *probably (must have)*. The choice of tense depends, as usual, on whether the verb is a specific action or a description or habitual condition.

Hier j'**ai dû** aller voir ma tante.	*Yesterday, I **had to** go see my aunt.*
En général, je **devais** faire mes devoirs avant de sortir.	*In general, I **had to** do my homework before going out.*
Il **a dû** oublier notre rendez-vous!	*He **probably** forgot our date! (He **must have** forgotten our date!)*
Il **devait** être très occupé.	*He was **probably** very busy. (He **must have** been very busy.)*

Note   When **devoir** means *was supposed to,* the imperfect is always used.

Nous **devions** dîner chez les Gilbert.	*We **were supposed to** have dinner at the Gilberts'.*

 C'est probable. Utilisez **devoir** au passé composé d'après le modèle pour modifier les phrases suivantes.

MODÈLE: Delphine n'a probablement pas fait ses devoirs.
Elle n'a pas dû faire ses devoirs.

> Remember that **sans doute** and **probablement** are synonyms.

1. Elle est sans doute sortie avec ses amis.
2. Elle n'a probablement pas étudié.
3. Elle a probablement eu une mauvaise note.
4. Elle a probablement pleuré.
5. Elle a sans doute parlé avec son professeur.
6. Elle a sans doute réussi la semaine d'après.

 Toutes ces obligations! Traduisez *(translate)* la forme verbale anglaise entre parenthèses pour compléter la phrase.

MODÈLE: Chantal _____ étudier pendant le week-end. *(was supposed to)*
Chantal devait étudier pendant le week-end.

1. Mes parents _____ venir nous chercher il y a 30 minutes. *(were supposed to)*
2. Ils _____ oublier. *(must have)*
3. Non, ils _____ être déjà en route. *(must)*
4. Nous _____ leur téléphoner, s'ils ne viennent pas bientôt. *(will have to)*
5. Il commence à faire froid. Tu _____ mettre ton manteau. *(must)*
6. Il est onze heures. Je _____ être chez moi avant cette heure-ci. *(was supposed to)*

C. Les pronoms interrogatifs

> Review **qui, que,** and **quel,** Ch. 4, p. 112.

■ Interrogative pronouns are used to ask questions. You have already learned to use several interrogative pronouns.

Qui est-ce?	*Who is that?*
Qu'est-ce que c'est?	*What is that?*

■ As in English, interrogative pronouns in French change form depending on whether they refer to people or to things.

Qui voyez-vous?	*Whom do you see?*
Que voyez-vous?	*What do you see?*

■ In addition, French interrogative pronouns change form depending on their function in the sentence. For example, the word *what* in English can take three different forms in French depending on whether it is the subject, the direct object, or the object of a preposition.

Qu'est-ce qui est à droite?	*What is on the right?*
Qu'est-ce que tu vois?	*What do you see?*
À **quoi** penses-tu?	*What are you thinking about?*

People

Subject

Qui	Qui parle?	*Who is speaking?*
Qui est-ce qui	Qui est-ce qui parle?	

Object

Qui (+ inversion)	Qui avez-vous vu?	*Whom did you see?*
Qui est-ce que	Qui est-ce que vous avez vu?	

After a preposition

... qui (+ inversion)	À qui écrivez-vous?	*To whom are you writing?*
... qui est-ce que	À qui est-ce que vous écrivez?	

Things

Subject

Qu'est-ce qui	Qu'est-ce qui fait ce bruit?	*What's making that noise?*

Object

Que (+ inversion)	Qu'avez-vous fait?	*What did you do?*
Qu'est-ce que	Qu'est-ce que vous avez fait?	

After a preposition

... quoi (+ inversion)	De quoi avez-vous besoin?	*What do you need?*
... quoi est-ce que	De quoi est-ce que vous avez besoin?	

■ If the question involves a person, the pronoun will always begin with **qui**. If it is a question about a thing, the pronoun will begin with **que** or **quoi**. There is no elision with **qui** or **quoi**, but **que** becomes **qu'** before a vowel.

Qui a parlé?	*Who spoke?*
De **quoi** a-t-il parlé?	*What did he talk about?*
Qu'est-ce **qu'**il a dit?	*What did he say?*

■ As shown in the charts above, there are two forms of each of these interrogative pronouns, except the subject pronoun **qu'est-ce qui**.

■ When interrogative pronouns are used as subjects, the verb is normally singular.

Mes parents ont téléphoné.   Qui **a** téléphoné?

QUOI DE NEUF, DOC?
SAVEZ-VOUS QUE BUGS BUNNY PARLE FRANÇAIS?

 Quelqu'un ou quelque chose? Utilisez un pronom interrogatif pour poser une question.

MODÈLES: Quelqu'un m'a téléphoné.
Qui vous a téléphoné?

Quelque chose m'intéresse.
Qu'est-ce qui vous intéresse?

J'ai téléphoné à quelqu'un.
À qui avez-vous téléphoné?

J'ai acheté quelque chose.
Qu'est-ce que vous avez acheté?

1. J'ai fait quelque chose le week-end dernier.
2. Quelque chose m'est arrivé.
3. J'ai vu quelqu'un.
4. Quelqu'un m'a parlé.
5. J'ai dansé avec quelqu'un.
6. Nous avons bu quelque chose.
7. J'ai dû payer pour quelqu'un.
8. J'ai dit au revoir à quelqu'un.

If this activity is done in pairs, you may wish to have students use **tu: Qui t'a téléphoné?**, etc.

Suggest that the partners respond with specific information of their own choosing, e.g., **Scott m'a téléphoné.**

7 **Comment? Je n'ai pas compris.** Votre partenaire vous a parlé mais vous n'avez pas bien entendu. Demandez qu'il (elle) répète. Remplacez l'expression en italique par un pronom interrogatif.

MODÈLES: *Mon frère* a acheté une voiture.

> VOUS: **Comment? Qui a acheté une voiture?**
> VOTRE PARTENAIRE: **Mon frère.**

J'ai lu *deux livres.*

> VOUS: **Comment? Qu'est-ce que tu as lu?**
> VOTRE PARTENAIRE: **Deux livres.**

1. *Sophie* a écrit une lettre à ses parents.
2. Elle avait besoin *d'argent.*
3. *Ses parents* ont lu la lettre.
4. Ils ont répondu *à Sophie.*
5. Ils lui ont envoyé *l'argent.*
6. Sa mère *lui* a téléphoné hier soir.
7. Elle lui a dit *que son frère était malade.*
8. Sophie aime beaucoup *son frère.*
9. *Sa maladie* lui fait peur.

Entre amis

Ma journée d'hier

1. Find out from your partner what happened yesterday.
2. Ask what s/he did.
3. Find out where s/he went and who was there.
4. Ask with whom s/he spoke.
5. What else can you find out?

D. *Ne ... personne* et *ne ... rien*

Qui avez-vous rencontré?	Je **n'**ai rencontré **personne.**
Qu'est-ce que vous avez fait?	Je **n'**ai **rien** fait.
Avec qui avez-vous dansé?	Je **n'**ai dansé avec **personne.**
De quoi avez-vous besoin?	Je **n'**ai besoin de **rien.**
Qui est venu?	**Personne n'**est venu.
Qu'est-ce qui est arrivé?	**Rien n'**est arrivé.

■ You have already learned that the opposite of **quelque chose** is **ne ... rien** *(nothing, not anything)*. The opposite of **quelqu'un** is **ne ... personne** *(no one, nobody, not anyone)*.

> Review **ne ... rien,** Ch. 6, p. 162.

■ When used as a *direct object*, **ne ... personne,** like **ne ... rien,** is placed around the conjugated verb.

Entendez-vous quelque chose?	Non, je **n'**entends **rien.**
Voyez-vous quelqu'un?	Non, je **ne** vois **personne.**

Remind students that all other negatives they have learned (**ne ... pas/plus/jamais**) are placed *before* the past participle.

Note Unlike **ne ... rien,** however, **ne ... personne** surrounds both the auxiliary verb *and* the past participle in the passé composé.

Avez-vous entendu quelque chose?	Non, je **n'**ai **rien** entendu.
But: Avez-vous vu quelqu'un?	Non, je **n'**ai vu **personne.**

■ Both **rien** and **personne** can be used as the *object of a preposition.*

Avez-vous besoin de quelque chose?   Non, je **n'**ai besoin *de* **rien.**
Parlez-vous avec quelqu'un?   Non, je **ne** parle *avec* **personne.**

■ **Personne** and **rien** can also serve as the *subject* of a verb. In this case, **personne** and **rien** come before **ne**. **Ne** still comes before the conjugated verb.

Personne n'a téléphoné.   *Nobody telephoned.*
Personne ne va à cet endroit.   *No one goes to that place.*
Rien ne m'intéresse.   *Nothing interests me.*

■ Like **jamais** and **rien, personne** can be used alone to answer a question.

Qui est venu?   **Personne.**
Qui avez-vous rencontré?   **Personne.**

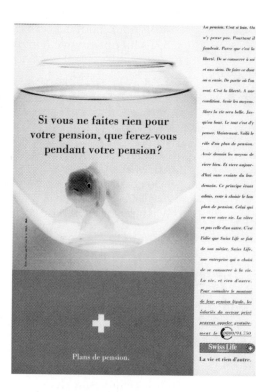

8 **Je n'ai rien fait à personne!** Utilisez **rien** ou **personne** pour répondre aux questions suivantes.

MODÈLES: Qui avez-vous vu?   Qu'avez-vous entendu?
Je n'ai vu personne.   **Je n'ai rien entendu.**

1. Avec qui êtes-vous sorti(e)?   6. À qui pensiez-vous?
2. Qu'est-ce que vous avez fait?   7. À quoi pensiez-vous?
3. Qu'est-ce que vous avez bu?   8. À qui est-ce que vous avez
4. Qui est-ce que vous avez vu?   téléphoné?
5. De quoi aviez-vous besoin?   9. Qu'avez-vous dit?

9 **Personne n'a rien fait.** Utilisez **rien** ou **personne** pour répondre aux questions suivantes.

> MODÈLES: Qui a vu l'accident? Qu'est-ce qui vous intéresse?
> **Personne n'a vu l'accident.** **Rien ne m'intéresse.**

1. Qui a pris ma voiture?
2. Qu'est-ce qui est arrivé hier soir?
3. Qui a écrit à Sylvie?
4. Qui lui a téléphoné?
5. Qu'est-ce qui lui est arrivé?
6. Qui est-ce qui est sorti avec elle?
7. Qui va faire ses devoirs ce soir?
8. Qu'est-ce qui va mal?
9. Qui a brûlé un stop?

10 **Ni rien ni personne.** Utilisez **rien** ou **personne** pour répondre aux questions suivantes.

1. Vous avez fait quelque chose le week-end dernier?
2. Quelque chose vous est arrivé?
3. Vous avez rencontré quelqu'un?
4. Quelqu'un vous a invité(e) à danser?
5. Vous avez dansé avec quelqu'un?
6. Après le bal quelqu'un vous a accompagné(e) au café?
7. Vous avez bu quelque chose?
8. Quelqu'un a payé pour vous?
9. Vous avez dit au revoir à quelqu'un?

Entre amis

Je préfère ne pas en parler

Your partner is very secretive and will answer **nothing** or **nobody** to all your questions.

1. Ask your partner who wrote to him/her.
2. Ask who called him/her on the telephone.
3. Find out with whom s/he went out.
4. Ask what happened.
5. Ask what s/he did.
6. Ask whom s/he saw.

PAR TELEPHONE

PAR COURRIER

2 Making Basic Hypotheses

Que feriez-vous[1] ...

	oui	non
... si vous n'aviez pas de devoirs?		
Je resterais dans ma chambre.	____	____
Je sortirais avec mes amis.	____	____
J'irais au cinéma.	____	____
Je m'amuserais.	____	____
... si, par hasard[2], vous gagniez à la loterie?		
J'achèterais une voiture.	____	____
Je paierais mes dettes[3].	____	____
Je donnerais de l'argent aux pauvres.	____	____
Je mettrais de l'argent à la banque.	____	____
... si vous n'étiez pas étudiant(e)?		
Je chercherais du travail.	____	____
Je gagnerais de l'argent.	____	____
Je voyagerais.	____	____
J'irais en France.	____	____

1. *What would you do*   2. *by chance*   3. *debts*

E. Le conditionnel

Je pourrais apporter quelque chose?	*Could I bring something?*
J'aimerais inviter les Martin.	*I would like to invite the Martins.*
Ils viendraient si tu leur téléphonais maintenant.	*They would come if you called them now.*

■ The conditional is used to express hypotheses and also politely stated requests or wishes.

■ The conditional is formed by adding the imperfect endings (**-ais, -ais, -ait, -ions, -iez, -aient**) to the future stem (see Ch. 12).

aimer		
j'	**aimer**	**ais**
tu	**aimer**	**ais**
il/elle/on	**aimer**	**ait**
nous	**aimer**	**ions**
vous	**aimer**	**iez**
ils/elles	**aimer**	**aient**

vendre		
je	**vendr**	**ais**
tu	**vendr**	**ais**
il/elle/on	**vendr**	**ait**
nous	**vendr**	**ions**
vous	**vendr**	**iez**
ils/elles	**vendr**	**aient**

■ Remember that a number of verbs have irregular future stems (see Ch. 12). These verbs use the same irregular stem in the conditional. The endings, however, are always regular.

être	**ser-**	je **serais**	*I would be*
avoir	**aur-**	j'**aurais**	*I would have*
faire	**fer-**	je **ferais**	*I would do*
aller	**ir-**	j'**irais**	*I would go*
venir	**viendr-**	je **viendrais**	*I would come*
devenir	**deviendr-**	je **deviendrais**	*I would become*
vouloir	**voudr-**	je **voudrais**	*I would like*
pouvoir	**pourr-**	je **pourrais**	*I could; I would be able*
devoir	**devr-**	je **devrais**	*I should; I ought to*
savoir	**saur-**	je **saurais**	*I would know*

■ Impersonal expressions also have conditional forms.

infinitive	present	conditional
pleuvoir	il pleut	**il pleuvrait**
falloir	il faut	**il faudrait**
valoir mieux	il vaut mieux	**il vaudrait mieux**

Review p. 410.

■ Since **-e-** is *pronounced* as [ə] before the sound combination [Rj], it is never dropped in the **nous** and **vous** forms of the conditional of **-er** verbs and of irregular verbs such as **vous feriez** and **nous serions**.

future	conditional
nous dansérons	nous dans**e**rions
vous chantérez	vous chant**e**riez
nous sérons	nous serions
vous férez	vous feriez

■ The conditional is used to make a polite request or suggestion because the present is often considered rather harsh or brusk. **Devoir** is often the verb used to make a polite suggestion.

Je **veux** une tasse de café.	*I **want** a cup of coffee.*
Je **voudrais** une tasse de café.	*I **would like** a cup of coffee.*

Vous **devez** faire attention.	*You **must** pay attention.*
Vous **devriez** faire attention.	*You **should (ought to)** pay attention.*

Tu devrais prendre le métro. C'est plus rapide.

 Quelle audace! *(What nerve!)* Mettez le verbe au conditionnel pour être plus poli(e).

MODÈLE: Vous devez parler plus fort *(loudly).*
Vous devriez parler plus fort.

1. Je peux vous poser une question?
2. Avez-vous l'heure?
3. Pouvez-vous me dire votre nom?
4. Faites-vous la cuisine ce soir, par hasard?
5. C'est très gentil de m'inviter.
6. Je veux un steak-frites.

Quel conseil donneriez-vous? Utilisez le verbe **devoir** au conditionnel pour suggérer ce qu'il faudrait faire. Pourriez-vous donner deux suggestions pour chaque phrase?

MODÈLE: Nous n'avons pas de bonnes notes.
Vous devriez étudier.
Vous ne devriez pas sortir tous les soirs.

1. Marc a très faim.
2. Nos amis ont soif.
3. Nous sommes en retard.
4. Robert et Anne sont malades.
5. Gertrude est fatiguée.
6. Je n'ai pas envie de sortir ce soir.
7. Notre professeur donne beaucoup de devoirs.

F. *Si* hypothétique

Review **si** + present, Ch. 12, p. 338.

Si je gagne à la loterie, **j'irai** en Europe et en Asie.
Si je ne gagne pas à la loterie, **je resterai** ici.

Review Hypothetical statements about the future can be made by using **si** plus the present tense in conjunction with a clause in the future. Such a hypothesis will become a virtual certainty *if* the event described in the **si** clause actually occurs.

Si ma mère me **téléphone** ce soir, je lui **raconterai** cette histoire.
Je n'**irai** pas avec toi **si** tu **continues** à me parler comme ça.

■ To *suggest* what someone *might* do, **si** can be used with the imperfect as a question.

Si vous veniez à 8 heures?	*How about coming at 8 o'clock?*
Si j'allais au supermarché?	*What if I went to the supermarket?*
Si nous jouions aux cartes?	*How about a game of cards?*

■ Hypothetical statements referring to what would happen if something else were also to take place can be made by using **si** + imperfect with a clause in the conditional. Such hypotheses are not as certain actually to occur as those expressed by **si** + present with a clause in the future.

Si j'étais libre, **je sortirais** avec mes amis.	*If I were free, I would go out with my friends.*
Que **feriez-vous si vous étiez** riche?	*What would you do, if you were rich?*

Synthèse: *Si* clauses used with the future or the conditional

Si + le présent, → le futur   **S'il pleut, nous ne sortirons pas.**
Si + l'imparfait, → le conditionnel   **S'il pleuvait, nous ne sortirions pas.**

 Deux solutions. Pour chaque «problème» vous devez suggérer deux solutions.

> **Modèle:** Nous avons faim.
> **Si vous mangiez quelque chose?**
> **Si nous allions au restaurant?**

1. Nous avons un examen demain.
2. Je suis malade.
3. Paul a besoin d'argent.
4. Je dois contacter mes amis.
5. J'ai soif.
6. Nous devons faire de l'exercice physique.
7. Nos amis sont tristes.

⑭ Que ferais-tu? Lisez ce questionnaire et répondez à chaque question. Interviewez ensuite votre partenaire en mettant les phrases à la forme interrogative avec **tu.** Comparez vos réponses.

> MODÈLE: VOUS: **Si tu avais besoin d'argent, est-ce que tu écrirais à tes parents?**
>
> VOTRE PARTENAIRE: **Non, je n'écrirais pas à mes parents. Et toi?**

1. Si j'avais besoin d'argent, ...   *oui*   *non*

   j'écrirais à mes parents.   ____   ____
   je chercherais du travail.   ____   ____
   je vendrais mon livre de français.   ____   ____
   j'irais voir mes amis.   ____   ____
   je pleurerais.   ____   ____

2. Si j'avais «F» à l'examen, ...

   je pleurerais.   ____   ____
   je serais fâché(e).   ____   ____
   je serais très triste.   ____   ____
   je téléphonerais à mes parents.   ____   ____
   je resterais dans ma chambre.   ____   ____
   j'arrêterais mes études.   ____   ____

3. Si on m'offrait une Mercédès, ...

   je l'accepterais.   ____   ____
   je la garderais.   ____   ____
   je la vendrais.   ____   ____
   je la donnerais à mes parents.   ____   ____

⑮ À vous. Répondez.

1. Si vous étiez professeur, qu'est-ce que vous enseigneriez?
2. Donneriez-vous beaucoup de devoirs à vos étudiants? Pourquoi ou pourquoi pas?
3. Que feriez-vous pendant les vacances?
4. Quelle marque de voiture auriez-vous?
5. Où iriez-vous dans cette voiture?

Entre amis

Des châteaux en Espagne *(Daydreams)*

1. Find out what your partner would do if s/he had a lot of money.
2. Ask where s/he would live.
3. Find out what s/he would buy.
4. Suggest two things your partner could do with the money.

Intégration

Révision

Have students work in pairs to try to guess each other's questions.

Give students 3–4 minutes. Who will have the longest list?

Have students review **si** + imparfait, p. 423.

 Suggestion: Have students do the Information Gap activity in the Instructor's Resource Manual.

A **Le témoin.** Un ami francophone a vu un accident. Faites une liste de questions que vous pourriez lui poser.

B **Un remue-méninges** *(Brainstorming).* Faites une liste de choses que vous pourriez faire avec cinquante dollars.

C **Quelques suggestions.**

1. Citez trois choses qu'on pourrait donner à un(e) ami(e) pour son anniversaire.
2. De quoi les étudiants ont-ils besoin pour être heureux sur votre campus? (trois choses)
3. Faites trois suggestions pour les prochaines vacances.
4. Quelles sont trois choses que vous feriez si vous étiez en France?

D **À vous.** Répondez.

1. Quelle sorte de maison aimeriez-vous avoir un jour?
2. Qu'est-ce qu'un étudiant devrait faire pour réussir au cours de français?
3. Que feriez-vous à la place du professeur? Pourquoi?
4. Qu'est-ce que vous apporteriez si vous étiez invité(e) chez une famille française?
5. Si vous alliez faire un long voyage et si vous deviez inviter quelqu'un, qui vous accompagnerait et pourquoi?

Pas de problème!

Preparation for the video:
1. Video worksheet in the *Cahier d'activités*
2. CD-ROM, *Module 12*

Cette activité est basée sur la vidéo, *Module 12*. Choisissez la bonne réponse pour compléter les phrases suivantes.

1. Jean-François invite _____ à la Fête de la musique.
   (Alissa, Betty, Marie-Christine)
2. La Fête de la musique est au mois de _____.
   (mai, juin, juillet)
3. La copine qu'ils vont retrouver à un autre concert s'appelle _____.
   (Alissa, Betty, Marie-Christine)
4. Moustapha a consulté son _____ pour savoir à quelle heure chaque concert devait avoir lieu.
   (livre, programme, ticket)
5. Les jeunes guitaristes vont faire _____.
   (une émission, un disque, une excursion)

Lecture I

A **Étude du vocabulaire.** Étudiez les phrases suivantes et choisissez les mots anglais qui correspondent aux mots français en caractères gras: *unavoidable, when, chase, darted out, stone throwing, was astonished, lived, young girls, imprisoned right away, around, court, cross, district.*

1. Il y avait plusieurs **fillettes** qui jouaient et riaient dans la cour de l'école.
2. Avant son mariage, Mme Dupont **demeurait** chez ses parents dans un **quartier** résidentiel.
3. Paul **s'est étonné** de ne pas voir beaucoup de gens dans les magasins **aux environs de** Noël.
4. Il fallait **traverser** la rue pour rentrer chez nous.
5. Après tous ses accidents, il était **inévitable** que cet homme perde son permis de conduire.
6. Le gendarme **s'est élancé** à la poursuite du criminel.
7. **Lorsque** le **tribunal** a condamné le criminel, on l'a **écroué sur le coup** dans une cellule de la prison.
8. Après une longue **course-poursuite** en voiture, les gendarmes ont réussi à arrêter le criminel.
9. Les **jets de pierre** sont formellement interdits par la police.

Use pp. 406–407 to help you prepare these questions.

B **Une interrogation.** Vous êtes gendarmes et vous devez questionner deux automobilistes. Lisez d'abord les articles qui suivent et ensuite composez huit questions qui commencent par des mots interrogatifs **Qui?, Qu'est-ce qui?,** etc., dont quatre questions pour Mme Walther et quatre pour M. Martin.

Follow up activity B by having students ask and answer their questions in pairs.

Deux accidents

Mulhouse. Sortie d'école tragique, hier, en fin de journée, à Habsheim, près de Mulhouse. Une fillette de onze ans a perdu la vie en rentrant à son domicile. Il était aux environs de 16 h 45. Monique Schoenhoffen se promenait le long de la route, lorsqu'elle s'est subitement élancée pour traverser la chaussée, devant la maison où elle demeurait, juste à l'entrée de la commune. Elle n'avait pas vu venir une voiture, qui arrivait de Mulhouse, et qui était pilotée par Mme Georgette Walther, domiciliée dans cette ville. Le choc était inévitable. La fillette a été tuée sur le coup. À l'arrivée des gendarmes, il n'y avait malheureusement plus rien à faire. À 20 h, la gendarmerie n'avait pas encore déterminé les circonstances exactes de ce drame.

Roanne. Un automobiliste de 25 ans, sans permis de conduire, qui avait engagé une course-poursuite avec la police à plus de 110 km/heure dans les rues de Roanne (Loire) et qui avait frappé les policiers après son arrestation, a été condamné mercredi à six mois de prison ferme par le tribunal correctionnel de la ville. M. Djaffar Martin, déjà condamné en mars dernier à quatre mois de prison, avait été reconnu, mardi après-midi, par une patrouille de police qui l'avait aussitôt pris en chasse. Le chauffard avait alors pris une rue du centre en sens interdit, à plus de 110 km/heure, puis brûlé cinq feux rouges, forçant les automobilistes à s'immobiliser, sans cependant provoquer d'accident. Il avait été finalement intercepté par la police dans son quartier. Il a alors violemment attaqué les policiers qui le questionnaient sous les jets de pierre d'une dizaine de jeunes du quartier. Le chauffard a été écroué à la prison de la Talaudière.

Une analyse des faits. Relisez les deux articles et comparez-les. Ensuite choisissez l'accident (Mulhouse ou Roanne) qui correspond mieux aux descriptions suivantes.

1. L'automobiliste n'avait sans doute rien fait de mauvais.
2. L'automobiliste avait déjà été en prison.
3. Une personne est morte dans cet accident.
4. D'autres ont voulu aider l'automobiliste.
5. L'automobiliste allait trop vite.
6. L'automobiliste n'avait pas pu s'arrêter à temps.
7. L'automobiliste habitait la ville où l'accident a eu lieu.

Suggestion: Have students enumerate the things that M. Martin did wrong.

 À votre avis. Relisez les deux articles. Ensuite décidez ce que vous feriez si vous étiez le juge (1) au procès *(lawsuit)* de Mme Walther; (2) au procès de M. Martin.

Lecture II

A **Étude du vocabulaire.** Étudiez les phrases suivantes. Essayez de deviner le sens des mots en caractères gras.

1. Est-ce qu'on peut camper ici? Je ne sais pas; demandez au **responsable** du camp.
2. **Je ne suis pas en mesure de** répondre à cette question. Posez-la à un spécialiste.
3. Marc étudie beaucoup et **pourtant** il ne réussit pas.
4. Paul a changé d'emploi. Il espère gagner **davantage** d'argent.
5. J'ai envie de lire; achetez-moi **n'importe quel** journal. Ça m'est égal.
6. Jacques est **nettement** plus grand que sa sœur. Mais il est aussi beaucoup plus âgé qu'elle.
7. Pour construire un grand bâtiment, on utilise du **béton.**
8. Tchernobyl était une **centrale** nucléaire russe.

B **Opinions.** Décidez si vous êtes d'accord avec les phrases suivantes.

1. L'énergie nucléaire est nécessaire pour l'indépendance économique de mon pays.
2. Toutes les centrales nucléaires sont dangereuses.
3. C'est aux États-Unis que les centrales nucléaires produisent le plus grand pourcentage d'électricité.
4. Il y a déjà eu un accident nucléaire aux États-Unis.
5. Il y a déjà eu un accident nucléaire en Russie.

Il existe de nombreuses centrales nucléaires en France. Il semble qu'elles soient mieux acceptées par le public français qu'elles ne le seraient aux États-Unis.

La France nucléaire

«Oui, je crois à la possibilité d'un accident. Ce qui serait dangereux, c'est que je n'y croie pas.» De la part du responsable de la sûreté nucléaire à EDF (Électricité de France), Pierre Tanguy, de tels propos[1] peuvent surprendre. Mais ils illustrent en fait une nouvelle attitude d'EDF après l'accident de Tchernobyl, où l'improbable est arrivé. «C'est en étant[2] sûr que l'accident peut arriver qu'on est le mieux en mesure de l'éviter[3], poursuit[4] Pierre Tanguy. De toute façon[5], je n'arrive pas à imaginer qu'on puisse avoir en France des rejets extérieurs tels[6] qu'une de nos centrales risque de faire des victimes dans la population.»

Pourtant, la France accumule davantage de risques statistiques que n'importe quel autre pays. Au nom de l'indépendance énergétique, elle a la première place pour la part du nucléaire dans l'électricité produite: 70%. Un record, comparé aux Américains, qui en sont à 16%, et aux Soviétiques, à 11%. De plus, la France possède 44 réacteurs électronucléaires qui se trouvent dans un espace[7] nettement plus restreint[8] et plus peuplé. En cas d'incident, pouvons-nous réussir une évacuation de 135.000 personnes, comme à Tchernobyl? Les experts français prévoient[9] l'évacuation des habitants dans un rayon[10] de seulement 5 kilomètres autour de la centrale et le confinement des habitants chez eux jusqu'à 10 kilomètres, mais il n'y a pas de plan de secours à grande échelle[11] plus loin. «Ce n'est pas du laxisme», explique Jean Petit, directeur adjoint de l'Institut de protection et de sûreté nucléaire. La raison de cette assurance? «Des fuites[12] radioactives dans l'atmosphère ne peuvent pas s'échapper[13] des centrales françaises, affirme-t-on à EDF. Car, à la différence de ceux des Soviétiques, nos réacteurs sont enfermés sous un dôme de béton de 90 centimètres d'épaisseur[14].» C'est ainsi que l'accident de Three Mile Island, aux États-Unis, n'a pas fait de victimes, car dans la centrale américaine les poisons radioactifs sont restés enfermés dans le dôme de béton.

Adapté de «Risques: le système France», *Le Point* (n° 761)

---

1. *such words* 2. *by being* 3. *avoid* 4. *continues* 5. *In any case* 6. *discharge to the degree* 7. *space*
8. *smaller* 9. *foresee* 10. *radius* 11. *large scale* 12. *leaks* 13. *escape* 14. *90 centimeters thick*

Vrai ou faux? Décidez si les phrases suivantes sont vraies ou fausses d'après la lecture. Si une phrase est fausse, corrigez-la.

1. Les centrales nucléaires françaises sont meilleures que celles des Russes.
2. La centrale nucléaire de Three Mile Island était exactement comme celle de Tchernobyl.
3. Pierre Tanguy est sûr qu'il n'y aura jamais de problème.
4. D'après Tanguy, personne ne sera tué s'il y a un accident nucléaire.
5. L'EDF est sûre qu'il n'y aura jamais de fuite.
6. S'il y a un problème, les Français ont l'intention d'évacuer tous les gens qui habitent très près de la centrale.

D **À votre avis**

1. Êtes-vous pour ou contre l'utilisation de l'énergie nucléaire? Expliquez votre réponse.
2. Que pensez-vous de la sûreté du système nucléaire français?

VOCABULAIRE ACTIF

Noms
un chauffard *bad driver*
un conducteur *driver (male)*
une conductrice *driver (female)*
une dette *debt*
les études *(f. pl.) studies*
une faute *fault; mistake*
un(e) idiot(e) *idiot*
un(e) imbécile *imbecile*
une marque *make, brand*

Adjectifs
pâle *pale*
physique *physical*

Verbes
accepter *to accept*
assurer *to assure; to insure*
entendre parler de *to hear about*

Pronom
personne (ne ... personne) *no one; nobody; not anyone*

Préposition
contre *against; (in exchange) for*

Expressions utiles
juste derrière *right behind*
par hasard *by chance*
parler plus fort *to speak more loudly*
puisque *since*

À propos d'un accident
un accident *accident*
un agent de police *police officer*
un(e) automobiliste *driver*
blessé(e) *wounded*

brûler un stop *to run a stop sign*
la chaussée *pavement*
une contravention *traffic ticket*
déraper *to skid*
entrer en collision *to hit; to collide*
freiner *to brake*
un gendarme *policeman*
glissant(e) *slippery*
heurter *to hit; to run into (something)*
ivre *drunk*
la mort *death*
rouler *to go; to roll*
un témoin *witness*
tuer *to kill*

escale 5
Les Antilles

Haïti

REPÈRES: HAÏTI

Statut politique:	république
Superficie:	27.750 km² (équivalente à celle du Maryland)
Population:	7.320.000 (95% noirs et 5% mulâtres); 72% rurale, 28% urbaine
Langue officielle:	français et créole (depuis 1987); 30% de la population comprend le français
Religion:	catholique, protestant, vaudou
Capitale:	Port-au-Prince
Ressources:	tourisme, agriculture (bananes, canne à sucre, café, mangues), minéraux (bauxite, magnésium)

CHRONOLOGIE

1492 Christophe Colomb découvre l'île où les Arawaks habitent depuis le VIIᵉ siècle. Il l'appelle Hispaniola.

1508 Une cargaison (*cargo*) d'Afrique dépose les premiers esclaves, introduits pour suppléer à la main-d'œuvre indigène, décimée par les maladies et de pénibles conditions de travail.

1697 La France occupe la partie ouest de l'île et en fait une riche colonie agricole.

1750–1801 Rébellions de plus en plus sanglantes contre les colonisateurs. Rivalités entre noirs et mulâtres.

1801 Toussaint Louverture, ancien esclave, devient gouverneur général à vie.

1802 Une armée envoyée par Napoléon reprend l'île. Toussaint est fait prisonnier et envoyé en France.

1803 L'armée haïtienne est victorieuse contre l'armée française, décimée par la maladie.

1804 Déclaration d'indépendance de l'île, qui devient la première république noire autonome moderne.

1825 La France réclame une indemnité de 50 millions de francs avant de reconnaître l'indépendance du pays.

Haïti et ses habitants

La dualité de l'héritage historique des Haïtiens, l'esclavage et la colonisation française, continue à marquer la structure sociale. Une élite riche et peu nombreuse se distingue par la couleur de sa peau, son éducation et l'adoption de la langue et de la culture françaises. La grande majorité du peuple est noire, pauvre, rurale, mais devient de plus en plus urbaine, et parle uniquement créole. Entre ces deux classes s'est créée une classe moyenne, aujourd'hui grandissante, de noirs qui se sont promus par l'éducation ou par une carrière dans l'armée, le gouvernement ou l'industrie. Certains sont très fiers de leurs origines africaines et font un effort pour établir l'usage officiel du créole, alors que les autres souhaitent faire partie de l'élite culturelle française.

Ce pays, qui était la plus riche des colonies françaises au XVIIIᵉ siècle, est devenu l'un des plus pauvres. L'instabilité politique, les rébellions, massacres et dictatures successives ont déchiré le pays. L'érosion, due à la déforestation nécessaire pour la monoculture imposée par le régime colonial, a appauvri la terre. La lourde indemnité exigée par la France comme prix de l'indépendance a contribué à atrophier l'économie du pays.

De même que le français reste la langue officielle et le créole la langue de tous les jours, la religion catholique, adoptée par 90% des habitants, coexiste avec les pratiques vaudoues d'origine africaine, qui influencent les attitudes et la culture de ce peuple. Haïti garde un caractère africain plus marqué que d'autres pays de l'Amérique latine par la majorité de sa population noire, descendant directement des esclaves africains, et par ses croyances vaudoues.

La religion vaudou

Bien que l'église catholique condamne les pratiques vaudou, la plupart des habitants d'Haïti ne perçoivent aucun conflit entre les deux religions. Ils iront souvent à une cérémonie vaudou le samedi soir et à la messe le lendemain matin. Mais qu'est-ce que la religion vaudou? Pour certains, il s'agit avant tout d'un culte des ancêtres; d'autres honorent aussi les esprits qui président aux différents aspects de la vie de tous les jours. Durant leurs cérémonies, les croyants cherchent à entretenir des rapports étroits avec les esprits par des offrandes rituelles. À l'origine, le mot «vaudou» désignait la danse donnée en l'honneur des esprits. Cette danse peut produire un état de trance où le danseur se sent possédé par un esprit. Des prêtres ou prêtresses jouent un rôle d'intermédiaire entre les croyants et les esprits et dirigent les rituels.

Les croyances vaudou apportent au peuple haïtien un certain réconfort dans leurs épreuves. Elles encouragent la joie de vivre et aident à surmonter la violence et les souffrances que ce pays a connues au cours de son histoire. Ce culte sert aussi d'inspiration aux peintres du pays.

La Peinture haïtienne

Venant des milieux les plus simples, souvent sans aucune éducation et sans formation artistique, les peintres haïtiens ne sont pas attachés aux conventions formelles. En 1943, grâce à l'établissement d'un centre d'art à Port-au-Prince, cette peinture devient connue et appréciée d'un public international. Elle représente un réalisme merveilleux. Plus elle se fait connaître, plus la richesse artistique du pays se révèle et se développe.

On distingue deux écoles dans cette tradition primitive. Dans le sud, Hector Hyppolite, le peintre haïtien le plus connu, était prêtre vaudou. Il peignait avec des plumes d'oiseaux et des restes de peinture de bâtiment. Ses tableaux, pleins de mouvement, de lignes audacieuses et de couleurs très vives, expriment une spiritualité et un charme particuliers. Ils intègrent souvent des thèmes ou des symboles vaudou. Au nord, Philomé Obin, employé de bureau, représente des thèmes historiques ou des scènes de la vie de tous les jours de manière plus statique et moins vive mais avec exactitude et minutie. Outre cette peinture dite primitive, qui connaît un grand succès à l'étranger, on trouve une peinture haïtienne moderne et très expressive, émanant de peintres qui ont eu une formation académique. Ainsi, Haïti, un des pays les plus pauvres du monde, est aussi un des plus riches dans le domaine de la peinture contemporaine.

L'œuvre d'un artiste haïtien

Vrai ou Faux?

1. La majorité des Haïtiens parlent français.
2. Les mulâtres sont les premiers habitants d'Haïti.
3. Napoléon voulait qu'Haïti reste française.
4. Les premiers peintres haïtiens n'avaient souvent pas d'éducation formelle.

Les Petites Antilles

CHRONOLOGIE

1493 Christophe Colomb découvre la Guadeloupe et en 1502, la Martinique.

1508 La première cargaison d'esclaves africains arrive.

1635 Occupation française de la Martinique et de la Guadeloupe.

1678 Le nombre d'esclaves aux Antilles françaises atteint 27.000.

1848 La France abolit l'esclavage.

1902 Éruption de la Montagne Pelée à la Martinique, qui détruit l'ancienne capitale, Saint-Pierre, et tue 29.000 personnes.

1946 La Martinique et la Guadeloupe deviennent départements français d'outre-mer, gouvernés par la France. Les habitants sont de nationalité française et ont le droit de vote.

REPÈRES:	LA MARTINIQUE	LA GUADELOUPE
Statut politique:	départements français d'outre-mer	
Superficie:	1.106 km^2	1.780 km^2
Population:	375.000	426.000
Groupes ethniques:	mulâtres, noirs, créoles, Indiens d'Asie	
Langue officielle:	français	français
Religion:	catholique	catholique
Chef-lieu:	Fort-de-France	Pointe-à-Pitre
Ressources:	subvention de l'État français, tourisme, industrie (rhum, sucre), agriculture (canne à sucre, bananes, ananas)	

Les Petites Antilles françaises: une évasion tropicale

Situées en zone tropicale, les Petites Antilles françaises sont un archipel en forme d'arc où se trouvent la Martinique (mot qui veut dire «île aux fleurs») et la Guadeloupe («île aux belles eaux»). Cette dernière est composée de deux îles principales, qui forment un papillon, Basse-Terre et Grande-Terre.

L'hospitalité des Antillais est célèbre et le touriste appréciera les baignades sous un doux soleil, les promenades dans les forêts tropicales ou les plongées sous-marines parmi des poissons de toutes les couleurs. On peut aussi, à bord d'un voilier, apprécier le calme et la beauté des plages sauvages bordées de palmiers, explorer des villages de pêcheurs ou visiter, à la Martinique, le village des Trois-Îlets où est née en 1763 Marie-Josèphe Rose Tascher de la Pagerie, la future impératrice, femme de Napoléon.

Mais ces îles de rêve ont leur côté sombre. Chaque année, des ouragans violents frappent la région. Ces îles volcaniques sont à la merci d'éruptions, comme celle qui en 1902 a détruit Saint-Pierre à la Martinique. Elles sont aussi menacées de tremblements de terre qui peuvent faire disparaître des portions d'île entières.

Au cours de leur histoire, ces îles ont connu l'exploitation, la violence et la misère. Aujourd'hui encore, le chômage (*unemployment*) est très élevé: 23,5% à la Martinique, plus élevé encore en Guadeloupe. Certains Antillais voudraient se séparer de la France. Aimé Césaire, célèbre poète de la négritude, qui est devenu maire de Fort-de-France, a déclaré que la Martinique «perdait son âme» en restant française et dépendante de la France. Par contre, une séparation de la France serait un désastre économique.

De nombreux Antillais choisissent d'émigrer, surtout en France. Certains vont y faire des études et retrouvent dans les universités françaises des francophones africains dont ils partagent souvent la pensée. Ceux qui restent aux Antilles font face courageusement à une vie très dure, qui s'illumine cependant d'une joie de vivre et d'un amour des fêtes, de la musique et de la danse.

Vrai ou Faux?

1. Il fait assez froid en hiver à la Martinique.
2. La Guadeloupe fait partie de la France.
3. Aimé Césaire a été maire de Fort-de-France.
4. Saint-Pierre avait une population de près de 100.000 habitants.
5. Il y a un volcan sur l'île de la Martinique.

Le carnaval

Dans les Antilles françaises, le carnaval est l'occasion d'une fête de plusieurs jours. À la Martinique, tout commence la dernière semaine avant le carême (*Lent*). Le vendredi soir, on danse jusque très tard dans la nuit. Le lendemain, les Antillais descendent dans les rues «courir le vidé». Les «vidés», immenses personnages habillés de rouge ou de noir, mènent les foules le long des rues en chantant et en dansant, pour qu'elles oublient leurs soucis quotidiens et les conventions sociales. Le dimanche aussi a lieu le défilé de Vaval, roi du carnaval, et l'élection de la reine du carnaval. Le lundi, troisième jour du carnaval, est plus calme. Des femmes déguisées en hommes et vice-versa se promènent dans les rues, figurant, en une parade burlesque, des couples mariés. La journée se termine par des mariages légitimes. Le jour suivant, mardi gras, on célèbre la fête du diable rouge. Vestige de l'influence africaine, ce personnage, habillé de satin rouge et la tête couverte d'un masque rouge et noir surmonté de cornes, danse au son de clochettes en brandissant un trident décoré. Enfin, le mercredi des cendres est jour de deuil. Les participants à la fête s'habillent en noir et blanc pour aller brûler le roi Vaval au milieu des pleurs et des cris, mais avec la certitude de le voir renaître l'année suivante.

Le zouk, musique populaire de la Martinique

Le mot «zouk» vient de la Martinique. Il signifie «danse» en créole. Pendant les années 80, ce mot désignait la danse exécutée au son de la musique du groupe «Kassav». Ce groupe, qui est en grande partie responsable du succès de ce genre de musique, se compose de musiciens et chanteurs de la Martinique et de la Guadeloupe, vivant actuellement en France. Aux Antilles, la popularité du zouk a fait naître de nouveaux groupes de musiciens. Musique composite à l'image du mélange des races antillaises, le zouk combine de nombreux styles, rythmes et mélodies sur synthétiseurs, batteries électroniques et instruments d'origines multiples: tambours, congas, maracas d'influence africaine, banjo et clarinette de La Nouvelle-Orléans, instruments à cordes venant d'Europe. Le zouk se danse sur place avec un mouvement rythmique des hanches (*hips*). Il se rattache au phénomène musical du «world beat» ou «world music». Il résulte de l'union de la musique folklorique et la chanson créole avec la technologie électronique moderne.

Le créole

Le créole est le produit d'une fusion de plusieurs langues. Aux Antilles françaises, il s'est développé au XVIIe siècle avec l'arrivée des esclaves africains. Ces derniers, originaires de communautés linguistiques différentes, devaient communiquer non seulement entre eux mais aussi avec leurs «maîtres». L'apprentissage en masse du français par les Africains ne ressemblait en rien à l'enseignement dans une salle de classe sous la tutelle d'un professeur. Les Africains apprenaient le français dans les champs de canne à sucre en écoutant le langage familier des colons français, qui ressemblait peu au français littéraire. De ces circonstances est née une langue nouvelle, le créole.

Vrai ou Faux?

1. Le carnaval a lieu après la fête de Pâques (*Easter*).
2. Le dernier jour avant le début du carême est un mardi.
3. Le zouk est la langue parlée par les Martiniquais.
4. À leur arrivée aux Antilles, les esclaves parlaient tous la même langue africaine.

Verbes

Infinitif	Présent		Passé Composé		Imparfait	
1. parler	je	parle	j'	ai parlé	je	parlais
	tu	parles	tu	as parlé	tu	parlais
	il/elle/on	parle	il/elle/on	a parlé	il/elle/on	parlait
	nous	parlons	nous	avons parlé	nous	parlions
	vous	parlez	vous	avez parlé	vous	parliez
	ils/elles	parlent	ils/elles	ont parlé	ils/elles	parlaient
2. finir	je	finis	j'	ai fini	je	finissais
	tu	finis	tu	as fini	tu	finissais
	il/elle/on	finit	il/elle/on	a fini	il/elle/on	finissait
	nous	finissons	nous	avons fini	nous	finissions
	vous	finissez	vous	avez fini	vous	finissiez
	ils/elles	finissent	ils/elles	ont fini	ils/elles	finissaient
3. attendre	j'	attends	j'	ai attendu	j'	attendais
	tu	attends	tu	as attendu	tu	attendais
	il/elle/on	attend	il/elle/on	a attendu	il/elle/on	attendait
	nous	attendons	nous	avons attendu	nous	attendions
	vous	attendez	vous	avez attendu	vous	attendiez
	ils/elles	attendent	ils/elles	ont attendu	ils/elles	attendaient
4. se laver	je	me lave	je	me suis lavé(e)	je	me lavais
	tu	te laves	tu	t'es lavé(e)	tu	te lavais
	il/on	se lave	il/on	s'est lavé	il/on	se lavait
	elle	se lave	elle	s'est lavée	elle	se lavait
	nous	nous lavons	nous	nous sommes lavé(e)s	nous	nous lavions
	vous	vous lavez	vous	vous êtes lavé(e)(s)	vous	vous laviez
	ils	se lavent	ils	se sont lavés	ils	se lavaient
	elles	se lavent	elles	se sont lavées	elles	se lavaient

Impératif	Futur		Conditionnel		Subjonctif	
parle	je	parlerai	je	parlerais	que je	parle
parlons	tu	parleras	tu	parlerais	que tu	parles
parlez	il/elle/on	parlera	il/elle/on	parlerait	qu'il/elle/on	parle
	nous	parlerons	nous	parlerions	que nous	parlions
	vous	parlerez	vous	parleriez	que vous	parliez
	ils/elles	parleront	ils/elles	parleraient	qu'ils/elles	parlent
finis	je	finirai	je	finirais	que je	finisse
finissons	tu	finiras	tu	finirais	que tu	finisses
finissez	il/elle/on	finira	il/elle/on	finirait	qu'il/elle/on	finisse
	nous	finirons	nous	finirions	que nous	finissions
	vous	finirez	vous	finiriez	que vous	finissiez
	ils/elles	finiront	ils/elles	finiraient	qu'ils/elles	finissent
attends	j'	attendrai	j'	attendrais	que j'	attende
attendons	tu	attendras	tu	attendrais	que tu	attendes
attendez	il/elle/on	attendra	il/elle/on	attendrait	qu'il/elle/on	attende
	nous	attendrons	nous	attendrions	que nous	attendions
	vous	attendrez	vous	attendriez	que vous	attendiez
	ils/elles	attendront	ils/elles	attendraient	qu'ils/elles	attendent
lave-toi	je	me laverai	je	me laverais	que je	me lave
lavons-nous	tu	te laveras	tu	te laverais	que tu	te laves
lavez-vous	il/on	se lavera	il/on	se laverait	qu'il/on	se lave
	elle	se lavera	elle	se laverait	qu'elle	se lave
	nous	nous laverons	nous	nous laverions	que nous	nous lavions
	vous	vous laverez	vous	vous laveriez	que vous	vous laviez
	ils	se laveront	ils	se laveraient	qu'ils	se lavent
	elles	se laveront	elles	se laveraient	qu'elles	se lavent

VERBES RÉGULIERS AVEC CHANGEMENTS ORTHOGRAPHIQUES

Infinitif	Présent		Passé Composé	Imparfait
1. manger	je mange tu manges il/elle/on mange	nous mangeons vous mangez ils/elles mangent	j'ai mangé	je mangeais
2. avancer	j' avance tu avances il/elle/on avance	nous avançons vous avancez ils/elles avancent	j'ai avancé	j'avançais
3. payer	je paie tu paies il/elle/on paie	nous payons vous payez ils/elles paient	j'ai payé	je payais
4. préférer	je préfère tu préfères il/elle/on préfère	nous préférons vous préférez ils/elles préfèrent	j'ai préféré	je préférais
5. acheter	j' achète tu achètes il/elle/on achète	nous achetons vous achetez ils/elles achètent	j'ai acheté	j'achetais
6. appeler	j' appelle tu appelles il/elle/on appelle	nous appelons vous appelez ils/elles appellent	j'ai appelé	j'appelais

Impératif	Futur	Conditionnel	Subjonctif	*Autres verbes*
mange mangeons mangez	je mangerai	je mangerais	que je mange que nous mangions	exiger nager neiger voyager
avance avançons avancez	j'avancerai	j'avancerais	que j'avance que nous avancions	commencer divorcer
paie payons payez	je paierai	je paierais	que je paie que nous payions	essayer
préfère préférons préférez	je préférerai	je préférerais	que je préfère que nous préférions	espérer exagérer répéter s'inquiéter
achète achetons achetez	j'achèterai	j'achèterais	que j'achète que nous achetions	lever se lever se promener
appelle appelons appelez	j'appellerai	j'appellerais	que j'appelle que nous appelions	épeler jeter s'appeler

VERBES IRRÉGULIERS

To conjugate the irregular verbs on the top of the opposite page, consult the verbs conjugated in the same manner, using the number next to the verbs. The verbs preceded by a bullet are conjugated with the auxiliary verb **être**. Of course, when the verbs in this chart are used with a reflexive pronoun (as reflexive verbs), the auxiliary verb **être** must be used in compound tenses.

Infinitif	Présent				Passé Composé	Imparfait
1. aller	je	vais	nous	allons	je suis allé(e)	j'allais
	tu	vas	vous	allez		
	il/elle/on	va	ils/elles	vont		
2. s'asseoir	je	m'assieds	nous	nous asseyons	je me suis assis(e)	je m'asseyais
	tu	t'assieds	vous	vous asseyez		
	il/elle/on	s'assied	ils/elles	s'asseyent		
3. avoir	j'	ai	nous	avons	j'ai eu	j'avais
	tu	as	vous	avez		
	il/elle/on	a	ils/elles	ont		
4. battre	je	bats	nous	battons	j'ai battu	je battais
	tu	bats	vous	battez		
	il/elle/on	bat	ils/elles	battent		
5. boire	je	bois	nous	buvons	j'ai bu	je buvais
	tu	bois	vous	buvez		
	il/elle/on	boit	ils/elles	boivent		
6. conduire	je	conduis	nous	conduisons	j'ai conduit	je conduisais
	tu	conduis	vous	conduisez		
	il/elle/on	conduit	ils/elles	conduisent		
7. connaître	je	connais	nous	connaissons	j'ai connu	je connaissais
	tu	connais	vous	connaissez		
	il/elle/on	connaît	ils/elles	connaissent		
8. croire	je	crois	nous	croyons	j'ai cru	je croyais
	tu	crois	vous	croyez		
	il/elle/on	croit	ils/elles	croient		
9. devoir	je	dois	nous	devons	j'ai dû	je devais
	tu	dois	vous	devez		
	il/elle/on	doit	ils/elles	doivent		

apprendre 25
comprendre 25
couvrir 21
découvrir 21
décrire 11

détruire 6
• devenir 28
dormir 22
élire 16
• s'endormir 22

offrir 21
permettre 17
promettre 17
réduire 6

• repartir 22
• revenir 28
revoir 29
sentir 22

• sortir 22
sourire 26
traduire 6
valoir mieux 15

Impératif	Futur	Conditionnel	Subjonctif
va allons allez	j'irai	j'irais	que j'aille que nous allions
assieds-toi asseyons-nous asseyez-vous	je m'assiérai	je m'assiérais	que je m'asseye que nous nous asseyions
aie ayons ayez	j'aurai	j'aurais	que j'aie que nous ayons
bats battons battez	je battrai	je battrais	que je batte que nous battions
bois buvons buvez	je boirai	je boirais	que je boive que nous buvions
conduis conduisons conduisez	je conduirai	je conduirais	que je conduise que nous conduisions
connais connaissons connaissez	je connaîtrai	je connaîtrais	que je connaisse que nous connaissions
crois croyons croyez	je croirai	je croirais	que je croie que nous croyions
dois devons devez	je devrai	je devrais	que je doive que nous devions

Infinitif	Présent				Passé Composé	Imparfait
10. dire	je	dis	nous	disons	j'ai dit	je disais
	tu	dis	vous	dites		
	il/elle/on	dit	ils/elles	disent		
11. écrire	j'	écris	nous	écrivons	j'ai écrit	j'écrivais
	tu	écris	vous	écrivez		
	il/elle/on	écrit	ils/elles	écrivent		
12. envoyer	j'	envoie	nous	envoyons	j'ai envoyé	j'envoyais
	tu	envoies	vous	envoyez		
	il/elle/on	envoie	ils/elles	envoient		
13. être	je	suis	nous	sommes	j'ai été	j'étais
	tu	es	vous	êtes		
	il/elle/on	est	ils/elles	sont		
14. faire	je	fais	nous	faisons	j'ai fait	je faisais
	tu	fais	vous	faites		
	il/elle/on	fait	ils/elles	font		
15. falloir		il faut			il a fallu	il fallait
16. lire	je	lis	nous	lisons	j'ai lu	je lisais
	tu	lis	vous	lisez		
	il/elle/on	lit	ils/elles	lisent		
17. mettre	je	mets	nous	mettons	j'ai mis	je mettais
	tu	mets	vous	mettez		
	il/elle/on	met	ils/elles	mettent		
18. mourir	je	meurs	nous	mourons	je suis mort(e)	je mourais
	tu	meurs	vous	mourez		
	il/elle/on	meurt	ils/elles	meurent		
19. naître	je	nais	nous	naissons	je suis né(e)	je naissais
	tu	nais	vous	naissez		
	il/elle/on	naît	ils/elles	naissent		
20. nettoyer	je	nettoie	nous	nettoyons	j'ai nettoyé	je nettoyais
	tu	nettoies	vous	nettoyez		
	il/elle/on	nettoie	ils/elles	nettoient		
21. ouvrir	j'	ouvre	nous	ouvrons	j'ai ouvert	j'ouvrais
	tu	ouvres	vous	ouvrez		
	il/elle/on	ouvre	ils/elles	ouvrent		

Impératif	Futur	Conditionnel	Subjonctif
dis disons dites	je dirai	je dirais	que je dise que nous disions
écris écrivons écrivez	j'écrirai	j'écrirais	que j'écrive que nous écrivions
envoie envoyons envoyez	j'enverrai	j'enverrais	que j'envoie que nous envoyions
sois soyons soyez	je serai	je serais	que je sois que nous soyons
fais faisons faites	je ferai	je ferais	que je fasse que nous fassions
—	il faudra	il faudrait	qu'il faille
lis lisons lisez	je lirai	je lirais	que je lise que nous lisions
mets mettons mettez	je mettrai	je mettrais	que je mette que nous mettions
meurs mourons mourez	je mourrai	je mourrais	que je meure que nous mourions
nais naissons naissez	je naîtrai	je naîtrais	que je naisse que nous naissions
nettoie nettoyons nettoyez	je nettoierai	je nettoierais	que je nettoie que nous nettoyions
ouvre ouvrons ouvrez	j'ouvrirai	j'ouvrirais	que j'ouvre que nous ouvrions

Infinitif	Présent				Passé Composé	Imparfait
22. partir*	je	pars	nous	partons	je suis parti(e)*	je partais
	tu	pars	vous	partez		
	il/elle/on	part	ils/elles	partent		
23. pleuvoir		il pleut			il a plu	il pleuvait
24. pouvoir	je	peux**	nous	pouvons	j'ai pu	je pouvais
	tu	peux	vous	pouvez		
	il/elle/on	peut	ils/elles	peuvent		
25. prendre	je	prends	nous	prenons	j'ai pris	je prenais
	tu	prends	vous	prenez		
	il/elle/on	prend	ils/elles	prennent		
26. rire	je	ris	nous	rions	j'ai ri	je riais
	tu	ris	vous	riez		
	il/elle/on	rit	ils/elles	rient		
27. savoir	je	sais	nous	savons	j'ai su	je savais
	tu	sais	vous	savez		
	il/elle/on	sait	ils/elles	savent		
28. venir	je	viens	nous	venons	je suis venu(e)	je venais
	tu	viens	vous	venez		
	il/elle/on	vient	ils/elles	viennent		
29. voir	je	vois	nous	voyons	j'ai vu	je voyais
	tu	vois	vous	voyez		
	il/elle/on	voit	ils/elles	voient		
30. vouloir	je	veux	nous	voulons	j'ai voulu	je voulais
	tu	veux	vous	voulez		
	il/elle/on	veut	ils/elles	veulent		

*****Servir, dormir,** and **sentir** are conjugated with **avoir** in the passé composé. **Partir, sortir,** and **s'endormir** are conjugated with **être.**

The inverted form of **je peux is **puis-je ... ?**

Impératif	Futur	Conditionnel	Subjonctif
pars partons partez	je partirai	je partirais	que je parte que nous partions
—	il pleuvra	il pleuvrait	qu'il pleuve
— — —	je pourrai	je pourrais	que je puisse que nous puissions
prends prenons prenez	je prendrai	je prendrais	que je prenne que nous prenions
ris rions riez	je rirai	je rirais	que je rie que nous riions
sache sachons sachez	je saurai	je saurais	que je sache que nous sachions
viens venons venez	je viendrai	je viendrais	que je vienne que nous venions
vois voyons voyez	je verrai	je verrais	que je voie que nous voyions
veuille veuillons veuillez	je voudrai	je voudrais	que je veuille que nous voulions

Appendices

A list of International Phonetic Alphabet symbols

Voyelles

Son	Exemples	Pages: *Entre amis*
[i]	il, y	93, 299
[e]	et, parlé, aimer, chez	33, 56, 382
[ɛ]	mère, neige, aime, tête, chère, belle	33, 57, 410
[a]	la, femme	57
[wa]	toi, trois, quoi, voyage	57
[ɔ]	folle, bonne	186
[o]	eau, chaud, nos, chose	186, 382
[u]	vous, août	155
[y]	une, rue, eu	155, 157
[ø]	deux, veut, bleu, ennuyeuse	352
[œ]	heure, veulent, sœur	352
[ə]	le, serons, faisons	57, 410
[ɑ̃]	an, lent, chambre, ensemble	92
[ɔ̃]	mon, nom, sont	92
[ɛ̃]	main, faim, examen, important, vin, chien symphonie, brun*, parfum*	92

*Some speakers pronounce written **un** and **um** as [œ̃].

Consonnes

[p]	père, jupe	382
[t]	toute, grand ami, quand est-ce que …	106, 143, 382
[k]	comment, qui	213
[b]	robe, bien	382
[d]	deux, rendent	382
[g]	gare, longue, second	335, 382
[f]	fou, pharmacie, neuf	64
[s]	merci, professeur, français, tennis, démocratie	63, 213

[ʃ]	**ch**at, **sh**ort	213
[v]	**v**ous, neu**f** ans	64
[z]	**z**éro, ro**s**e	106, 213
[ʒ]	**j**e, â**g**e, na**ge**ons	37, 213
[l]	**l**ire, vi**ll**e	323
[R]	**r**ue, sœu**r**	242
[m]	**m**es, ai**m**e, co**mm**ent	92
[n]	**n**on, américai**n**e, bo**nn**e	92
[ɲ]	monta**gn**e	213

Semiconsonnes

[j]	f**ill**e, trava**il**, ch**i**en, vo**y**ez, **y**eux, h**i**er	299, 323
[w]	**ou**i, **w**eek-end	
[ɥ]	h**u**it, t**u**er	

A P P E N D I X   B

Professions

The following professions are in addition to those taught in Ch. 4, p. 111.

agent *m.* **d'assurances** insurance agent
agent *m.* **de police** police officer
agent *m.* **de voyages** travel agent
agent *m.* **immobilier** real-estate agent
artisan *m.* craftsperson
assistant(e) social(e) social worker
avocat(e) lawyer
banquier *m.* banker
boucher/bouchère butcher
boulanger/boulangère baker
caissier/caissière cashier
chanteur/chanteuse singer
charcutier/charcutière pork butcher, delicatessen owner
chauffeur *m.* driver
chercheur/chercheuse researcher
chirurgien(ne) surgeon
commerçant(e) shopkeeper
conférencier/conférencière lecturer
conseiller/conseillère counsellor; advisor
dentiste *m./f.* dentist
douanier/douanière customs officer
électricien(ne) electrician
épicier/épicière grocer
expert-comptable *m.* CPA
facteur/factrice mail deliverer
femme de ménage *f.* cleaning lady
fleuriste *m./f.* florist
garagiste *m./f.* garage owner; mechanic
homme/femme politique politician
hôtelier/hôtelière hotelkeeper
hôtesse de l'air *f.* stewardess
informaticien(ne) data processor

instituteur/institutrice elementary-school teacher
jardinier/jardinière gardener
maire *m.* mayor
mannequin *m.* fashion model
mécanicien(ne) mechanic
ménagère *f.* housewife
militaire *m.* serviceman/servicewoman
moniteur/monitrice (de ski) *(ski) instructor*
musicien(ne) musician
opticien(ne) optician
PDG *m./f.* CEO (chairperson)
pasteur *m.* (Protestant) minister
peintre *m./f.* painter
photographe *m./f.* photographer
pilote *m.* pilot
plombier *m.* plumber
pompier *m.* firefighter
prêtre *m.* priest
psychologue *m./f.* psychologist
rabbin *m.* rabbi
religieuse *f.* nun
reporter *m.* reporter
représentant(e) de commerce traveling salesperson
restaurateur/restauratrice restaurant owner
savant *m.* scientist; scholar
sculpteur *m.* sculptor
serveur/serveuse waiter/waitress
traducteur/traductrice translator
vétérinaire *m./f.* vet

Reference: Robert–Collins dictionary.

A P P E N D I X   C

Glossary of Grammatical Terms

Term	Definition	Example(s)
accord (*agreement*) 15–16, 22, 68	Articles, adjectives, pronouns, etc. are said to agree with the noun they modify when they "adopt" the gender and number of the noun.	*La **voisine** de Patrick est **allemande**. C'est **une** jeune **fille** très gen**tille**. **Elle** est partie en vacances.*
adjectif (*adjective*) 15, 22, 95	A word that describes or modifies a noun or a pronoun, specifying size, color, number, or other qualities.	*Lori Becker n'est pas **mariée**. Nous sommes **américains**. Le professeur a une voiture **noire**. C'est une **belle** voiture.* (See **adjectif démonstratif, adjectif interrogatif, adjectif possessif.**)
adjectif démonstratif (*demonstrative adjective*) 103	A noun determiner (see **déterminant**) that identifies and *demonstrates* a person or a thing.	*Regarde les couleurs de **cette** robe et de **ce** blouson!*
adjectif interrogatif (*interrogative adjective*) 112, 392	An adjective that introduces a question. In French, the word **quel** (*which* or *what*) is used as an interrogative adjective and agrees in gender and number with the noun it modifies.	***Quelle** heure est-il? **Quels** vêtements portez-vous?*
adjectif possessif (*possessive adjective*) 68, 75	A noun determiner that indicates *possession* or *ownership*. Agreement depends on the gender of the noun and not on the sex of the possessor, as in English (*his/her*).	*Où est **mon** livre? Comment s'appelle **son** père?*
adverbe (*adverb*) 96, 288	An invariable word that describes a verb, an adjective, or another adverb. It answers the question *when?* (time), *where?* (place), or *how? how much?* (manner).	*Mon père conduit **lentement**. (how?) On va regarder un match de foot **demain**. (when?) J'habite **ici**. (where?)*
adverbe interrogatif (*interrogative adverb*) 143	An adverb that introduces a question about time, location, manner, number, or cause.	***Où** sont mes lunettes? **Comment** est-ce que Lori a trouvé le film? **Pourquoi** est-ce que tu fumes?*

Term	Definition	Example(s)
article *(article)* 41, 59, 216	A word used to signal that a noun follows, and to specify the noun as to its *gender* and *number,* as well as whether it is general, particular, or part of a larger whole. (See **article défini, article indéfini,** and **article partitif**.)	
article défini *(definite article)* 41, 43, 311	The definite articles in French are **le, la, l',** and **les.** They are used to refer to a specific noun, or to things in general, in an abstract sense.	*Le professeur est dans la salle de classe. Le lait est bon pour la santé. J'aime les concerts de jazz.*
article indéfini *(indefinite article)* 59	The indefinite articles in French are **un, une,** and **des.** They are used to designate unspecified nouns.	*Lori Becker a un frère et une sœur. J'ai des amis qui habitent à Paris.*
article partitif *(partitive article)* 216	The partitive articles in French are **du, de la, de l',** and **des.** They are used to refer to *part* of a larger whole, or to things that cannot be counted.	*Je vais acheter du fromage. Tu veux de la soupe?*
comparatif *(comparison)* 308, 310	When comparing people or things, these comparative forms are used: **plus** *(more),* **moins** *(less),* **aussi** *(as ... as),* and **autant** *(as much as).*	*Le métro est plus rapide que le bus. Il neige moins souvent en Espagne qu'en France. Ma sœur parle aussi bien le français que moi. Elle gagne autant d'argent que moi.*
conditionnel *(conditional)* 420	A verb form used when stating hypotheses or expressing polite requests.	*Tu devrais faire attention. Je voudrais une tasse de café.*
conjugaison *(conjugation)* 36	An expression used to refer to the various forms of a verb that reflect *person* (1st, 2nd, or 3rd person), *number* (singular or plural), *tense* (present, past, or future), and *mood* (indicative, subjunctive, imperative, conditional). Each conjugated form consists of a *stem* and an *ending.*	Présent: *Nous parlons français en classe.* Passé composé: *Je suis allé à Paris l'année dernière.* Imparfait: *Quand il était jeune, mon frère s'amusait beaucoup.* Futur: *Je ferai le devoir de français ce soir.* Impératif: *Ouvrez vos livres!* Subjonctif: *Il faut qu'on fasse la lessive tout de suite.* Conditionnel: *Je voudrais un verre de coca.*

Term	Definition	Example(s)
contraction *(contraction)* 74, 125, 393	The condensing of two words to form one.	*C'est une photo **du** professeur* [**de + le**]. *Nous allons **au** café* [**à + le**].
déterminant *(determiner)* 333	A word that precedes a noun and *determines* its quality *(definite, indefinite, partitive,* etc.). In French, nouns are usually accompanied by one of these determiners.	Article *(**le** livre);* demonstrative adjective *(**cette** table);* possessive adjective *(**sa** voiture);* interrogative adjective *(**Quelle** voiture?);* number *(**trois** crayons).*
élision *(elision)* 14, 20, 41, 246	The process by which some words drop their final vowel and replace it with an apostrophe before words beginning with a vowel sound.	*Je **m'**appelle Martin et **j'**habite près de **l'**église.*
futur *(future)* 128, 336	A tense used to express what *will* happen. The construction **aller** + *infinitive* often replaces the future tense, especially when making more immediate plans.	*Un jour, nous **irons** en France. Nous **allons partir** cet après-midi.*
genre *(gender)* 4, 14, 41	The term used to designate whether a noun, article, pronoun, or adjective is masculine or feminine. All nouns in French have a grammatical *gender.*	***la** table, **le** livre, **le** garçon, **la** mère*
imparfait *(imperfect)* 301, 411	A past tense used to describe a setting (background information), a condition (physical or emotional), or a habitual action.	*Il **faisait** beau quand je suis parti. Je **prenais** beaucoup de médicaments quand j'**étais** jeune.*
impératif *(imperative)* 139, 281	The verb form used to give commands or to make suggestions.	***Répétez** après moi! **Allons** faire une promenade.*
indicatif *(indicative)* 14, 157, 301	A class of tenses, used to relate facts or supply information. **Le présent, le passé composé, l'imparfait, le futur** all belong to the indicative mood.	*Je ne **prends** pas le petit déjeuner. Le directeur **partira** en vacances le mois prochain. Il **faisait** beau quand je **suis parti**.*
infinitif *(infinitive)* 36, 43	The plain form of the verb, showing the general meaning of the verb without reflecting *tense, person,* or *number.* French verbs are often classified according to the last two letters of their infinitive forms: **-er** verbs, **-ir** verbs, or **-re** verbs.	*étudi**er**, chois**ir**, vend**re***

Term	Definition	Example(s)
inversion *(inversion)* 46, 62, 143, 158	An expression used to refer to the reversal of the subject pronoun-verb order in the formation of questions.	*Parlez-vous français? Chantez-vous bien?*
liaison *(liaison)* 11, 15, 37, 59–61, 124	The term used to describe the spoken linking of the final and usually silent consonant of a word with the beginning vowel sound of the following word.	*Vous [z]êtes américain? Ma sœur a un petit [t]ami.*
mot apparenté *(cognate)* 25, 91, 380	Words from different languages that are related in origin and that are similar are referred to as *cognates*.	***question*** [Fr.] = *question* [Eng.]; ***semestre*** [Fr.] = *semester* [Eng.]
négation *(negation)* 20, 96, 157, 285, 417	The process of transforming a positive sentence into a negative one. In negative sentences the verb is placed between two words, **ne** and another word defining the nature of the negation.	*On **ne** parle **pas** anglais ici. Il **ne** neige **jamais** à Casablanca. Mon grand-père **ne** travaille **plus**. Il n'y a **personne** dans la salle de classe. Mon fils **n**'a **rien** dit.*
nombre *(number)* 14, 16, 41	The form of a noun, article, pronoun, adjective, or verb that indicates whether it is *singular* or *plural*. When an adjective is said to agree with the noun it modifies in *number*, it means that the adjective will be singular if the noun is singular, and plural if the noun is plural.	***La*** *voiture de James **est** très petite.* ***Les*** *livres de français ne **sont** pas aussi chers que **les** livres de biologie.*
nom *(noun)* 16	The name of a person, place, thing, idea, etc. All nouns in French have a grammatical gender and are usually preceded by a determiner.	*le **livre**, la **vie**, les **étudiants**, ses **parents**, cette **photo**.*
objet direct *(direct object)* 226, 278	A thing or a person bearing directly the action of a verb. (See **pronom objet direct.**)	*Thierry écrit **un poème**.* *Il aime **Céline**.*

Term	Definition	Example(s)
objet indirect *(indirect object)* 385	A person (or persons) to or for whom something is done. The indirect object is often preceded by the preposition **à** because it receives the action of the verb *indirectly*. (See **pronom objet indirect.**)	*Thierry donne une rose à **Céline**. Le professeur raconte des histoires drôles **aux étudiants**.*
participe passé *(past participle)* 157, 189, 243	The form of a verb used with an auxiliary to form two-part (compound) past tenses such as **le passé composé.**	*Vous êtes **allés** au cinéma. Moi, j'ai **lu** un roman policier.*
passé composé 157, 188, 417	A past tense used to narrate an event in the past, to tell what happened, etc. It is used to express actions *completed* in the past. The **passé composé** is composed of two parts: an auxiliary **(avoir** or **être)** conjugated in the present tense, and the past participle form of the verb.	*Le président **a parlé** de l'économie. Nous **sommes arrivés** à 5h.*
personne *(person)* 13	The notion *person* indicates whether the subject of the verb is speaking *(1st person)*, spoken to *(2nd person)*, or spoken about *(3rd person)*. Verbs and pronouns are designated as being in the singular or plural of one of the three persons.	First person singular: *Je n'ai rien compris.* Second person plural: *Avez-**vous** de l'argent?* Third person plural: ***Elles** sont toutes les deux sénégalaises.*
plus-que-parfait *(pluperfect)* 412	A past tense used to describe an event that took place prior to some other past event. The **plus-que-parfait** is composed of two parts: an auxiliary **(avoir** or **être)** conjugated in the imperfect tense, and the past participle form of the verb.	*Il était ivre parce qu'il **avait** trop **bu**.*
préposition *(preposition)* 138, 142, 195	A word (or a small group of words) preceding a noun or a pronoun that shows position, direction, time, etc. relative to another word in the sentence.	*Mon oncle qui habite **à** Boston est allé **en** France. L'hôtel est **en face de** la gare.*
présent *(present)* 14, 36	A tense that expresses an action taking place at the moment of speaking, an action that one does habitually, or an action that began earlier and is still going on.	*Il **fait** très beau aujourd'hui. Je me **lève** à 7h tous les jours.*

Term	Definition	Example(s)
pronom *(pronoun)* 13, 112, 192, 226, 278, 385, 398	A word used in place of a noun or a noun phrase. Its form depends on the *number* (singular or plural), *gender* (masculine or feminine), *person* (1st, 2nd, 3rd), and *function* (subject, object, etc.) of the noun it replaces.	*Tu aimes les fraises? Oui, **je les** adore. Irez-**vous** à Paris cet été? Non, **je** n'**y** vais pas. Prenez-**vous** du sucre? Oui, **j'en** prends. Qui **t'**a dit de partir? **Lui.***
pronom accentué *(stress pronoun)* 168, 302	A pronoun that is separated from the verb and appears in different positions in the sentence.	*Voilà son livre à **elle**. Viens avec **moi!***
pronom interrogatif *(interrogative pronoun)* 112, 392–393, 414–416	Interrogative pronouns are used to ask questions. They change form depending upon whether they refer to people or things and also whether they function as the subject, the direct object, or the object of a preposition of a sentence.	***Qui** est là? **Que** voulez-vous faire dans la vie? **Qu'est-ce que** vous faites? **Qu'est-ce qui** est arrivé?*
pronom objet direct *(direct object pronoun)* 226, 278, 387	A pronoun that replaces a direct object noun.	*Thierry aime Céline et elle **l'**aime aussi.*
pronom objet indirect *(indirect object pronoun)* 385	A pronoun that replaces an indirect object noun.	*Thierry **lui** a donné une rose.*
pronom relatif *(relative pronoun)* 57, 256, 394	A pronoun that refers or "relates" to a preceding noun *(antécédent)* and connects two clauses into a single sentence.	*Le professeur a des amis **qui** habitent à Paris. J'ai lu le livre **que** tu m'as donné.*
pronom sujet *(subject pronoun)* 13	A pronoun that replaces a noun subject.	***Ils** attendent le train. **On** parle français ici.*
sujet *(subject)* 13	The person or thing that performs the action of the verb. (See **pronom sujet**.)	***Les étudiants** font souvent les devoirs à la bibliothèque. **Vous** venez d'où?*
subjonctif *(subjunctive)* 282, 365, 396	A class of tenses, used under specific conditions: (1) the verb is in the second (or subordinate) clause of a sentence; (2) the second clause is introduced by **que**; and (3), the verb of the first clause expresses advice, will, necessity, emotion, etc.	*Mon père préfère que je n'**aie** pas de voiture. Le professeur veut que nous **parlions** français. Ma mère est contente que vous **soyez** ici.*

Term	Definition	Example(s)
superlatif *(superlative)* 311	The superlative is used to express the superior or inferior degree or quality of a person or a thing.	*Le TGV est le train **le plus** rapide du monde. L'eau minérale est la boisson **la moins** chère.*
temps *(tense)* 36, 157, 301, 336	The particular form of a verb that indicates the time frame in which an action occurs: present, past, future, etc.	*La tour Eiffel **est** le monument le plus haut de Paris. Nous **sommes arrivés** à 5h à la gare. Je **ferai** de mon mieux.*
verbe *(verb)* 14, 36, 243	A word expressing action or condition of the subject. The verb consists of a *stem* and an *ending,* the form of which depends on the *subject* (singular, plural, 1st, 2nd, or 3rd person), the *tense* (present, past, future), and the *mood* (indicative, subjunctive, imperative, conditional).	
verbe auxiliaire *(auxiliary verb)* 157, 188	The two auxiliary (or helping) verbs in French are **avoir** and **être.** They are used in combination with a past participle to form **le passé composé.**	*Nous **sommes** allés au cinéma hier. Nous **avons** vu un très bon film.*
verbes pronominaux *(reflexive verbs)* 165, 190, 357	Verbs whose subjects and objects are the same. A reflexive pronoun will precede the verb and act as either the direct or indirect object of the verb. The reflexive pronoun has the same *number, gender,* and *person* as the subject.	*Lori **se réveille**. Elle et James **se sont** bien **amusés** hier soir.*

Vocabulaire

This vocabulary list includes all of the words and phrases included in the *Vocabulaire actif* sections of *Entre amis*, as well as the passive vocabulary used in the text. The definitions given are limited to the context in which the words are used in this book. Entries for active vocabulary are followed by the number of the chapter in which they are introduced for the first time. If a word is formally activated in more than one chapter, a reference is given for each chapter. Some entries are followed by specific examples from the text. Expressions are listed according to their key word. In subentries, the symbol ~ indicates the repetition of the key word.

Regular adjectives are given in the masculine form, with the feminine ending in parentheses. For irregular adjectives, the full feminine form is given in parentheses.

The gender of each noun is indicated after the noun. Irregular feminine or plural forms are also noted beside the singular form.

The following abbreviations are used.

CP   Chapitre préliminaire

adj.	adjective	*m.*	masculine
adv.	adverb	*m.pl.*	masculine plural
art.	article	*n.*	noun
conj.	conjunction	*pl.*	plural
f.	feminine	*prep.*	preposition
f.pl.	feminine plural	*pron.*	pronoun
inv.	invariable	*v.*	verb

à at, in, to   1
  ~ côté next door; to the side   5
  ~ côté de next to, beside   5
  ~ droite (de) to the right (of)   7
  ~ gauche (de) to the left (of)   7
  ~ ... heure(s) at ... o'clock   1
  ~ la vôtre! (here's) to yours!   2
  ~ l'heure on time   7
  ~ l'intérieur de inside   6
  ~ midi at noon   5
  ~ minuit at midnight   5
  ~ toute vitesse at top speed   10
  ~ travers throughout
  être ~ to belong to   6

abord: d' ~ at first   5
absolument absolutely   10
accepter to accept   15
accident *m.* accident   15
accompagner to accompany   6
accord *m.* agreement
  d' ~ okay   5
  être d' ~ (avec) to agree (with)   1, 11
accordéon *m.* accordion   6
accueillant(e) friendly
achat *m.* purchase   9
acheter to buy   9
acteur/actrice *m./f.* actor/actress   1
activité *f.* activity   11
actuellement now   14; nowadays

addition *f.* (restaurant) bill, check   8; addition
adieu *m.* (*pl.* **adieux**) farewell
adjoint au maire *m.* deputy mayor
adorer to adore; to love   2
adresse *f.* address   4
aéroport *m.* airport   5
affaires *f.pl.* business   4
  homme/femme d' ~ *m./f.* businessman/woman   4
affreux (affreuse) horrible   8
âge *m.* age   3
  quel ~ avez-vous? how old are you?   3
âgé(e) old   11
agent (de police) *m.* (police) officer   15

agir: il s'agit de it's a (*lit.* it's a matter of)

agrumes *m.pl.* citrus fruits

aider to help 4

aïe! ouch! 6

ail *m.* garlic 8

aimable kind; nice 9

aimer to like; to love 2

  s' ~ to love each other 14

air: avoir l' ~ to seem, to appear, to look 9

album *m.* album 11

alcool *m.* alcohol

Allemagne *f.* Germany 5

allemand(e) German 1

aller to go 5

  ~ en ville to go into town 5

  ~ -retour *m.* round-trip ticket 12

  ~ simple *m.* one-way (ticket) 12

  allez à la porte! go to the door! CP

  allez-y go ahead, let's go 12

  je vais très bien I'm fine 2

allô! hello! (*on the phone*) 12

alors then, therefore; so 2

amener to bring

américain(e) American 1

ami/amie *m./f.* friend 2

amusant(e) amusing, funny; fun 11

s'amuser to have fun; to have a good time 6

  je veux m'amuser I want to have fun 10

an *m.* year 3

  Jour de l' ~ *m.* New Year's Day 7

ananas *m.* pineapple

anchois *m.* anchovy 8

ancien (ancienne) former; old 4

anglais(e) English 1

Angleterre *f.* England 5

année *f.* year 6

  ~ scolaire *f.* school year 10

anniversaire *m.* birthday 7

  ~ de mariage wedding anniversary 10

annonce *f.* advertisement 14

  petites annonces want ads

annuler to cancel

août *m.* August 7

apéritif *m.* before-dinner drink 8

appareil *m.* appliance; phone 7

appartement *m.* apartment 3

s'appeler to be named, be called 13

  comment vous appelez-vous? what is your name? 1

  je m'appelle ... my name is ... 1

appétit *m.* appetite

  Bon ~! Have a good meal! 13

apporter to bring 8

apprendre to learn; to teach 8

après after 5

après-demain day after tomorrow 12

après-midi *m.* afternoon 1

  de l' ~ in the afternoon 5

  Bon ~. Have a good afternoon.

arabe *m.* Arabic 5; Arab

arachide *f.* peanut

arbre *m.* tree

argent *m.* money 9

armée *f.* army

arrêt (d'autobus) *m.* (bus) stop 10

arrêter to stop 10

arrière- great- 3

arriver to arrive; to happen 7

  qu'est-ce qui est arrivé? what happened? 14

artiste *m./f.* artist 4

aspirine *f.* aspirin 9

s'asseoir to sit down 13

  Asseyez-vous! Sit down! CP

assez sort of, rather, enough 1

  ~ bien fairly well 2

  ~ mal rather poorly 2

  en avoir ~ to be fed up 11

assiette *f.* plate 8

assister (à) to attend 14

assurer to assure; to insure 15

attacher to attach; to put on 10

attendre to wait (for) 9

attentif (attentive) attentive 10

attention: faire ~ to pay attention 4

au contraire to the contrary 4

au revoir good-bye 1

aujourd'hui today 4

aussi also, too 1; as 11

  ~ ... que as ... as ... 11

autant (de) as much 11

autocar *m.* tour bus 12

automne *m.* fall 7

automobiliste *m./f.* driver 15

autoroute *f.* turnpike; throughway, highway 12

autour de around 5

autre other 3

avance *f.* advance

  en ~ early 7

avancer to advance 10

avant before 5

avare miserly 4

avec with 2

avenir *m.* future

avertissement *m.* warning 14

avion *m.* airplane 7

avis *m.* opinion, advice

  à mon (à ton, etc.) ~ in my (your, etc.) opinion 11

avoir to have 3

  ~ besoin de to need 9

  ~ chaud to be hot 8

  ~ envie de to want to; to feel like 5

  ~ faim to be hungry 8

  ~ froid to be cold 8

  ~ l'air to seem, to appear, to look 9

  ~ lieu to take place 11

  ~ l'intention de to plan to 5

  ~ mal (à) to be sore, to have a pain (in) 9

  ~ peur to be afraid 8

  ~ pitié (de) to have pity (on), to feel sorry (for) 10

  ~ raison to be right 8

  ~ rendez-vous to have an appointment, meeting 4

  ~ soif to be thirsty 8

  ~ sommeil to be sleepy 8

  ~ tendance à to tend to 12

  ~ tort to be wrong; to be unwise 8

  en ~ assez to be fed up 11

  qu'est-ce que tu as? what's the matter with you? 9

avril *m.* April 7

bagages *m.pl.* luggage 7

bague *f.* ring 14

bande dessinée *f.* comic strip 6

banque *f.* bank 5

barquette *f.* small box; mini crate 9

basket-ball (basket) *m.* basketball 6

baskets *f.pl.* high-top sneakers 4

bâtiment *m.* building 5

batterie *f.* drums 6

bavard(e) talkative 4

beau/bel/belle/beaux/belles handsome, beautiful 1
  il fait ~ it's nice out CP, 7

beau-frère *m* brother-in-law 3

beau-père *m.* (*pl.* **beaux-pères**) stepfather (or father-in-law) 3

beaucoup a lot 2; much, many

beaujolais *m.* Beaujolais (*wine*) 8

beaux-parents *m.pl.* stepparents (or in-laws) 3

bébé *m.* baby 7

beige beige 4

belge Belgian 1

Belgique *f.* Belgium 5

belle-mère *f.* (*pl.* **belles-mères**) stepmother (or mother-in-law) 3

belle-sœur *f.* sister-in-law 3

berk! yuck! awful! 8

besoin *m.* need
  avoir ~ de to need 9

beurre *m.* butter 8
  ~ d'arachide *m.* peanut butter 8

bibliothèque *f.* library 5

bien well; fine 2
  ~ que although
  ~ sûr of course 8

bientôt soon
  À bientôt. See you soon. 5

Bienvenue! Welcome! 3

bière *f.* beer 2

billet *m.* bill (*paper money*) 9; ticket 12

bise *f.* kiss 5

bistro *m.* bar and café; bistro 5

bizarre weird; funny looking 4

blague *f.* joke
  sans ~! no kidding! 14

blanc (blanche) white 4

blessé(e) wounded 15

bleu(e) blue 4

bleuet *m.* blueberry (*French-Canadian*)

blond(e) blond 4

blouson *m.* windbreaker, jacket 4

bœuf *m.* beef 8

boire to drink 8
  voulez-vous ~ quelque chose? do you want to drink something? 2

boisson *f.* drink, beverage 2

boîte *f.* box, can 8

bol *m.* bowl 13

bon (bonne) good 2
  bon marché *adj. inv.* inexpensive 4
  bonne journée have a good day 1

bonbon *m.* candy 8

bonjour hello 1

bonsoir good evening 1

bordeaux *m.* Bordeaux (*wine*) 8

bottes *f.pl.* boots 4

bouche *f.* mouth 9

boucherie *f.* butcher shop 9

boulangerie *f.* bakery 5

boum *f.* party 10

bouquet *m.* bouquet 9

bout *m.* end, goal

bouteille *f.* bottle 8

boutique *f.* (gift, clothing) shop 9

bras *m.* arm 9

bridge *m.* bridge (*game*) 6

brie *m.* Brie (*cheese*) 8

brocoli *m.* broccoli 8

brosse *f.* brush
  ~ à cheveux *f.* hairbrush 13
  ~ à dents *f.* toothbrush 13

se brosser (les dents) to brush (one's teeth) 13

bruit *m.* noise 9

brûler to burn; to run through (light) 15

brun(e) brown(-haired) 4

bureau *m.* (*pl.* **bureaux**) desk; office 3
  ~ de poste *m.* post office 5
  ~ de tabac *m.* tobacco shop 5

but *m.* goal

ça (cela) that 4
  ~ dépend It depends 9
  ~ va? How's it going? 2
  ~ va bien (I'm) fine 2
  ~ veut dire … it means … CP

cachet (d'aspirine) *m.* (aspirin) tablet 9

cadeau *m.* gift 9

cadre *m.* executive 4

café *m.* coffee 2; café 5
  ~ crème *m.* coffee with cream 2

cafétéria *f.* cafeteria 5

calculatrice *f.* calculator 3

calme calm 4

camarade de chambre *m./f.* roommate 3

camembert *m.* Camembert (*cheese*) 8

campagne *f.* country(side)

campus *m.* campus 5

Canada *m.* Canada 5

canadien(ne) Canadian 1

car because

carte *f.* map 12; menu 13
  ~ de crédit *f.* credit card 9
  ~ postale *f.* postcard 4

cartes *f.pl.* cards (*game*) 6

cas: en tout ~ in any case

cassis *m.* blackcurrant

ce/cet/cette/ces this, that, these, those 4

ceinture *f.* belt 4
  ~ de sécurité *f.* safety belt, seat belt 10

cela (ça) that 9

célèbre famous 14

célibataire single, unmarried 1

celui *m.* this (that) one

celle *f.* this (that) one

celles *f.pl.* these; those

cendre *f.* ash 8

cent one hundred 3

centime *m.* centime (*1/100 of a euro*) 3

centre commercial *m.* shopping center, mall 5

cependant however

céréales *f.pl.* cereal; grains 8

certainement surely, of course 1

c'est it is, this is 1
  c'est-à-dire that is to say
  ~ gentil à vous that's nice of you 2
  ~ pour vous it's for you 1

ceux *m.pl.* these; those

CFA (=Communauté financière africaine) African Financial Community

chacun(e) each

chaîne (de télé) *f.* (TV) channel 14

chaise *f.* chair 3
chambre *f.* bedroom 3; room
  camarade de ~ *m./f.* roommate 3
champignons *m.pl.* mushrooms 8
chance *f.* luck
  Bonne ~! Good luck! 12
changer (de) to change 10
chanson *f.* song 2
chanter to sing 2
chanteur/chanteuse *m./f.* singer 11
chapeau *m.* (*pl.* **chapeaux**) hat 4
chaque each 7
charcuterie *f.* pork butcher's; delicatessen 9
charmant(e) charming 3
chat *m.* cat 3
château *m.* castle 5
chaud(e) hot 2
  avoir ~ to be hot 8
  il fait ~ it's hot (warm) CP, 4, 7
chauffage *m.* heat 13
chauffard *m.* bad driver 15
chauffeur *m.* driver 10
chaussée *f.* pavement 15
chaussettes *f.pl.* socks 4
chaussures *f.pl.* shoes 4
chauve bald 4
chef *m.* head *(person in charge)*; boss; chef
chemise *f.* shirt 4
chemisier *m.* blouse 4
chèque *m.* check 9
  ~ de voyage *m.* traveler's check 9
cher (chère) dear 2; expensive 4
chercher to look for 2
chéri(e) *m./f.* dear, honey 10
cheveux *m.pl.* hair 4
chèvre *m.* goat cheese 8
chewing-gum *m.* chewing gum 9
chez at the home of 3
  ~ moi at my house 3
  ~ vous at your house 3
chic *adj. inv.* chic; stylish 4
chien *m.* dog 3
chimie *f.* chemistry 5
Chine *f.* China 5
chinois(e) Chinese 1

chocolat chaud *m.* hot chocolate 2
choisir to choose 12
choix *m.* choice 8
chose *f.* thing 4
  quelque ~ *m.* something 2
  pas grand- ~ not much 5
chouette great *(fam.)* 14
chut! shh! 10
cigare *m.* cigar 6
cinéma *m.* movie theater 5
cinq five CP
cinquante fifty 3
circulation *f.* traffic 15
citron pressé *m.* lemonade 2
classe *f.* class
  en ~ in class; to class 4
clé *f.* key 12
climatisation *f.* air conditioning 13
coca *m.* Coca-Cola 2
code postal *m.* zip code 9
coin *m.* corner
collège *m.* jr. high school
combien (de) how many, how much 3
commander to order 8
comme like, as 2; how; since
  ~ ci, ~ ça so-so 2
  ~ il (elle) était ...! how ... he (she) was! 11
  ~ si ... as if ...
commencer to begin 7
  commencez! begin! CP
comment how; what 3
  ~ ? what (did you say?) CP, 2
  ~ allez-vous? how are you? 2
  ~ ça va? how is it going? 2
  ~ dit-on ...? how do you say ...? CP
  ~ est (sont) ...? what is (are) ... like? 4
  ~ est-ce qu'on écrit ...? how do you spell ...? 2
  ~ je vais faire? what am I going to do? 12
  ~ trouvez-vous ...? what do you think of ...? 2
  ~ vous appelez-vous? what is your name? 1
commentaire *m.* commentary 10
commerce *m.* business 5

communication *f.* communication
  votre ~ de ... your call from ... 1
complet *m.* suit 4
complet (complète) full; complete 12
composter (un billet) to punch (a ticket) 12
compréhensif/compréhensive understanding 4
  je ne comprends pas I don't understand CP
comprendre to understand; to include 8
compris(e) included; understood 8
comptabilité *f.* accounting 5
compter to count
condamner: être condamné(e) to be sentenced
conducteur/conductrice driver 15
conduire to drive 10
confirmer to confirm 12
confiture *f.* jam 8
confortable comfortable 4
confus(e) ashamed; embarrassed 14
connaître to know; to be acquainted with, to be familiar with 10
conseil *m.* (piece of) advice 10
se consoler to console oneself 14
content(e) happy 5
constamment constantly 10
constant(e) constant 10
continuer to continue
  continuez continue CP
contraire *m.* contrary, opposite
  au ~ on the contrary 4, 8
contravention *f.* traffic ticket 15
contre against; in exchange for 15
  par ~ on the other hand
corps *m.* body 9
côté *m.* side
  à ~ next door; to the side 5
  à ~ de next to, beside 5
se coucher to go to bed 6
couci-couça so-so
couleur *f.* color 4
  de quelle ~ est (sont) ...? what color is (are) ...? 4

couloir *m.* hall; corridor 5
coup *m.*: **~ d'envoi** kick-off
couper to cut 13
cour *f.* court
couramment fluently 11
coureur/coureuse runner; cyclist
courir to run
cours *m.* course; class 5
course *f.* race
courses *f.pl.* errands, shopping 4
cousin/cousine *m./f.* cousin 3
couteau *m.* (*pl.* **couteaux**) knife 13
coûter to cost 9
coutume *f.* custom
craie *f.* chalk CP
cravate *f.* tie 4
crédit: carte de ~ *f.* credit card 9
crème *f.* cream 2
crêpe *f.* crepe; French pancake 8
croire to believe, to think 14
  je crois que oui I think so 14
  je ne crois pas I don't think so 14
croissance *f.* increase, growth
croissant *m.* croissant 8
crudités *f.pl.* raw vegetables 8
cuiller *f.* spoon 13
cuisine *f.* cooking; food 4; kitchen 3
cuisinière *f.* stove 3

d'abord at first 5
d'accord okay 5
  être ~ (avec) to agree (with) 5
dame *f.* lady 13
dames *f.pl.* checkers 6
dangereux (dangereuse) dangerous 11
dans in 2
  ~ une heure one hour from now 5
danser to dance 2
d'après according to
davantage additional, more
de (d') from, of 1
de rien you're welcome 12
décalage horaire *m.* time difference 5
décembre *m.* December 7
décider to decide
décombres *m.pl.* ruins
décrire to describe 6

déçu(e) disappointed 9
dehors outside
déjà already 6
déjeuner *m.* lunch 8
  petit ~ breakfast 8
déjeuner *v.* to have lunch 5
délicieux (délicieuse) delicious 8
demain tomorrow 5
  après- ~ day after tomorrow 12
demande *f.* request 12
  faire une ~ to make a request 12
demander to ask 6
démarrer to start 10
demi(e) half
  et ~ half past (the hour) 5
demi- (frère, sœur) step (brother, sister) 3
demi-heure *f.* half hour 7
dent *f.* tooth 9
dentifrice *m.* toothpaste 9
départ *m.* departure 12
départementale *f.* departmental (local) highway 12
dépasser to pass
se dépêcher to hurry 13
dépendre to depend 9
  ça dépend (de …) it (that) depends (on …) 9
déprimé(e) depressed 9
depuis for 6; since 9
déranger to bother 1
  Excusez-moi de vous ~ Excuse me for bothering you. 1
déraper to skid 15
dernier (dernière) last 6
  la dernière fois the last time 6
derrière behind 5
  juste ~ right behind 15
des some; any 3; of the
descendre to go down, get out of 7
désirer to want 2
désolé(e) sorry 9
dessert *m.* dessert 8
dessin animé *m.* cartoon 11
se détendre to relax 9
détester to hate, to detest 2
détruire to destroy
dette *f.* debt 15
deux two CP, 1
  tous (toutes) les ~ both 12

devant in front of 5
devenir to become 7
deviner to guess
devoir *m.* obligation
  devoirs *m.pl.* homework 4
devoir *v.* must, to have to, to probably be, to be supposed to; to owe 5
d'habitude usually 4
Dieu *m.* God
  Mon Dieu! My goodness! 2
dimanche *m.* Sunday 5
dîner *m.* dinner 4
dîner *v.* to eat dinner 4
diplôme *m.* diploma 12
dire to say; to tell 14
  … veut ~ … … means … 6
  vous dites you say 3
discret (discrète) discreet, reserved 4
se disputer to argue 14
dissertation *f.* (term) paper 6
divorce *m.* divorce 14
divorcé(e) divorced 1
divorcer to get a divorce 14
dix ten CP
dix-huit eighteen CP
dix-neuf nineteen CP
dix-sept seventeen CP
doigt *m.* finger
dollar *m.* dollar 9
DOM (=Département d'outre-mer) overseas department *(equivalent of a state)*
dommage *m.* pity, shame
  c'est ~ that's (it's) too bad 14
donc then; therefore
donner to give 4
  donnez-moi … give me … CP
dont about/of which (whom); whose 14
dormir to sleep 6
dos *m.* back 9
d'où: vous êtes ~? where are you from? 2
douche *f.* shower 12
  prendre une douche to shower
doute *m.* doubt
  sans ~ probably 3
doux (douce) mild
douzaine *f.* dozen 8
douze twelve CP
droit *m.* right *(entitlement)*

droit(e) *adj.* right
  à ~ (de) to the right (of)   5
  tout ~ straight ahead   5
drôle funny   14
durcir to harden
durée *f.* duration; length

eau *f.* (*pl.* **eaux**) water   2
  ~ minérale mineral water   2
échanger (contre) to trade (for)
  15
échecs *m.pl.* chess   6
éclater to burst
école *f.* school   5
écouter to listen (to)   2
  écoutez! listen!   CP
écrire to write   6
  **comment est-ce qu'on écrit
    … ?** how do you
    spell … ?   2
  écrivez votre nom! write your
    name!   CP
  … s'écrit … … is spelled …   2
écrivain *m.* writer   4
égal(e) (*m.pl.* **égaux**) equal
  cela (ça) m'est ~ I don't care   5
église *f.* church   5
Eh bien … Well then …
élève *m./f.* pupil   4
élire to elect
elle she, it   1; her   6
elles they   1; them   6
s'éloigner to move away
s'embrasser to kiss   14
émission (de télé) *f.* (TV) show
  11
emmenthal *f.* Swiss cheese   8
emploi du temps *m.* schedule
  5
employé/employée *m./f.*
  employee   4
emprunter to borrow   14
en *prep.* in   1; by, through
  ~ avance early   7
  ~ première (seconde) in first
    (second) class   12
  ~ retard late   7
  ~ tout cas in any case   5
  ~ voiture by car   7
en *pron.* some, of it (them); about
  it (them)   14
  je vous ~ prie don't mention
    it; you're welcome; please do
    7

vous n' ~ avez pas? don't you
  have any?   9
encore again   CP; still, more   3
  ~ à boire (manger)? more to
    drink (eat)?   8
  ~ de …? more …?   8
  pas ~ not yet   2
s'endormir to fall asleep   13
endroit *m.* place   5
enfant *m./f.* child   3
enfin finally   5
ennuyeux (ennuyeuse) boring
  4
enseigne *f.* sign
enseigner to teach   2
ensemble together   CP, 2
ensoleillé(e) sunny
ensuite next, then   5
entendre to hear   9
  ~ parler de to hear about   15
  s' ~ (avec) to get along (with)
    14
  entendu agreed; understood
    12
entre between, among   5
  ~ amis between (among) friends
    1
entrée *m.* first course, appetizer
entreprise *f.* business
entrer to enter   7
  ~ en collision to hit, collide   15
  entrez! come in!   CP
envie: avoir ~ de to want to; to
  feel like   5
environ approximately
envoyer to send   6
épaule *f.* shoulder   9
épeler to spell   12
épicerie *f.* grocery store   5
épinards *m.pl.* spinach   8
époque *f.* time, period   11
  à cette ~ at that time; back
    then   11
épouser to marry   11
équilibré(e) stable
équipe *f.* team   11
escale *f.* stop(over)
escargot *m.* snail   10
esclave *m./f.* slave
Espagne *f.* Spain   5
espagnol(e) Spanish   1
espérer to hope   8
essayer to try
essentiel: il est ~ que it is essential that   10

est *m.* east
est-ce que (*question marker*)   2
estomac *m.* stomach   9
et and   1
étage *m.* floor   12
état *m.* state   5
  ~ civil marital status   1
États-Unis *m.pl.* United States   5
été *m.* summer   7
étranger/étrangère *m./f.*
  foreigner
étranger (étrangère) foreign
  12
étroit(e) narrow; close
études *f.pl.* studies   15
étudiant(e) *m./f.* student   3
étudier to study   2
être to be   1
  ~ à to belong to   6
  ~ d'accord (avec) to agree
    (with)   5
  ~ en train de to be in the
    process of   11
  ~ originaire de to be a native
    of   7
  vous êtes d'où? where are
    you from?   2
eux *m.pl. pron.* they, them   6
exact(e) exact, correct
  c'est ~ that's right   13
exagérer to exaggerate   2
examen *m.* test, exam   6
  à un ~ on an exam   6
excellent(e) excellent   2
excuser to excuse
  excusez-moi excuse me   1
  **excusez-moi (nous, etc.)
    d'être en retard** excuse me
    (us, etc.) for being late   13
exemple *m.* example
  par ~ for example   6
exercice *m.* exercise   6
exiger (que) to demand (that)
  13
expédier to send
extroverti(e) outgoing   4

fâché(e) angry   14
se fâcher to get angry   14
facile easy   9
façon *f.* way, manner   8
  sans ~ honestly, no kidding   8
faim *f.* hunger
  avoir ~ to be hungry   8

faculté *f*.: ~ **des lettres** College of Liberal Arts
faire to do, to make 4
  ~ **attention** to pay attention 4
  ~ **du pouce** to hitchhike *(French-Canadian)*
  ~ **du sport** to play sports 6
  ~ **la cuisine** to cook 4
  ~ **la lessive** to do laundry 4
  ~ **la sieste** to take a nap 4
  ~ **les provisions** to do the grocery shopping 4
  ~ **un voyage** to take a trip 5
  ~ **une demande** to make a request 12
  ~ **une promenade** to take a walk; to take a ride 4
  il fait chaud it's hot out CP, 4, 7
  se ~ des amis to make friends 14
fait *m*. fact
  au ~ ... by the way ... 2
falloir (il faut) to be necessary 4, 10
famille *f*. family 3
fatigué(e) tired 2
faut: il ~ ... it is necessary ... 4
  il ~ que it is necessary that, (someone) must 10
  il ne ~ pas que (someone) must not 10
faute *f*. fault; mistake 15
fauteuil *m*. armchair 3
faux (fausse) false; wrong 2
femme *f*. woman 1; wife 3
  ~ **d'affaires** businesswoman 4
  ~ **politique** (female) politician 4
fermé(e) closed 6
fermer to close 6
  fermez le livre! close the book! CP
  fermez la porte! close the door! CP
fermier/fermière *m./f.* farmer 4
fête *f*. holiday 7
feu *m*. (*pl*. **feux**) traffic light 10; fire
feuille *f*. leaf/sheet (of paper) 9
feuilleton *m*. soap opera; series 14
février *m*. February 7

fiançailles *f.pl.* engagement 14
fiancé(e) engaged 1
fier (fière) proud
fièvre *f*. fever 9
fille *f*. girl 3; daughter 3
film *m*. film, movie 5
fils *m*. son 3
fin *f*. end
finir to finish 12
flamand *m*. Flemish 5
fleur *f*. flower 9
fleuriste *m./f.* florist 9
fleuve *m*. river
flûte *f*. flute 6
  ~ **!** darn!; shucks! 12
fois *f*. one time 6; times, multiplied by
  à la ~ at the same time
  la dernière ~ the last time 6
  deux ~ twice
follement in a crazy manner 10
fonctionnaire *m./f.* civil servant 4
football (foot) *m*. soccer 6
  ~ **américain** *m*. football 6
formidable great, fantastic 14
fort *adv*. loudly, with strength 15
fou/folle *m./f.* fool; crazy person 10
fou (folle) (*m.pl.* **fous**) crazy 10
foulard *m*. scarf 4
fourchette *f*. fork 13
frais: il fait ~ it's cool 7
fraises *f.pl.* strawberries 8
franc *m*. franc 9
français(e) French 1
  à la française in the French style 13
  en français in French CP
France *f*. France 5
francophone French-speaking
frapper to knock
  Frappez à la porte! Knock on the door! CP
freiner to brake 15
fréquenter (quelqu'un) to date (someone) 11
frère *m*. brother 3
frites *f.pl.* French fries 8
  steak- ~ *m*. steak with French fries 15
froid(e) cold 2
  avoir ~ to be cold 8
  il fait ~ it's cold CP, 7

fromage *m*. cheese 5
frontière *f*. border
fruit *m*. a piece of fruit 8
fumer to smoke 6
fumeur/fumeuse *m./f.* smoker
  non- ~ nonsmoker
fumeur *m*. smoking car 12;
  non ~ nonsmoking car 12
fumeur/fumeuse *adj*. smoking

gagner to win; to earn
  ~ **(à la loterie)** to win (the lottery) 12
gants *m.pl.* gloves 4
garage *m*. garage 3
garçon *m*. boy 3; waiter 8
garder to keep; to look after 4
gare *f*. (train) station 3
gâteau *m*. (*pl*. **gâteaux**) cake 8
  petit ~ cookie
gauche *adj*. left
  à ~ (de) to the left (of) 5
gendarme *m*. (state) policeman 15
général: en ~ in general 2
généralement generally 4
généreux (généreuse) generous
genou *m*. knee 9
  genoux *m.pl.* lap, knees 13
gens *m.pl.* people 4
gentil(le) nice 3
  c'est ~ à vous that's nice of you 2
gestion *f*. management 5
glace *f*. ice cream 8
glissant(e) slippery 15
golf *m*. golf 6
gorge *f*. throat 9
goudron *m*. tar
goûter to taste 13
grand(e) big, tall 1
  ~ **magasin** *m*. department store 9
  pas grand-chose not much 5
grand-mère *f*. (*pl*. **grands-mères**) grandmother 3
grand-père *m*. (*pl*. **grands-pères**) grandfather 3
grands-parents *m.pl.* grandparents 3
gras (grasse) fat
  faire la ~ matinée to sleep in, to sleep late

gratuit(e) free
grippe *f.* flu 6
gris(e) grey 4
gros(se) fat; large 1
grossir to put on weight 12
guerre *f.* war 7
  en temps de ~ in wartime
guitare *f.* guitar 6
gymnase *m.* gymnasium 5
gymnastique *f.* gymnastics 5

*An asterisk indicates that no liaison
or elision is made at the beginning of
the word.*
habile skilful
s'habiller to get dressed 13
habiter to live; to reside 2
  où habitez-vous? where do
    you live? 1
habitude *f.* habit
  d' ~ usually 4
  avoir l' ~ de to be used to
    5
*__*haricots verts__ *m.pl.* green beans
  8
*__*hasard__ *m.* chance, luck
  par ~ by chance 15
heure *f.* hour CP, 1; (clock)
    time 5
  à l' ~ on time 7
  dans une ~ one hour from
    now 5
  il est … heure(s) it is …
    o'clock CP, 5
  tout à l' ~ in a little while 5;
    a little while ago 6
heureusement fortunately 6
heureux (heureuse) happy 4
*__*heurter__ to hit, run into 15
hier yesterday 6
histoire *f.* story 14
  quelle ~! what a story! 14
hiver *m.* winter 7
*__*hockey__ *m.* hockey 6
homme *m.* man 1
  ~ d'affaires businessman 4
  ~ politique politician 4
horaire *m.* timetable 12
*__*hors-d'œuvre__ *m. inv.* appetizer
  8
hôtel *m.* hotel 1
hôtesse de l'air *f.* (female) flight
    attendant 11
*__*huit__ eight CP

hypermarché *m.* giant super-
    market 9

ici here 2
  par ~ this way, follow me 13
idiot/idiote *m./f.* idiot 15
il he, it 1
il y a there is (are) 3
  il n'y a pas de quoi you're
    welcome 13
  il n'y en a plus there is (are)
    no more 12
  ~ … jours … days ago 6
  qu'est-ce qu' ~ ? what's the
    matter? 3
île *f.* island
ils they 1
imbécile *m./f.* imbecile 15
immeuble *m.* building
impair: nombre ~ *m.* odd
    number
impatience *f.* impatience 9
impatient(e) impatient 4
imperméable *m.* raincoat 4
important(e) important
  il est ~ que it is important that
    10
incroyable *adj.* unbelievable, in-
    credible 14
indications *f.pl.* directions 10
indiquer to tell; to indicate; to
    point out 12
indispensable indispensable,
    essential
  il est ~ que it is essential that
    10
infirmier/infirmière *m./f.* nurse
  4
informations *f.pl.* news 14
informatique *f.* computer sci-
    ence 5
ingénieur *m.* engineer 4
inondation *f.* flood
s'inquiéter to worry 13
insister to insist
  je n'insiste pas I won't insist
    8
  si vous insistez if you insist 8
s'installer to move (into)
instrument *m.* instrument 6
intelligent(e) intelligent 4
intellectuel(le) intellectual 4
intention: avoir l' ~ de to plan
    to 5

interdit(e) forbidden
  sens ~ *m.* one-way street 10
intéressant(e) interesting 4
s'intéresser à to be interested in
    14
intérêt *m.* interest 9
intérieur *m.* inside
  à l' ~ de inside of 6
interprète *m./f.* interpreter 4
intolérant(e) intolerant 4
inutile useless 12
inviter to invite 10
Irlande *f.* Ireland 5
Israël *m.* Israel 5
Italie *f.* Italy 5
italien(ne) Italian 1
ivre drunk 15

jamais ever, never
  ne … ~ never 4
jambe *f.* leg 9
jambon *m.* ham 8
janvier *m.* January 7
Japon *m.* Japan 5
japonais(e) Japanese 1
jaune yellow 4
je I 1
jean *m.* jeans 4
jeu *m.(pl.* **jeux)** game 6
jeudi *m.* Thursday 5
jeune young 1
jogging *m.* jogging 2
joli(e) pretty 1
jouer to play 2
  à quoi jouez-vous? what
    (game) do you play? 6
  de quoi jouez-vous? what
    (instrument) do you play? 6
jour *m.* day 1
  ~ de l'An New Year's Day 7
  quinze jours two weeks 11
journal *m.* newspaper 6
journée *f.* day
  bonne ~! have a nice day! 1
juillet *m.* July 7
juin *m.* June 7
jupe *f.* skirt 4
jurer to swear
  je te le jure I swear (to you) 14
jus *m.* juice
  ~ d'orange orange juice 2
jusqu'à *prep.* until 10
  jusqu'au bout right up till the
    end

juste *adv.* just; right
  ~ **derrière moi** right behind
    me 15

kilo *m.* kilogram 8
kiosque *m.* newsstand 9
kir *m.* kir 2

la (*see* **le**)
là there 4
laid(e) ugly 1
laisser to leave; to let 10
  laisse-moi (laissez-moi) tran-
    quille! leave me alone! 10
lait *m.* milk 2
langue *f.* language 5
laquelle (*see* **lequel**)
las(se) tired
lave-vaisselle *m.* dishwasher 3
laver to wash 13
  se ~ to get washed; to wash up
    13
le/la/l'/les the 2; him, her, it,
    them 8
légume *m.* vegetable 8
lent(e) slow 10
lentement slowly 10
lequel/laquelle/lesquels/
    lesquelles which? which
    one(s)? 14
les (*see* **le**)
lesquel(le)s (*see* **lequel**)
lessive *f.* wash; laundry 4
lettre *f.* letter 6
leur *pron.* (to) them 14
leur(s) *adj.* their 3
lever to lift; to raise 13
  se ~ to get up; to stand up 6
  Levez-vous! Get up! CP
librairie *f.* bookstore 5
libre free 5; vacant
lien *m.* tie; bind
lieu *m.* (*pl.* **lieux**) place 5
  avoir ~ to take place 11
limonade *f.* lemon-lime soda 2
lire to read 6
  lisez! read! CP
lit *m.* bed 3
litre *m.* liter 9
littérature *f.* literature 5
livre *f.* pound 9
livre *m.* book 3
loi *f.* law

loin (de) far (from) 5
loisir *m.* leisure activity
long (longue) long 9
longtemps a long time 6
louer to rent 12
lui he, him 6; (to) him; (to) her
    14
lundi *m.* Monday 5
lunettes *f.pl.* eyeglasses 4
lycée *m.* high school

ma (*see* **mon**)
machine à laver *f.* washing ma-
    chine 3
Madame (Mme) Mrs., ma'am;
    woman 1
Mademoiselle (Mlle) Miss;
    young woman 1
magasin *m.* store 4
  grand ~ department store 9
magazine *m.* magazine 6
Maghreb *m.* the three North
    African countries of Algeria,
    Morocco, and Tunisia.
mai *m.* May 7
maigrir to lose weight 12
maillot de bain *m.* bathing suit
    13
main *f.* hand 9
maintenant now 5
maire *m.* mayor 11
  adjoint au ~ deputy mayor
mairie *f.* town (city) hall 11
mais but 2
maison *f.* house 3
mal *m.*: **avoir ~ (à)** to be sore, to
    have a pain (in) 9
mal *adv.* poorly 2; badly
malade sick 2
malgré in spite of
manger to eat 2
manquer to miss
manteau *m.* (*pl.* **manteaux**) coat
    4
marchand/marchande *m./f.*
    merchant 9
marché *m.* (open-air) market 9
  ~ aux puces flea market 9
mardi *m.* Tuesday 5
mari *m.* husband 3
mariage *m.* marriage; wedding
    11
marié(e) married 1
se marier (avec) to marry 14

marine *f.* navy
Maroc *m.* Morocco 5
marocain(e) Moroccan 1
marque *f.* make, brand 15
marron *adj. inv.* brown 4
mars *m.* March 7
match *m.* game 10
matin *m.* morning 1
matinée: faire la grasse ~ to
    sleep in late
mauvais(e) bad 4
  il fait ~ the weather is bad 7
mayonnaise *f.* mayonnaise 8
me me 10; (to) me 14
méchant(e) nasty; mean 4
méchoui *m.* roast lamb (*North-*
    African specialty)
médecin *m.* doctor 4
médicament *m.* medicine 9
se méfier de to watch out for
meilleur(e) better 11
  ~ ami(e) *m./f.* best friend 1
  le/la ~ best 11
  Avec mon ~ souvenir
    With my best regards 4
membre *m.* member 3
même even 14; same
  -~(s) -self (-selves) 2
ménage *m.* housework 4
menu *m.* (fixed price) menu 13
merci thank you 1; (no) thanks
    2
  non, ~ no, thank you 2
mercredi *m.* Wednesday 5
mère *f.* mother 2, 3
mes (*see* **mon**)
mesdames *f.pl.* ladies 13
message *m.* message
  ~ électronique email 6
messieurs *m.pl.* gentlemen 13
mesure *f.* (unit of) measure
météo(rologie) *f.* weather 14
météorologique *adj.* weather
mettre to put; to place; to lay
    13
  ~ la table to set the table 13
  ~ le chauffage to turn on the
    heat 13
  se ~ à table to sit down to eat
    13
  Mettez …! Put …! CP
mexicain(e) Mexican 1
Mexico Mexico City
Mexique *m.* Mexico 5
miam! yum! 8

midi noon 5
le mien/la mienne mine 5
mieux better 11
   il vaut ~ que it is preferable that, it is better that 10
   j'aime le ~ I like best 11
mille *inv.* one thousand 3
milliard *m.* billion 3
million *m.* million 3
mince thin 1
   ~ ! darn it! 12
minuit midnight 5
minute *f.* minute 5
mobylette *f.* moped, motorized bicycle 3
moi me 1; I, me 6
   ~ aussi me too 2
   ~ non plus me neither 2
moins less 11
   au ~ at least 6
   j'aime le ~ I like least 11
   ~ le quart quarter to (the hour) 5
mois *m.* month 6
mon, ma, mes my 3
monde *m.* world 7
   tout le ~ everybody 4
monnaie *f.* change, coins 9
Monsieur (M.) Mr., Sir; man 1
monter to go up; to get into 7
montre *f.* watch 4
montrer to show 14
morceau *m.* (*pl.* **morceaux**) piece 8
mort *f.* death 15
mort(e) dead
mot *m.* word 6
   plus un ~ not one more word 10
moto *f.* motorcycle 3
mourir to die 7
moutarde *f.* mustard 8
musée *m.* museum 5
musique *f.* music 6
myrtille *f.* blueberry

nager to swim 2
naïf (naïve) naive 4
naître to be born 7
   je suis né(e) I was born 3
   né(e) born
nappe *f.* tablecloth 13
nationalité *f.* nationality 1

naturellement naturally 8
navire *m.* ship
ne (n') not 1
   ~ ... jamais never 4
   ~ ... pas not 1
   ~ ... personne no one, nobody, not anyone 15
   ~ ... plus no more, no longer 8
   ~ ... que only 11
   ~ ... rien nothing, not anything 6
   n'est-ce pas? right?; are you?; don't they?; etc. 2
nécessaire: il est ~ que it is necessary that 10
négritude *f.* negritude *(system of black cultural and spiritual values)*
neiger to snow 7
   il neige it's snowing CP, 7
nerveux (nerveuse) nervous 4
nettoyer to clean 6
neuf nine CP
neuf (neuve) brand-new 10
   quoi de neuf? what's new? 5
neveu *m.* (*pl.* **neveux**) nephew 3
nez *m.* nose 9
   le ~ qui coule runny nose 9
nièce *f.* niece 3
Noël *m.* Christmas 7
   le père ~ Santa Claus 1
noir(e) black 4
nom *m.* name CP, 1
   ~ de famille last name 1
   à quel ~ ...? in whose name ...? 12
nombre *m.* number 1
nommer to name
non no 1
non plus neither 6
nord *m.* north
note *f.* note; grade, mark 4
notre, nos our 3
nourrir to feed, to nourish
nous we 1; us 10; (to) us 14
nouveau/nouvel (nouvelle) (*m.pl.* **nouveaux**) new 4
novembre *m.* November 7
nuit *f.* night 1
   Bonne nuit. Pleasant dreams. 5
numéro (de téléphone) *m.* (telephone) number 4

obéir to obey 12
occidental(e) western
occupé(e) busy 6
s'occuper de to be busy with, to take care of 7
   occupe-toi de tes oignons! mind your own business! 11
octobre *m.* October 7
œil *m.* (*pl.* **yeux**) eye 9
   mon ~! my eye!, I don't believe it! 10
œuf *m.* egg 8
œuvre *f.* work
offrir to offer
oh là là! oh dear!, wow! 9
oignon *m.* onion 8
   occupe-toi de tes oignons! mind your own business! 11
oiseau *m.* bird 5
omelette *f.* omelet 8
on one, people, we, they, you 1
oncle *m.* uncle 3
onze eleven CP
or *m.* gold
orange *f.* orange *(fruit)* 4
   jus d' ~ *m.* orange juice 2
orange *adj. inv.* orange 4
orangina *m.* orange soda 2
ordinaire ordinary, everyday 4
ordinateur *m.* computer 3
ordre *m.* order
oreille *f.* ear 9
oriental(e) eastern
original(e) (*m.pl.* **originaux**) different; novel; original 14
ou or 1
où where 1
oublier to forget 6
ouest *m.* west
oui yes 1
ouvert(e) open 12
ouverture *f.* opening
   heures d'~ hours of business
ouvrier/ouvrière *m./f.* laborer 4
ouvrir to open
ouvrez la porte! open the door! CP

pain *m.* bread 8
   ~ grillé toast 8
pâle pale 15

pantalon *m.* (pair of) pants   4
papier *m.* paper   9
paquet *m.* package   9
par by; through   6
  ~ contre on the other hand
  ~ exemple for example   6
  ~ ici (come) this way, follow
    me   13
  ~ jour per day   5
parce que because   6
pardon: ~? pardon?, what did
    you say?   CP
  je vous demande ~ please ex-
    cuse me; I beg your pardon
    9
parents *m.pl.* parents; relatives
    3
paresseux (paresseuse) lazy   4
parfait(e) perfect   5
parking *m.* parking lot   5
parler to speak   2
  ~ de to tell about   7
  ~ fort to speak loudly   15
partie *f.* part
partir (de) to leave (from)   6
  à partir de from that time on
pas no, not
  ne ... ~ not   1
  ~ du tout! not at all!   1
  ~ encore not yet   2
  ~ grand-chose not much   5
  ~ trop bien not too well   2
passer to pass
  ~ un an to spend a year   3
  ~ un test to take a test   5
se passer to happen; to take place
passionnant(e) exciting   14
pastille *f.* lozenge   9
pâte dentifrice *f.* toothpaste   9
pâté *m.* pâté *(meat spread)*   8
patiemment patiently   10
patient(e) patient   4
patiner to skate   2
patinoire *f.* skating rink   10
pâtisserie *f.* pastry shop; pastry
    9
patrie *f.* homeland
patron/patronne *m./f.* boss   4
pauvre poor   4, 11
payer to pay (for)   9
pays *m.* country   5
Pays-Bas *m.pl.* Netherlands   5
pêche *f.* fishing
pédagogie *f.* education, teacher
    preparation   5

pendant for; during   6
  ~ que while   6
  ~ combien de temps ...? how
    long ...?   6
penser to think   8
  qu'en penses-tu? what do you
    think of it (of them)?   8
perdre to lose   9
  ~ patience to lose (one's) pa-
    tience   9
père *m.* father   2, 3
père Noël *m.* Santa Claus   1
permettre to allow
  **permettez-moi de me
    présenter** allow me to in-
    troduce myself   1
  vous permettez? may I?   1
permis de conduire *m.* driver's
    license   10
personnage *m.* character;
    individual
personne *f.* person *(male or
    female)*   1
  ne ... ~ no one, nobody, not
    anyone   15
personnellement personally
    10
pétanque *f.* lawn bowling   6
petit(e) small, short   1
  ~ ami(e) *m./f.* boyfriend/
    girlfriend   3
  petit déjeuner *m.* breakfast   8
  petite fille *f.* little girl   3
  petits pois *m.pl.* peas   8
petite-fille *f.* (*pl.* **petites-filles**)
    granddaughter   3
petit-fils *m.* (*pl.* **petits-fils**)
    grandson   3
petits-enfants *m.pl.* grand-
    children   3
peu (de) little, few   8
  un ~ a little bit   2
peuple *m.* people
peur *f.* fear
  avoir ~ to be afraid   8
peut-être maybe; perhaps   2
pharmacie *f.* pharmacy   5, 9
pharmacien/pharmacienne
    m./f. pharmacist
photo *f.* photograph   3
  sur la ~ in the picture   3
physique physical   15
piano *m.* piano   6
pièce *f.* room   3
pièce *f.* play   6

  ~ (de monnaie) coin   9
pied *m.* foot   9
pilote *m.* pilot   11
pilule *f.* pill   9
pique-nique *m.* picnic   12
piscine *f.* swimming pool   5
pitié *f.* pity
  avoir ~ (de) to have pity, to
    feel sorry (for)   10
pizza *f.* pizza   2
place *f.* seat; room; place   7
plaire to please
  s'il vous plaît please   2
plaisir *m.* pleasure
  Au plaisir. See you again.   5
  avec ~ with pleasure   2
plan *m.* map (city; house)
plancher *m.* floor   13
plat *m.* course, dish   8
plein(e) full
pleurer to cry   2
pleuvoir to rain   7
  il pleut it's raining   CP, 7
  il pleuvait it was raining   11
plupart *f.* majority
  la ~ (de) most (of)   6
plus more   11
  il n'y en a ~ there is (are) no
    more   12
  le/la/les ~ ... the most ...   11
  moi non ~ nor I, me neither
    6
  ne ... ~ no more, no longer   8
plusieurs several
poème *m.* poem   6
pois *m.pl.*: **petits ~** peas   8
poisson *m.* fish   2
poivre *m.* pepper   13
police *f.* police (force)
  agent de ~ police officer   15
politique *f.* politics   2; policy
politique: homme/femme ~
    m./f. politician   4
pomme *f.* apple   8
pomme de terre *f.* potato   8
populaire popular   11
porc *m.* pork   8
porte *f.* door   1
porter to wear; to carry   4
portugais(e) Portuguese   5
poser une question to ask a
    question   12
possession *f.* possession   3
postale: carte ~ *f.* postcard   4
poste *f.* post office; mail

bureau de ~ *m.* post office 5
poster to mail 7
pouce *m.* thumb
  faire du ~ to hitchhike *(French-Canadian)*
poulet *m.* chicken 8
pour for, in order to 2
  ~ ce qui est de with respect to
pourquoi why 2
  ~ pas? why not? 6
pourvoir to provide
pouvoir *m.* power
pouvoir *v.* to be able; to be allowed 10; can
  je peux I can 9
  on peut one can 9
  pouvez-vous me dire …? can you tell me …? 9
  pourriez-vous …? could you …? 12
  puis-je …? may I …? 12
préciser to specify
préféré(e) favorite 11
préférence *f.*: **de ~** preferably
préférer to prefer 8
  je préfère que I prefer that 10
premier (première) first 5
  en première in first class 12
prendre to take; to eat, to drink 8
  prenez …! take …! CP
prénom *m.* first name 1
préparer (un cours) to prepare (a lesson) 6
près (de) near 1
  tout ~ very near 12
présenter to introduce
  je vous présente … let me introduce you to … 3
presque almost 14
prêter to lend 14
prie: je vous en ~ you're welcome 7
printemps *m.* spring 7
prise de conscience *f.* awareness
prix *m.* price 12
problème *m.* problem
  Pas de problème! No problem!
prochain(e) next 5
  À la prochaine. Until next time. 5
proche near; close
produit *m.* product; article

professeur (prof) *m.* teacher *(male or female)* 1
profession *f.* profession, occupation
promenade *f.* walk; ride 4
  faire une ~ to take a walk; to take a ride 4
se promener to take a walk, ride 13
promettre to promise
  c'est promis it's a promise 10
propos: à ~ de regarding, on the subject of 8
propre clean 4; specific; own
propriétaire *m./f.* owner 10
provisions *f.pl.* groceries 4
  faire les ~ to do the grocery shopping 4
provoquer to cause
prudemment prudently 10
prudent(e) cautious 10
publicité *f.* publicity; commercial 14
puis then; next 4
puis-je …? may I …? 12
puisque since
pull-over (pull) *m.* sweater 4
pyjama *m.* (pair of) pajamas 13

quand when 4
quantité *f.* quantity
quarante forty 3
quart quarter
  et ~ quarter past, quarter after 5
  moins le ~ quarter to, quarter till 5
quatorze fourteen CP
quatre four CP, 1
quatre-vingt-dix ninety 3
quatre-vingt-onze ninety-one 3
quatre-vingt-un eight-one 3
quatre-vingts eighty 3
que that
  ~ …? what …? 4
  ne … ~ only 11
quel(le) …? which …? 4
  quel âge avez-vous? how old are you? 3
  quel jour est-ce? what day is it? 5
  quelle …! what a …! 2

quelle est votre nationalité? what is your nationality? 1
quelle heure est-il? what time is it? 5
quelque chose *m.* something 2
quelquefois sometimes 4
quelques a few; some 8
quelqu'un someone 2
qu'est-ce que/qui what? 4
  qu'est-ce que c'est? what is this? what is it? 4
  qu'est-ce que vous avez comme …? what do you have for (in the way of) …? 8
  qu'est-ce qu'il y a …? what is there …? what's the matter? 3
  qu'est-ce que tu aimes? what do you like? 2
  qu'est-ce que vous voulez? what do you want? 2
qui who 1
  qu'est-ce ~ …? what …? 4
quinze fifteen CP
  ~ jours two weeks 11
quoi what
  il n'y a pas de ~ don't mention it, you're welcome 13
  ~ de neuf? what's new? 5

raconter to tell 14
radio *f.* radio 2
raison *f.* reason
  avoir ~ to be right 8
raisonnable reasonable 10
ralentir to slow down 12
rapide rapid, fast 10
rapidement rapidly 10
rarement rarely 4
ravi(e) delighted 14
récemment recently 6
recette *f.* recipe
recommander to recommend 12
reculer to back up 10
récuser to exclude; to challenge
réduire to reduce
réfrigérateur *m.* refrigerator 3
refuser to refuse
regarder to watch; to look at 2
regretter to be sorry 14
  je regrette I'm sorry 8

relief *m.* relief, hilly area
remarquer to notice   6
remercier to thank   12
remplacer to replace
rencontrer to meet   5, 14
rendez-vous *m.* meeting; date   5
  avoir ~ to have an appointment, meeting
rendre to give back   9
  ~ visite à qqn to visit someone   9
renseignement *m.* item of information   12
(se) renseigner to inform (oneself); to find out about
rentrer to go (come) back; to go (come) home   7
repas *m.* meal   8
répéter to repeat; to practice   8
  répétez, s'il vous plaît please repeat   CP
répondre (à) to answer   9
  répondez answer   CP
se reposer to rest   13
RER *m.* train to Paris suburbs   2
réserver to reserve   9
résidence (universitaire) *f.* dormitory   5
responsabilité *f.* responsibility   11
restaurant *m.* restaurant   5
rester to stay   5; to remain
  il vous reste ...? do you still have ...?   12
résultat *m.* result; outcome
retard *m.* delay
  en ~ late   7
retour *m.* return
  aller- ~ round-trip ticket   12
retourner to go back, to return   7
rétroviseur *m.* rearview mirror   10
réunion *f.* meeting   13
réussir (à) to succeed; to pass (a test)   12
se réveiller to wake up   13
revenant *m.* ghost   14
revenir to come back   7
revoir to see again
  au ~ good-bye   1
rez-de-chaussée *m.* ground floor   12
rhume *m.* cold *(illness)*   9
riche rich   12

ridicule ridiculous   14
rien nothing
  de ~ you're welcome; don't mention it, not at all   12
  ne ... ~ nothing, not anything   6
riz *m.* rice   8
robe *f.* dress   4
  ~ de mariée wedding dress   11
robinet *m.* faucet   6
roi *m.* king
roman *m.* novel   6
  ~ policier detective story   6
rose *adj.* pink   4
rôti (de bœuf) *m.* (beef) roast   9
rouge red   4
rouler to roll; to move *(vehicle)*; to go   15
route *f.* route, way, road   10, 12
roux (rousse) red(-haired)   4
rue *f.* street   9
rugby *m.* rugby   6
russe Russian   1
Russie *f.* Russia   5

sa *(see* **son***)*
s'agir to be about
il s'agit de it's a matter of
s'amuser to have a good time; to have fun   6
saison *f.* season   7
salade *f.* salad   8
  ~ (verte) (green) salad   8
sale dirty   4
salle *f.* room
  ~ à manger dining room   3
  ~ de bain(s) bathroom   3
  ~ de classe classroom   P, 5
  ~ de séjour living room; den   3
salon *m.* living room   3
salut! hi!   1; bye (-bye)   5
salutation *f.* greeting
samedi *m.* Saturday   5
sandwich *m.* sandwich   8
sans without   6
  ~ blague! no kidding   14
  ~ doute probably   3
  ~ façon honestly, no kidding   8
santé *f.* health
  à votre ~! (here's) to your health!; cheers!   2

sardine *f.* sardine   9
saucisse *f.* sausage   9
saumon *m.* salmon   8
savoir to know   12
  je ne sais pas I don't know   2
saxophone *m.* saxophone   6
sciences *f.pl.* science   5
  ~ économiques economics   5
scolaire *adj.* school
  année ~ *f.* school year   10
se oneself   6
sec (sèche) dry
second(e) second
  en seconde in (by) second class   12
seize sixteen   CP
séjour *m.* stay
sel *m.* salt   13
semaine *f.* week   5
semestre *m.* semester   6
Sénégal *m.* Senegal   5
sénégalais(e) Senegalese   1
sens interdit *m.* one-way street   10
(se) sentir to feel
se séparar to separate (from each other)   14
sept seven   CP
septembre *m.* September   7
sérieusement seriously   10
sérieux (sérieuse) serious   10
serveur/serveuse *m./f.* waiter/waitress   8
service *m.* service
  à votre ~ at your service
serviette *f.* towel   12; napkin   13
ses *(see* **son***)*
seul(e) alone; only   5
  un ~ a single
seulement only   2
short *m.* (pair of) shorts   4
si *conj.* if   3
  s'il vous plaît please   2
si *adv.* so   10
si! yes!   3
siècle *m.* century   10
sieste *f.* nap   4
  faire la ~ to take a nap   4
simple simple, plain   4
  c'est bien simple it's quite easy
simple: aller ~ one-way ticket   12
sincère sincere   11

se situer to be situated
six six   CP
skier to ski   2
skis *m.pl.* skis   13
smoking *m.* tuxedo   11
SNCF *f.* French railroad system   2
sœur *f.* sister   3
sofa *m.* sofa   3
soif: avoir ~ to be thirsty   8
soir *m.* evening   1
  ce ~ tonight   5
  tous les soirs every night   6
soirée *f.* party   13; evening
soixante sixty   3
soixante et onze seventy-one   3
soixante-dix seventy   3
soixante-douze seventy-two   3
soleil *m.* sun   7
  Il fait du soleil. It's sunny.   CP
son, sa, ses his, her, its   3
sorte *f.* kind   8
  quelle(s) sorte(s) de ...? what kind(s) of ...?   8
  toutes sortes de choses all kinds of things   9
sortir to go out   6
  je vais ~ I'm going to go out   5
  sortez! leave!   CP
souci *m.* worry; care   11
souffler to blow
souhaiter (que) to wish; to hope (that)   13
soupe *f.* soup   8
sourire *m.* smile   13
sourire *v.* to smile   13
souris *f.* mouse   5
sous under   5
sous-sol *m.* basement   3
se souvenir (de) to remember   13
souvent often   2
sportif (sportive) athletic   4
statue *f.* statue   11
steak *m.* steak
  ~ -frites steak with French fries   15
stéréo *f.* stereo   3
stop *m.* stop sign   10
sucre *m.* sugar   13
sud *m.* south
Suède *f.* Sweden   5
suédois(e) Swedish   1

Suisse *f.* Switzerland   5
suisse *adj.* Swiss   1
suite: tout de ~ right away   1
suivant(e) following, next   7
superficie *f.* area
supermarché *m.* supermarket   9
supplément *m.* extra charge; supplement   12
sur on   3
sûr(e) sure
  bien ~ of course   8
sûrement surely, definitely   14
surveiller to watch
sweat-shirt *m.* sweatshirt   4

TGV *m.* very fast train   7
tabac *m.* tobacco; tobacco shop   9
  bureau de ~ tobacco shop   5
table *f.* table   1
  à ~ at dinner, at the table   6
tableau *m.* chalkboard   CP
se taire to be quiet
  tais-toi! (taisez-vous!) keep quiet!   10
tant so much; so many   6
tante *f.* aunt   3
tard late   6
tarder to be a long time coming   13
tarte *f.* pie   8
tasse *f.* cup   2
taux *m.* rate
tchao bye   5
te you   10; (to) you   14
tee-shirt *m.* tee-shirt   4
téléphone *m.* telephone   1
  au ~ on the telephone   6
téléphoner (à) to telephone   6
télévision (télé) *f.* television   2
témoin *m.* witness   15
temps *m.* time   6; weather   4
  emploi du ~ *m.* schedule   4
  quel ~ fait-il? what is the weather like?   4
tendance *f.* tendency, trend
  avoir ~ à to tend to   12
tennis *m.* tennis   2
  jouer au ~ to play tennis   2
  tennis *f.pl.* tennis shoes   4
tentation *f.* temptation
terre *f.* earth   9
tête *f.* head   9
thé *m.* tea   2

théâtre *m.* theater
Tiens! Well! Gee!   3
timbre *m.* stamp   9
toi you   4
toilettes *f.pl.* restroom   3, 5
toit *m.* roof   5
tomate *f.* tomato   8
tomber to fall   2
ton, ta, tes your   3
tort *m.* wrong
  avoir ~ to be wrong; to be unwise   8
tôt early   6
toujours always   4; still
toupet *m.* nerve
tour *f.* tower   11
tour *m.* turn, tour   11
tourner to turn   7
Toussaint *f.* All Saints' Day
tousser to cough   9
tout/toute/tous/toutes *adj.* all; every; the whole   12
  tous les deux (toutes les deux) both   12
  tous les soirs every night   6
  toute la famille the whole family   11
  tout le monde everybody   CP, 4
  tout le week-end all weekend (long)   5
tout *adv.* completely; very   12
  ~ à l'heure a little while ago, in a little while   5
  ~ de suite right away   12
  À ~ de suite. See you very soon.
  ~ près very near   7
tout *pron. inv.* all, everything
  pas du ~ ! not at all!   1
train *m.* train   3
  être en ~ de to be in the process of   11
tranche *f.* slice   8
tranquille calm   10
travail (manuel) *m.* (manual) work   4
travailler to work   2
travailleur (travailleuse) hardworking   4
travers: à ~ throughout
treize thirteen   CP
tremblement de terre *m.* earthquake
trente thirty   3

très very 1
triste sad 4
trois three CP, 1
trompette *f.* trumpet 6
trop (de) too much, too many 3
trouver to find, to be of the opinion 2
  se ~ to be located
  où se trouve (se trouvent) ...? where is (are) ...? 5
  vous trouvez? do you think so? 2
truite *f.* trout 8
tu you *(familiar)* 1
tuer to kill 15

un(e) one CP, 1; one, a, an 3
union *f.:* **~ douanière** customs union
unique unique
  enfant ~ *m./f.* only child
université *f.* university 1
universitaire *(adj.)* university 5

vacances *f.pl.* vacation 6
  bonnes ~! have a good vacation! 6
  en ~ on vacation 6
vaisselle *f.* dishes 4
valeur *f.* value
valise *f.* suitcase
valoir mieux (il vaut mieux) to be better 10
valse *f.* waltz 6
vanille *f.:* **glace à la ~** *f.* vanilla ice cream 8
vaut: il ~ mieux que it is preferable that, it is better that 10
vélo *m.* bicycle 3
vendeur/vendeuse *m./f.* salesman/saleswoman 4
vendre to sell 9
vendredi *m.* Friday 5
venir to come 7

  ~ de ... to have just ... 7
d'où venez-vous? where do you come from? 7
je viens de ... I come from ... 2
vent *m.* wind
  il fait du ~ it's windy CP, 7
véranda *f.* porch 3
vérité *f.* truth 14
verre *m.* glass 2
vers toward 5
  ~ (8 heures) approximately, around (8 o'clock) 5
verser to pour 13
vert(e) green 4
veste *f.* sportcoat 4
vêtement *m.* article of clothing 4
veuf/veuve *m./f.* widower/widow 1
veux *(see* **vouloir***)*
viande *f.* meat 8
victime *f.* victim 7
vie *f.* life 4
  c'est la ~ that's life 6
  gagner sa ~ to earn one's living
vieux/vieil (vieille) old 1
ville *f.* city 4, 5; town
vin *m.* wine 2
vingt twenty CP
vingt et un twenty-one CP
vingt-deux twenty-two CP
violet(te) purple 4
violon *m.* violin 6
visite: rendre ~ à to visit (a person) 9
visiter to visit (a place)
vite quickly 10
vitesse *f.* speed 10
  à toute ~ at top speed 10
vivement eagerly
voici here is; here are 3
voilà there is; there are 1
voir to see 14
  tu vas voir you're going to see 5

tu vois you see 11
voisin/voisine *m./f.* neighbor 11
voiture *f.* automobile 3
  en ~ by car 7
voix *f.* voice 7
vol *m.* flight 12
volant *m.* steering wheel 10
volontiers gladly 2
votre, vos your 1
vôtre: à la ~! (here's) to yours! (to your health!) 2
vouloir to want, to wish 10
  ... veut dire ... ... means ... CP, 6
  je veux bien gladly; yes, thanks 2
  je veux que I want 10
  je voudrais I would like 2, 10
vous you *(formal)* 1; (to) you 14
voyage *m.* trip, voyage 5
  chèque de ~ *m.* traveler's check 9
  faire un ~ to take a trip 5
voyager to travel 2
vrai(e) true 2
vraiment really 2

week-end *m.* weekend 5
  tout le ~ all weekend (long) 5
wolof *m.* Wolof *(language)* 5

y there 7
  allez- ~ go ahead 12
  il y a there is (are) 3
yeux *m.pl.* eyes 4, 9

zéro zero CP, 3
Zut! Darn! 12, 15

Vocabulaire

This vocabulary list includes only the active words and phrases listed in the *Vocabulaire actif* sections. Only those French equivalents that occur in the text are given. Expressions are listed according to the key word. The symbol ~ indicates repetition of the key word.

The following abbreviations are used.

adj.	adjective	*m.pl.*	masculine plural
adv.	adverb	*n.*	noun
conj.	conjunction	*pl.*	plural
f.	feminine	*prep.*	preposition
f.pl.	feminine plural	*pron.*	pronoun
inv.	invariable	*v.*	verb
m.	masculine		

a, an un(e)
able: be ~ pouvoir
about de; environ
   ~ 8:00 vers 8 heures
   ~ it (them) en
   hear ~ entendre parler de
absolutely absolument
accept accepter
accident accident *m.*
accompany accompagner
according to d'après
accordion accordéon *m.*
accounting comptabilité *f.*
acquainted: be ~ with connaître
activity activité *f.*
actor/actress acteur/actrice *m./f.*
address *n.* adresse *f.*
adore adorer
advance *v.* avancer
advertisement annonce *f.*
advice (piece of) conseil *m.*
afraid: be ~ avoir peur
after après
afternoon après-midi *m.*
  in the ~ de l'après-midi
again encore
against contre
age âge *m.*

ago il y a ...
agree (with) être d'accord (avec)
   agreed entendu
ahead: go ~ allez-y
   straight ~ tout droit
air conditioning climatisation *f.*
airplane avion *m.*
airport aéroport *m.*
all *pron./adj.* tout (toute/tous/toutes)
   ~ weekend (long) tout le weekend
   not at ~! pas du tout!
allow permettre
   ~ me to introduce myself permettez-moi de me présenter
almost presque
alone seul(e)
   leave me ~! laisse-moi (laissez-moi) tranquille!
already déjà
also aussi
always toujours
   not ~ pas toujours
American *adj.* américain(e)
amusing *adj.* amusant(e)
anchovy anchois *m.*

and et
angry fâché(e)
   get ~ se fâcher
answer répondre (à)
anyone quelqu'un
   not ~ ne ... personne
anything quelque chose *m.*
   not ~ ne ... rien
apartment appartement *m.*
appear avoir l'air
appetizer hors-d'œuvre *m.inv.*
apple pomme *f.*
appointment rendez-vous *m.*
   have an ~ avoir rendez-vous
approximately environ; vers *(time)*
April avril *m.*
Arabic arabe *m.*
argue se disputer
arm bras *m.*
armchair fauteuil *m.*
around environ; vers *(time)*; autour de *(place)*
   ~ (8 o'clock) vers (huit heures)
arrive arriver
artist artiste *m./f.*
as aussi, comme
   ~ ... ~ aussi ... que

~ **much** autant (de)
ashamed confus(e)
ask demander
  ~ **a question** poser une
    question
asleep: fall ~ s'endormir
aspirin tablet cachet d'aspirine
  m.
assure assurer
at à
  ~ **first** d'abord
  ~ **midnight** à minuit
  ~ **noon** à midi
  ~ **... o'clock** à ... heure(s)
  ~ **the home of** chez
athletic sportif (sportive)
attach attacher
attend assister (à)
attention: pay ~ faire attention
attentive attentif (attentive)
August août *m.*
aunt tante *f.*
automobile voiture *f.*
away: right ~ tout de suite
awful! berk!

baby bébé *m.*
back *n.* dos *m.*
back *adv.*: **go** ~ retourner; rentrer
  ~ **then** à cette époque
  come ~ revenir
  give ~ rendre
back up reculer
bad mauvais(e)
  ~ **driver** chauffard *m.*
  that's (it's) too ~ c'est
    dommage
  the weather is ~ il fait
    mauvais
badly mal
bakery boulangerie *f.*
bald chauve
ball (dance) bal *m.*
bank banque *f.*
bar and café bistro *m.*
basement sous-sol *m.*
basketball basket-ball (basket) *m.*
bathing suit maillot de bain *m.*
bathroom salle de bain *f.*
be être
  ~ **a long time coming** tarder
  ~ **able** pouvoir
  ~ **acquainted with, familiar**
    with connaître
  ~ **afraid** avoir peur

~ **born** naître
~ **cold** avoir froid
~ **fed up** en avoir assez
~ **hot** avoir chaud
~ **hungry** avoir faim
~ **in the process of** être en
  train de
~ **interested in** s'intéresser à
~ **located** se trouver
~ **necessary** falloir (il faut)
~ **of the opinion** trouver
~ **probably, supposed** devoir
~ **right** avoir raison
~ **sleepy** avoir sommeil
~ **sore** avoir mal (à)
~ **sorry** regretter
~ **thirsty** avoir soif
~ **wrong, unwise** avoir tort
beans haricots *m.pl.*
Beaujolais *(wine)* beaujolais *m.*
beautiful beau/bel/belle/beaux/
  belles
because parce que
become devenir
bed lit *m.*
  go to ~ se coucher
bedroom chambre *f.*
beef bœuf *m.*
beer bière *f.*
before avant
begin commencer
behind derrière; en retard
  right ~ juste derrière
beige beige
Belgian belge
Belgium Belgique *f.*
believe (in) croire (à)
  I don't ~ **it!** mon œil!
belong to être à
belt ceinture *f.*
  safety ~, **seat** ~ ceinture de
    sécurité *f.*
beside à côté (de)
best *adv.* mieux; *adj.* le/la
  meilleur(e)
  ~ **friend** meilleur(e) ami(e)
    m./f.
  I like ~ j'aime le mieux (le
    plus); je préfère
  ~ **regards** avec mon meilleur
    souvenir
better *adv.* mieux; *adj.*
  meilleur(e)
  it is ~ **that** il vaut mieux que
between entre

~ **friends** entre amis
beverage boisson *f.*
bicycle vélo *m.*
big grand(e), gros(se)
bill *n.* *(paper money)* billet *m.*;
  (restaurant check) addition *f.*
billion milliard *m.*
bird oiseau *m.*
birthday anniversaire *m.*
bistro bistro *m.*
black noir(e)
  ~ **currant liqueur** crème de
    cassis *f.*
blond blond(e)
blouse chemisier *m.*
blue bleu(e)
body corps *m.*
book livre *m.*
bookstore librairie *f.*
boots bottes *f.pl.*
Bordeaux *(wine)* bordeaux *m.*
boring ennuyeux (ennuyeuse)
born né(e)
  be ~ naître
borrow emprunter
boss patron (patronne) *m./f.*
both tous les deux (toutes les
  deux)
bother déranger
bottle bouteille *f.*
bowl *n.* bol *m.*
bowling: lawn ~ pétanque *f.*
box boîte *f.*
boy garçon *m.*
boyfriend petit ami *m.*
brake *v.* freiner
brand *n.* marque *f.*
brand-new neuf (neuve)
bread pain *m.*
breakfast petit déjeuner *m.*
bridge *(game)* bridge *m.*
Brie *(cheese)* brie *m.*
bring apporter
broccoli brocoli *m.*
brother frère *m.*
brother-in-law beau-frère *m.* *(pl.*
  beaux-frères)
brown brun(e); marron
brush *n.* brosse *f.*
  tooth ~ brosse à dents *f.*
brush *v.* se brosser
building bâtiment *m.*
burn brûler
business affaires *f.pl.*, commerce
  m.

mind your own ~! occupe-toi de tes oignons!
businessman/woman homme/femme d'affaires *m./f.*
busy occupé(e)
  be ~ with s'occuper de
but mais
butcher shop boucherie *f.*
  pork butcher's charcuterie *f.*
butter beurre *m.*
  peanut ~ beurre d'arachide *m.*
buy acheter
by par
  ~ car en voiture
  ~ chance par hasard
  ~ the way ... au fait ...
bye salut; tchao

café café *m.*, bistro *m.*
cafeteria cafétéria *f.*
cake gâteau *m.* (*pl.* gâteaux)
calculator calculatrice *f.*
call appeler, téléphoner
  your ~ from ... votre communication de ...
called: be ~ s'appeler
calm calme, tranquille
Camembert (*cheese*) camembert *m.*
campus campus *m.*
can *n.* boîte *f.*
can (be able to) *v.* pouvoir
Canada Canada *m.*
Canadian canadien(ne)
candy bonbon *m.*
car voiture *f.*
  by ~ en voiture
card carte *f.*
  credit ~ carte de crédit
  post ~ carte postale
cards (*game*) cartes *f.pl.*
care *n.* souci *m.*
  take ~ of s'occuper de
care *v.*: **I don't ~** cela (ça) m'est égal
carry porter
cartoon dessin animé *m.*
cat chat *m.*
cautious prudent(e)
centime centime *m.*
century siècle *m.*
cereal céréales *f.pl.*
certain sûr(e)
certainly tout à fait; certainement

chair chaise *f.*
chalk craie *f.*
chalkboard tableau *m.*
chance hasard *m.*
  by ~ par hasard
change *n.* monnaie *f.*
change *v.* changer (de)
channel: TV ~ chaîne (de télé) *f.*
charge: extra ~ supplément *m.*
charming charmant(e)
cheap bon marché *adj. inv.*
check chèque *m.*
  traveler's ~ chèque de voyage *m.*
  ~ (restaurant bill) addition *f.*
checkers dames *f.pl.*
cheese fromage *m.*
chemistry chimie *f.*
chess échecs *m.pl.*
chewing gum chewing-gum *m.*
chic chic *adj. inv.*
chicken poulet *m.*
child enfant *m./f.*
China Chine *f.*
Chinese chinois(e)
chocolate: hot ~ chocolat chaud *m.*
choice choix *m.*
choose choisir
Christmas Noël *m.*
church église *f.*
cigar cigare *m.*
cigarette cigarette *f.*
city ville *f.*
civil servant fonctionnaire *m./f.*
class cours *m.*, classe *f.*
  in ~ en classe
  in first ~ en première classe
classroom salle de classe *f.*
clean *v.* nettoyer
clean propre
close *adj.* près (de)
close *v.* fermer
closed fermé(e)
clothing (article of) vêtement *m.*
coat manteau *m.* (*pl.* manteaux)
Coca-Cola coca *m.*
coffee café *m.*
coin pièce (de monnaie) *f.*
cold (*illness*) *n.* rhume *m.*
cold *adj.* froid(e)
  be ~ avoir froid
  it's ~ il fait froid
collide entrer en collision
color couleur *f.*

what ~ is (are) ...? de quelle couleur est (sont) ...?
come venir
  ~ back revenir, rentrer
  ~ in! entrez!
  where do you ~ from? d'où venez-vous?
comfortable confortable
comic strip bande dessinée *f.*
commentary commentaire *m.*
commercial *n.* publicité *f.*
complete complet (complète)
completely tout *inv. adv.*; complètement
computer ordinateur *m.*
  ~ science informatique *f.*
confirm confirmer
console oneself se consoler
constant constant(e)
constantly constamment
contrary contraire *m.*
  on the ~ au contraire
cooking cuisine *f.*
cool: it's ~ il fait frais
corner coin *m.*
corridor couloir *m.*
cost *v.* coûter
cough *v.* tousser
could you ...? pourriez-vous ...?
country pays *m.*
course (*classroom*) cours *m.*; (*meal*) plat *m.*
  of ~ certainement, bien sûr
cousin cousin/cousine *m./f.*
crazy fou (folle)
  ~ person fou/folle *m./f.*
  in a ~ manner follement
cream crème *f.*
credit card carte de crédit *f.*
croissant croissant *m.*
cry *v.* pleurer
cup tasse *f.*
custom coutume *f.*
cut *v.* couper
cyclist coureur (cycliste)

dance *n.* bal *m.*
dance *v.* danser
dangerous dangereux (dangereuse)
darn it! mince!; zut!
date *n.* date *f.*; rendez-vous *m.*
date (someone) *v.* fréquenter (quelqu'un)

daughter fille *f.*
day jour *m.*
   ~ after tomorrow après-
     demain
   have a good ~ bonne journée
   New Year's ~ Jour de l'An *m.*
   what ~ is it? quel jour est-ce?
dead mort(e)
dear *n.* chéri/chérie *m./f.*
dear *adj.* cher (chère)
death mort *f.*
debt dette *f.*
December décembre *m.*
definitely sûrement,
   certainement
delicatessen charcuterie *f.*
delicious délicieux (délicieuse)
delighted ravi(e)
demand (that) exiger (que)
department store grand
   magasin *m.*
departmental (local) highway
   départementale *f.*
departure départ *m.*
depend dépendre
   it (that) depends ça dépend
depressed déprimé(e)
describe décrire
desk bureau *m.* (*pl.* bureaux)
dessert dessert *m.*
detective story roman policier
   m.
detest détester
die mourir
different original(e) (*m.pl.*
   originaux); différent(e)
dining room salle à manger *f.*
dinner dîner *m.*
   at ~ à table
   have ~ dîner
diploma diplôme *m.*
directions indications *f.pl.*
dirty sale
disappointed déçu(e)
discreet discret (discrète)
dish plat *m.*
dishes vaisselle *f.*
   do the ~ faire la vaisselle
dishwasher lave-vaisselle *m.*
divorce *n.* divorce *m.*
divorce *v.* divorcer
divorced divorcé(e)
do faire
   ~ the grocery shopping faire
     les provisions

what am I going to ~?
   comment je vais faire?
doctor médecin *m.*, docteur *m.*
dog chien *m.*
dollar dollar *m.*
door porte *f.*
dormitory résidence
   (universitaire) *f.*
dozen douzaine *f.*
dress *n.* robe *f.*
   wedding ~ robe de mariée *f.*
dressed: get ~ s'habiller
drink *n.* boisson *f.*
   before-dinner ~ apéritif *m.*
drink *v.* boire, prendre
   do you want to ~ something?
     voulez-vous boire quelque
     chose?; quelque chose à
     boire?
drive *n.:* **to take a ~** faire une
   promenade en voiture   4
drive conduire
driver automobiliste *m./f.*,
   conducteur/conductrice *m./f.*,
   chauffeur *m.*
   ~ 's license permis de conduire
     m.
drums batterie *f.*
drunk *adj.* ivre
during pendant

each chaque
each one chacun(e)
ear oreille *f.*
early tôt, en avance
earn one's living gagner sa vie
earth terre *f.*
easy facile; simple
eat manger, prendre
   ~ dinner dîner
   ~ lunch déjeuner
economics sciences économiques
   f.pl.
education pédagogie *f.*
egg œuf *m.*
eight huit
eighteen dix-huit
eighty quatre-vingts
eighty-one quatre-vingt-un
eleven onze
embarrassed confus(e)
employee employé/employée
   m./f.
end *n.* fin *f.*

engaged fiancé(e)
engagement fiançailles *f.pl.*
engineer ingénieur *m.*
England Angleterre *f.*
English anglais(e)
enough assez
enter entrer
errands courses *f.pl.*
essential essentiel(le)
   it is ~ that il est essentiel que
even même
evening soir *m.*
   good ~ bonsoir
ever jamais
every chaque; tout (toute/tous/
   toutes)
   ~ night tous les soirs
everybody tout le monde
everything tout *pron. inv.*
exaggerate exagérer
exam examen *m.*
   on an ~ à un examen
example exemple *m.*
   for ~ par exemple
excellent excellent(e)
exciting passionnant(e)
excuse: ~ me je vous demande
   pardon; excusez-moi
executive cadre *m.*
exercise exercice *m.*
expensive cher (chère)
eye œil *m.* (*pl.* yeux)
   my ~! mon œil!
eyeglasses lunettes *f.pl.*

fall *n.* automne *m.*
fall *v.* tomber
   ~ asleep s'endormir
false faux (fausse)
familiar: be ~ with connaître
family famille *f.*
famous célèbre
fantastic formidable
far (from) loin (de)
farmer fermier/fermière *m./f.*
fast rapide
fat gros(se), gras(se)
father père *m.*
father-in-law beau-père *m.* (*pl.*
   beaux-pères)
faucet robinet *m.*
fault faute *f.*
favorite préféré(e)
fear peur

February février *m.*
fed up: be ~ en avoir assez
feel sentir, se sentir
　~ like avoir envie de
　~ sorry (for someone) avoir
　　pitié (de)
fever fièvre *f.*
few peu (de)
　a ~ quelques
fifteen quinze
fifty cinquante
film film *m.*
finally enfin
find *v.* trouver
fine bien
　I'm ~ je vais très bien; ça va
　　bien
finish finir
first premier (première)
　~ name prénom *m.*
　at ~ d'abord
　in ~ class en première classe
fish *n.* poisson *m.*
five cinq
flea market marché aux puces
　m.
Flemish flamand *m.*
flight vol *m.*
flight attendant (female) hôtesse
　de l'air *f.*
floor (of a building) étage *m.*; (of a
　room) plancher *m.*
　ground ~ rez-de-chaussée *m.*
florist fleuriste *m./f.*
flower fleur *f.*
flu grippe *f.*
fluently couramment
flute flûte *f.*
follow: ~ me par ici
following suivant(e)
food cuisine *f.*
fool fou/folle *m./f.*
foot pied *m.*
football football américain *m.*
for depuis; pendant; pour
foreign étranger (étrangère)
forget oublier
fork fourchette *f.*
fortunately heureusement
forty quarante
four quatre
fourteen quatorze
franc franc *m.*
France France *f.*
free libre

French français(e)
　~ fries frites *f.pl.*
　in ~ en français
　in the ~ style à la française
　steak with ~ fries steak-frites
　　m.
Friday vendredi
friend ami/amie *m./f.*
　make friends se faire des amis
from de
front: in ~ of devant
fruit fruit *m.*
fun amusant(e)
　have ~ s'amuser
funny amusant(e), drôle

game jeu *m.* (*pl.* jeux), match *m.*
garage garage *m.*
garlic ail *m.*
Gee! Tiens!
general: in ~ en général
generally généralement
generous généreux (généreuse)
German allemand(e)
Germany Allemagne *f.*
get obtenir, recevoir
　~ along (with) s'entendre
　　(avec)
　~ angry se fâcher
　~ dressed s'habiller
　~ into monter
　~ out of descendre
　~ up, stand up se lever
　~ washed, wash up se laver
ghost revenant *m.*
gift cadeau *m.*
girl fille *f.*
girlfriend petite amie *f.*
give donner
　~ back rendre
gladly volontiers; je veux bien
glass (drinking) verre *m.*
glasses (eye) lunettes *f.pl.*
gloves gants *m.pl.*
go aller, rouler (in a vehicle)
　~ across traverser
　~ ahead allez-y
　~ back retourner, rentrer
　~ down descendre
　~ into town aller en ville
　~ out sortir
　~ to bed se coucher
　~ up monter
goat cheese chèvre *m.*

golf golf *m.*
good bon (bonne)
　~ evening bonsoir
　~ morning bonjour
　have a ~ day bonne journée
　have a ~ time s'amuser
good-bye au revoir
grade note *f.*
grains céréales *f.pl.*
grandchildren petits-enfants
　m.pl.
granddaughter petite-fille *f.* (*pl.*
　petites-filles)
grandfather grand-père *m.* (*pl.*
　grands-pères)
grandmother grand-mère *f.* (*pl.*
　grands-mères)
grandparents grands-parents
　m.pl.
grandson petit-fils *m.* (*pl.* petits-
　fils)
great formidable; chouette (*fam.*)
great-grandfather arrière-
　grand-père *m.*
green vert(e)
　~ beans haricots verts *m.pl.*
grey gris(e)
groceries provisions *f.pl.*
　do the grocery shopping faire
　　les provisions
guess deviner
grocery store épicerie *f.*
guitar guitare *f.*
gymnasium gymnase *m.*
gymnastics gymnastique *f.*

hair cheveux *m.pl.*
　hairbrush brosse à cheveux *f.*
half *adj.* demi(e)
　~ past ... il est ... heure(s) et
　　demie
hall couloir *m.*
ham jambon *m.*
hand main *f.*
handsome beau/bel/belle/beaux/
　belles
happen arriver, se passer
happy heureux (heureuse);
　content(e)
hard-working travailleur
　(travailleuse)
hat chapeau *m.*
hate *v.* détester
have avoir

~ an appointment, date avoir rendez-vous

~ a pain (in) avoir mal (à)

~ dinner dîner

~ fun s'amuser

~ just venir de

~ lunch déjeuner

~ pity avoir pitié (de)

~ to devoir

do you still ~ ...? il vous reste ...?

what do you ~ for (in the way of) ...? qu'est-ce que vous avez comme ...?

he *pron.* il; lui

head tête *f.*

health: (here's) to your ~! à votre santé!

hear entendre

~ about entendre parler de

heat chauffage *m.*

hello bonjour; bonsoir; salut

~ ! *(on the phone)* allô!

help aider

her *pron.* elle; lui

her *adj.* son, sa, ses

here ici

~ is, ~ are voici

hi! salut!

high-top sneakers baskets *f.pl.*

highway autoroute *f.*

departmental (local) ~ départementale *f.*

him *pron.* lui

his *adj.* son, sa, ses

hockey hockey *m.*

holiday fête *f.*

home maison *f.*

at the ~ of chez

go (come) ~ rentrer

homework devoirs *m.pl.*

honestly sans façon

hope espérer; souhaiter (que)

horrible affreux (affreuse)

hot chaud(e)

~ chocolate chocolat chaud *m.*

be ~ avoir chaud

it is ~ il fait chaud

hotel hôtel *m.*

hour heure *f.*

one ~ ago il y a une heure

one ~ from now dans une heure

house maison *f.*

at your ~ chez toi

housework ménage *m.*

do ~ faire le ménage

how comment

~ are you? comment allez-vous?; (comment) ça va?

~ do you say ...? comment dit-on ...?

~ do you spell ...? comment est-ce qu'on écrit ...?

~ long? pendant combien de temps ...?

~ many, much combien (de)

~ old are you? quel âge avez-vous?

~ ... he (she) was! comme il (elle) était ...!

hundred cent

hungry: be ~ avoir faim

hurry se dépêcher

husband mari *m.*

I *pron.* je; moi

ice cream glace *f.*

vanilla ~ glace à la vanille *f.*

idiot idiot (idiote) *m./f.*

if si

imbecile imbécile *m./f.*

impatience impatience *f.*

impatient impatient(e)

important important(e)

it is ~ that il est important que

in à; dans; en

~ a crazy manner follement

~ a little while tout à l'heure

~ exchange for contre

~ general en général

~ order to pour

~ the afternoon de l'après-midi

included compris(e)

incredible incroyable

indeed tout à fait

indicate indiquer

indispensable indispensable

inexpensive bon marché *inv.*

inform (se) renseigner

information renseignement *m.*

inside intérieur *m.*

~ of à l'intérieur de

insist insister

instrument instrument *m.*

insure assurer

intellectual *adj.* intellectuel(le)

intelligent intelligent(e)

interest intérêt *m.*

interested: be ~ in s'intéresser à

interesting intéressant(e)

interpreter interprète *m./f.*

introduce présenter

allow me to ~ myself permettez-moi de me présenter

invite inviter

Ireland Irlande *f.*

Israel Israël *m.*

it *pron.* cela, ça; il, elle

it is il est, c'est

is it ...? est-ce que ...?

~ better that il vaut mieux que

~ cold il fait froid

~ cool il fait frais

~ essential il est essentiel

~ nice out il fait beau

~ preferable il vaut mieux

~ raining il pleut

~ snowing il neige

~ windy il fait du vent

Italian italien(ne)

Italy Italie *f.*

its *adj.* son, sa, ses

jacket blouson *m.*

jam confiture *f.*

January janvier *m.*

Japan Japon *m.*

Japanese japonais(e)

jeans jean *m.*

jogging jogging *m.*

juice jus *m.*

orange ~ jus d'orange *m.*

July juillet *m.*

June juin *m.*

just: to have ~ ... venir de ...

just *adv.* juste

keep garder

key clé *f.*

kidding: no ~ sans façon; sans blague!

kilogram kilo *m.*

kind *n.* sorte *f.*

all ~s of things toutes sortes de choses

what ~(s) of ... quelle(s) sorte(s) de ...

kind *adj.* aimable, gentil(le)

kir kir *m.*

kiss *v.* s'embrasser
kitchen cuisine *f.*
knee genou *m.* (*pl.* genoux)
knife couteau *m.* (*pl.* couteaux)
knock frapper
know connaître, savoir
   I don't ~ je ne sais pas

laborer ouvrier/ouvrière *m./f.*
lady dame *f.*
language langue *f.*
lap *n.* genoux *m.pl.*
last dernier (dernière)
   ~ name nom de famille *m.*
   the ~ time la dernière fois
late tard, en retard
   be ~ être en retard
   it is ~ il est tard
lawn bowling pétanque *f.*
lay mettre
lazy paresseux (paresseuse)
leaf (*of paper*) feuille *f.*
learn apprendre (à)
least le/la/les moins
   at ~ au moins
   I like ~ j'aime le moins
leave laisser, partir
   ~ from partir (de)
   ~ me alone! laisse-moi
     (laissez-moi) tranquille!
   there's one left il en reste un(e)
left: to the ~ (of) à gauche (de)
leg jambe *f.*
leisure activity loisir *m.*
lemon-lime soda limonade *f.*
lemonade citron pressé *m.*
lend prêter
length (*of time*) durée *f.*
less moins
let laisser
   let's go allez-y, allons-y
letter lettre *f.*
library bibliothèque *f.*
license: driver's ~ permis de
   conduire *m.*
life vie *f.*
   that's ~ c'est la vie
lift lever
like *v.* aimer
   I would ~ je voudrais
like *conj.* comme
listen (to) écouter
liter litre *m.*
literature littérature *f.*

little *adj.* petit(e)
   ~ girl petite fille *f.*
little *adv.* peu (de)
   a ~ un peu (de)
live habiter
living room salon *m.*
long long (longue)
   a ~ time longtemps
   be a ~ time coming tarder
   how ~ …? pendant combien de
     temps …?
   no longer ne … plus
look regarder; (*seem*) avoir l'air
   ~ after garder
   ~ for chercher
lose perdre
   ~ (one's) patience perdre
     patience
   ~ weight maigrir
lot: a ~ (of) beaucoup (de)
love *v.* adorer, aimer
   ~ each other s'aimer
lozenge pastille *f.*
luck chance *f.*
   good ~! bonne chance!
   what ~! quelle chance!
lunch déjeuner *m.*
   have ~ déjeuner

magazine magazine *m.*
mail *v.* poster
make *n.* marque *f.*
make *v.* faire
   ~ a request faire une demande
   ~ friends se faire des amis
mall centre commercial *m.*
man homme *m.*, monsieur *m.*
management gestion *f.*
manner façon *f.*
manners étiquette *f.*
many beaucoup
   how ~ combien
   so ~ tant
   too ~ trop (de)
map carte *f.*
map (city) plan *m.*
March mars *m.*
market marché *m.*
   flea ~ marché aux puces *m.*
   super ~ supermarché *m.*
marriage mariage *m.*
married marié(e)
marry se marier (avec); épouser
matter: what's the ~ with you?
   qu'est-ce que tu as?

May mai *m.*
may (be able to) pouvoir
   ~ I? vous permettez?, puis-je?
maybe peut-être
mayonnaise mayonnaise *f.*
mayor maire *m.*
me *pron.* me, moi
   ~ neither, nor I moi non plus
meal repas *m.*
   have a good ~! bon appétit!
mean *v.* vouloir dire
mean *adj.* méchant(e)
meat viande *f.*
medicine médicament *m.*
meet rencontrer
   to have met avoir connu
meeting réunion *f.*, rendez-vous
   m.
   have a ~ avoir rendez-vous
member membre *m.*
mention: don't ~ it il n'y a pas
   de quoi; de rien
menu carte *f.* (*à la carte*); menu *m.*
   (*fixed price*)
merchant marchand/marchande
   m./f.
Mexican mexicain(e)
Mexico Mexique *m.*
midnight minuit *m.*
milk lait *m.*
million million *m.*
mind your own business!
   occupe-toi de tes oignons!
mine le mien/la mienne
minute minute *f.*
mirror: rearview ~ rétroviseur
   m.
miserly avare
Miss Mademoiselle (Mlle)
mistake faute *f.*
Monday lundi *m.*
money argent *m.*
month mois *m.*
moped mobylette *f.*
more encore, plus
   ~ …? encore de …?
   ~ to drink (eat)? encore à
     boire (manger)?
   there is no ~ il n'y en a plus
morning matin *m.*
Moroccan marocain(e)
Morocco Maroc *m.*
most (of) la plupart (de);
   the ~ le/la/les plus
mother mère *f.*

mother-in-law belle-mère (*pl.* belles-mères)
motorcycle moto *f.*
motorized bicycle mobylette *f.*
mouse souris *f.*
mouth bouche *f.*
movie film *m.*
  ~ theater cinéma *m.*
Mr. Monsieur (M.)
Mrs. Madame (Mme)
much beaucoup
  how ~ combien
  not ~ pas grand-chose
  so ~ tant (de)
  too ~ trop (de)
museum musée *m.*
mushrooms champignons *m.pl.*
music musique *f.*
must devoir, il faut
  (someone) ~ not il ne faut pas
mustard moutarde *f.*
my *adj.* mon, ma, mes

naive naïf (naïve)
name *n.* nom *m.*
  family (last) ~ nom de famille
  in whose ~ ...? à quel nom ...?
  my ~ is ... je m'appelle ...
  what is your ~? comment vous appelez-vous?
named: be ~ s'appeler
nap sieste *f.*
  take a ~ faire la sieste
napkin serviette *f.*
nasty méchant(e)
nationality nationalité *f.*
  what is your ~? quelle est votre nationalité?
naturally naturellement
near près (de)
  very ~ tout près
necessary nécessaire
  it is ~ il faut, il est nécessaire (que)
need avoir besoin de
neighbor voisin/voisine *m./f.*
neither: me ~ moi non plus
nephew neveu *m.* (*pl.* neveux)
nervous nerveux (nerveuse)
never jamais (ne ... jamais)
new nouveau/nouvel (nouvelle) (*m.pl.* nouveaux); neuf (neuve)
  ~ Year's Day Jour de l'An *m.*
  what's ~? quoi de neuf?

news informations *f.pl.*
newspaper journal *m.*
newsstand kiosque *m.*
next *adv.* ensuite, puis; *adj.* prochain(e); suivant(e)
  ~ door à côté
  ~ to à côté de
nice aimable, gentil(le)
  have a ~ day bonne journée
  it's ~ out il fait beau
  that's ~ of you c'est gentil à vous
niece nièce *f.*
night nuit *f.*
nine neuf
nineteen dix-neuf
ninety quatre-vingt-dix
ninety-one quatre-vingt-onze
no non
  ~ kidding! sans blague!; sans façon
  ~ longer ne ... plus
  ~ more ne ... plus
  ~ one ne ... personne
nobody ne ... personne
noise bruit *m.*
noon midi
nor: ~ I moi non plus
nose nez *m.*
  runny ~ le nez qui coule
not ne (n') ... pas
  ~ anyone ne ... personne
  ~ anything ne ... rien
  ~ at all il n'y a pas de quoi, de rien; pas du tout
  ~ much pas grand-chose
  ~ yet pas encore
note note *f.*
nothing ne ... rien
notice remarquer
novel *n.* roman *m.*
novel *adj.* original(e) (*m.pl.* originaux)
November novembre *m.*
now maintenant, actuellement
number nombre *m.*, numéro *m.*
  telephone ~ numéro de téléphone *m.*
nurse infirmier/infirmière *m./f.*

obey obéir
o'clock heure(s)
  at ... ~ à ... heure(s)
  it is ... ~ il est ... heure(s)
October octobre *m.*

of de
  ~ course bien sûr
office bureau *m.* (*pl.* bureaux)
  post ~ bureau de poste *m.*
officer: police ~ agent de police *m.*
often souvent
oh dear! oh là là!
okay d'accord
  if that's ~ si ça va
old âgé(e), vieux/vieil (vieille)
  how ~ are you? quel âge avez-vous?
omelet omelette *f.*
on sur
one *pron.* on
  no ~ ne ... personne
one (*number*) un (une)
one-way: ~ street sens interdit *m.*
  ~ ticket aller simple *m.*
onion oignon *m.*
only *adj.* seul(e); *adv.* seulement; ne ... que
open *v.* ouvrir
open *adj.* ouvert(e)
opening ouverture *f.*
opinion avis *m.*
  be of the ~ trouver, penser
  in my (your, etc.) ~ à mon (à ton, etc.) avis
opposite contraire *m.*
or ou
orange *n.* orange *m.*
  ~ juice jus d'orange *m.*
  ~ soda orangina *m.*
orange *adj.* orange *inv.*
order *v.* commander
order: in ~ to pour
ordinary *adj.* ordinaire
original original(e) (*m.pl.* originaux)
other autre
ouch! aïe!
our notre, nos
outgoing extroverti(e)
outside dehors
owe devoir
owner propriétaire *m./f.*

package paquet *m.*
pain: have a ~ (in) avoir mal (à)
pajamas (pair of) pyjama *m.*
pale pâle
pants (pair of) pantalon *m.*

paper papier *m.*; journal *m.*
  term ~ dissertation *f.*
pardon: I beg your ~ je vous demande pardon; excusez-moi
parents parents *m.pl.*
parents-in-law beaux-parents *m.pl.*
party boum *f.*, soirée *f.*
pass *(an exam)* réussir
pass *(a car)* dépasser
pastry pâtisserie *f.*
  ~ shop pâtisserie *f.*
patience: lose (one's) ~ perdre patience
patient *adj.* patient(e)
patiently patiemment
pavement chaussée *f.*
pay (for) payer
  ~ attention faire attention
peanut arachide *f.*
  ~ butter beurre d'arachide *m.*
peas petits pois *m.pl.*
people gens *m.pl.*; on
pepper poivre *m.*
per par
perfect parfait(e)
perhaps peut-être
period époque *f.*
person *(male or female)* personne *f.*
personally *adv.* personnellement
pharmacy pharmacie *f.*
photograph photo *f.*
physical physique
piano piano *m.*
picnic pique-nique *m.*
pie tarte *f.*
piece morceau *m.* *(pl.* morceaux*)*
pill pilule *f.*, cachet *m.*
pilot pilote *m.*
pink rose
pity pitié *f.*
pizza pizza *f.*
place *n.* endroit *m.*, lieu *m.*
  take ~ avoir lieu
place *v.* mettre
plain simple
plan to avoir l'intention de
plate assiette *f.*
play *n.* pièce *f.*
play *v.* jouer
  ~ a game jouer à
  ~ an instrument jouer de
  ~ sports faire du sport
  ~ tennis jouer au tennis

please s'il vous plaît (s'il te plaît)
  ~ do je vous en prie
pleasure plaisir *m.*
  with ~ avec plaisir
poem poème *m.*
point out indiquer
police officer agent de police *m.*, gendarme *m.*
politician homme/femme politique *m./f.*
politics politique *f.*
poor *adj.* pauvre
poorly mal
popular populaire
porch véranda *f.*
pork porc *m.*
  ~ butcher's charcuterie *f.*
post office bureau de poste *m.*
postcard carte postale *f.*
potato pomme de terre *f.*
pound livre *f.*
pour verser
practice répéter
prefer préférer
  I ~ that je préfère que
preferable: it is ~ that il vaut mieux que
prepare (a lesson) préparer (un cours)
pretty joli(e)
price prix *m.*
probably sans doute
process: be in the ~ of être en train de
program programme *m.*
  TV ~ émission (de télé) *f.*
promise promettre
  it's a ~ c'est promis
prudently prudemment
publicity publicité *f.*
punch (a ticket) composter (un billet)
pupil élève *m./f.*
purchase achat *m.*
purple violet(te)
put mettre
  ~ on attacher; mettre *(clothes)*
  ~ on weight grossir

quarter *m.* quart
  ~ past, ~ after et quart
  ~ to, ~ till moins le quart
question question *f.*
  ask a ~ poser une question

quickly vite; rapidement
quiet: keep ~! tais-toi! (taisez-vous!)

race course *f.*
radio radio *f.*
rain pleuvoir
  it's raining il pleut
raincoat imperméable *m.*
raise lever
rapid rapide
rapidly rapidement
rare *(undercooked)* saignant(e)
rarely rarement
rather assez
  ~ poorly assez mal
read lire
really vraiment; sans façon
reasonable raisonnable
recently récemment
recommend recommander
red rouge
  ~ -haired roux (rousse)
refrigerator réfrigérateur *m.*
regarding à propos de
relatives parents *m.pl.*
remain rester
remember se souvenir (de)
rent *v.* louer
repeat répéter
request *n.* demande *f.*
  make a ~ faire une demande
reserve réserver
reside habiter
responsibility responsabilité *f.*
rest se reposer
restaurant restaurant *m.*
restroom toilettes *f.pl.*
return retourner, revenir, rentrer
rice riz *m.*
rich riche
ride: take a ~ se promener, faire une promenade en voiture
ridiculous ridicule
right *n.* droit *m.*
right *adj.* droit(e); exact(e)
  ~ ? n'est-ce pas?
  ~ away tout de suite
  ~ behind juste derrière
  be ~ avoir raison
  that's ~ c'est exact
  to the ~ (of) à droite (de)
ring *n.* bague *f.*
road route *f.*

roast (of beef) rôti (de bœuf) *m.*
roll *v.* rouler
roof toit *m.*
room chambre *f.;* salle *f.;* pièce *f.*
   bath ~ salle de bain(s) *f.*
   bed ~ chambre *f.*
   class ~ salle de classe *f.*
   dining ~ salle à manger *f.*
roommate camarade de chambre
   m./f.
round-trip ticket aller-retour *m.*
rugby rugby *m.*
run courir
run a stop sign brûler un stop
run into heurter
runner coureur/coureuse
Russia Russie *f.*
Russian russe

sad triste
salad salade *f.*
   (green) ~ salade (verte) *f.*
salesman/saleswoman
   vendeur/vendeuse *m./f.*
salmon saumon *m.*
salt sel *m.*
sandwich sandwich *m.*
Santa Claus le père Noël
sardine sardine *f.*
Saturday samedi *m.*
sausage saucisse *f.*
saxophone saxophone *m.*
say dire
scarf foulard *m.*
schedule emploi du temps *m.*
school école *f.*
   high ~ lycée *m.*
science sciences *f.pl.*
   computer ~ informatique *f.*
season saison *f.*
second second(e), deuxième
   in ~ class en seconde
see voir
seem avoir l'air
-self(-selves) -même(s)
sell vendre
semester semestre *m.*
send envoyer
Senegal Sénégal *m.*
Senegalese sénégalais(e)
separate *v.* séparer
   ~ from each other se séparer
September septembre *m.*
series *(TV)* feuilleton *m.*

serious sérieux (sérieuse)
seriously sérieusement
service: at your ~ à votre service
set: ~ the table mettre la table
seven sept
seventeen dix-sept
seventy soixante-dix
seventy-one soixante et onze
seventy-two soixante-douze
she *pron.* elle
sheet (of paper) feuille *f.*
shh! chut!
shirt chemise *f.*
shoes chaussures *f.pl.*
shop *(clothing)* boutique *f.*
   tobacco ~ (bureau de) tabac *m.*
shopping courses *f.pl.*
   ~ center centre commercial *m.*
short petit(e)
shorts (pair of) short *m.*
shoulder épaule *f.*
show montrer
shower *n.* douche *f.*
shower *v.* se doucher
sick malade
since depuis
sincere sincère
sing chanter
singer chanteur/chanteuse *m./f.*
single célibataire
Sir Monsieur (M.)
sister sœur *f.*
sister-in-law belle-sœur *f.* *(pl.*
   belles-sœurs)
sit down s'asseoir
   ~ to eat se mettre à table
six six
sixteen seize
sixty soixante
skate patiner
skating rink patinoire *f.*
ski skier
skid déraper
skirt jupe *f.*
skis skis *m.pl.*
sleep dormir
sleepy: be ~ avoir sommeil
slice tranche *f.*
slippery glissant(e)
slow *adj.* lent(e)
slow down ralentir
slowly lentement
small petit(e)
smile *n.* sourire *m.*
smile *v.* sourire

smoke fumer
smoking (car) fumeur
   non- ~ non-fumeur
snail escargot *m.*
snow neiger
   it's snowing il neige
so alors, si
   ~ many tant
   ~ much tant
soap opera feuilleton *m.*
soccer football (foot) *m.*
socks chaussettes *f.pl.*
soda: lemon-lime ~ limonade *f.;*
      orange ~ orangina *m.*
sofa sofa *m.*
some *adj.* des, quelques; *pron.* en
someone quelqu'un
something quelque chose *m.*
sometimes quelquefois
son fils *m.*
song chanson *f.*
soon bientôt
sore: be ~ avoir mal (à)
sorry désolé(e)
   be ~ regretter
   feel ~ (for) avoir pitié (de)
sort of assez
so-so comme ci, comme ça
soup soupe *f.*
Spain Espagne *f.*
Spanish espagnol(e)
speak parler
specify préciser
speed vitesse *f.*
   at top ~ à toute vitesse
spell épeler
   how do you ~ ...? comment
      est-ce qu'on écrit ...?
   ... is spelled ... ... s'écrit ...
spend (a year) passer (un an)
spinach épinards *m.pl.*
spoon cuiller *f.*
sportcoat veste *f.*
spring *n.* printemps *m.*
stamp timbre *m.*
stand up se lever
start commencer; démarrer
   it's starting to get cold il
      commence à faire froid
state état *m.*
statue statue *f.*
stay rester
steak steak *m.*
   ~ with French fries steak-
      frites *m.*

steering wheel volant *m.*
stepbrother demi-frère *m.*
stepfather beau-père *m.* (*pl.* beaux-pères)
stepmother belle-mère *f.* (*pl.* belles-mères)
stepparents beaux-parents *m.pl.*
stepsister demi-sœur *f.*
stereo stéréo *f.*
still encore; toujours
stomach estomac *m.*
stop *n.* arrêt *m.*
  ~ sign stop *m.*
  bus ~ arrêt d'autobus *m.*
stop *v.* (s')arrêter
store magasin *m.*
  department ~ grand magasin *m.*
  grocery ~ épicerie *f.*
story histoire *f.*
  detective ~ roman policier *m.*
stove cuisinière *f.*
strawberries fraises *f.pl.*
street rue *f.*
  one-way ~ sens interdit *m.*
student étudiant/étudiante *m./f.*
studies *n.* études *f.pl.*
study *v.* étudier
stylish chic *adj. inv.*
succeed réussir
sugar sucre *m.*
suit *n.* complet *m.*
  bathing ~ maillot de bain *m.*
suitcase valise *f.*
summer été *m.*
sun soleil *m.*
Sunday dimanche *m.*
supermarket supermarché *m.*
  giant ~ hypermarché *m.*
supplement supplément *m.*
supposed: be ~ to devoir
surely certainement, sûrement
surprise surprise *f.*
  what a good ~! quelle bonne surprise!
swear jurer
  I ~ (to you) je te le jure
sweater pull-over (pull) *m.*
sweatshirt sweat-shirt *m.*
Sweden Suède *f.*
Swedish suédois(e)
swim nager
swimming pool piscine *f.*
Swiss suisse
  ~ cheese emmenthal *m.*

Switzerland Suisse *f.*

table table *f.*
  at the ~ à table
  set the ~ mettre la table
tablecloth nappe *f.*
tablet cachet *m.*
  aspirin ~ cachet d'aspirine *m.*
take prendre
  ~ a nap faire la sieste
  ~ a test passer (un examen)
  ~ a trip faire un voyage
  ~ a walk, a ride faire une promenade
  ~ place avoir lieu
talkative bavard(e)
tall grand(e)
taste goûter
tea thé *m.*
teach enseigner
teacher professeur *m.*
  ~ preparation pédagogie *f.*
team équipe *f.*
tee-shirt tee-shirt *m.*
telephone *n.* téléphone *m.*
  ~ number numéro de téléphone *m.*
  on the ~ au téléphone
telephone *v.* téléphoner (à)
television télévision (télé) *f.*
tell indiquer, raconter, dire, parler
  can you ~ me ...? pouvez-vous me dire ...?
  ~ a story raconter une histoire
ten dix
tend to avoir tendance à
tennis tennis *m.*
  ~ shoes tennis *f.pl.*
  play ~ jouer au tennis
term paper dissertation *f.*
test examen *m.*
thank *v.* remercier
thanks merci
  yes, ~ je veux bien
that *adj.* ce/cet, cette, ces; *conj.* que; *pron.* ce, cela, ça; *relative pron.* qui, que
the le/la/les
theater théâtre *m.*
their leur(s)
them elles, eux; les, leur
then alors, ensuite, puis
there là, y
  ~ is (are) il y a, voilà

  over ~ là-bas
therefore alors; donc
they *pron.* ils, elles, on, eux
thin mince
thing chose *f.*
think croire, penser, trouver
  do you ~ so? vous trouvez?
  I don't ~ so je ne crois pas
  what do you ~ of it (of them)? qu'en penses-tu?
  what do you ~ of ...? comment trouvez-vous ...?
thirsty: be ~ avoir soif
thirteen treize
thirty trente
this *adj.* ce/cet, cette, ces
  ~ way par ici
those *adj.* ces
thousand mille *inv.*
three trois
throat gorge *f.*
throughway autoroute *f.*
Thursday jeudi *m.*
ticket billet *m.*
  one-way ~ aller simple *m.*
  round-trip ~ aller-retour *m.*
  traffic ~ contravention *f.*
tie *n.* cravate *f.*
time temps *m.*; heure *f.*; fois *f.*
  ~ difference décalage horaire *m.*
  a long ~ longtemps
  at that ~ à cette époque
  on ~ à l'heure
  the last ~ la dernière fois
  what ~ is it? quelle heure est-il?
tired fatigué(e)
to à
  ~ the side à côté
toast pain grillé *m.*
tobacco tabac *m.*
  ~ shop (bureau de) tabac *m.*
today aujourd'hui
together ensemble
tomato tomate *f.*
tomorrow demain
  day after ~ après-demain
tonight ce soir
too aussi
  ~ many trop (de)
  ~ much trop (de)
  you ~ vous aussi
tooth dent *f.*
toothbrush brosse à dents *f.*

toothpaste dentifrice *m.*
tour tour *m.*
   ~ bus autocar *m.*
towel serviette *f.*
tower tour *f.*
town ville *f.*
   ~ hall mairie *f.*
trade ... for échanger ... contre
traffic circulation *f.*
traffic light feu *m.* (*pl.* feux)
train train *m.*
   ~ station gare *f.*
travel voyager
traveler's check chèque de
   voyage *m.*
trip voyage *m.*
trout truite *f.*
true vrai(e)
truly vraiment
   yours ~ amicalement
trumpet trompette *f.*
truth vérité *f.*
try essayer
   may I ~ ...? puis-je ...?
Tuesday mardi *m.*
turn *n.* tour *m.*
turn *v.* tourner
   ~ on (*the TV*) mettre
   ~ on the heat mettre le
      chauffage
turnpike autoroute *f.*
tuxedo smoking *m.*
twelve douze
twenty vingt
twenty-one vingt et un
twenty-two vingt-deux
two deux

ugly laid(e)
unbelievable incroyable
uncle oncle *m.*
under sous
understand comprendre
understanding compréhensif/
   compréhensive
United States États-Unis *m.pl.*
university université *f.*
unmarried célibataire
until *prep.* jusqu'à
unwise: be ~ avoir tort
up: get ~ se lever
us nous
useless inutile
usually d'habitude

vacation vacances *f.pl.*
   have a good ~! bonnes
      vacances!
   on ~ en vacances
vanilla vanille *f.*
   ~ ice cream glace à la vanille *f.*
vegetable légume *m.*
   raw vegetables crudités *f.pl.*
very tout; très
violin violon *m.*
visit visiter
   ~ someone rendre visite
      à qqn
voyage voyage *m.*

wait (for) attendre
waiter garçon *m.*, serveur *m.*
waitress serveuse *f.*
wake up se réveiller
walk *n.* promenade *f.*
   take a ~ se promener, faire une
      promenade
walk *v.* se promener
waltz valse *f.*
want vouloir, désirer, avoir envie
   de
war guerre *f.*
warning avertissement *m.*
wash laver; se laver
washing machine machine à
   laver *f.*
watch *n.* montre *f.*
watch *v.* regarder
water eau *f.* (*pl.* eaux)
   mineral ~ eau minérale
way route *f.*; façon *f.*
   by the ~ au fait
we nous
wear porter
weather météo(rologie) *f.*, temps
   m.
   the ~ is bad il fait mauvais
   what is the ~ like? quel temps
      fait-il?
wedding mariage *m.*
   ~ anniversary anniversaire de
      mariage *m.*
   ~ dress robe de mariée *f.*
Wednesday mercredi *m.*
week semaine *f.*
   per ~ par semaine
   two weeks quinze jours
weekend week-end *m.*
weight: put on ~ grossir

   lose ~ maigrir
welcome: you're ~ de rien, je
   vous en prie, il n'y a pas de
   quoi
Welcome! Bienvenue!
well *adv.* bien
   are you ~? vous allez bien?
   fairly ~ assez bien
   not very ~ pas très bien
Well! Tiens!
Well then ... Eh bien ...
what *pron.* qu'est-ce que/qu'est-
   ce qui, que; *adj.* quel(le)
   ~? comment?
   ~ am I going to do? comment
      je vais faire?
   ~ day is it? quel jour est-ce?
   ~ (did you say)? comment?
   ~ is (are) ... like? comment est
      (sont) ...?
   ~ is there ...? qu'est-ce qu'il y
      a ...?
   ~ is this? qu'est-ce que c'est?
   ~ is your name? comment
      vous appelez-vous?
   ~'s new? quoi de neuf?
   ~'s the matter? qu'est-ce qu'il
      y a?
   ~ time is it? quelle heure
      est-il?
wheel: steering ~ volant *m.*
weird bizarre
when quand
where où
   ~ are you from? vous êtes
      d'où?; d'où venez-vous?
   ~ is (are) ...? où se trouve (se
      trouvent) ...?
which *adj.* quel(le); *pron.* lequel
while pendant que
   a little ~ tout à l'heure
white blanc (blanche)
who qui
why pourquoi
   ~ not? pourquoi pas?
widower/widow veuf/veuve
   m./f.
wife femme *f.*
win gagner
   ~ the lottery gagner à la
      loterie
wind vent *m.*
   it's windy il fait du vent
windbreaker blouson *m.*
wine vin *m.*

winter hiver *m.*
wish vouloir; souhaiter
  I want je veux (que)
  I would like je voudrais (que)
with avec
without sans
witness témoin *m.*
Wolof *(language)* wolof *m.*
woman femme *f.*, dame *f.*
word mot *m.*
work *n.* travail *m.*
  manual ~ travail manuel *m.*
work *v.* travailler
world monde *m.*

worry *n.* souci *m.*
worry *v.* s'inquiéter
wounded *adj.* blessé(e)
wow! oh là là!
write écrire
wrong faux (fausse)
  be ~ avoir tort

year an *m.;* année *f.*
  school ~ année scolaire
yellow jaune
yes oui; si!
yesterday hier

yet encore
  not ~ pas encore
you *pron.* tu, vous; te, vous; toi, vous
young jeune
your *adj.* ton, ta, tes; votre, vos
  (here's) to yours! à la vôtre!
yuck! berk!
yum! miam!

zero zéro
zip code code postal *m.*

Index

In the following index, the symbol (v) refers to lists of vocabulary within the lessons. The symbol (g) refers to the sections titled *Il y a un geste* that explain gestures used with the indicated phrase.

Permissions and Credits

The authors and editors wish to thank the following persons and publishers for permission to include the works or excerpts mentioned.

Photos; p. 178, © Yves Marcoux/Stone 414505-001Q; p. 179, © Beryl Goldberg; p. 179, © Focus on Sports; p. 180, © Voscar/ The Maine Photographer; p. 181, © Bob Krist/ eStock Photography (Leo de Wys); p. 182, © Voge/Figaro Magazine/Liaison Agency; p.185, © Owen Franken; p. 188, © Robert Fried; p. 205, © Jean Bernard Vernier/Sygma; p. 208, © Kevin Galvin; p. 211, © David R. Frazier Photolibrary; p. 214, © Richard Passmore/Stone; p. 217, © Cathlyn Melloan/Stone; p. 232, © David Simson/Stock Boston; p. 237, © Judy Poe; p. 240, © Beryl Goldberg; p. 251, © Owen Franken; p. 264, © C.M. Hardt/Liason Agency; p. 265, © W. Campbell/Sygma; p. 265, © Charlotte Miller; p. 267, © Beryl Goldberg; p. 267, © Jeremy Hartley/Panos Pictures; p. 268, © Owen Franken; p. 271, © Kevin Galvin; p. 292, © Reuters/Charles Platiau/Archive Photos; p. 295, © Owen Franken; p. 298, © Owen Franken/Stock Boston; p. 302, © Dennis Stock/ Magnum; p. 307, © Stu Rosner/Stock Boston; p. 319, © Bob Krist/eStock Photography (Leo de Wys); p. 322, © Owen Franken; p. 335, © Beryl Goldberg ; p. 338 © Owen Franken; p. 342, © Monkmeyer/Press; p. 344, © Kees van den Berg/Photo Researchers; p. 345, © J. Boisberranger/Liason Agency; p. 346, © AP/Wide World Photos; p. 347, © Bernard Wolf/Monkhmeyer; p. 348, © Richard Kalvar/Magnum; p. 364, © Beryl Goldberg; p. 368, © Chad Ehlers/Stone; p. 372, © Michael Busselle/Stone; p. 377, © Owen Franken; p. 380, © Beryl Goldberg; p. 385, © Charles Nes/Liason Agency; p. 405, © Kevin Galvin; p. 408, © Mark Burnett/David R. Frazier Photolibrary; p. 411, © Andrew Brilliant; p. 422, © Beryl Goldberg; p. 428, © Ulrike Welsch; p. 430, © Owen Franken; p. 431, © Archivo Iconografico/S.A./Corbis; p. 432, © T. Gilou/Ask Images/Viesti Associates; p. 433, © Hoa-Qui/Liason Agency.

Gesture photos by Jennifer Waddell.

Realia

p. 8:   Ibis Hotel
p. 29:   Orangina
p. 29:   Perrier
p. 32:   La Belle Époque
p. 114: Air France
p. 136: Galeries Lafayette
p. 146: Courtesy of Angers Tourisme
p. 163: Lire magazine
p. 210: Vieux Fagots
p. 238: Galeries Lafayette
p. 241: Laboratoires homéopathiques de France
p. 252: Téléfleurs France
p. 306: Léon de Brussels 1893
p. 320: Courtesy of Holiday Inn Worldwide
p. 328: Esig l'école
p. 332: Société Générale
p. 418: Swiss Life (Belgium)

Illustrations by G. S. Weiland.

Computer Art by Catherine Hawkes.

Maps by Patty Isaacs.

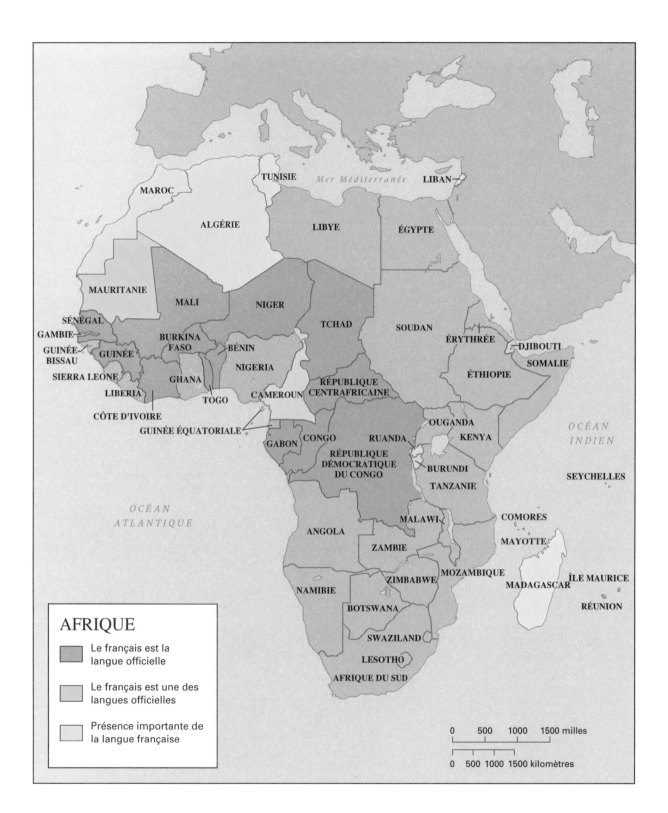

AFRIQUE

Le français est la langue officielle

Le français est une des langues officielles

Présence importante de la langue française

MAROC
TUNISIE
Mer Méditerranée
LIBAN
ALGÉRIE
LIBYE
ÉGYPTE
MAURITANIE
MALI
NIGER
SÉNÉGAL
TCHAD
SOUDAN
GAMBIE
ÉRYTHRÉE
DJIBOUTI
GUINÉE-BISSAU
BURKINA FASO
BÉNIN
GUINÉE
SOMALIE
SIERRA LEONE
GHANA
NIGERIA
ÉTHIOPIE
LIBERIA
TOGO
CAMEROUN
RÉPUBLIQUE CENTRAFRICAINE
CÔTE D'IVOIRE
GUINÉE ÉQUATORIALE
OUGANDA
GABON
CONGO
RUANDA
KENYA
RÉPUBLIQUE DÉMOCRATIQUE DU CONGO
BURUNDI
TANZANIE
OCÉAN INDIEN
SEYCHELLES
OCÉAN ATLANTIQUE
MALAWI
COMORES
ANGOLA
MAYOTTE
ZAMBIE
MOZAMBIQUE
ZIMBABWE
ÎLE MAURICE
NAMIBIE
MADAGASCAR
RÉUNION
BOTSWANA
SWAZILAND
LESOTHO
AFRIQUE DU SUD

0   500   1000   1500 milles

0   500   1000   1500 kilomètres